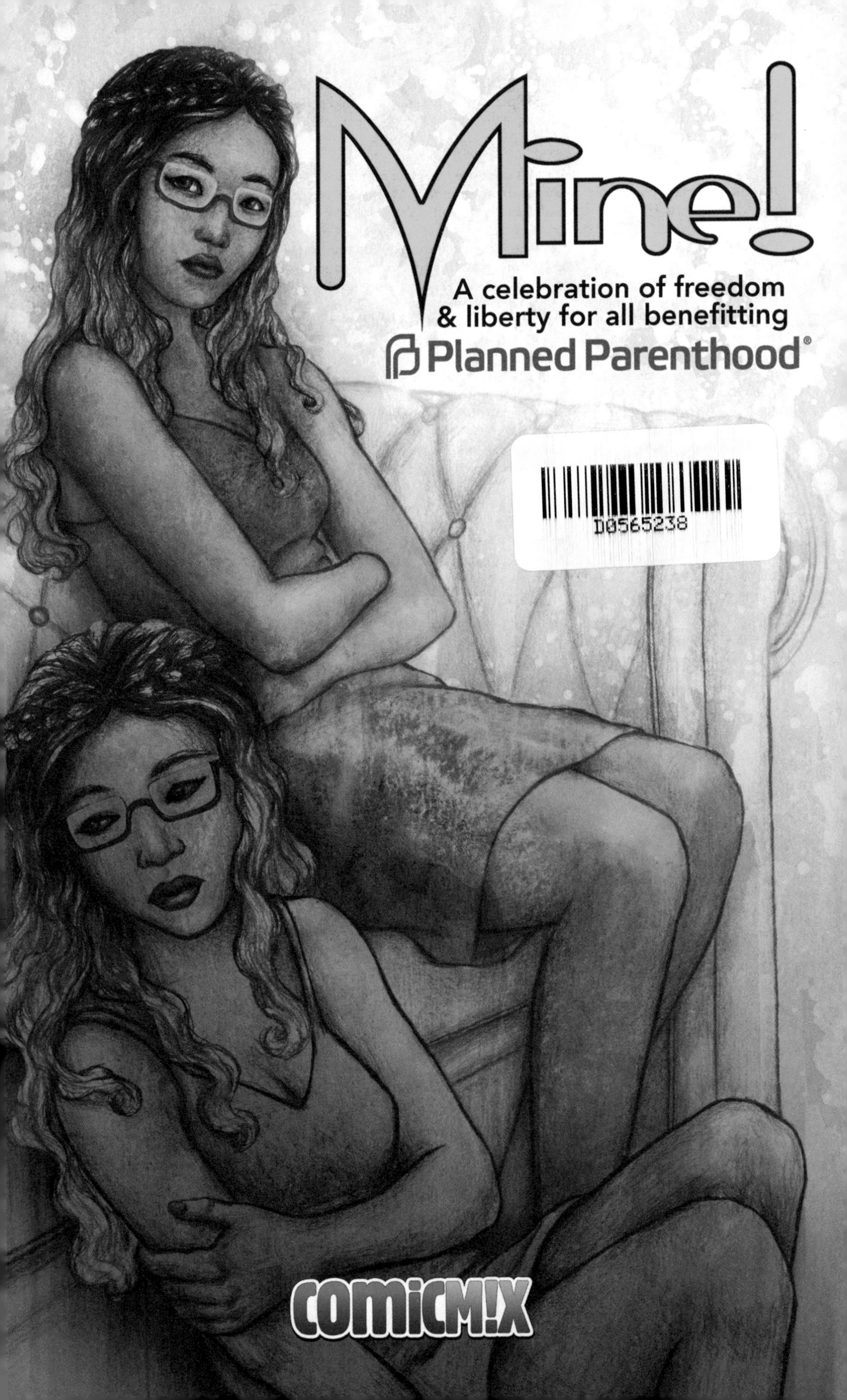
Mine!
A celebration of freedom & liberty for all benefitting
Planned Parenthood®
comicM!X

The book you're holding in your hands first manifested in December of 2015 when both of us were sitting in a small pizzeria in Astoria on a cold night. We talked about how we had both been writing columns for ComicMix for a bit, but wanted to do a comic anthology through them. That night we were still figuring out what it would be.

We spoke about a lot of different ideas over the next few months. These included anthologies about Golden-Age style comics, crime noir, or a western style comic. Mostly, we wanted to avoid the oversaturated superhero genre. However, none of these ideas felt right for us. We wanted this book to be more.

By March of 2016, we settled on a benefit comic anthology to support Planned Parenthood. It's an organization that everyone at ComicMix agreed was important and should be supported. Joe had a contact he reached out to and over the course of many e-mails, phone calls, conference calls, and contracts, we were close to locking it in. It was an exciting time, and we were so eager to get started.

Then the election on November 8th, 2016 happened.

People might assume that the election is what got this anthology moving; it wasn't. It actually threw a wrench into everything. Planned Parenthood was rightfully focused on their survival. It would be many months before contracts were signed off on and we could officially move forward.

In that time we were able to line up much of the impressive talent on display in this book. So many creators were excited to be part of this project and ready to show their support. While this has been a challenging and complicated process, it has also been rewarding and humbling. This book represents two years of our lives and the work of over 150 incredibly talented individuals all agreeing that Planned Parenthood is vital to millions of people. We are so proud to be a part of this group, and standing for body autonomy for all.

Thank you for picking up this book. We both hope you enjoy experiencing all of the fun, wonderful, and sobering stories this volume contains. Most of all, thank you for supporting Planned Parenthood. They need it, but so do we all.

—Joe Corallo and Molly Jackson
Project Editors, ComicMix, LLC

Cover art: Soo Lee • Title page art: Alice Meichi Li
Back cover art : Dean Haspiel, Barbara Haspiel, & Leah Garrett

Special thanks to...

Mike Gold
Adriane Nash
Evelyn Kriete
Leia Calderon
Andrea Levine
Matthew Kaplowitz
Jason Scott Jones
Jill Thompson
Mike Grell
Vito Delsante
Beth Rimmels
Yona Harvey
Patrick J. Kennedy
Tee Franklin

Margot Atwell
Mariko Tamaki
Gerard Way
Sean Von Gorman
Jamal Igle
Yuri Lowenthal
Catrina Brighton
Adrianne Palicki
Amanda Palmer
Caren Spruch
Rachel Craw
Stephanie Bryant
The Corallo Family
The Jackson Family

So What? Press
Geeks OUT
Jay Spence
Megan Cosman
Jim Patterson
James Killen
Backerkit
All our backers...
   ...and especially
all the creators we
   didn't have room
   for in this edition,
   but who will be in
      Mine, Too!

MINE! A Celebration of Liberty And Freedom For All Benefiting Planned Parenthood. DECEMBER 2017.

The stories in this volume reflect the opinions of their creators, and should not be considered official statements of Planned Parenthood.

Joe Corallo & Molly Jackson – Editors
John Workman – Logo Design
Glenn Hauman – Production & Book Design
Martha Thomases – Media Goddess
Shann Dornhecker – Chief Executive Officer

Hardcover ISBN: 978-1-939888-66-2
Softcover ISBN: 978-1-939888-65-5

Planned Parenthood®

Find a health center by calling 1-800-230-PLAN
or online at www.plannedparenthood.org

Need Help? Chat Now.

Chat online or text "PPNOW" to 774636 (PPINFO) to get answers about pregnancy, birth control, emergency contraception, STDs, and abortion.

Standard message and data rates may apply.
Text STOP to quit at anytime, and HELP for info.

http://www.comicmix.com

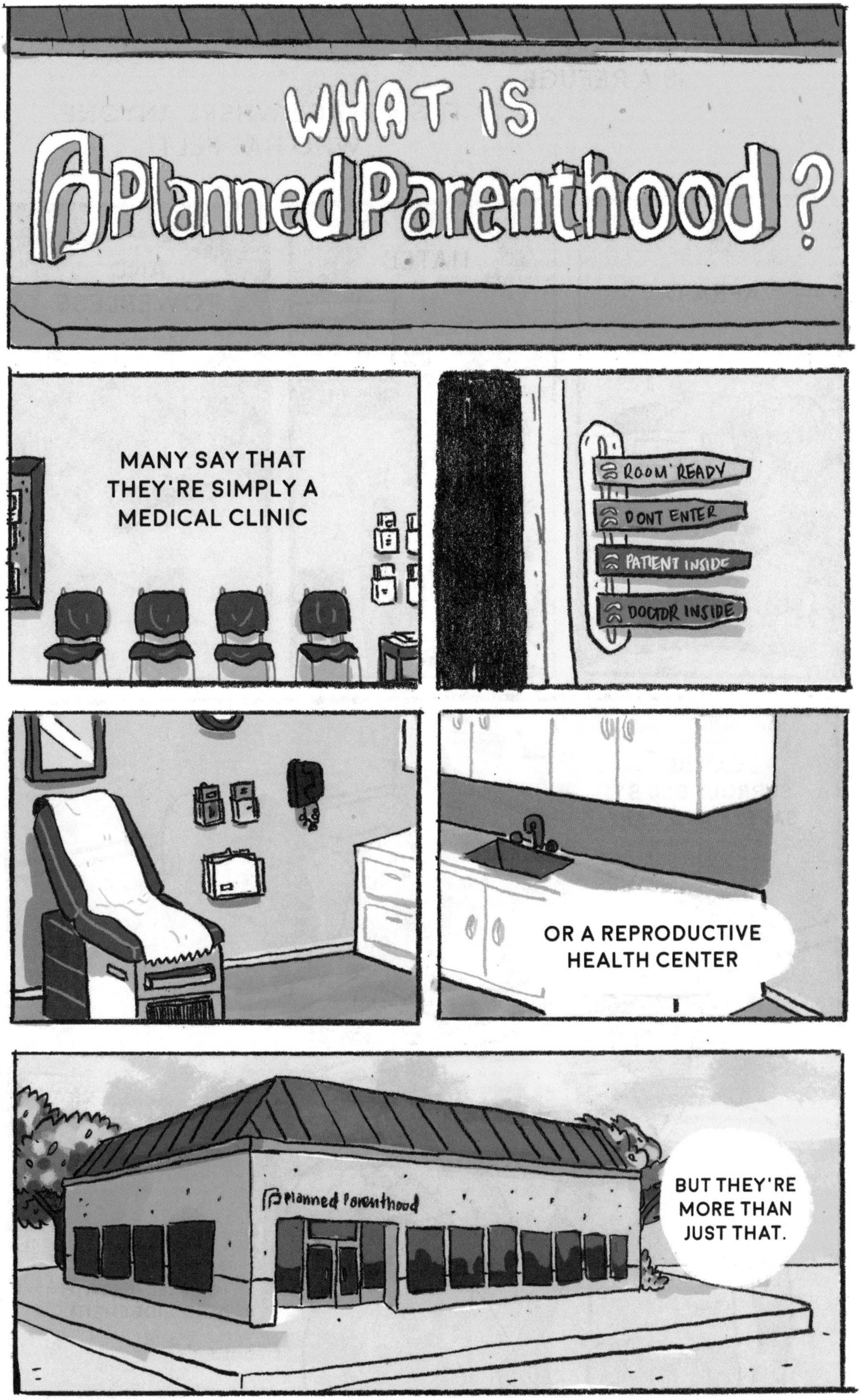

WHAT IS
Planned Parenthood?
MANY SAY THAT THEY'RE SIMPLY A MEDICAL CLINIC
ROOM READY
DONT ENTER
PATIENT INSIDE
DOCTOR INSIDE
OR A REPRODUCTIVE HEALTH CENTER
Planned Parenthood
BUT THEY'RE MORE THAN JUST THAT.

PLANNED PARENTHOOD
IS A REFUGE.

IT'S A PLACE WHERE ANYONE
WHO HAS FELT

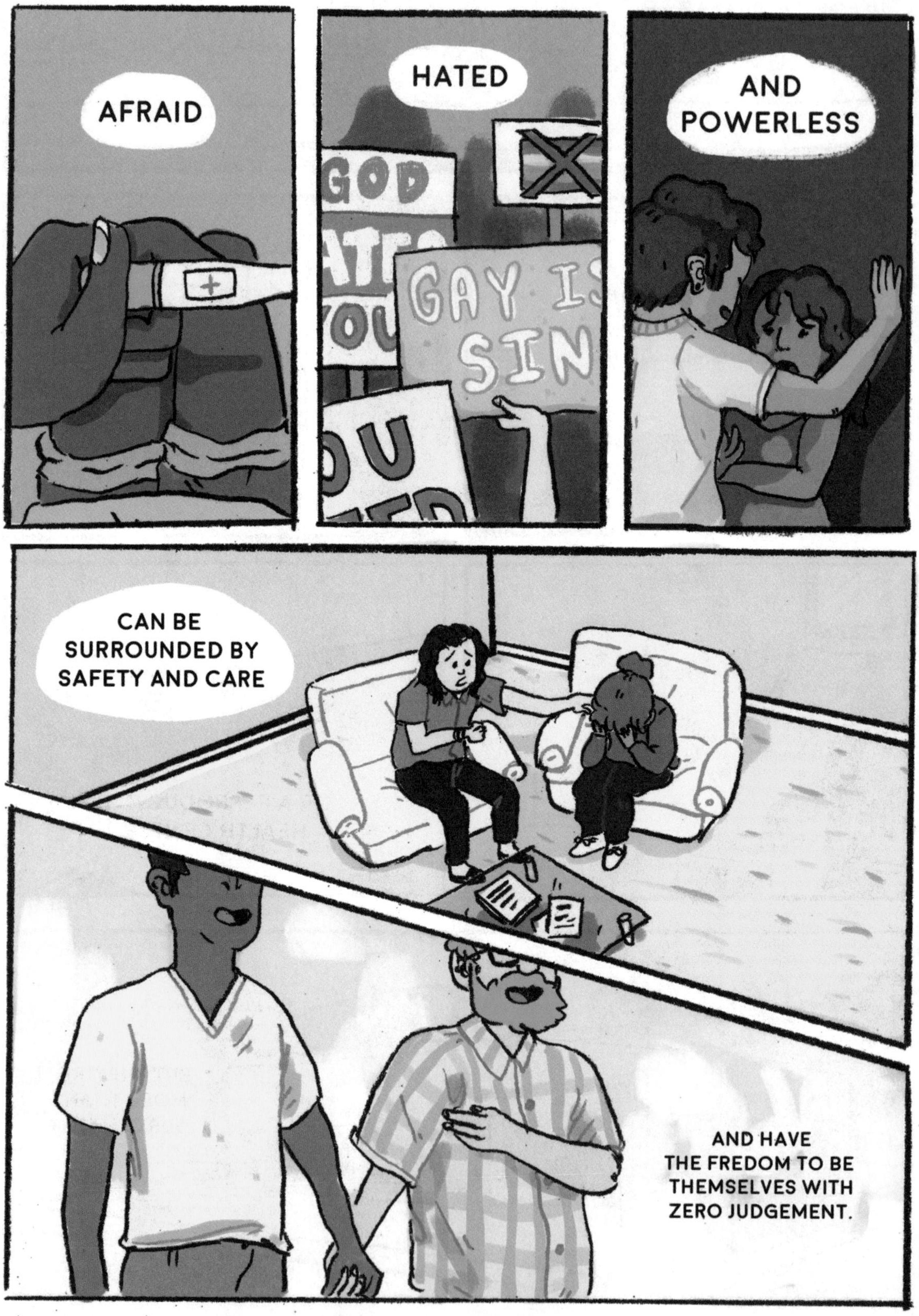
AFRAID
HATED
GOD
GAY IS
SIN
AND
POWERLESS
CAN BE
SURROUNDED BY
SAFETY AND CARE
AND HAVE
THE FREDOM TO BE
THEMSELVES WITH
ZERO JUDGEMENT.

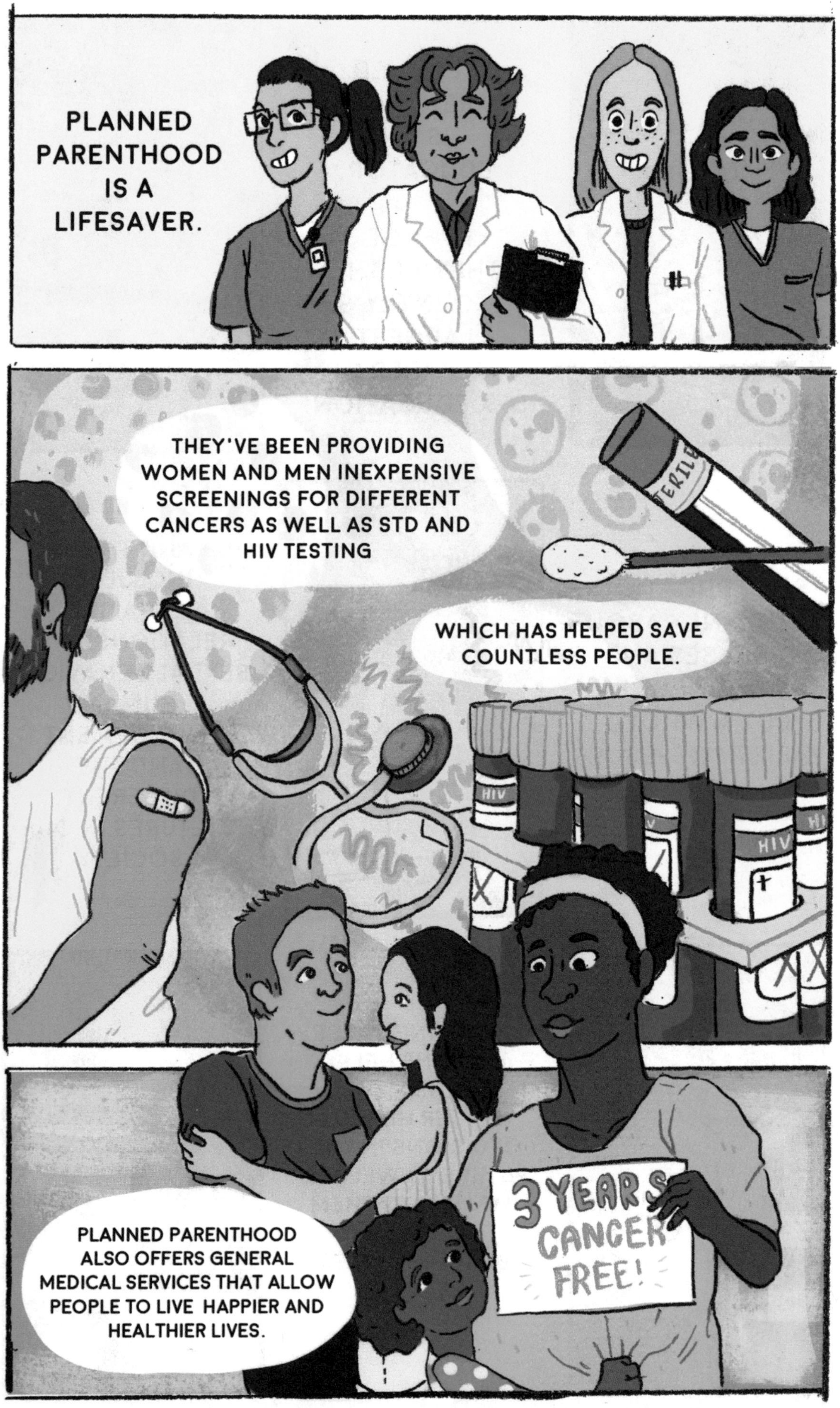
PLANNED PARENTHOOD IS A LIFESAVER.
THEY'VE BEEN PROVIDING WOMEN AND MEN INEXPENSIVE SCREENINGS FOR DIFFERENT CANCERS AS WELL AS STD AND HIV TESTING
WHICH HAS HELPED SAVE COUNTLESS PEOPLE.
HIV
HIV
3 YEARS CANCER FREE!
PLANNED PARENTHOOD ALSO OFFERS GENERAL MEDICAL SERVICES THAT ALLOW PEOPLE TO LIVE HAPPIER AND HEALTHIER LIVES.

LEARN
TEENS
PARENTS

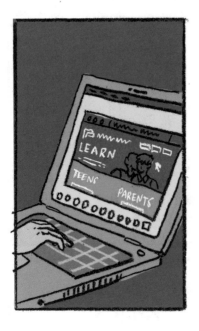

PLANNED PARENTHOOD IS AN EDUCATOR.

IN FACT, THEY'RE THE COUNTRY'S LARGEST PROVIDER OF SEX EDUCATION.

REPRODUCTI
STEM
uterus
cervix
vagina

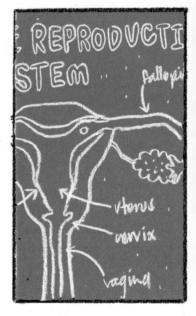

SEX EDUCATION ISN'T ONLY ABOUT DISEASES AND ABSTINENCE BUT A WHOLE VARIETY OF ISSUES

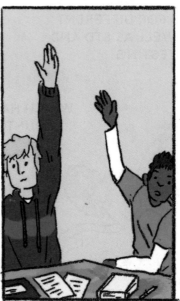

AND THAT INCLUDES SEXUALITY, RELATIONSHIPS, SEXUAL BEHAVIOR, HUMAN DEVELOPMENT, AND THE DIFFERENT CULTURES IN OUR SOCIETY

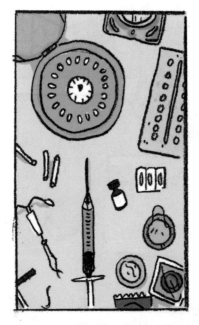

TEACHING THESE LESSONS HELPS TEENS MAKE BETTER HEALTH DECISIONS IN THE FUTURE AS WELL AS IMPARTS TO THEM THE SKILLS TO BECOME BETTER PEOPLE.

CONSE

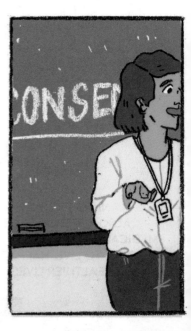

PLANNED PARENTHOOD HAS BEEN MORE THAN JUST A REPRODUCTIVE HEALTH CENTER FOR 100 YEARS.

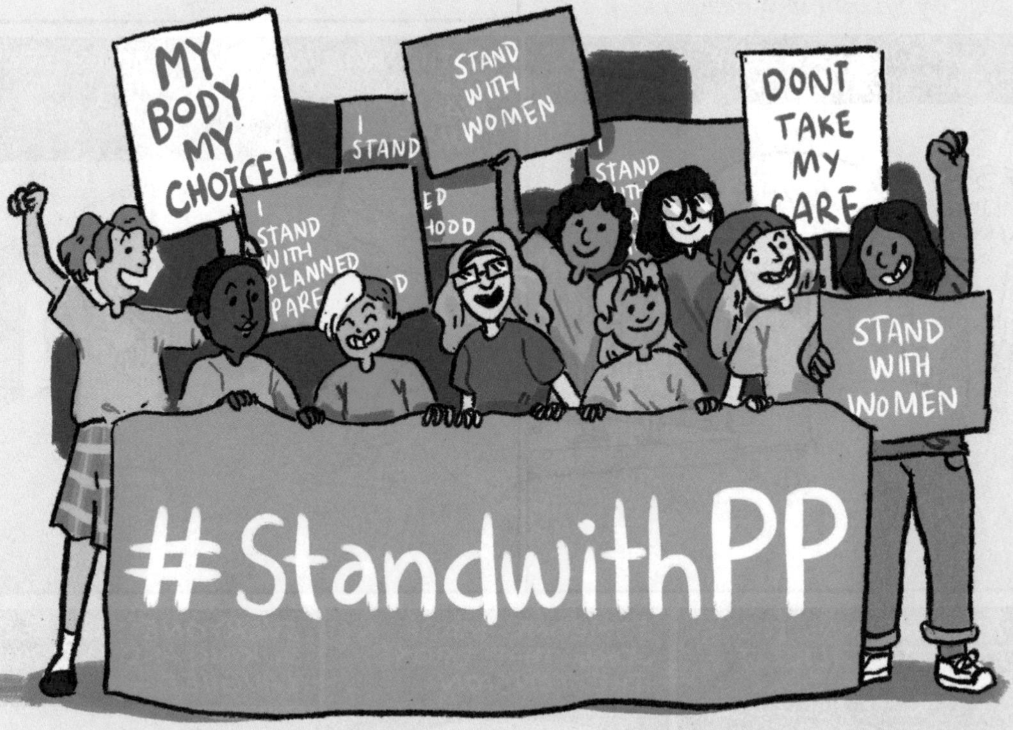
MY BODY MY CHOICE!
STAND WITH WOMEN
I STAND
I STAND WITH PLANNED
DONT TAKE MY CARE
STAND WITH WOMEN
#StandwithPP

HERE'S TO THE NEXT 100.

Story & Art: **Micha Cruz**

I TOOK A GIRLFRIEND TO GET AN ABORTION

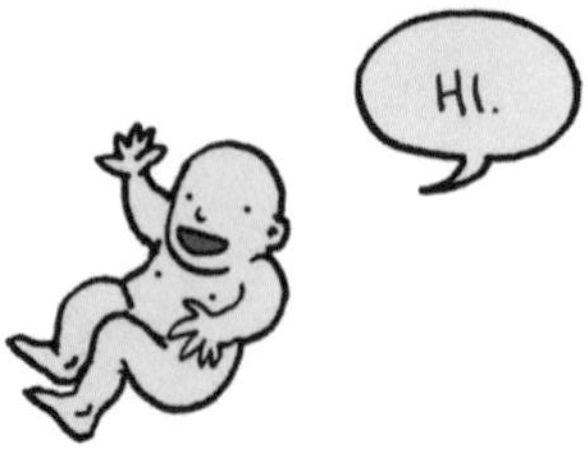
HI.

by Shannon Wheeler

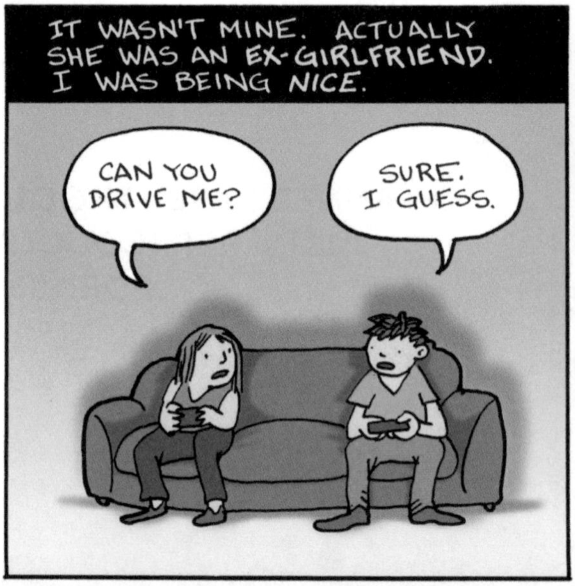
IT WASN'T MINE. ACTUALLY SHE WAS AN EX-GIRLFRIEND. I WAS BEING NICE.
CAN YOU DRIVE ME?
SURE. I GUESS.

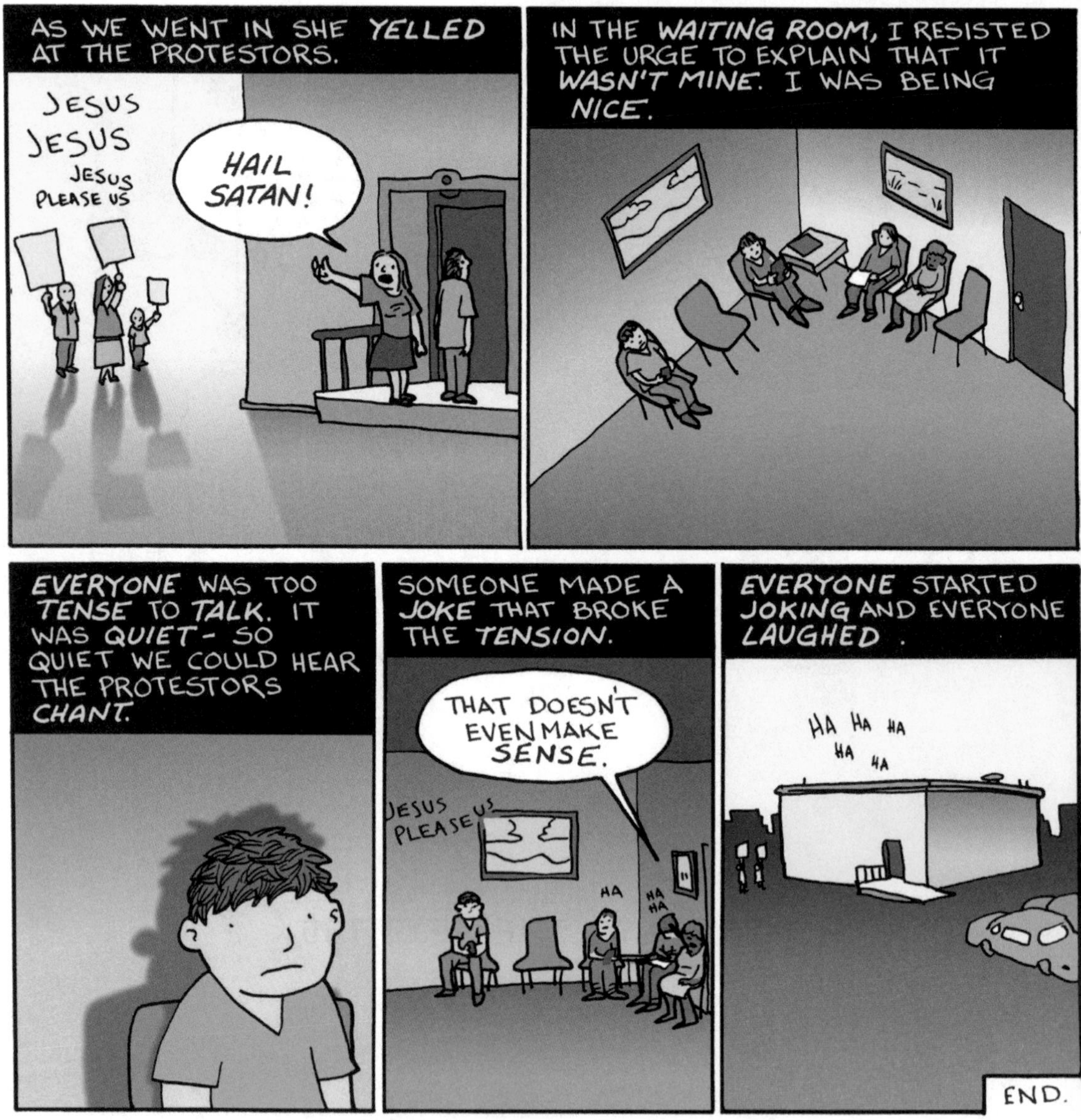
AS WE WENT IN SHE YELLED AT THE PROTESTORS.
JESUS
JESUS
JESUS PLEASE US
HAIL SATAN!
IN THE WAITING ROOM, I RESISTED THE URGE TO EXPLAIN THAT IT WASN'T MINE. I WAS BEING NICE.
EVERYONE WAS TOO TENSE TO TALK. IT WAS QUIET- SO QUIET WE COULD HEAR THE PROTESTORS CHANT.
SOMEONE MADE A JOKE THAT BROKE THE TENSION.
THAT DOESN'T EVEN MAKE SENSE.
JESUS PLEASE US
HA
HA HA
EVERYONE STARTED JOKING AND EVERYONE LAUGHED.
HA HA HA
HA HA
END.

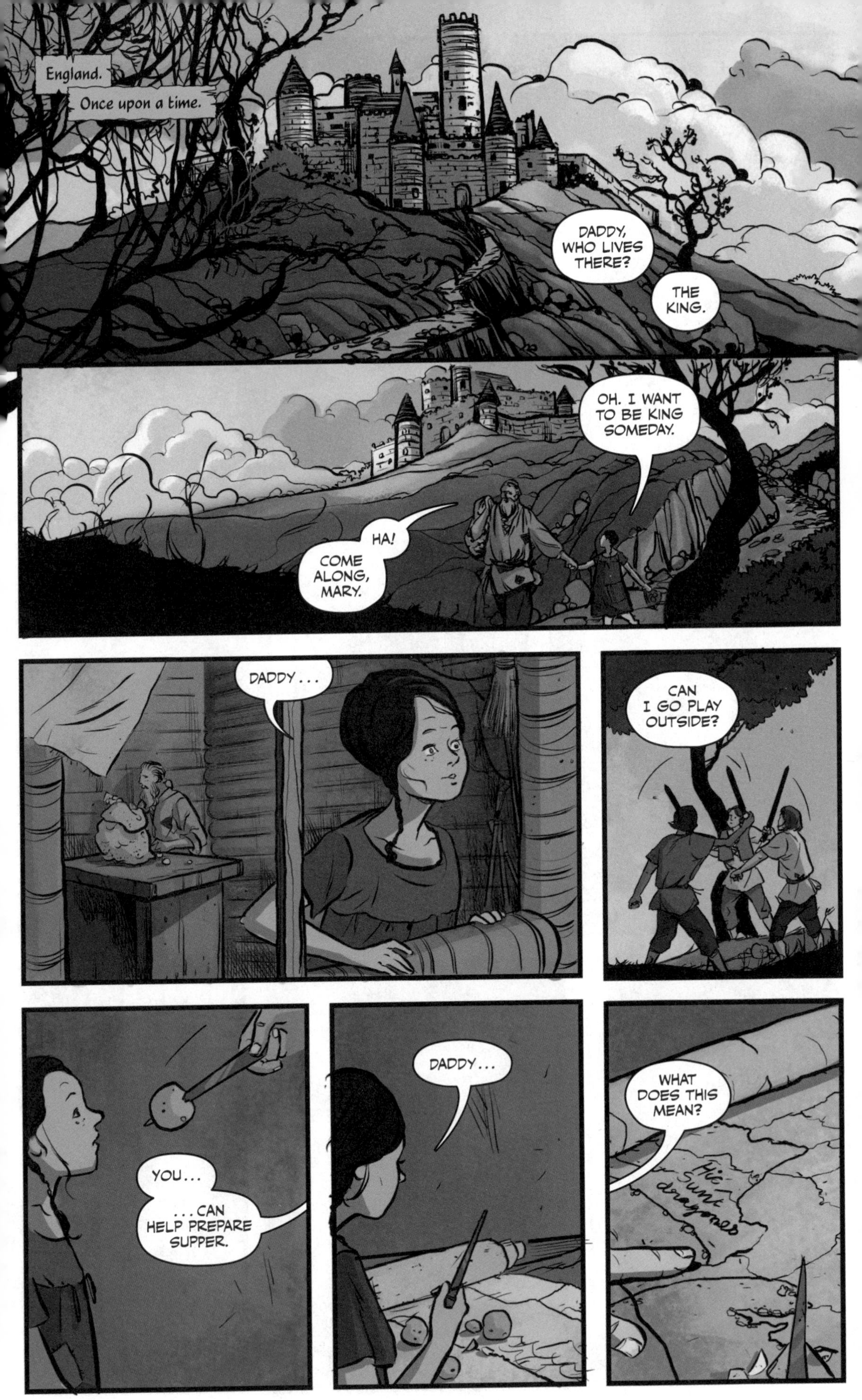
England.
Once upon a time.
DADDY, WHO LIVES THERE?
THE KING.
OH. I WANT TO BE KING SOMEDAY.
HA!
COME ALONG, MARY.
DADDY . . .
CAN I GO PLAY OUTSIDE?
YOU . . .
. . . CAN HELP PREPARE SUPPER.
DADDY . . .
WHAT DOES THIS MEAN?
Hic Sunt dragones

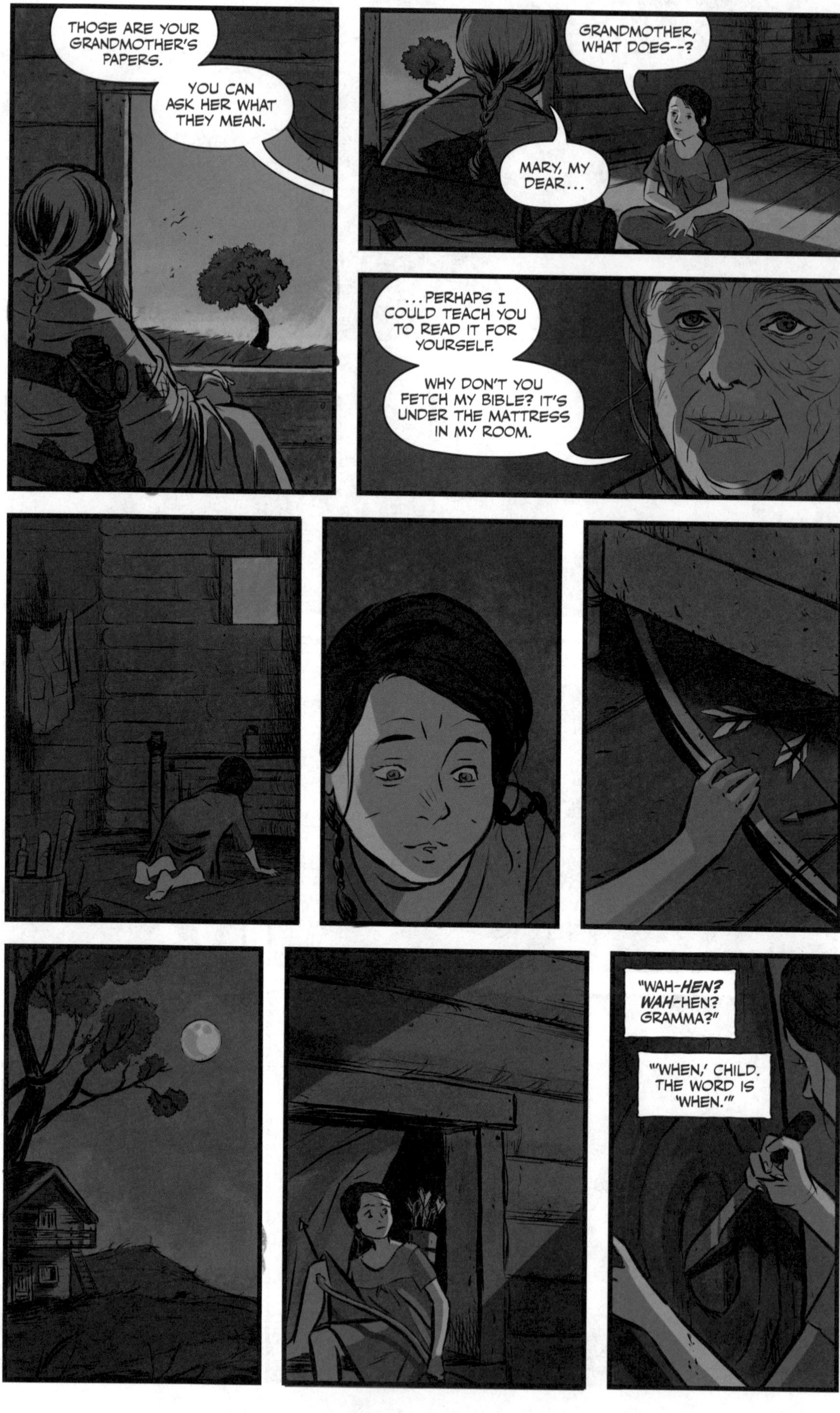
THOSE ARE YOUR GRANDMOTHER'S PAPERS.
YOU CAN ASK HER WHAT THEY MEAN.
GRANDMOTHER, WHAT DOES--?
MARY, MY DEAR...
...PERHAPS I COULD TEACH YOU TO READ IT FOR YOURSELF.
WHY DON'T YOU FETCH MY BIBLE? IT'S UNDER THE MATTRESS IN MY ROOM.
"WAH-HEN? WAH-HEN? GRAMMA?"
"'WHEN,' CHILD. THE WORD IS 'WHEN.'"

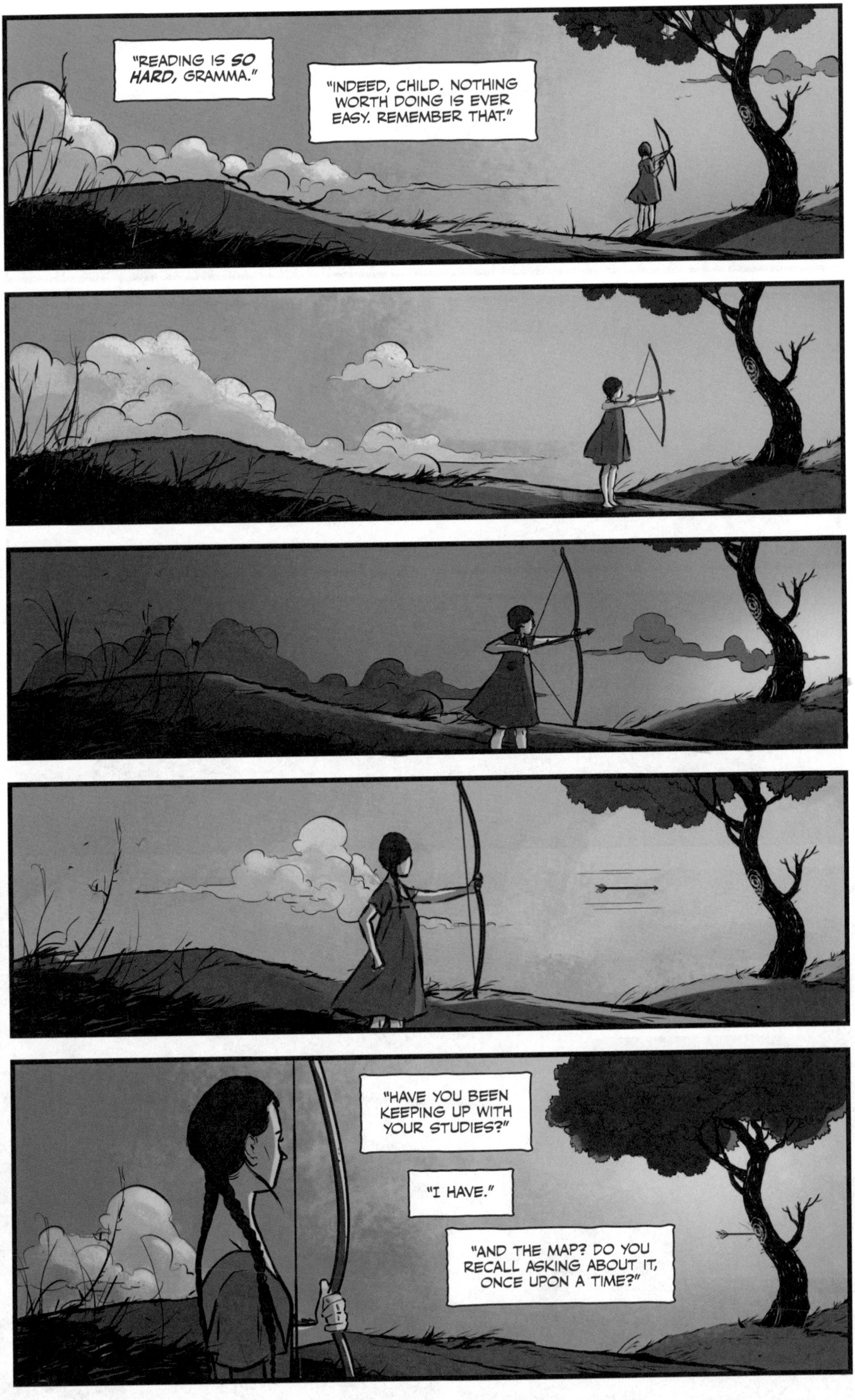
"READING IS *SO HARD,* GRAMMA."
"INDEED, CHILD. NOTHING WORTH DOING IS EVER EASY. REMEMBER THAT."
"HAVE YOU BEEN KEEPING UP WITH YOUR STUDIES?"
"I HAVE."
"AND THE MAP? DO YOU RECALL ASKING ABOUT IT, ONCE UPON A TIME?"

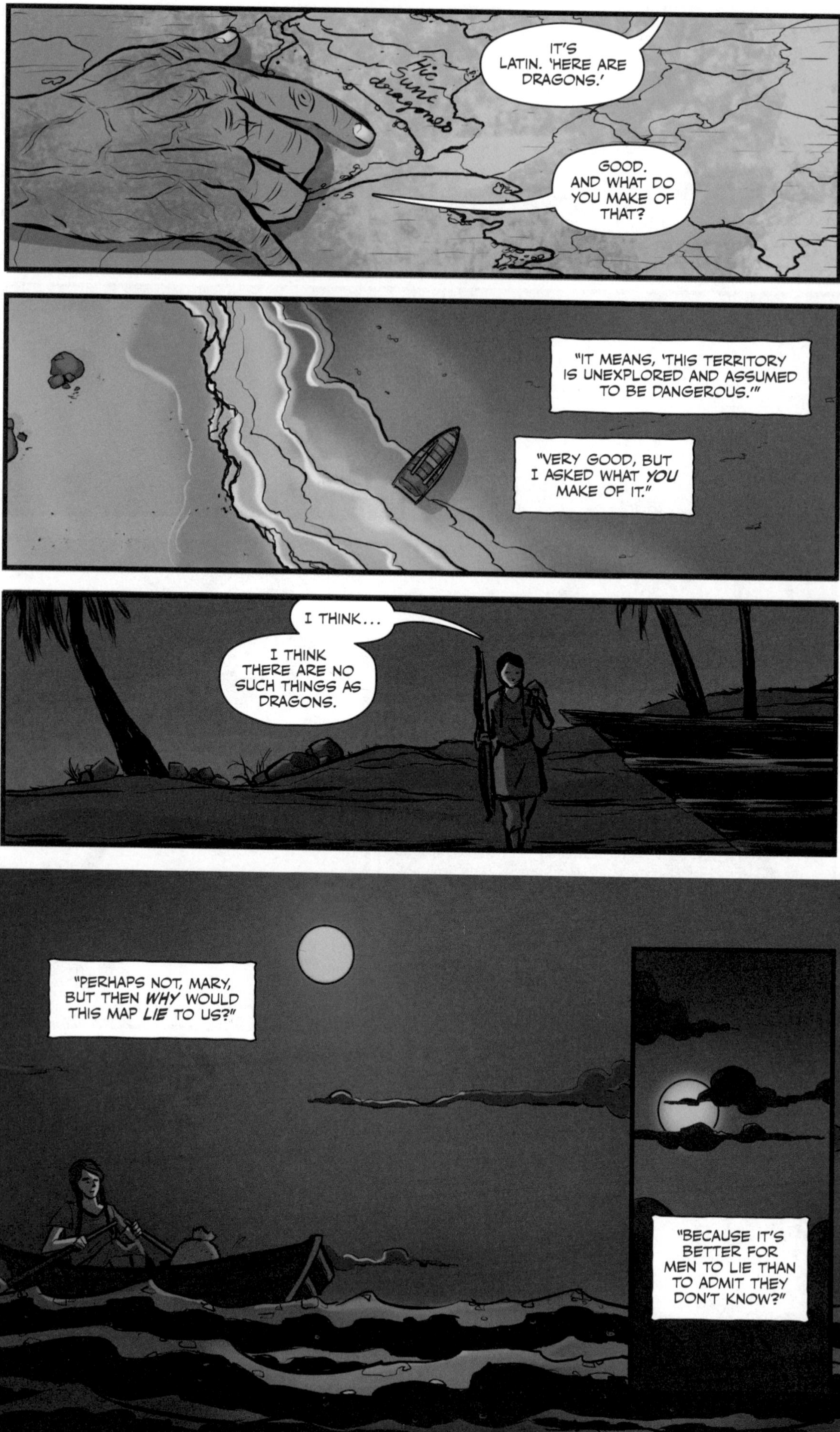
Hic Sunt dragones
IT'S LATIN. 'HERE ARE DRAGONS.'
GOOD. AND WHAT DO YOU MAKE OF THAT?
"IT MEANS, 'THIS TERRITORY IS UNEXPLORED AND ASSUMED TO BE DANGEROUS.'"
"VERY GOOD, BUT I ASKED WHAT *YOU* MAKE OF IT."
I THINK...
I THINK THERE ARE NO SUCH THINGS AS DRAGONS.
"PERHAPS NOT, MARY, BUT THEN *WHY* WOULD THIS MAP *LIE* TO US?"
"BECAUSE IT'S BETTER FOR MEN TO LIE THAN TO ADMIT THEY DON'T KNOW?"

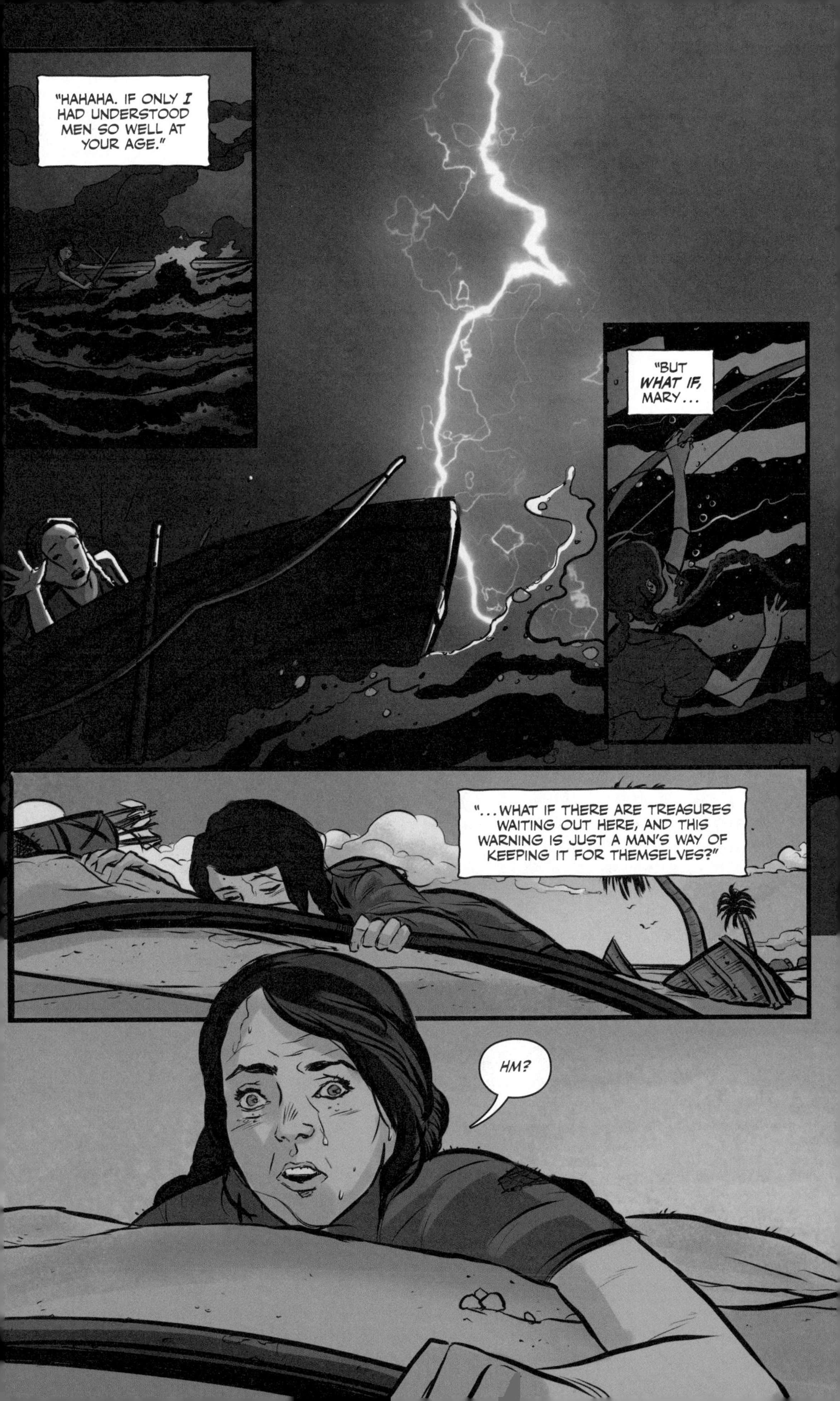
"HAHAHA. IF ONLY *I* HAD UNDERSTOOD MEN SO WELL AT YOUR AGE."
"BUT *WHAT IF,* MARY...
"...WHAT IF THERE ARE TREASURES WAITING OUT HERE, AND THIS WARNING IS JUST A MAN'S WAY OF KEEPING IT FOR THEMSELVES?"
HM?

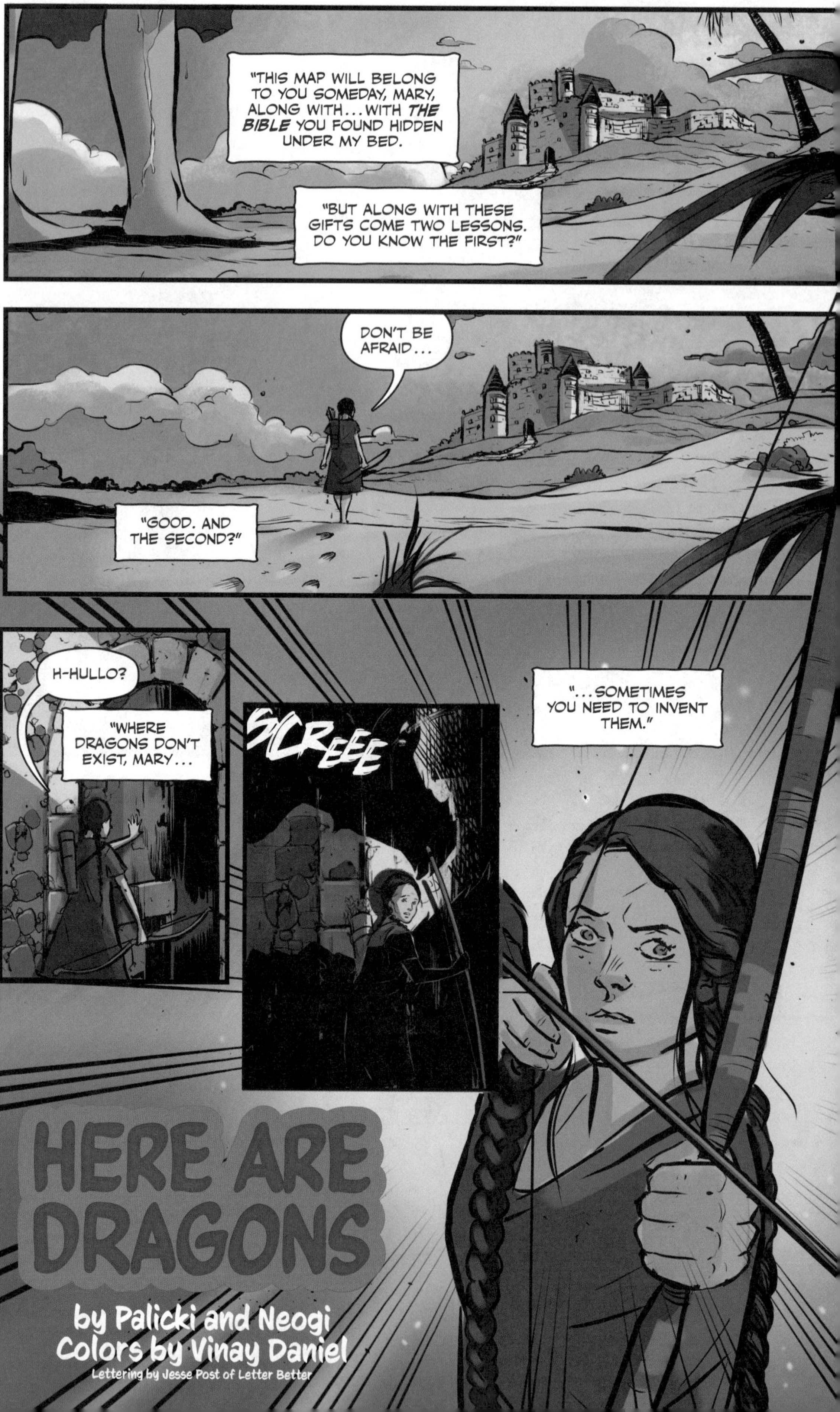
"THIS MAP WILL BELONG TO YOU SOMEDAY, MARY, ALONG WITH...WITH *THE BIBLE* YOU FOUND HIDDEN UNDER MY BED.
"BUT ALONG WITH THESE GIFTS COME TWO LESSONS. DO YOU KNOW THE FIRST?"
DON'T BE AFRAID...
"GOOD. AND THE SECOND?"
H-HULLO?
"WHERE DRAGONS DON'T EXIST, MARY...
SCREEE
"...SOMETIMES YOU NEED TO INVENT THEM."
HERE ARE DRAGONS
by Palicki and Neogi
Colors by Vinay Daniel
Lettering by Jesse Post of Letter Better

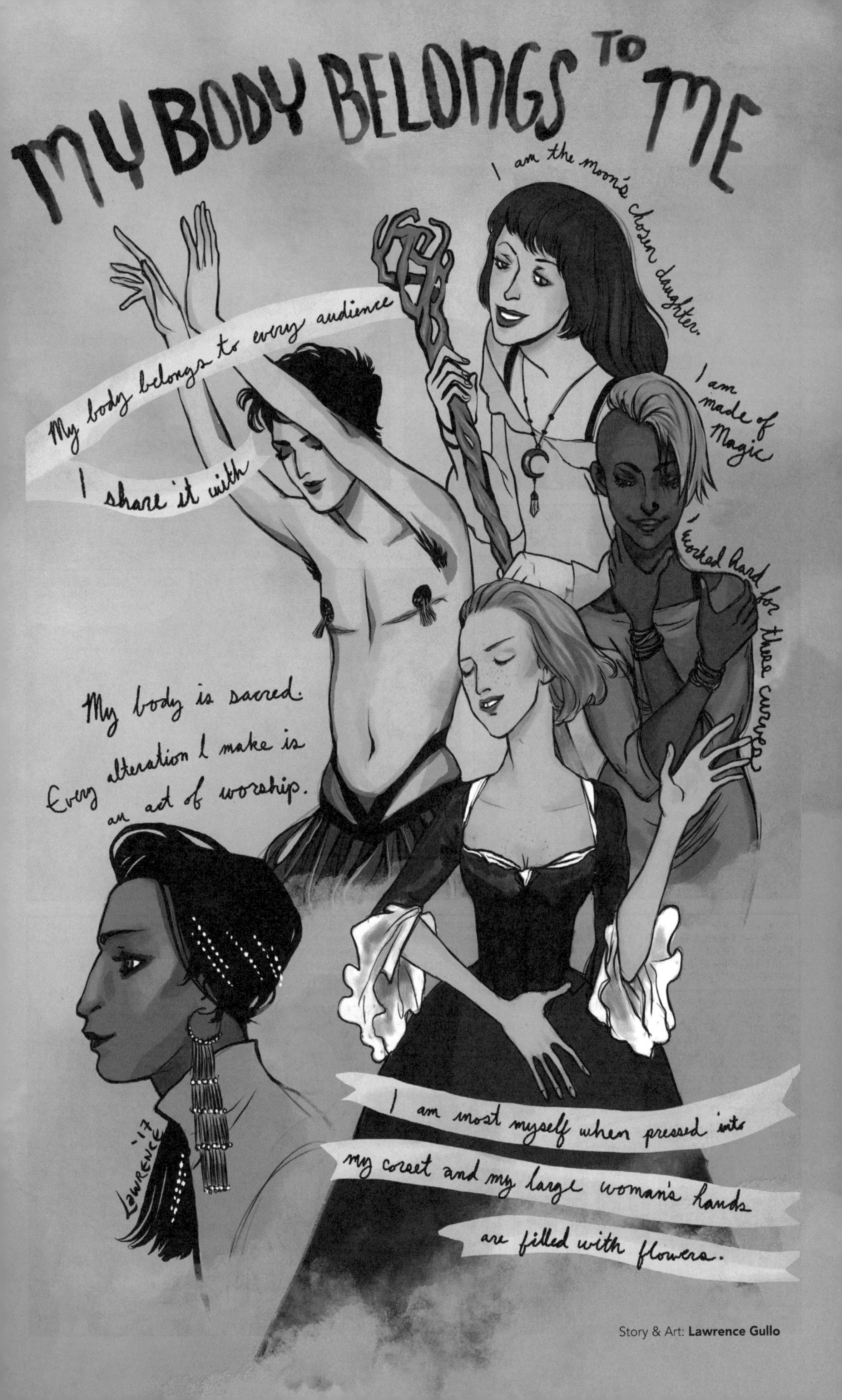
MY BODY BELONGS TO ME
I am the moon's chosen daughter.
My body belongs to every audience
I share it with
I am made of Magic
I worked hard for these curves
My body is sacred.
Every alteration I make is an act of worship.
I am most myself when pressed into my corset and my large woman's hands are filled with flowers.
LAWRENCE -17

Story & Art: **Lawrence Gullo**

MATILDA WHO?

WRITTEN AND DRAWN BY ERIC SHANOWER
COLOR BY LAURA MARTIN

DURING THE LATE NINE-TEENTH CENTURY WHEN AMERICAN WOMEN HAD LITTLE LEGAL CONTROL OVER THEIR LIVES, MATILDA JOSLYN GAGE WAS A TIRELESS FIGHTER FOR EQUAL RIGHTS FOR WOMEN.

GAGE WAS PART OF THE GREAT TRIUMVIRATE OF THE *NATIONAL WOMAN'S SUFFRAGE ASSOCIATION*.

SUSAN BROWNELL ANTHONY

MATILDA JOSLYN GAGE

ELIZABETH CADY STANTON

ANTHONY AND STANTON ARE STILL WIDELY RE-MEMBERED. BUT MATILDA GAGE WAS NEARLY WIPED FROM THE HISTORICAL RECORD.

WHY?

MATILDA ELECTA JOSLYN WAS BORN MARCH 24, 1826, IN CICERO, NEW YORK, AND RAISED TO THINK FOR HERSELF. SHE ENJOYED LISTENING TO HER FATHER'S CIRCLE OF ANTI-SLAVERY SPEAKERS AND ADVANCED THINKERS.

NOW, CONSIDERING THE DOCTRINAL POINT OF ORIGINAL SIN...

IN 1845 SHE MARRIED HENRY HILL GAGE. IN FAYETTEVILLE, NEW YORK, THEY RAISED FOUR CHILDREN IN A HOME THAT SERVED AS A STOP ON THE UNDERGROUND RAILROAD.

IN SEPTEMBER 1852, MATILDA GAGE BURST INTO WIDER PUBLIC VIEW AT THE THIRD NATIONAL WOMAN'S RIGHTS CONVENTION, HELD IN NEARBY SYRACUSE. UNKNOWN AND UNSCHEDULED, SHE GAVE HER FIRST PUBLIC SPEECH.

ALTHOUGH SO MUCH HAS BEEN SAID OF WOMAN'S UNFITNESS FOR PUBLIC LIFE, IT CAN BE SEEN, FROM SEMIRAMIS TO VICTORIA, THAT SHE HAS A PECULIAR FITNESS FOR GOVERNING...

WOMAN'S RIGHTS CONVENTION

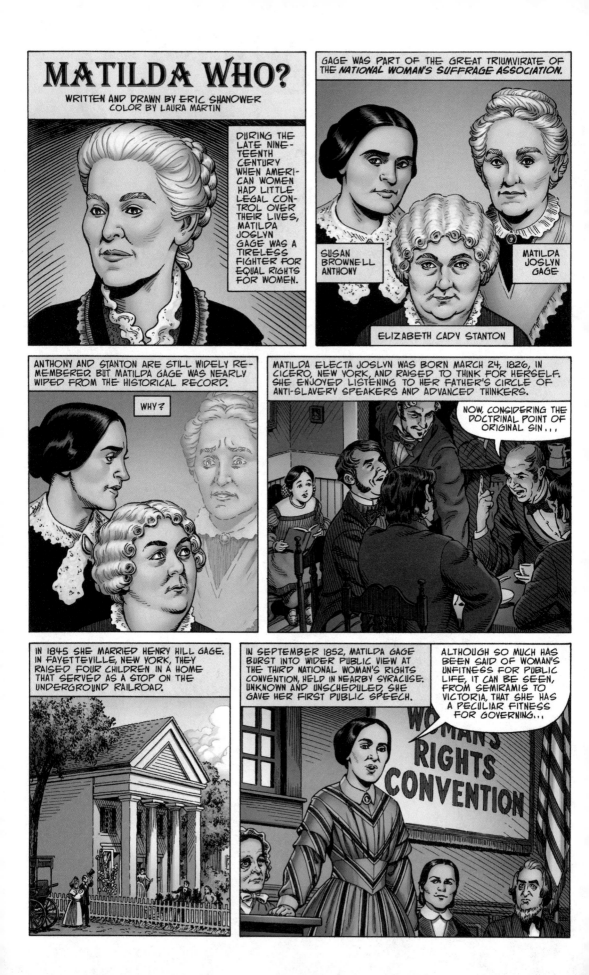

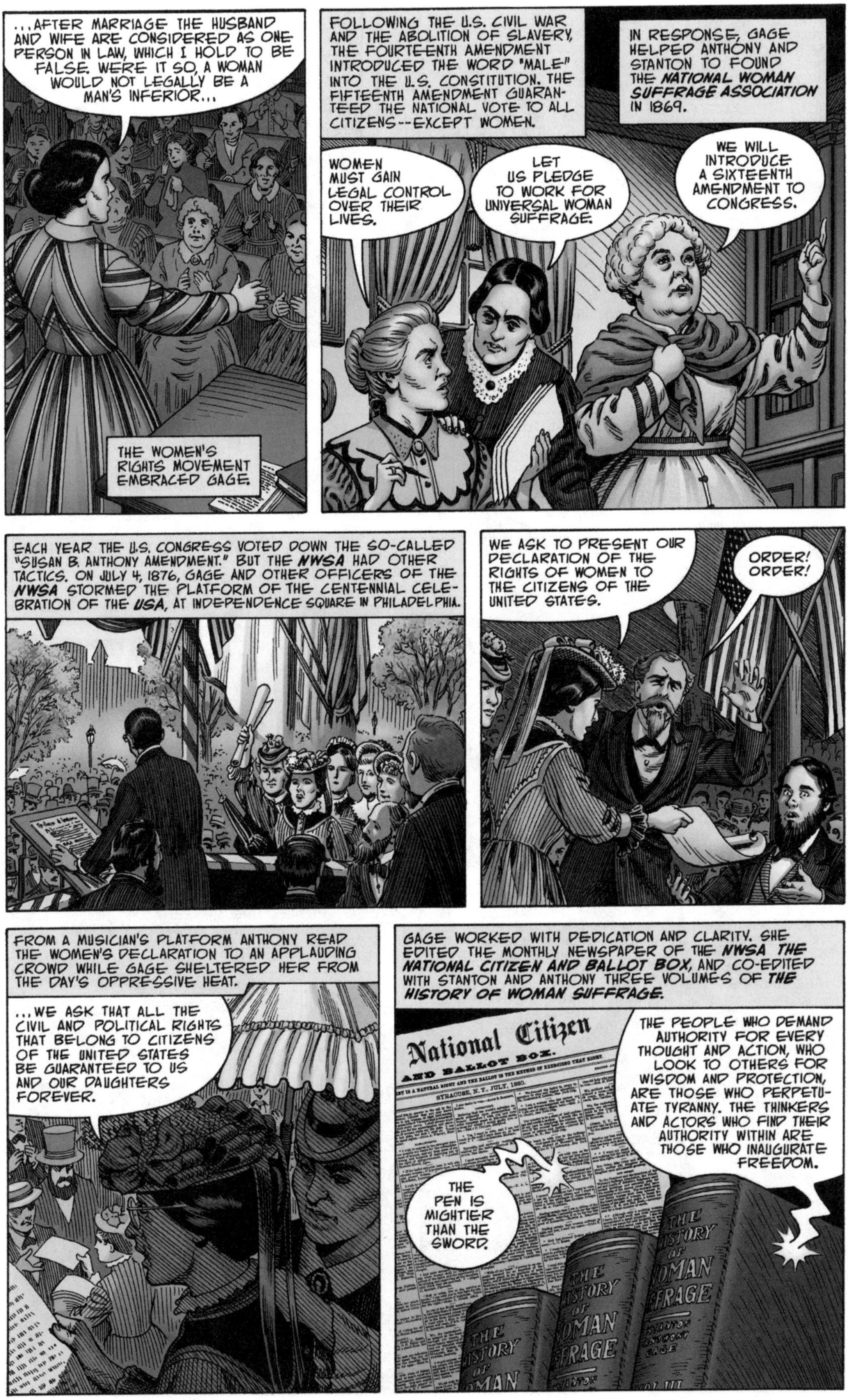
...AFTER MARRIAGE THE HUSBAND AND WIFE ARE CONSIDERED AS ONE PERSON IN LAW, WHICH I HOLD TO BE FALSE. WERE IT SO, A WOMAN WOULD NOT LEGALLY BE A MAN'S INFERIOR...
THE WOMEN'S RIGHTS MOVEMENT EMBRACED GAGE.
FOLLOWING THE U.S. CIVIL WAR AND THE ABOLITION OF SLAVERY, THE FOURTEENTH AMENDMENT INTRODUCED THE WORD "MALE" INTO THE U.S. CONSTITUTION. THE FIFTEENTH AMENDMENT GUARANTEED THE NATIONAL VOTE TO ALL CITIZENS--EXCEPT WOMEN.
IN RESPONSE, GAGE HELPED ANTHONY AND STANTON TO FOUND THE NATIONAL WOMAN SUFFRAGE ASSOCIATION IN 1869.
WOMEN MUST GAIN LEGAL CONTROL OVER THEIR LIVES.
LET US PLEDGE TO WORK FOR UNIVERSAL WOMAN SUFFRAGE.
WE WILL INTRODUCE A SIXTEENTH AMENDMENT TO CONGRESS.
EACH YEAR THE U.S. CONGRESS VOTED DOWN THE SO-CALLED "SUSAN B. ANTHONY AMENDMENT." BUT THE NWSA HAD OTHER TACTICS. ON JULY 4, 1876, GAGE AND OTHER OFFICERS OF THE NWSA STORMED THE PLATFORM OF THE CENTENNIAL CELEBRATION OF THE USA, AT INDEPENDENCE SQUARE IN PHILADELPHIA.
WE ASK TO PRESENT OUR DECLARATION OF THE RIGHTS OF WOMEN TO THE CITIZENS OF THE UNITED STATES.
ORDER! ORDER!
FROM A MUSICIAN'S PLATFORM ANTHONY READ THE WOMEN'S DECLARATION TO AN APPLAUDING CROWD WHILE GAGE SHELTERED HER FROM THE DAY'S OPPRESSIVE HEAT.
...WE ASK THAT ALL THE CIVIL AND POLITICAL RIGHTS THAT BELONG TO CITIZENS OF THE UNITED STATES BE GUARANTEED TO US AND OUR DAUGHTERS FOREVER.
GAGE WORKED WITH DEDICATION AND CLARITY. SHE EDITED THE MONTHLY NEWSPAPER OF THE NWSA THE NATIONAL CITIZEN AND BALLOT BOX, AND CO-EDITED WITH STANTON AND ANTHONY THREE VOLUMES OF THE HISTORY OF WOMAN SUFFRAGE.
National Citizen
AND BALLOT BOX.
SYRACUSE, N.Y., JULY, 1880.
THE PEOPLE WHO DEMAND AUTHORITY FOR EVERY THOUGHT AND ACTION, WHO LOOK TO OTHERS FOR WISDOM AND PROTECTION, ARE THOSE WHO PERPETUATE TYRANNY. THE THINKERS AND ACTORS WHO FIND THEIR AUTHORITY WITHIN ARE THOSE WHO INAUGURATE FREEDOM.
THE PEN IS MIGHTIER THAN THE SWORD.

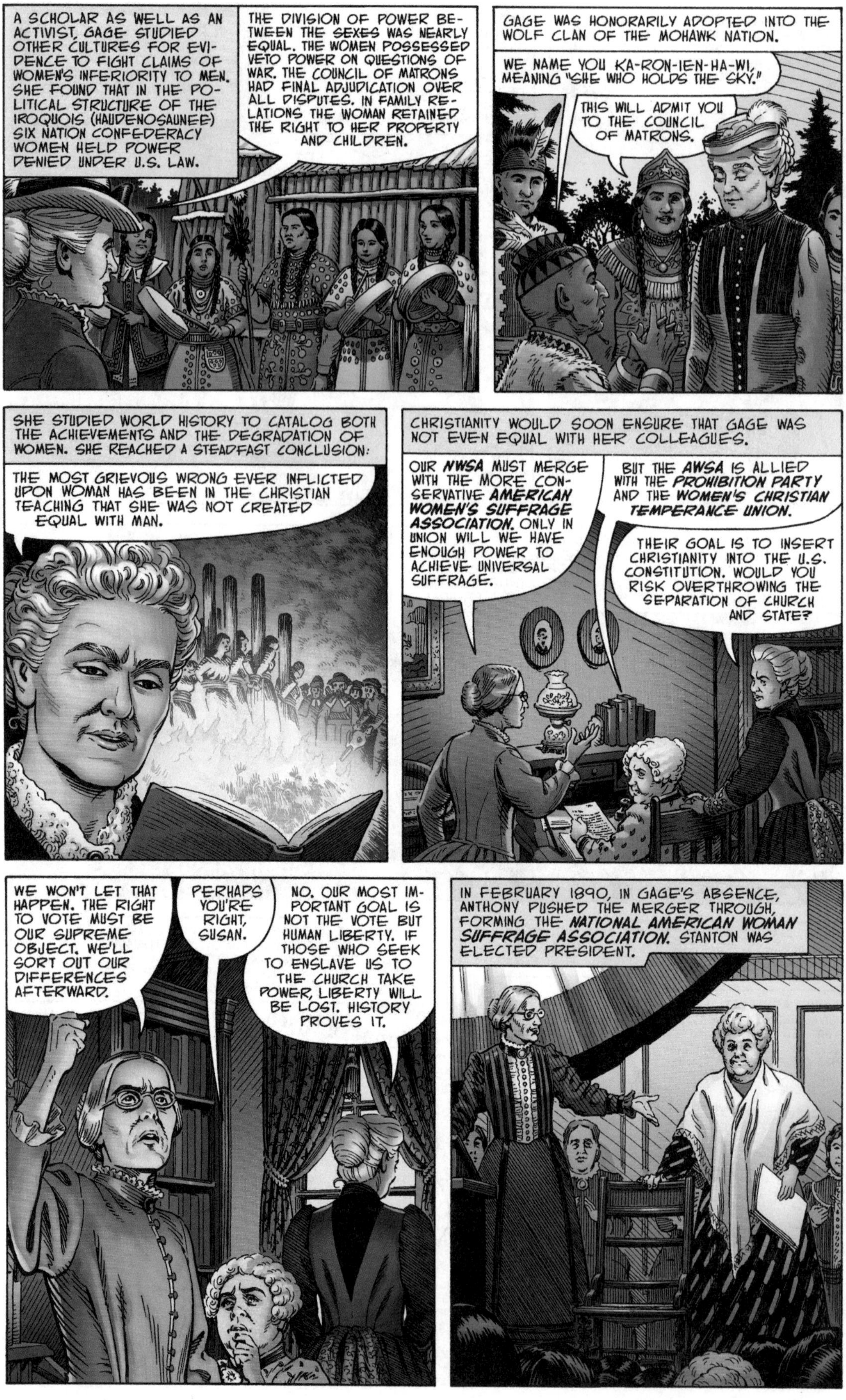

A SCHOLAR AS WELL AS AN ACTIVIST, GAGE STUDIED OTHER CULTURES FOR EVIDENCE TO FIGHT CLAIMS OF WOMEN'S INFERIORITY TO MEN. SHE FOUND THAT IN THE POLITICAL STRUCTURE OF THE IROQUOIS (HAUDENOSAUNEE) SIX NATION CONFEDERACY WOMEN HELD POWER DENIED UNDER U.S. LAW.
THE DIVISION OF POWER BETWEEN THE SEXES WAS NEARLY EQUAL. THE WOMEN POSSESSED VETO POWER ON QUESTIONS OF WAR. THE COUNCIL OF MATRONS HAD FINAL ADJUDICATION OVER ALL DISPUTES. IN FAMILY RELATIONS THE WOMAN RETAINED THE RIGHT TO HER PROPERTY AND CHILDREN.
GAGE WAS HONORARILY ADOPTED INTO THE WOLF CLAN OF THE MOHAWK NATION.
WE NAME YOU KA-RON-IEN-HA-WI, MEANING "SHE WHO HOLDS THE SKY."
THIS WILL ADMIT YOU TO THE COUNCIL OF MATRONS.
SHE STUDIED WORLD HISTORY TO CATALOG BOTH THE ACHIEVEMENTS AND THE DEGRADATION OF WOMEN. SHE REACHED A STEADFAST CONCLUSION:
THE MOST GRIEVOUS WRONG EVER INFLICTED UPON WOMAN HAS BEEN IN THE CHRISTIAN TEACHING THAT SHE WAS NOT CREATED EQUAL WITH MAN.
CHRISTIANITY WOULD SOON ENSURE THAT GAGE WAS NOT EVEN EQUAL WITH HER COLLEAGUES.
OUR **NWSA** MUST MERGE WITH THE MORE CONSERVATIVE ***AMERICAN WOMEN'S SUFFRAGE ASSOCIATION.*** ONLY IN UNION WILL WE HAVE ENOUGH POWER TO ACHIEVE UNIVERSAL SUFFRAGE.
BUT THE **AWSA** IS ALLIED WITH THE ***PROHIBITION PARTY*** AND THE ***WOMEN'S CHRISTIAN TEMPERANCE UNION.***
THEIR GOAL IS TO INSERT CHRISTIANITY INTO THE U.S. CONSTITUTION. WOULD YOU RISK OVERTHROWING THE SEPARATION OF CHURCH AND STATE?
WE WON'T LET THAT HAPPEN. THE RIGHT TO VOTE MUST BE OUR SUPREME OBJECT. WE'LL SORT OUT OUR DIFFERENCES AFTERWARD.
PERHAPS YOU'RE RIGHT, SUSAN.
NO. OUR MOST IMPORTANT GOAL IS NOT THE VOTE BUT HUMAN LIBERTY. IF THOSE WHO SEEK TO ENSLAVE US TO THE CHURCH TAKE POWER, LIBERTY WILL BE LOST. HISTORY PROVES IT.
IN FEBRUARY 1890, IN GAGE'S ABSENCE, ANTHONY PUSHED THE MERGER THROUGH, FORMING THE ***NATIONAL AMERICAN WOMAN SUFFRAGE ASSOCIATION.*** STANTON WAS ELECTED PRESIDENT.

FEELING BETRAYED, GAGE FORMED THE RIVAL **WOMAN'S NATIONAL LIBERAL UNION**. AT ITS FOUNDING CONVENTION IN WASHINGTON, DC, SHE SPOKE ON "THE DANGERS OF THE HOUR."

...THE STRONGHOLD OF THE CHURCH HAS EVER BEEN THE IGNORANCE AND DEGRADATION OF WOMEN. ITS CONTROL OVER WOMAN IN THE TWO QUESTIONS OF MARRIAGE AND EDUCATION HAVE GIVEN IT KEYS OF POWER MORE POTENT THAN THOSE OF PETER...

ANTHONY LASHED OUT.

MRS. GAGE'S ORGANIZATION IS RIDICULOUS, ABSURD, SECTARIAN, BIGOTED, AND TOO HORRIBLE FOR ANYTHING!

THE MARGINALIZATION OF MATILDA JOSLYN GAGE WAS IN FULL GEAR.

BUT GAGE COULDN'T BE COMPLETELY ERASED. IN 1893 SHE PUBLISHED THE FULLEST EXPRESSION OF HER VIEWS, THE BOOK **WOMAN, CHURCH AND STATE**. CONTROVERSIAL AT THE TIME -- EVEN RADICAL -- IT REMAINS COMPELLING READING TODAY.

THE WHOLE THEORY REGARDING WOMAN, UNDER CHRISTIANITY, HAS BEEN BASED UPON THE CONCEPTION THAT SHE HAD NO RIGHT TO LIVE FOR HERSELF ALONE.

HER DUTY TO OTHERS HAS CONTINUOUSLY BEEN PLACED BEFORE HER AND HER TRAINING HAS EVER BEEN THAT OF SELF-SACRIFICE.

FIVE YEARS LATER, ON MARCH 18, 1898, GAGE DIED. HER MEMORIAL STONE IN THE FAYETTEVILLE CEMETERY BEARS HER FAVORITE MOTTO.

THERE IS A WORD SWEETER THAN MOTHER, HOME, OR HEAVEN; THAT WORD IS LIBERTY.

GAGE
MATILDA JOSLYN
1826 GAGE 1898
THERE IS A WORD
SWEETER THAN MOTHER
HOME OR HEAVEN
THAT WORD IS LIBERTY

PERHAPS GAGE'S INFLUENCE SURVIVED MOST STRONGLY IN THE WRITINGS OF HER SON-IN-LAW, L. FRANK BAUM, WHOSE OZ BOOKS FOR CHILDREN PRESENTED AN IMMORTAL LAND OF HARMONY WHERE WOMEN RULE SUPREME, RELIGION HOLDS NO SWAY, AND ALL CITIZENS -- EVEN THOSE NOT ACTUALLY HUMAN -- ARE RESPECTED.

THE REDISCOVERY OF GAGE HERSELF BEGAN WITHIN THE WOMEN'S MOVEMENT OF THE LATE TWENTIETH CENTURY. THANKS LARGELY TO THE EFFORTS OF HER BIOGRAPHER, SALLY ROESCH WAGNER, GAGE'S HOME IN FAYETTEVILLE IS NOW A CENTER FOR SOCIAL JUSTICE DIALOGUE, WHERE HER LEGACY IS A BEACON TO ALL WHO VALUE THE EMPOWERMENT OF WOMEN AND OF HUMANITY AS A WHOLE.

A BRIGHTER DAY IS TO COME FOR THE WORLD, A DAY WHEN THE INTUITIONS OF WOMAN'S SOUL SHALL BE ACCEPTED AS PART OF HUMANITY'S SPIRITUAL WEALTH.

MATILDA JOSLYN GAGE
NATIONALLY KNOWN ABOLITIONIST
AND WOMEN'S RIGHTS ADVOCATE
LIVED HERE FROM 1854
UNTIL HER DEATH IN 1898

GAGE CENTER

THE END

SPECIAL THANKS TO DR. SALLY ROESCH WAGNER AND TO DR. GITA MORENA.

THE MORALITY OF BIRTH CONTROL

STORY: OCTOBER CRIFASI ART: JAMES ROMBERGER AND MARGUERITE VAN COOK

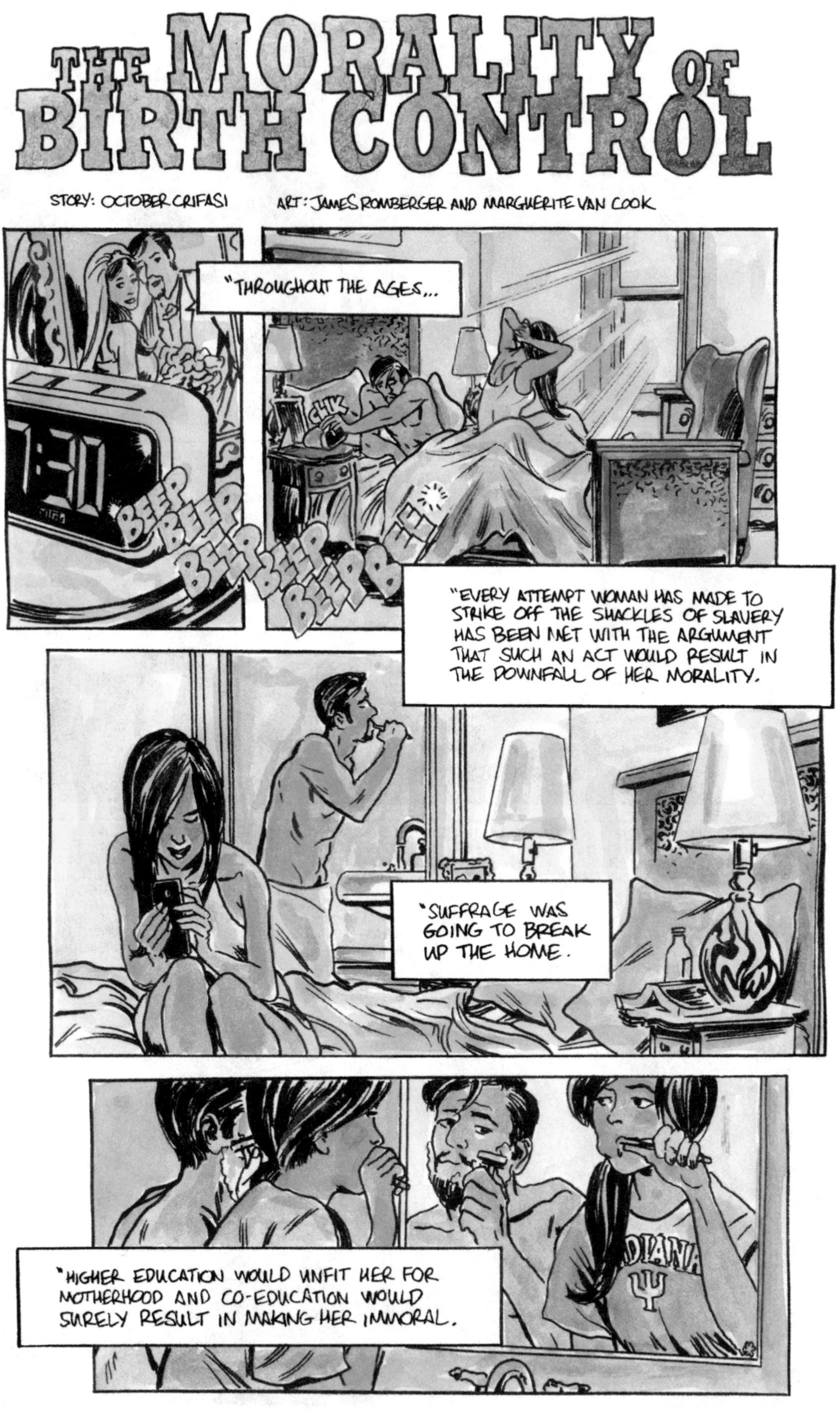

"THROUGHOUT THE AGES...
BEEP BEEP BEEP BEEP BEEP
CHK
"EVERY ATTEMPT WOMAN HAS MADE TO STRIKE OFF THE SHACKLES OF SLAVERY HAS BEEN MET WITH THE ARGUMENT THAT SUCH AN ACT WOULD RESULT IN THE DOWNFALL OF HER MORALITY.
"SUFFRAGE WAS GOING TO BREAK UP THE HOME.
"HIGHER EDUCATION WOULD UNFIT HER FOR MOTHERHOOD AND CO-EDUCATION WOULD SURELY RESULT IN MAKING HER IMMORAL.

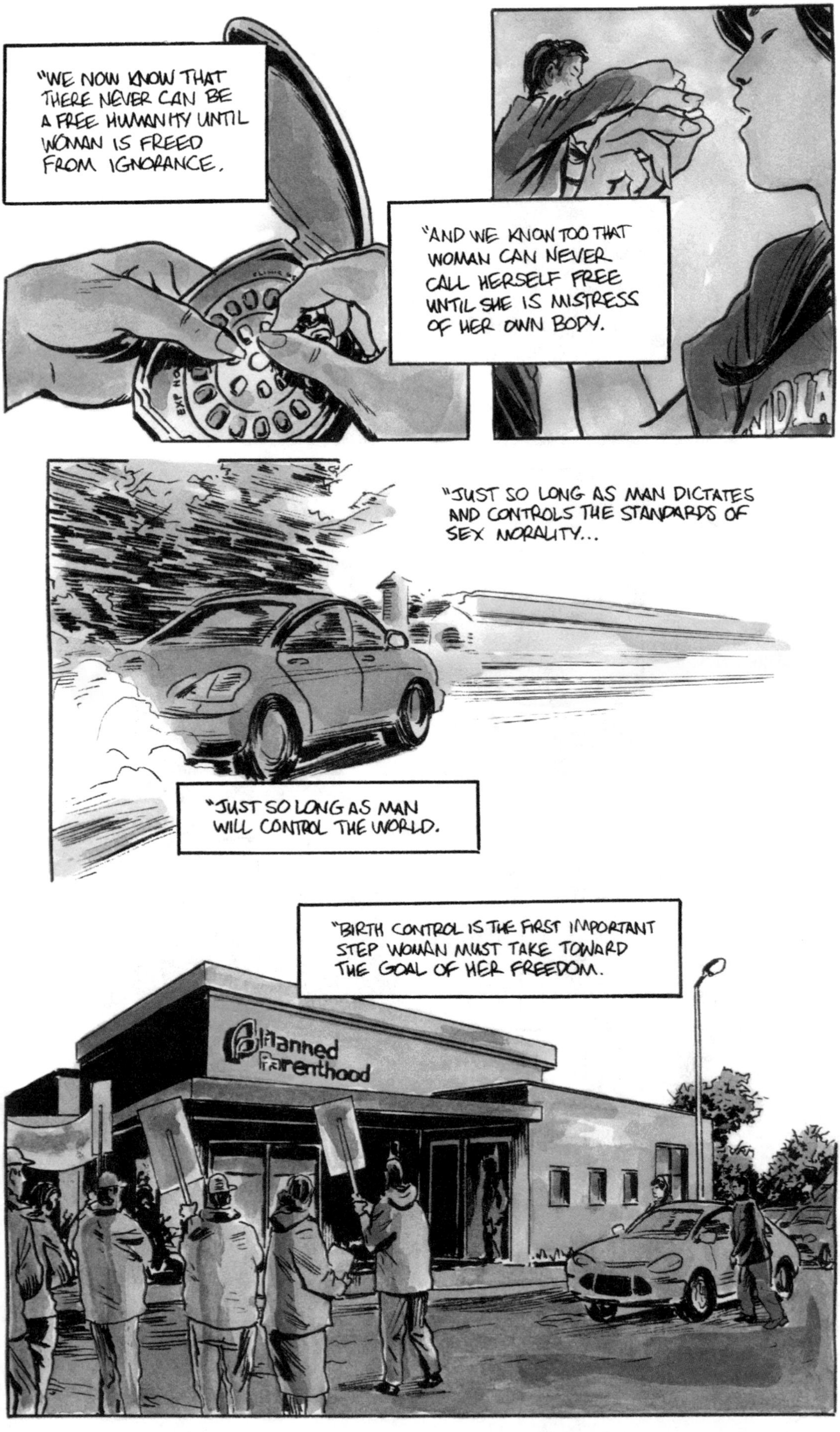
"WE NOW KNOW THAT THERE NEVER CAN BE A FREE HUMANITY UNTIL WOMAN IS FREED FROM IGNORANCE.
"AND WE KNOW TOO THAT WOMAN CAN NEVER CALL HERSELF FREE UNTIL SHE IS MISTRESS OF HER OWN BODY.
"JUST SO LONG AS MAN DICTATES AND CONTROLS THE STANDARDS OF SEX MORALITY...
"JUST SO LONG AS MAN WILL CONTROL THE WORLD.
"BIRTH CONTROL IS THE FIRST IMPORTANT STEP WOMAN MUST TAKE TOWARD THE GOAL OF HER FREEDOM.
Planned Parenthood

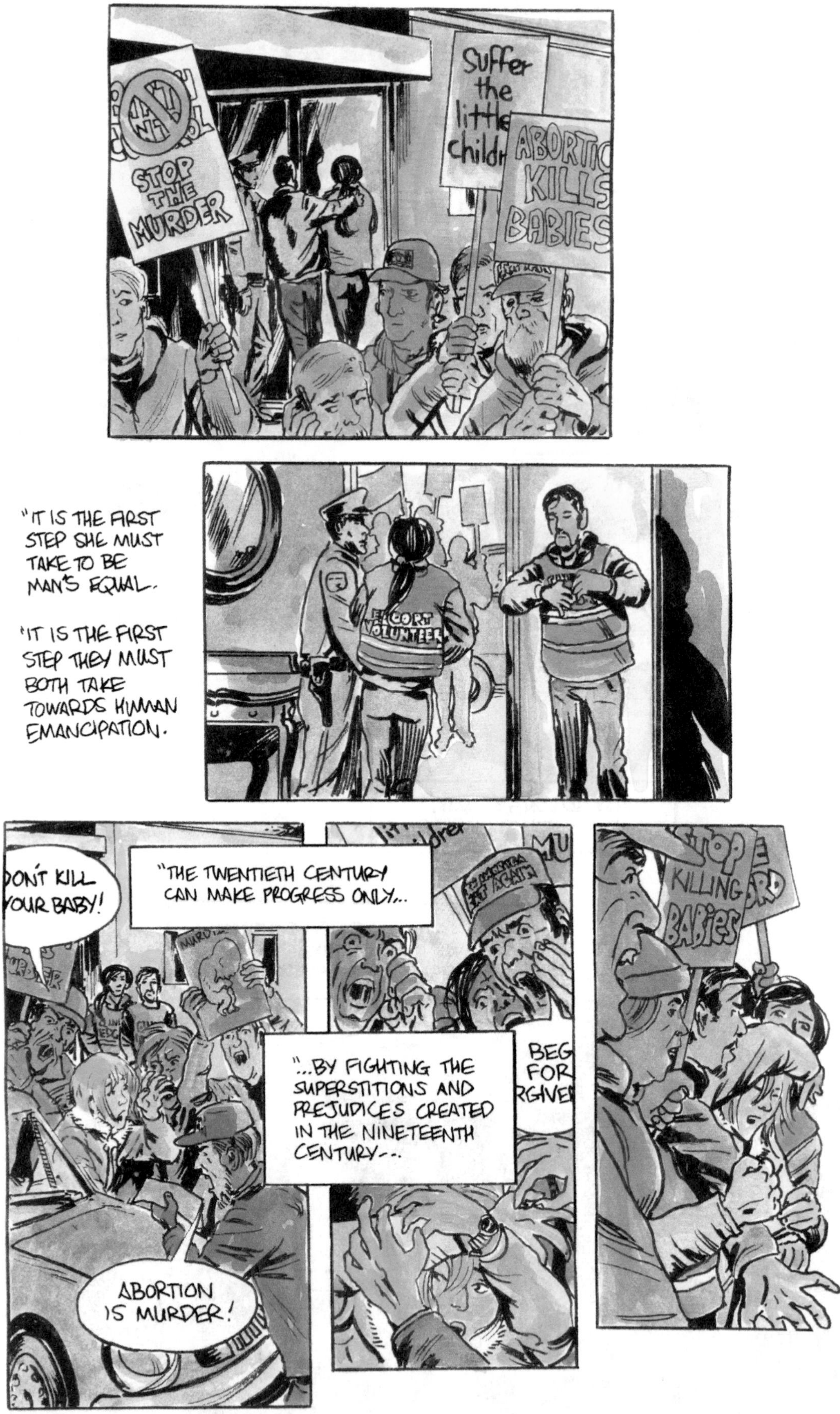
STOP THE MURDER
Suffer the little childr
ABORTIO KILLS BABIES
"IT IS THE FIRST STEP SHE MUST TAKE TO BE MAN'S EQUAL.
"IT IS THE FIRST STEP THEY MUST BOTH TAKE TOWARDS HUMAN EMANCIPATION.
ESCORT VOLUNTEER
DON'T KILL YOUR BABY!
"THE TWENTIETH CENTURY CAN MAKE PROGRESS ONLY...
ABORTION IS MURDER!
"...BY FIGHTING THE SUPERSTITIONS AND PREJUDICES CREATED IN THE NINETEENTH CENTURY...
BEG FOR RGIVE
STOP KILLING BABIES

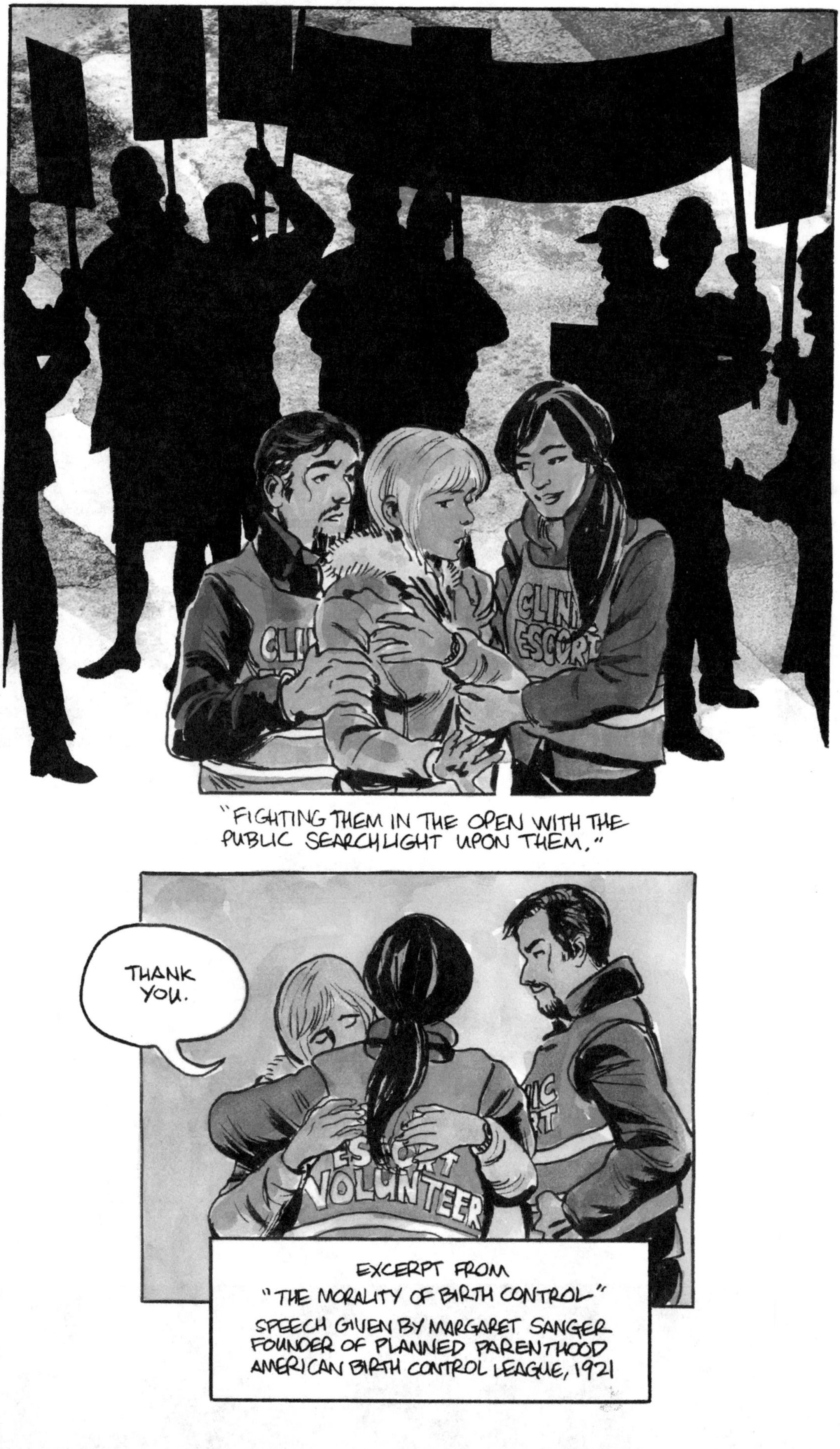
"FIGHTING THEM IN THE OPEN WITH THE PUBLIC SEARCHLIGHT UPON THEM."
THANK YOU.
VOLUNTEER
EXCERPT FROM
"THE MORALITY OF BIRTH CONTROL"
SPEECH GIVEN BY MARGARET SANGER
FOUNDER OF PLANNED PARENTHOOD
AMERICAN BIRTH CONTROL LEAGUE, 1921

EPIDEMIC

NIKI SMITH

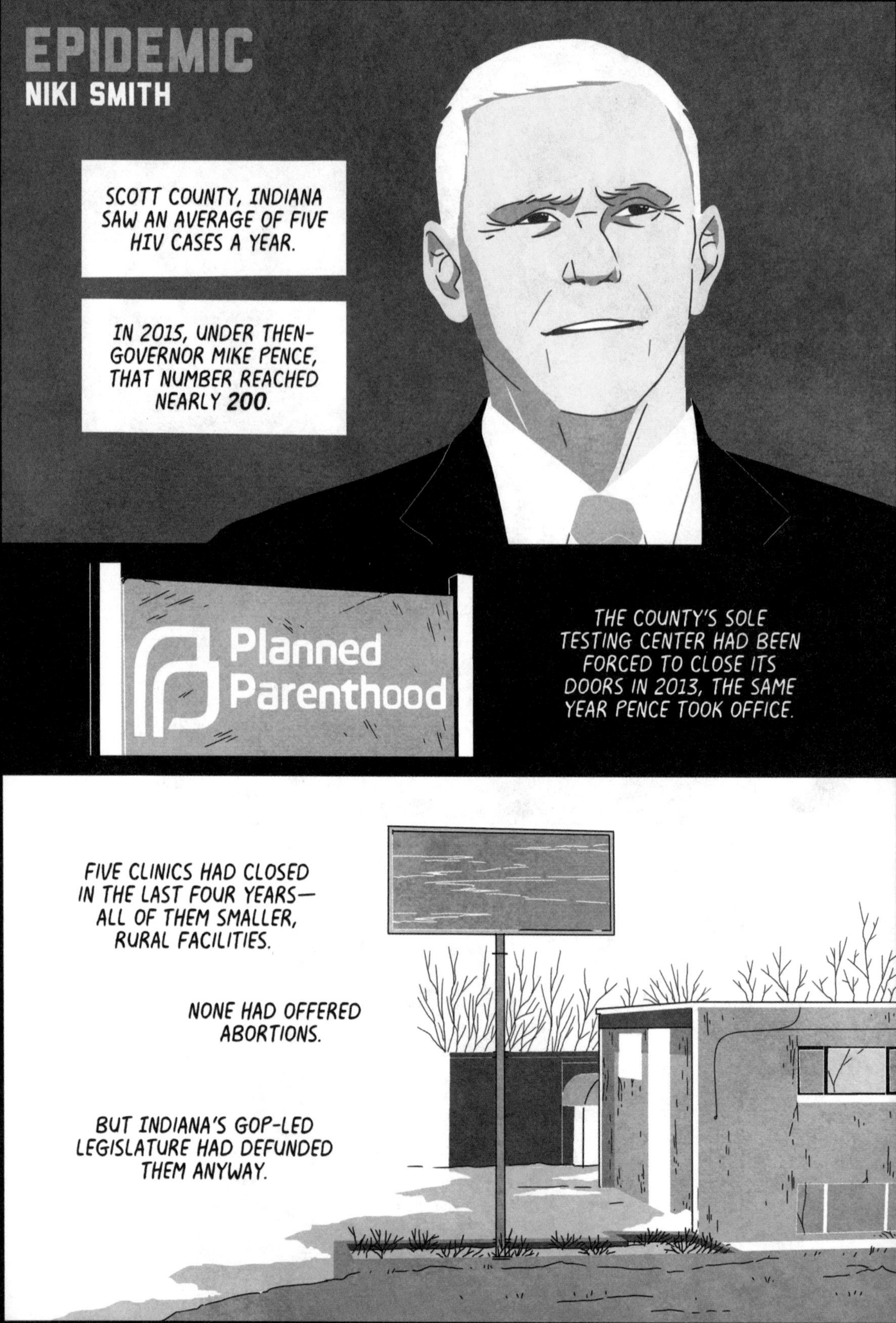

SCOTT COUNTY, INDIANA SAW AN AVERAGE OF FIVE HIV CASES A YEAR.
IN 2015, UNDER THEN-GOVERNOR MIKE PENCE, THAT NUMBER REACHED NEARLY **200**.
Planned Parenthood
THE COUNTY'S SOLE TESTING CENTER HAD BEEN FORCED TO CLOSE ITS DOORS IN 2013, THE SAME YEAR PENCE TOOK OFFICE.
FIVE CLINICS HAD CLOSED IN THE LAST FOUR YEARS—ALL OF THEM SMALLER, RURAL FACILITIES.
NONE HAD OFFERED ABORTIONS.
BUT INDIANA'S GOP-LED LEGISLATURE HAD DEFUNDED THEM ANYWAY.

THIS WAS MY MOTHER, IN 1986.

AND THIS WAS ME.

THE HEIGHT OF THE AIDS EPIDEMIC.
BIOSAFETY LEVEL 3.

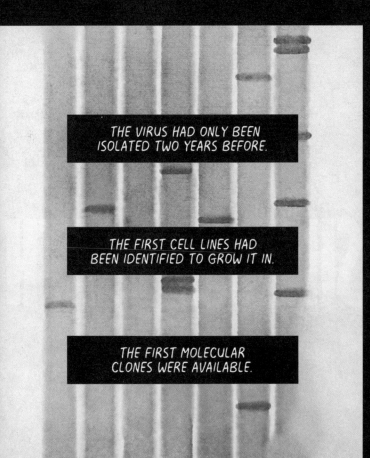

THE VIRUS HAD ONLY BEEN ISOLATED TWO YEARS BEFORE.

THE FIRST CELL LINES HAD BEEN IDENTIFIED TO GROW IT IN.

THE FIRST MOLECULAR CLONES WERE AVAILABLE.

AND EVERY YEAR, THOUSANDS DIED.

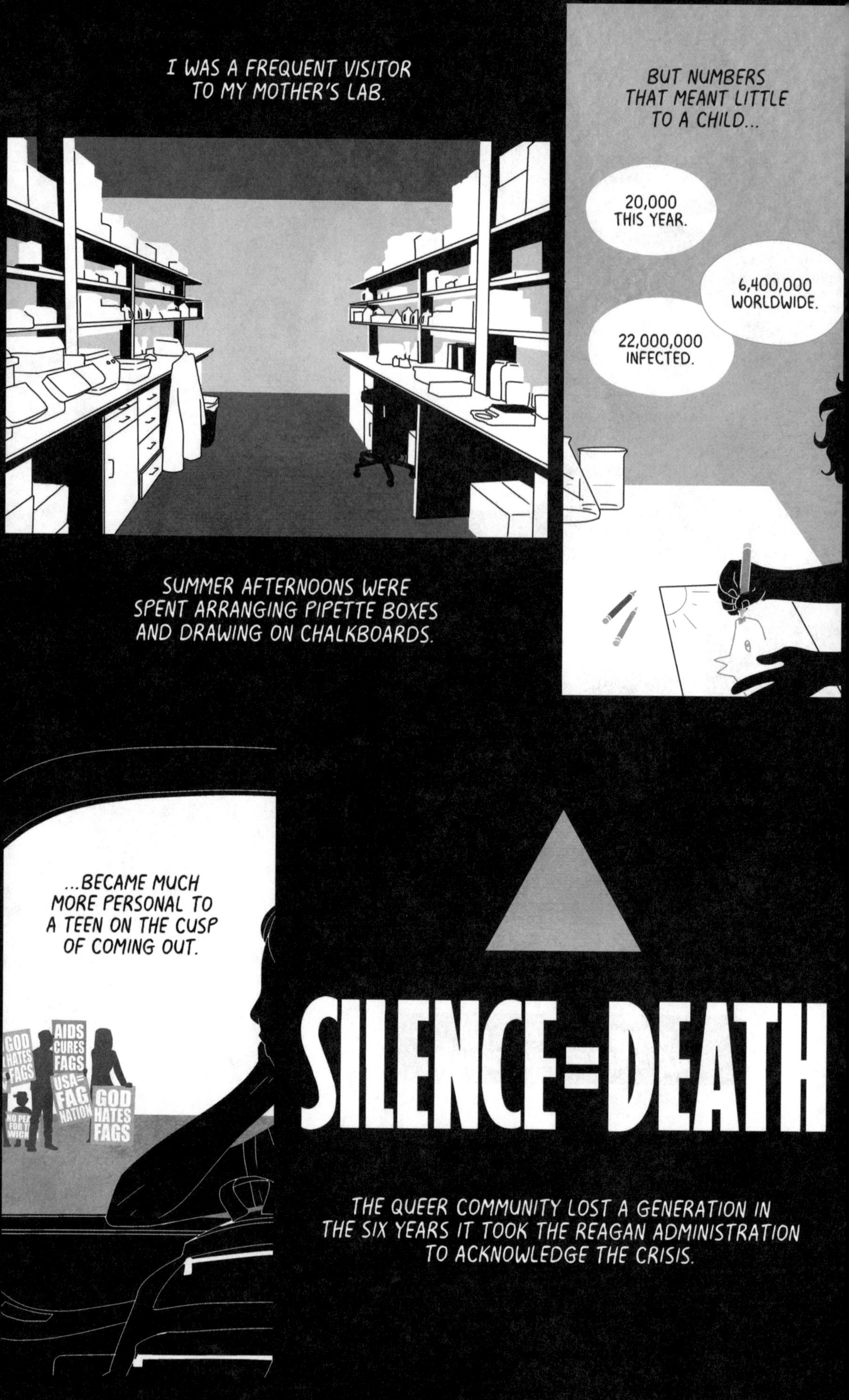
I WAS A FREQUENT VISITOR TO MY MOTHER'S LAB.
SUMMER AFTERNOONS WERE SPENT ARRANGING PIPETTE BOXES AND DRAWING ON CHALKBOARDS.
BUT NUMBERS THAT MEANT LITTLE TO A CHILD...
20,000 THIS YEAR.
6,400,000 WORLDWIDE.
22,000,000 INFECTED.
...BECAME MUCH MORE PERSONAL TO A TEEN ON THE CUSP OF COMING OUT.
GOD HATES FAGS
AIDS CURES FAGS
USA= FAG NATION
GOD HATES FAGS
SILENCE=DEATH
THE QUEER COMMUNITY LOST A GENERATION IN THE SIX YEARS IT TOOK THE REAGAN ADMINISTRATION TO ACKNOWLEDGE THE CRISIS.

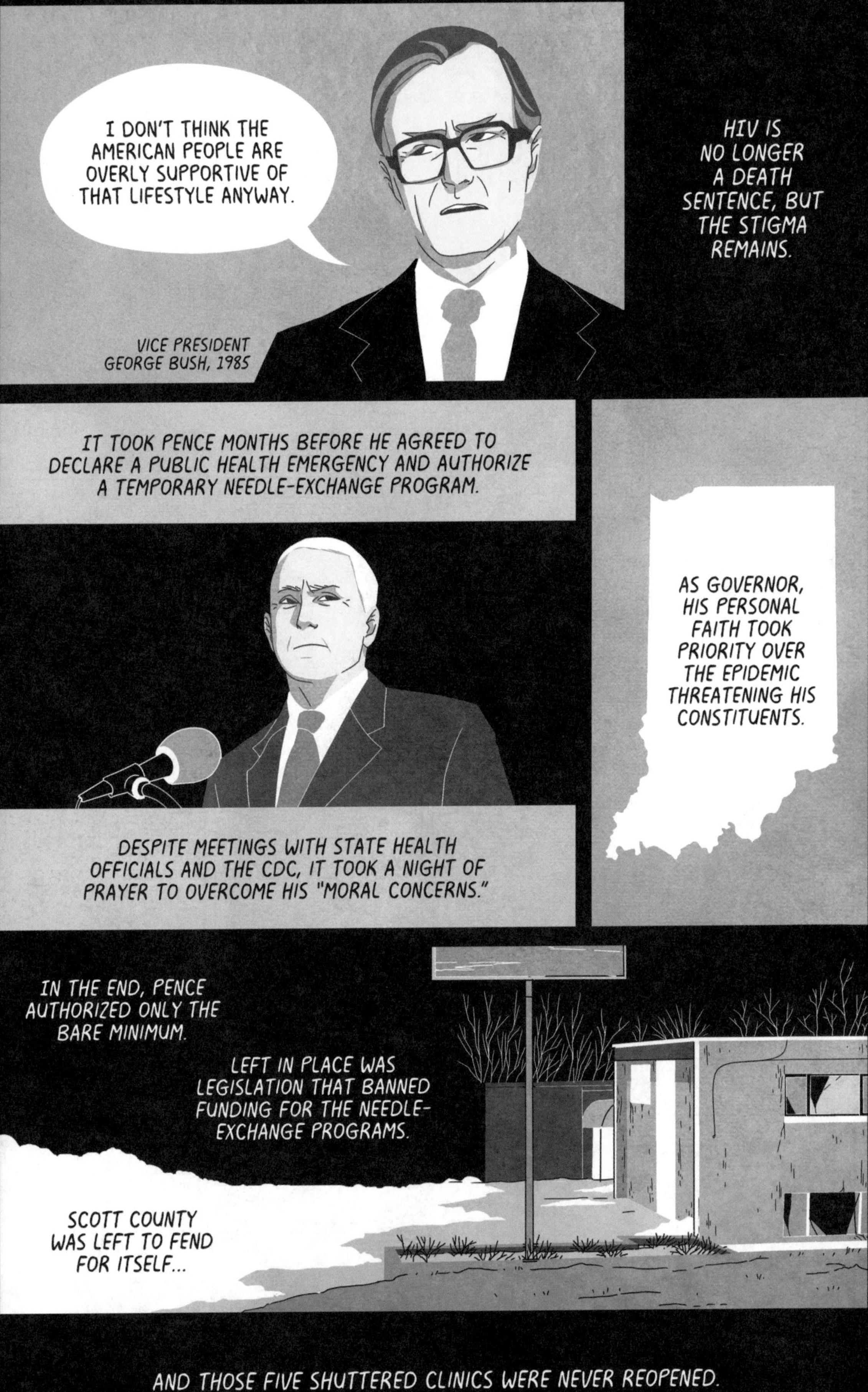
I DON'T THINK THE AMERICAN PEOPLE ARE OVERLY SUPPORTIVE OF THAT LIFESTYLE ANYWAY.
VICE PRESIDENT GEORGE BUSH, 1985
HIV IS NO LONGER A DEATH SENTENCE, BUT THE STIGMA REMAINS.
IT TOOK PENCE MONTHS BEFORE HE AGREED TO DECLARE A PUBLIC HEALTH EMERGENCY AND AUTHORIZE A TEMPORARY NEEDLE-EXCHANGE PROGRAM.
DESPITE MEETINGS WITH STATE HEALTH OFFICIALS AND THE CDC, IT TOOK A NIGHT OF PRAYER TO OVERCOME HIS "MORAL CONCERNS."
AS GOVERNOR, HIS PERSONAL FAITH TOOK PRIORITY OVER THE EPIDEMIC THREATENING HIS CONSTITUENTS.
IN THE END, PENCE AUTHORIZED ONLY THE BARE MINIMUM.
LEFT IN PLACE WAS LEGISLATION THAT BANNED FUNDING FOR THE NEEDLE-EXCHANGE PROGRAMS.
SCOTT COUNTY WAS LEFT TO FEND FOR ITSELF...
AND THOSE FIVE SHUTTERED CLINICS WERE NEVER REOPENED.

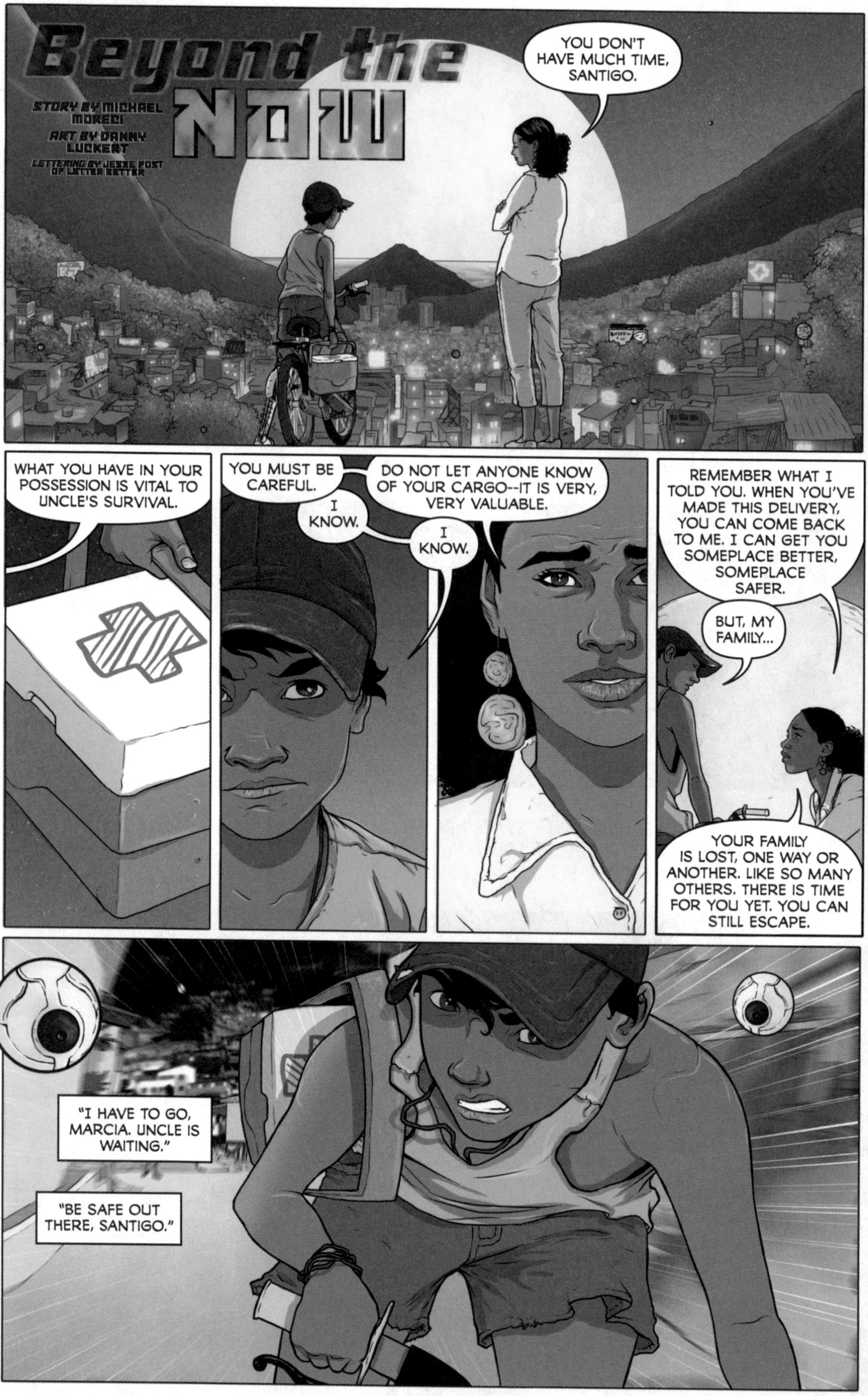
Beyond the NOW
STORY BY MICHAEL MORECI
ART BY DANNY LUCKERT
LETTERING BY JESSE POST OF LETTER BETTER
YOU DON'T HAVE MUCH TIME, SANTIGO.
WHAT YOU HAVE IN YOUR POSSESSION IS VITAL TO UNCLE'S SURVIVAL.
YOU MUST BE CAREFUL.
I KNOW.
DO NOT LET ANYONE KNOW OF YOUR CARGO--IT IS VERY, VERY VALUABLE.
I KNOW.
REMEMBER WHAT I TOLD YOU. WHEN YOU'VE MADE THIS DELIVERY, YOU CAN COME BACK TO ME. I CAN GET YOU SOMEPLACE BETTER, SOMEPLACE SAFER.
BUT, MY FAMILY...
YOUR FAMILY IS LOST, ONE WAY OR ANOTHER. LIKE SO MANY OTHERS. THERE IS TIME FOR YOU YET. YOU CAN STILL ESCAPE.
"I HAVE TO GO, MARCIA. UNCLE IS WAITING."
"BE SAFE OUT THERE, SANTIGO."

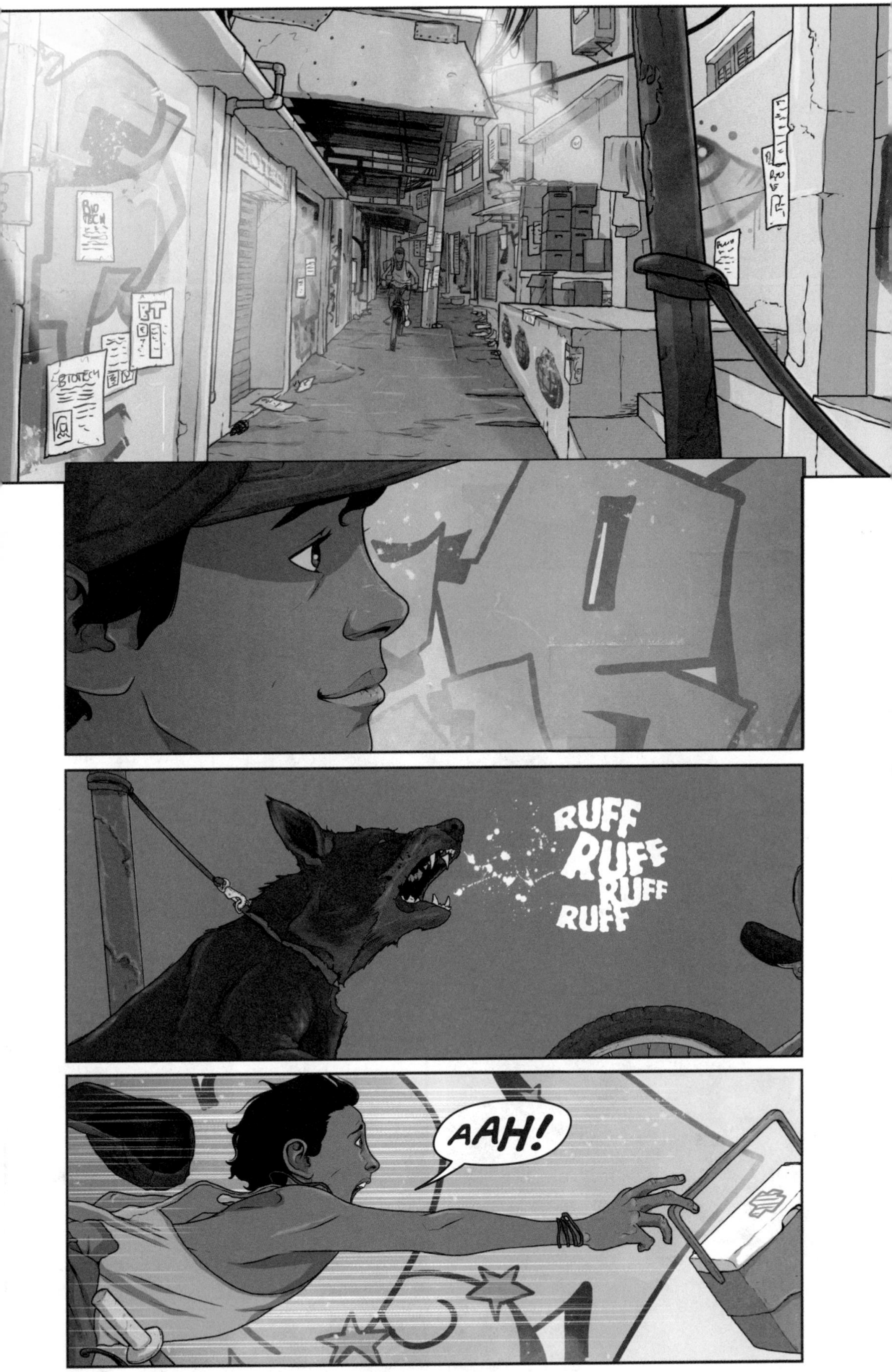
BIOTECH
RUFF
RUFF
RUFF
RUFF
AAH!

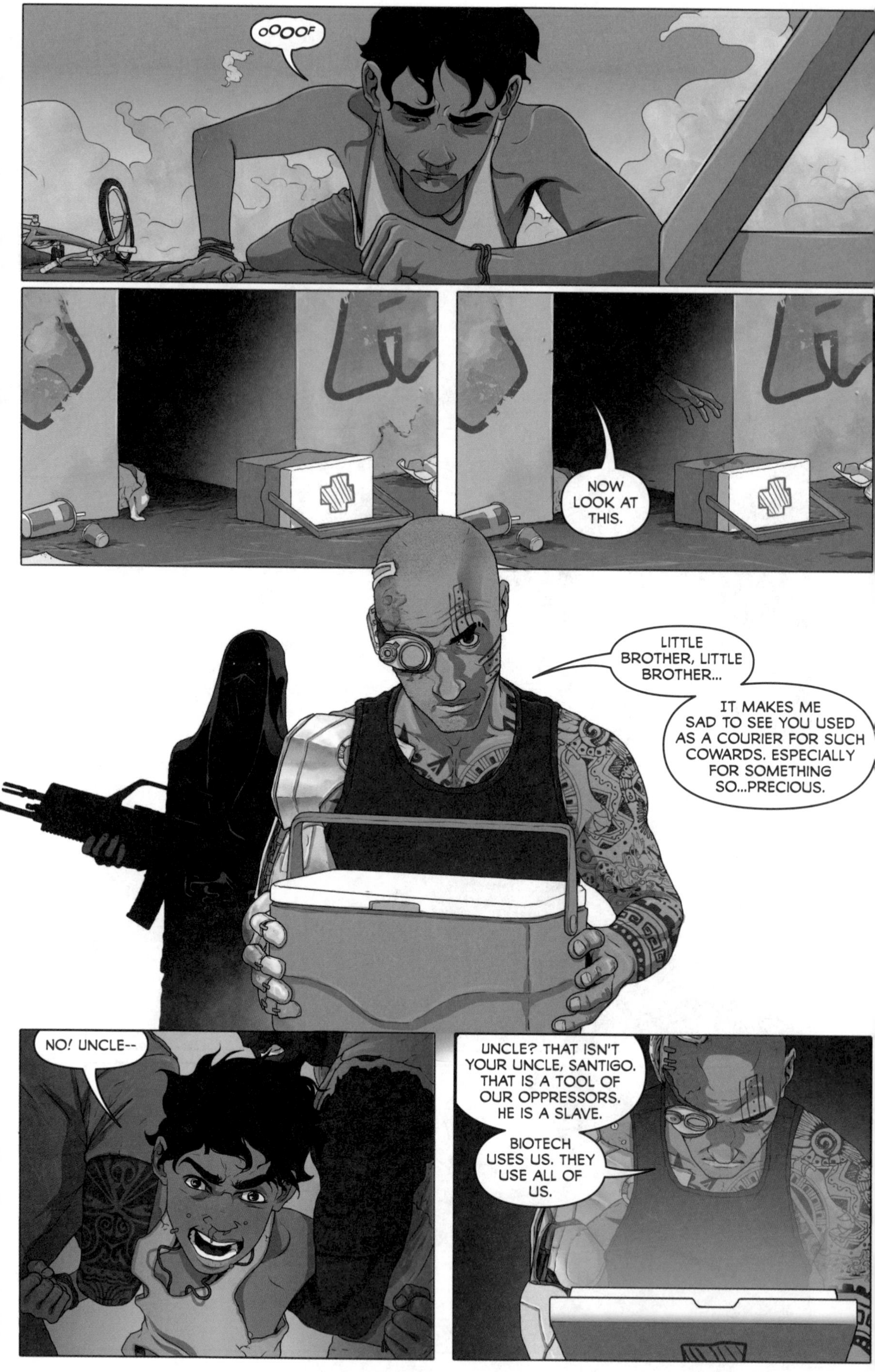
OOOOF
NOW LOOK AT THIS.
LITTLE BROTHER, LITTLE BROTHER...
IT MAKES ME SAD TO SEE YOU USED AS A COURIER FOR SUCH COWARDS. ESPECIALLY FOR SOMETHING SO...PRECIOUS.
NO! UNCLE--
UNCLE? THAT ISN'T YOUR UNCLE, SANTIGO. THAT IS A TOOL OF OUR OPPRESSORS. HE IS A SLAVE.
BIOTECH USES US. THEY USE ALL OF US.

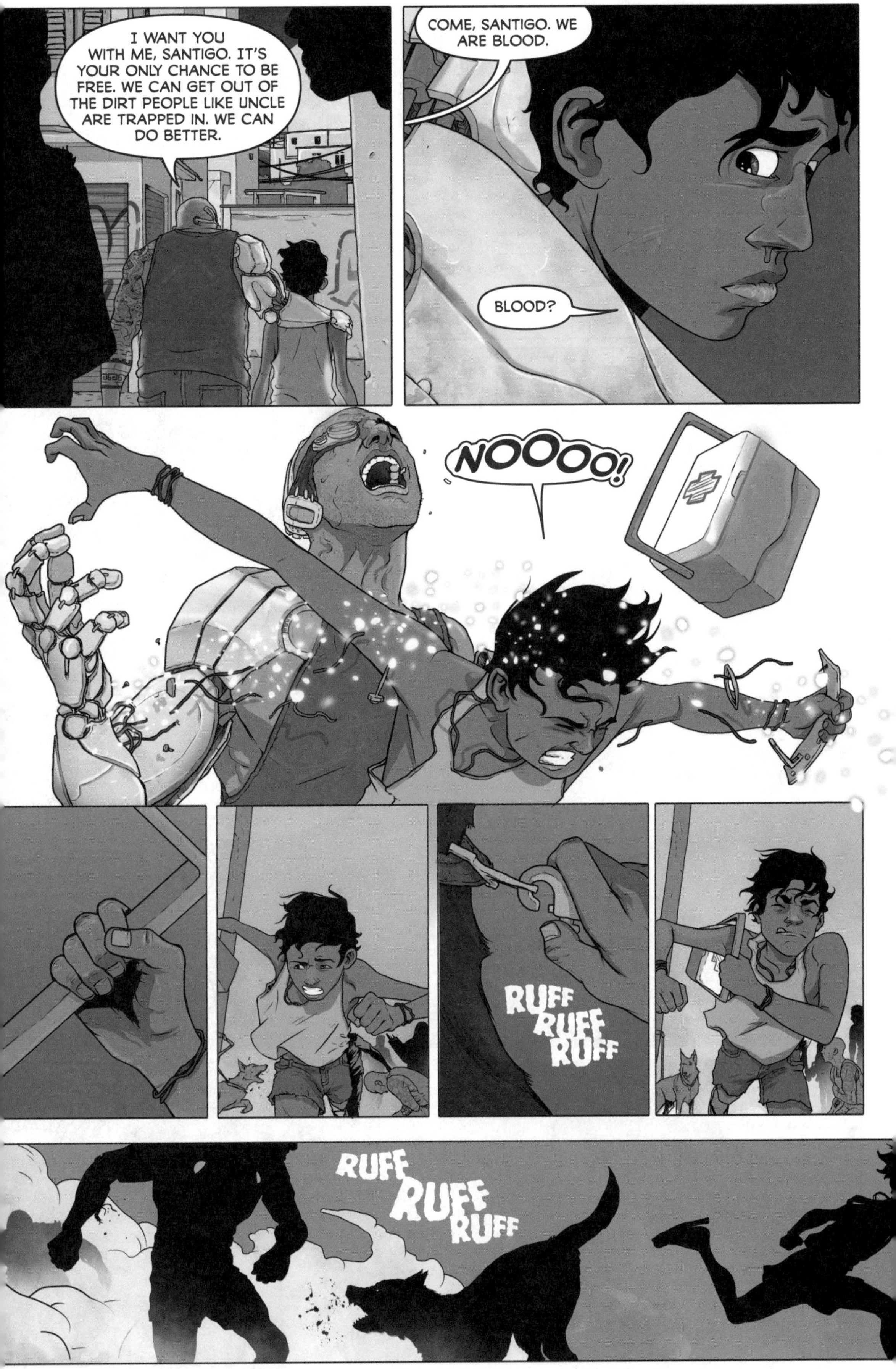
I WANT YOU WITH ME, SANTIGO. IT'S YOUR ONLY CHANCE TO BE FREE. WE CAN GET OUT OF THE DIRT PEOPLE LIKE UNCLE ARE TRAPPED IN. WE CAN DO BETTER.
COME, SANTIGO. WE ARE BLOOD.
BLOOD?
NOOOO!
RUFF RUFF RUFF
RUFF RUFF RUFF

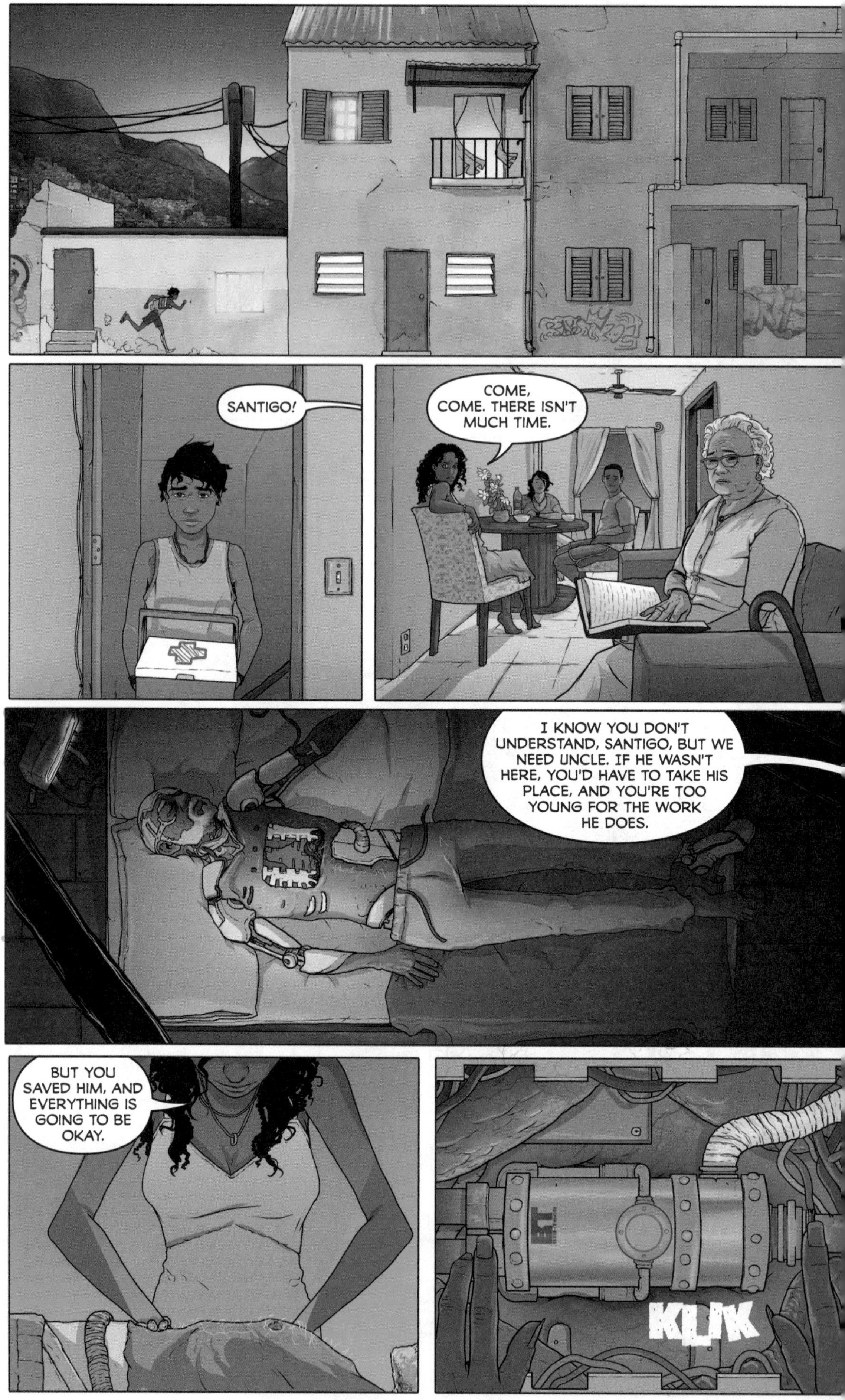
SANTIGO!
COME, COME. THERE ISN'T MUCH TIME.
I KNOW YOU DON'T UNDERSTAND, SANTIGO, BUT WE NEED UNCLE. IF HE WASN'T HERE, YOU'D HAVE TO TAKE HIS PLACE, AND YOU'RE TOO YOUNG FOR THE WORK HE DOES.
BUT YOU SAVED HIM, AND EVERYTHING IS GOING TO BE OKAY.
KLIK

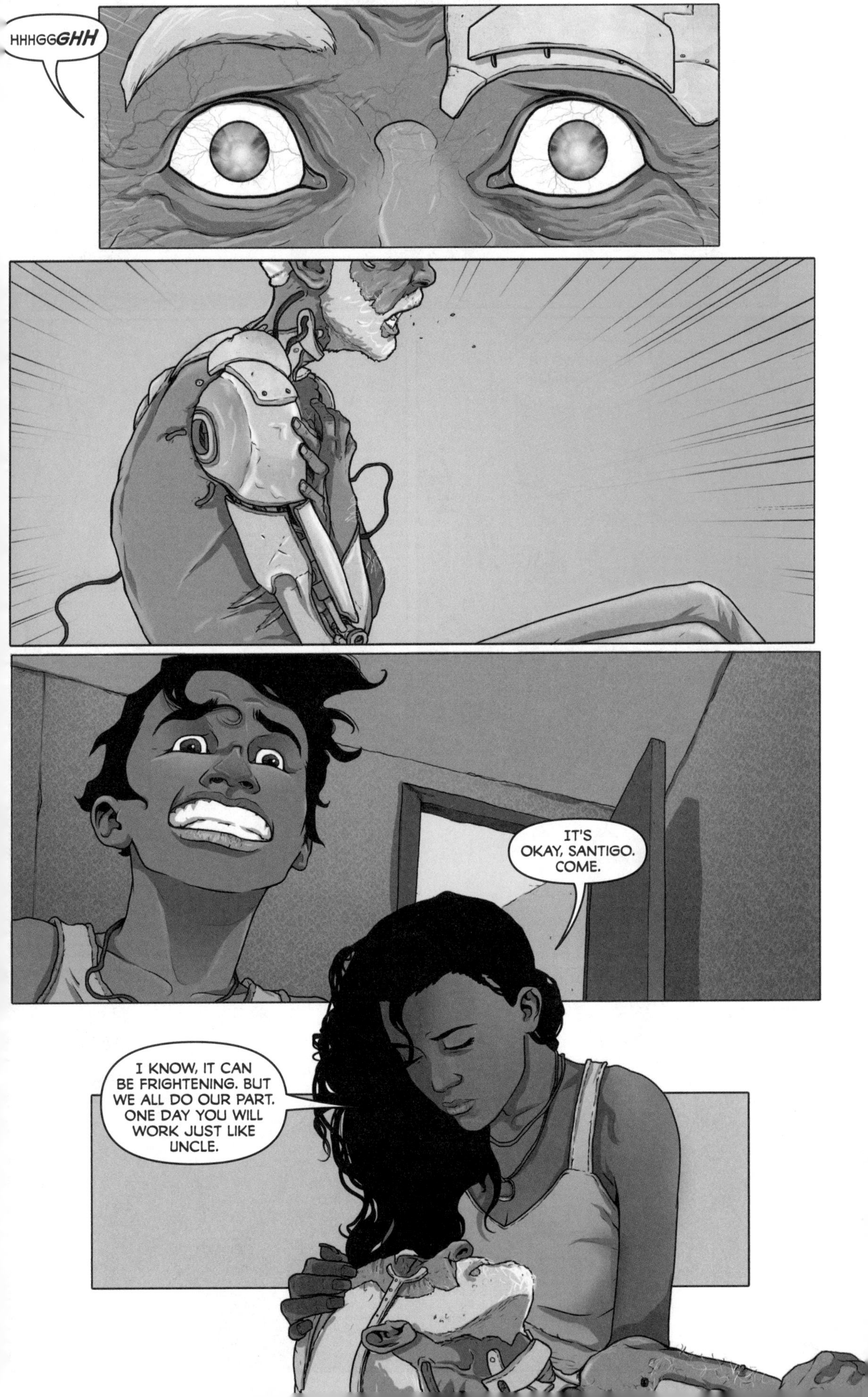
HHHGGGHH
IT'S OKAY, SANTIGO. COME.
I KNOW, IT CAN BE FRIGHTENING. BUT WE ALL DO OUR PART. ONE DAY YOU WILL WORK JUST LIKE UNCLE.

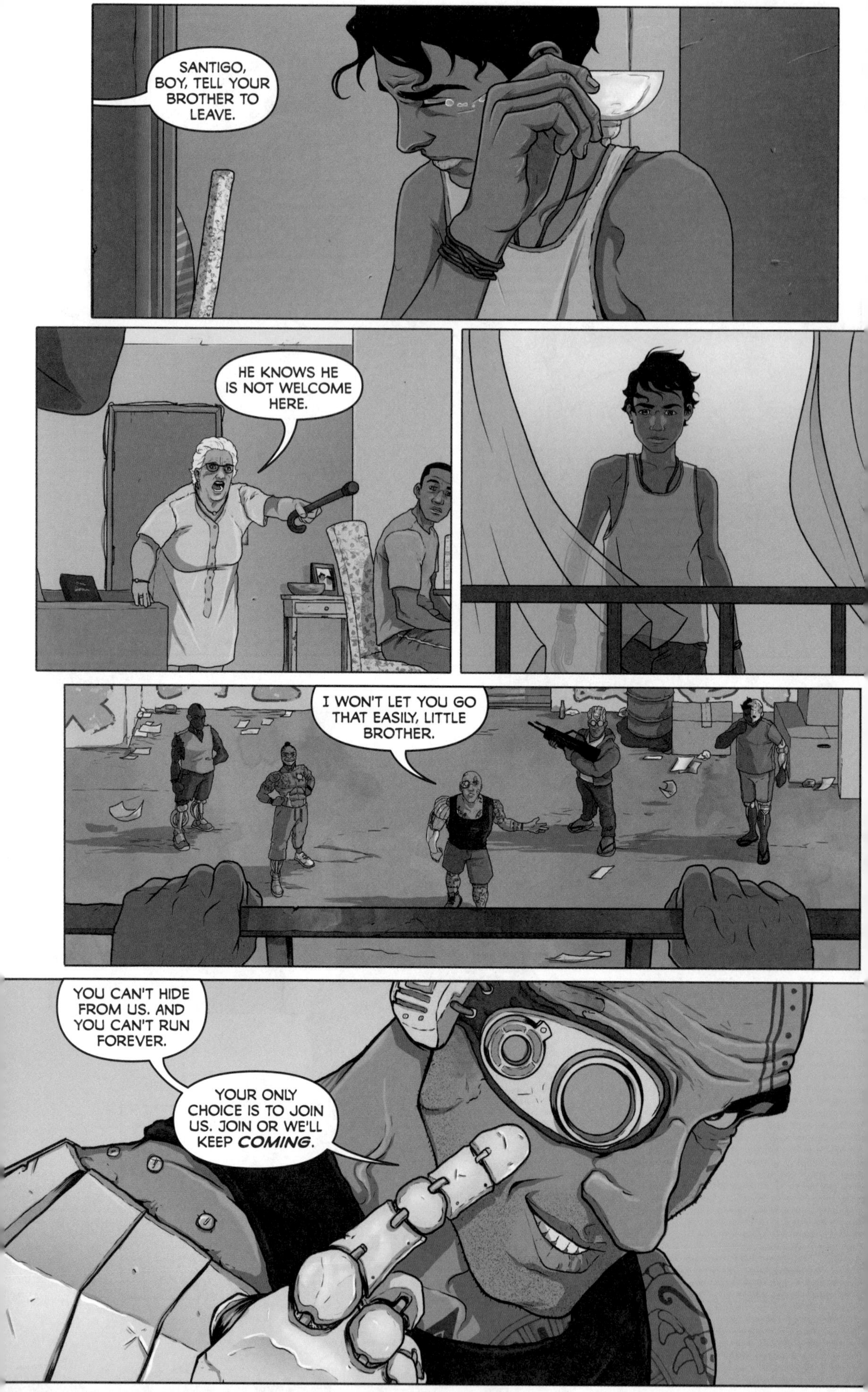
SANTIGO, BOY, TELL YOUR BROTHER TO LEAVE.
HE KNOWS HE IS NOT WELCOME HERE.
I WON'T LET YOU GO THAT EASILY, LITTLE BROTHER.
YOU CAN'T HIDE FROM US. AND YOU CAN'T RUN FOREVER.
YOUR ONLY CHOICE IS TO JOIN US. JOIN OR WE'LL KEEP COMING.

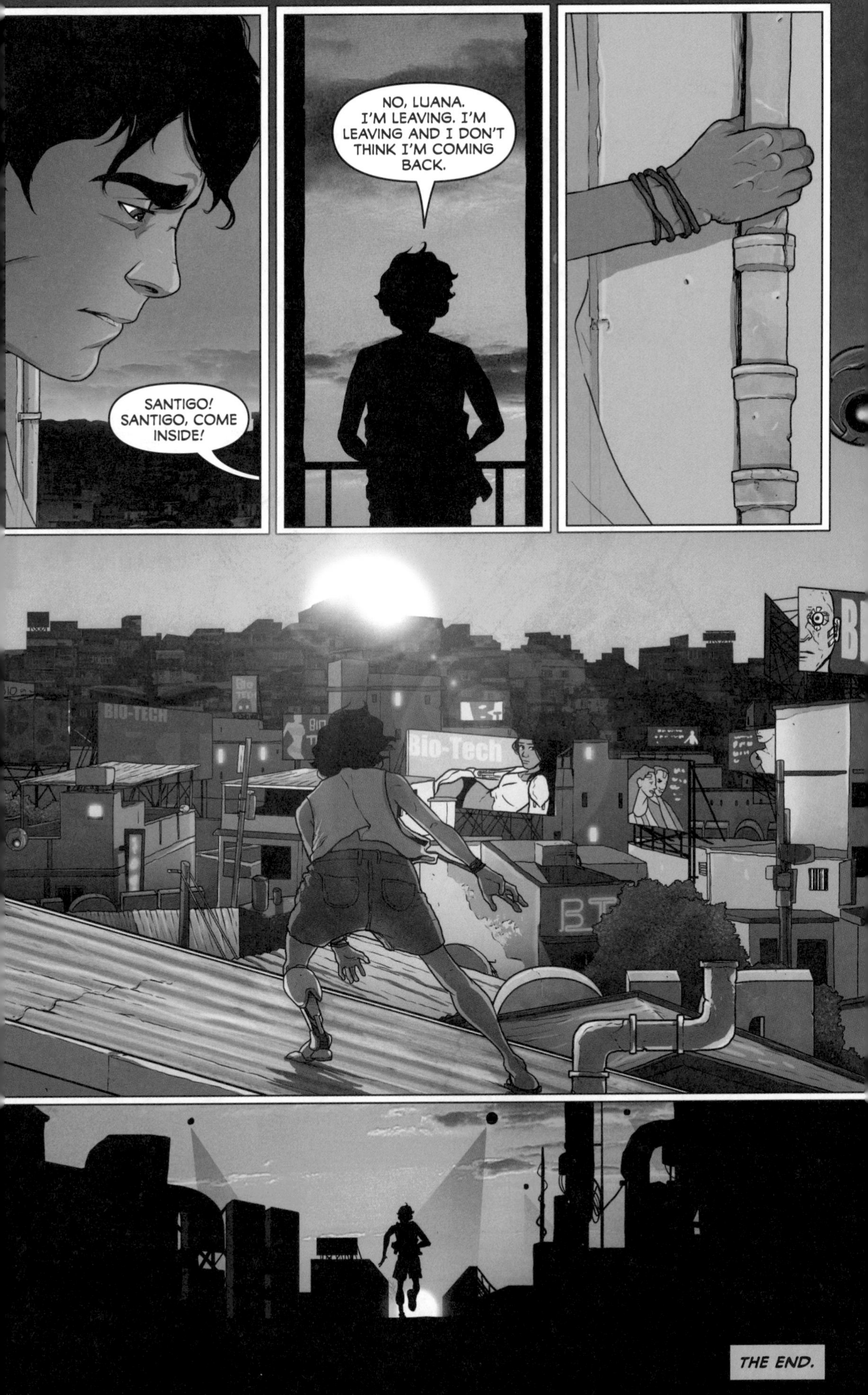
SANTIGO! SANTIGO, COME INSIDE!
NO, LUANA. I'M LEAVING. I'M LEAVING AND I DON'T THINK I'M COMING BACK.
BIO-TECH
Bio-Tech
BT
THE END.

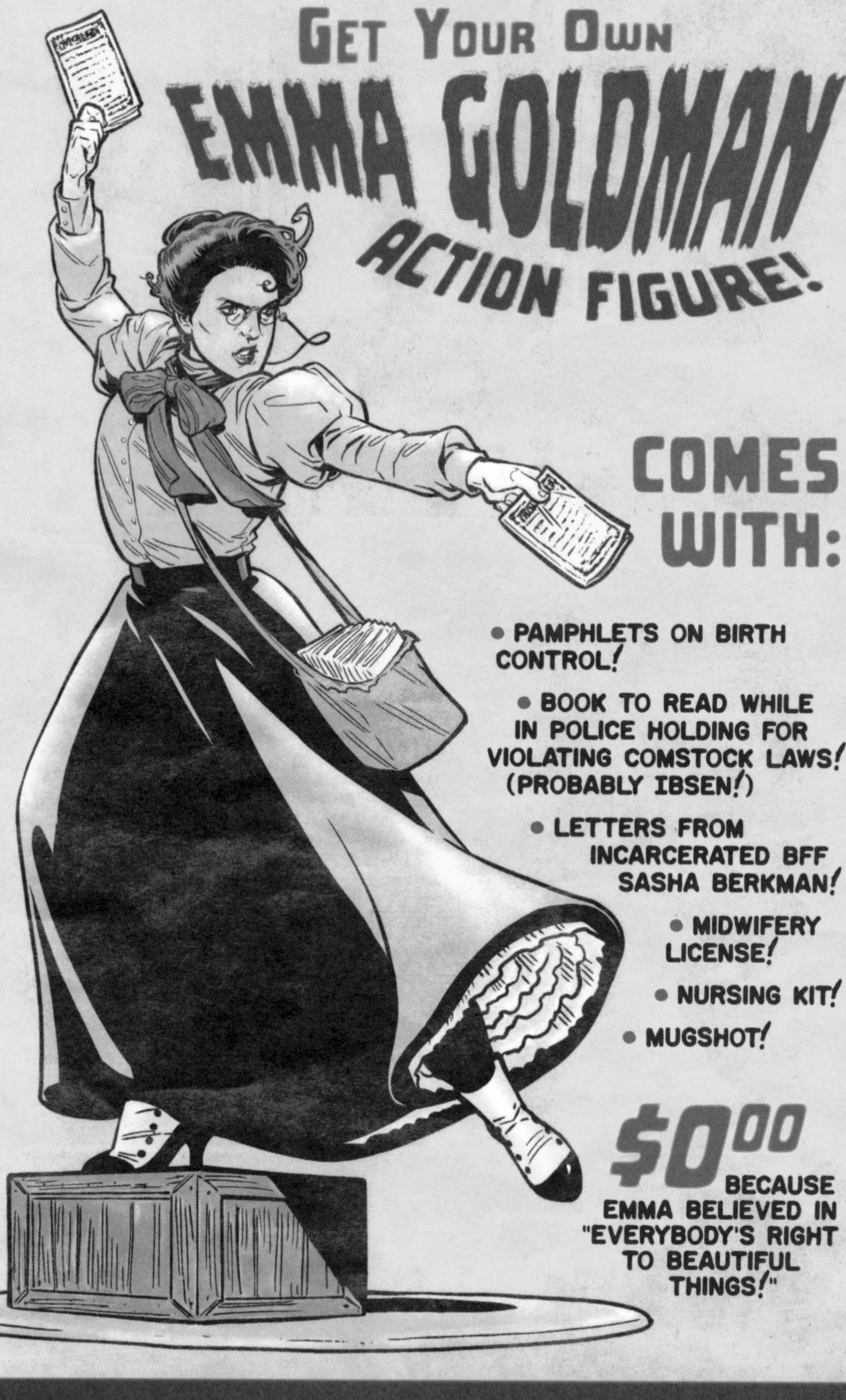
GET YOUR OWN
EMMA GOLDMAN
ACTION FIGURE!
COMES WITH:
• PAMPHLETS ON BIRTH CONTROL!
• BOOK TO READ WHILE IN POLICE HOLDING FOR VIOLATING COMSTOCK LAWS! (PROBABLY IBSEN!)
• LETTERS FROM INCARCERATED BFF SASHA BERKMAN!
• MIDWIFERY LICENSE!
• NURSING KIT!
• MUGSHOT!
$0.00
BECAUSE EMMA BELIEVED IN "EVERYBODY'S RIGHT TO BEAUTIFUL THINGS!"

"It is not because woman is **LACKING** in responsibility, but because she has **TOO MUCH** of the latter that she demands to know how to prevent conception."

WRITER: MARA WILSON • ARTIST: REBEKAH ISSACS • COLORIST: GLENN HAUMAN • LETTERER: JESSE POST OF LETTER BETTER

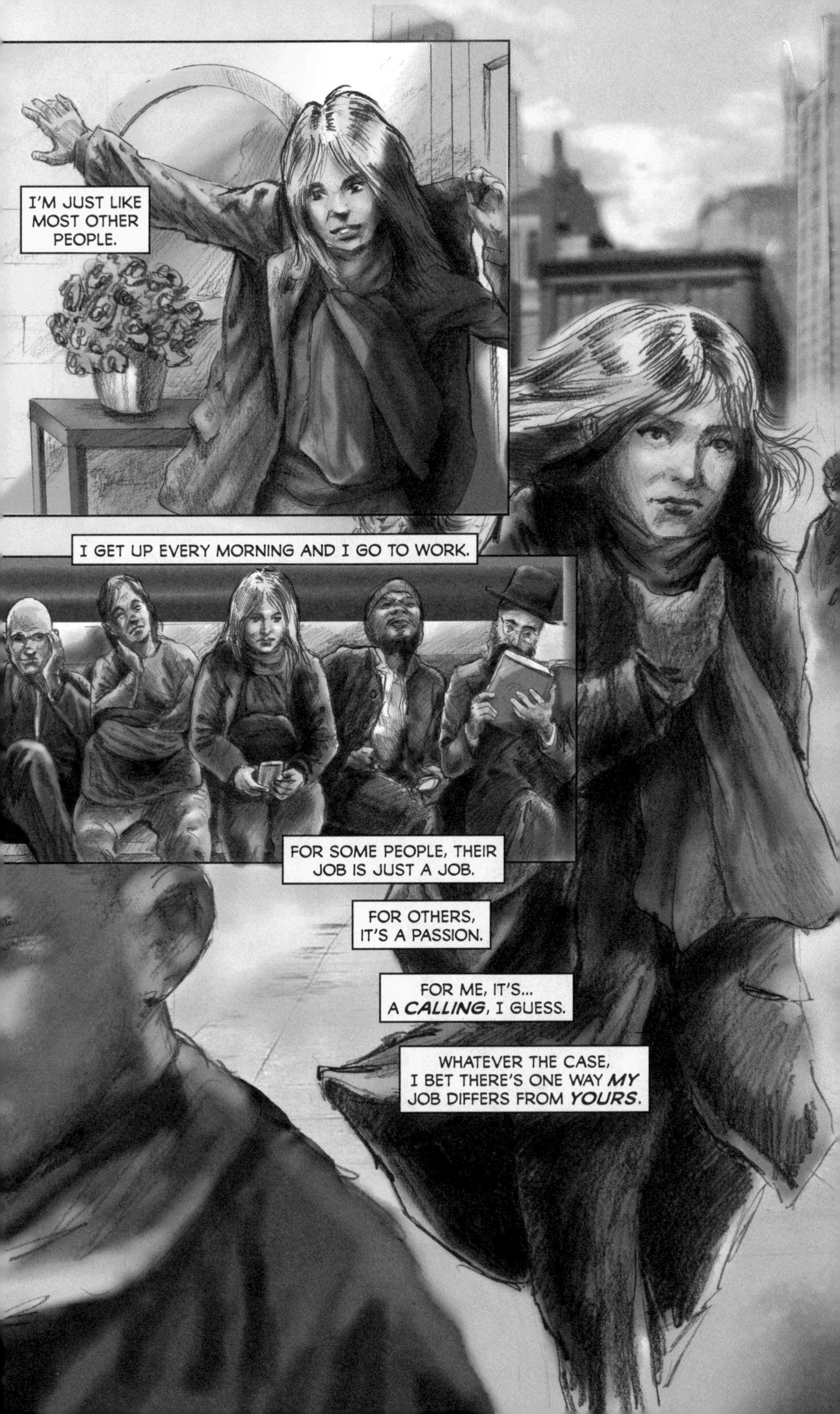
I'M JUST LIKE MOST OTHER PEOPLE.
I GET UP EVERY MORNING AND I GO TO WORK.
FOR SOME PEOPLE, THEIR JOB IS JUST A JOB.
FOR OTHERS, IT'S A PASSION.
FOR ME, IT'S... A ***CALLING***, I GUESS.
WHATEVER THE CASE, I BET THERE'S ONE WAY ***MY*** JOB DIFFERS FROM ***YOURS***.

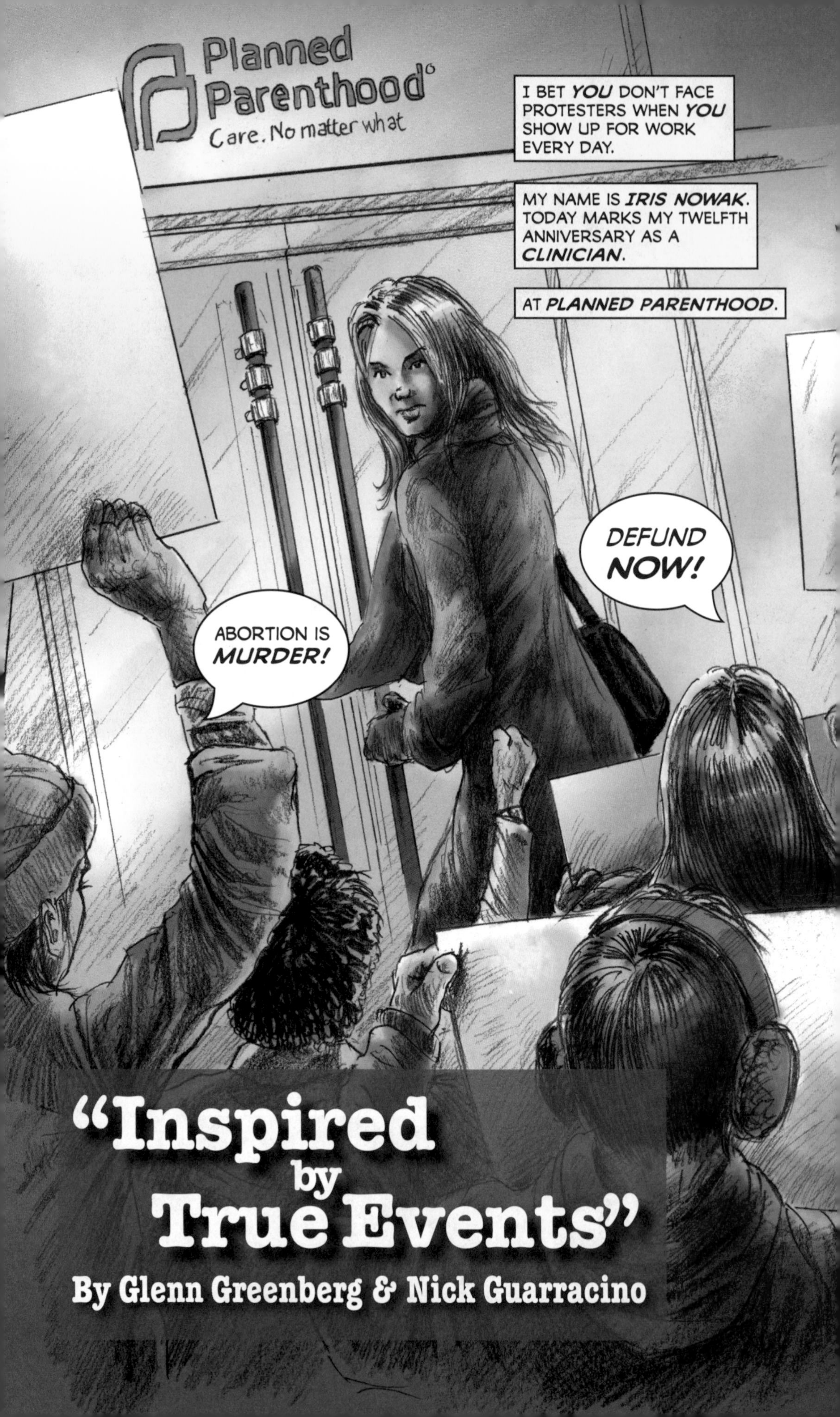
Planned Parenthood
Care. No matter what
I BET *YOU* DON'T FACE PROTESTERS WHEN *YOU* SHOW UP FOR WORK EVERY DAY.
MY NAME IS ***IRIS NOWAK***. TODAY MARKS MY TWELFTH ANNIVERSARY AS A ***CLINICIAN***.
AT ***PLANNED PARENTHOOD***.
ABORTION IS ***MURDER!***
DEFUND ***NOW!***
"Inspired by True Events"
By Glenn Greenberg & Nick Guarracino

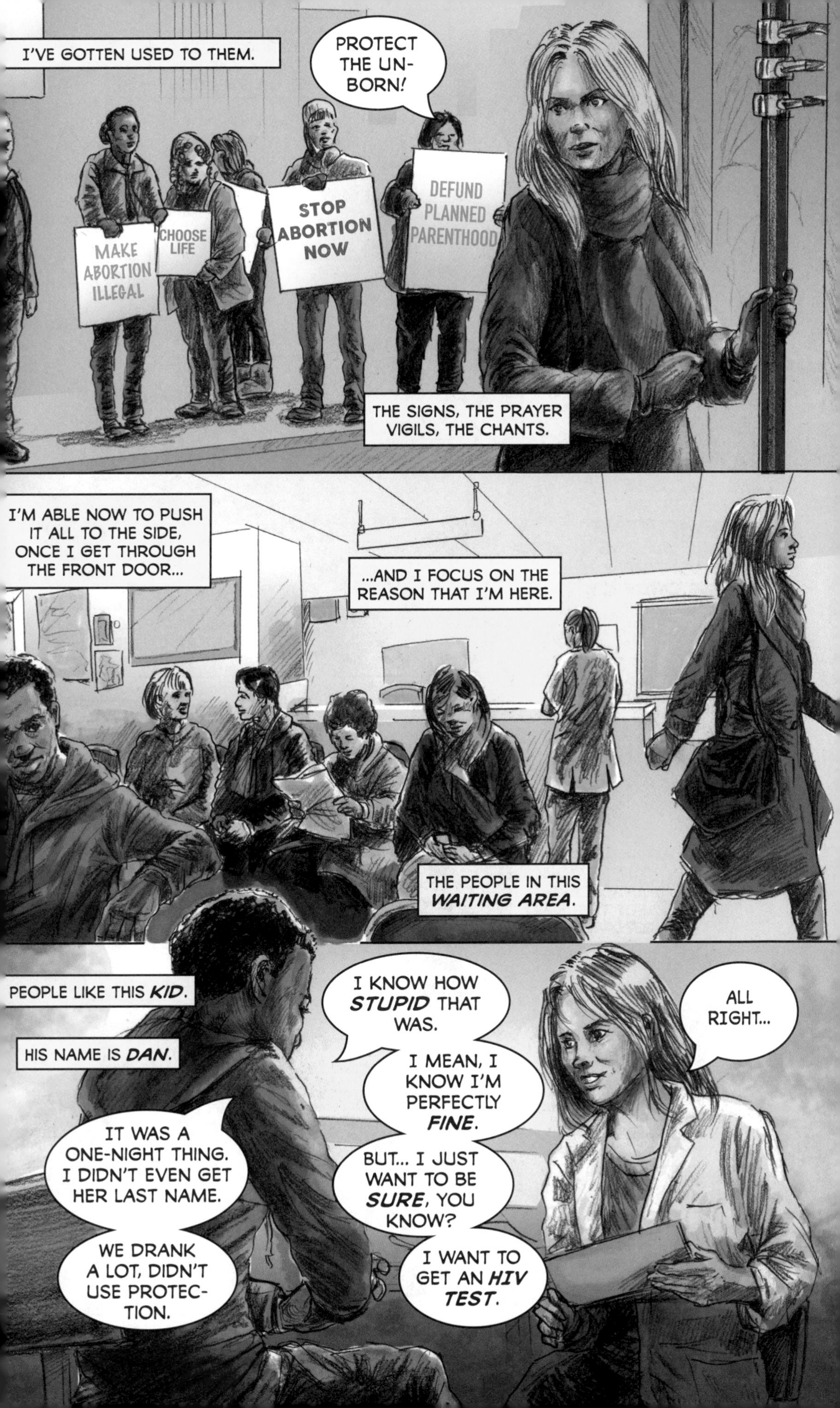
I'VE GOTTEN USED TO THEM.
PROTECT THE UN-BORN!
MAKE ABORTION ILLEGAL
CHOOSE LIFE
STOP ABORTION NOW
DEFUND PLANNED PARENTHOOD
THE SIGNS, THE PRAYER VIGILS, THE CHANTS.
I'M ABLE NOW TO PUSH IT ALL TO THE SIDE, ONCE I GET THROUGH THE FRONT DOOR...
...AND I FOCUS ON THE REASON THAT I'M HERE.
THE PEOPLE IN THIS *WAITING AREA*.
PEOPLE LIKE THIS *KID*.
HIS NAME IS *DAN*.
IT WAS A ONE-NIGHT THING. I DIDN'T EVEN GET HER LAST NAME.
WE DRANK A LOT, DIDN'T USE PROTEC-TION.
I KNOW HOW *STUPID* THAT WAS.
I MEAN, I KNOW I'M PERFECTLY *FINE*.
BUT... I JUST WANT TO BE *SURE*, YOU KNOW?
I WANT TO GET AN *HIV TEST*.
ALL RIGHT...

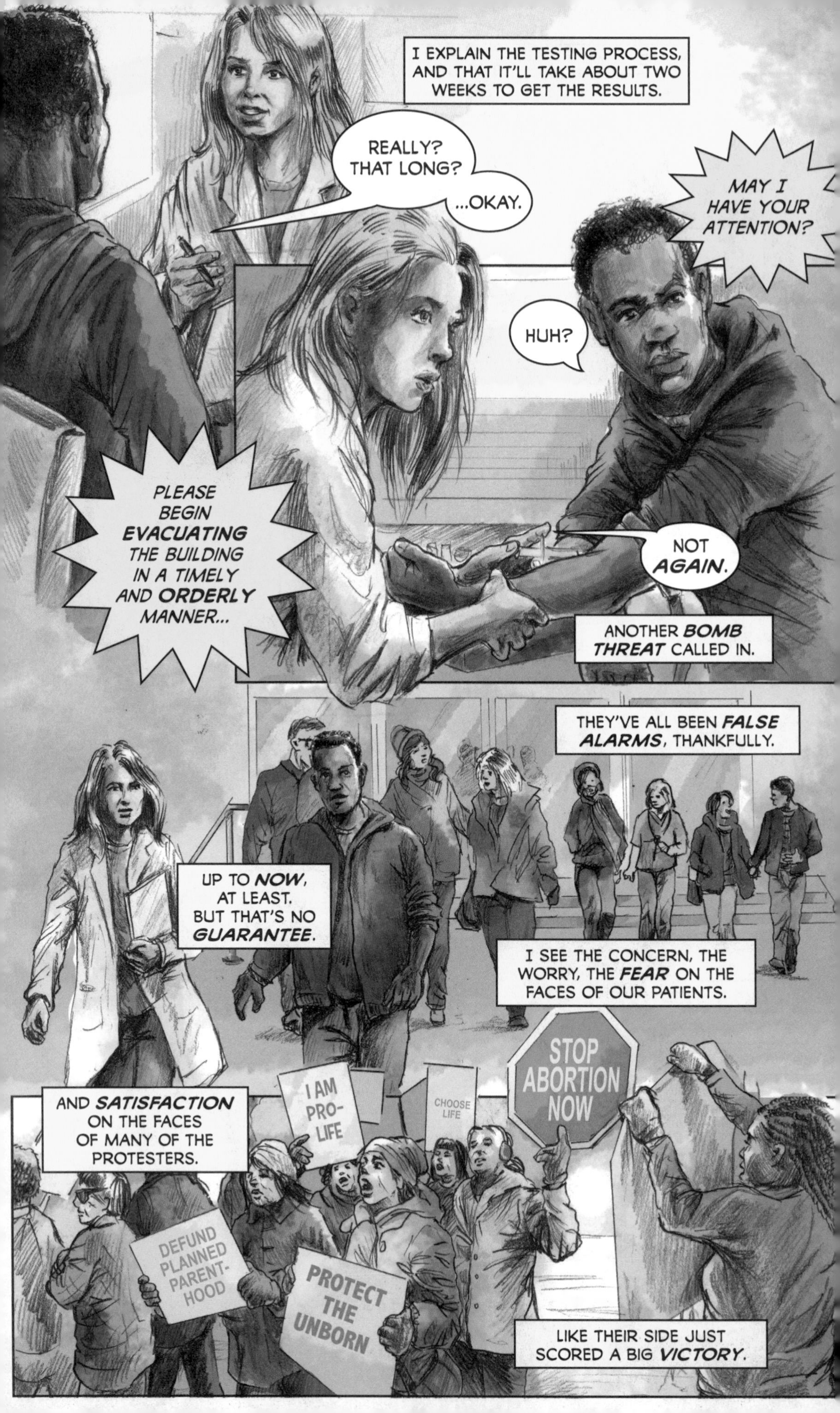
I EXPLAIN THE TESTING PROCESS, AND THAT IT'LL TAKE ABOUT TWO WEEKS TO GET THE RESULTS.
REALLY? THAT LONG?
...OKAY.
MAY I HAVE YOUR ATTENTION?
HUH?
PLEASE BEGIN EVACUATING THE BUILDING IN A TIMELY AND ORDERLY MANNER...
NOT AGAIN.
ANOTHER BOMB THREAT CALLED IN.
THEY'VE ALL BEEN FALSE ALARMS, THANKFULLY.
UP TO NOW, AT LEAST. BUT THAT'S NO GUARANTEE.
I SEE THE CONCERN, THE WORRY, THE FEAR ON THE FACES OF OUR PATIENTS.
AND SATISFACTION ON THE FACES OF MANY OF THE PROTESTERS.
I AM PRO-LIFE
CHOOSE LIFE
STOP ABORTION NOW
DEFUND PLANNED PARENT-HOOD
PROTECT THE UNBORN
LIKE THEIR SIDE JUST SCORED A BIG VICTORY.

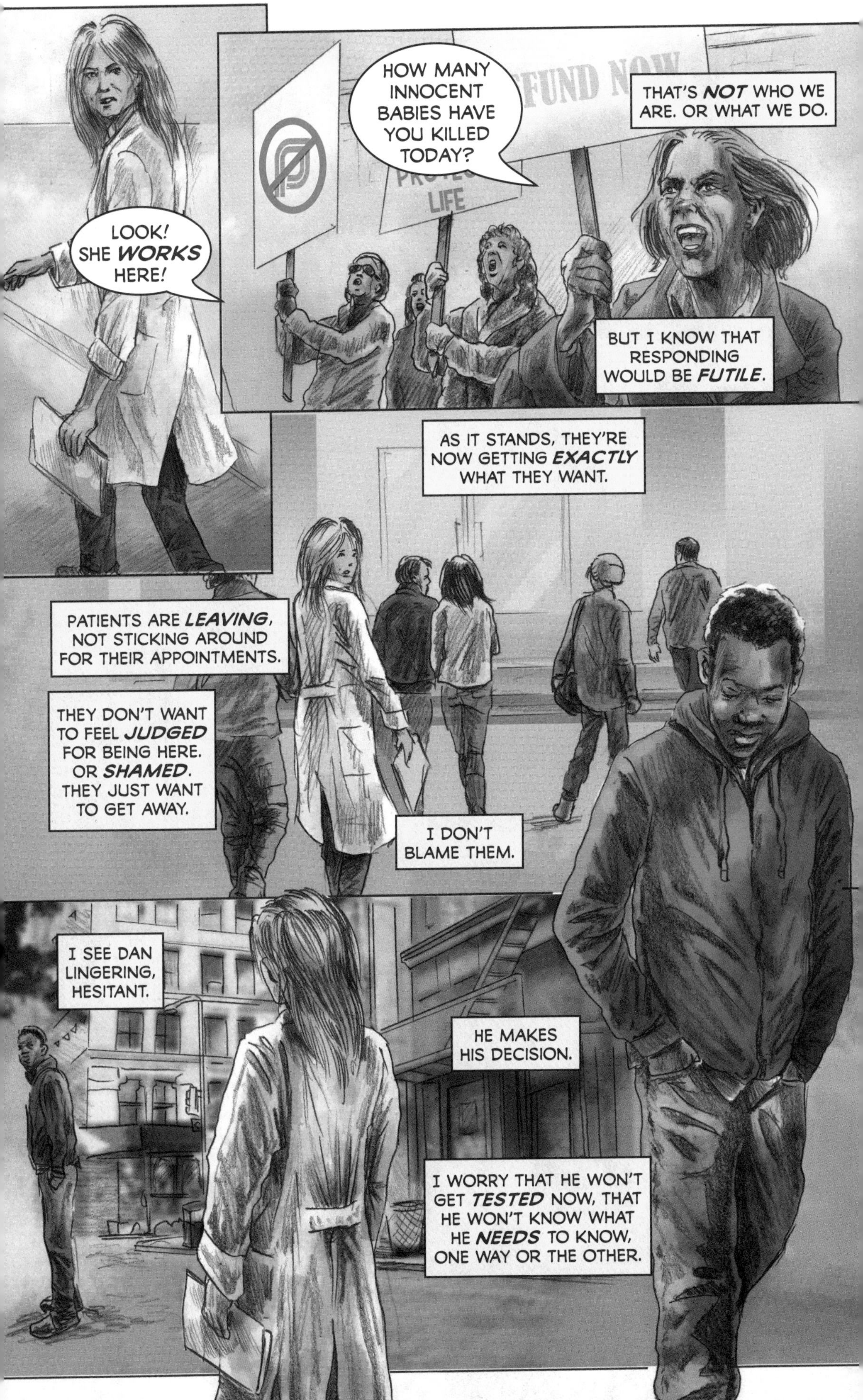

LOOK! SHE *WORKS* HERE!
HOW MANY INNOCENT BABIES HAVE YOU KILLED TODAY?
LIFE
THAT'S *NOT* WHO WE ARE. OR WHAT WE DO.
BUT I KNOW THAT RESPONDING WOULD BE *FUTILE*.
AS IT STANDS, THEY'RE NOW GETTING *EXACTLY* WHAT THEY WANT.
PATIENTS ARE *LEAVING*, NOT STICKING AROUND FOR THEIR APPOINTMENTS.
THEY DON'T WANT TO FEEL *JUDGED* FOR BEING HERE. OR *SHAMED*. THEY JUST WANT TO GET AWAY.
I DON'T BLAME THEM.
I SEE DAN LINGERING, HESITANT.
HE MAKES HIS DECISION.
I WORRY THAT HE WON'T GET *TESTED* NOW, THAT HE WON'T KNOW WHAT HE *NEEDS* TO KNOW, ONE WAY OR THE OTHER.

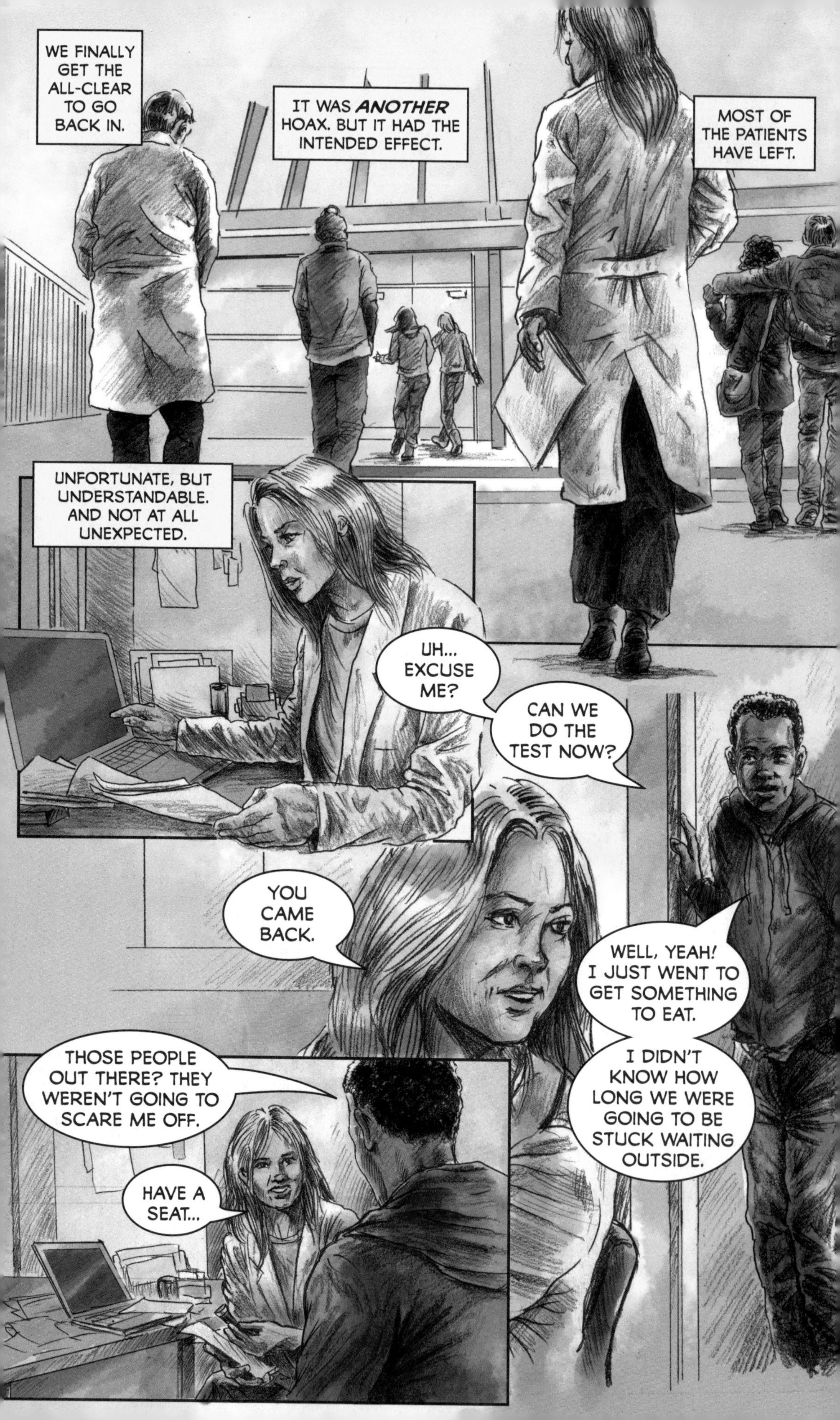
WE FINALLY GET THE ALL-CLEAR TO GO BACK IN.
IT WAS *ANOTHER* HOAX. BUT IT HAD THE INTENDED EFFECT.
MOST OF THE PATIENTS HAVE LEFT.
UNFORTUNATE, BUT UNDERSTANDABLE. AND NOT AT ALL UNEXPECTED.
UH... EXCUSE ME?
CAN WE DO THE TEST NOW?
YOU CAME BACK.
WELL, YEAH! I JUST WENT TO GET SOMETHING TO EAT.
I DIDN'T KNOW HOW LONG WE WERE GOING TO BE STUCK WAITING OUTSIDE.
THOSE PEOPLE OUT THERE? THEY WEREN'T GOING TO SCARE ME OFF.
HAVE A SEAT...

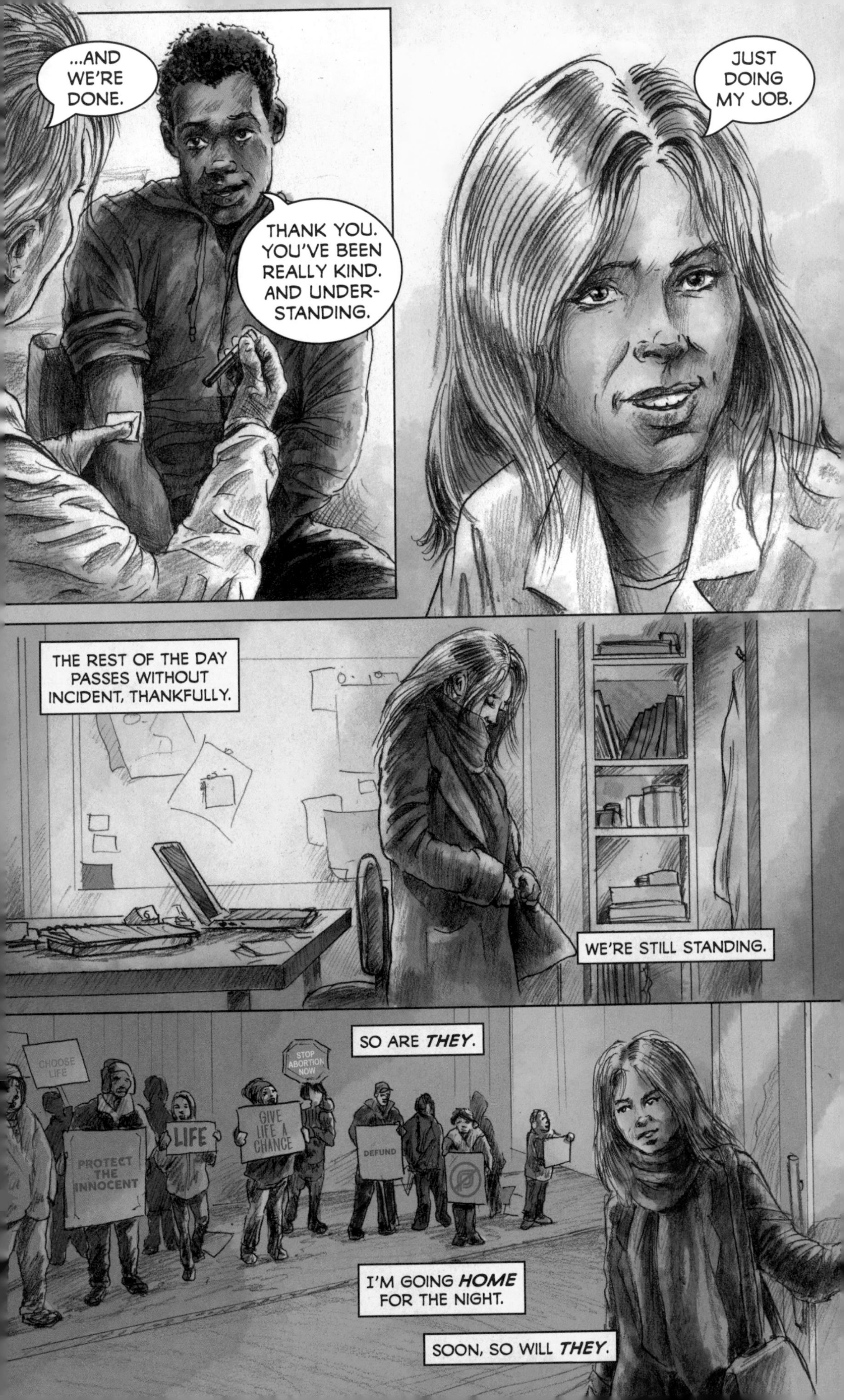

...AND WE'RE DONE.
THANK YOU. YOU'VE BEEN REALLY KIND. AND UNDER-STANDING.
JUST DOING MY JOB.
THE REST OF THE DAY PASSES WITHOUT INCIDENT, THANKFULLY.
WE'RE STILL STANDING.
SO ARE *THEY*.
CHOOSE LIFE
STOP ABORTION NOW
GIVE LIFE A CHANCE
LIFE
PROTECT THE INNOCENT
DEFUND
I'M GOING *HOME* FOR THE NIGHT.
SOON, SO WILL *THEY*.

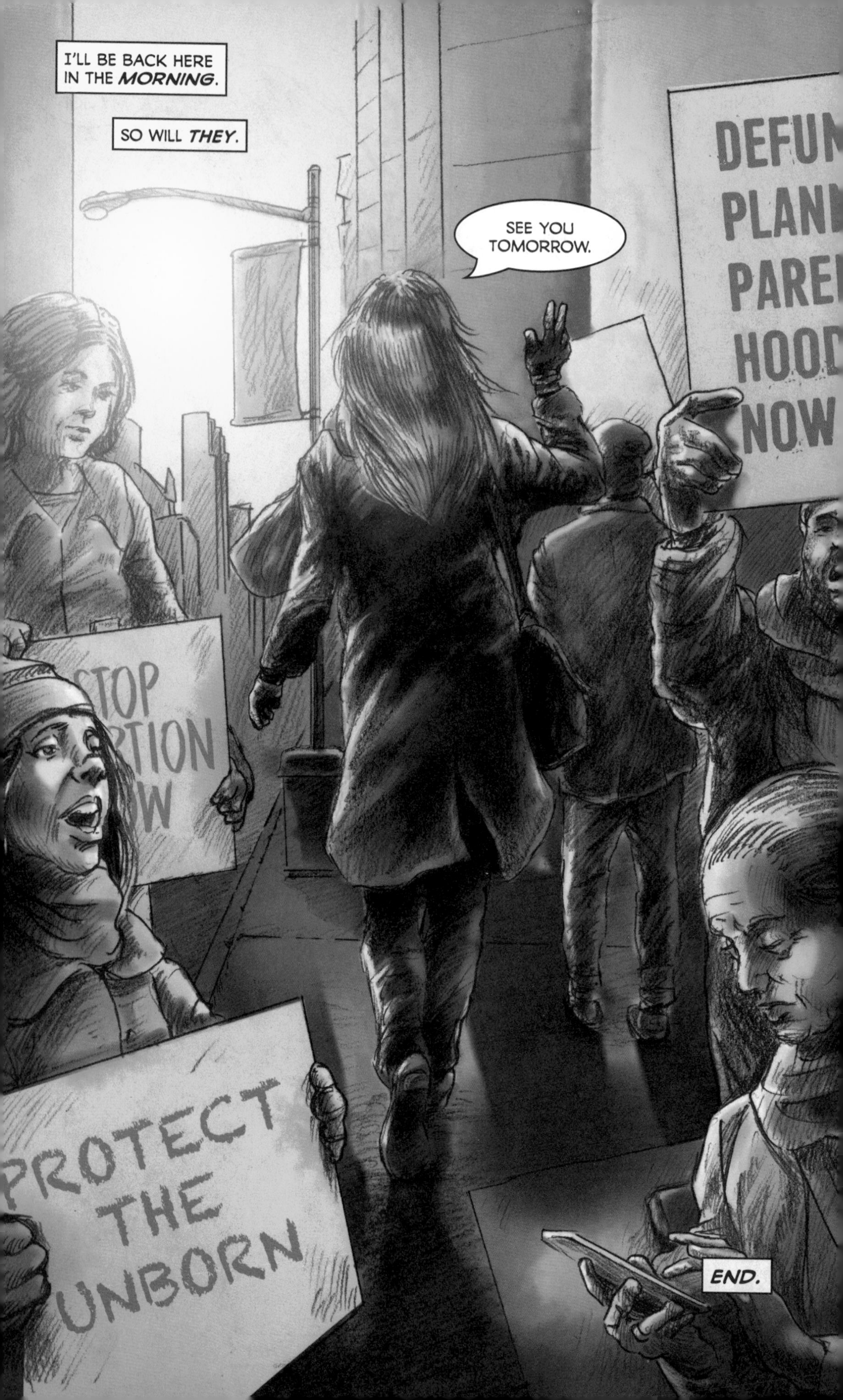
I'LL BE BACK HERE IN THE *MORNING*.
SO WILL *THEY*.
SEE YOU TOMORROW.
PROTECT THE UNBORN
END.

THE FUTURE DYSTOPIA REPUBLICANS ARE TRYING TO PREVENT

STORY: FRANK CONNIFF   ART: MARGUERITE DABAIE

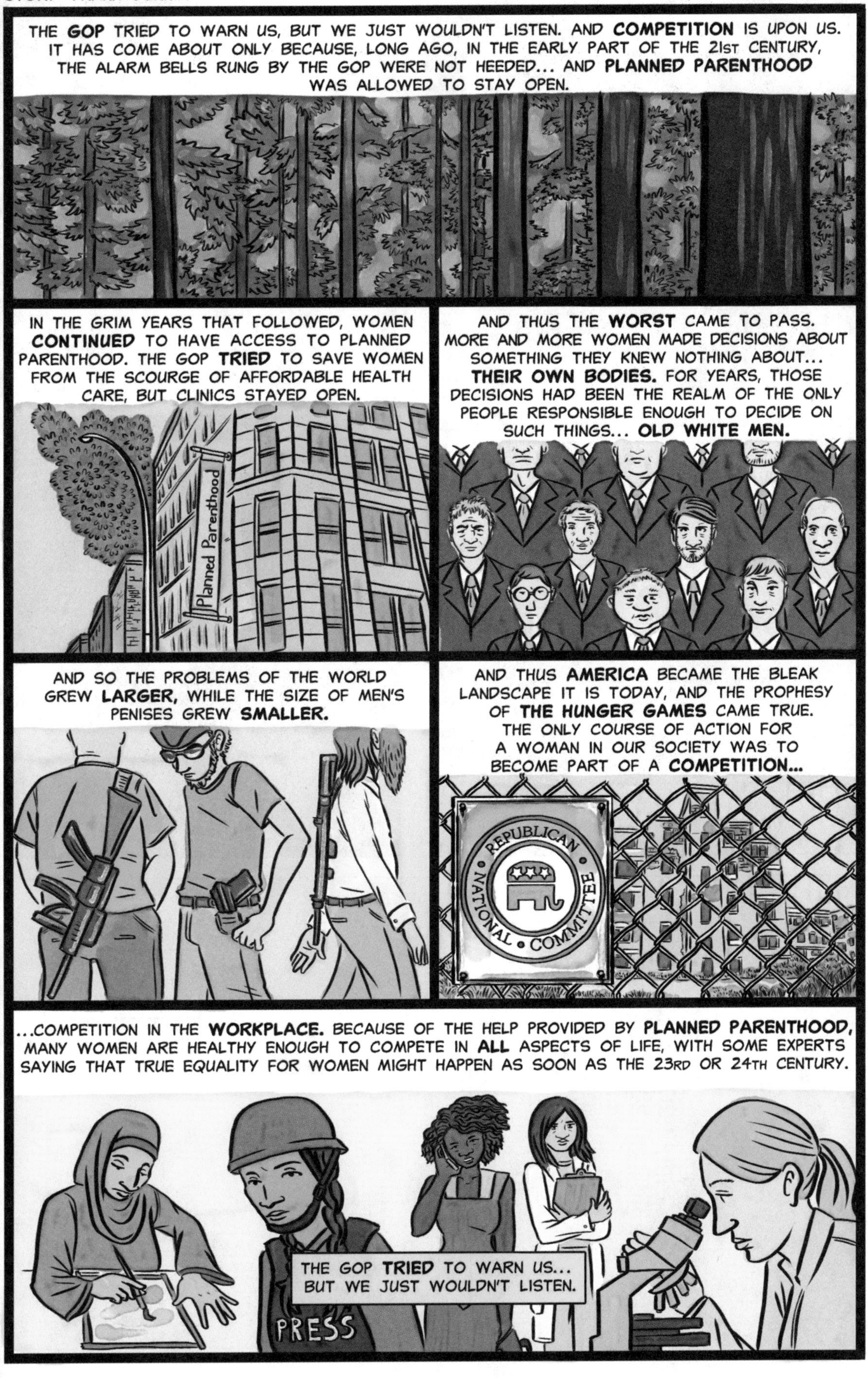

THE GOP TRIED TO WARN US, BUT WE JUST WOULDN'T LISTEN. AND COMPETITION IS UPON US. IT HAS COME ABOUT ONLY BECAUSE, LONG AGO, IN THE EARLY PART OF THE 21ST CENTURY, THE ALARM BELLS RUNG BY THE GOP WERE NOT HEEDED... AND PLANNED PARENTHOOD WAS ALLOWED TO STAY OPEN.
IN THE GRIM YEARS THAT FOLLOWED, WOMEN CONTINUED TO HAVE ACCESS TO PLANNED PARENTHOOD. THE GOP TRIED TO SAVE WOMEN FROM THE SCOURGE OF AFFORDABLE HEALTH CARE, BUT CLINICS STAYED OPEN.
Planned Parenthood
AND THUS THE WORST CAME TO PASS. MORE AND MORE WOMEN MADE DECISIONS ABOUT SOMETHING THEY KNEW NOTHING ABOUT... THEIR OWN BODIES. FOR YEARS, THOSE DECISIONS HAD BEEN THE REALM OF THE ONLY PEOPLE RESPONSIBLE ENOUGH TO DECIDE ON SUCH THINGS... OLD WHITE MEN.
AND SO THE PROBLEMS OF THE WORLD GREW LARGER, WHILE THE SIZE OF MEN'S PENISES GREW SMALLER.
AND THUS AMERICA BECAME THE BLEAK LANDSCAPE IT IS TODAY, AND THE PROPHESY OF THE HUNGER GAMES CAME TRUE. THE ONLY COURSE OF ACTION FOR A WOMAN IN OUR SOCIETY WAS TO BECOME PART OF A COMPETITION...
REPUBLICAN NATIONAL • COMMITTEE
...COMPETITION IN THE WORKPLACE. BECAUSE OF THE HELP PROVIDED BY PLANNED PARENTHOOD, MANY WOMEN ARE HEALTHY ENOUGH TO COMPETE IN ALL ASPECTS OF LIFE, WITH SOME EXPERTS SAYING THAT TRUE EQUALITY FOR WOMEN MIGHT HAPPEN AS SOON AS THE 23RD OR 24TH CENTURY.
THE GOP TRIED TO WARN US... BUT WE JUST WOULDN'T LISTEN.
PRESS

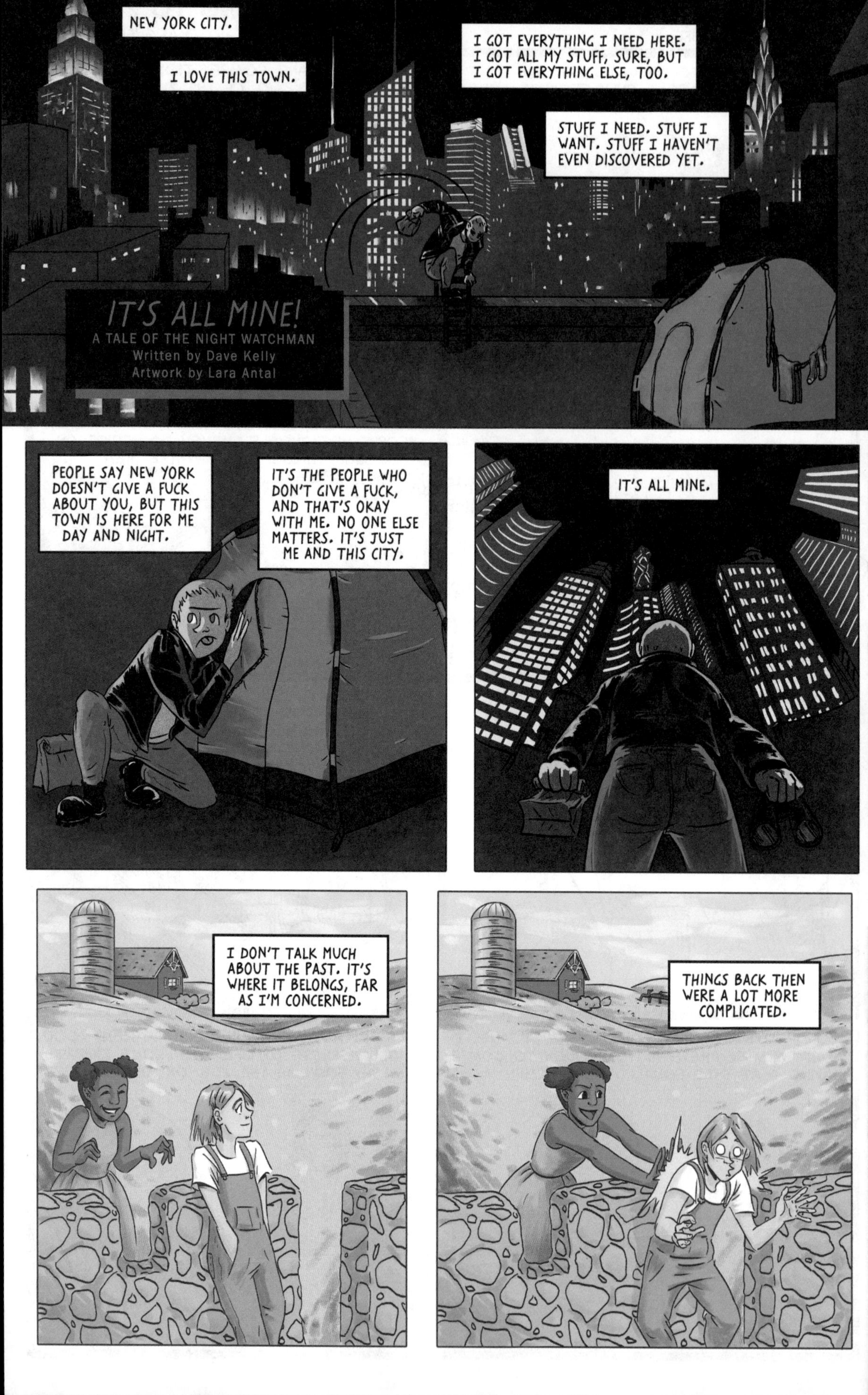
NEW YORK CITY.
I LOVE THIS TOWN.
I GOT EVERYTHING I NEED HERE. I GOT ALL MY STUFF, SURE, BUT I GOT EVERYTHING ELSE, TOO.
STUFF I NEED. STUFF I WANT. STUFF I HAVEN'T EVEN DISCOVERED YET.
IT'S ALL MINE!
A TALE OF THE NIGHT WATCHMAN
Written by Dave Kelly
Artwork by Lara Antal
PEOPLE SAY NEW YORK DOESN'T GIVE A FUCK ABOUT YOU, BUT THIS TOWN IS HERE FOR ME DAY AND NIGHT.
IT'S THE PEOPLE WHO DON'T GIVE A FUCK, AND THAT'S OKAY WITH ME. NO ONE ELSE MATTERS. IT'S JUST ME AND THIS CITY.
IT'S ALL MINE.
I DON'T TALK MUCH ABOUT THE PAST. IT'S WHERE IT BELONGS, FAR AS I'M CONCERNED.
THINGS BACK THEN WERE A LOT MORE COMPLICATED.

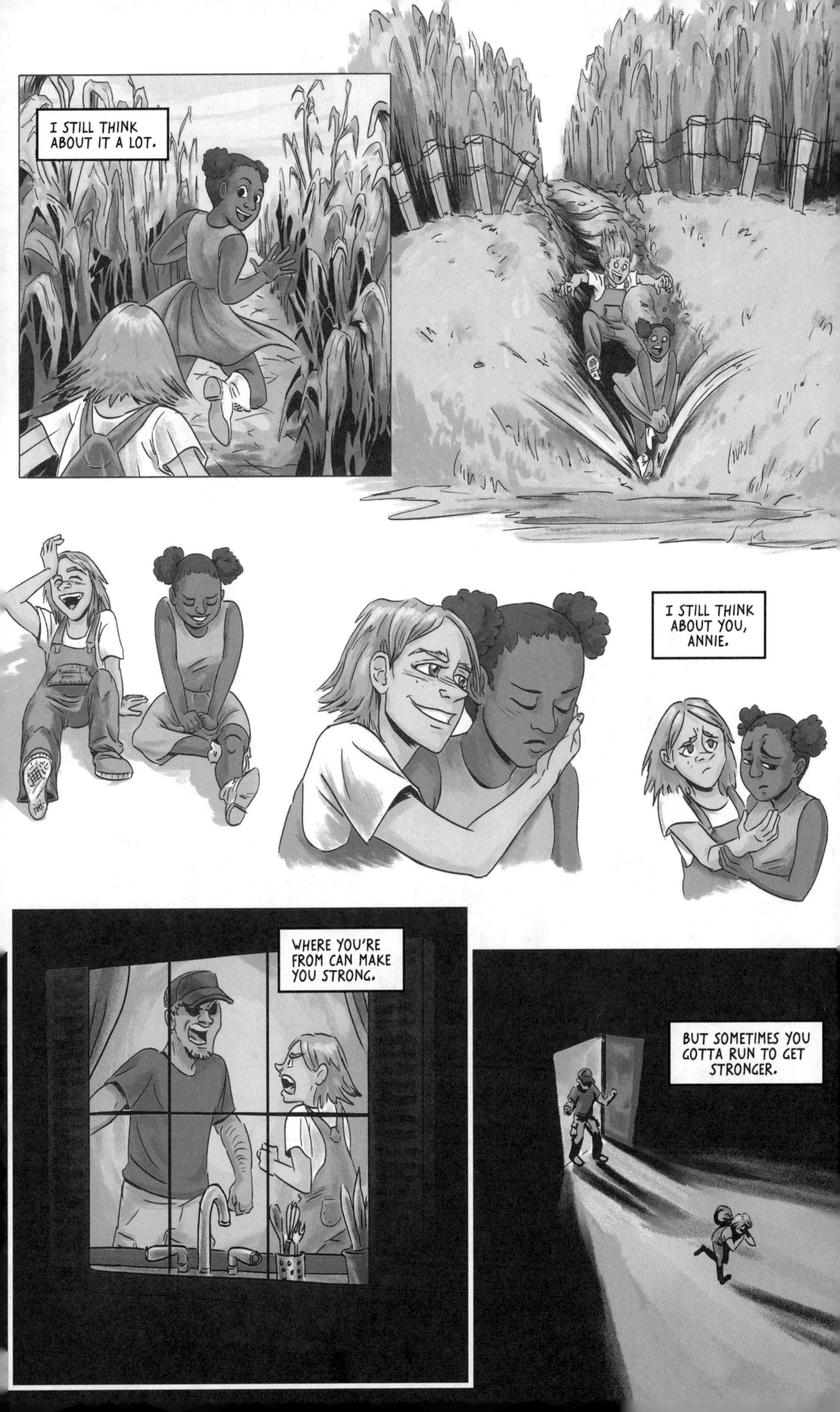
I STILL THINK ABOUT IT A LOT.
I STILL THINK ABOUT YOU, ANNIE.
WHERE YOU'RE FROM CAN MAKE YOU STRONG.
BUT SOMETIMES YOU GOTTA RUN TO GET STRONGER.

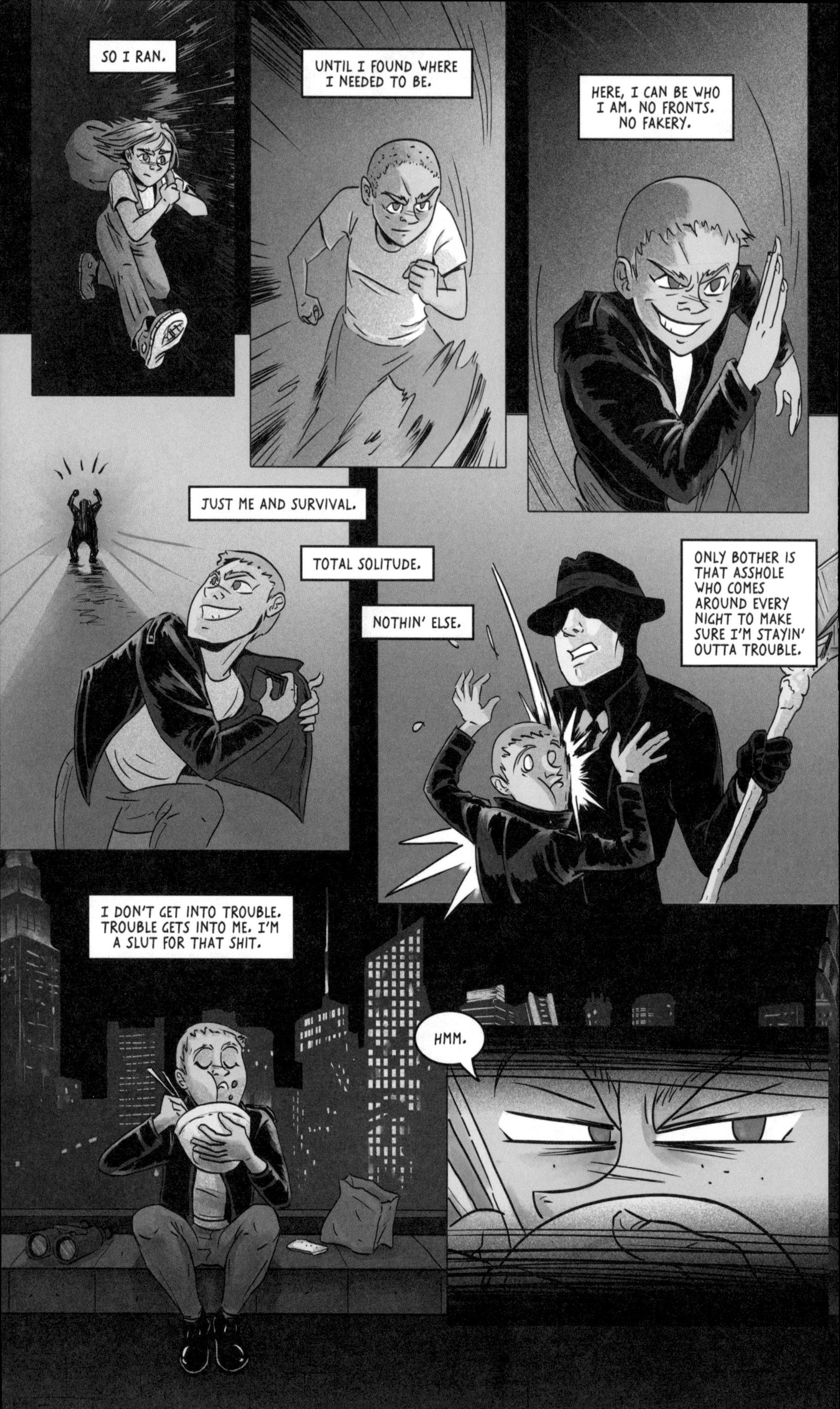

SO I RAN.
UNTIL I FOUND WHERE I NEEDED TO BE.
HERE, I CAN BE WHO I AM. NO FRONTS. NO FAKERY.
JUST ME AND SURVIVAL.
TOTAL SOLITUDE.
NOTHIN' ELSE.
ONLY BOTHER IS THAT ASSHOLE WHO COMES AROUND EVERY NIGHT TO MAKE SURE I'M STAYIN' OUTTA TROUBLE.
I DON'T GET INTO TROUBLE. TROUBLE GETS INTO ME. I'M A SLUT FOR THAT SHIT.
HMM.

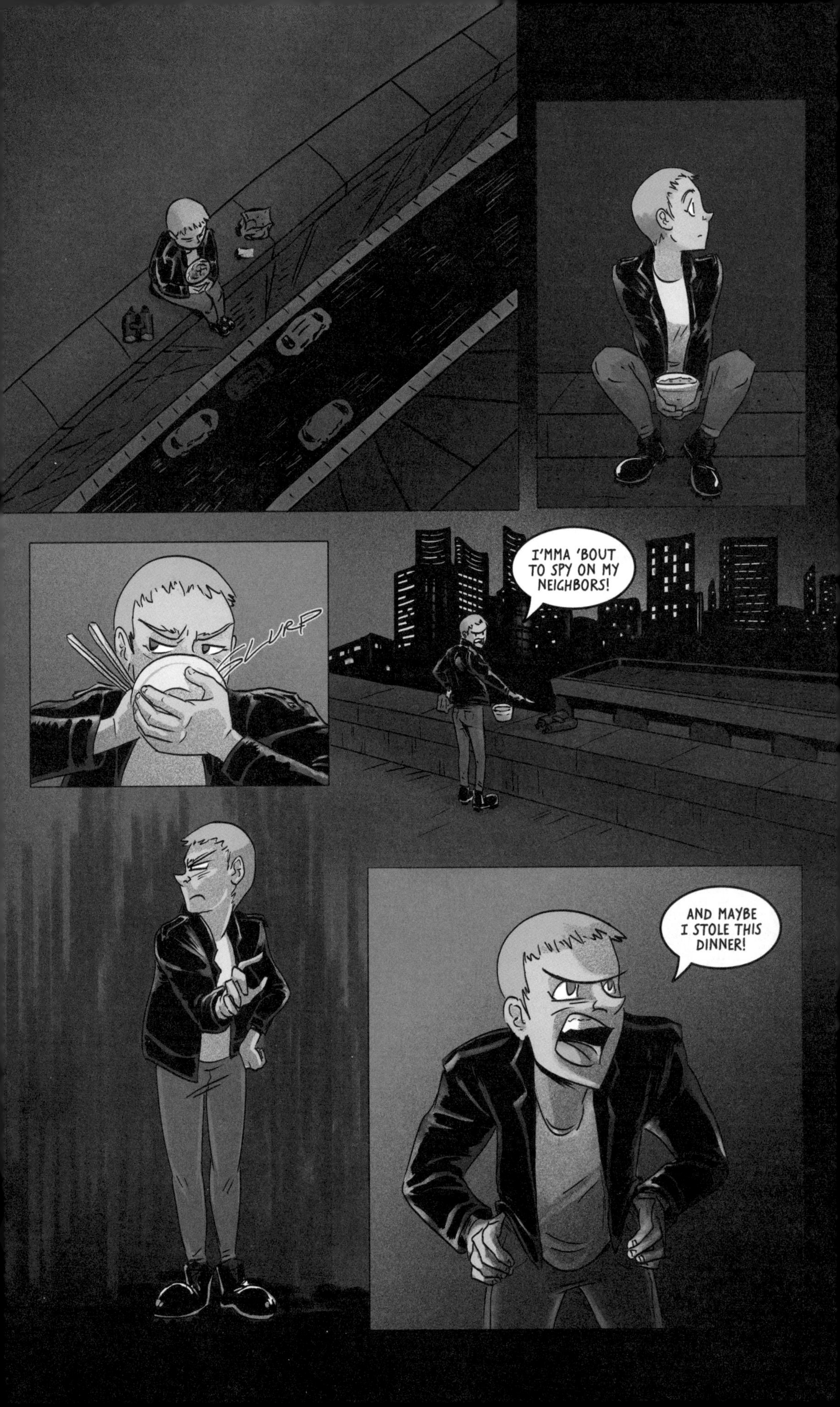
SLURP
I'MMA 'BOUT TO SPY ON MY NEIGHBORS!
AND MAYBE I STOLE THIS DINNER!

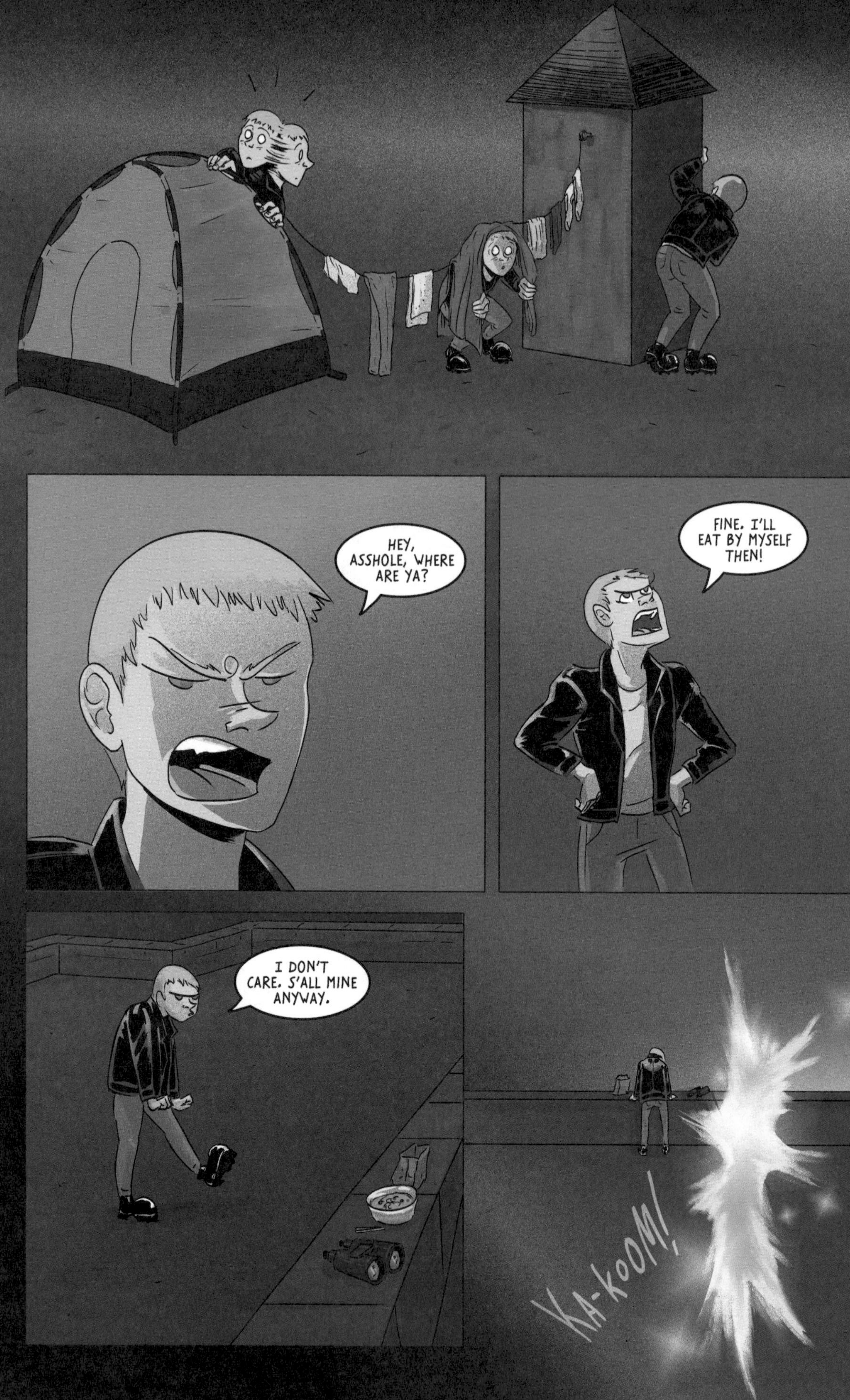
HEY, ASSHOLE, WHERE ARE YA?
FINE. I'LL EAT BY MYSELF THEN!
I DON'T CARE. S'ALL MINE ANYWAY.
KA-KOOM!

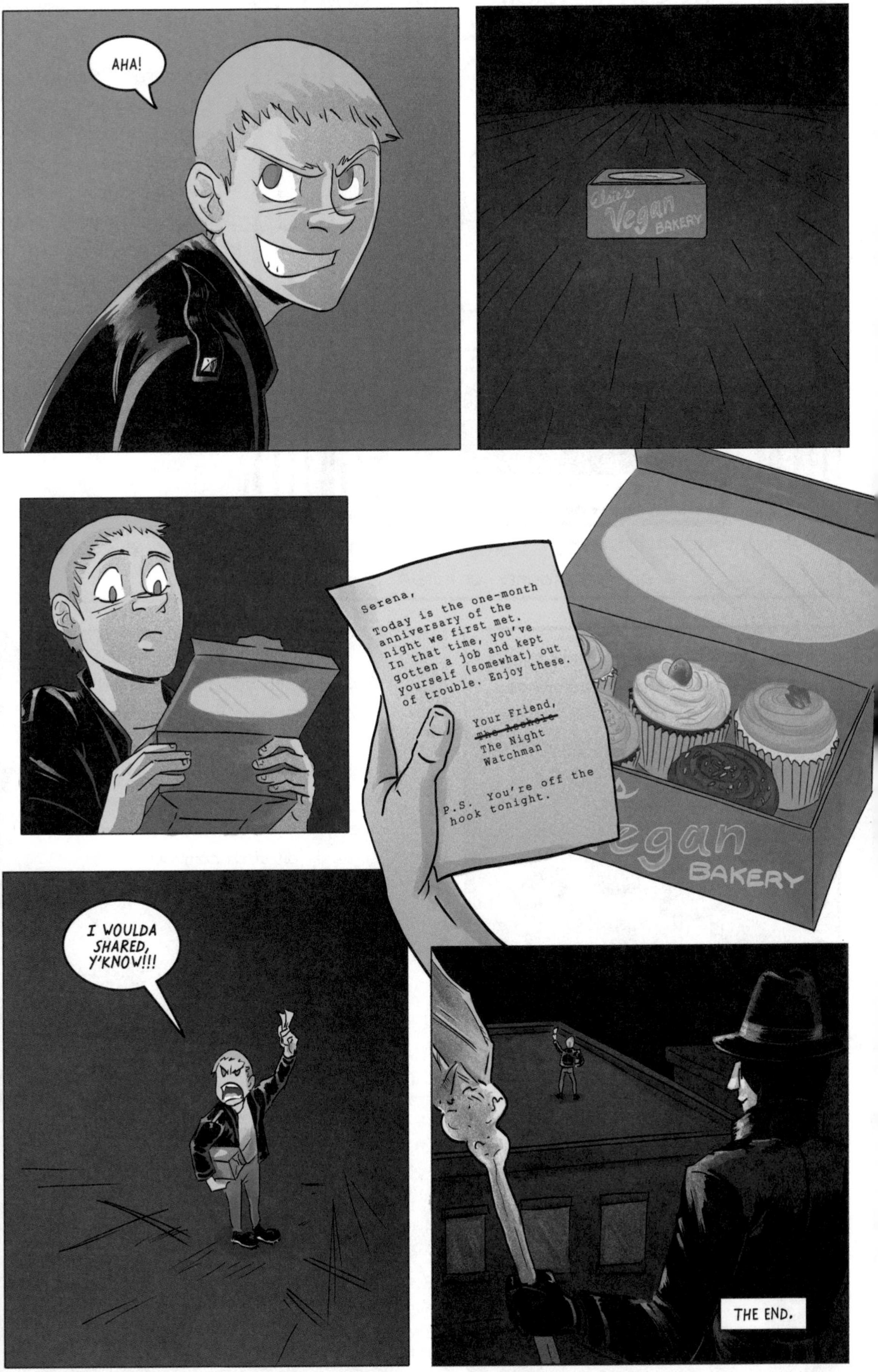
AHA!
Elsie's Vegan BAKERY
Serena,
Today is the one-month anniversary of the night we first met. In that time, you've gotten a job and kept yourself (somewhat) out of trouble. Enjoy these.
Your Friend,
~~The Asshole~~
The Night Watchman
P.S. You're off the hook tonight.
Vegan BAKERY
I WOULDA SHARED, Y'KNOW!!!
THE END.

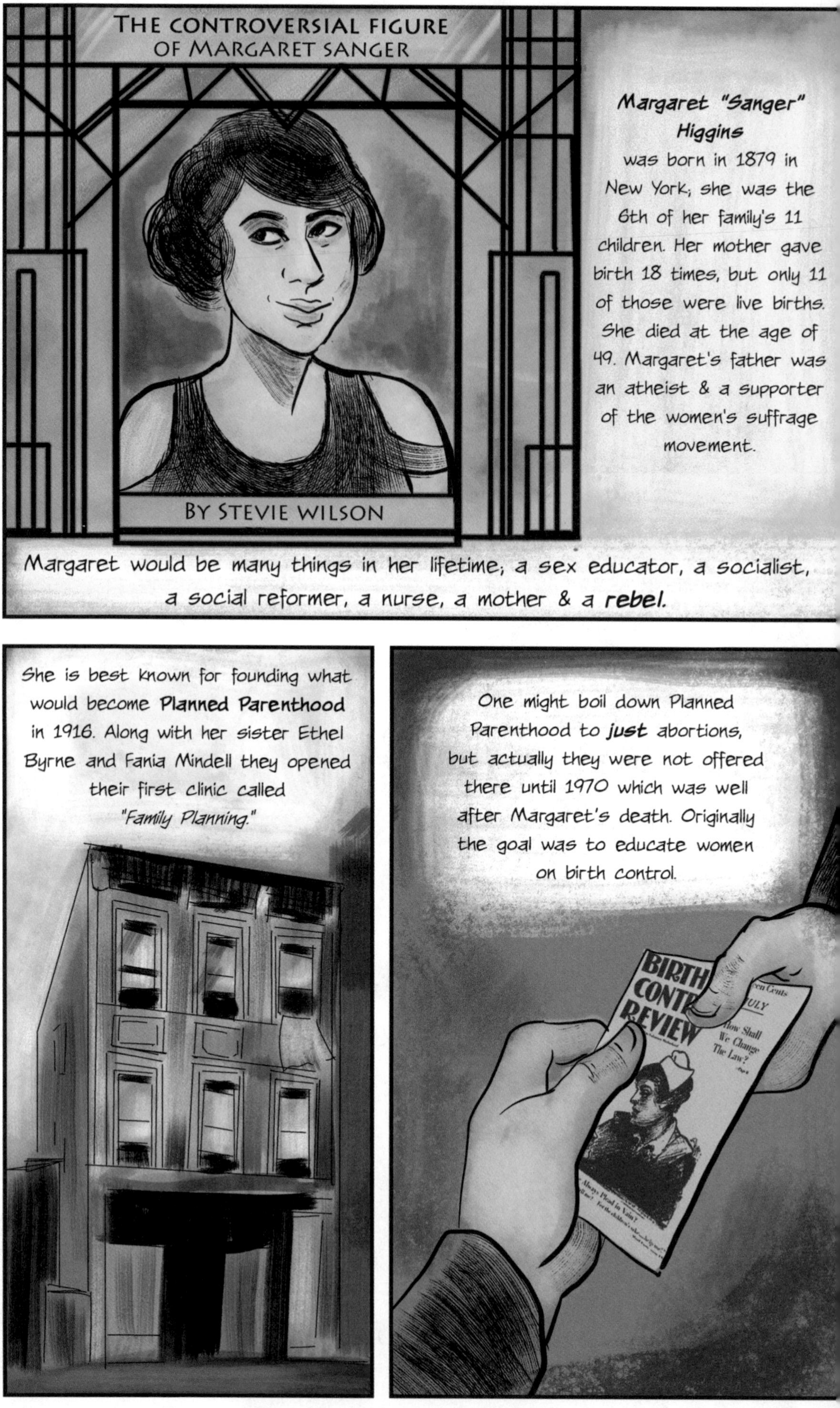

THE CONTROVERSIAL FIGURE OF MARGARET SANGER
BY STEVIE WILSON
Margaret "Sanger" Higgins was born in 1879 in New York; she was the 6th of her family's 11 children. Her mother gave birth 18 times, but only 11 of those were live births. She died at the age of 49. Margaret's father was an atheist & a supporter of the women's suffrage movement.
Margaret would be many things in her lifetime; a sex educator, a socialist, a social reformer, a nurse, a mother & a **rebel.**
She is best known for founding what would become **Planned Parenthood** in 1916. Along with her sister Ethel Byrne and Fania Mindell they opened their first clinic called *"Family Planning."*
One might boil down Planned Parenthood to ***just*** abortions, but actually they were not offered there until 1970 which was well after Margaret's death. Originally the goal was to educate women on birth control.
BIRTH
CONTR
REVIEW
How Shall We Change The Law?

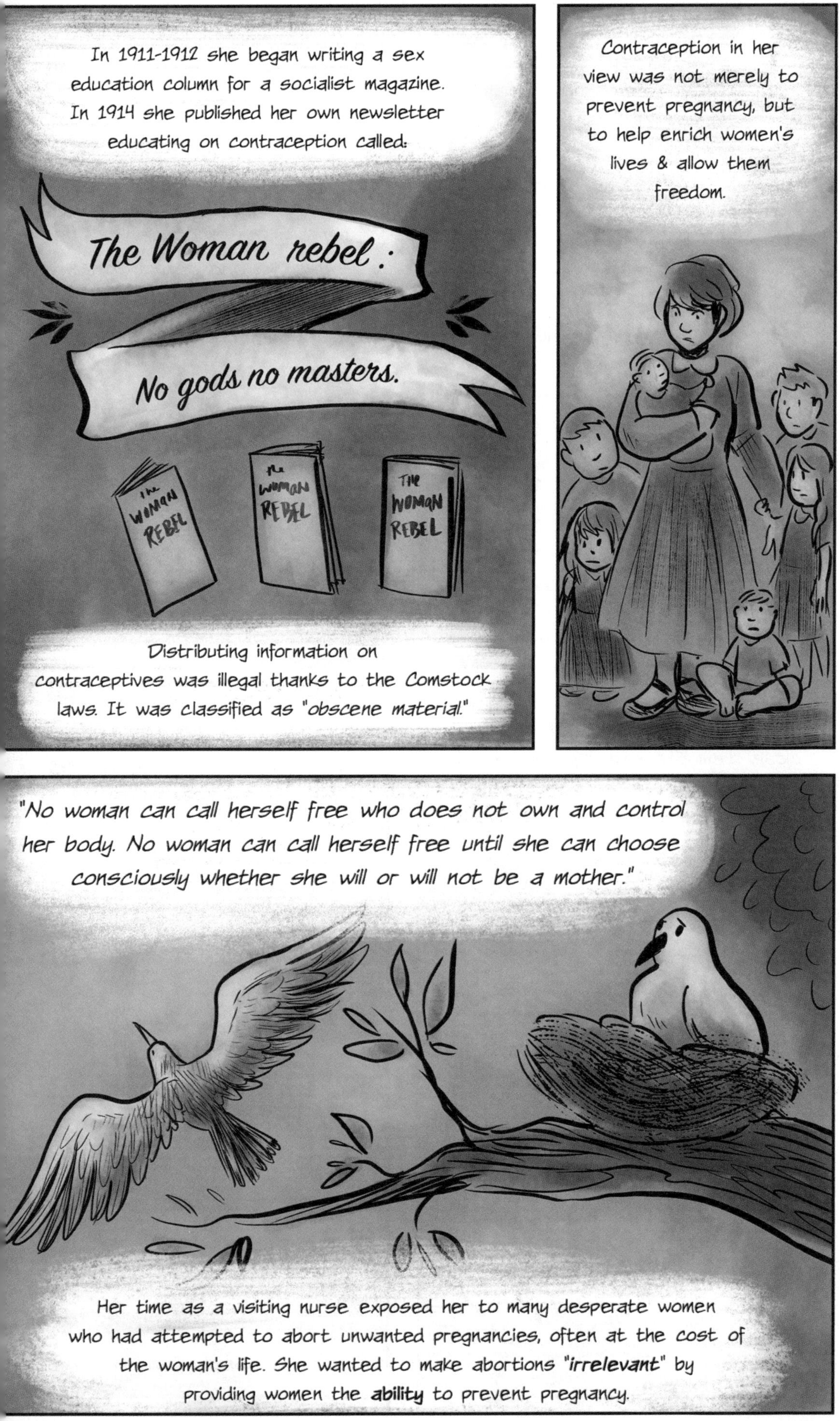
In 1911-1912 she began writing a sex education column for a socialist magazine. In 1914 she published her own newsletter educating on contraception called:
The Woman rebel:
No gods no masters.
THE WOMAN REBEL
THE WOMAN REBEL
THE WOMAN REBEL
Distributing information on contraceptives was illegal thanks to the Comstock laws. It was classified as "obscene material."
Contraception in her view was not merely to prevent pregnancy, but to help enrich women's lives & allow them freedom.
"No woman can call herself free who does not own and control her body. No woman can call herself free until she can choose consciously whether she will or will not be a mother."
Her time as a visiting nurse exposed her to many desperate women who had attempted to abort unwanted pregnancies, often at the cost of the woman's life. She wanted to make abortions "irrelevant" by providing women the ability to prevent pregnancy.

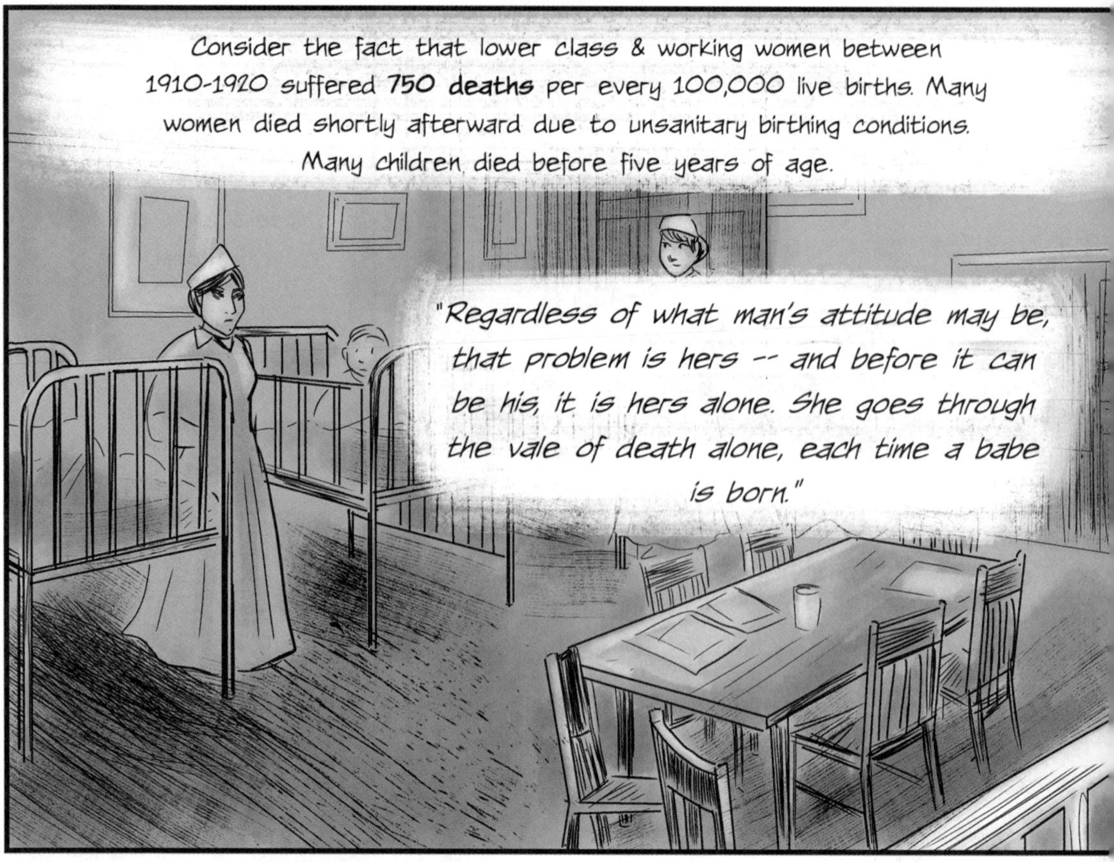
Consider the fact that lower class & working women between 1910-1920 suffered **750 deaths** per every 100,000 live births. Many women died shortly afterward due to unsanitary birthing conditions. Many children died before five years of age.
"Regardless of what man's attitude may be, that problem is hers -- and before it can be his, it is hers alone. She goes through the vale of death alone, each time a babe is born."

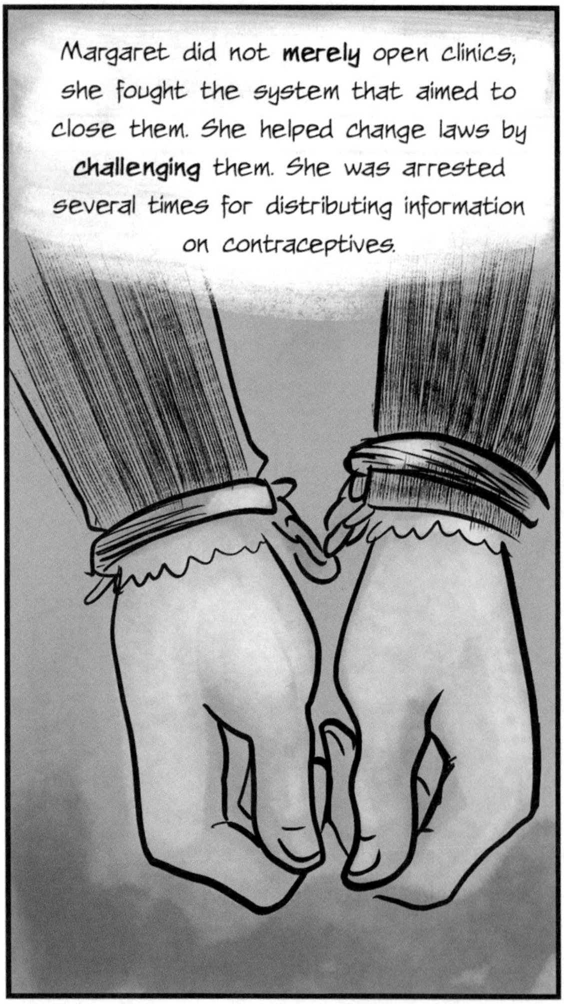
Margaret did not **merely** open clinics; she fought the system that aimed to close them. She helped change laws by **challenging** them. She was arrested several times for distributing information on contraceptives.

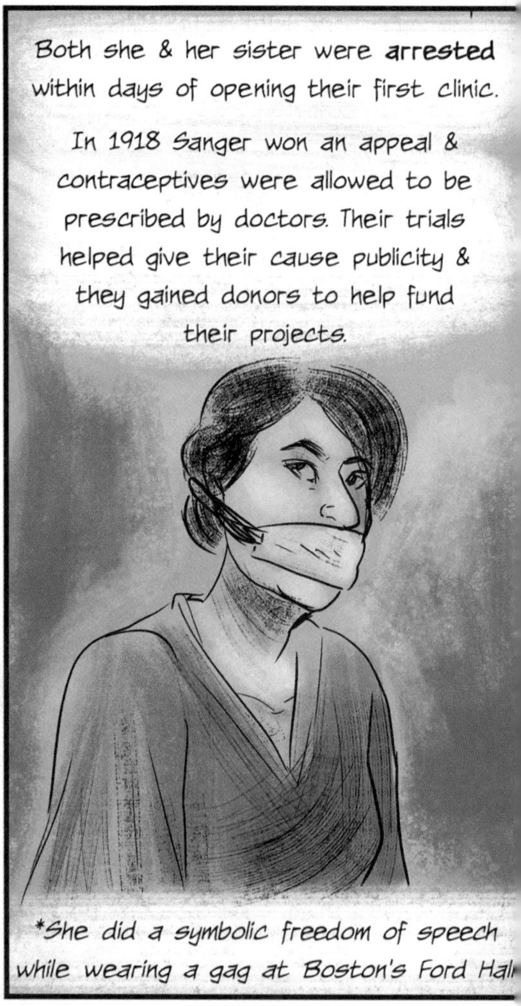
Both she & her sister were **arrested** within days of opening their first clinic.
In 1918 Sanger won an appeal & contraceptives were allowed to be prescribed by doctors. Their trials helped give their cause publicity & they gained donors to help fund their projects.
**She did a symbolic freedom of speech while wearing a gag at Boston's Ford Hal*

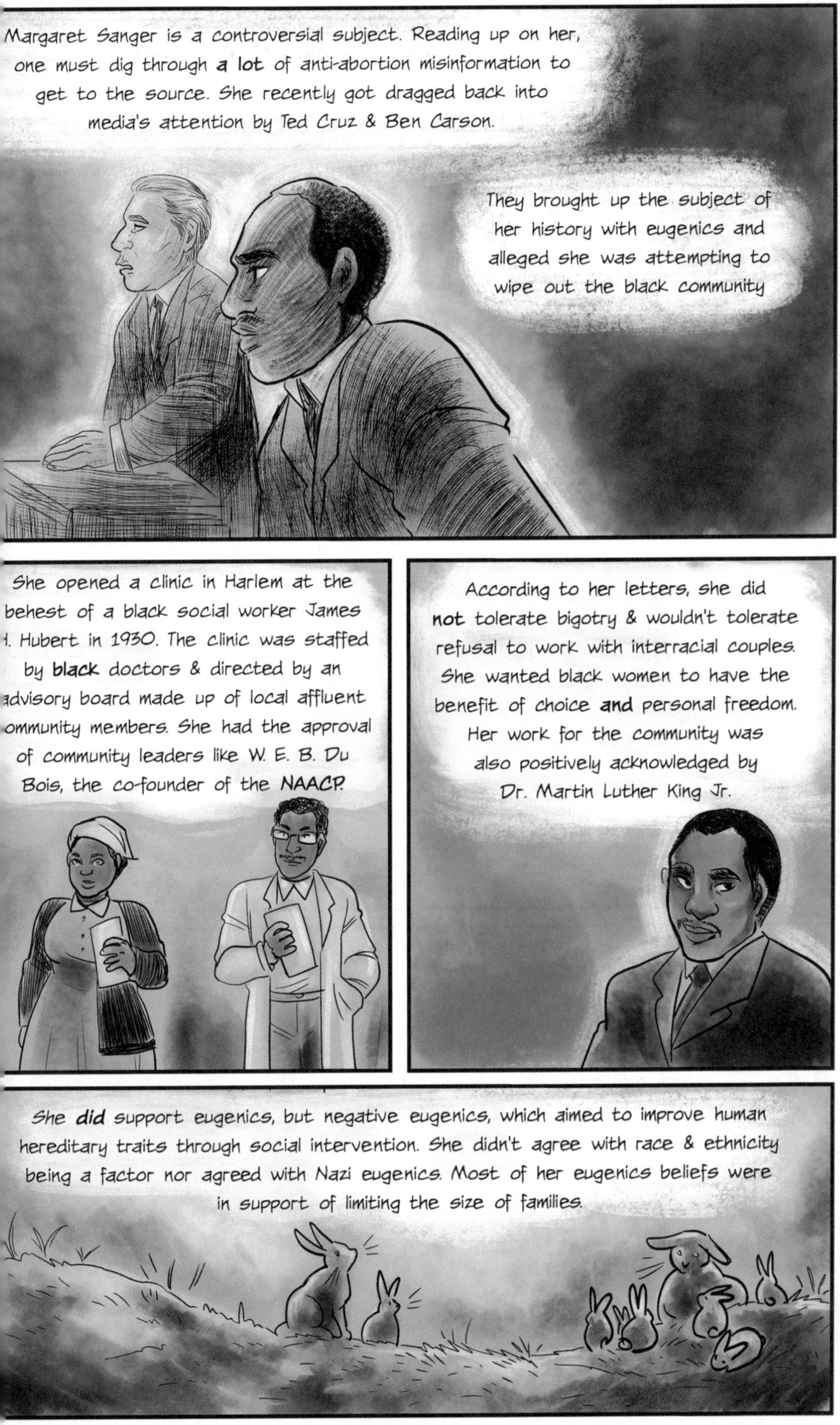
Margaret Sanger is a controversial subject. Reading up on her, one must dig through **a lot** of anti-abortion misinformation to get to the source. She recently got dragged back into media's attention by Ted Cruz & Ben Carson.
They brought up the subject of her history with eugenics and alleged she was attempting to wipe out the black community
She opened a clinic in Harlem at the behest of a black social worker James . Hubert in 1930. The clinic was staffed by **black** doctors & directed by an dvisory board made up of local affluent ommunity members. She had the approval of community leaders like W. E. B. Du Bois, the co-founder of the **NAACP**.
According to her letters, she did **not** tolerate bigotry & wouldn't tolerate refusal to work with interracial couples. She wanted black women to have the benefit of choice **and** personal freedom. Her work for the community was also positively acknowledged by Dr. Martin Luther King Jr.
She **did** support eugenics, but negative eugenics, which aimed to improve human hereditary traits through social intervention. She didn't agree with race & ethnicity being a factor nor agreed with Nazi eugenics. Most of her eugenics beliefs were in support of limiting the size of families.

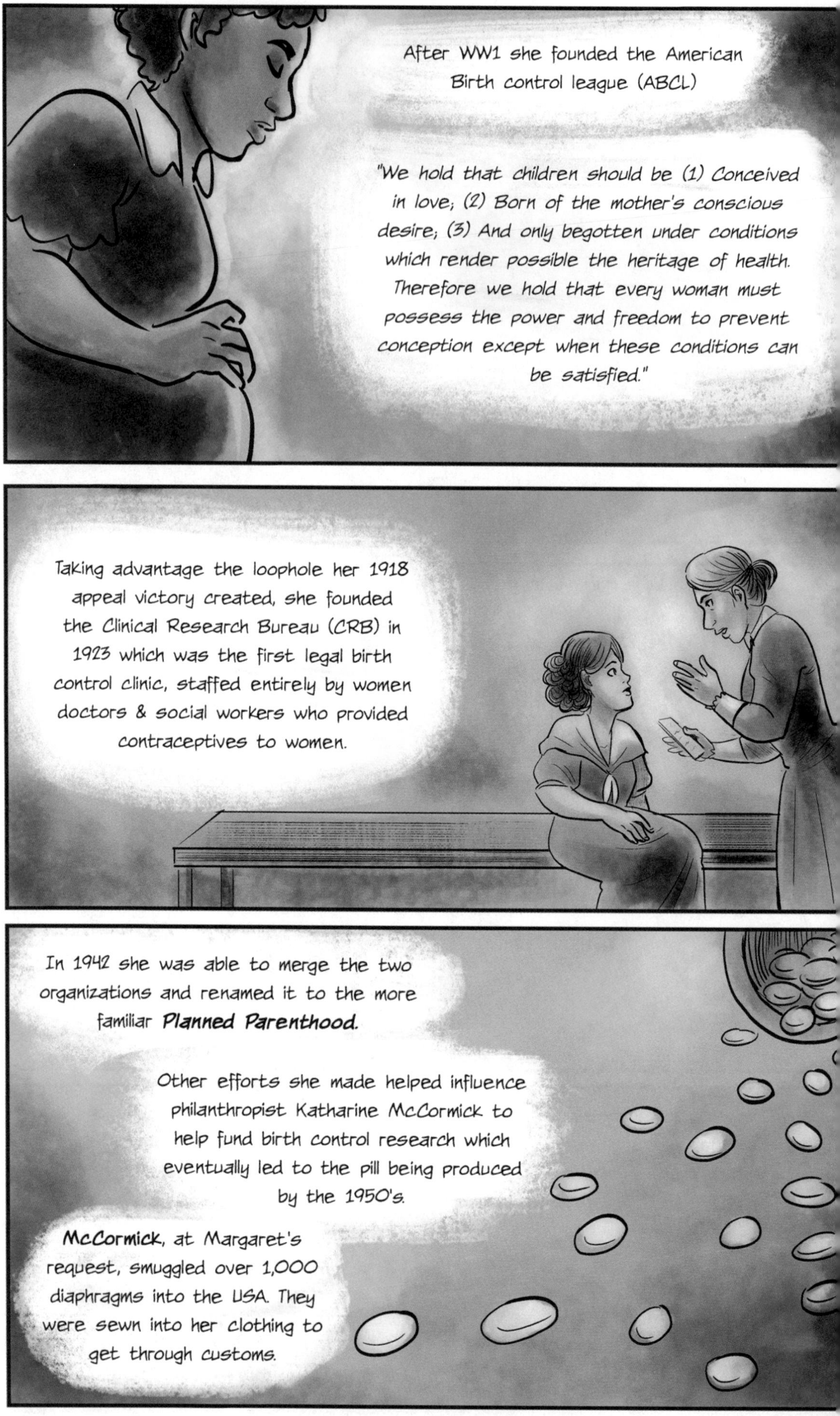
After WW1 she founded the American Birth control league (ABCL)
"We hold that children should be (1) Conceived in love; (2) Born of the mother's conscious desire; (3) And only begotten under conditions which render possible the heritage of health. Therefore we hold that every woman must possess the power and freedom to prevent conception except when these conditions can be satisfied."
Taking advantage the loophole her 1918 appeal victory created, she founded the Clinical Research Bureau (CRB) in 1923 which was the first legal birth control clinic, staffed entirely by women doctors & social workers who provided contraceptives to women.
In 1942 she was able to merge the two organizations and renamed it to the more familiar **Planned Parenthood.**
Other efforts she made helped influence philanthropist Katharine McCormick to help fund birth control research which eventually led to the pill being produced by the 1950's.
McCormick, at Margaret's request, smuggled over 1,000 diaphragms into the USA. They were sewn into her clothing to get through customs.

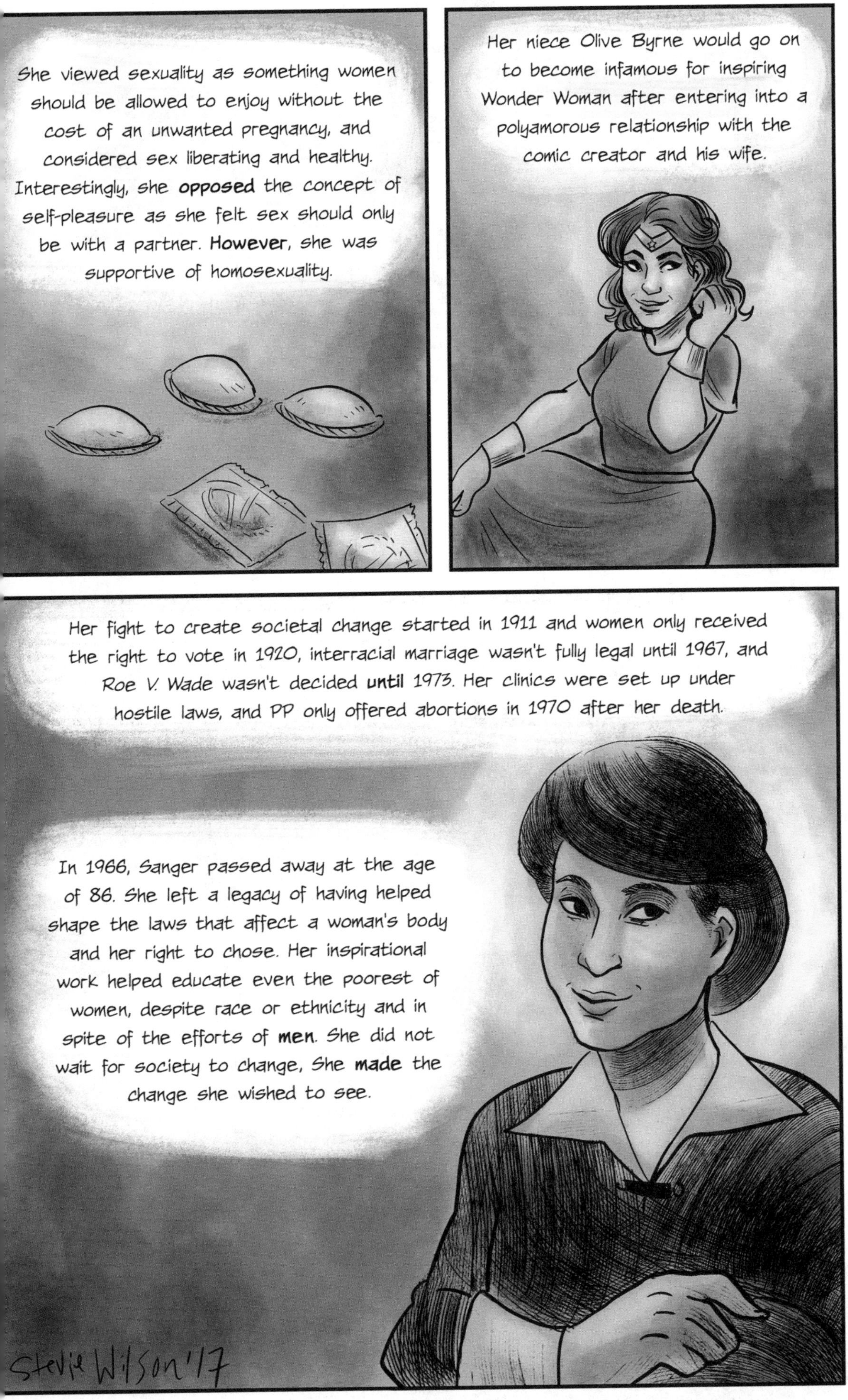
She viewed sexuality as something women should be allowed to enjoy without the cost of an unwanted pregnancy, and considered sex liberating and healthy. Interestingly, she **opposed** the concept of self-pleasure as she felt sex should only be with a partner. **However**, she was supportive of homosexuality.
Her niece Olive Byrne would go on to become infamous for inspiring Wonder Woman after entering into a polyamorous relationship with the comic creator and his wife.
Her fight to create societal change started in 1911 and women only received the right to vote in 1920, interracial marriage wasn't fully legal until 1967, and Roe V. Wade wasn't decided **until** 1973. Her clinics were set up under hostile laws, and PP only offered abortions in 1970 after her death.
In 1966, Sanger passed away at the age of 86. She left a legacy of having helped shape the laws that affect a woman's body and her right to chose. Her inspirational work helped educate even the poorest of women, despite race or ethnicity and in spite of the efforts of **men**. She did not wait for society to change, She **made** the change she wished to see.
Stevie Wilson '17

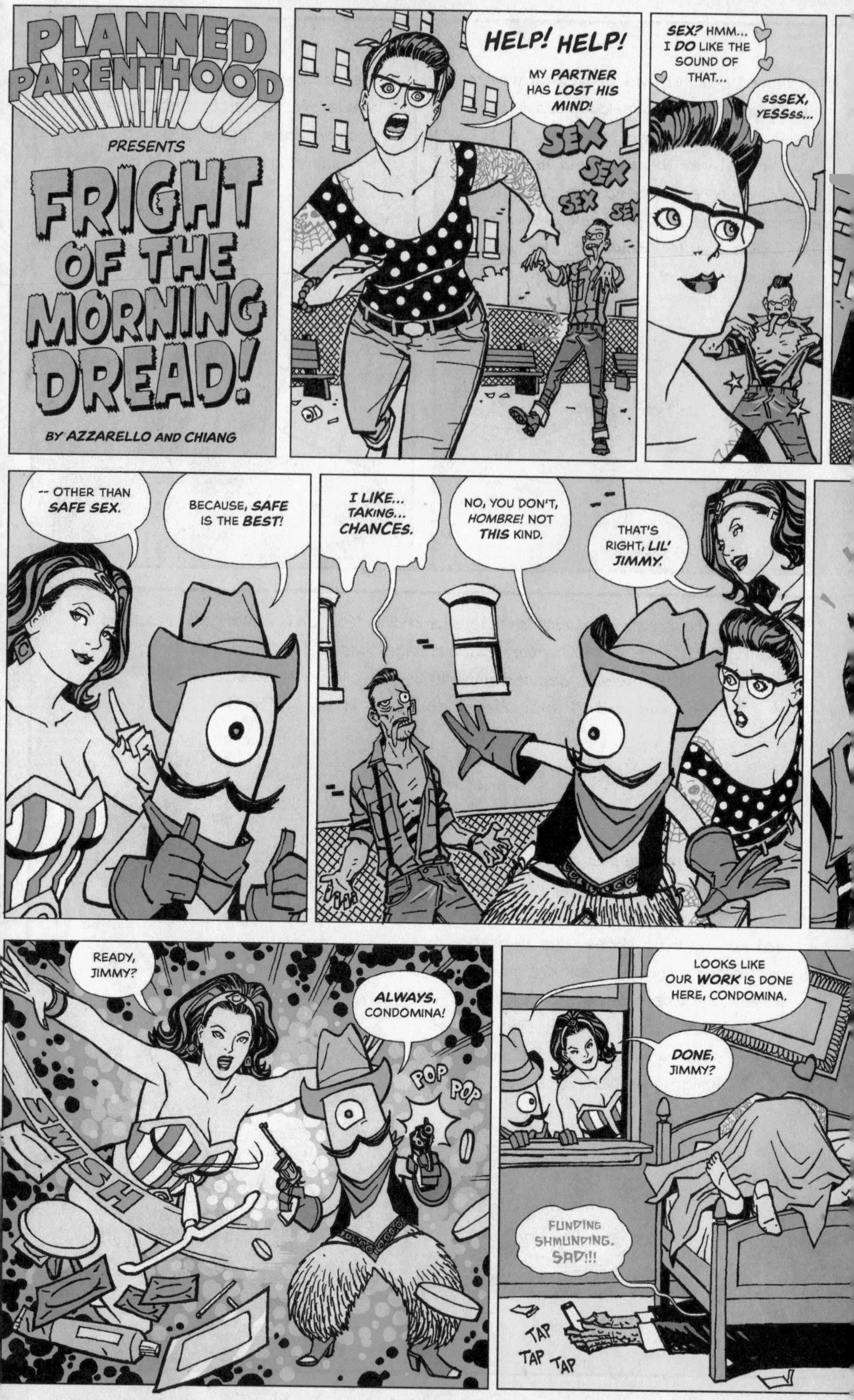
PLANNED PARENTHOOD
PRESENTS
FRIGHT OF THE MORNING DREAD!
BY AZZARELLO AND CHIANG
HELP! HELP!
MY PARTNER HAS LOST HIS MIND!
SEX
SEX
SEX
SEX? HMM... I DO LIKE THE SOUND OF THAT...
SSSEX, YESSSS...
-- OTHER THAN SAFE SEX.
BECAUSE, SAFE IS THE BEST!
I LIKE... TAKING... CHANCES.
NO, YOU DON'T, HOMBRE! NOT THIS KIND.
THAT'S RIGHT, LIL' JIMMY.
READY, JIMMY?
ALWAYS, CONDOMINA!
POP POP
SWISH
LOOKS LIKE OUR WORK IS DONE HERE, CONDOMINA.
DONE, JIMMY?
FUNDING SHMUNDING. SAD!!!
TAP TAP TAP

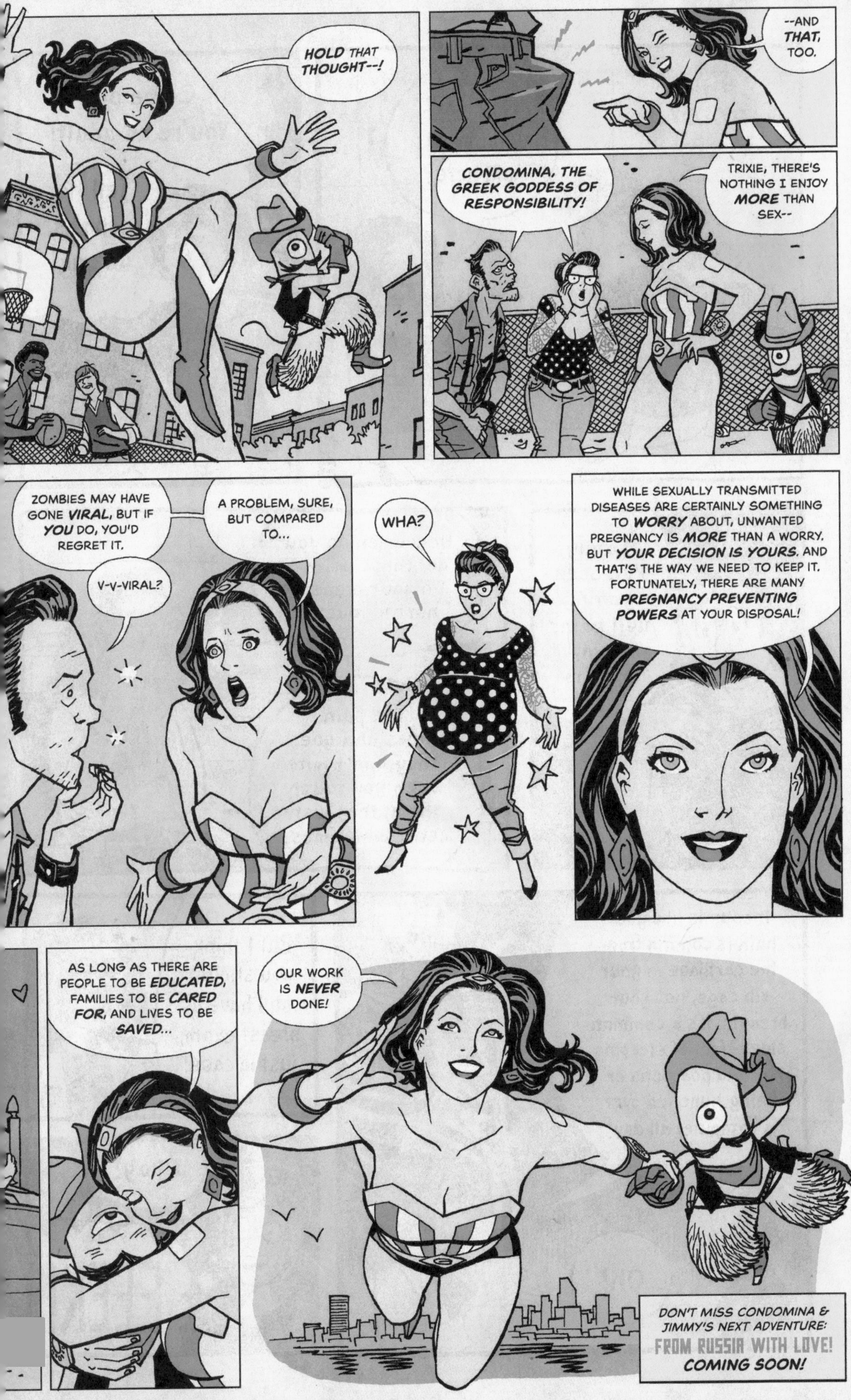
HOLD THAT THOUGHT--!
--AND THAT, TOO.
CONDOMINA, THE GREEK GODDESS OF RESPONSIBILITY!
TRIXIE, THERE'S NOTHING I ENJOY MORE THAN SEX--
ZOMBIES MAY HAVE GONE VIRAL, BUT IF YOU DO, YOU'D REGRET IT.
V-V-VIRAL?
A PROBLEM, SURE, BUT COMPARED TO...
WHA?
WHILE SEXUALLY TRANSMITTED DISEASES ARE CERTAINLY SOMETHING TO WORRY ABOUT, UNWANTED PREGNANCY IS MORE THAN A WORRY. BUT YOUR DECISION IS YOURS, AND THAT'S THE WAY WE NEED TO KEEP IT. FORTUNATELY, THERE ARE MANY PREGNANCY PREVENTING POWERS AT YOUR DISPOSAL!
AS LONG AS THERE ARE PEOPLE TO BE EDUCATED, FAMILIES TO BE CARED FOR, AND LIVES TO BE SAVED...
OUR WORK IS NEVER DONE!
DON'T MISS CONDOMINA & JIMMY'S NEXT ADVENTURE:
FROM RUSSIA WITH LOVE!
COMING SOON!

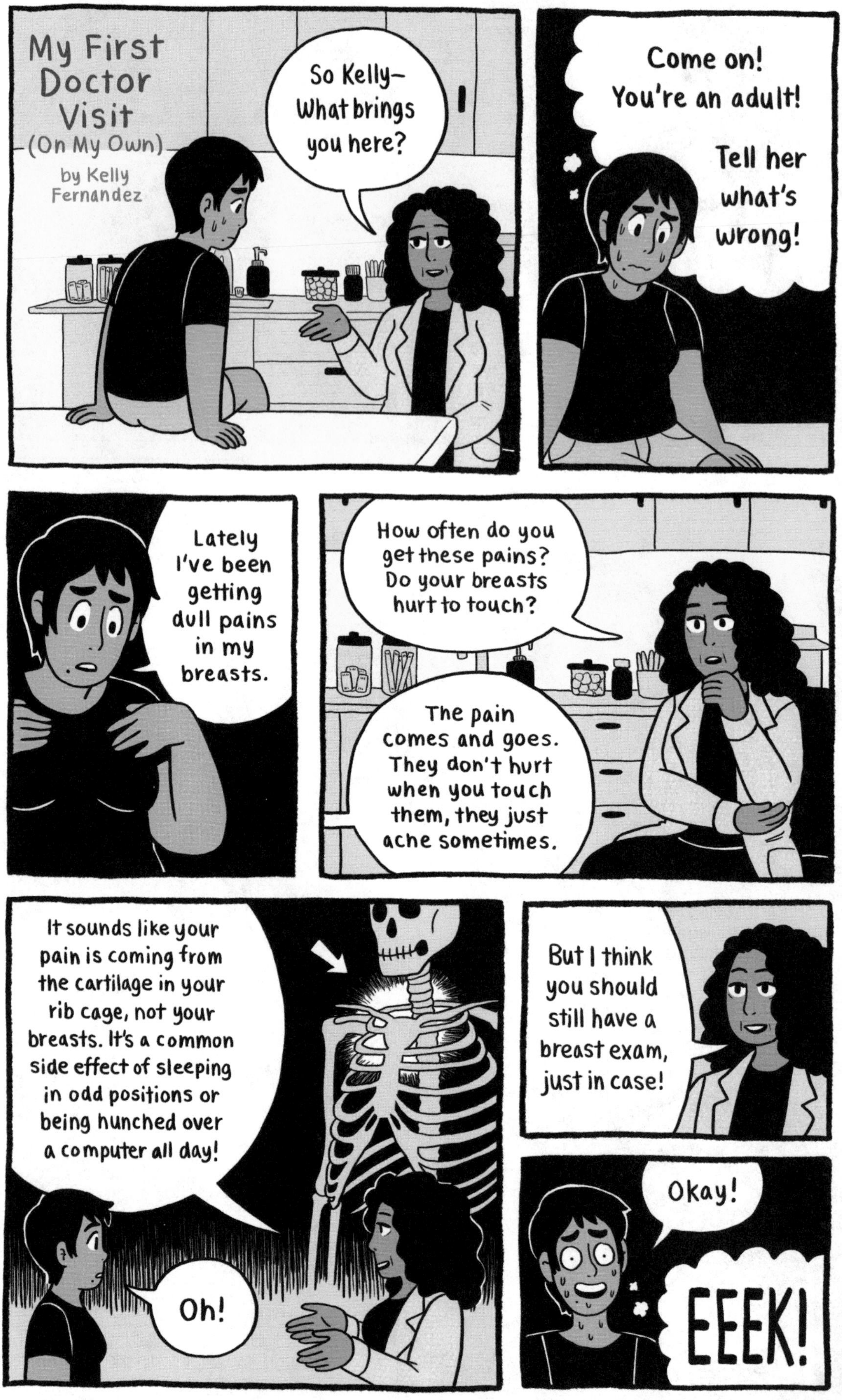
My First Doctor Visit (On My Own)
by Kelly Fernandez
So Kelly— What brings you here?
Come on! You're an adult!
Tell her what's wrong!
Lately I've been getting dull pains in my breasts.
How often do you get these pains? Do your breasts hurt to touch?
The pain comes and goes. They don't hurt when you touch them, they just ache sometimes.
It sounds like your pain is coming from the cartilage in your rib cage, not your breasts. It's a common side effect of sleeping in odd positions or being hunched over a computer all day!
Oh!
But I think you should still have a breast exam, just in case!
Okay!
EEEK!

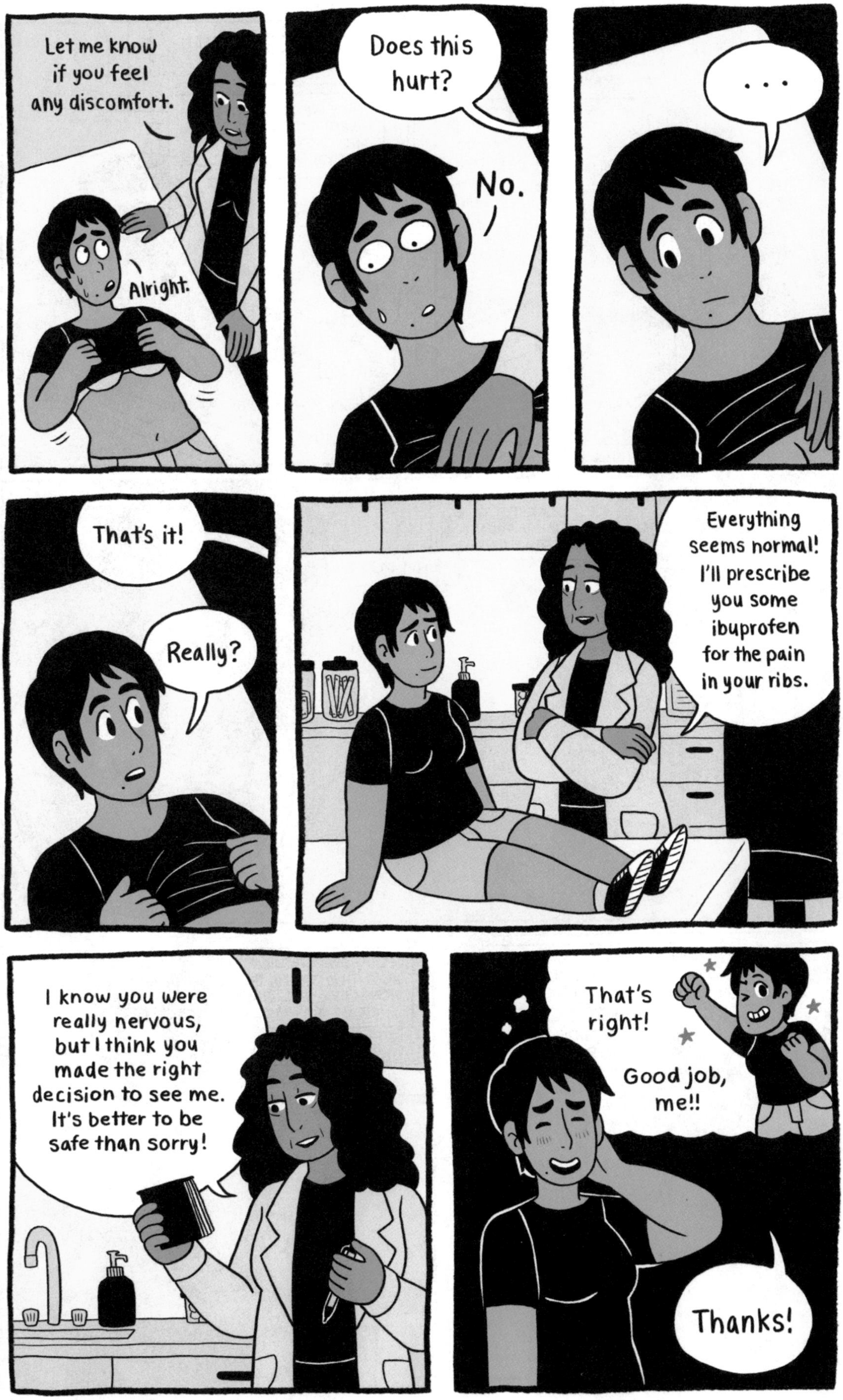
Let me know if you feel any discomfort.
Alright.
Does this hurt?
No.
. . .
That's it!
Really?
Everything seems normal! I'll prescribe you some ibuprofen for the pain in your ribs.
I know you were really nervous, but I think you made the right decision to see me. It's better to be safe than sorry!
That's right!
Good job, me!!
Thanks!

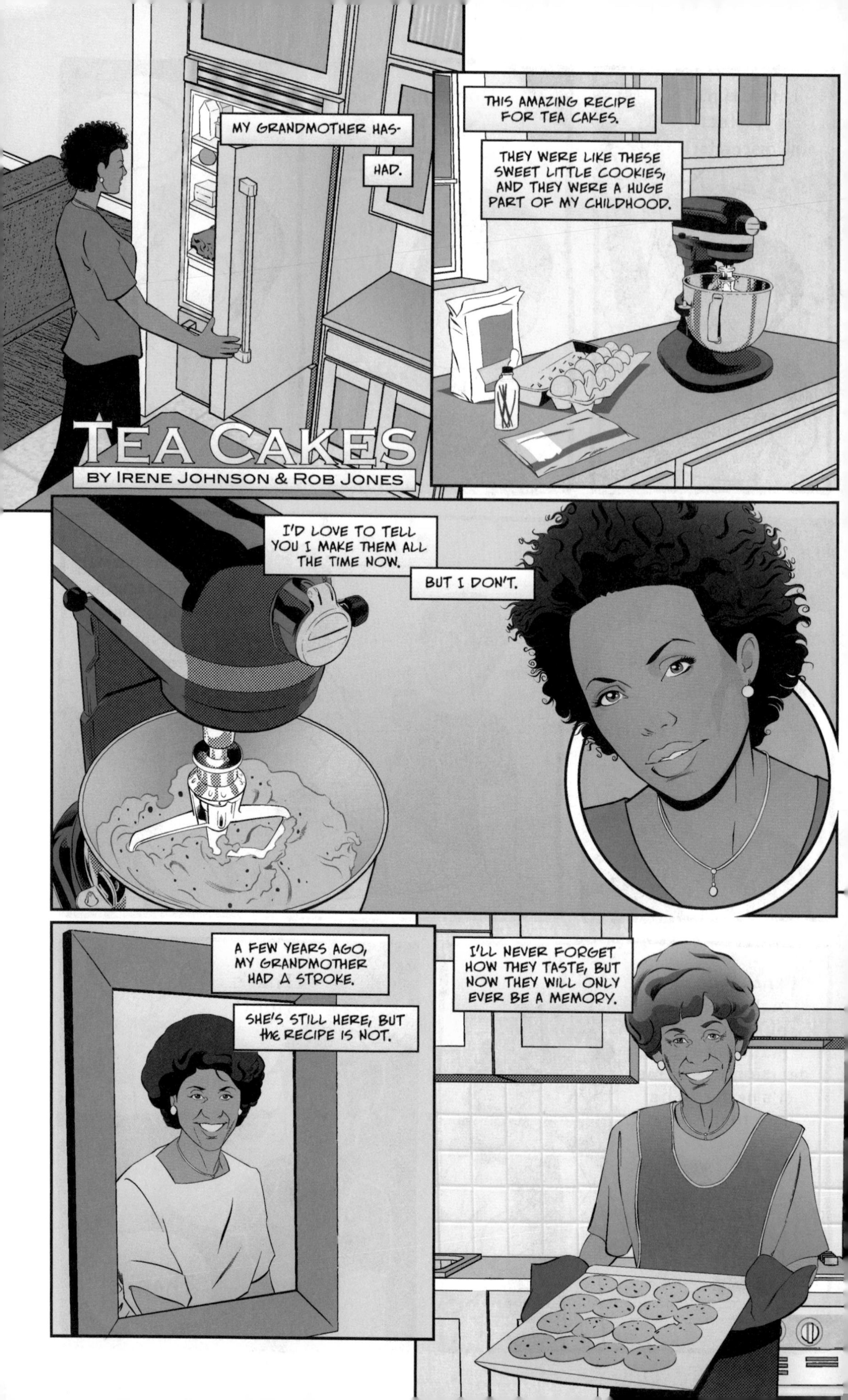

TEA CAKES
BY IRENE JOHNSON & ROB JONES
MY GRANDMOTHER HAS-
HAD.
THIS AMAZING RECIPE FOR TEA CAKES.
THEY WERE LIKE THESE SWEET LITTLE COOKIES, AND THEY WERE A HUGE PART OF MY CHILDHOOD.
I'D LOVE TO TELL YOU I MAKE THEM ALL THE TIME NOW.
BUT I DON'T.
A FEW YEARS AGO, MY GRANDMOTHER HAD A STROKE.
SHE'S STILL HERE, BUT THE RECIPE IS NOT.
I'LL NEVER FORGET HOW THEY TASTE, BUT NOW THEY WILL ONLY EVER BE A MEMORY.

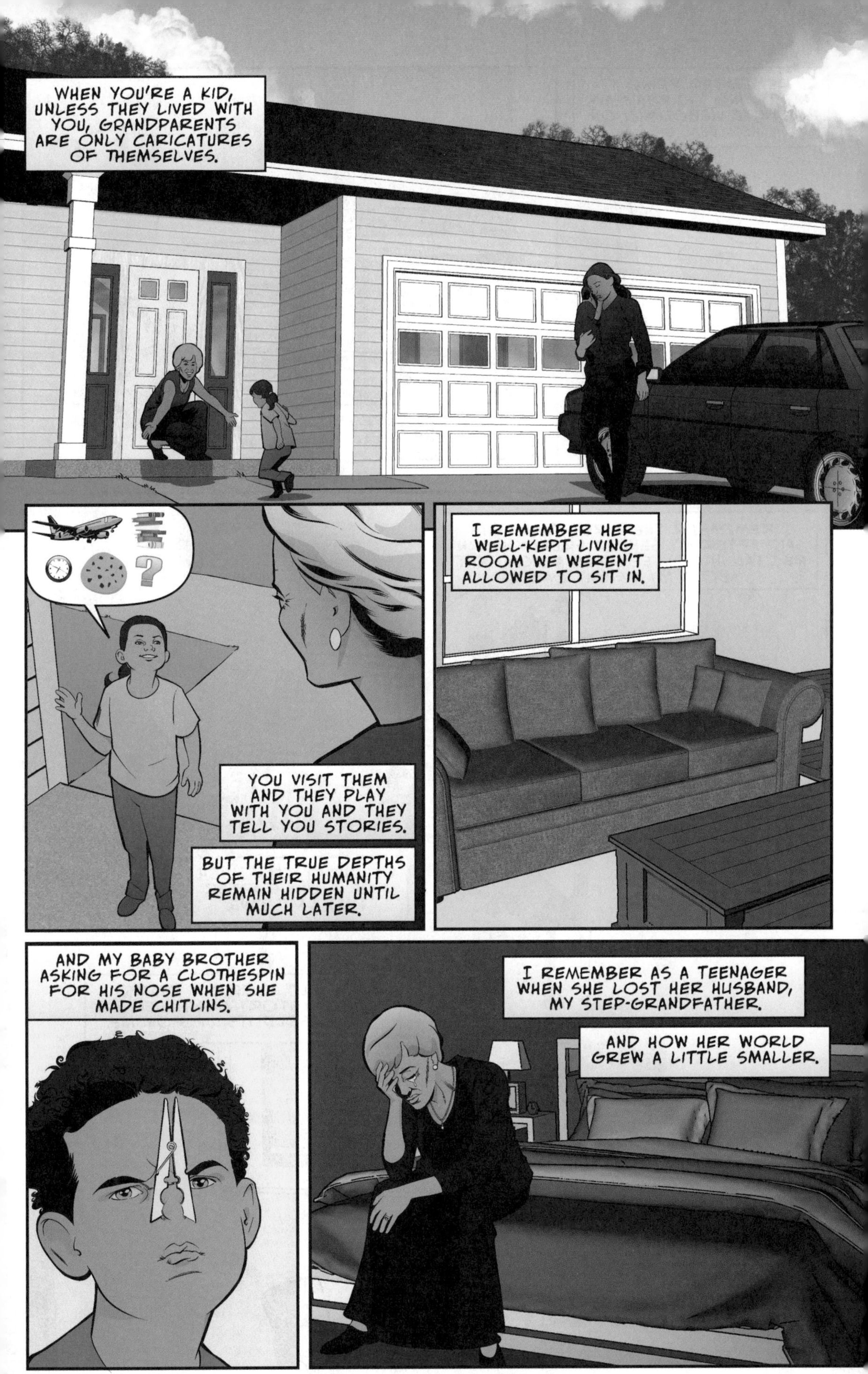
WHEN YOU'RE A KID, UNLESS THEY LIVED WITH YOU, GRANDPARENTS ARE ONLY CARICATURES OF THEMSELVES.
YOU VISIT THEM AND THEY PLAY WITH YOU AND THEY TELL YOU STORIES.
BUT THE TRUE DEPTHS OF THEIR HUMANITY REMAIN HIDDEN UNTIL MUCH LATER.
I REMEMBER HER WELL-KEPT LIVING ROOM WE WEREN'T ALLOWED TO SIT IN.
AND MY BABY BROTHER ASKING FOR A CLOTHESPIN FOR HIS NOSE WHEN SHE MADE CHITLINS.
I REMEMBER AS A TEENAGER WHEN SHE LOST HER HUSBAND, MY STEP-GRANDFATHER.
AND HOW HER WORLD GREW A LITTLE SMALLER.

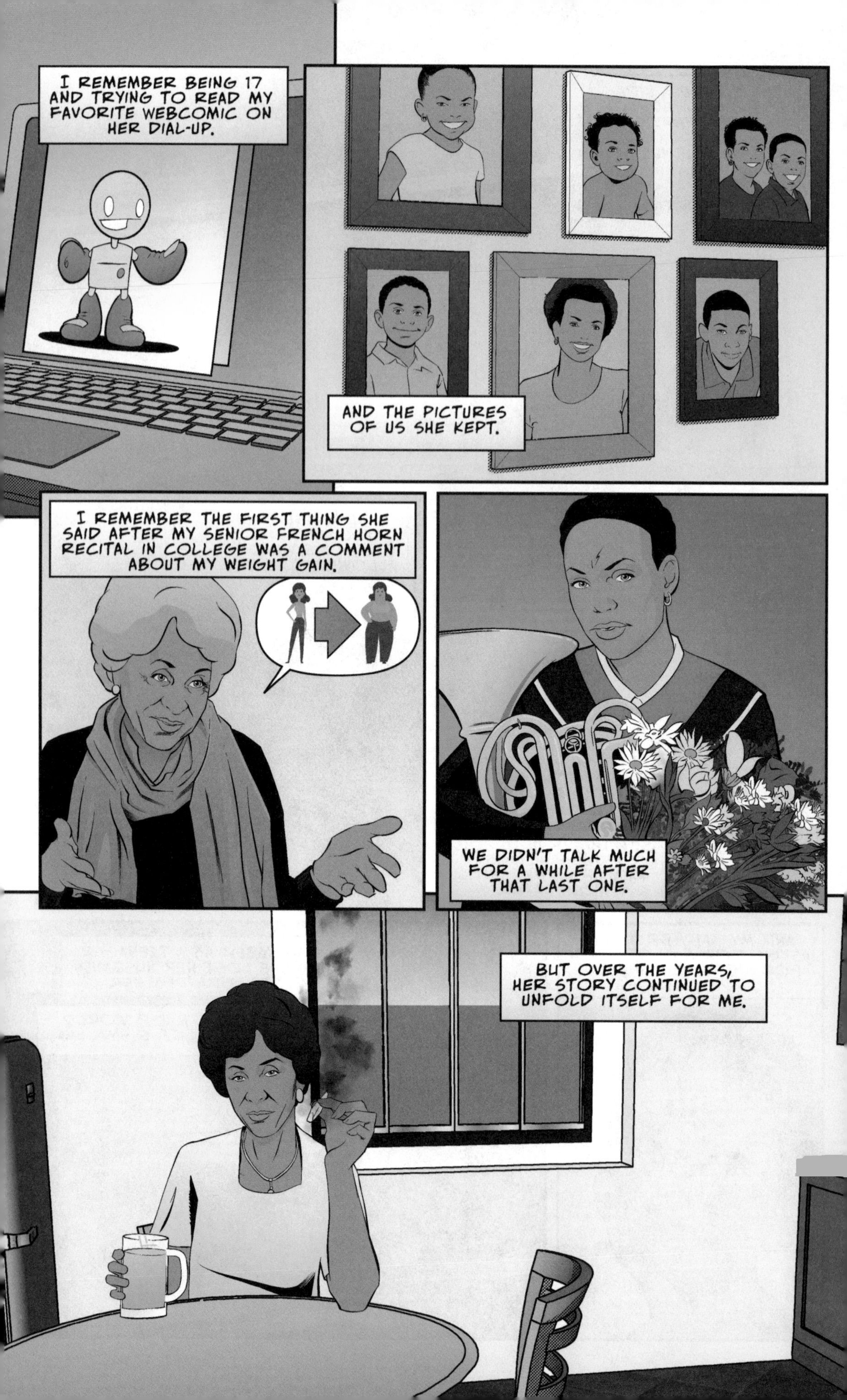
I REMEMBER BEING 17 AND TRYING TO READ MY FAVORITE WEBCOMIC ON HER DIAL-UP.
AND THE PICTURES OF US SHE KEPT.
I REMEMBER THE FIRST THING SHE SAID AFTER MY SENIOR FRENCH HORN RECITAL IN COLLEGE WAS A COMMENT ABOUT MY WEIGHT GAIN.
WE DIDN'T TALK MUCH FOR A WHILE AFTER THAT LAST ONE.
BUT OVER THE YEARS, HER STORY CONTINUED TO UNFOLD ITSELF FOR ME.

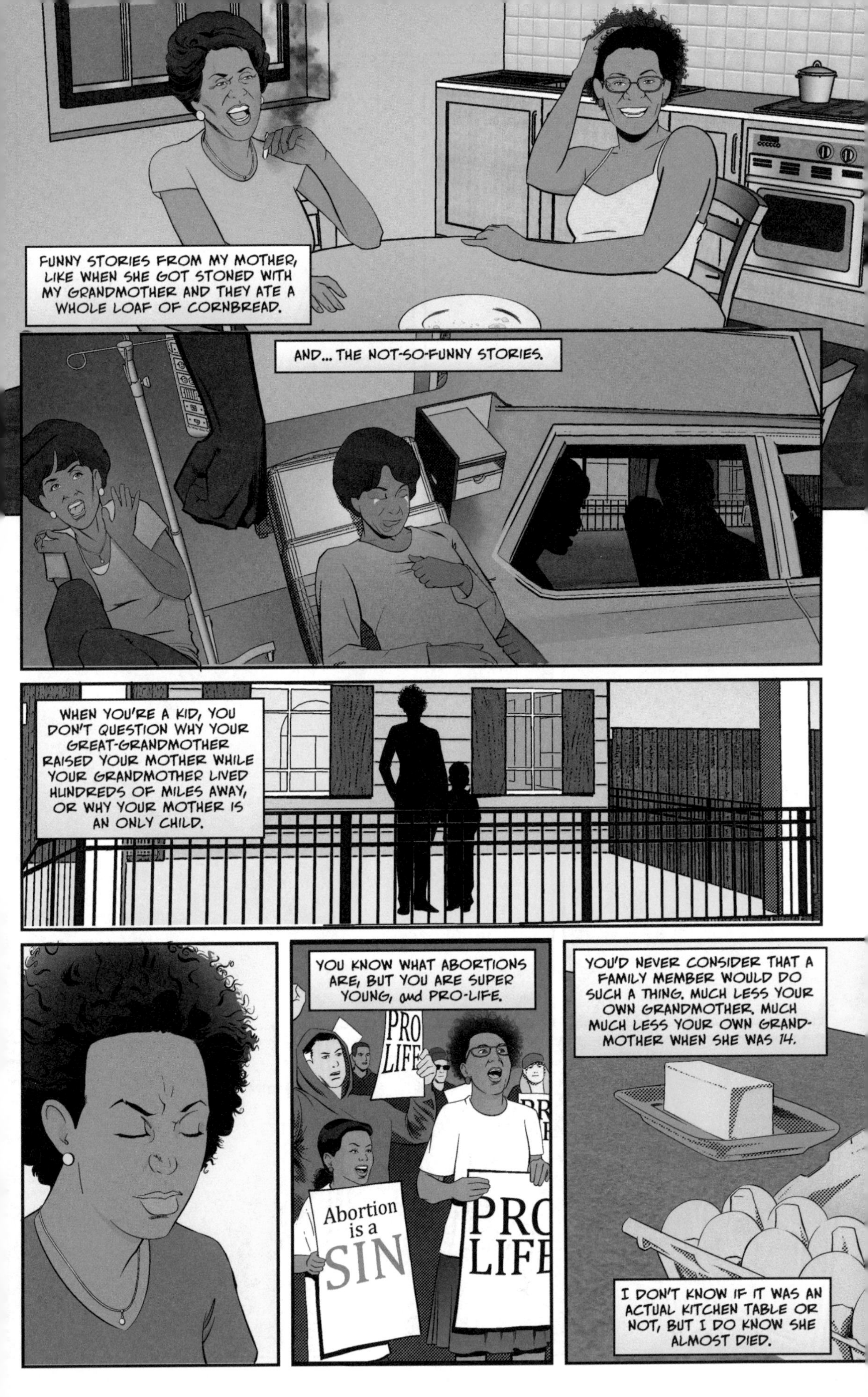
FUNNY STORIES FROM MY MOTHER, LIKE WHEN SHE GOT STONED WITH MY GRANDMOTHER AND THEY ATE A WHOLE LOAF OF CORNBREAD.
AND... THE NOT-SO-FUNNY STORIES.
WHEN YOU'RE A KID, YOU DON'T QUESTION WHY YOUR GREAT-GRANDMOTHER RAISED YOUR MOTHER WHILE YOUR GRANDMOTHER LIVED HUNDREDS OF MILES AWAY, OR WHY YOUR MOTHER IS AN ONLY CHILD.
YOU KNOW WHAT ABORTIONS ARE, BUT YOU ARE SUPER YOUNG, and PRO-LIFE.
PRO LIFE
Abortion is a SIN
PRO LIFE
YOU'D NEVER CONSIDER THAT A FAMILY MEMBER WOULD DO SUCH A THING. MUCH LESS YOUR OWN GRANDMOTHER. MUCH MUCH LESS YOUR OWN GRAND-MOTHER WHEN SHE WAS 14.
I DON'T KNOW IF IT WAS AN ACTUAL KITCHEN TABLE OR NOT, BUT I DO KNOW SHE ALMOST DIED.

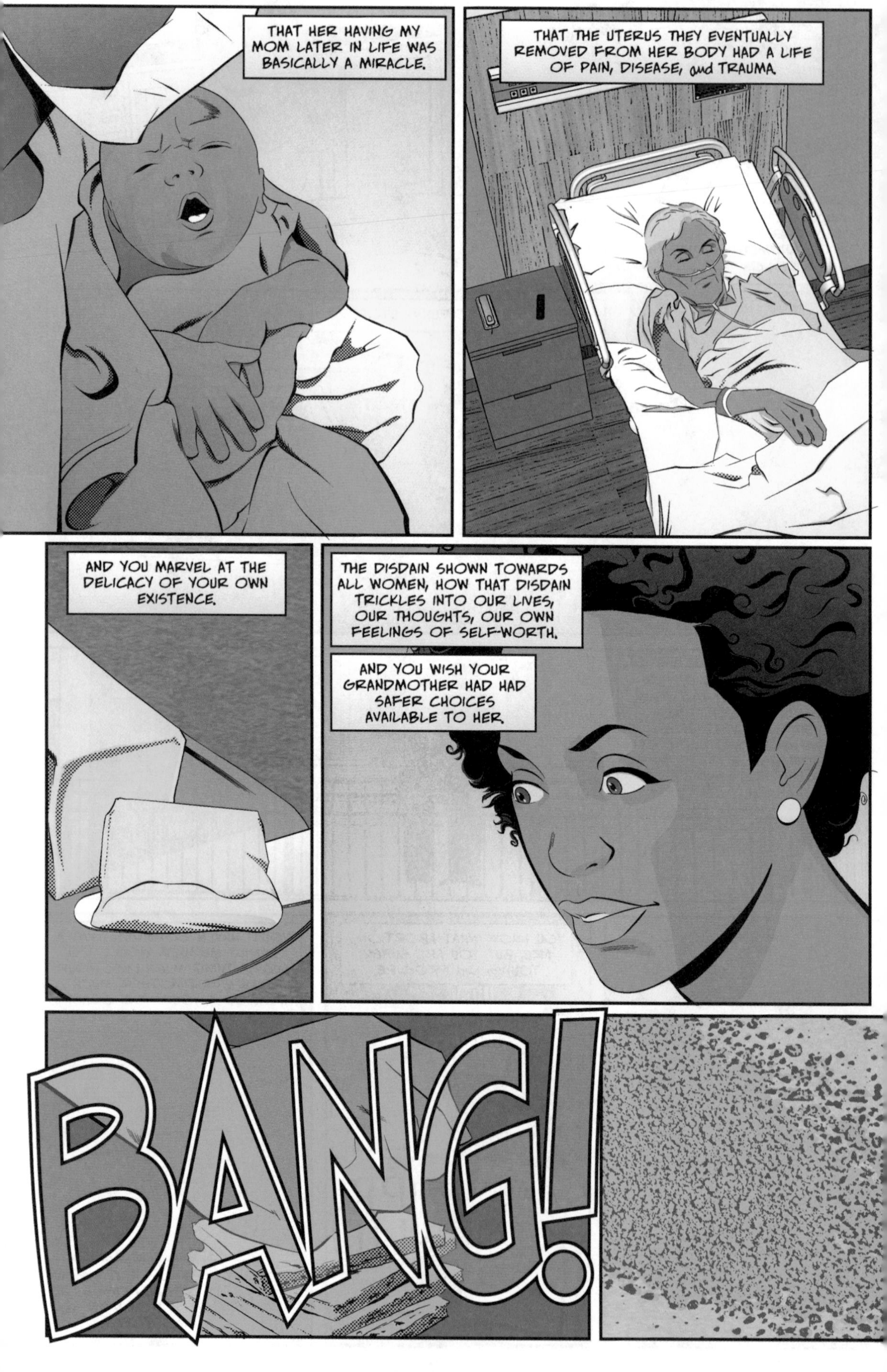
THAT HER HAVING MY MOM LATER IN LIFE WAS BASICALLY A MIRACLE.
THAT THE UTERUS THEY EVENTUALLY REMOVED FROM HER BODY HAD A LIFE OF PAIN, DISEASE, and TRAUMA.
AND YOU MARVEL AT THE DELICACY OF YOUR OWN EXISTENCE.
THE DISDAIN SHOWN TOWARDS ALL WOMEN, HOW THAT DISDAIN TRICKLES INTO OUR LIVES, OUR THOUGHTS, OUR OWN FEELINGS OF SELF-WORTH.
AND YOU WISH YOUR GRANDMOTHER HAD HAD SAFER CHOICES AVAILABLE TO HER.
BANG!

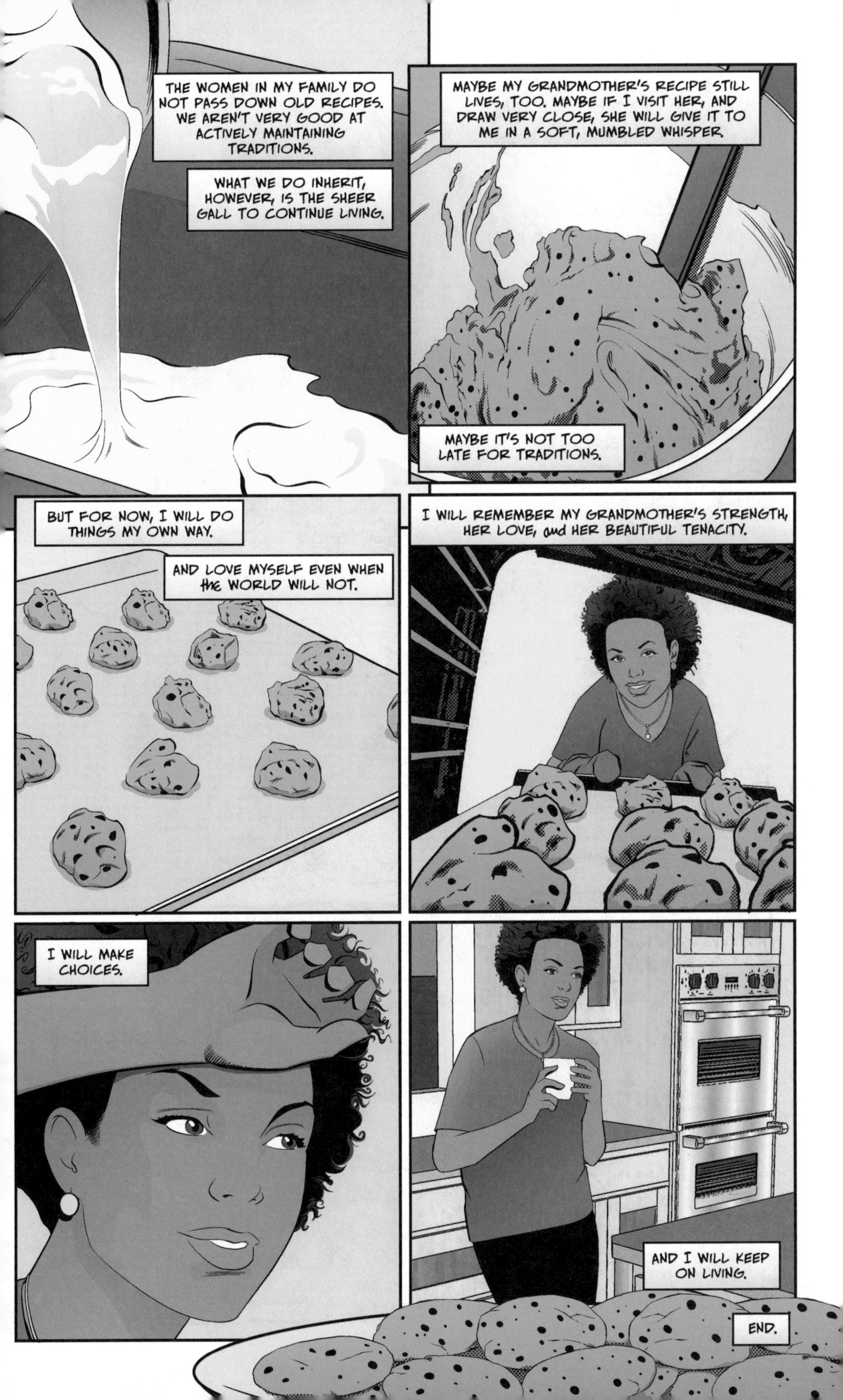
THE WOMEN IN MY FAMILY DO NOT PASS DOWN OLD RECIPES. WE AREN'T VERY GOOD AT ACTIVELY MAINTAINING TRADITIONS.
WHAT WE DO INHERIT, HOWEVER, IS THE SHEER GALL TO CONTINUE LIVING.
MAYBE MY GRANDMOTHER'S RECIPE STILL LIVES, TOO. MAYBE IF I VISIT HER, AND DRAW VERY CLOSE, SHE WILL GIVE IT TO ME IN A SOFT, MUMBLED WHISPER.
MAYBE IT'S NOT TOO LATE FOR TRADITIONS.
BUT FOR NOW, I WILL DO THINGS MY OWN WAY.
AND LOVE MYSELF EVEN WHEN the WORLD WILL NOT.
I WILL REMEMBER MY GRANDMOTHER'S STRENGTH, HER LOVE, and HER BEAUTIFUL TENACITY.
I WILL MAKE CHOICES.
AND I WILL KEEP ON LIVING.
END.

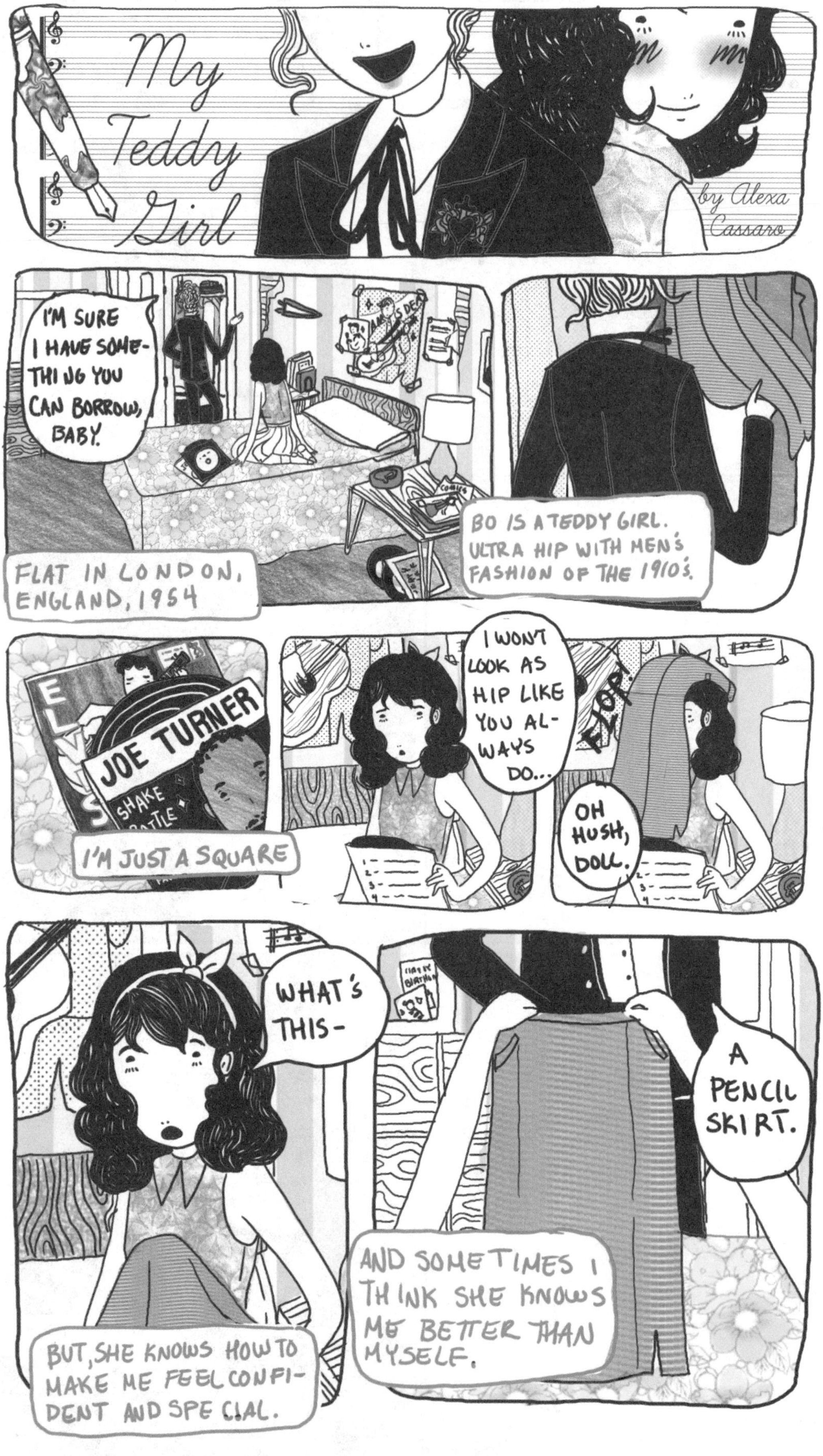

My Teddy Girl
by Alexa Cassaro
I'M SURE I HAVE SOME-THING YOU CAN BORROW, BABY.
FLAT IN LONDON, ENGLAND, 1954
BO IS A TEDDY GIRL. ULTRA HIP WITH MEN'S FASHION OF THE 1910'S.
JOE TURNER
SHAKE
I'M JUST A SQUARE
I WON'T LOOK AS HIP LIKE YOU AL-WAYS DO...
FLOP!
OH HUSH, DOLL.
WHAT'S THIS-
A PENCIL SKIRT.
BUT, SHE KNOWS HOW TO MAKE ME FEEL CONFI-DENT AND SPECIAL.
AND SOMETIMES I THINK SHE KNOWS ME BETTER THAN MYSELF.

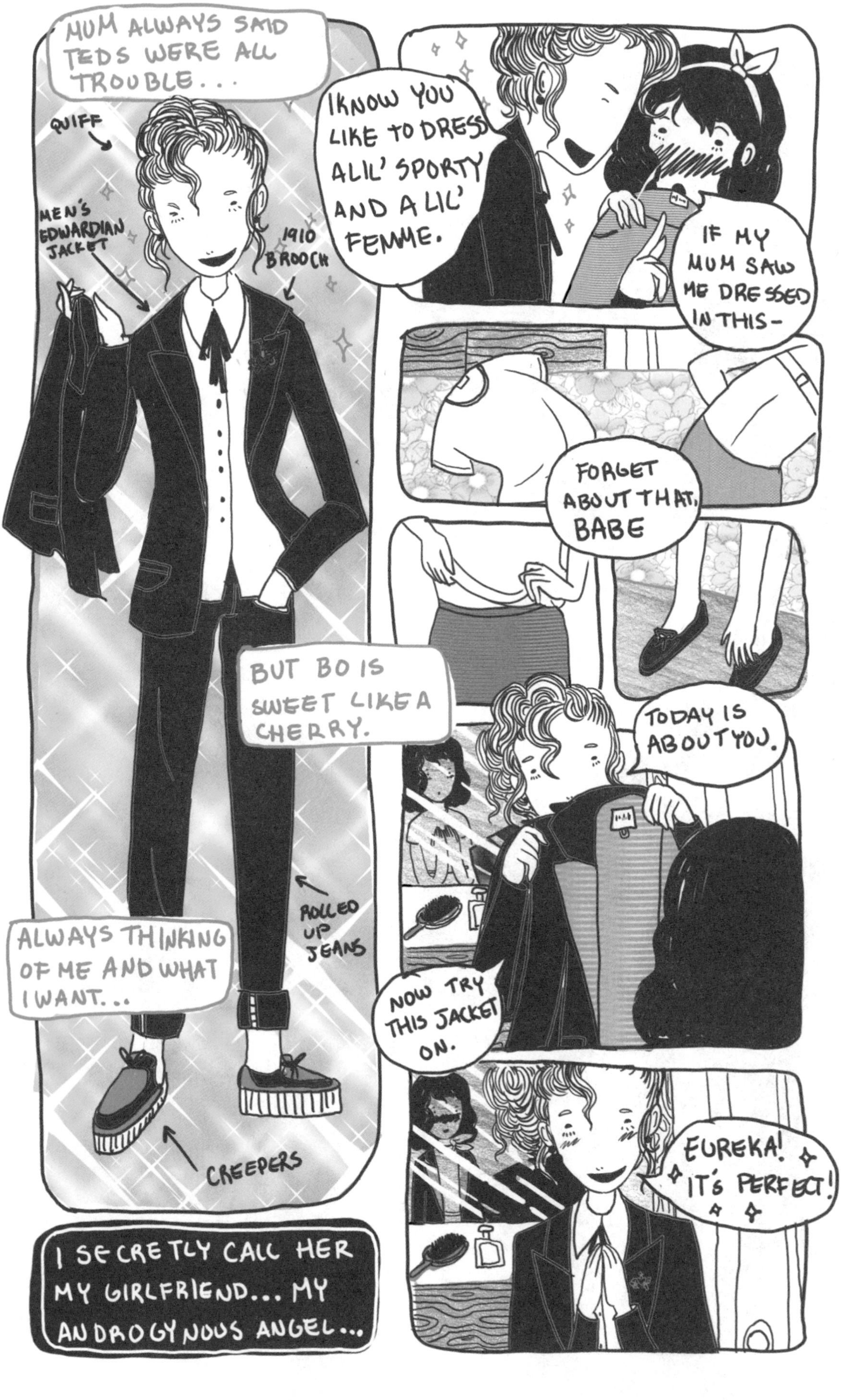
MUM ALWAYS SAID TEDS WERE ALL TROUBLE...
QUIFF
MEN'S EDWARDIAN JACKET
1910 BROOCH
BUT BO IS SWEET LIKE A CHERRY.
ROLLED UP JEANS
ALWAYS THINKING OF ME AND WHAT I WANT...
CREEPERS
I SECRETLY CALL HER MY GIRLFRIEND... MY ANDROGYNOUS ANGEL...
I KNOW YOU LIKE TO DRESS A LIL' SPORTY AND A LIL' FEMME.
IF MY MUM SAW ME DRESSED IN THIS-
FORGET ABOUT THAT, BABE
TODAY IS ABOUT YOU.
NOW TRY THIS JACKET ON.
EUREKA! IT'S PERFECT!

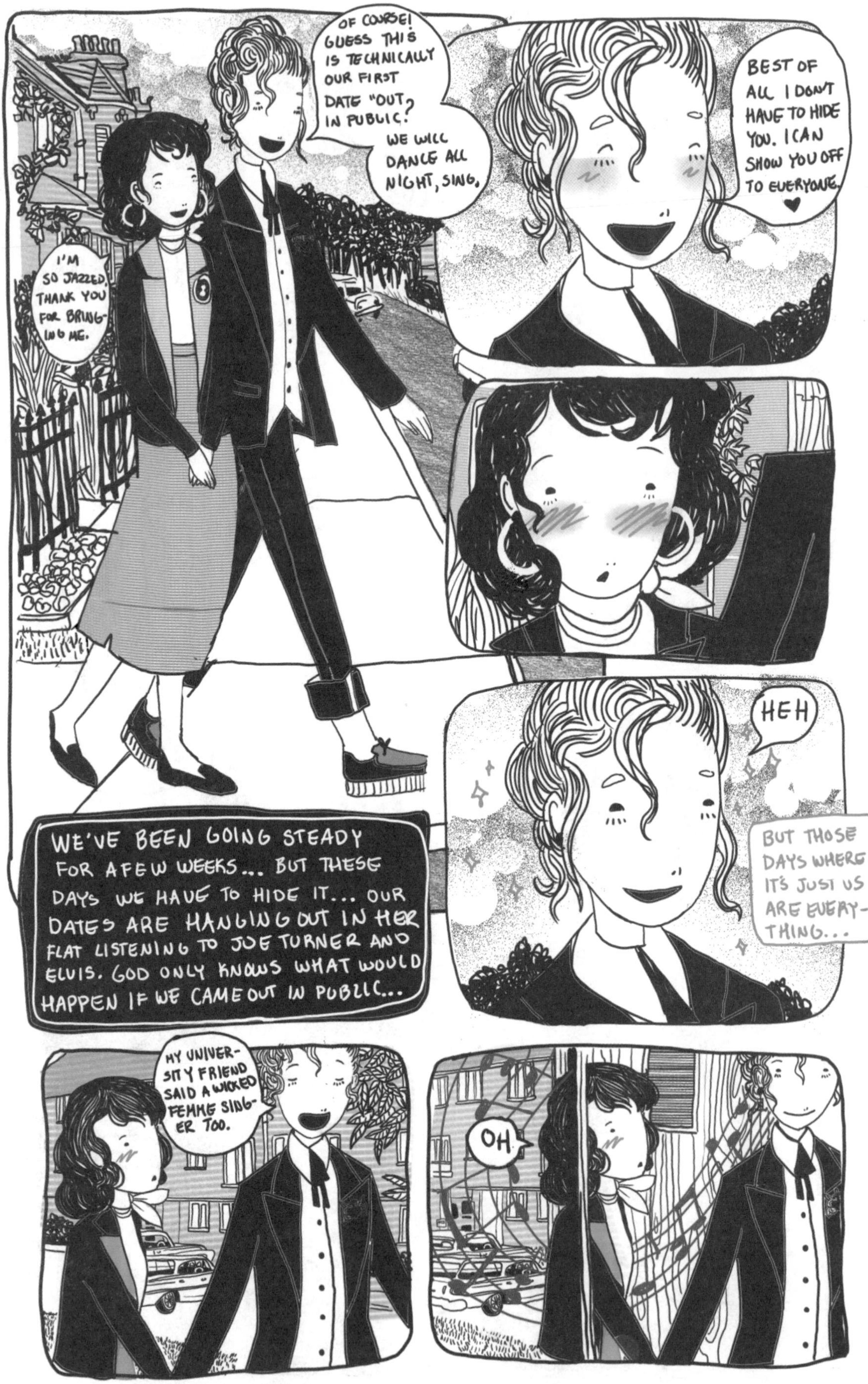
I'M SO JAZZED, THANK YOU FOR BRING-ING ME.
OF COURSE! GUESS THIS IS TECHNICALLY OUR FIRST DATE "OUT IN PUBLIC"?
WE WILL DANCE ALL NIGHT, SING.
BEST OF ALL I DON'T HAVE TO HIDE YOU. I CAN SHOW YOU OFF TO EVERYONE. ♥
WE'VE BEEN GOING STEADY FOR A FEW WEEKS... BUT THESE DAYS WE HAVE TO HIDE IT... OUR DATES ARE HANGING OUT IN HER FLAT LISTENING TO JOE TURNER AND ELVIS. GOD ONLY KNOWS WHAT WOULD HAPPEN IF WE CAME OUT IN PUBLIC...
HEH
BUT THOSE DAYS WHERE IT'S JUST US ARE EVERY-THING...
MY UNIVER-SITY FRIEND SAID A WICKED FEMME SING-ER TOO.
OH.

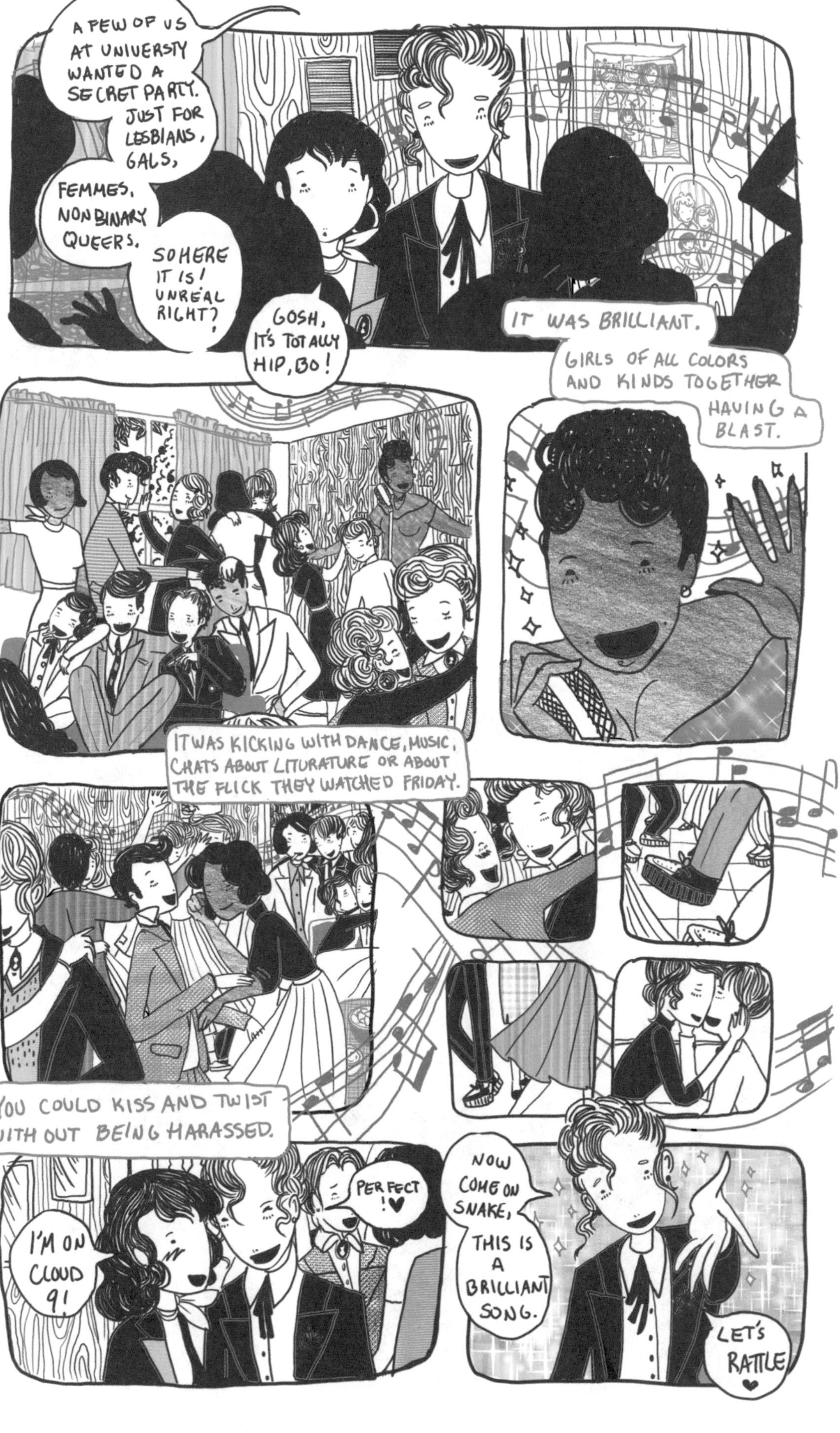
A FEW OF US AT UNIVERSITY WANTED A SECRET PARTY. JUST FOR LESBIANS, GALS,
FEMMES, NONBINARY QUEERS.
SO HERE IT IS! UNREAL RIGHT?
GOSH, IT'S TOTALLY HIP, BO!
IT WAS BRILLIANT.
GIRLS OF ALL COLORS AND KINDS TOGETHER HAVING A BLAST.
IT WAS KICKING WITH DANCE, MUSIC, CHATS ABOUT LITURATURE OR ABOUT THE FLICK THEY WATCHED FRIDAY.
YOU COULD KISS AND TWIST WITH OUT BEING HARASSED.
I'M ON CLOUD 9!
PERFECT!♥
NOW COME ON SNAKE,
THIS IS A BRILLIANT SONG.
LET'S RATTLE ♥

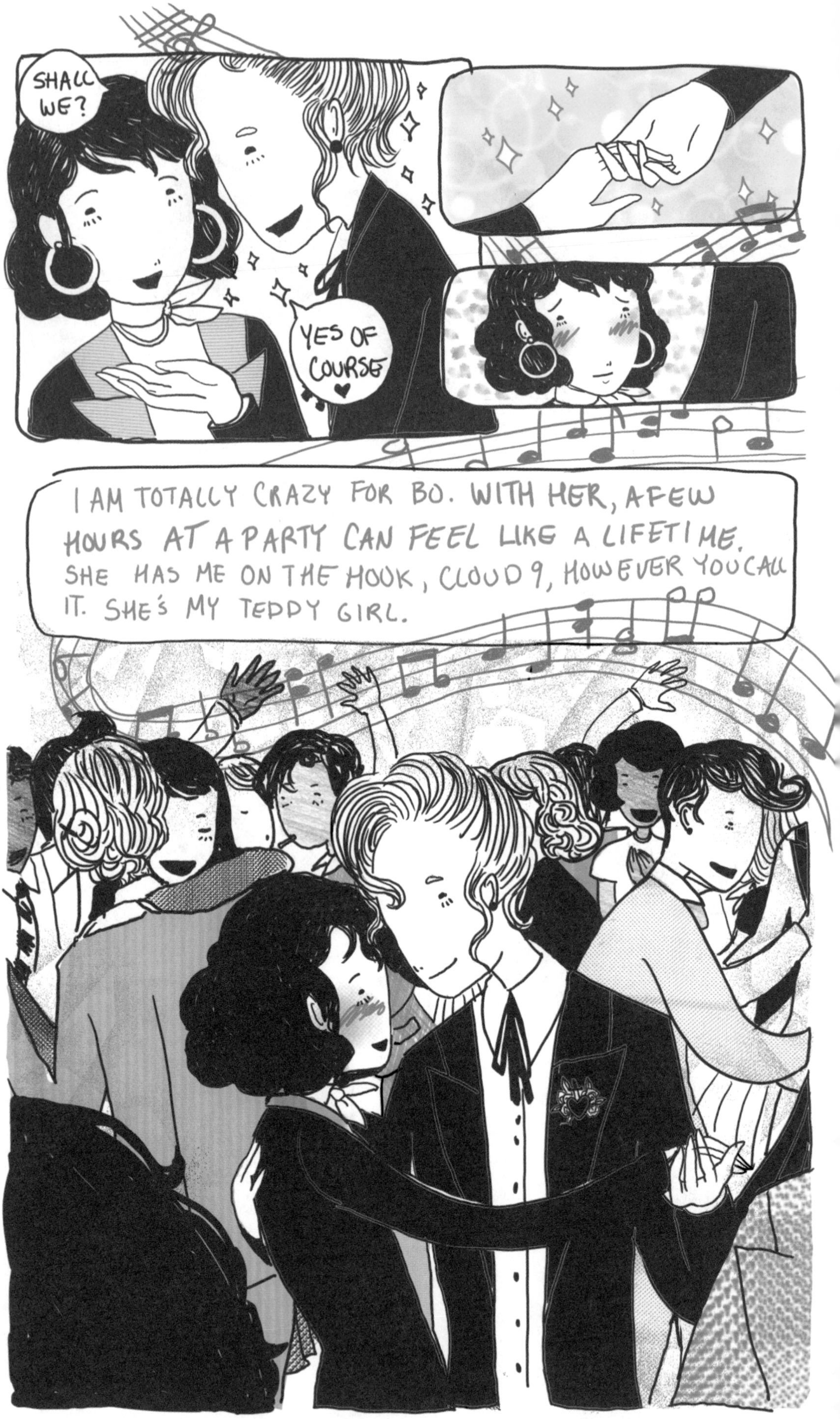
SHALL WE?
YES OF COURSE ♥
I AM TOTALLY CRAZY FOR BO. WITH HER, A FEW HOURS AT A PARTY CAN FEEL LIKE A LIFETIME. SHE HAS ME ON THE HOOK, CLOUD 9, HOWEVER YOU CALL IT. SHE'S MY TEDDY GIRL.

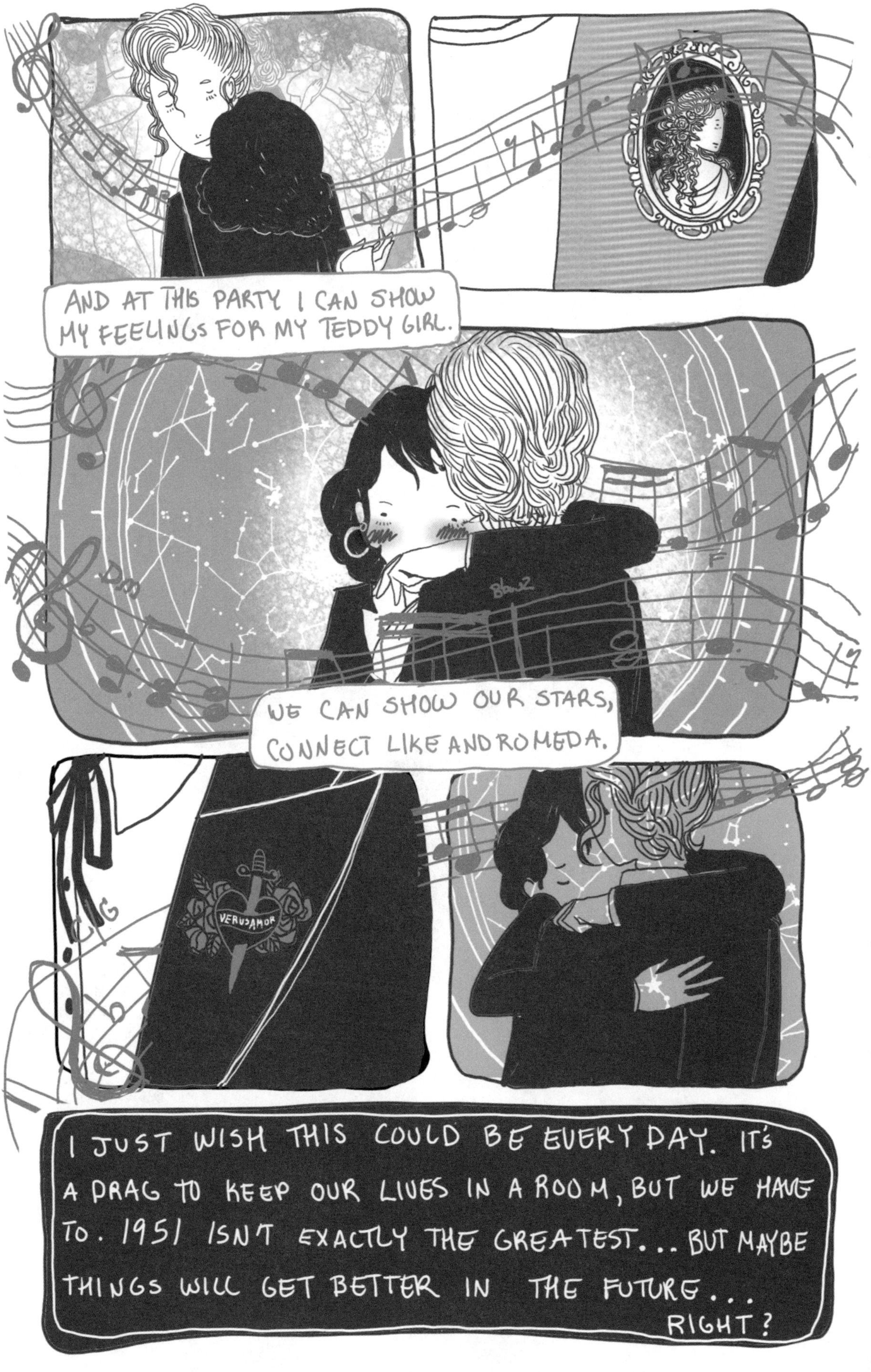
AND AT THIS PARTY I CAN SHOW MY FEELINGS FOR MY TEDDY GIRL.
WE CAN SHOW OUR STARS, CONNECT LIKE ANDROMEDA.
VERUSAMOR
I JUST WISH THIS COULD BE EVERY DAY. IT'S A DRAG TO KEEP OUR LIVES IN A ROOM, BUT WE HAVE TO. 1951 ISN'T EXACTLY THE GREATEST... BUT MAYBE THINGS WILL GET BETTER IN THE FUTURE... RIGHT?

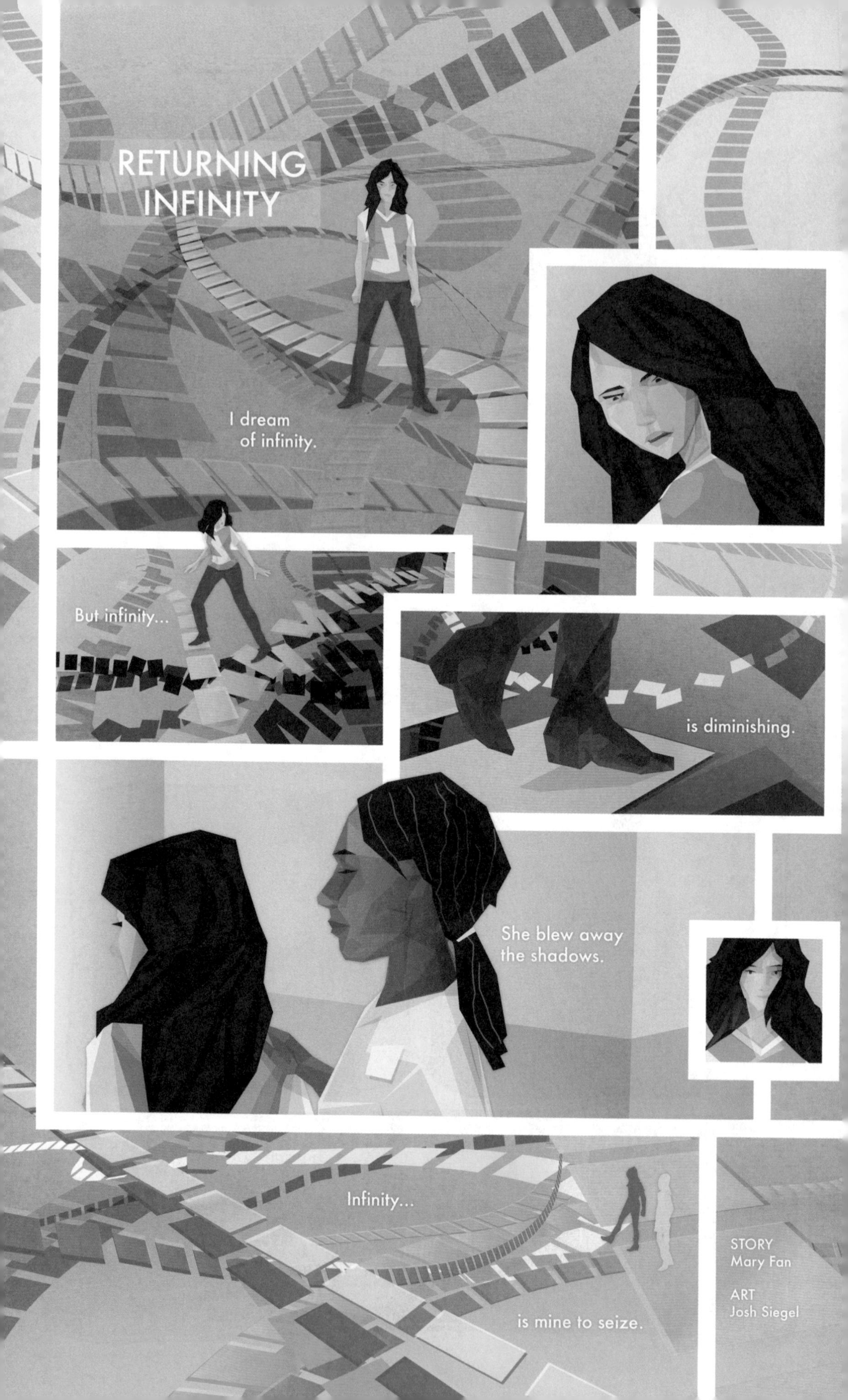
RETURNING INFINITY
I dream of infinity.
But infinity...
is diminishing.
She blew away the shadows.
Infinity...
is mine to seize.
STORY
Mary Fan
ART
Josh Siegel

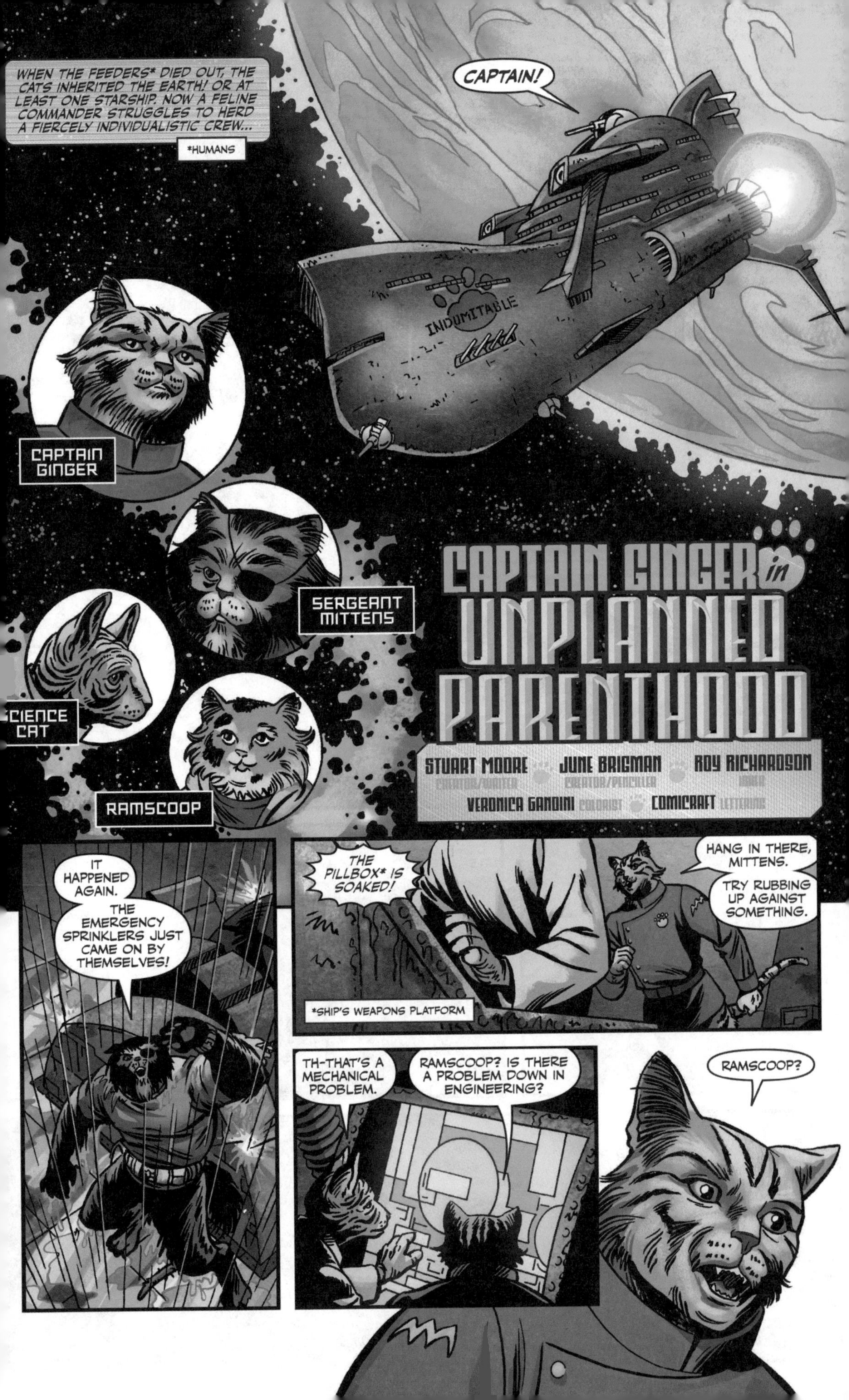

WHEN THE FEEDERS* DIED OUT, THE CATS INHERITED THE EARTH! OR AT LEAST ONE STARSHIP. NOW A FELINE COMMANDER STRUGGLES TO HERD A FIERCELY INDIVIDUALISTIC CREW...
*HUMANS
CAPTAIN!
INDOMITABLE
CAPTAIN GINGER
SERGEANT MITTENS
CIENCE CAT
RAMSCOOP
CAPTAIN GINGER in
UNPLANNED PARENTHOOD
STUART MOORE CREATOR/WRITER
JUNE BRIGMAN CREATOR/PENCILLER
ROY RICHARDSON INKER
VERONICA GANDINI COLORIST
COMICRAFT LETTERING
IT HAPPENED AGAIN.
THE EMERGENCY SPRINKLERS JUST CAME ON BY THEMSELVES!
THE PILLBOX* IS SOAKED!
HANG IN THERE, MITTENS.
TRY RUBBING UP AGAINST SOMETHING.
*SHIP'S WEAPONS PLATFORM
TH-THAT'S A MECHANICAL PROBLEM.
RAMSCOOP? IS THERE A PROBLEM DOWN IN ENGINEERING?
RAMSCOOP?

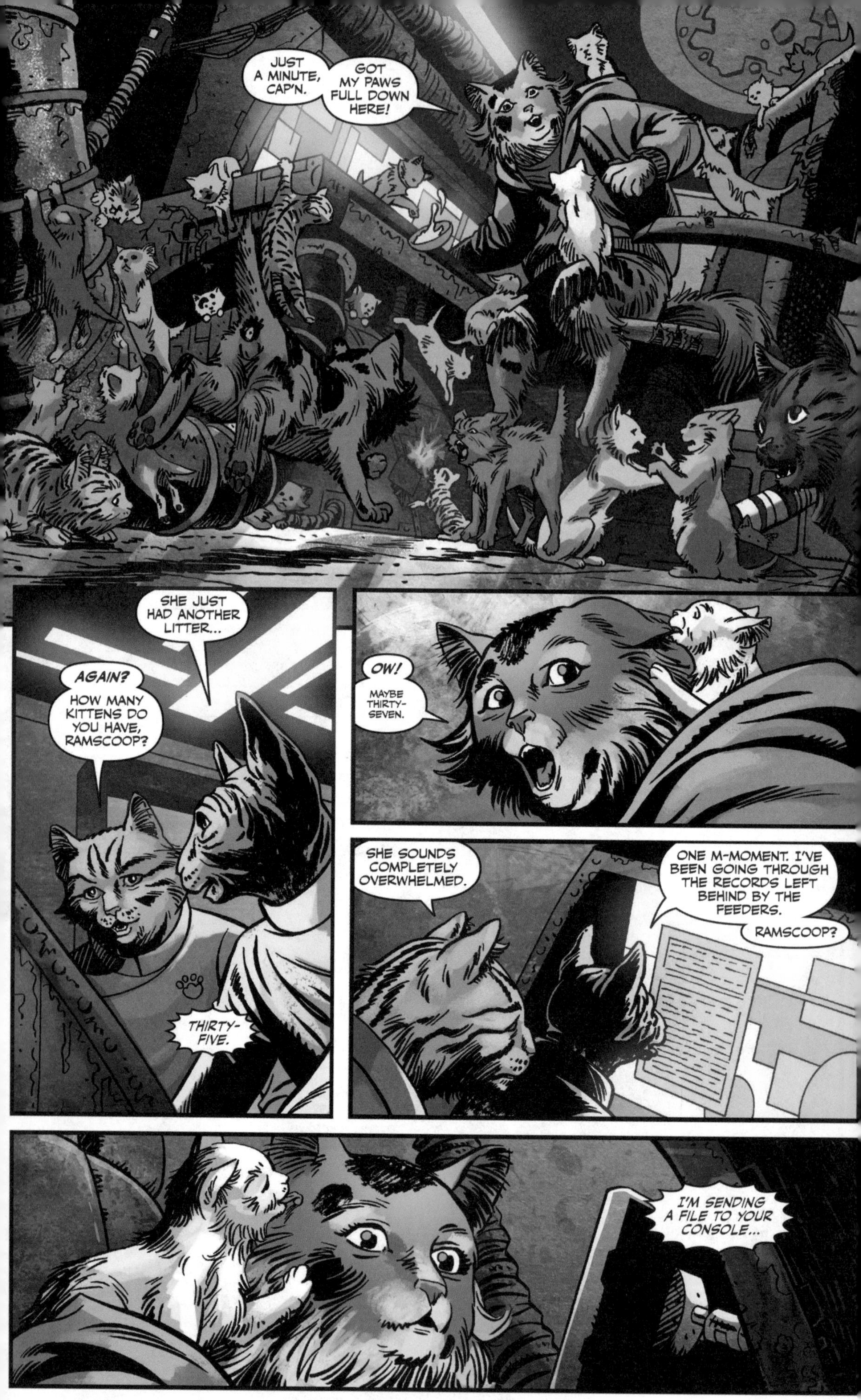

JUST A MINUTE, CAP'N.
GOT MY PAWS FULL DOWN HERE!
SHE JUST HAD ANOTHER LITTER...
AGAIN? HOW MANY KITTENS DO YOU HAVE, RAMSCOOP?
THIRTY-FIVE.
OW! MAYBE THIRTY-SEVEN.
SHE SOUNDS COMPLETELY OVERWHELMED.
ONE M-MOMENT. I'VE BEEN GOING THROUGH THE RECORDS LEFT BEHIND BY THE FEEDERS.
RAMSCOOP?
I'M SENDING A FILE TO YOUR CONSOLE...

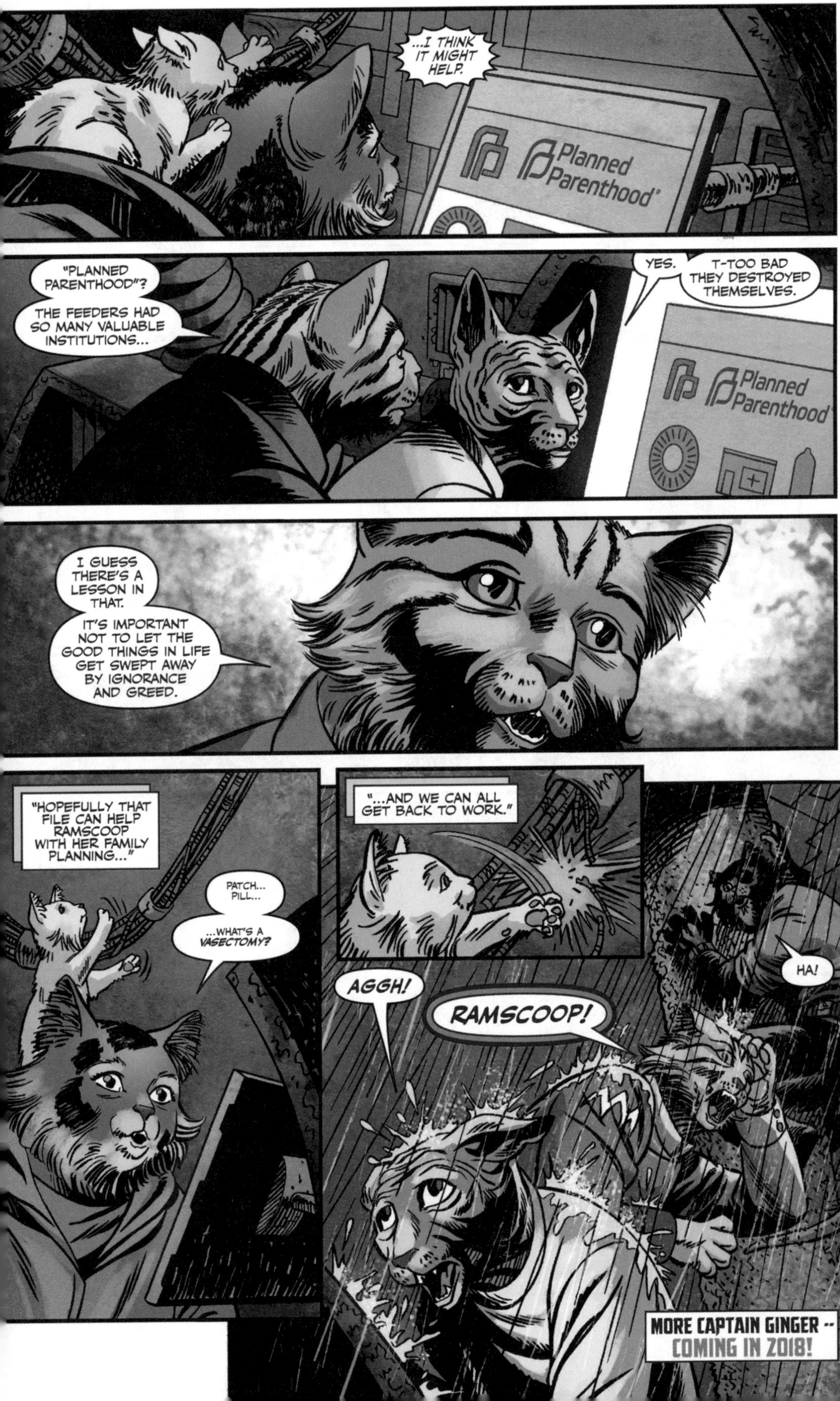

...I THINK IT MIGHT HELP.
Planned Parenthood
"PLANNED PARENTHOOD"?
THE FEEDERS HAD SO MANY VALUABLE INSTITUTIONS...
YES.
T-TOO BAD THEY DESTROYED THEMSELVES.
Planned Parenthood
I GUESS THERE'S A LESSON IN THAT.
IT'S IMPORTANT NOT TO LET THE GOOD THINGS IN LIFE GET SWEPT AWAY BY IGNORANCE AND GREED.
"HOPEFULLY THAT FILE CAN HELP RAMSCOOP WITH HER FAMILY PLANNING..."
PATCH... PILL...
...WHAT'S A VASECTOMY?
"...AND WE CAN ALL GET BACK TO WORK."
HA!
AGGH!
RAMSCOOP!
MORE CAPTAIN GINGER -- COMING IN 2018!

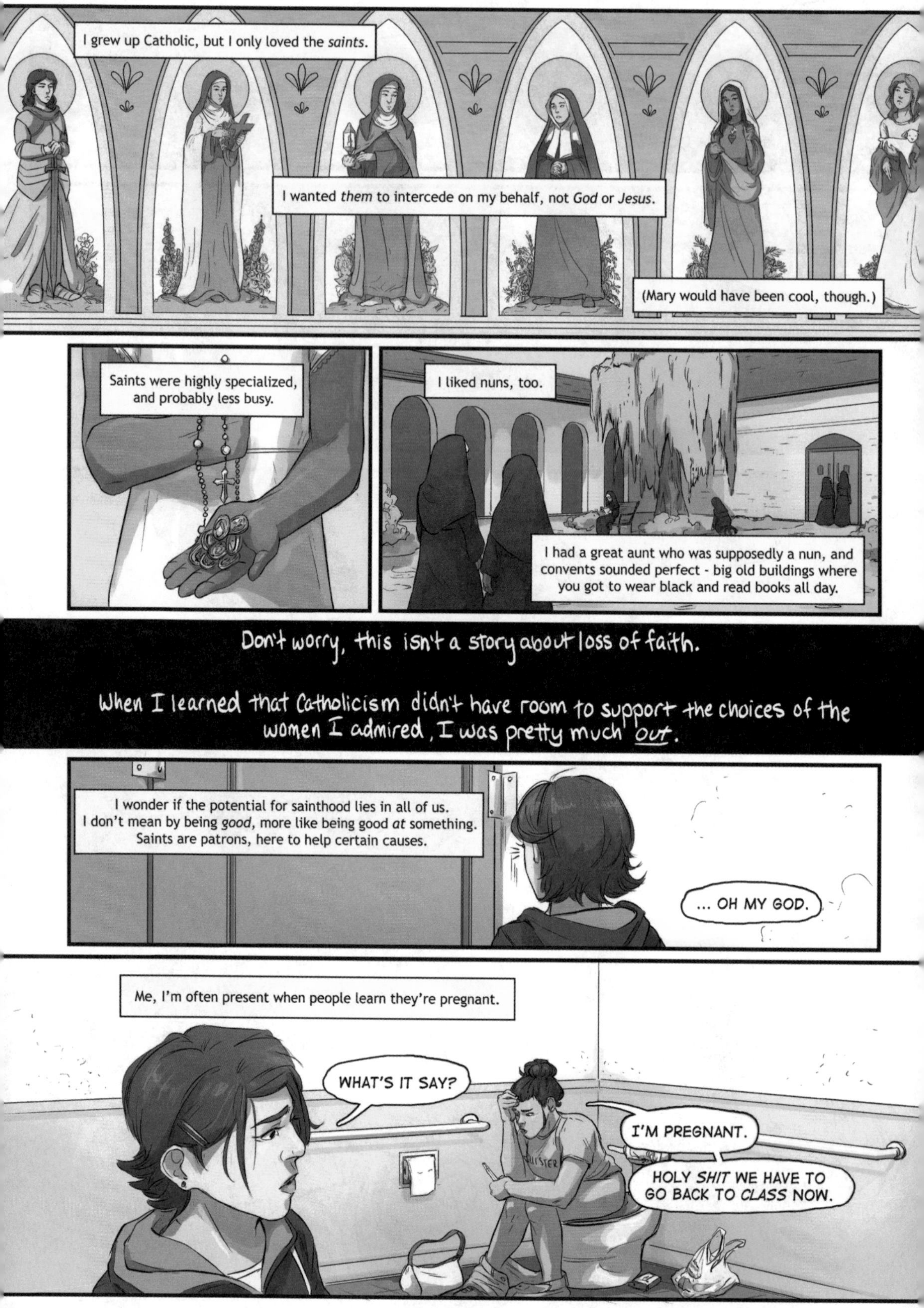
I grew up Catholic, but I only loved the *saints*.
I wanted *them* to intercede on my behalf, not *God* or *Jesus*.
(Mary would have been cool, though.)
Saints were highly specialized, and probably less busy.
I liked nuns, too.
I had a great aunt who was supposedly a nun, and convents sounded perfect - big old buildings where you got to wear black and read books all day.
Don't worry, this isn't a story about loss of faith.
When I learned that Catholicism didn't have room to support the choices of the women I admired, I was pretty much out.
I wonder if the potential for sainthood lies in all of us. I don't mean by being *good*, more like being good *at* something. Saints are patrons, here to help certain causes.
... OH MY GOD.
Me, I'm often present when people learn they're pregnant.
WHAT'S IT SAY?
I'M PREGNANT.
HOLY *SHIT* WE HAVE TO GO BACK TO *CLASS* NOW.

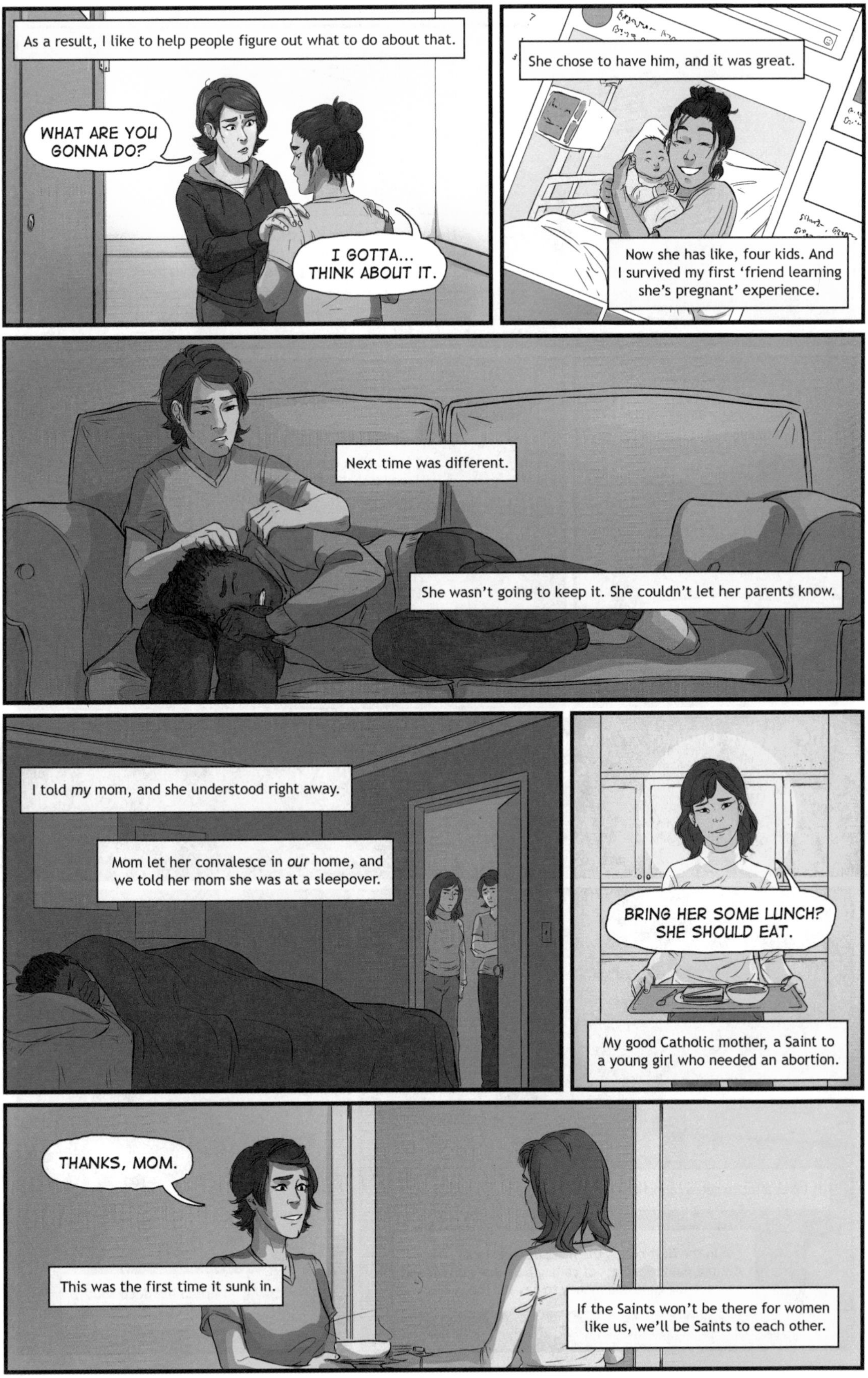
As a result, I like to help people figure out what to do about that.
WHAT ARE YOU GONNA DO?
I GOTTA... THINK ABOUT IT.
She chose to have him, and it was great.
Now she has like, four kids. And I survived my first 'friend learning she's pregnant' experience.
Next time was different.
She wasn't going to keep it. She couldn't let her parents know.
I told *my* mom, and she understood right away.
Mom let her convalesce in *our* home, and we told her mom she was at a sleepover.
BRING HER SOME LUNCH? SHE SHOULD EAT.
My good Catholic mother, a Saint to a young girl who needed an abortion.
THANKS, MOM.
This was the first time it sunk in.
If the Saints won't be there for women like us, we'll be Saints to each other.

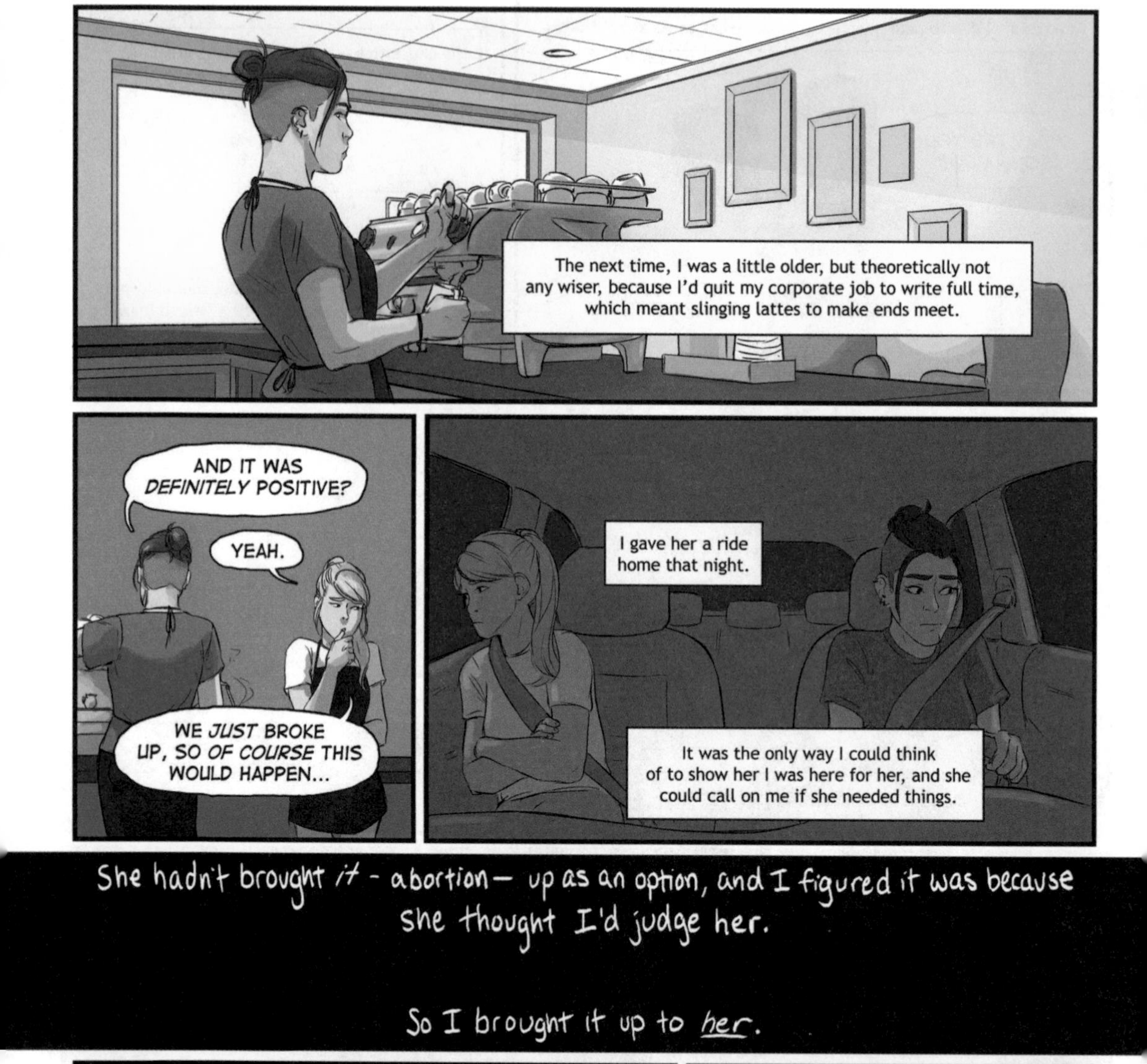
The next time, I was a little older, but theoretically not any wiser, because I'd quit my corporate job to write full time, which meant slinging lattes to make ends meet.
AND IT WAS *DEFINITELY* POSITIVE?
YEAH.
WE *JUST* BROKE UP, SO *OF COURSE* THIS WOULD HAPPEN...
I gave her a ride home that night.
It was the only way I could think of to show her I was here for her, and she could call on me if she needed things.

She hadn't brought *it* - abortion - up as an option, and I figured it was because she thought I'd judge her.

So I brought it up to <u>her</u>.

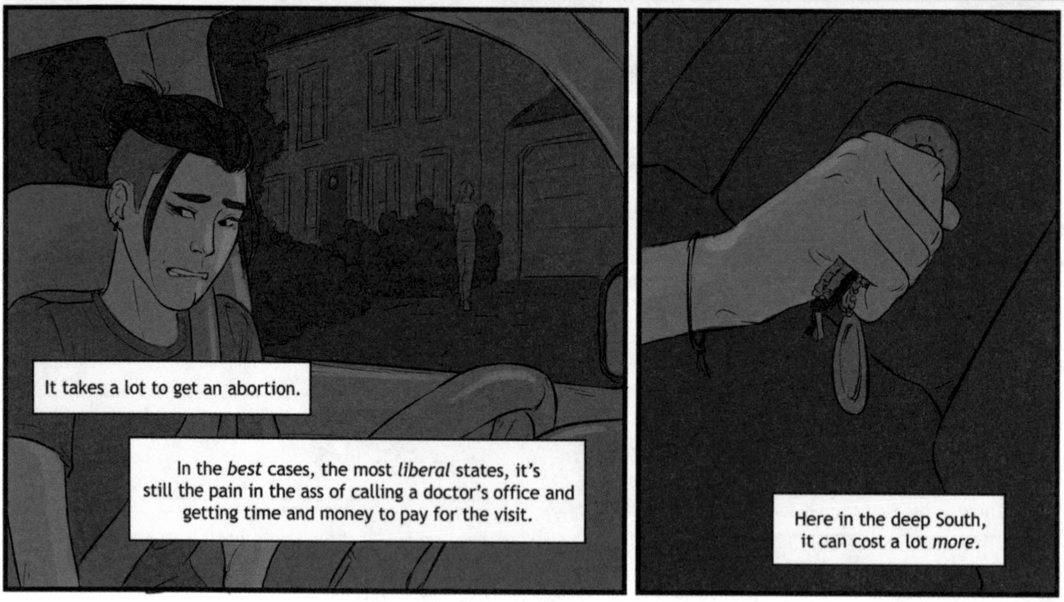
It takes a lot to get an abortion.
In the *best* cases, the most *liberal* states, it's still the pain in the ass of calling a doctor's office and getting time and money to pay for the visit.
Here in the deep South, it can cost a lot *more*.

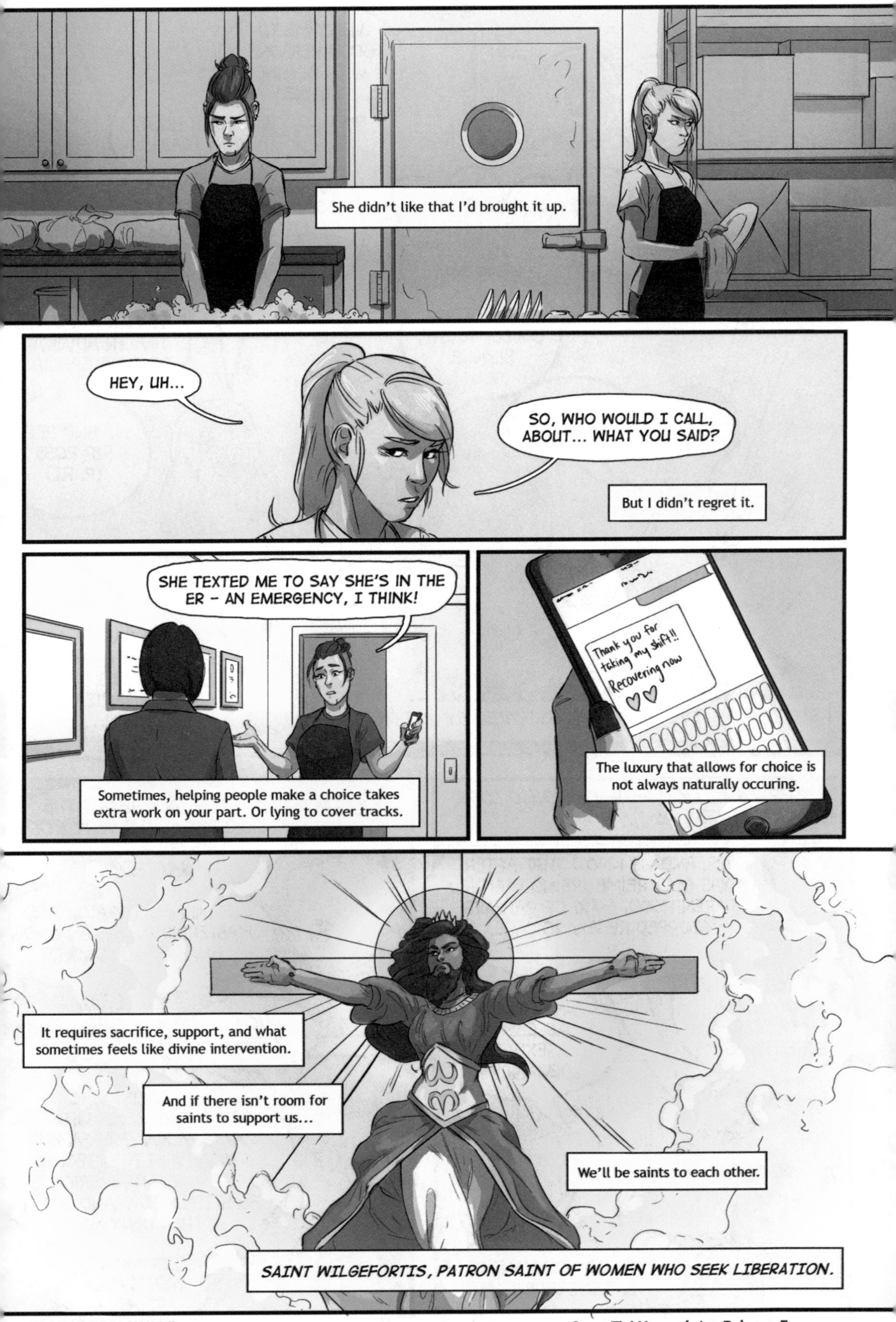
She didn't like that I'd brought it up.
HEY, UH...
SO, WHO WOULD I CALL, ABOUT... WHAT YOU SAID?
But I didn't regret it.
SHE TEXTED ME TO SAY SHE'S IN THE ER – AN EMERGENCY, I THINK!
Sometimes, helping people make a choice takes extra work on your part. Or lying to cover tracks.
Thank you for taking my shift!! Recovering now
The luxury that allows for choice is not always naturally occuring.
It requires sacrifice, support, and what sometimes feels like divine intervention.
And if there isn't room for saints to support us...
We'll be saints to each other.
SAINT WILGEFORTIS, PATRON SAINT OF WOMEN WHO SEEK LIBERATION.

"SAINT TERMINIA" Story: **Tini Howard** Art: **Rebecca Farrow**

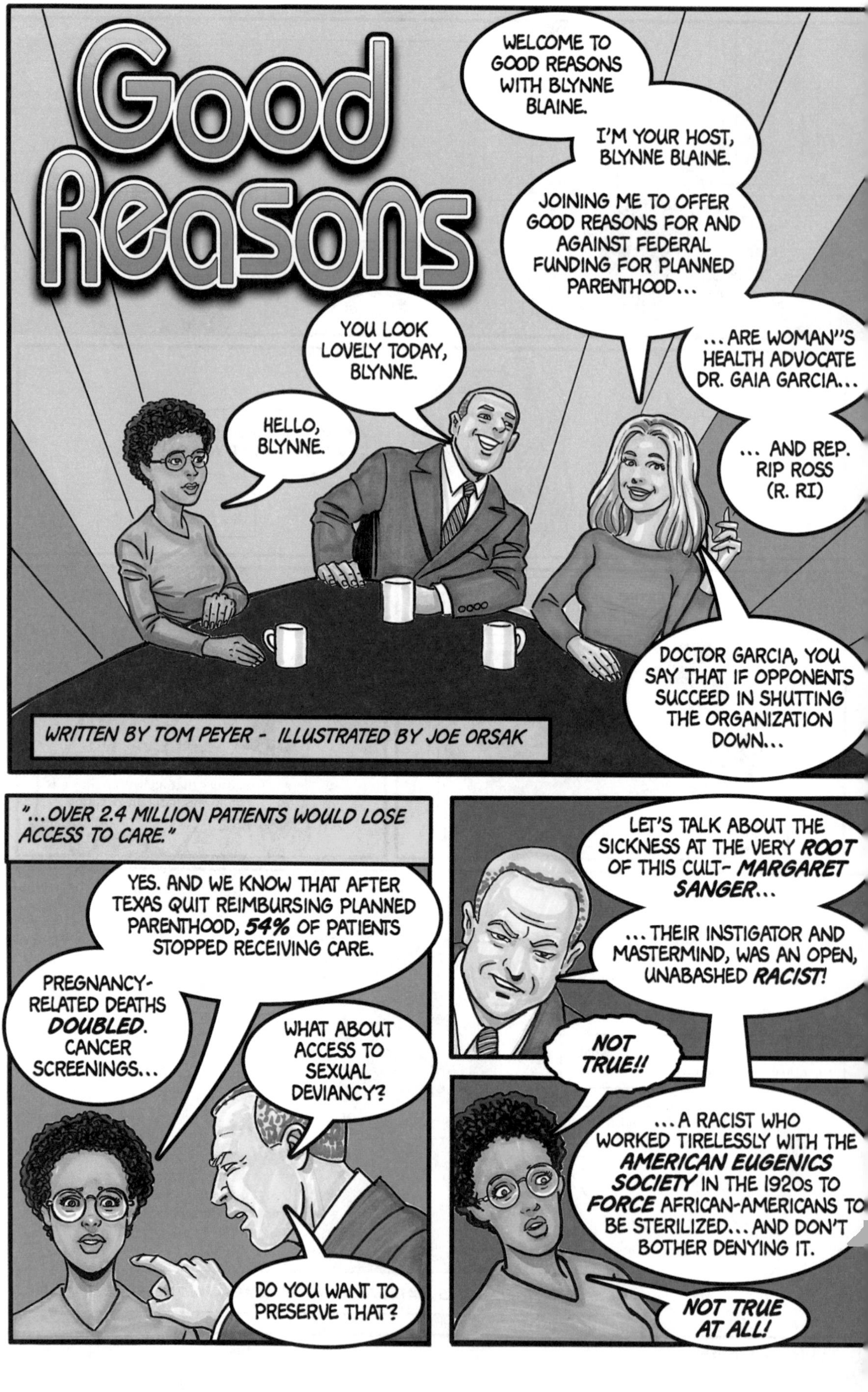
Good Reasons
WELCOME TO GOOD REASONS WITH BLYNNE BLAINE.
I'M YOUR HOST, BLYNNE BLAINE.
JOINING ME TO OFFER GOOD REASONS FOR AND AGAINST FEDERAL FUNDING FOR PLANNED PARENTHOOD...
...ARE WOMAN''S HEALTH ADVOCATE DR. GAIA GARCIA...
... AND REP. RIP ROSS (R. RI)
HELLO, BLYNNE.
YOU LOOK LOVELY TODAY, BLYNNE.
DOCTOR GARCIA, YOU SAY THAT IF OPPONENTS SUCCEED IN SHUTTING THE ORGANIZATION DOWN...
WRITTEN BY TOM PEYER - ILLUSTRATED BY JOE ORSAK
"...OVER 2.4 MILLION PATIENTS WOULD LOSE ACCESS TO CARE."
YES. AND WE KNOW THAT AFTER TEXAS QUIT REIMBURSING PLANNED PARENTHOOD, 54% OF PATIENTS STOPPED RECEIVING CARE.
PREGNANCY-RELATED DEATHS DOUBLED. CANCER SCREENINGS...
WHAT ABOUT ACCESS TO SEXUAL DEVIANCY?
DO YOU WANT TO PRESERVE THAT?
LET'S TALK ABOUT THE SICKNESS AT THE VERY ROOT OF THIS CULT- MARGARET SANGER...
...THEIR INSTIGATOR AND MASTERMIND, WAS AN OPEN, UNABASHED RACIST!
NOT TRUE!!
...A RACIST WHO WORKED TIRELESSLY WITH THE AMERICAN EUGENICS SOCIETY IN THE 1920s TO FORCE AFRICAN-AMERICANS TO BE STERILIZED... AND DON'T BOTHER DENYING IT.
NOT TRUE AT ALL!

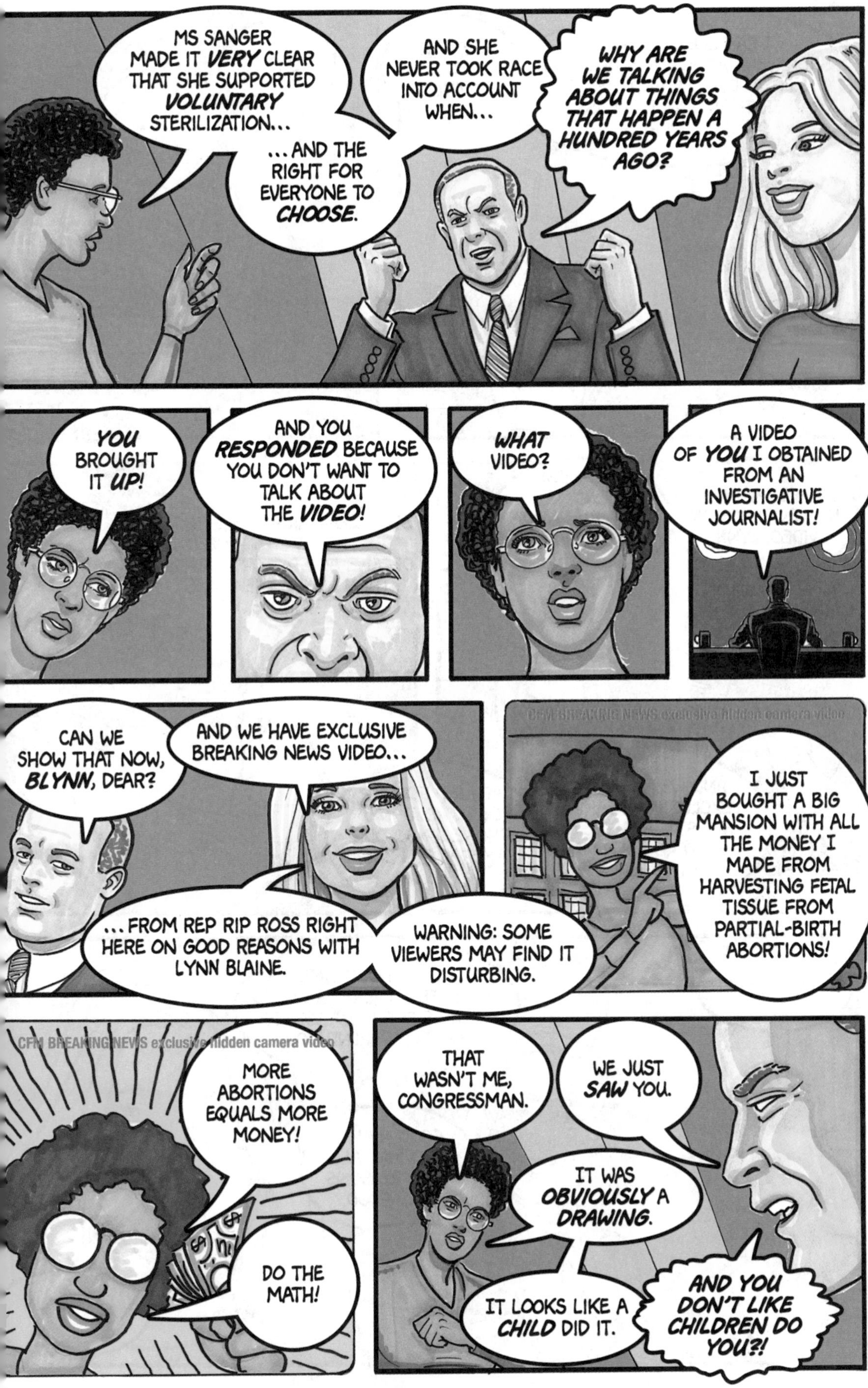
MS SANGER MADE IT VERY CLEAR THAT SHE SUPPORTED VOLUNTARY STERILIZATION...
...AND THE RIGHT FOR EVERYONE TO CHOOSE.
AND SHE NEVER TOOK RACE INTO ACCOUNT WHEN...
WHY ARE WE TALKING ABOUT THINGS THAT HAPPEN A HUNDRED YEARS AGO?
YOU BROUGHT IT UP!
AND YOU RESPONDED BECAUSE YOU DON'T WANT TO TALK ABOUT THE VIDEO!
WHAT VIDEO?
A VIDEO OF YOU I OBTAINED FROM AN INVESTIGATIVE JOURNALIST!
CAN WE SHOW THAT NOW, BLYNN, DEAR?
AND WE HAVE EXCLUSIVE BREAKING NEWS VIDEO...
...FROM REP RIP ROSS RIGHT HERE ON GOOD REASONS WITH LYNN BLAINE.
WARNING: SOME VIEWERS MAY FIND IT DISTURBING.
CFN BREAKING NEWS exclusive hidden camera video
I JUST BOUGHT A BIG MANSION WITH ALL THE MONEY I MADE FROM HARVESTING FETAL TISSUE FROM PARTIAL-BIRTH ABORTIONS!
CFN BREAKING NEWS exclusive hidden camera video
MORE ABORTIONS EQUALS MORE MONEY!
DO THE MATH!
THAT WASN'T ME, CONGRESSMAN.
WE JUST SAW YOU.
IT WAS OBVIOUSLY A DRAWING.
IT LOOKS LIKE A CHILD DID IT.
AND YOU DON'T LIKE CHILDREN DO YOU?!

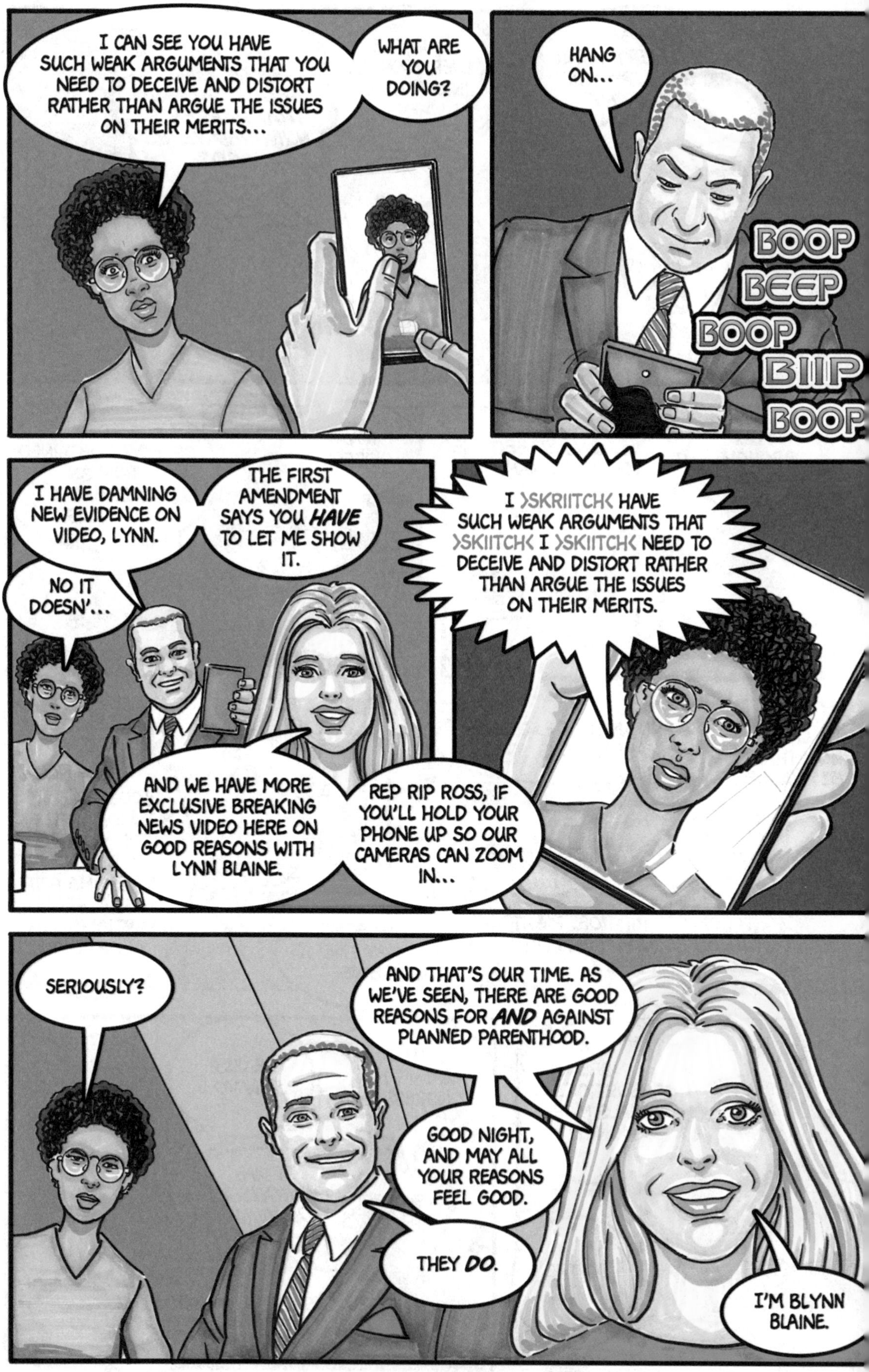
I CAN SEE YOU HAVE SUCH WEAK ARGUMENTS THAT YOU NEED TO DECEIVE AND DISTORT RATHER THAN ARGUE THE ISSUES ON THEIR MERITS...
WHAT ARE YOU DOING?
HANG ON...
BOOP
BEEP
BOOP
BIIP
BOOP
I HAVE DAMNING NEW EVIDENCE ON VIDEO, LYNN.
THE FIRST AMENDMENT SAYS YOU *HAVE* TO LET ME SHOW IT.
NO IT DOESN'...
AND WE HAVE MORE EXCLUSIVE BREAKING NEWS VIDEO HERE ON GOOD REASONS WITH LYNN BLAINE.
REP RIP ROSS, IF YOU'LL HOLD YOUR PHONE UP SO OUR CAMERAS CAN ZOOM IN...
I >SKRIITCH< HAVE SUCH WEAK ARGUMENTS THAT >SKIITCH< I >SKIITCH< NEED TO DECEIVE AND DISTORT RATHER THAN ARGUE THE ISSUES ON THEIR MERITS.
SERIOUSLY?
AND THAT'S OUR TIME. AS WE'VE SEEN, THERE ARE GOOD REASONS FOR *AND* AGAINST PLANNED PARENTHOOD.
GOOD NIGHT, AND MAY ALL YOUR REASONS FEEL GOOD.
THEY *DO*.
I'M BLYNN BLAINE.

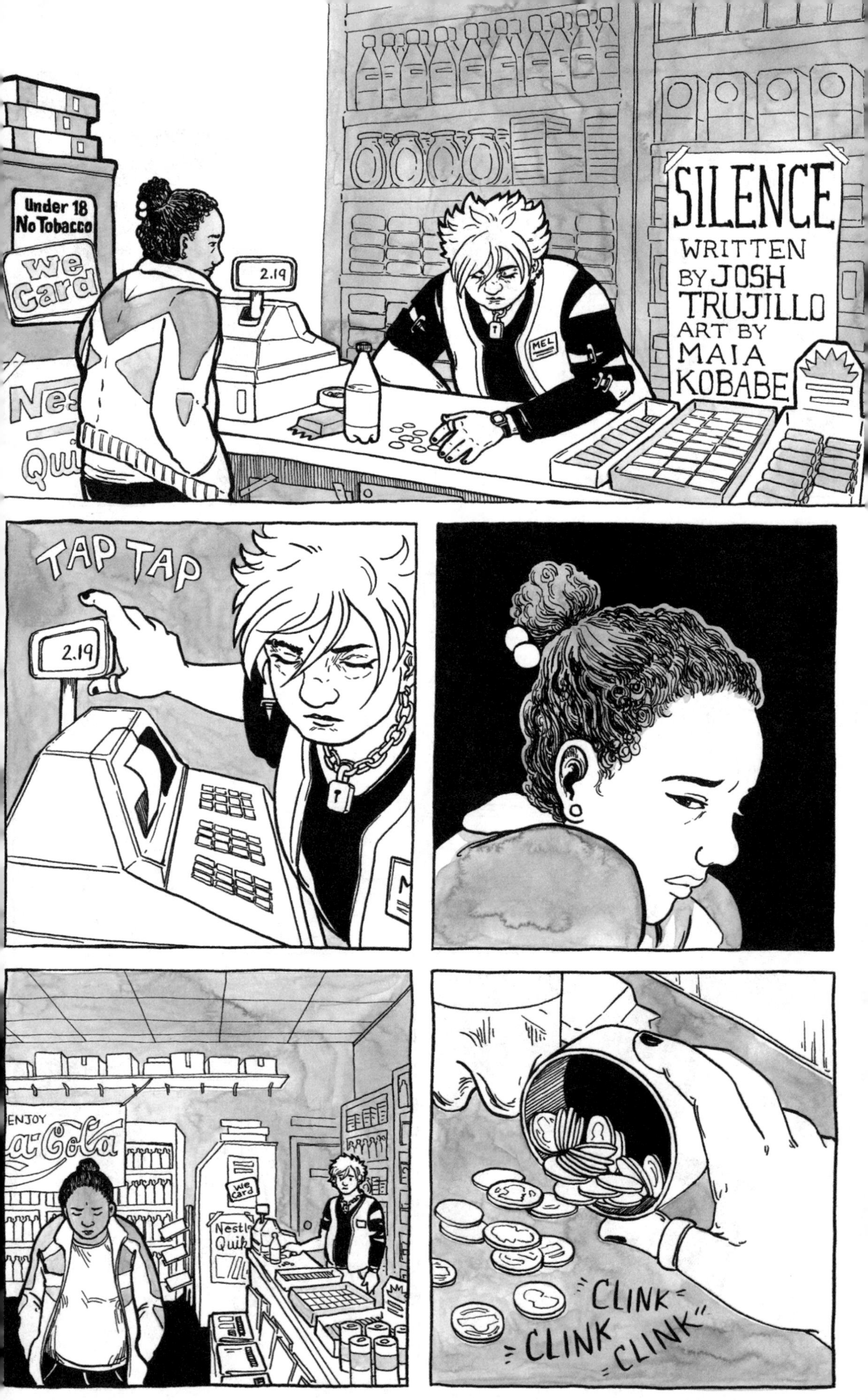
Under 18
No Tobacco
We Card
Nes
Qui
2.19
MEL
SILENCE
WRITTEN BY JOSH TRUJILLO
ART BY MAIA KOBABE
TAP TAP
2.19
ENJOY
Coca-Cola
We Card
Nestle
Quik
CLINK
CLINK
CLINK

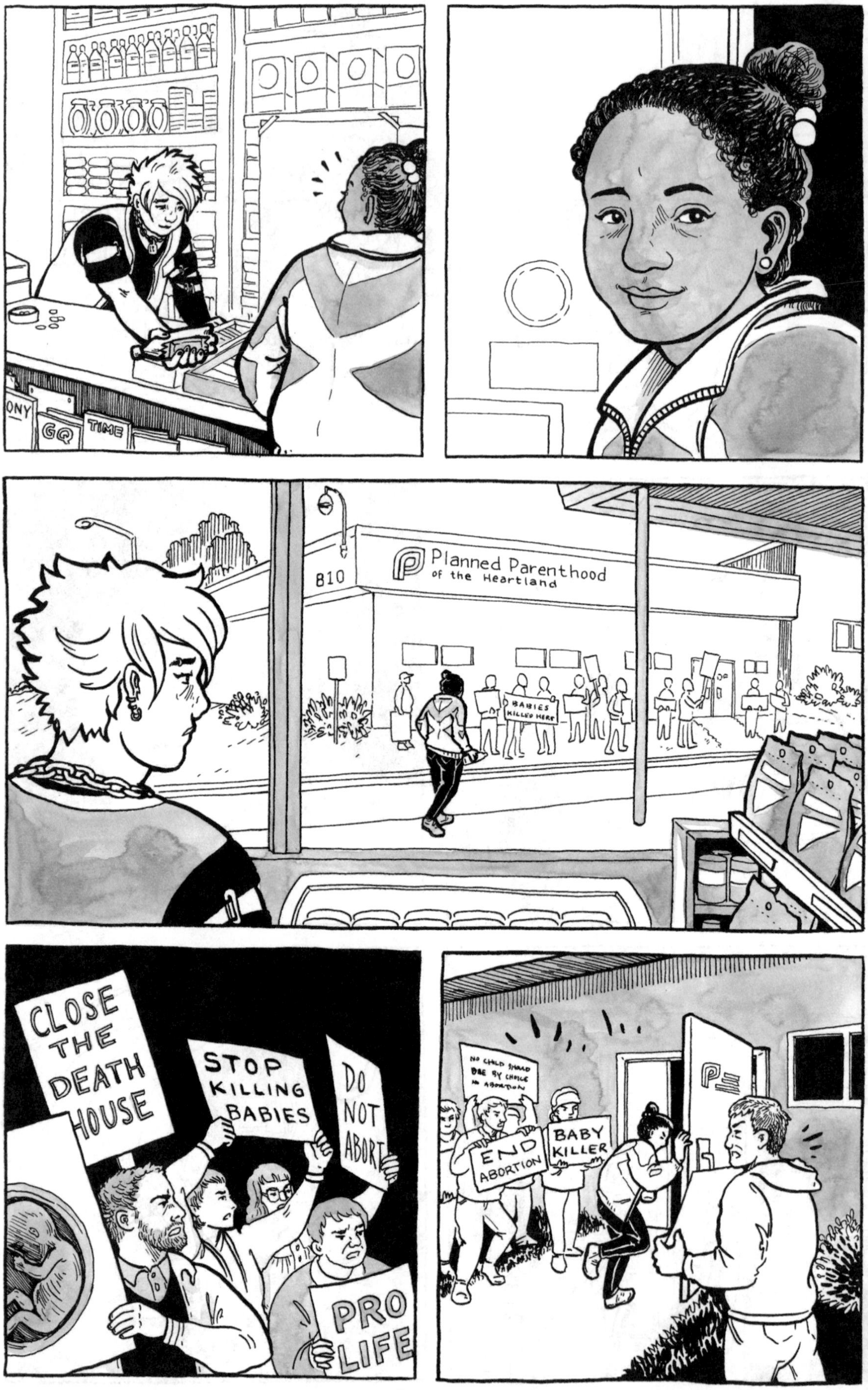
ONY
GQ
TIME
810
Planned Parenthood
of the Heartland
BABIES KILLED HERE
CLOSE THE DEATH HOUSE
STOP KILLING BABIES
DO NOT ABORT
PRO LIFE
NO CHILD SHOULD DIE BY CHOICE NO ABORTION
END ABORTION
BABY KILLER

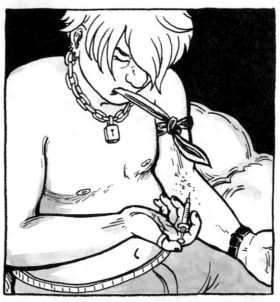

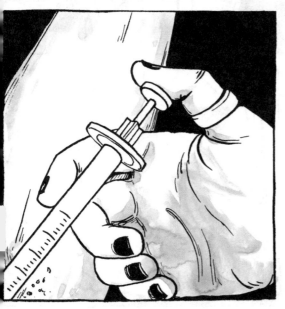

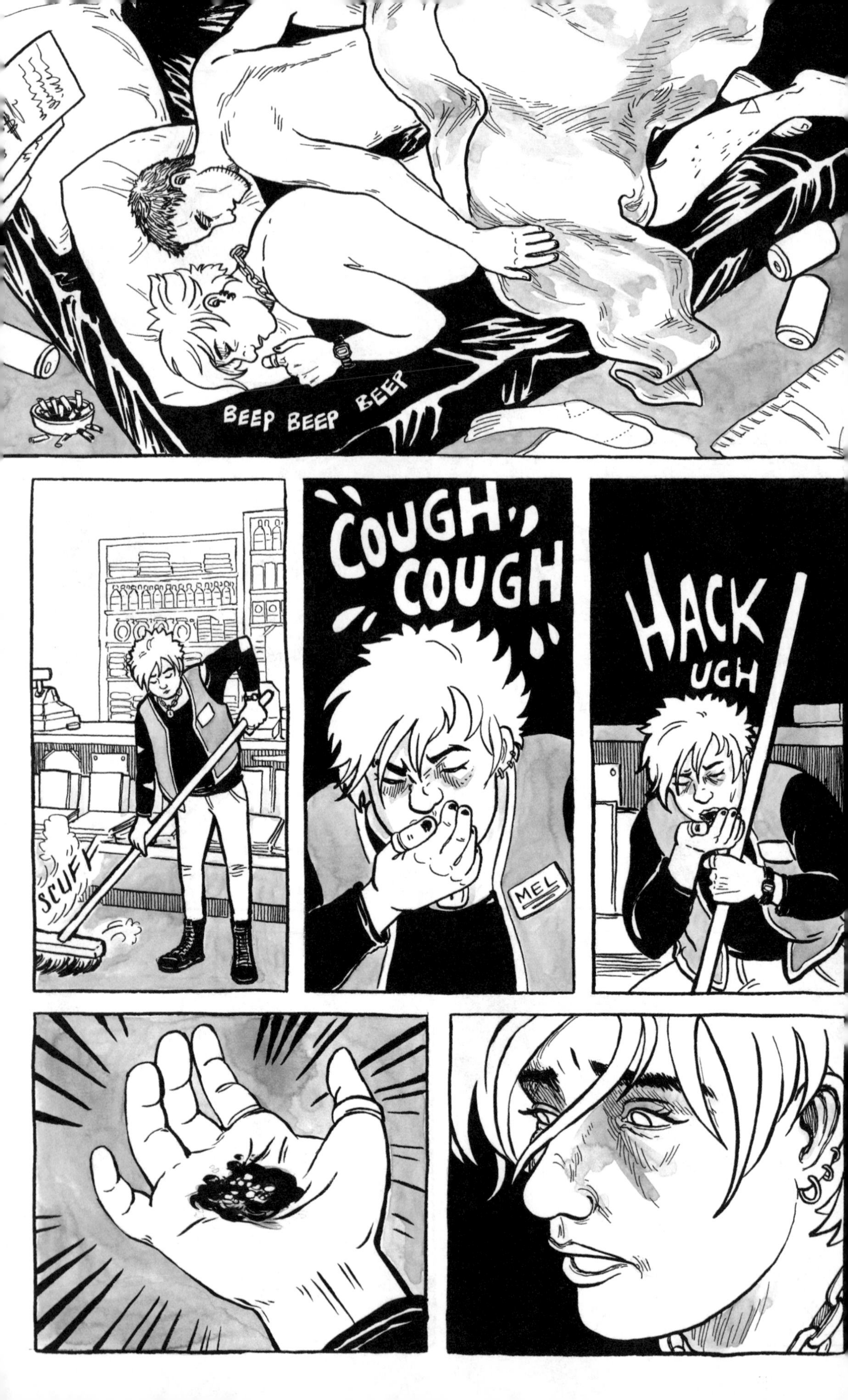
BEEP BEEP BEEP
SCUFF
COUGH, COUGH
HACK
UGH
MEL

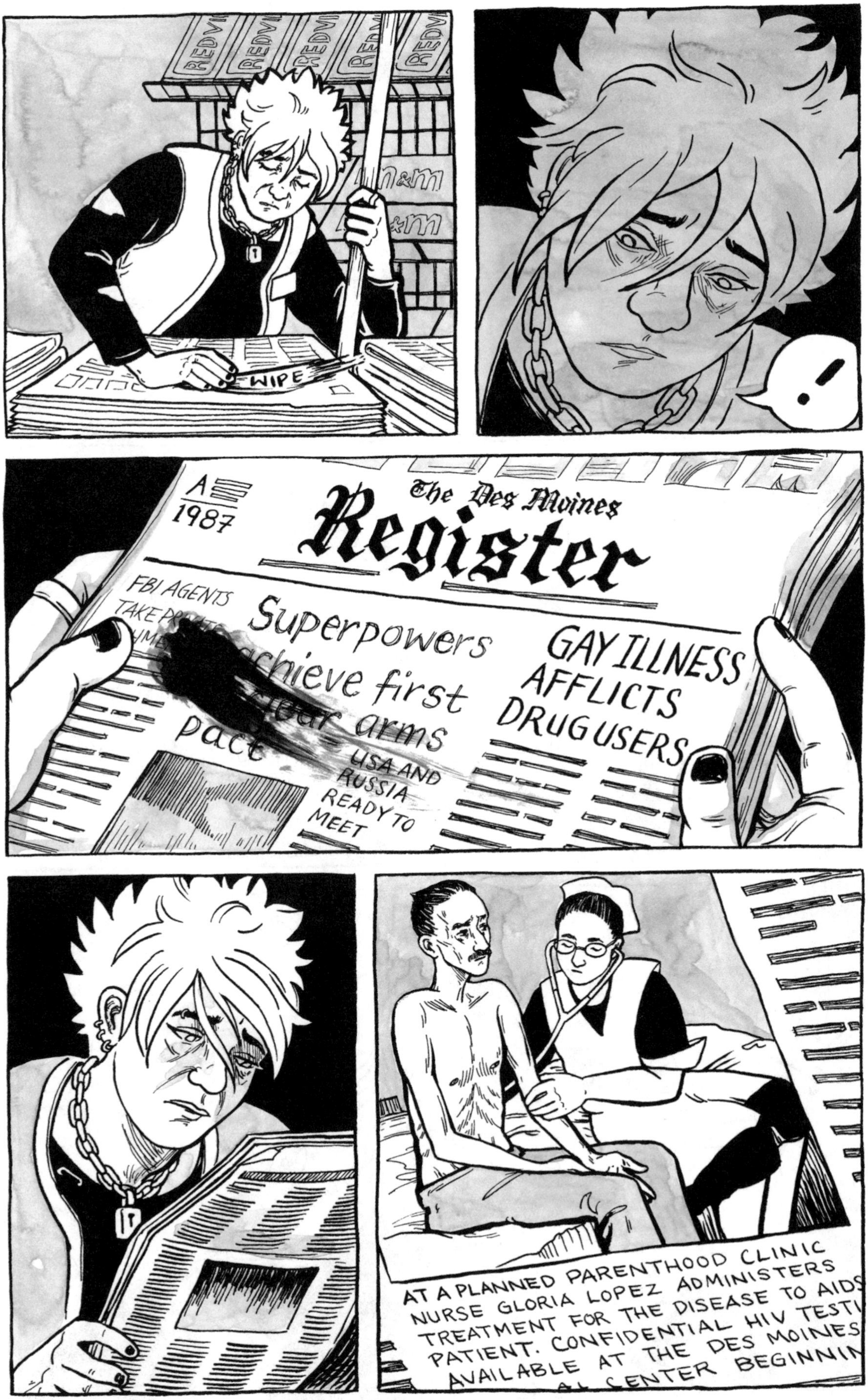
WIPE
!
A
1987
The Des Moines Register
FBI AGENTS
Superpowers
achieve first
arms
pact
USA AND RUSSIA READY TO MEET
GAY ILLNESS AFFLICTS DRUG USERS
AT A PLANNED PARENTHOOD CLINIC
NURSE GLORIA LOPEZ ADMINISTERS
TREATMENT FOR THE DISEASE TO AIDS
PATIENT. CONFIDENTIAL HIV TESTI
AVAILABLE AT THE DES MOINES
CENTER BEGINNIN

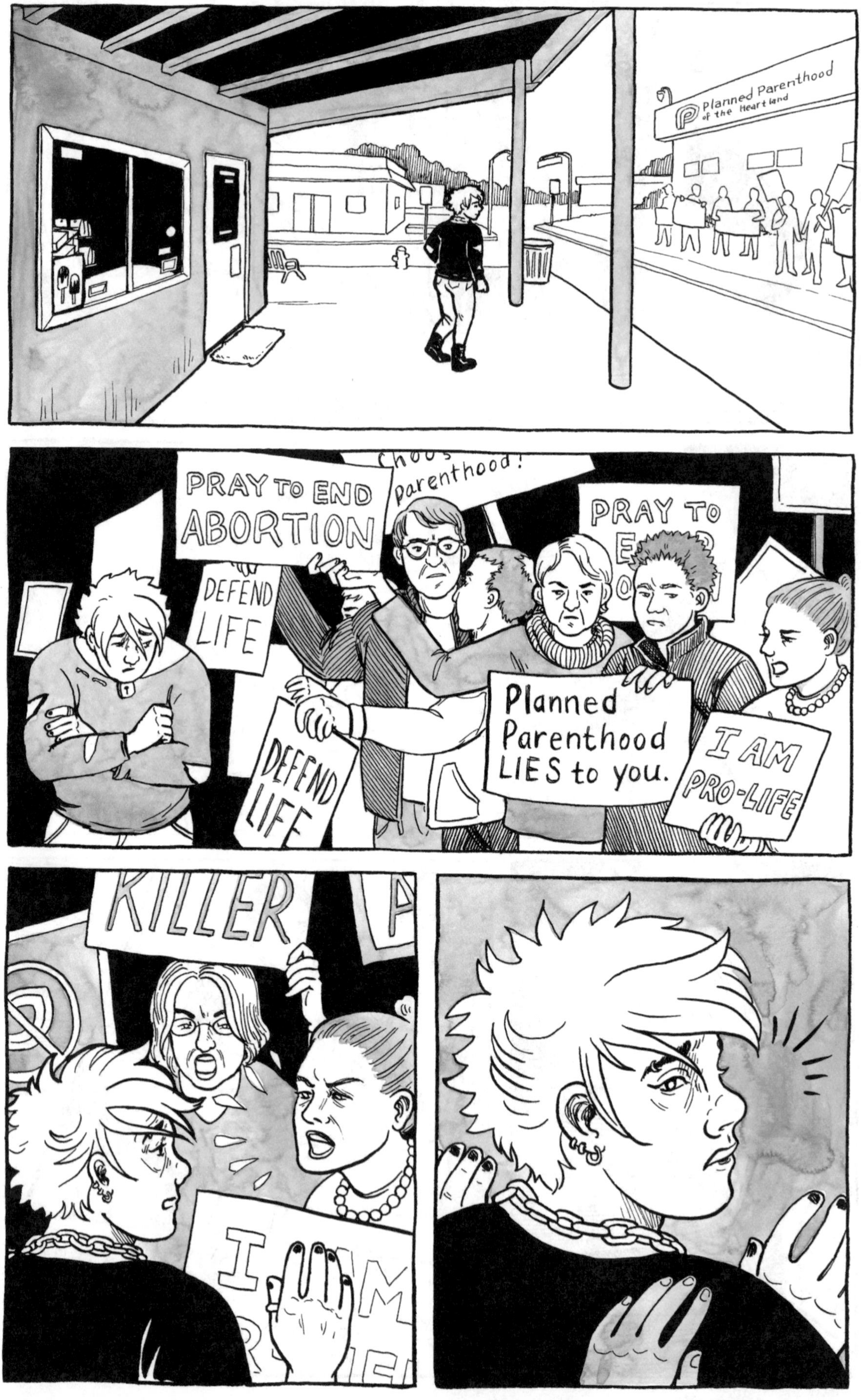
Planned Parenthood
of the Heartland
PRAY TO END ABORTION
parenthood!
DEFEND LIFE
PRAY TO
Planned Parenthood LIES to you.
DEFEND LIFE
I AM PRO-LIFE
KILLER

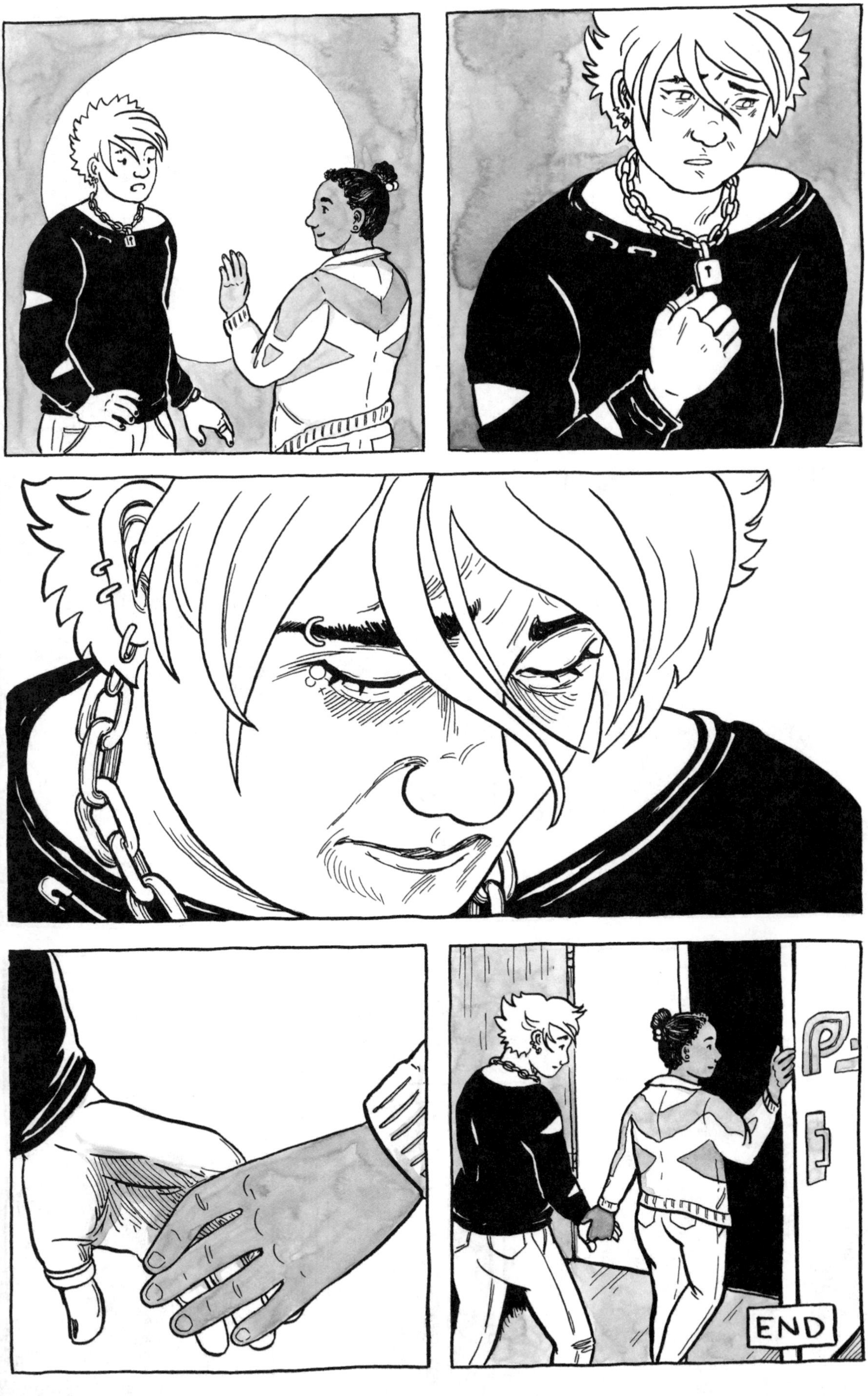
END

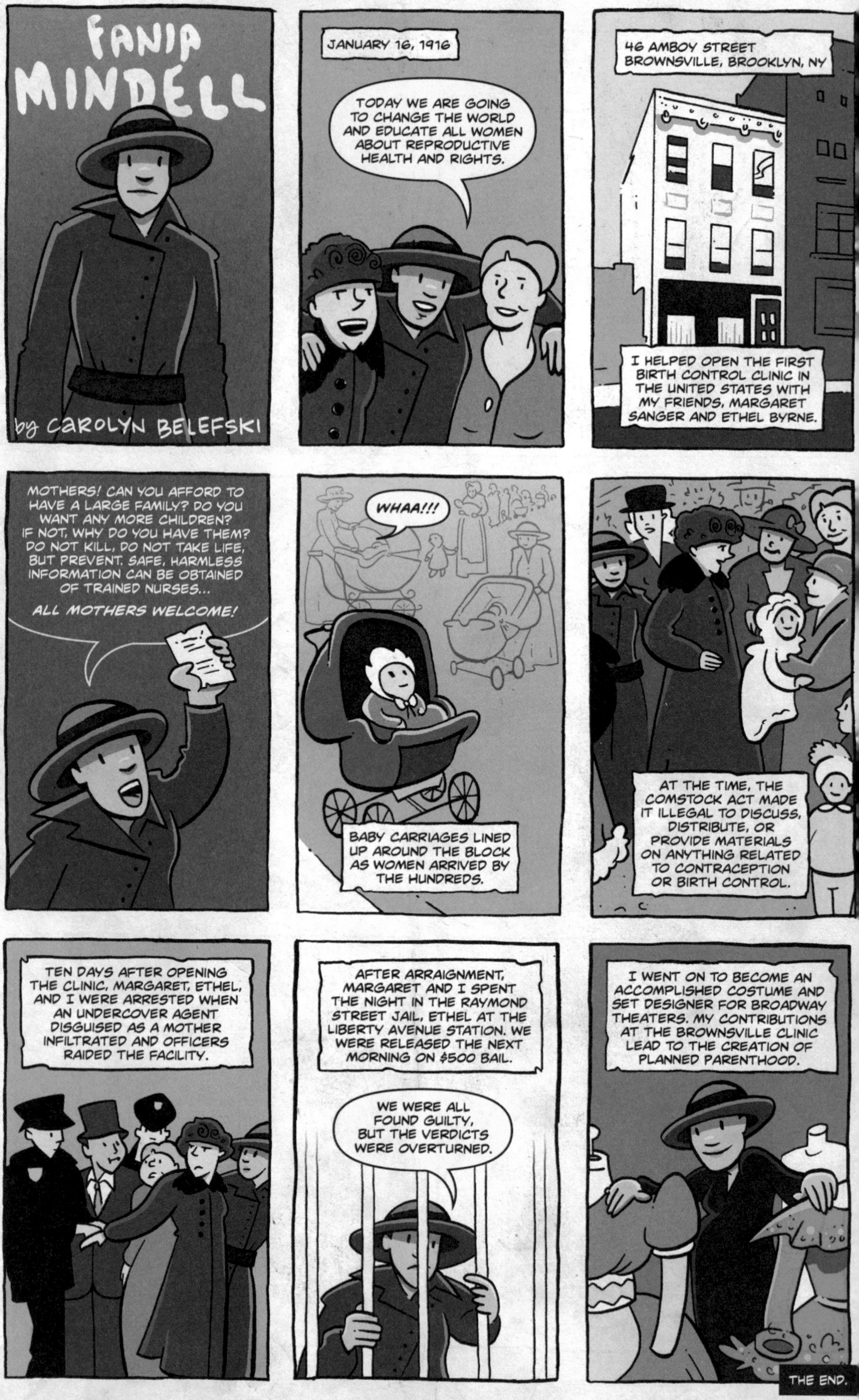
FANIA MINDELL
by CAROLYN BELEFSKI
JANUARY 16, 1916
TODAY WE ARE GOING TO CHANGE THE WORLD AND EDUCATE ALL WOMEN ABOUT REPRODUCTIVE HEALTH AND RIGHTS.
46 AMBOY STREET BROWNSVILLE, BROOKLYN, NY
I HELPED OPEN THE FIRST BIRTH CONTROL CLINIC IN THE UNITED STATES WITH MY FRIENDS, MARGARET SANGER AND ETHEL BYRNE.
MOTHERS! CAN YOU AFFORD TO HAVE A LARGE FAMILY? DO YOU WANT ANY MORE CHILDREN? IF NOT, WHY DO YOU HAVE THEM? DO NOT KILL, DO NOT TAKE LIFE, BUT PREVENT. SAFE, HARMLESS INFORMATION CAN BE OBTAINED OF TRAINED NURSES... ALL MOTHERS WELCOME!
WHAA!!!
BABY CARRIAGES LINED UP AROUND THE BLOCK AS WOMEN ARRIVED BY THE HUNDREDS.
AT THE TIME, THE COMSTOCK ACT MADE IT ILLEGAL TO DISCUSS, DISTRIBUTE, OR PROVIDE MATERIALS ON ANYTHING RELATED TO CONTRACEPTION OR BIRTH CONTROL.
TEN DAYS AFTER OPENING THE CLINIC, MARGARET, ETHEL, AND I WERE ARRESTED WHEN AN UNDERCOVER AGENT DISGUISED AS A MOTHER INFILTRATED AND OFFICERS RAIDED THE FACILITY.
AFTER ARRAIGNMENT, MARGARET AND I SPENT THE NIGHT IN THE RAYMOND STREET JAIL, ETHEL AT THE LIBERTY AVENUE STATION. WE WERE RELEASED THE NEXT MORNING ON $500 BAIL.
WE WERE ALL FOUND GUILTY, BUT THE VERDICTS WERE OVERTURNED.
I WENT ON TO BECOME AN ACCOMPLISHED COSTUME AND SET DESIGNER FOR BROADWAY THEATERS. MY CONTRIBUTIONS AT THE BROWNSVILLE CLINIC LEAD TO THE CREATION OF PLANNED PARENTHOOD.
THE END.

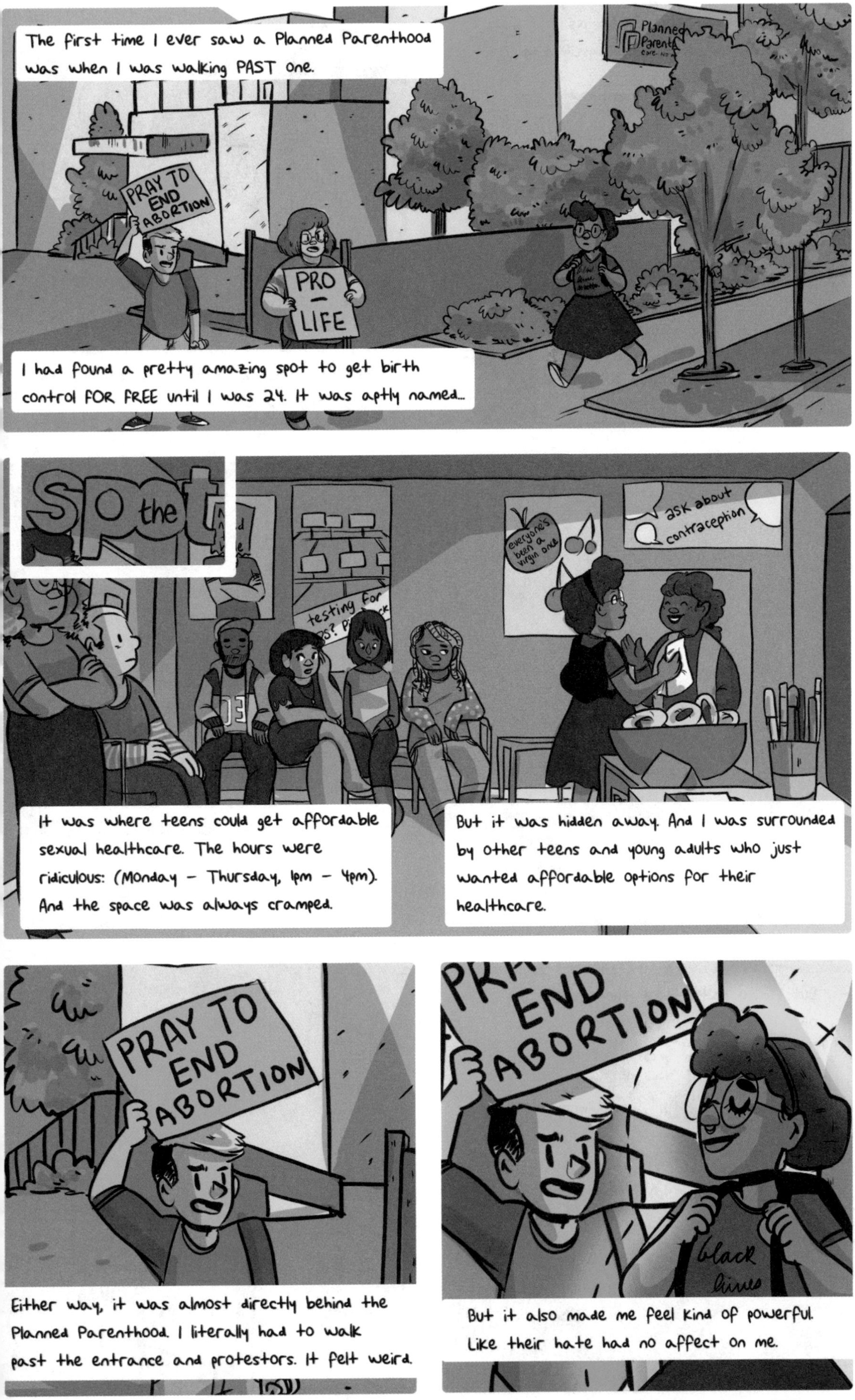

The first time I ever saw a Planned Parenthood was when I was walking PAST one.
PRAY TO END ABORTION
PRO – LIFE
I had found a pretty amazing spot to get birth control FOR FREE until I was 24. It was aptly named...
spot the
everyone's been a virgin once
ask about contraception
It was where teens could get affordable sexual healthcare. The hours were ridiculous: (Monday – Thursday, 1pm – 4pm). And the space was always cramped.
But it was hidden away. And I was surrounded by other teens and young adults who just wanted affordable options for their healthcare.
PRAY TO END ABORTION
Either way, it was almost directly behind the Planned Parenthood. I literally had to walk past the entrance and protestors. It felt weird.
END ABORTION
black lives
But it also made me feel kind of powerful. Like their hate had no affect on me.

But on the other hand, I felt as if I was keeping a secret for myself and not sharing the wealth.

What was to happen to the people over 24 who still couldn't afford healthcare?

They still had to deal with people yelling at them every month as if they were criminals and sinners. For what?

PRAY TO END ABORTION

Because they wanted to get tested? Because they wanted a way out of an unwanted pregnancy?

I'm grateful that places like The Spot exist. I know I wouldn't be able to deal with having to walk past people yelling at me when all I wanted was birth control.

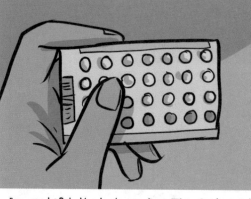

But I also hate that those were my only two choices.

testing for
S? p

Maybe if there were more places like The Spot, there would be less of a concentraction of Pro-Life protestors at ONE establishment...

NE LIFE
AKEN
STOP
FEND BORTION Y
IFE NOW

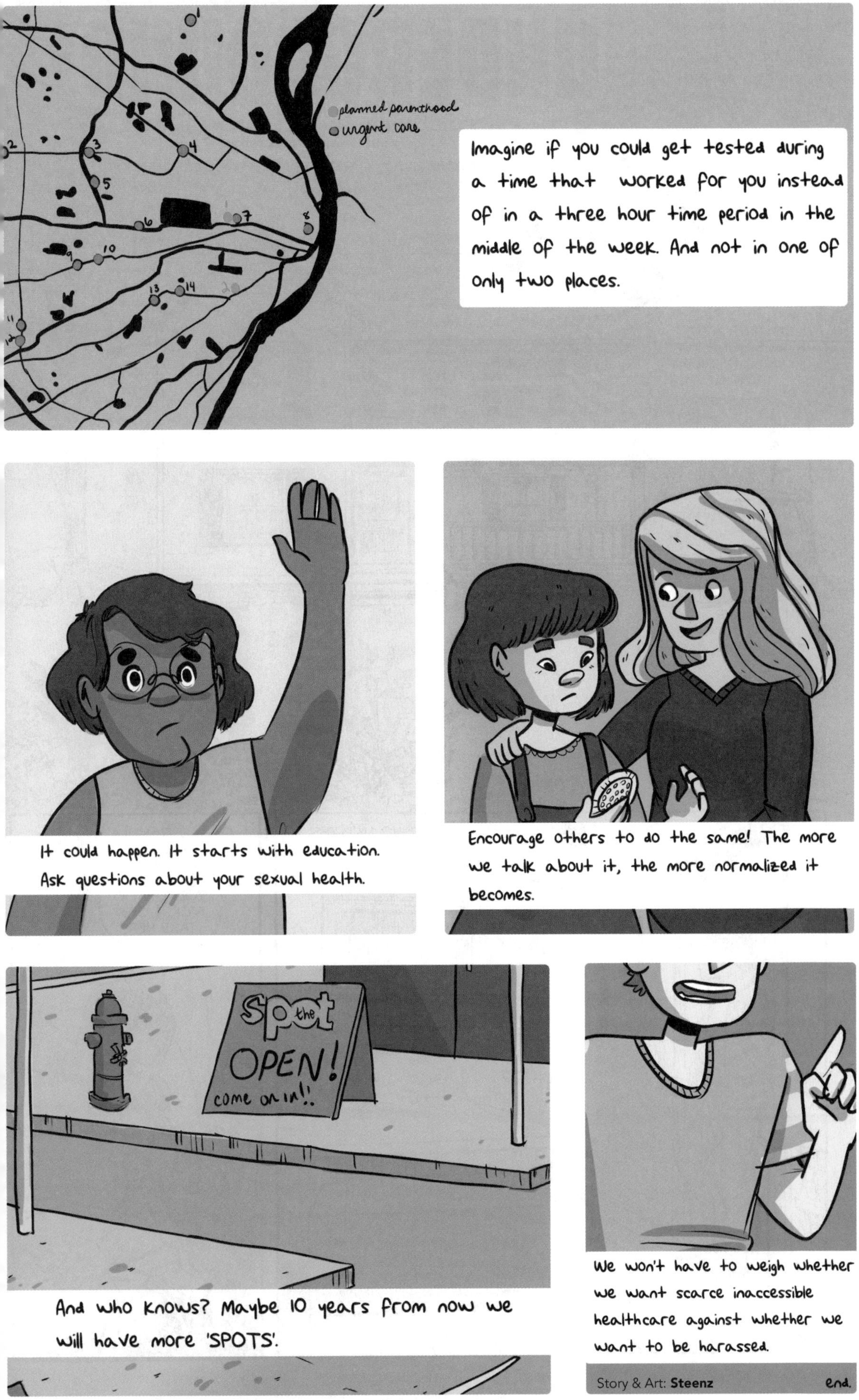
planned parenthood
urgent care
Imagine if you could get tested during a time that worked for you instead of in a three hour time period in the middle of the week. And not in one of only two places.
It could happen. It starts with education. Ask questions about your sexual health.
Encourage others to do the same! The more we talk about it, the more normalized it becomes.
Spot the
OPEN!
come on in!!
And who knows? Maybe 10 years from now we will have more 'SPOTS'.
We won't have to weigh whether we want scarce inaccessible healthcare against whether we want to be harassed.
Story & Art: Steenz
end.

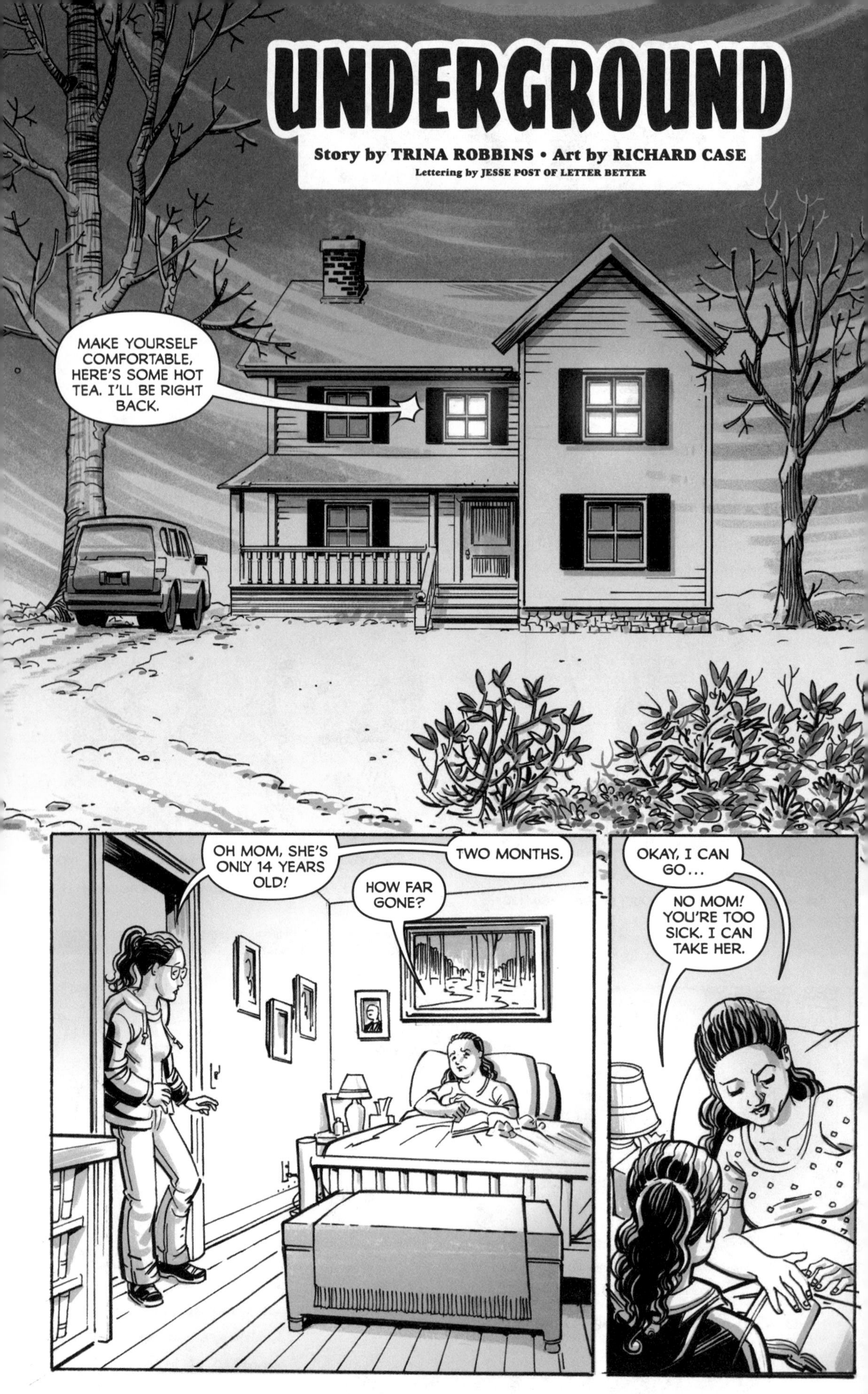
UNDERGROUND
Story by TRINA ROBBINS • Art by RICHARD CASE
Lettering by JESSE POST OF LETTER BETTER
MAKE YOURSELF COMFORTABLE, HERE'S SOME HOT TEA. I'LL BE RIGHT BACK.
OH MOM, SHE'S ONLY 14 YEARS OLD!
HOW FAR GONE?
TWO MONTHS.
OKAY, I CAN GO...
NO MOM! YOU'RE TOO SICK. I CAN TAKE HER.

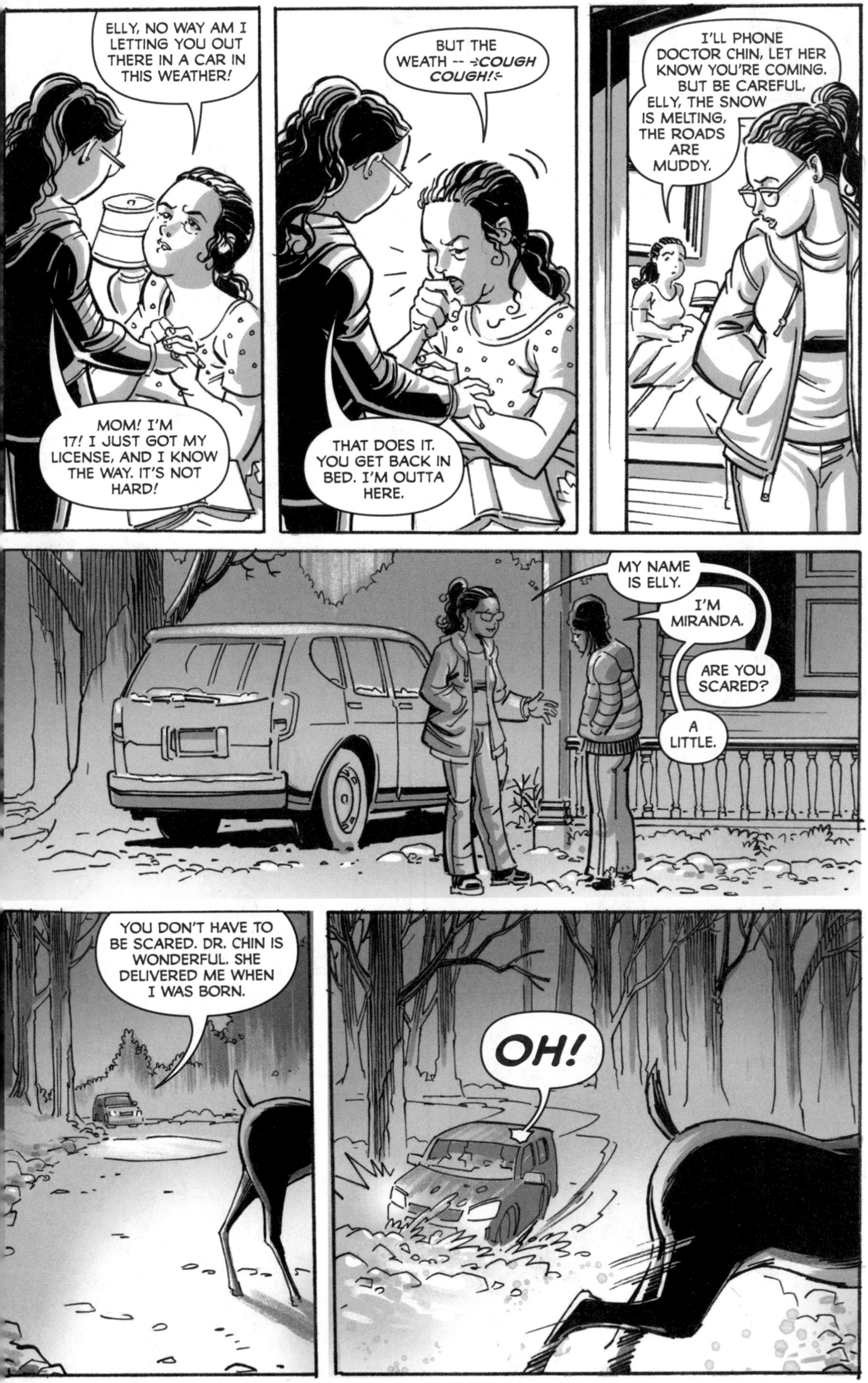
ELLY, NO WAY AM I LETTING YOU OUT THERE IN A CAR IN THIS WEATHER!
MOM! I'M 17! I JUST GOT MY LICENSE, AND I KNOW THE WAY. IT'S NOT HARD!
BUT THE WEATH -- COUGH COUGH!
THAT DOES IT. YOU GET BACK IN BED. I'M OUTTA HERE.
I'LL PHONE DOCTOR CHIN, LET HER KNOW YOU'RE COMING. BUT BE CAREFUL, ELLY, THE SNOW IS MELTING, THE ROADS ARE MUDDY.
MY NAME IS ELLY.
I'M MIRANDA.
ARE YOU SCARED?
A LITTLE.
YOU DON'T HAVE TO BE SCARED. DR. CHIN IS WONDERFUL. SHE DELIVERED ME WHEN I WAS BORN.
OH!

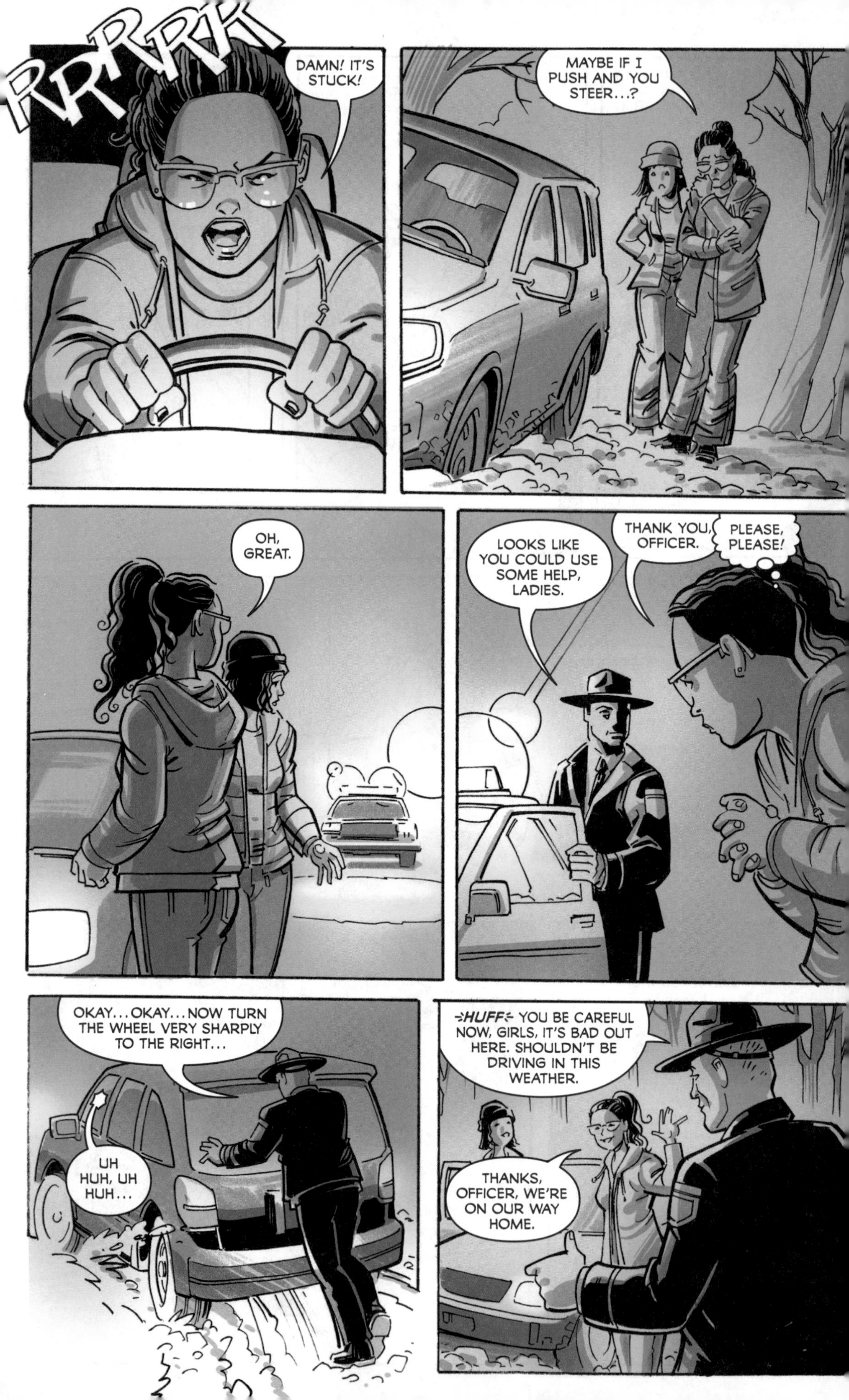
RRRRK
DAMN! IT'S STUCK!
MAYBE IF I PUSH AND YOU STEER...?
OH, GREAT.
LOOKS LIKE YOU COULD USE SOME HELP, LADIES.
THANK YOU, OFFICER.
PLEASE, PLEASE!
OKAY...OKAY...NOW TURN THE WHEEL VERY SHARPLY TO THE RIGHT...
UH HUH, UH HUH...
HUFF YOU BE CAREFUL NOW, GIRLS, IT'S BAD OUT HERE. SHOULDN'T BE DRIVING IN THIS WEATHER.
THANKS, OFFICER, WE'RE ON OUR WAY HOME.

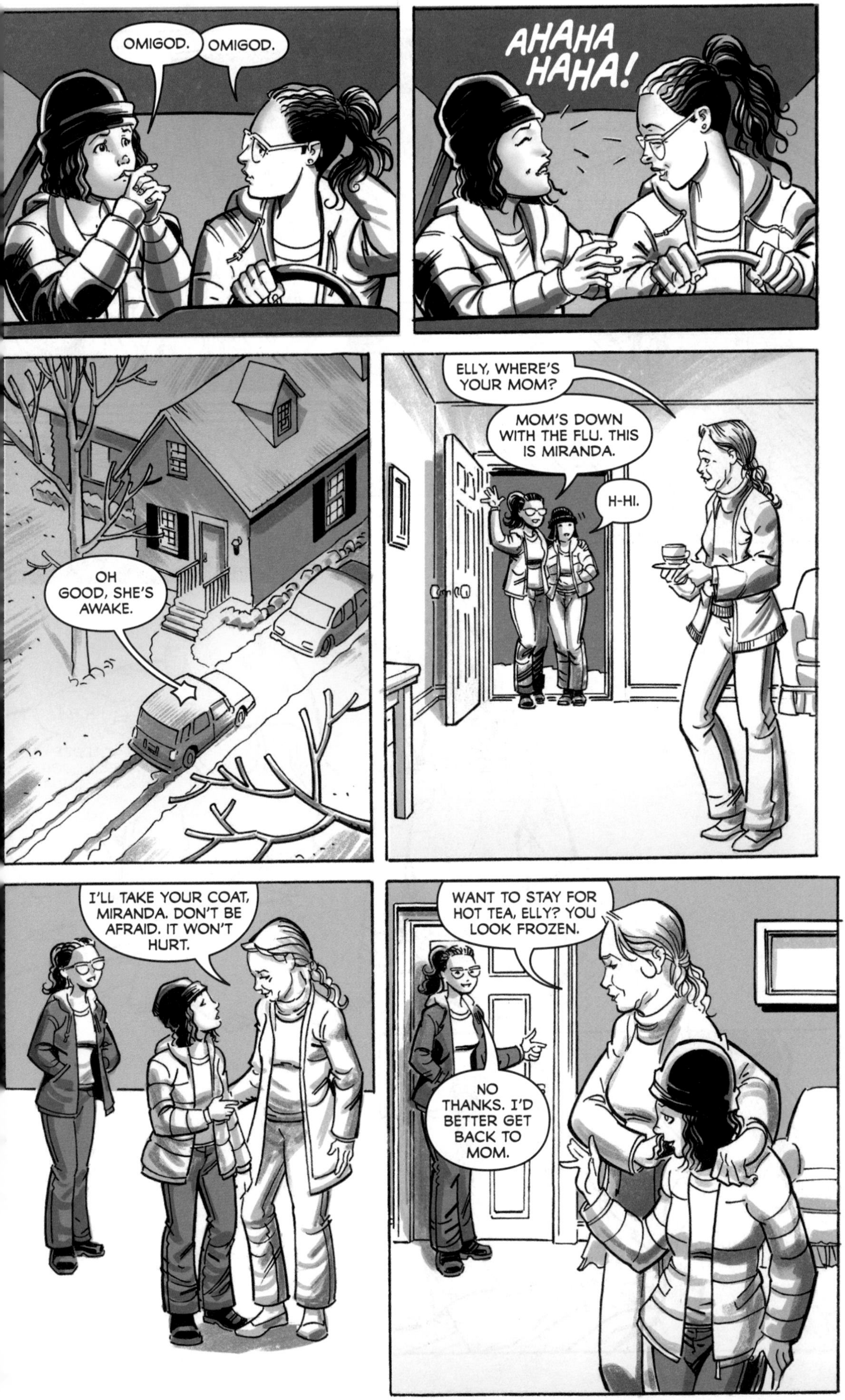
OMIGOD.
OMIGOD.
AHAHA HAHA!
OH GOOD, SHE'S AWAKE.
ELLY, WHERE'S YOUR MOM?
MOM'S DOWN WITH THE FLU. THIS IS MIRANDA.
H-HI.
I'LL TAKE YOUR COAT, MIRANDA. DON'T BE AFRAID. IT WON'T HURT.
WANT TO STAY FOR HOT TEA, ELLY? YOU LOOK FROZEN.
NO THANKS. I'D BETTER GET BACK TO MOM.

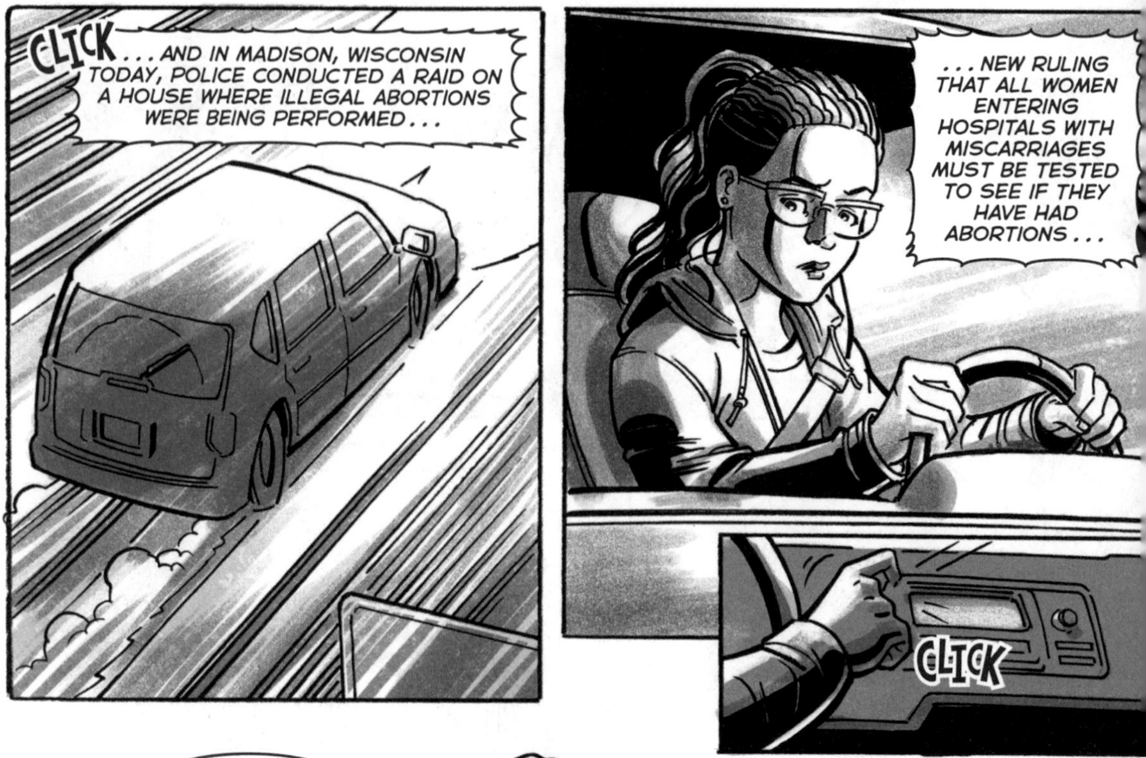
CLICK
. . . AND IN MADISON, WISCONSIN TODAY, POLICE CONDUCTED A RAID ON A HOUSE WHERE ILLEGAL ABORTIONS WERE BEING PERFORMED . . .
. . . NEW RULING THAT ALL WOMEN ENTERING HOSPITALS WITH MISCARRIAGES MUST BE TESTED TO SEE IF THEY HAVE HAD ABORTIONS . . .
CLICK

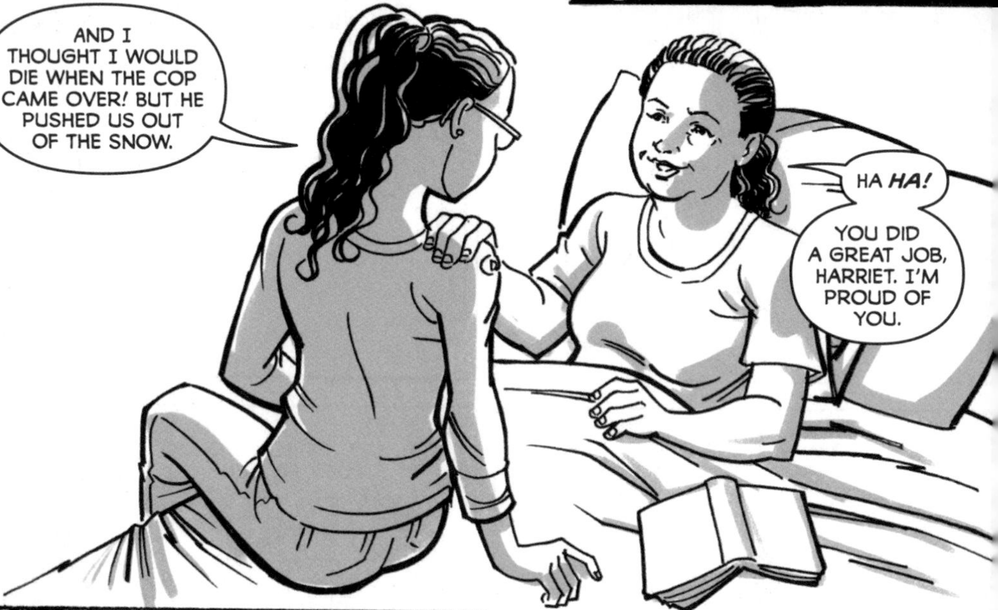
AND I THOUGHT I WOULD DIE WHEN THE COP CAME OVER! BUT HE PUSHED US OUT OF THE SNOW.
HA *HA!*
YOU DID A GREAT JOB, HARRIET. I'M PROUD OF YOU.

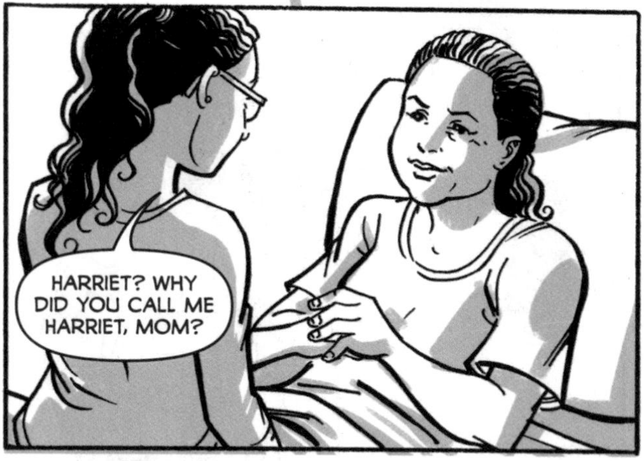
HARRIET? WHY DID YOU CALL ME HARRIET, MOM?

Born a slave, *Harriet Tubman* was the most famous conductor of the *Underground Railroad.* During 19 trips from the slave states to the free North, she led over 300 slaves to freedom.

family first

by clarissa

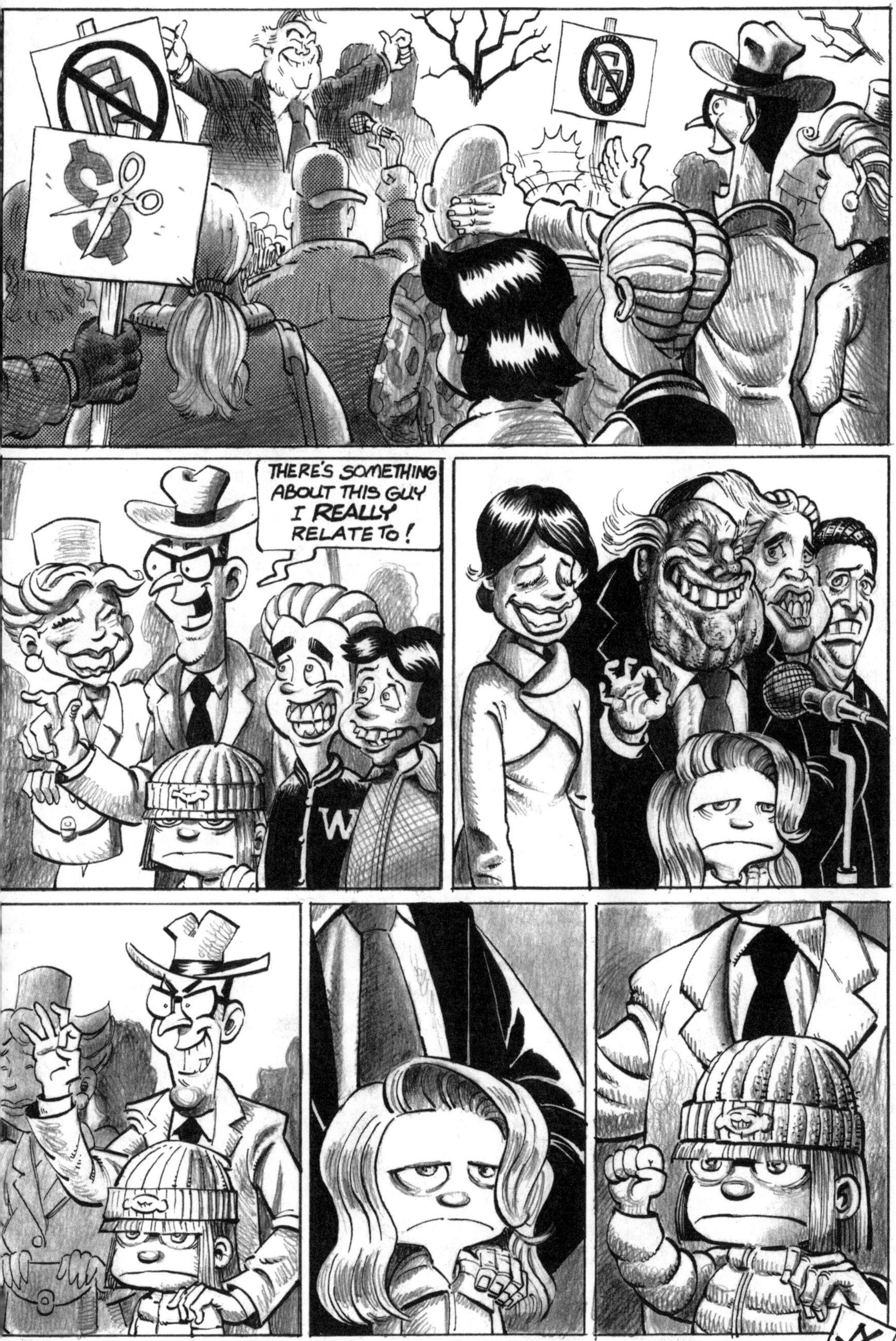
THERE'S SOMETHING ABOUT THIS GUY I REALLY RELATE TO!

Story & Art: **Jason Yungbluth**

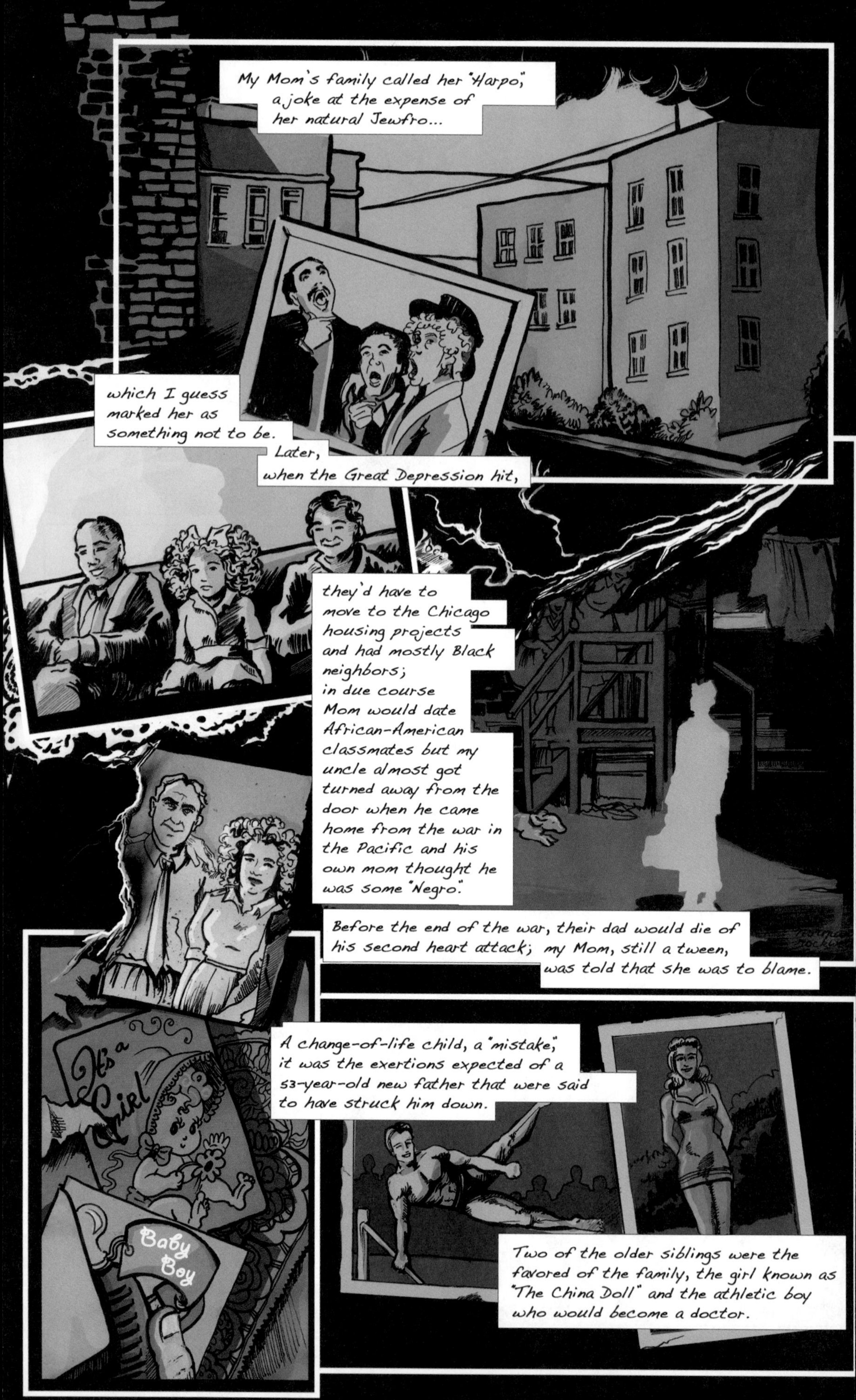
My Mom's family called her "Harpo," a joke at the expense of her natural Jewfro...
which I guess marked her as something not to be.
Later, when the Great Depression hit,
they'd have to move to the Chicago housing projects and had mostly Black neighbors; in due course Mom would date African-American classmates but my uncle almost got turned away from the door when he came home from the war in the Pacific and his own mom thought he was some "Negro."
Before the end of the war, their dad would die of his second heart attack; my Mom, still a tween, was told that she was to blame.
A change-of-life child, a "mistake," it was the exertions expected of a 53-year-old new father that were said to have struck him down.
It's a Girl
Baby Boy
Two of the older siblings were the favored of the family, the girl known as "The China Doll" and the athletic boy who would become a doctor.

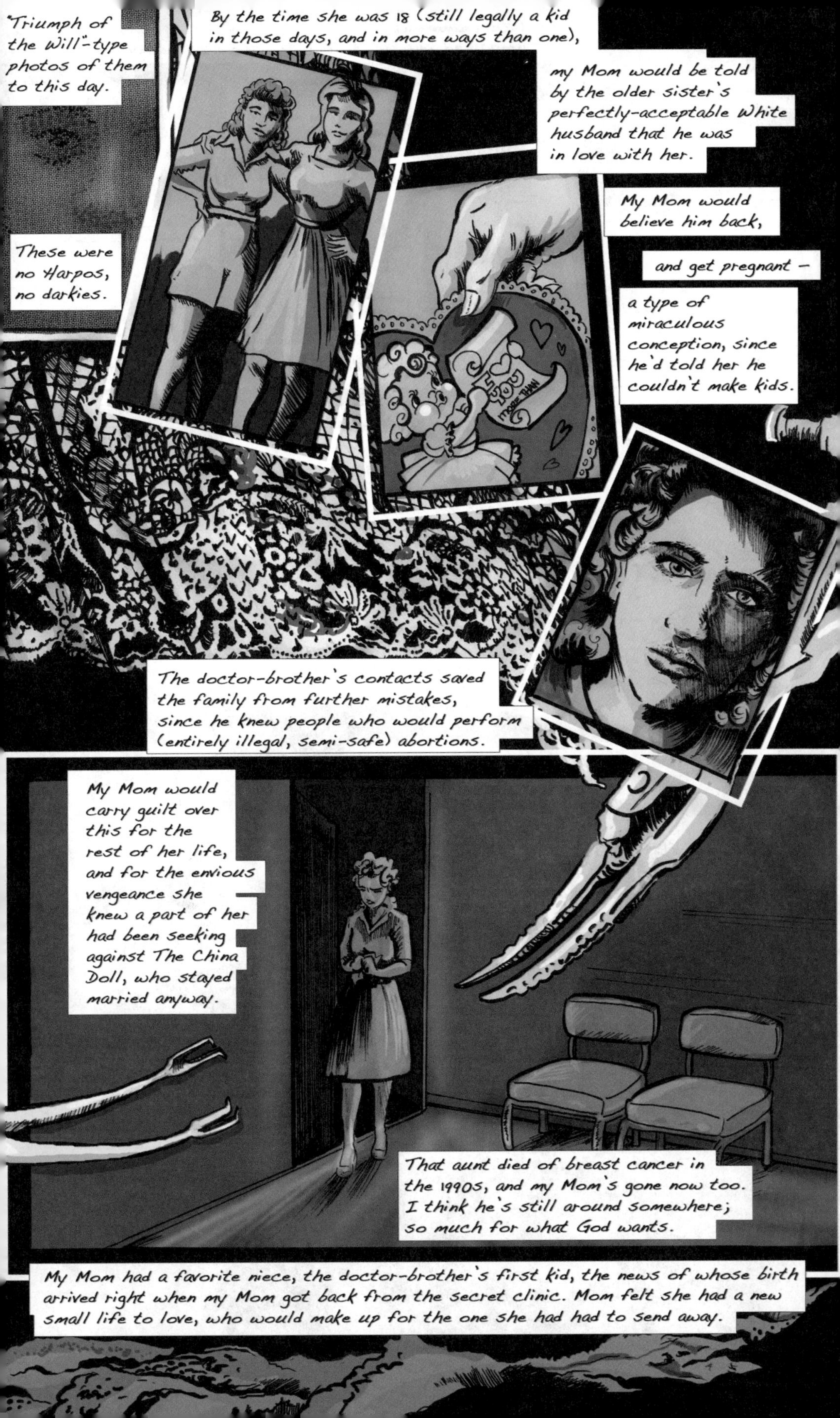
"Triumph of the Will"-type photos of them to this day.
These were no Harpos, no darkies.
By the time she was 18 (still legally a kid in those days, and in more ways than one),
my Mom would be told by the older sister's perfectly-acceptable White husband that he was in love with her.
My Mom would believe him back,
and get pregnant –
a type of miraculous conception, since he'd told her he couldn't make kids.
The doctor-brother's contacts saved the family from further mistakes, since he knew people who would perform (entirely illegal, semi-safe) abortions.
My Mom would carry guilt over this for the rest of her life, and for the envious vengeance she knew a part of her had been seeking against The China Doll, who stayed married anyway.
That aunt died of breast cancer in the 1990s, and my Mom's gone now too. I think he's still around somewhere; so much for what God wants.
My Mom had a favorite niece, the doctor-brother's first kid, the news of whose birth arrived right when my Mom got back from the secret clinic. Mom felt she had a new small life to love, who would make up for the one she had had to send away.

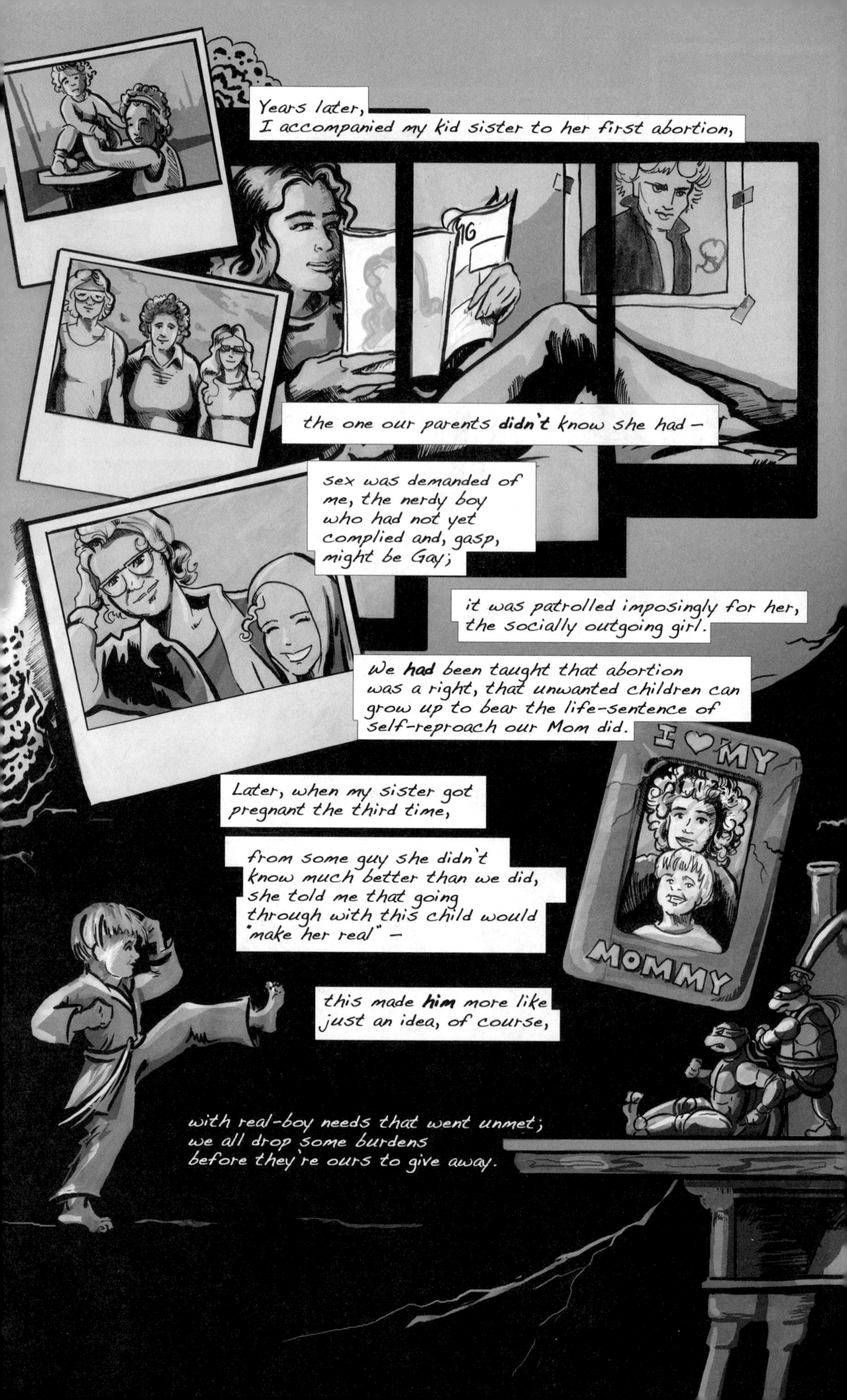
Years later, I accompanied my kid sister to her first abortion,
16
the one our parents **didn't** know she had—
sex was demanded of me, the nerdy boy who had not yet complied and, gasp, might be Gay;
it was patrolled imposingly for her, the socially outgoing girl.
We **had** been taught that abortion was a right, that unwanted children can grow up to bear the life-sentence of self-reproach our Mom did.
I ♥ MY MOMMY
Later, when my sister got pregnant the third time,
from some guy she didn't know much better than we did, she told me that going through with this child would "make her real"—
this made **him** more like just an idea, of course,
with real-boy needs that went unmet; we all drop some burdens before they're ours to give away.

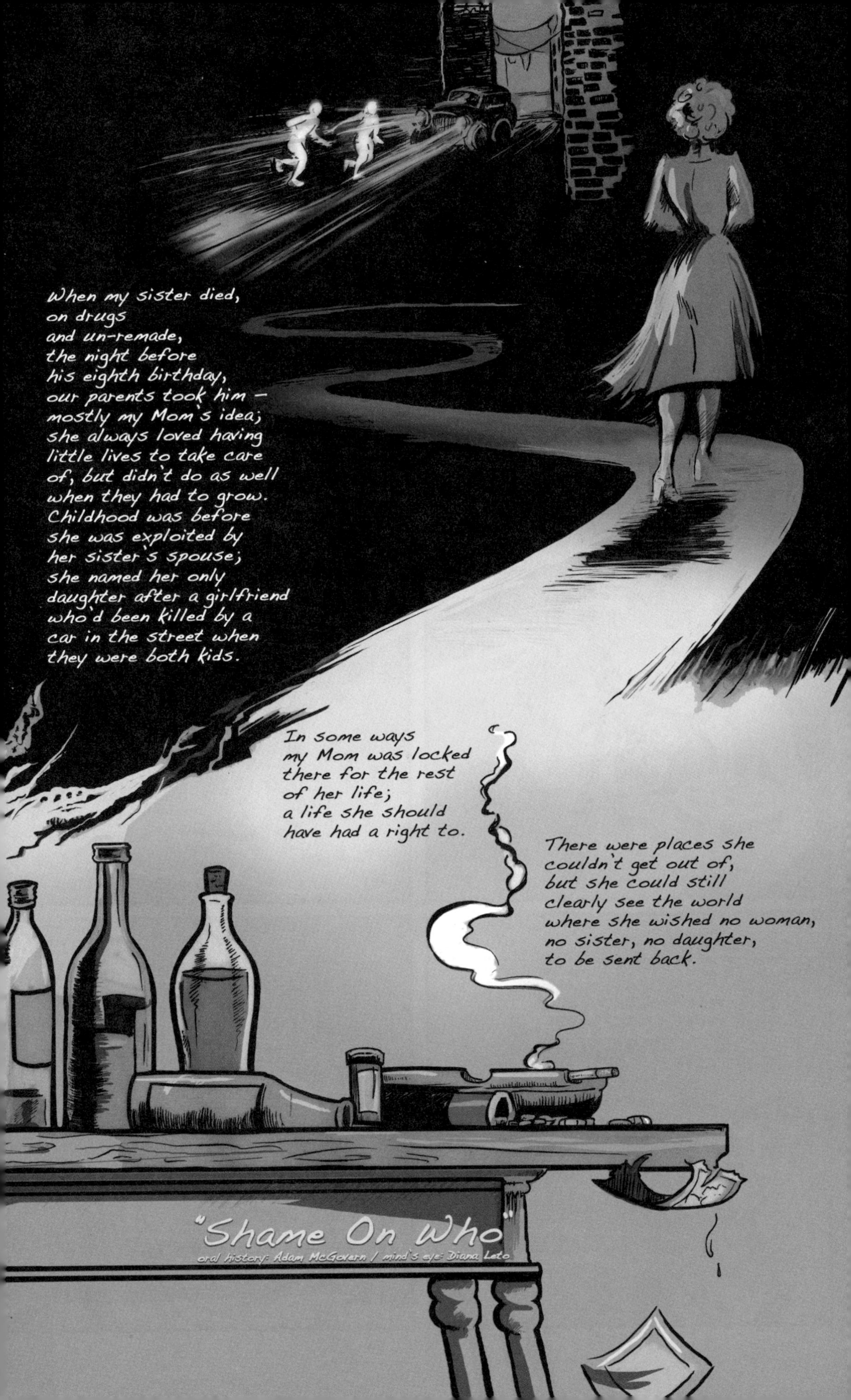
When my sister died, on drugs and un-remade, the night before his eighth birthday, our parents took him — mostly my Mom's idea; she always loved having little lives to take care of, but didn't do as well when they had to grow. Childhood was before she was exploited by her sister's spouse; she named her only daughter after a girlfriend who'd been killed by a car in the street when they were both kids.
In some ways my Mom was locked there for the rest of her life; a life she should have had a right to.
There were places she couldn't get out of, but she could still clearly see the world where she wished no woman, no sister, no daughter, to be sent back.
"Shame On Who"
oral history: Adam McGovern / mind's eye: Diana Leto

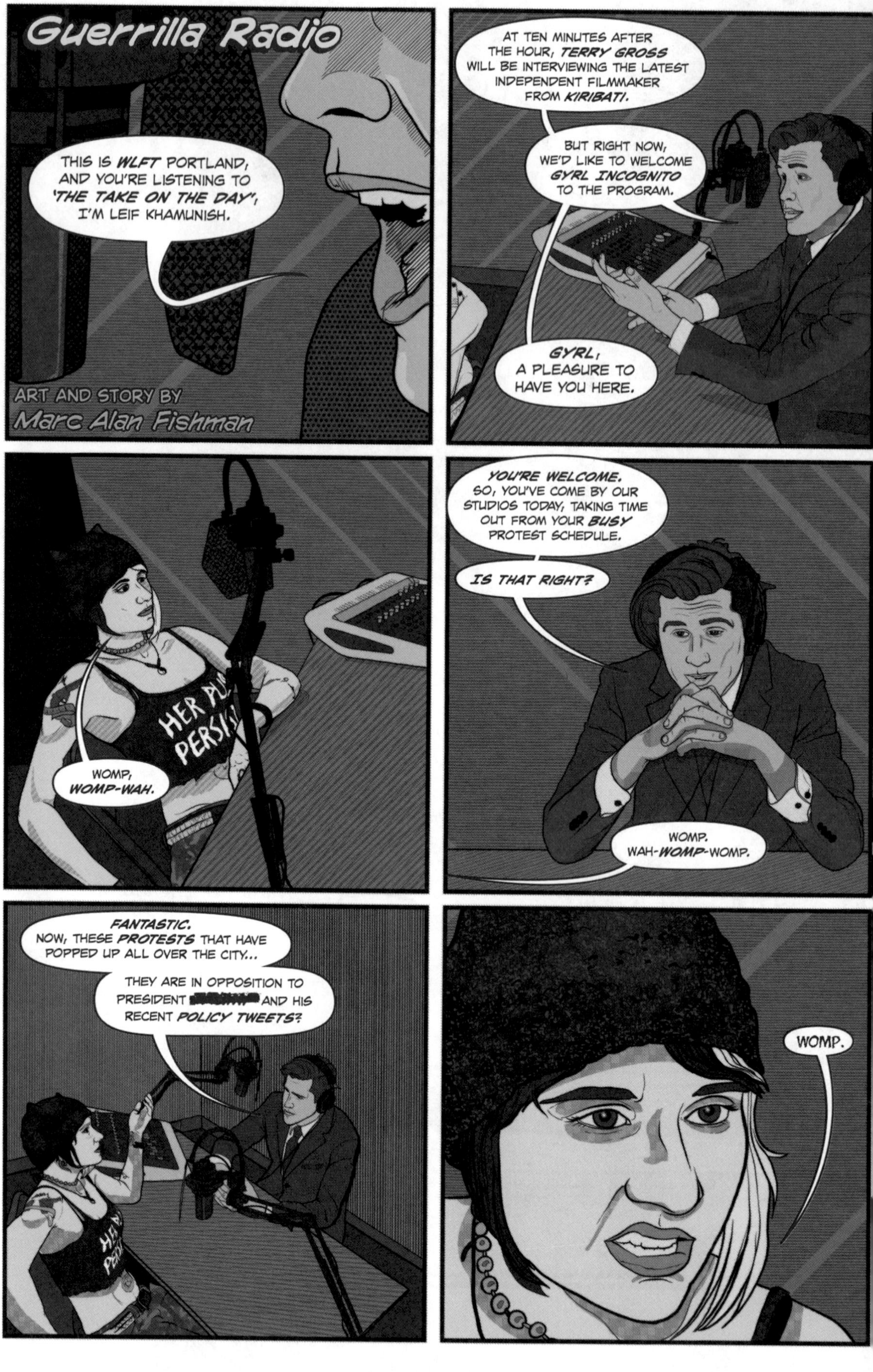
Guerrilla Radio
THIS IS WLFT PORTLAND, AND YOU'RE LISTENING TO 'THE TAKE ON THE DAY', I'M LEIF KHAMUNISH.
ART AND STORY BY
Marc Alan Fishman
AT TEN MINUTES AFTER THE HOUR, TERRY GROSS WILL BE INTERVIEWING THE LATEST INDEPENDENT FILMMAKER FROM KIRIBATI.
BUT RIGHT NOW, WE'D LIKE TO WELCOME GYRL INCOGNITO TO THE PROGRAM.
GYRL, A PLEASURE TO HAVE YOU HERE.
WOMP, WOMP-WAH.
YOU'RE WELCOME. SO, YOU'VE COME BY OUR STUDIOS TODAY, TAKING TIME OUT FROM YOUR BUSY PROTEST SCHEDULE.
IS THAT RIGHT?
WOMP. WAH-WOMP-WOMP.
FANTASTIC. NOW, THESE PROTESTS THAT HAVE POPPED UP ALL OVER THE CITY...
THEY ARE IN OPPOSITION TO PRESIDENT [redacted] AND HIS RECENT POLICY TWEETS?
WOMP.

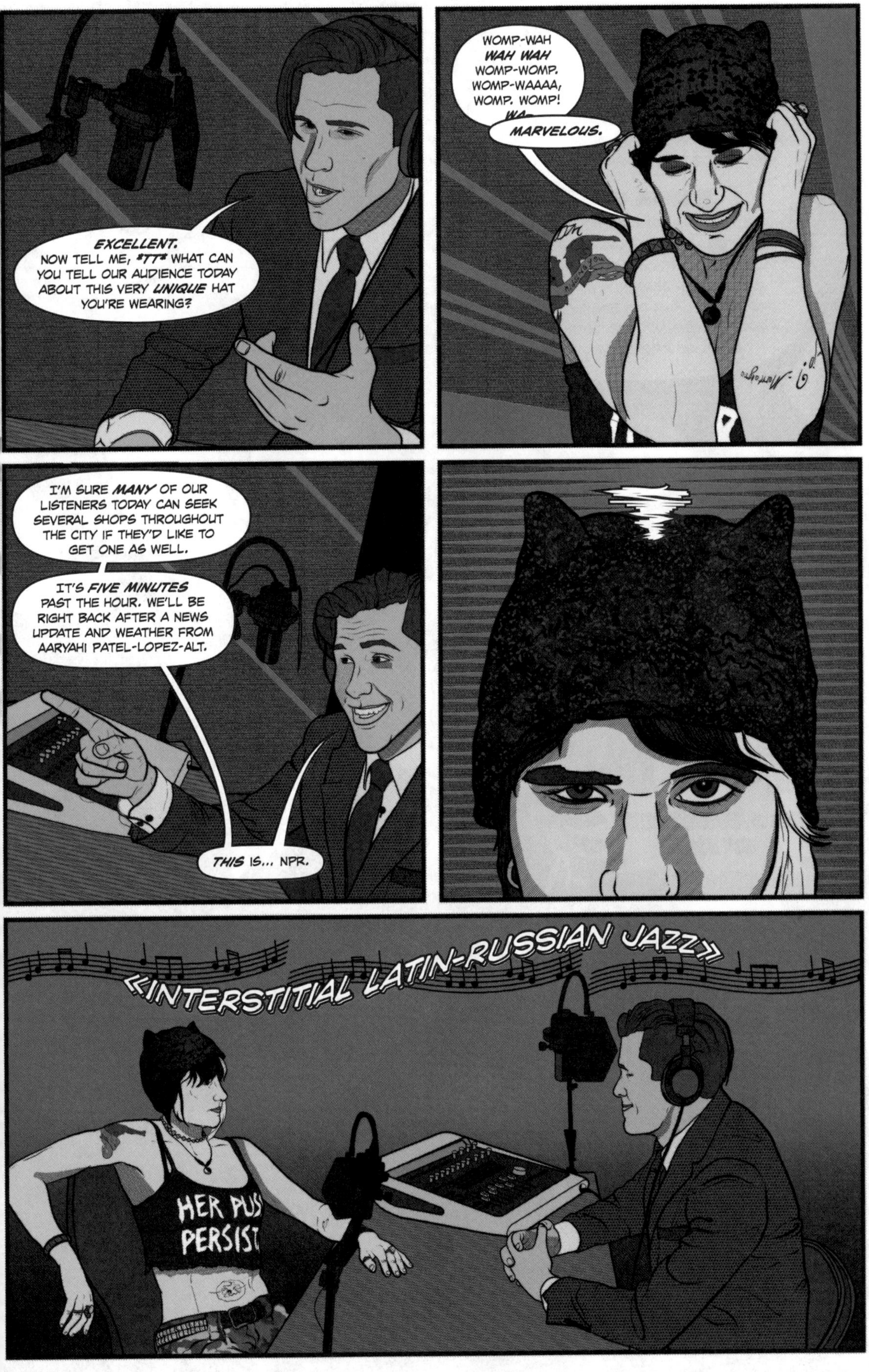
EXCELLENT.
NOW TELL ME, *TT* WHAT CAN YOU TELL OUR AUDIENCE TODAY ABOUT THIS VERY UNIQUE HAT YOU'RE WEARING?
WOMP-WAH WAH WAH WOMP-WOMP. WOMP-WAAAA, WOMP. WOMP! WA-
MARVELOUS.
I'M SURE MANY OF OUR LISTENERS TODAY CAN SEEK SEVERAL SHOPS THROUGHOUT THE CITY IF THEY'D LIKE TO GET ONE AS WELL.
IT'S FIVE MINUTES PAST THE HOUR. WE'LL BE RIGHT BACK AFTER A NEWS UPDATE AND WEATHER FROM AARYAHI PATEL-LOPEZ-ALT.
THIS IS... NPR.
«INTERSTITIAL LATIN-RUSSIAN JAZZ»
HER PUS
PERSIS

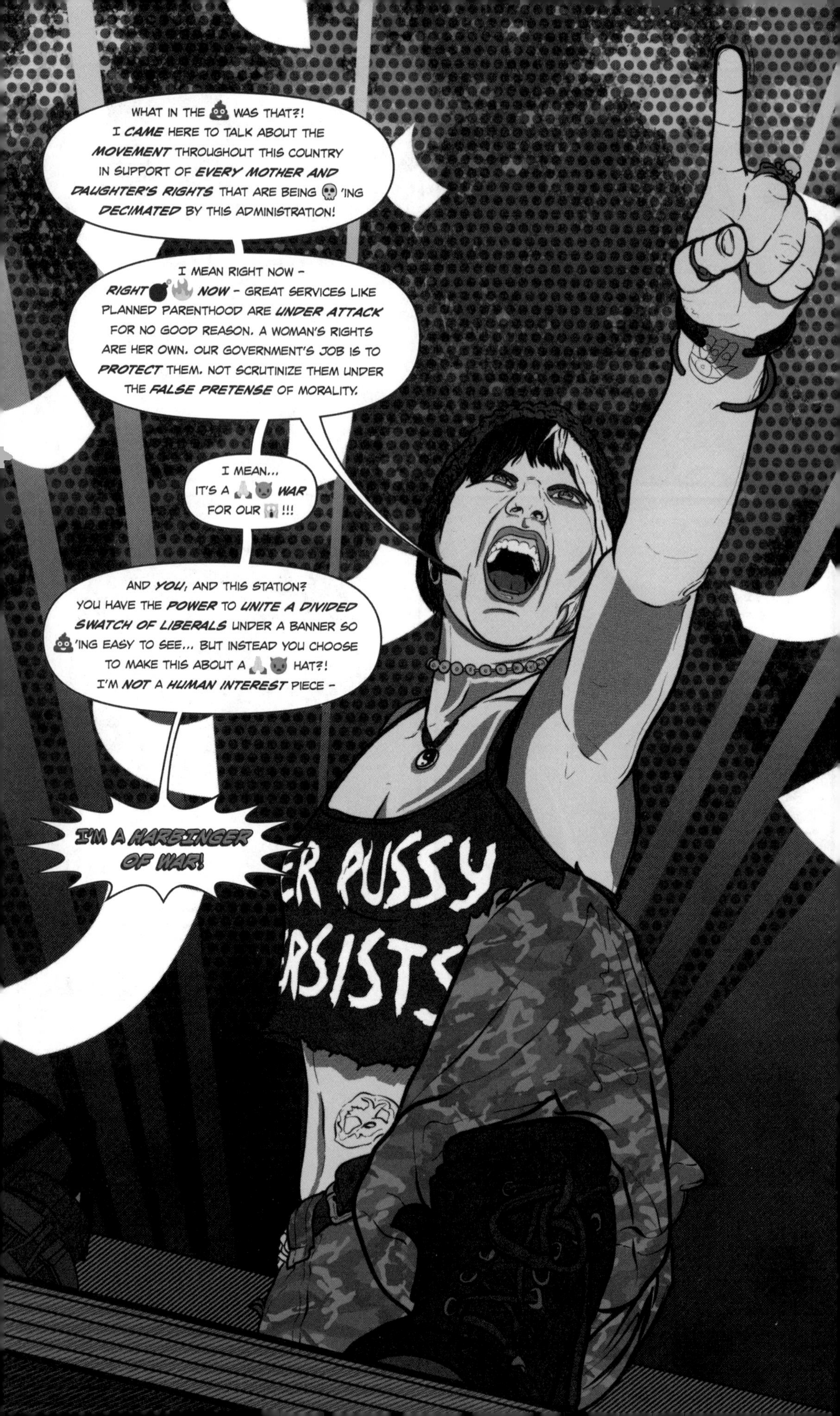
WHAT IN THE 💩 WAS THAT?! I CAME HERE TO TALK ABOUT THE MOVEMENT THROUGHOUT THIS COUNTRY IN SUPPORT OF EVERY MOTHER AND DAUGHTER'S RIGHTS THAT ARE BEING 💀'ING DECIMATED BY THIS ADMINISTRATION!
I MEAN RIGHT NOW – RIGHT 💣🔥 NOW – GREAT SERVICES LIKE PLANNED PARENTHOOD ARE UNDER ATTACK FOR NO GOOD REASON. A WOMAN'S RIGHTS ARE HER OWN. OUR GOVERNMENT'S JOB IS TO PROTECT THEM. NOT SCRUTINIZE THEM UNDER THE FALSE PRETENSE OF MORALITY.
I MEAN... IT'S A 🙏😈 WAR FOR OUR 😱!!!
AND YOU, AND THIS STATION? YOU HAVE THE POWER TO UNITE A DIVIDED SWATCH OF LIBERALS UNDER A BANNER SO 💩'ING EASY TO SEE... BUT INSTEAD YOU CHOOSE TO MAKE THIS ABOUT A 🙏😈 HAT?! I'M NOT A HUMAN INTEREST PIECE –
I'M A HARBINGER OF WAR!
ER PUSSY
RSISTS

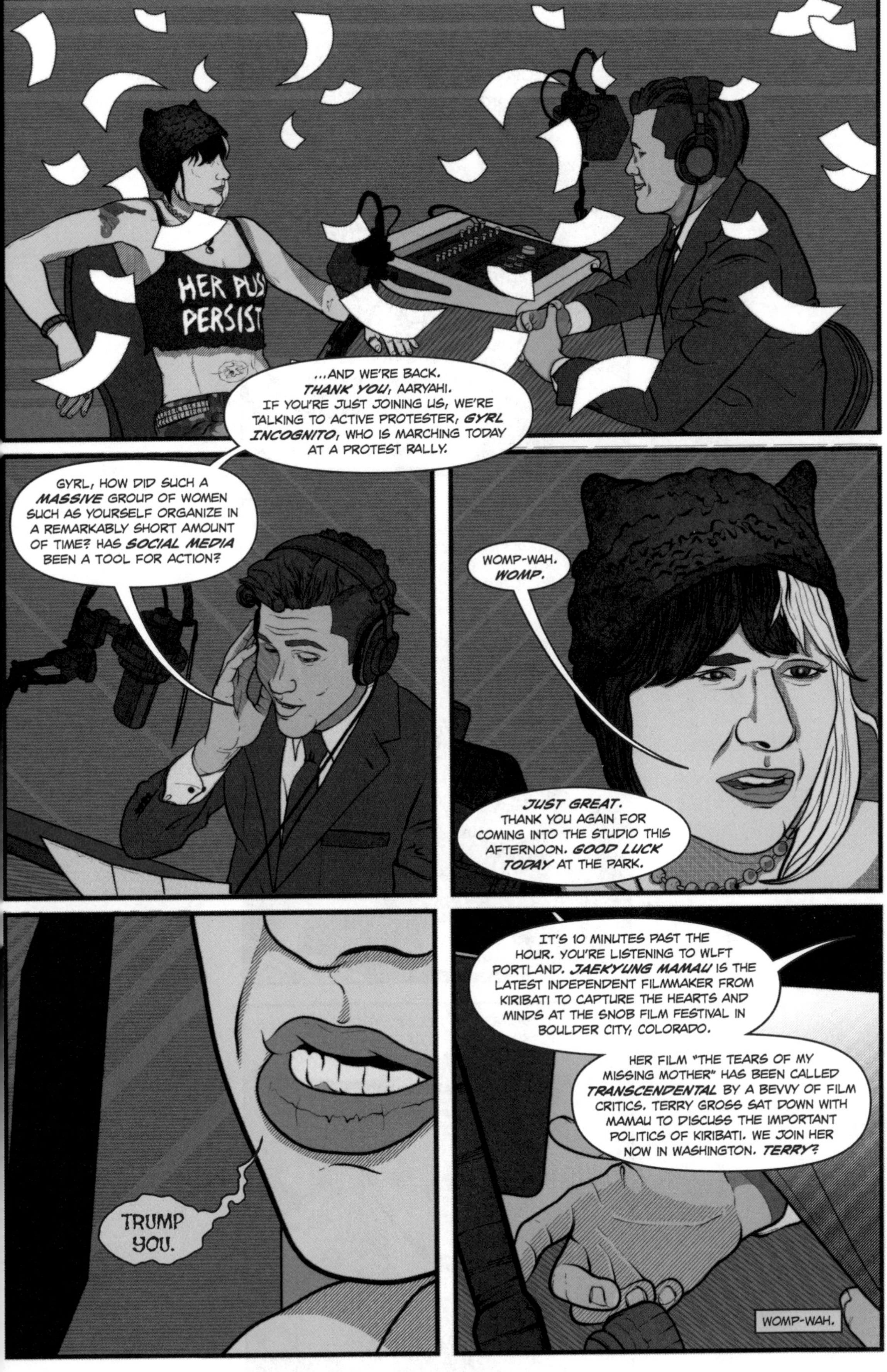

HER PUS
PERSIST
...AND WE'RE BACK. THANK YOU, AARYAHI. IF YOU'RE JUST JOINING US, WE'RE TALKING TO ACTIVE PROTESTER, GYRL INCOGNITO, WHO IS MARCHING TODAY AT A PROTEST RALLY.
GYRL, HOW DID SUCH A MASSIVE GROUP OF WOMEN SUCH AS YOURSELF ORGANIZE IN A REMARKABLY SHORT AMOUNT OF TIME? HAS SOCIAL MEDIA BEEN A TOOL FOR ACTION?
WOMP-WAH. WOMP.
JUST GREAT. THANK YOU AGAIN FOR COMING INTO THE STUDIO THIS AFTERNOON. GOOD LUCK TODAY AT THE PARK.
TRUMP YOU.
IT'S 10 MINUTES PAST THE HOUR. YOU'RE LISTENING TO WLFT PORTLAND. JAEKYUNG MAMAU IS THE LATEST INDEPENDENT FILMMAKER FROM KIRIBATI TO CAPTURE THE HEARTS AND MINDS AT THE SNOB FILM FESTIVAL IN BOULDER CITY, COLORADO.
HER FILM "THE TEARS OF MY MISSING MOTHER" HAS BEEN CALLED TRANSCENDENTAL BY A BEVVY OF FILM CRITICS. TERRY GROSS SAT DOWN WITH MAMAU TO DISCUSS THE IMPORTANT POLITICS OF KIRIBATI. WE JOIN HER NOW IN WASHINGTON. TERRY?
WOMP-WAH.

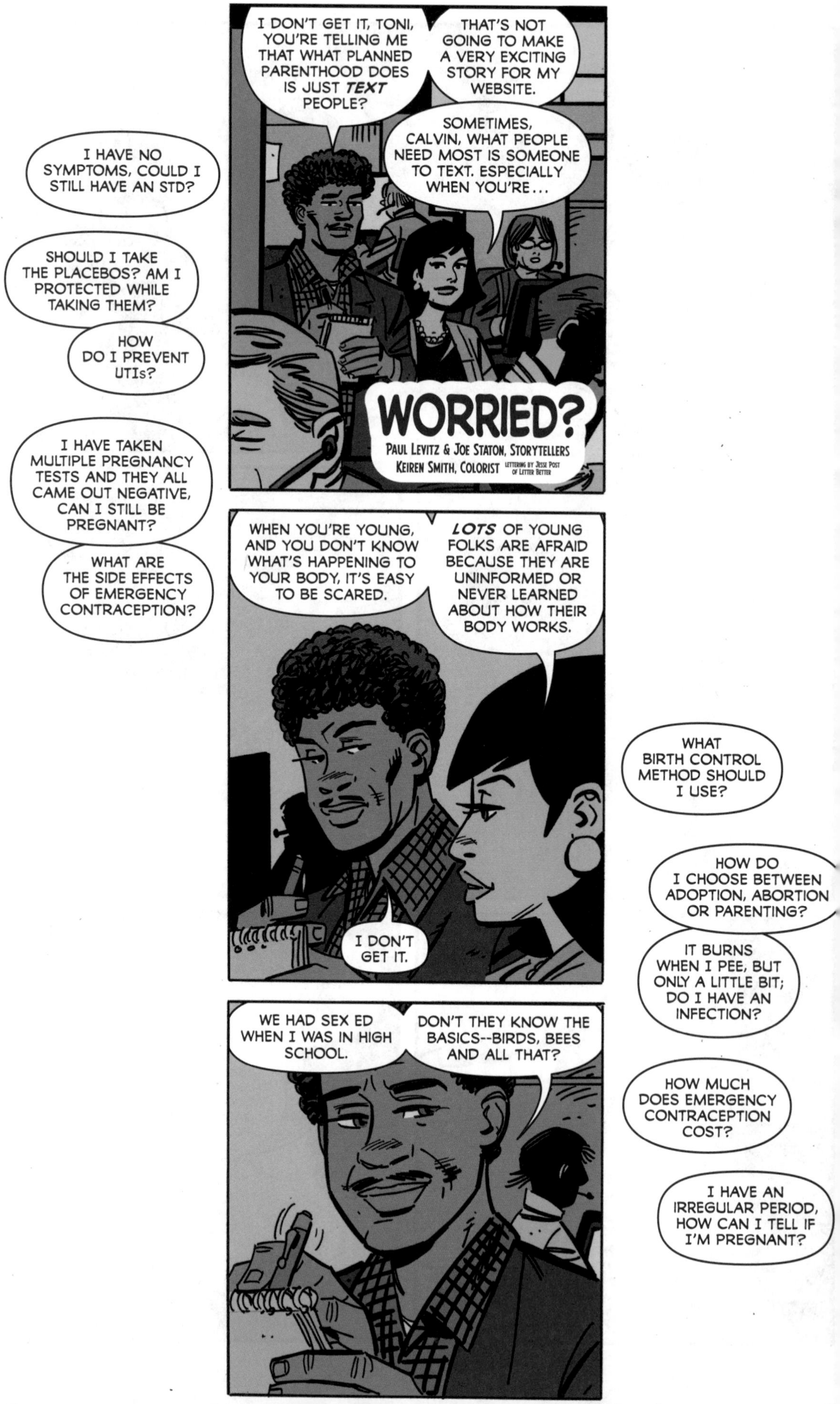
I DON'T GET IT, TONI, YOU'RE TELLING ME THAT WHAT PLANNED PARENTHOOD DOES IS JUST *TEXT* PEOPLE?
THAT'S NOT GOING TO MAKE A VERY EXCITING STORY FOR MY WEBSITE.
SOMETIMES, CALVIN, WHAT PEOPLE NEED MOST IS SOMEONE TO TEXT. ESPECIALLY WHEN YOU'RE...
WORRIED?
PAUL LEVITZ & JOE STATON, STORYTELLERS
KEIREN SMITH, COLORIST
LETTERING BY JESSE POST OF LETTER BETTER
I HAVE NO SYMPTOMS, COULD I STILL HAVE AN STD?
SHOULD I TAKE THE PLACEBOS? AM I PROTECTED WHILE TAKING THEM?
HOW DO I PREVENT UTIs?
I HAVE TAKEN MULTIPLE PREGNANCY TESTS AND THEY ALL CAME OUT NEGATIVE, CAN I STILL BE PREGNANT?
WHAT ARE THE SIDE EFFECTS OF EMERGENCY CONTRACEPTION?
WHEN YOU'RE YOUNG, AND YOU DON'T KNOW WHAT'S HAPPENING TO YOUR BODY, IT'S EASY TO BE SCARED.
LOTS OF YOUNG FOLKS ARE AFRAID BECAUSE THEY ARE UNINFORMED OR NEVER LEARNED ABOUT HOW THEIR BODY WORKS.
I DON'T GET IT.
WHAT BIRTH CONTROL METHOD SHOULD I USE?
HOW DO I CHOOSE BETWEEN ADOPTION, ABORTION OR PARENTING?
IT BURNS WHEN I PEE, BUT ONLY A LITTLE BIT; DO I HAVE AN INFECTION?
WE HAD SEX ED WHEN I WAS IN HIGH SCHOOL.
DON'T THEY KNOW THE BASICS--BIRDS, BEES AND ALL THAT?
HOW MUCH DOES EMERGENCY CONTRACEPTION COST?
I HAVE AN IRREGULAR PERIOD, HOW CAN I TELL IF I'M PREGNANT?

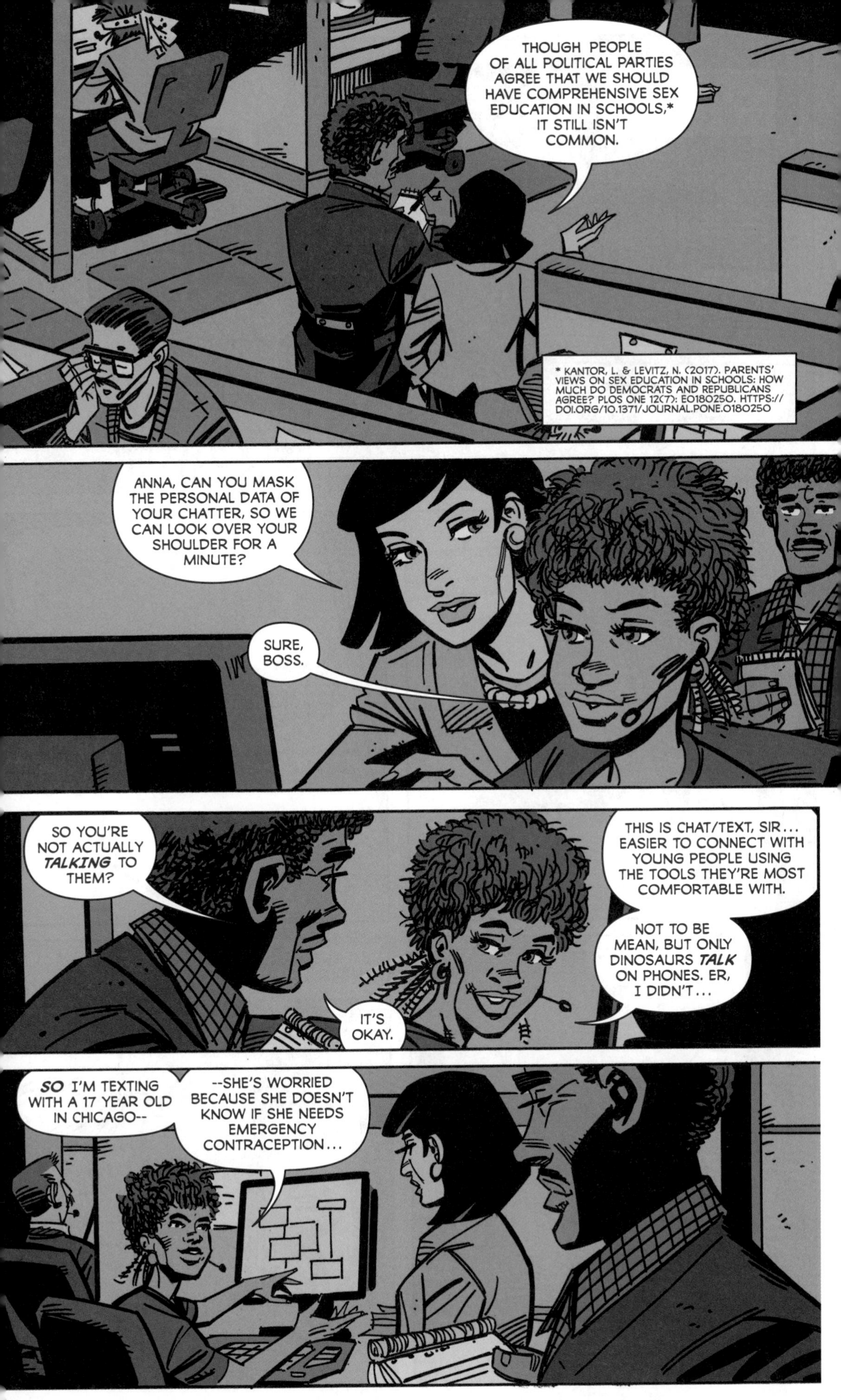
THOUGH PEOPLE OF ALL POLITICAL PARTIES AGREE THAT WE SHOULD HAVE COMPREHENSIVE SEX EDUCATION IN SCHOOLS,* IT STILL ISN'T COMMON.
* KANTOR, L. & LEVITZ, N. (2017). PARENTS' VIEWS ON SEX EDUCATION IN SCHOOLS: HOW MUCH DO DEMOCRATS AND REPUBLICANS AGREE? PLOS ONE 12(7): E0180250. HTTPS://DOI.ORG/10.1371/JOURNAL.PONE.0180250
ANNA, CAN YOU MASK THE PERSONAL DATA OF YOUR CHATTER, SO WE CAN LOOK OVER YOUR SHOULDER FOR A MINUTE?
SURE, BOSS.
SO YOU'RE NOT ACTUALLY *TALKING* TO THEM?
THIS IS CHAT/TEXT, SIR... EASIER TO CONNECT WITH YOUNG PEOPLE USING THE TOOLS THEY'RE MOST COMFORTABLE WITH.
NOT TO BE MEAN, BUT ONLY DINOSAURS *TALK* ON PHONES. ER, I DIDN'T...
IT'S OKAY.
SO I'M TEXTING WITH A 17 YEAR OLD IN CHICAGO--
--SHE'S WORRIED BECAUSE SHE DOESN'T KNOW IF SHE NEEDS EMERGENCY CONTRACEPTION...

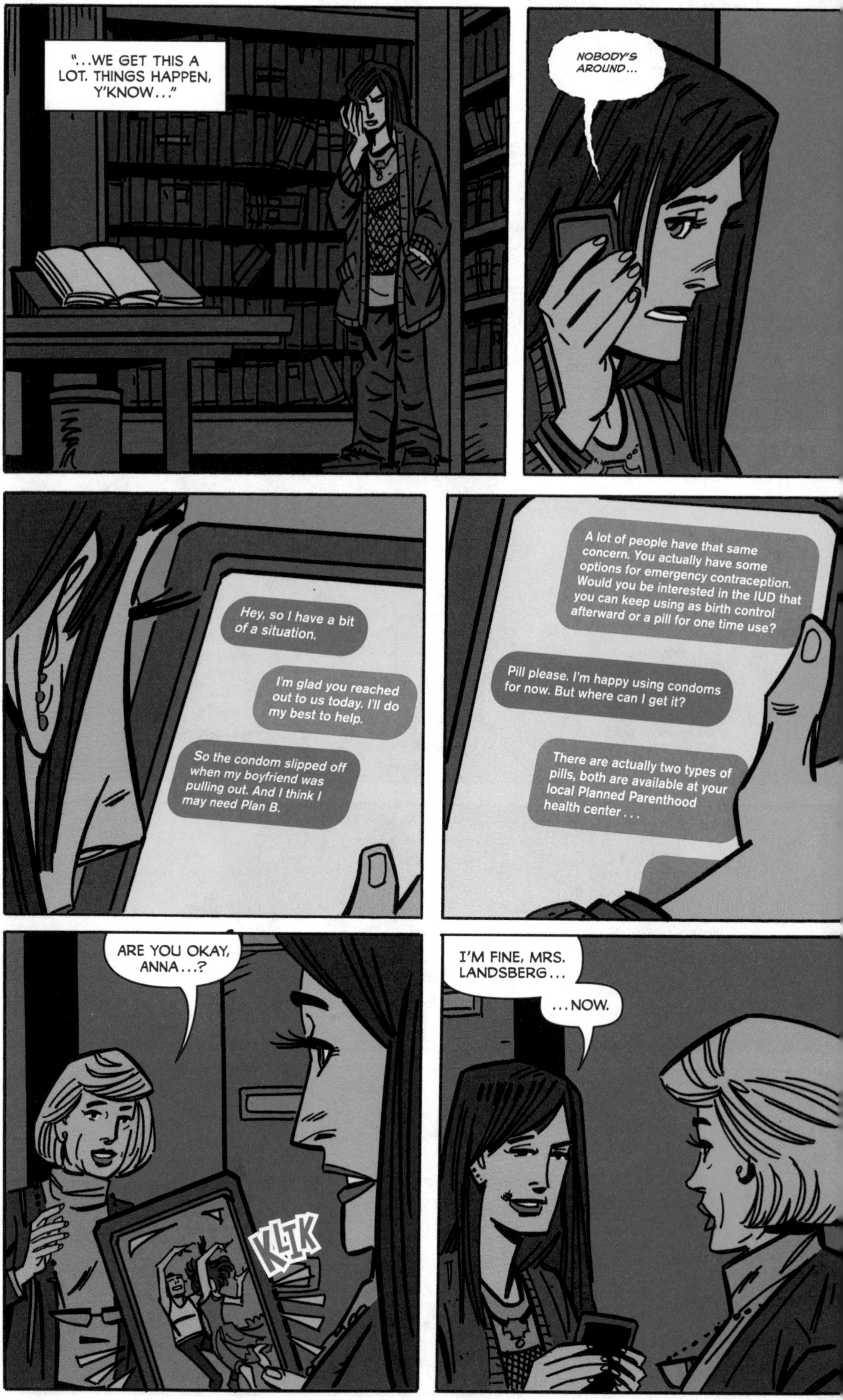
"...WE GET THIS A LOT. THINGS HAPPEN, Y'KNOW..."
NOBODY'S AROUND...
Hey, so I have a bit of a situation.
I'm glad you reached out to us today. I'll do my best to help.
So the condom slipped off when my boyfriend was pulling out. And I think I may need Plan B.
A lot of people have that same concern. You actually have some options for emergency contraception. Would you be interested in the IUD that you can keep using as birth control afterward or a pill for one time use?
Pill please. I'm happy using condoms for now. But where can I get it?
There are actually two types of pills, both are available at your local Planned Parenthood health center...
ARE YOU OKAY, ANNA...?
KLIK
I'M FINE, MRS. LANDSBERG...
...NOW.

Planned Parenthood has 20,000 conversations per month via Chat/Text, answering questions, helping users come up with an action plan and connecting them to the help they need.

1 in 5 American women utilize the services of a Planned Parenthood n their lifetime. Over 2 million people will go to a Planned Parenthood health center every year.

1.5 million people are reached in-person through Planned Parenthood sex education.

Each month there are 6 million visitors to the Planned Parenthood website.

A pregnancy is a $250,000 investment in the future (the average cost of raising a child to age 18, so that doesn't include the heavy costs of a college education). Hardly a decision to be make without planning.

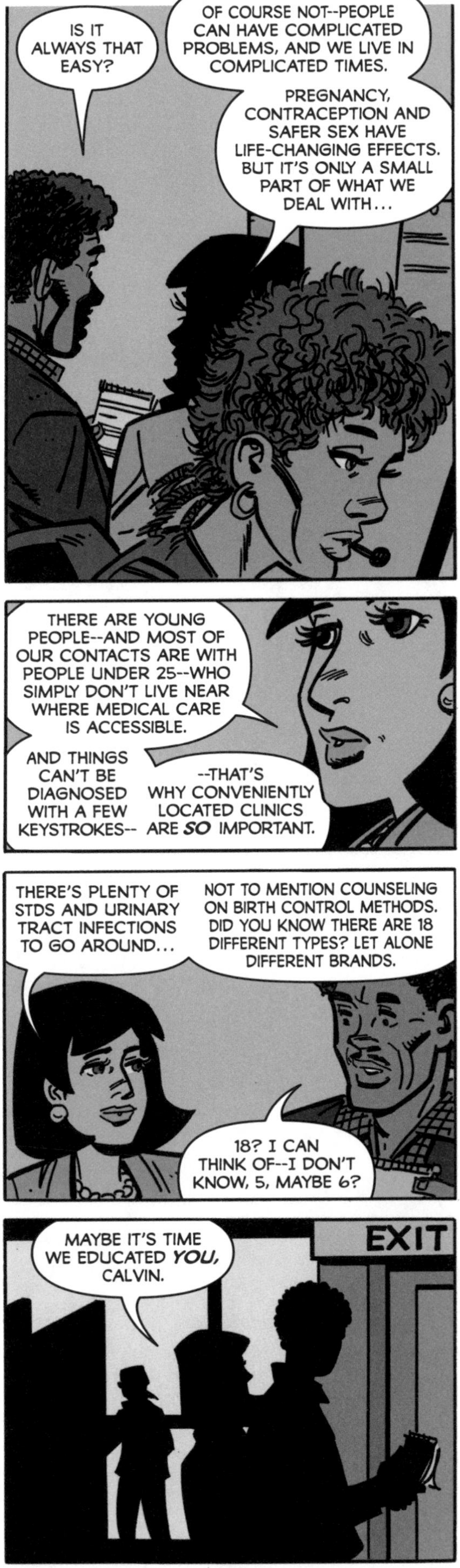

IS IT ALWAYS THAT EASY?
OF COURSE NOT--PEOPLE CAN HAVE COMPLICATED PROBLEMS, AND WE LIVE IN COMPLICATED TIMES.
PREGNANCY, CONTRACEPTION AND SAFER SEX HAVE LIFE-CHANGING EFFECTS. BUT IT'S ONLY A SMALL PART OF WHAT WE DEAL WITH...
THERE ARE YOUNG PEOPLE--AND MOST OF OUR CONTACTS ARE WITH PEOPLE UNDER 25--WHO SIMPLY DON'T LIVE NEAR WHERE MEDICAL CARE IS ACCESSIBLE.
AND THINGS CAN'T BE DIAGNOSED WITH A FEW KEYSTROKES--
--THAT'S WHY CONVENIENTLY LOCATED CLINICS ARE *SO* IMPORTANT.
THERE'S PLENTY OF STDS AND URINARY TRACT INFECTIONS TO GO AROUND...
NOT TO MENTION COUNSELING ON BIRTH CONTROL METHODS. DID YOU KNOW THERE ARE 18 DIFFERENT TYPES? LET ALONE DIFFERENT BRANDS.
18? I CAN THINK OF--I DON'T KNOW, 5, MAYBE 6?
MAYBE IT'S TIME WE EDUCATED *YOU,* CALVIN.
EXIT

In these politically charged times, we ask that you support Planned Parenthood for the sake of the millions of women who depend on their services for their health, well-being and peace of mind.

Let your political representatives know that you support Planned Parenthood.

Talk to people about your experiences if you've benefited from Planned Parenthood's services.

If you can, when you can, consider donating to your local Planned Parenthood affiliate to help them provide services at low or no cost.

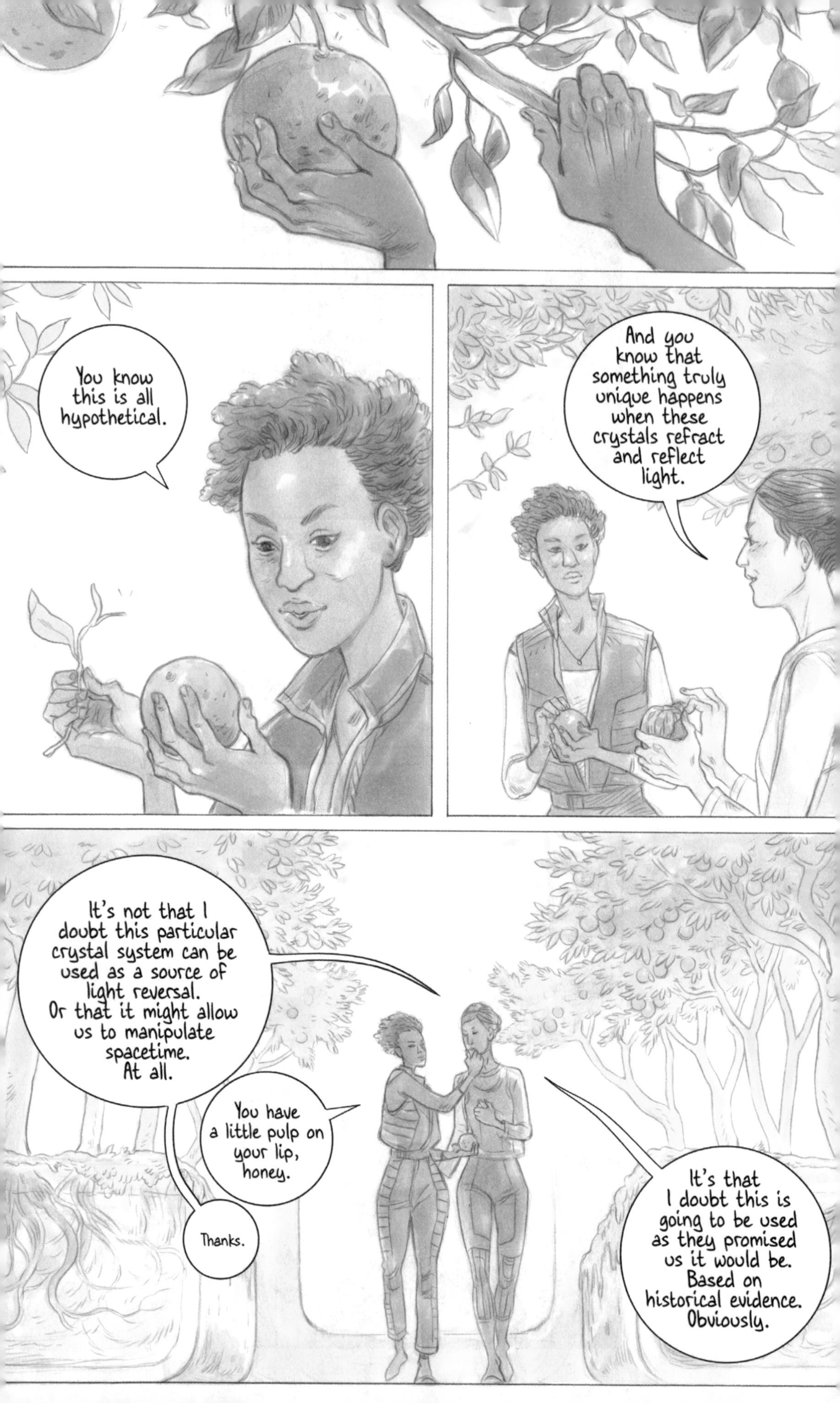
You know this is all hypothetical.
And you know that something truly unique happens when these crystals refract and reflect light.
It's not that I doubt this particular crystal system can be used as a source of light reversal. Or that it might allow us to manipulate spacetime. At all.
You have a little pulp on your lip, honey.
Thanks.
It's that I doubt this is going to be used as they promised us it would be. Based on historical evidence. Obviously.

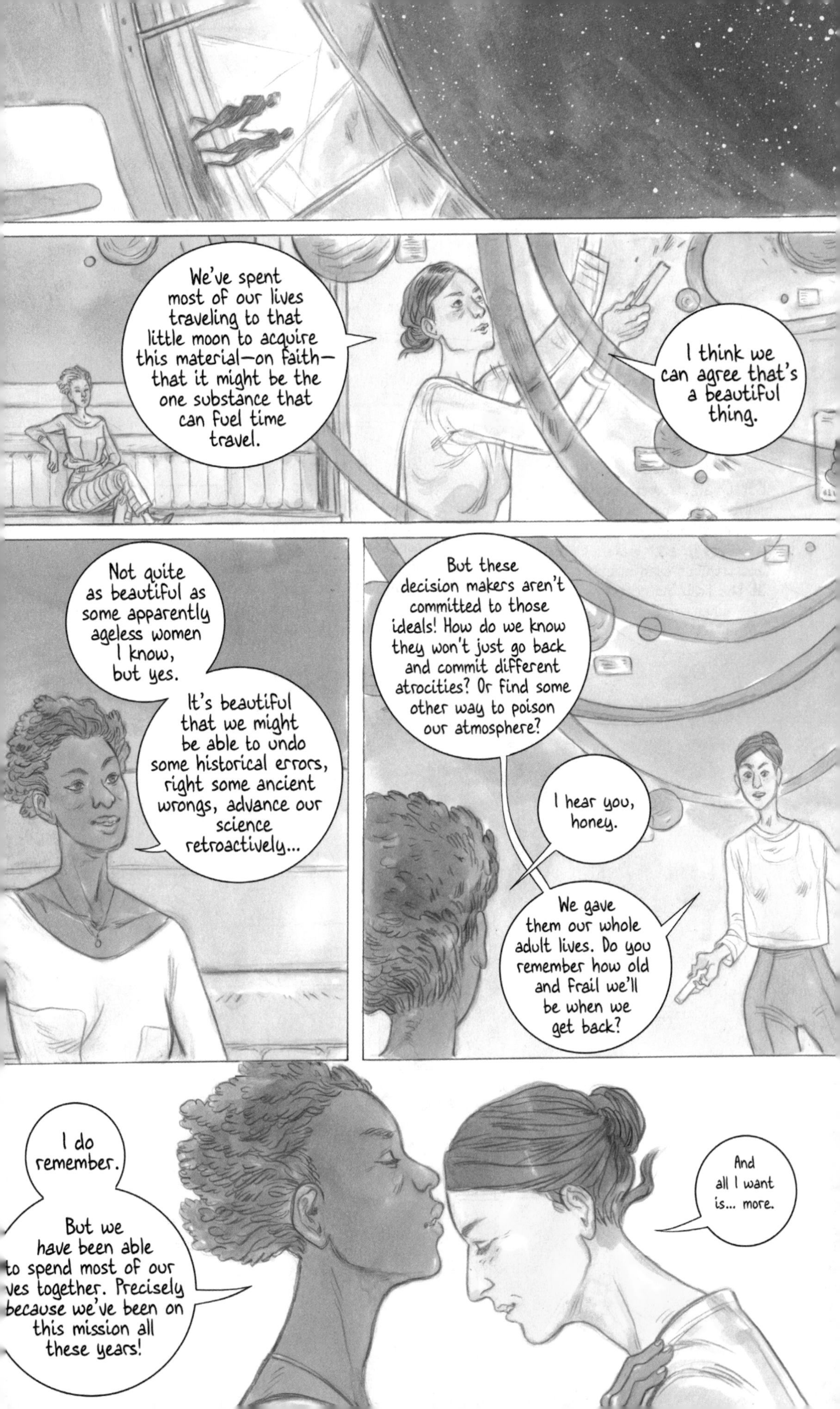
We've spent most of our lives traveling to that little moon to acquire this material—on faith—that it might be the one substance that can fuel time travel.
I think we can agree that's a beautiful thing.
Not quite as beautiful as some apparently ageless women I know, but yes.
It's beautiful that we might be able to undo some historical errors, right some ancient wrongs, advance our science retroactively...
But these decision makers aren't committed to those ideals! How do we know they won't just go back and commit different atrocities? Or find some other way to poison our atmosphere?
I hear you, honey.
We gave them our whole adult lives. Do you remember how old and frail we'll be when we get back?
I do remember.
But we have been able to spend most of our ves together. Precisely because we've been on this mission all these years!
And all I want is... more.

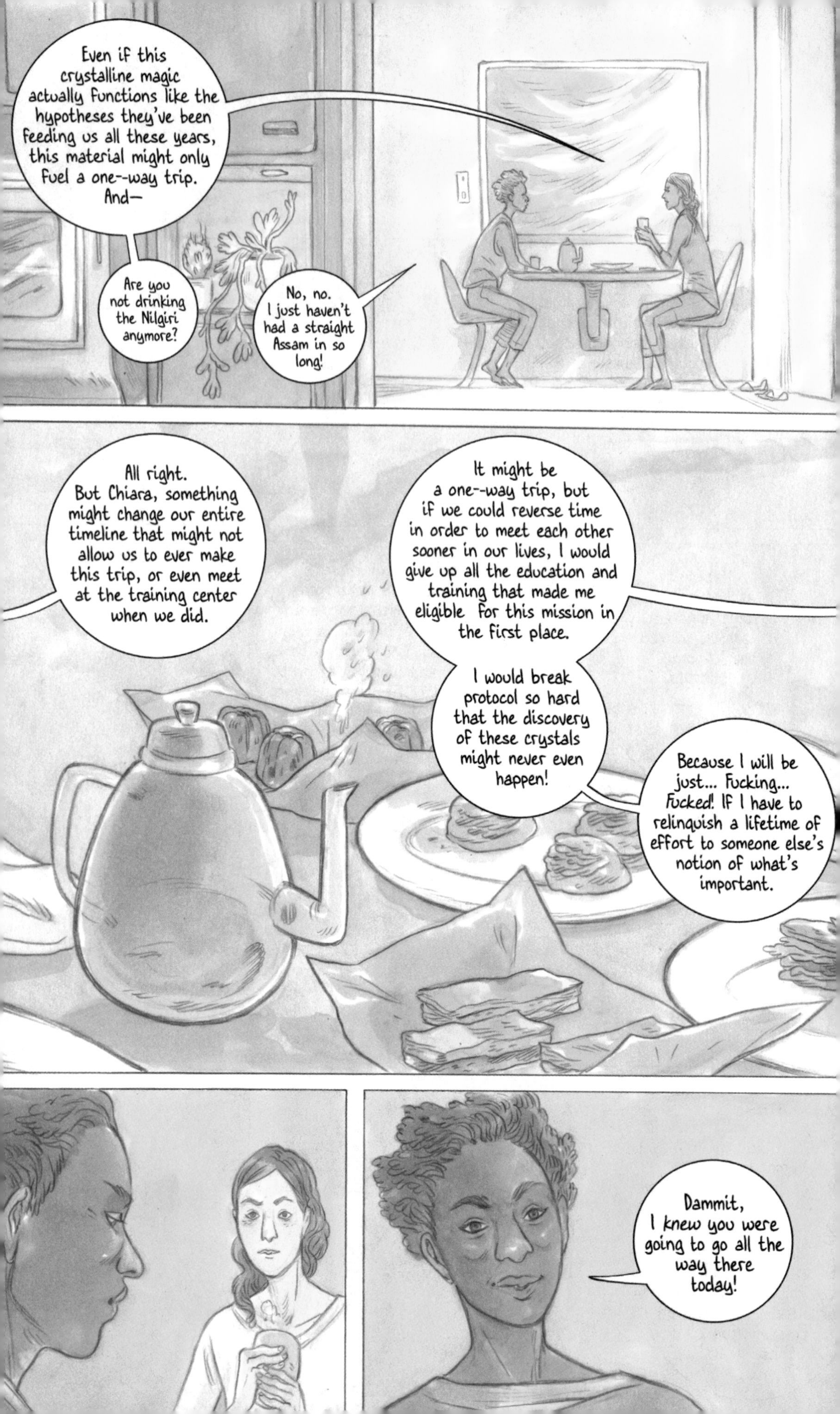
Even if this crystalline magic actually functions like the hypotheses they've been feeding us all these years, this material might only fuel a one--way trip. And—
Are you not drinking the Nilgiri anymore?
No, no. I just haven't had a straight Assam in so long!
All right. But Chiara, something might change our entire timeline that might not allow us to ever make this trip, or even meet at the training center when we did.
It might be a one--way trip, but if we could reverse time in order to meet each other sooner in our lives, I would give up all the education and training that made me eligible for this mission in the first place.
I would break protocol so hard that the discovery of these crystals might never even happen!
Because I will be just... Fucking... Fucked! If I have to relinquish a lifetime of effort to someone else's notion of what's important.
Dammit, I knew you were going to go all the way there today!

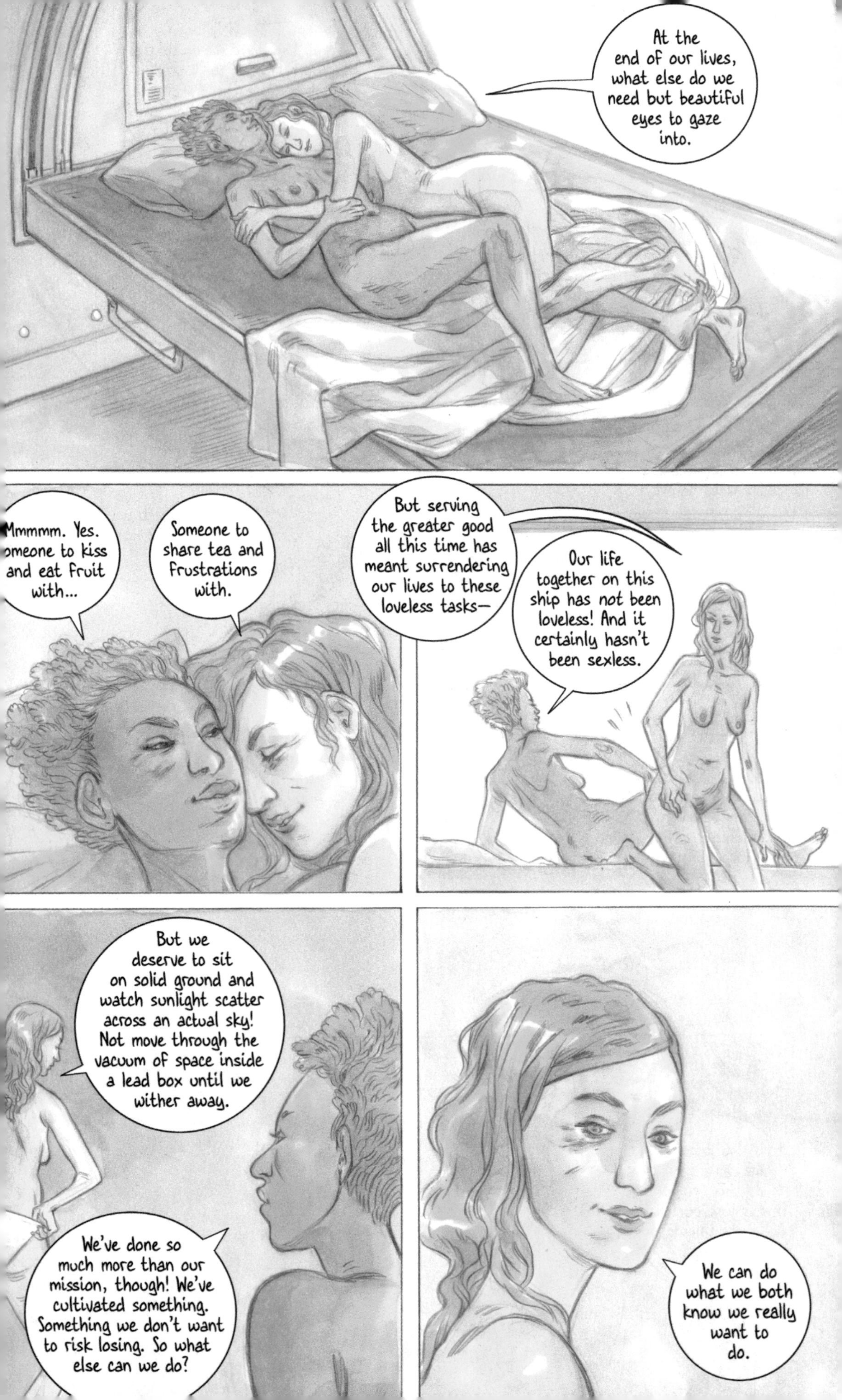
At the end of our lives, what else do we need but beautiful eyes to gaze into.
Mmmmm. Yes. omeone to kiss and eat fruit with...
Someone to share tea and frustrations with.
But serving the greater good all this time has meant surrendering our lives to these loveless tasks—
Our life together on this ship has not been loveless! And it certainly hasn't been sexless.
But we deserve to sit on solid ground and watch sunlight scatter across an actual sky! Not move through the vacuum of space inside a lead box until we wither away.
We've done so much more than our mission, though! We've cultivated something. Something we don't want to risk losing. So what else can we do?
We can do what we both know we really want to do.

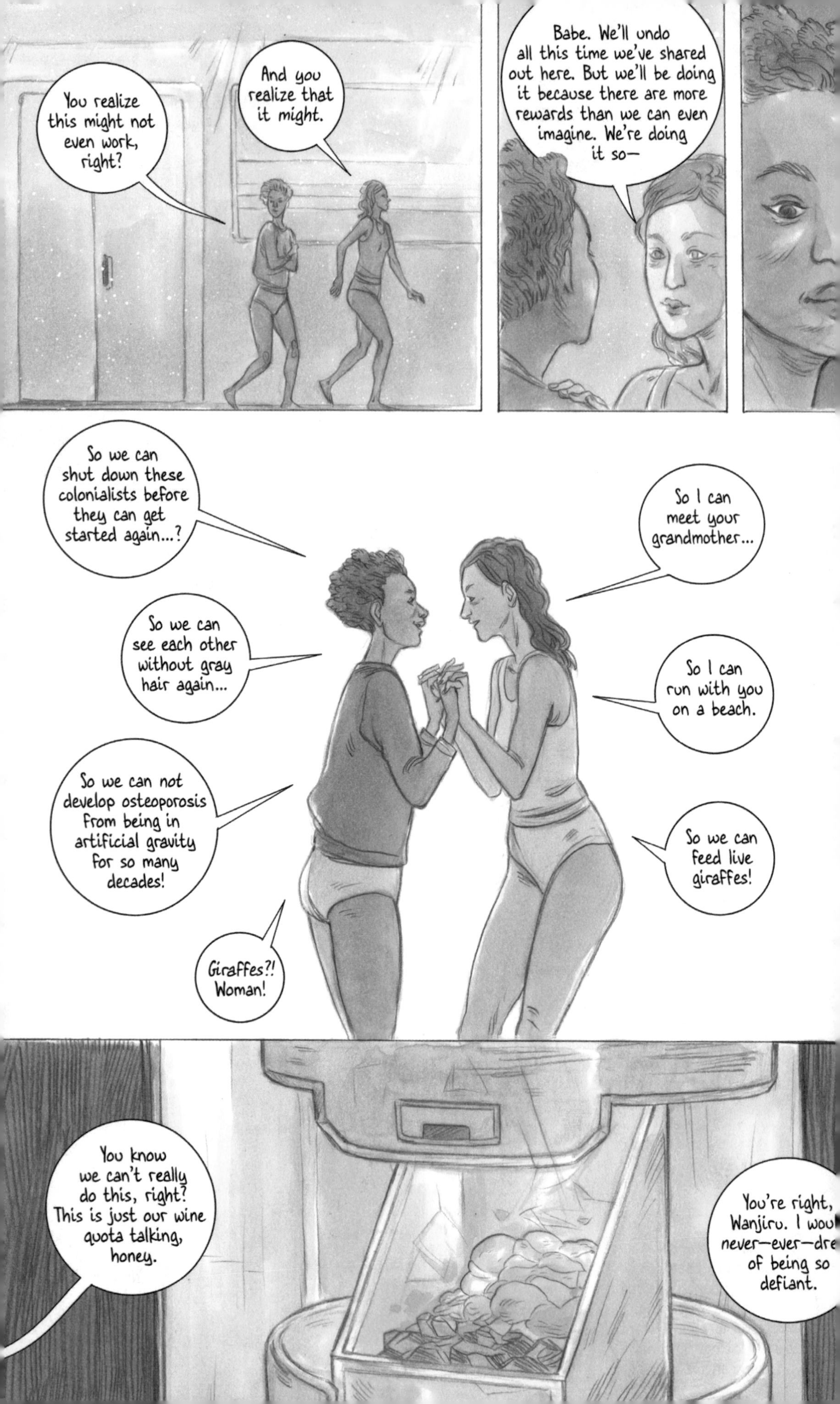
You realize this might not even work, right?
And you realize that it might.
Babe. We'll undo all this time we've shared out here. But we'll be doing it because there are more rewards than we can even imagine. We're doing it so—
So we can shut down these colonialists before they can get started again...?
So I can meet your grandmother...
So we can see each other without gray hair again...
So I can run with you on a beach.
So we can not develop osteoporosis from being in artificial gravity for so many decades!
So we can feed live giraffes!
Giraffes?! Woman!
You know we can't really do this, right? This is just our wine quota talking, honey.

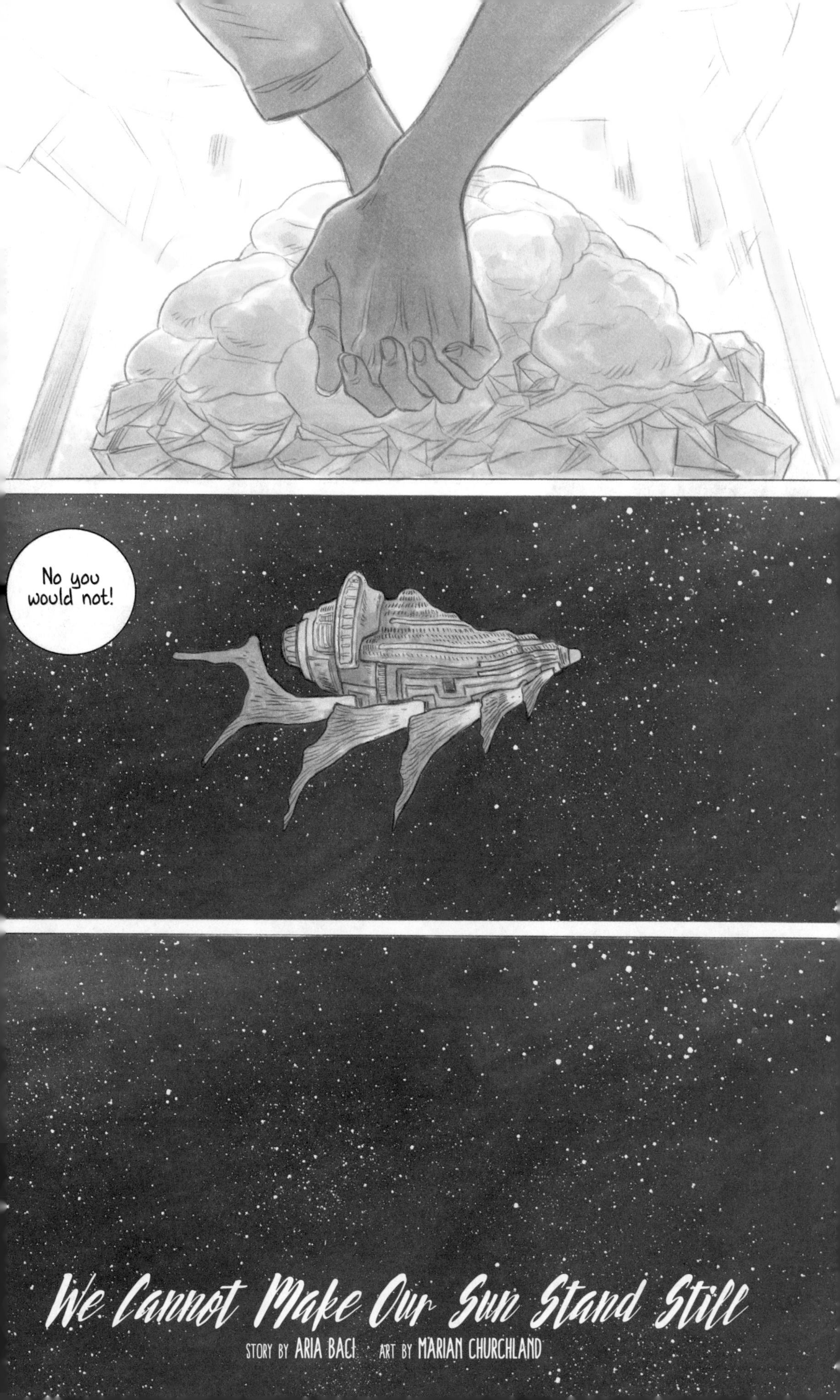
No you would not!
We Cannot Make Our Sun Stand Still
STORY BY ARIA BACI ART BY MARIAN CHURCHLAND

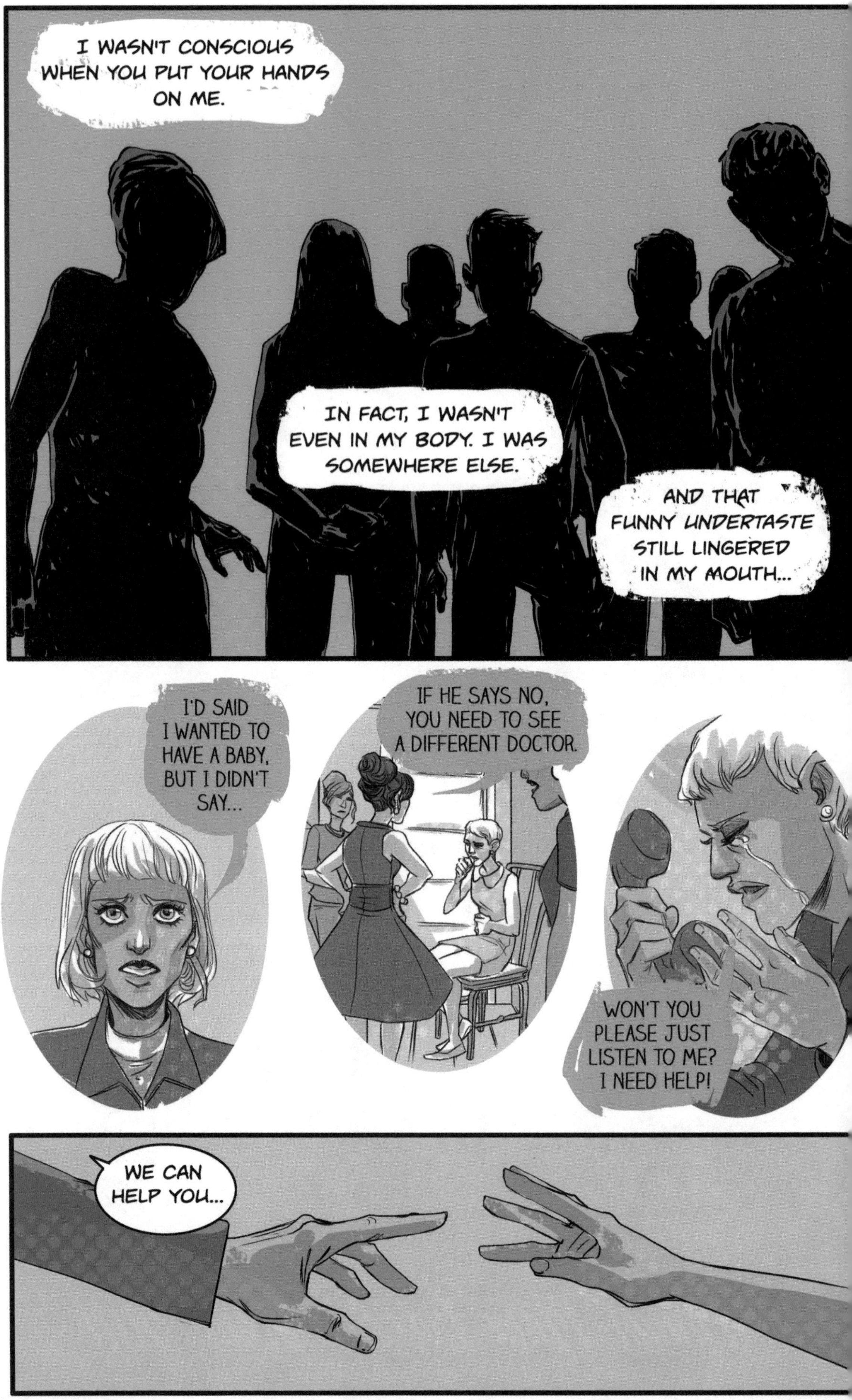
I WASN'T CONSCIOUS WHEN YOU PUT YOUR HANDS ON ME.
IN FACT, I WASN'T EVEN IN MY BODY. I WAS SOMEWHERE ELSE.
AND THAT FUNNY UNDERTASTE STILL LINGERED IN MY MOUTH...
I'D SAID I WANTED TO HAVE A BABY, BUT I DIDN'T SAY...
IF HE SAYS NO, YOU NEED TO SEE A DIFFERENT DOCTOR.
WON'T YOU PLEASE JUST LISTEN TO ME? I NEED HELP!
WE CAN HELP YOU...

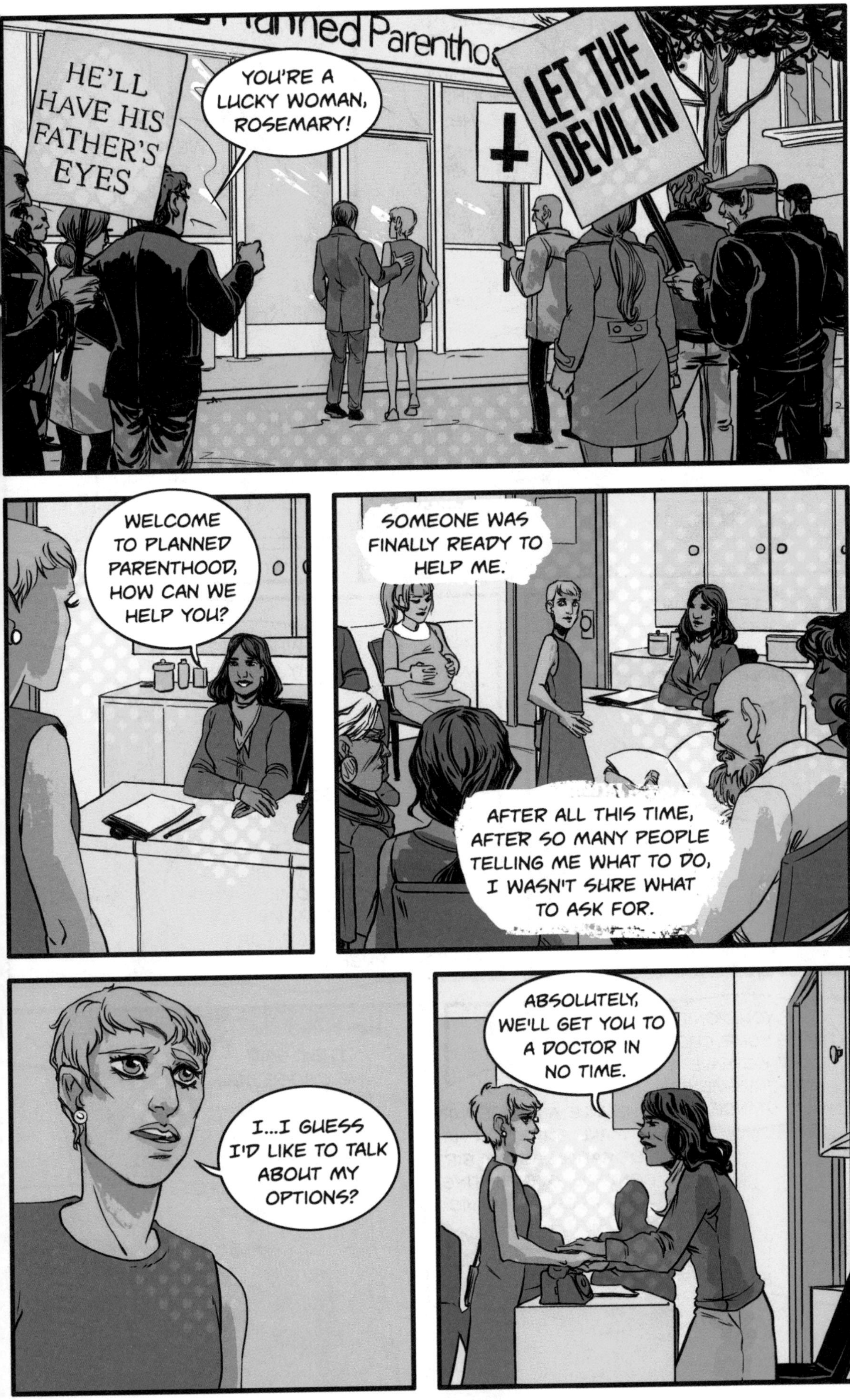
Planned Parenthoo
HE'LL HAVE HIS FATHER'S EYES
YOU'RE A LUCKY WOMAN, ROSEMARY!
LET THE DEVIL IN
WELCOME TO PLANNED PARENTHOOD, HOW CAN WE HELP YOU?
SOMEONE WAS FINALLY READY TO HELP ME.
AFTER ALL THIS TIME, AFTER SO MANY PEOPLE TELLING ME WHAT TO DO, I WASN'T SURE WHAT TO ASK FOR.
I...I GUESS I'D LIKE TO TALK ABOUT MY OPTIONS?
ABSOLUTELY, WE'LL GET YOU TO A DOCTOR IN NO TIME.

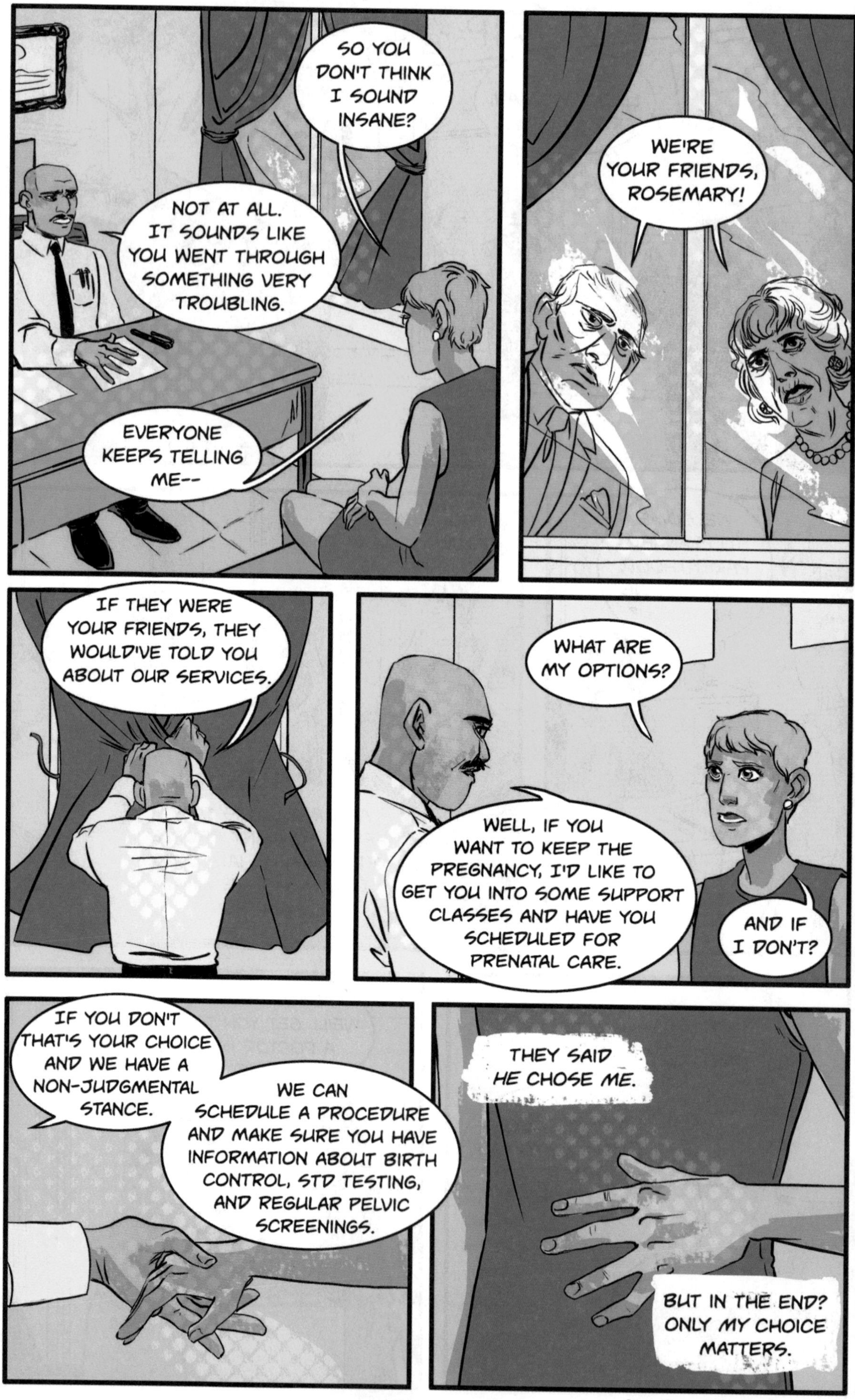
SO YOU DON'T THINK I SOUND INSANE?
NOT AT ALL. IT SOUNDS LIKE YOU WENT THROUGH SOMETHING VERY TROUBLING.
EVERYONE KEEPS TELLING ME--
WE'RE YOUR FRIENDS, ROSEMARY!
IF THEY WERE YOUR FRIENDS, THEY WOULD'VE TOLD YOU ABOUT OUR SERVICES.
WHAT ARE MY OPTIONS?
WELL, IF YOU WANT TO KEEP THE PREGNANCY, I'D LIKE TO GET YOU INTO SOME SUPPORT CLASSES AND HAVE YOU SCHEDULED FOR PRENATAL CARE.
AND IF I DON'T?
IF YOU DON'T THAT'S YOUR CHOICE AND WE HAVE A NON-JUDGMENTAL STANCE.
WE CAN SCHEDULE A PROCEDURE AND MAKE SURE YOU HAVE INFORMATION ABOUT BIRTH CONTROL, STD TESTING, AND REGULAR PELVIC SCREENINGS.
THEY SAID *HE* CHOSE ME.
BUT IN THE END? ONLY *MY* CHOICE MATTERS.

Story: **Casey Gilly** Art: **Jen Hickman**

ETHEL BYRNE *by* CECIL CASTELLUCCI & SCOTT CHANTLER

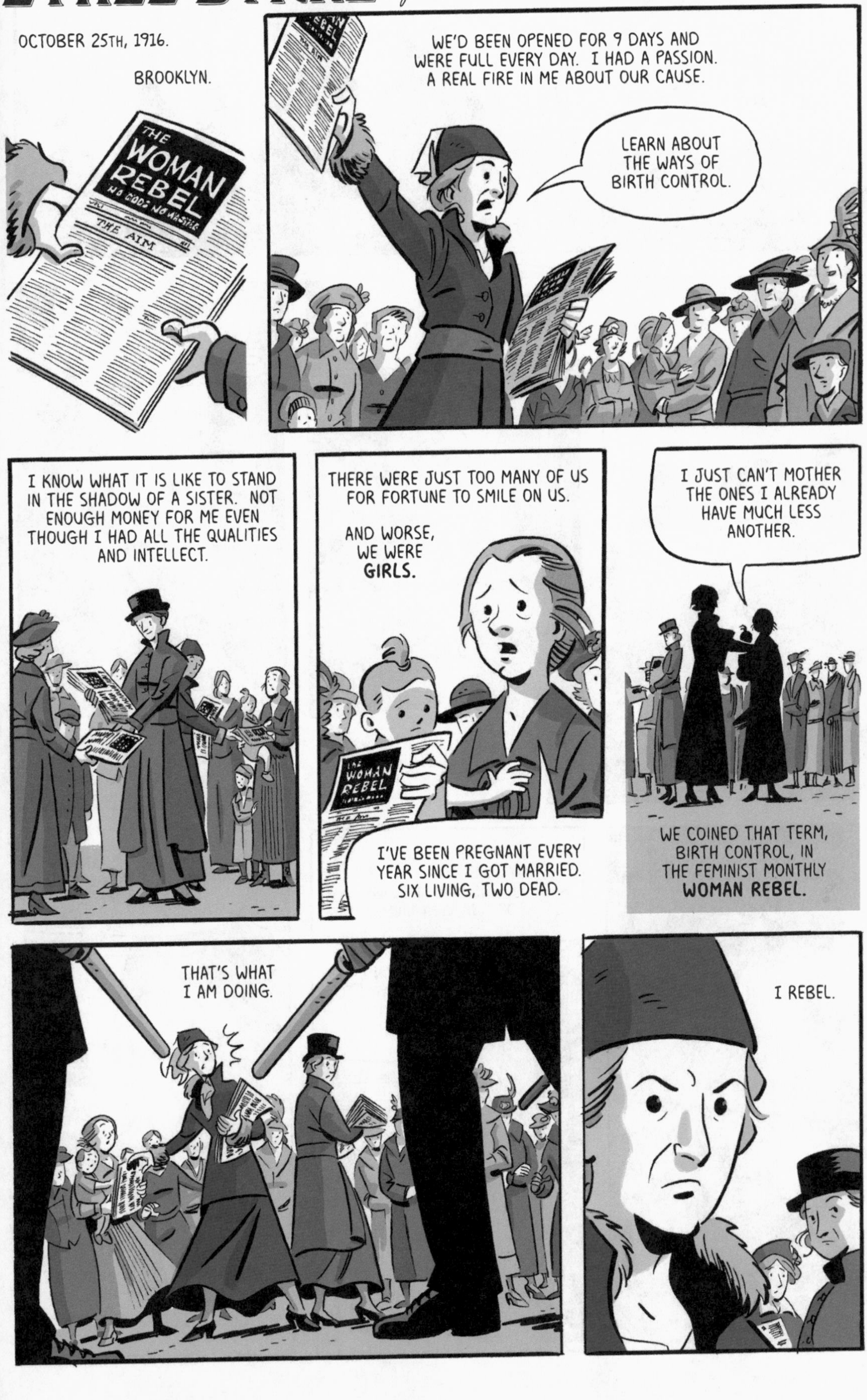

OCTOBER 25TH, 1916.
BROOKLYN.
THE WOMAN REBEL
THE AIM
WE'D BEEN OPENED FOR 9 DAYS AND WERE FULL EVERY DAY. I HAD A PASSION. A REAL FIRE IN ME ABOUT OUR CAUSE.
LEARN ABOUT THE WAYS OF BIRTH CONTROL.
I KNOW WHAT IT IS LIKE TO STAND IN THE SHADOW OF A SISTER. NOT ENOUGH MONEY FOR ME EVEN THOUGH I HAD ALL THE QUALITIES AND INTELLECT.
THERE WERE JUST TOO MANY OF US FOR FORTUNE TO SMILE ON US.
AND WORSE, WE WERE **GIRLS.**
THE WOMAN REBEL
I'VE BEEN PREGNANT EVERY YEAR SINCE I GOT MARRIED. SIX LIVING, TWO DEAD.
I JUST CAN'T MOTHER THE ONES I ALREADY HAVE MUCH LESS ANOTHER.
WE COINED THAT TERM, BIRTH CONTROL, IN THE FEMINIST MONTHLY **WOMAN REBEL.**
THAT'S WHAT I AM DOING.
I REBEL.

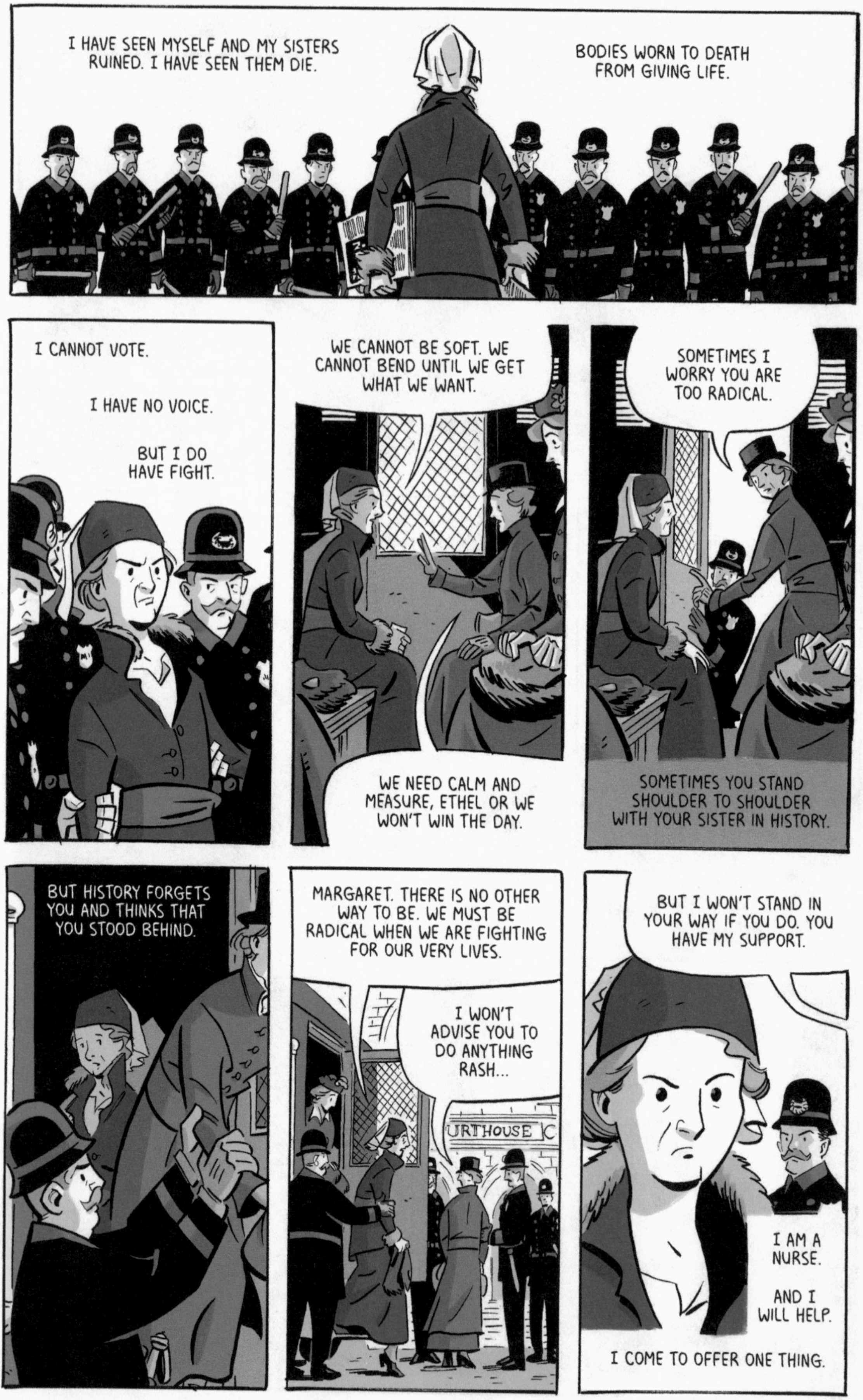
I HAVE SEEN MYSELF AND MY SISTERS RUINED. I HAVE SEEN THEM DIE.
BODIES WORN TO DEATH FROM GIVING LIFE.
I CANNOT VOTE.
I HAVE NO VOICE.
BUT I DO HAVE FIGHT.
WE CANNOT BE SOFT. WE CANNOT BEND UNTIL WE GET WHAT WE WANT.
WE NEED CALM AND MEASURE, ETHEL OR WE WON'T WIN THE DAY.
SOMETIMES I WORRY YOU ARE TOO RADICAL.
SOMETIMES YOU STAND SHOULDER TO SHOULDER WITH YOUR SISTER IN HISTORY.
BUT HISTORY FORGETS YOU AND THINKS THAT YOU STOOD BEHIND.
MARGARET. THERE IS NO OTHER WAY TO BE. WE MUST BE RADICAL WHEN WE ARE FIGHTING FOR OUR VERY LIVES.
I WON'T ADVISE YOU TO DO ANYTHING RASH...
URTHOUSE C
BUT I WON'T STAND IN YOUR WAY IF YOU DO. YOU HAVE MY SUPPORT.
I AM A NURSE.
AND I WILL HELP.
I COME TO OFFER ONE THING.

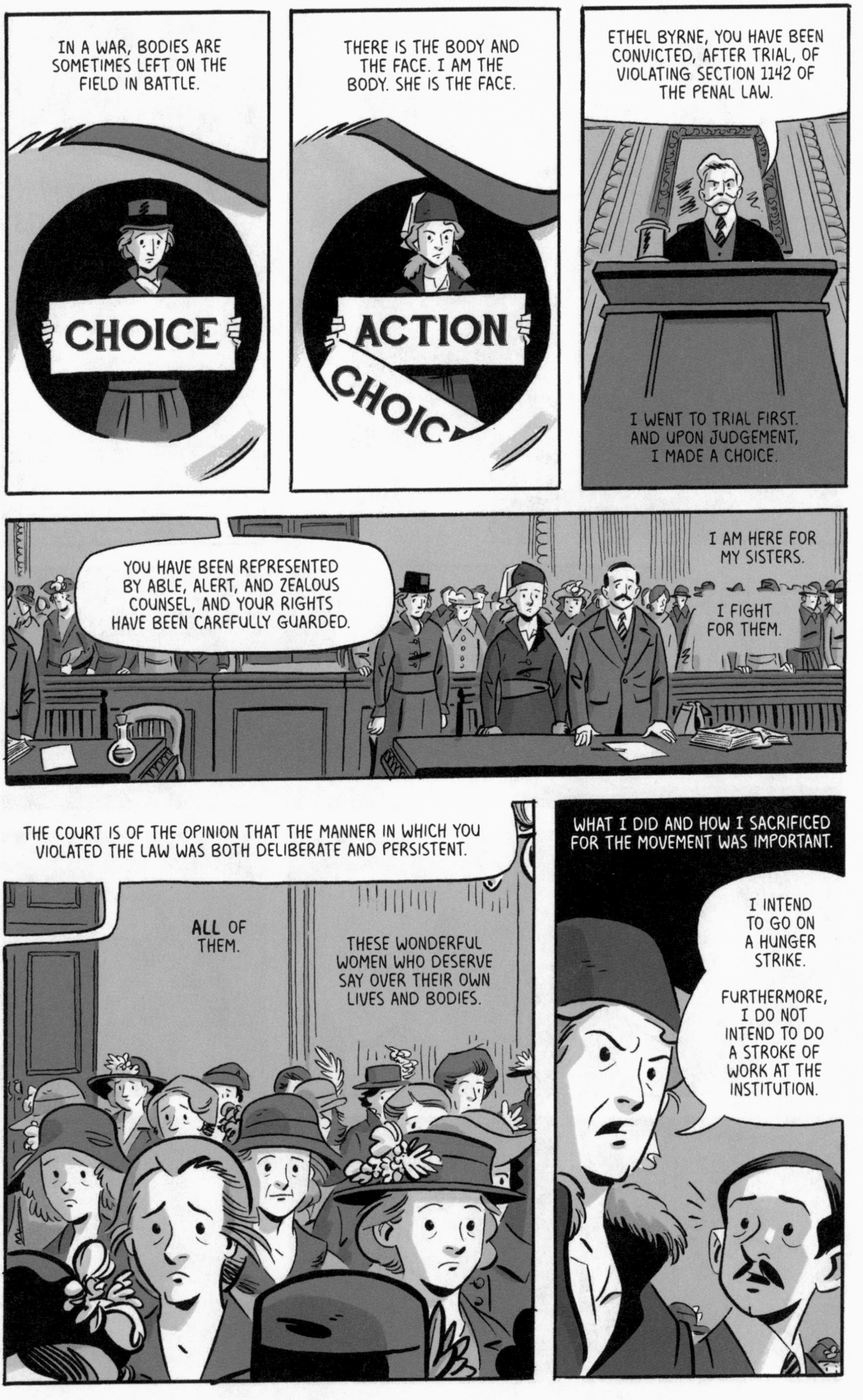

IN A WAR, BODIES ARE SOMETIMES LEFT ON THE FIELD IN BATTLE.
CHOICE
THERE IS THE BODY AND THE FACE. I AM THE BODY. SHE IS THE FACE.
ACTION
CHOIC
ETHEL BYRNE, YOU HAVE BEEN CONVICTED, AFTER TRIAL, OF VIOLATING SECTION 1142 OF THE PENAL LAW.
I WENT TO TRIAL FIRST. AND UPON JUDGEMENT, I MADE A CHOICE.
YOU HAVE BEEN REPRESENTED BY ABLE, ALERT, AND ZEALOUS COUNSEL, AND YOUR RIGHTS HAVE BEEN CAREFULLY GUARDED.
I AM HERE FOR MY SISTERS.
I FIGHT FOR THEM.
THE COURT IS OF THE OPINION THAT THE MANNER IN WHICH YOU VIOLATED THE LAW WAS BOTH DELIBERATE AND PERSISTENT.
ALL OF THEM.
THESE WONDERFUL WOMEN WHO DESERVE SAY OVER THEIR OWN LIVES AND BODIES.
WHAT I DID AND HOW I SACRIFICED FOR THE MOVEMENT WAS IMPORTANT.
I INTEND TO GO ON A HUNGER STRIKE.
FURTHERMORE, I DO NOT INTEND TO DO A STROKE OF WORK AT THE INSTITUTION.

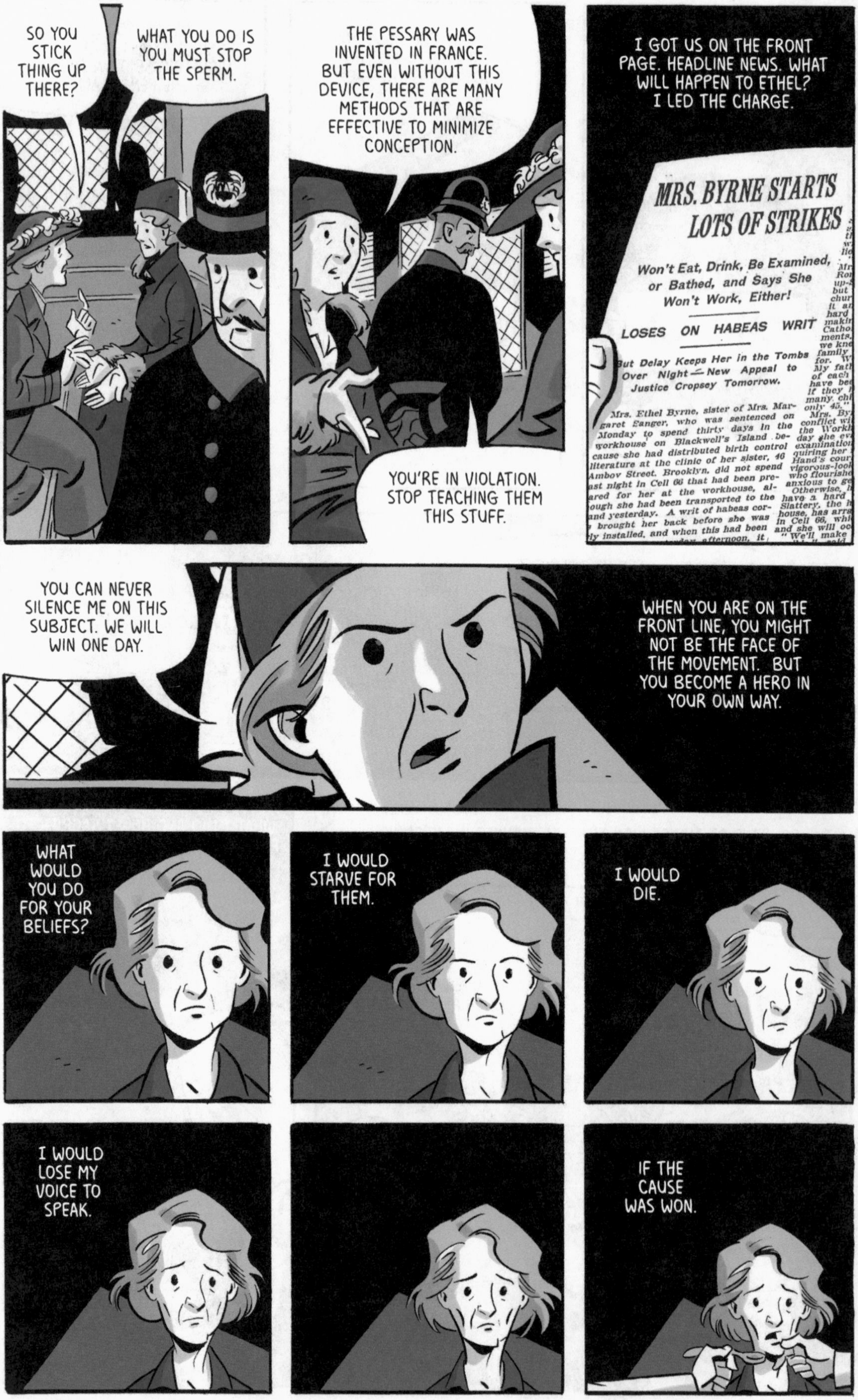

SO YOU STICK THING UP THERE?
WHAT YOU DO IS YOU MUST STOP THE SPERM.
THE PESSARY WAS INVENTED IN FRANCE. BUT EVEN WITHOUT THIS DEVICE, THERE ARE MANY METHODS THAT ARE EFFECTIVE TO MINIMIZE CONCEPTION.
YOU'RE IN VIOLATION. STOP TEACHING THEM THIS STUFF.
I GOT US ON THE FRONT PAGE. HEADLINE NEWS. WHAT WILL HAPPEN TO ETHEL? I LED THE CHARGE.
MRS. BYRNE STARTS LOTS OF STRIKES
Won't Eat, Drink, Be Examined, or Bathed, and Says She Won't Work, Either!
LOSES ON HABEAS WRIT
But Delay Keeps Her in the Tombs Over Night—New Appeal to Justice Cropsey Tomorrow.
YOU CAN NEVER SILENCE ME ON THIS SUBJECT. WE WILL WIN ONE DAY.
WHEN YOU ARE ON THE FRONT LINE, YOU MIGHT NOT BE THE FACE OF THE MOVEMENT. BUT YOU BECOME A HERO IN YOUR OWN WAY.
WHAT WOULD YOU DO FOR YOUR BELIEFS?
I WOULD STARVE FOR THEM.
I WOULD DIE.
I WOULD LOSE MY VOICE TO SPEAK.
IF THE CAUSE WAS WON.

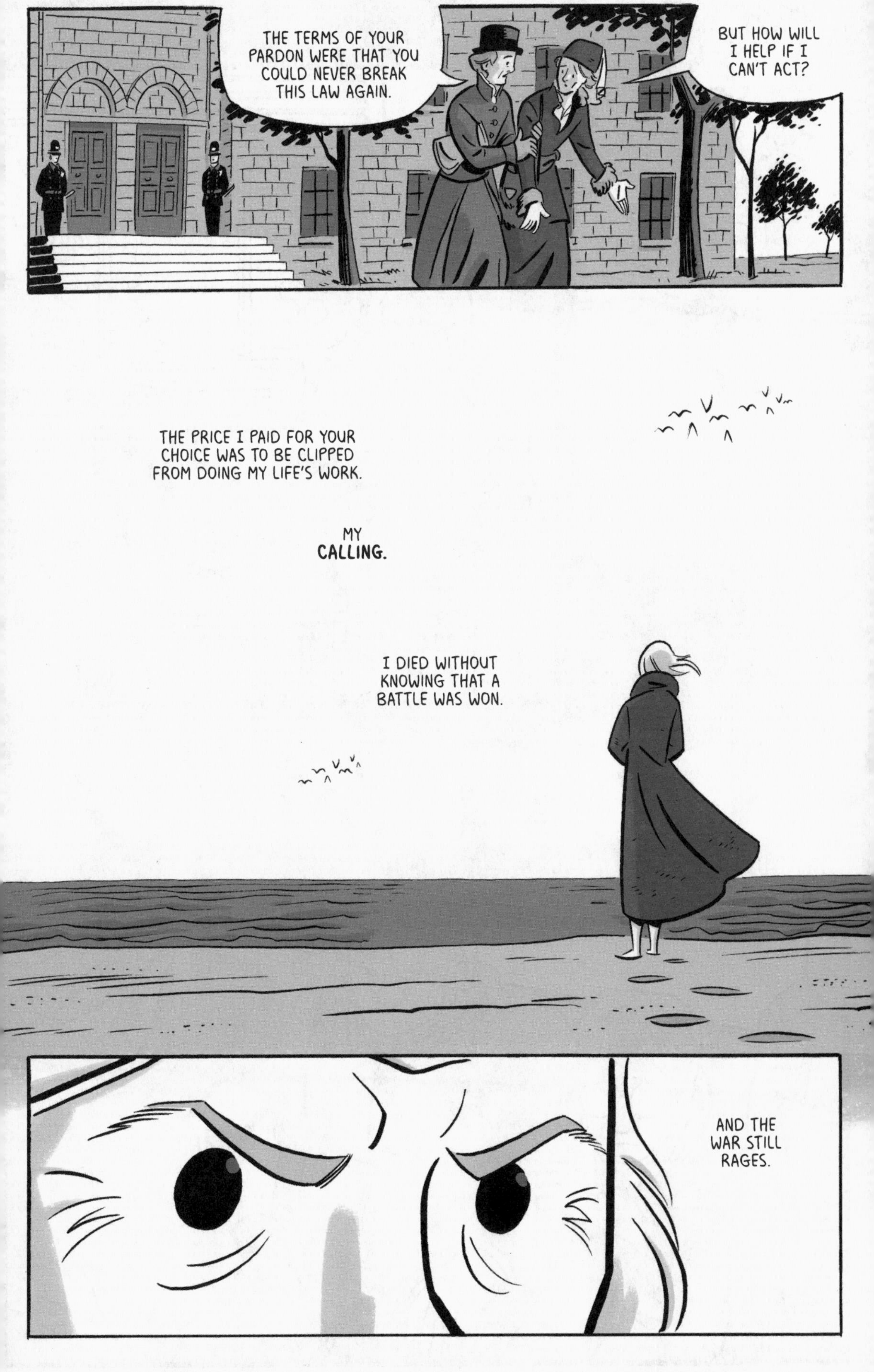

THE TERMS OF YOUR PARDON WERE THAT YOU COULD NEVER BREAK THIS LAW AGAIN.
BUT HOW WILL I HELP IF I CAN'T ACT?
THE PRICE I PAID FOR YOUR CHOICE WAS TO BE CLIPPED FROM DOING MY LIFE'S WORK.
MY CALLING.
I DIED WITHOUT KNOWING THAT A BATTLE WAS WON.
AND THE WAR STILL RAGES.

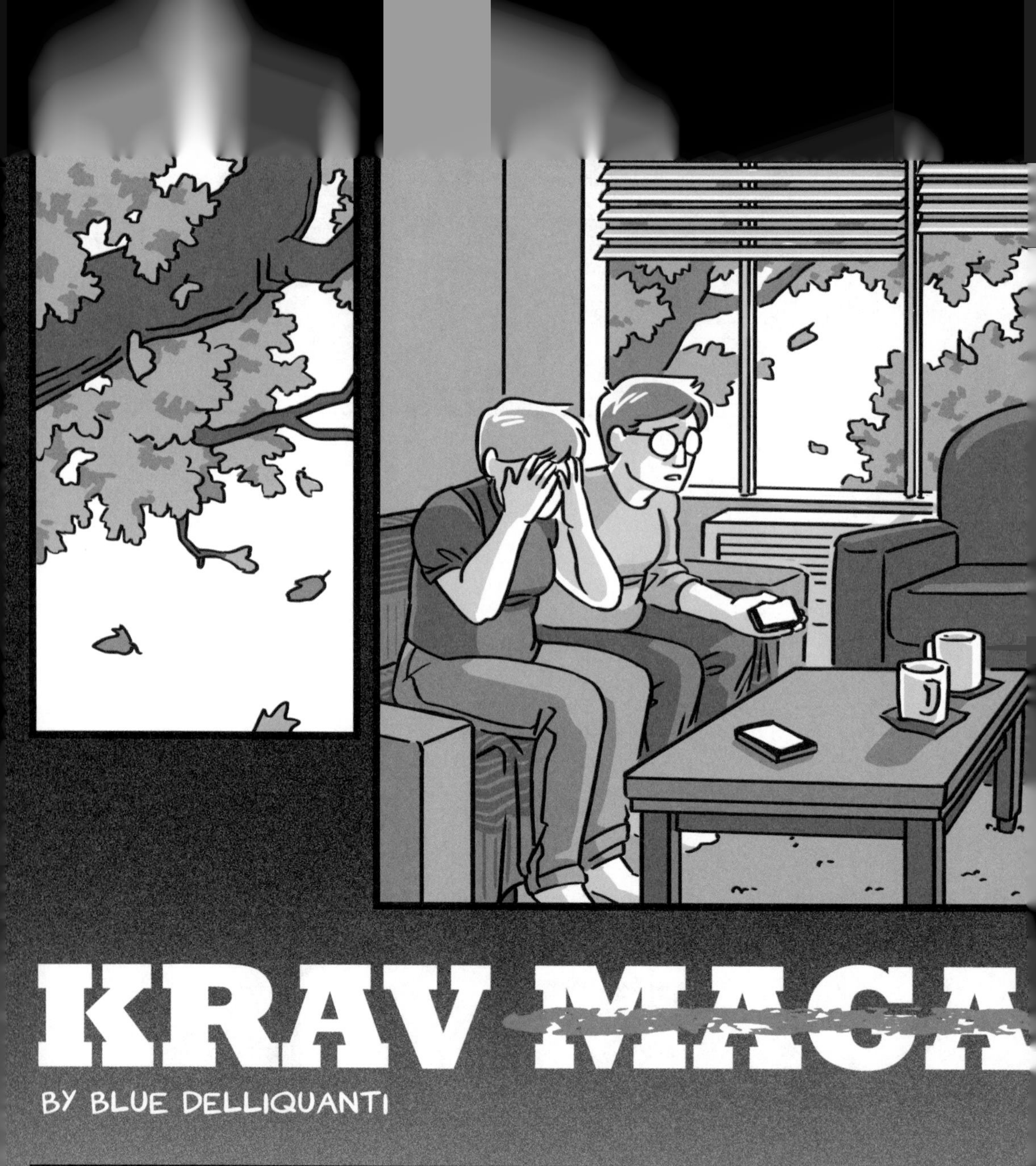

KRAV MAGA

BY BLUE DELLIQUANTI

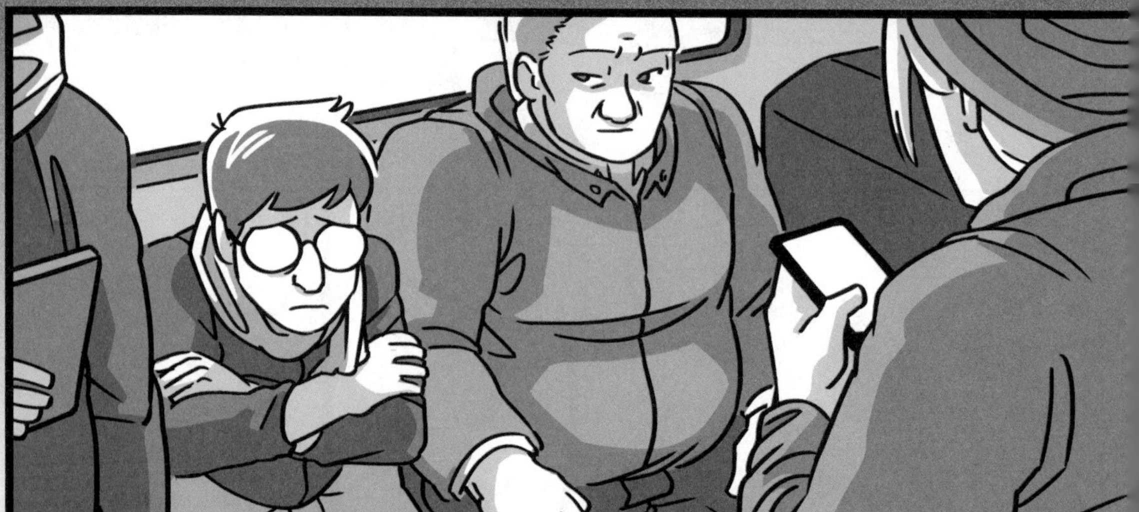

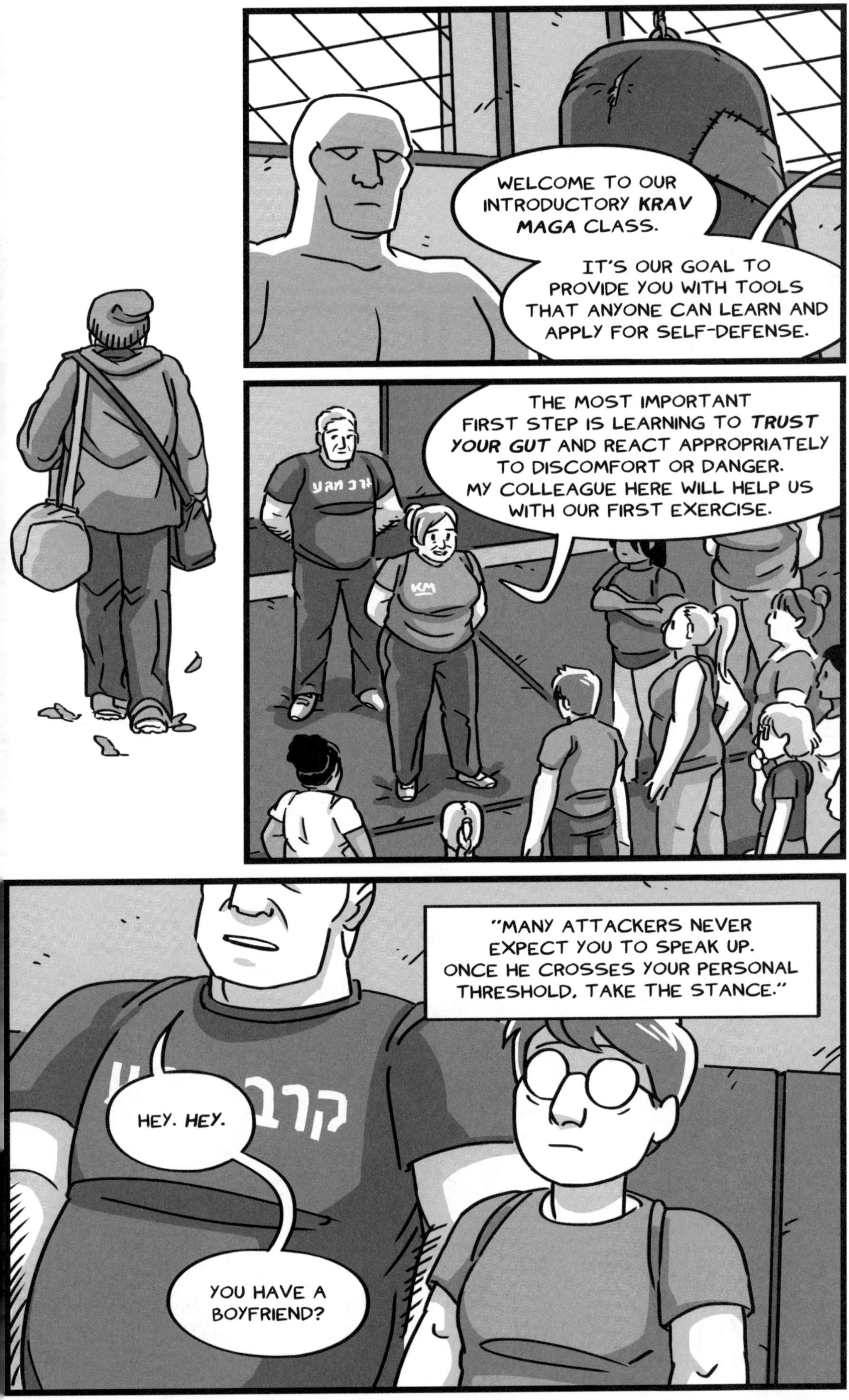

WELCOME TO OUR INTRODUCTORY KRAV MAGA CLASS.
IT'S OUR GOAL TO PROVIDE YOU WITH TOOLS THAT ANYONE CAN LEARN AND APPLY FOR SELF-DEFENSE.
THE MOST IMPORTANT FIRST STEP IS LEARNING TO TRUST YOUR GUT AND REACT APPROPRIATELY TO DISCOMFORT OR DANGER. MY COLLEAGUE HERE WILL HELP US WITH OUR FIRST EXERCISE.
"MANY ATTACKERS NEVER EXPECT YOU TO SPEAK UP. ONCE HE CROSSES YOUR PERSONAL THRESHOLD, TAKE THE STANCE."
HEY. HEY.
YOU HAVE A BOYFRIEND?

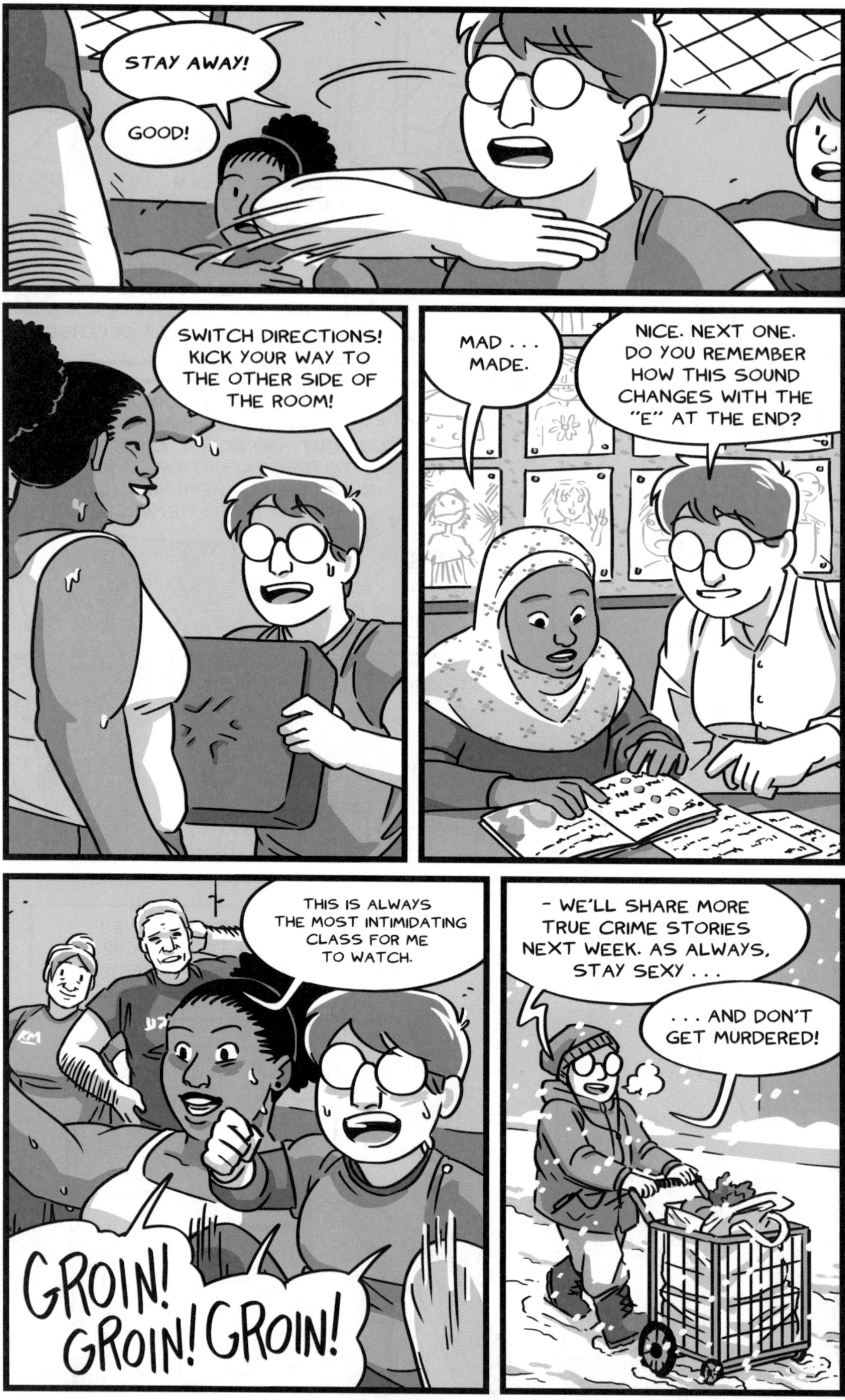
STAY AWAY!
GOOD!
SWITCH DIRECTIONS! KICK YOUR WAY TO THE OTHER SIDE OF THE ROOM!
MAD . . . MADE.
NICE. NEXT ONE. DO YOU REMEMBER HOW THIS SOUND CHANGES WITH THE "E" AT THE END?
THIS IS ALWAYS THE MOST INTIMIDATING CLASS FOR ME TO WATCH.
GROIN! GROIN! GROIN!
- WE'LL SHARE MORE TRUE CRIME STORIES NEXT WEEK. AS ALWAYS, STAY SEXY . . .
. . . AND DON'T GET MURDERED!

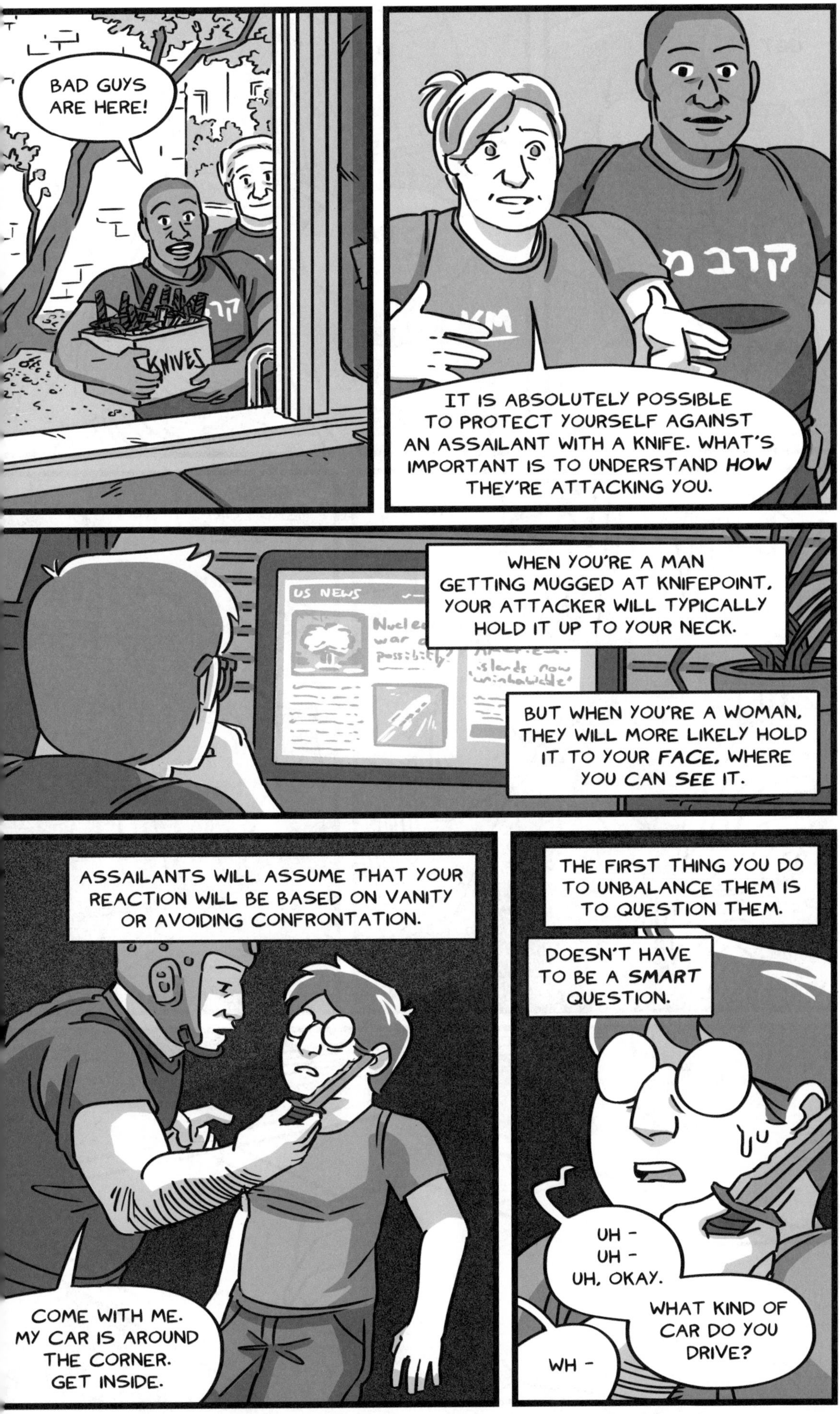
BAD GUYS ARE HERE!
KNIVES
קרב מ
KM
IT IS ABSOLUTELY POSSIBLE TO PROTECT YOURSELF AGAINST AN ASSAILANT WITH A KNIFE. WHAT'S IMPORTANT IS TO UNDERSTAND HOW THEY'RE ATTACKING YOU.
US NEWS
WHEN YOU'RE A MAN GETTING MUGGED AT KNIFEPOINT, YOUR ATTACKER WILL TYPICALLY HOLD IT UP TO YOUR NECK.
BUT WHEN YOU'RE A WOMAN, THEY WILL MORE LIKELY HOLD IT TO YOUR FACE, WHERE YOU CAN SEE IT.
ASSAILANTS WILL ASSUME THAT YOUR REACTION WILL BE BASED ON VANITY OR AVOIDING CONFRONTATION.
COME WITH ME. MY CAR IS AROUND THE CORNER. GET INSIDE.
THE FIRST THING YOU DO TO UNBALANCE THEM IS TO QUESTION THEM.
DOESN'T HAVE TO BE A SMART QUESTION.
UH - UH - UH, OKAY.
WHAT KIND OF CAR DO YOU DRIVE?
WH -

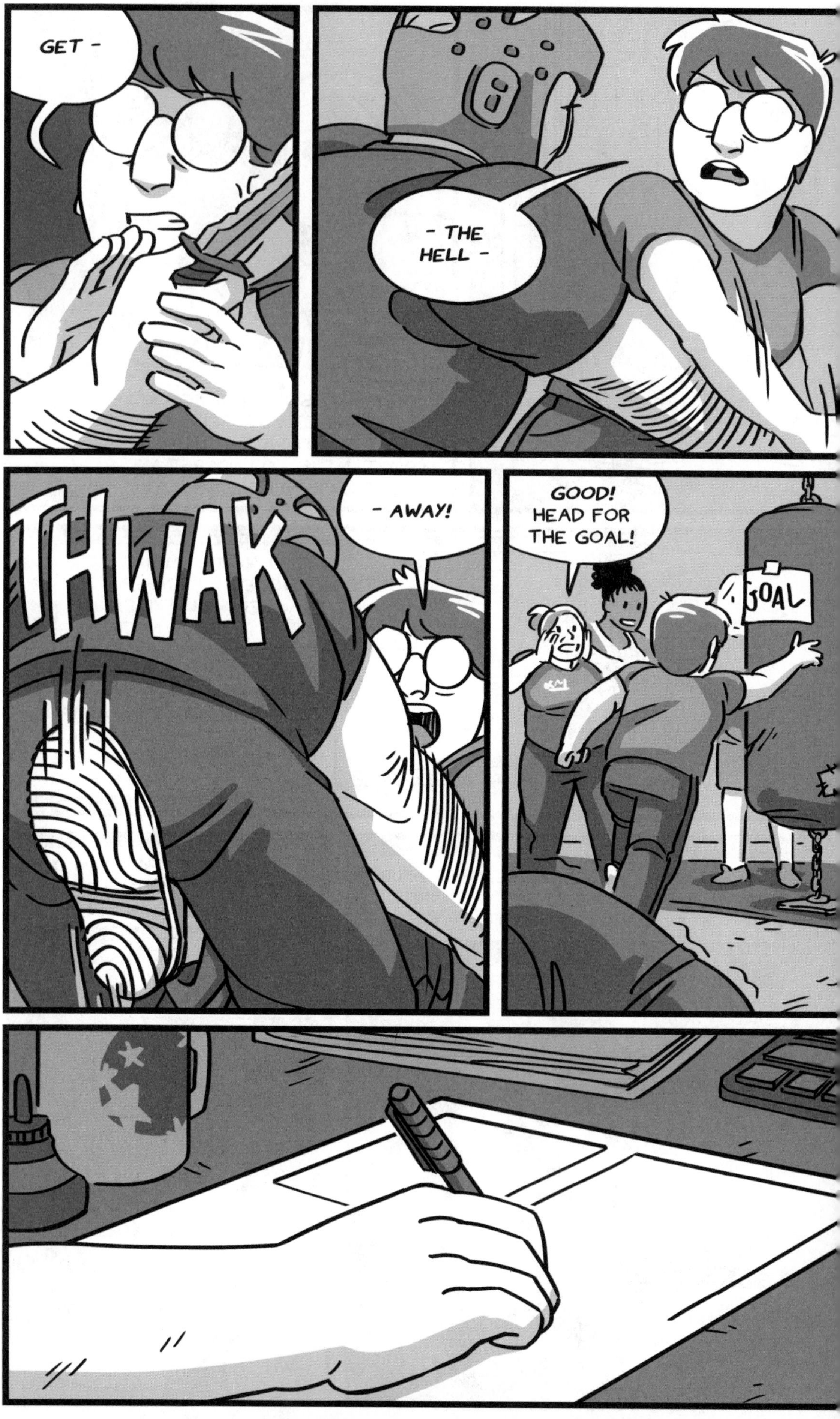
GET -
- THE HELL -
THWAK
- AWAY!
GOOD! HEAD FOR THE GOAL!
GOAL

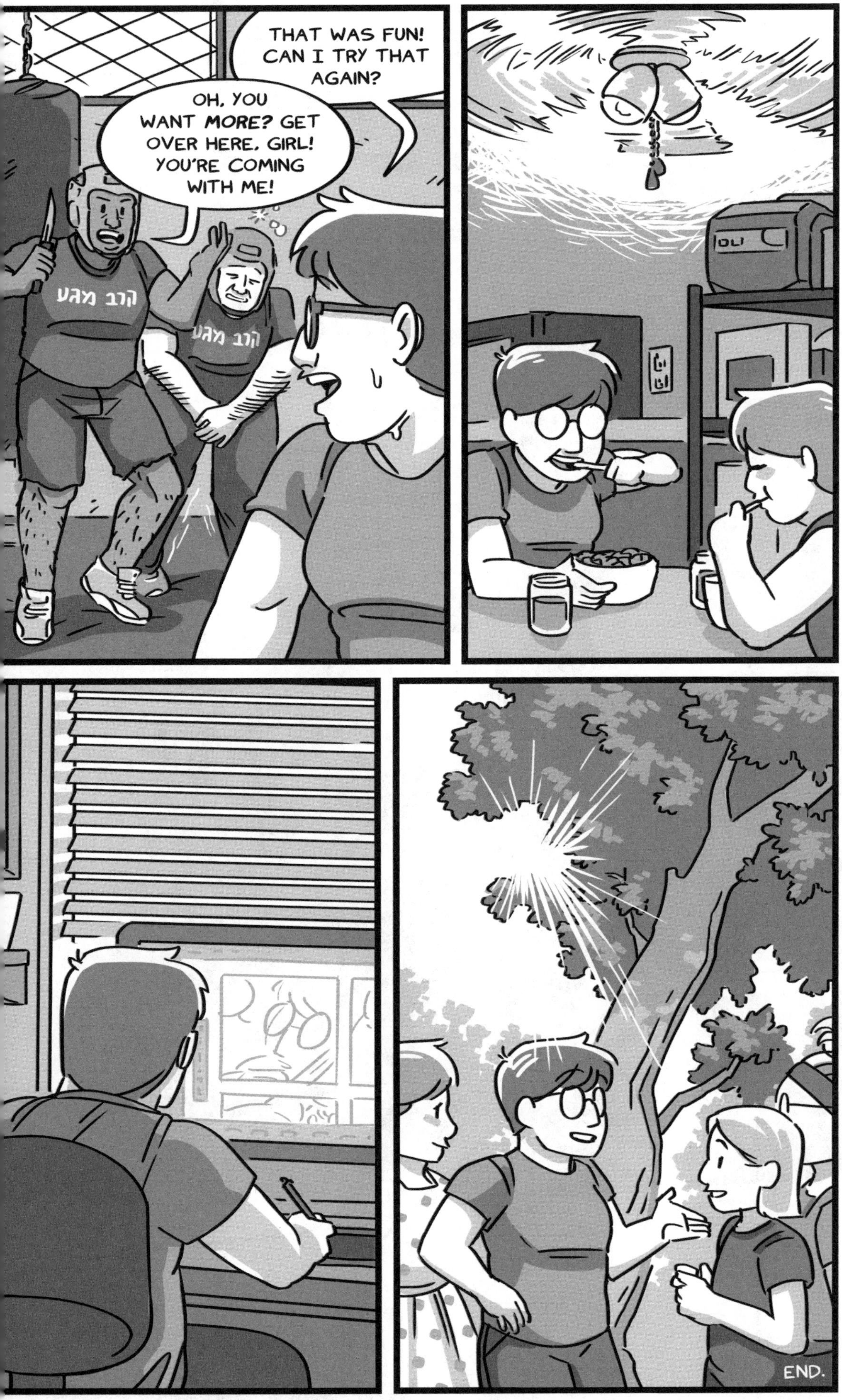
THAT WAS FUN! CAN I TRY THAT AGAIN?
OH, YOU WANT MORE? GET OVER HERE, GIRL! YOU'RE COMING WITH ME!
קרב מגע
קרב מגע
END.

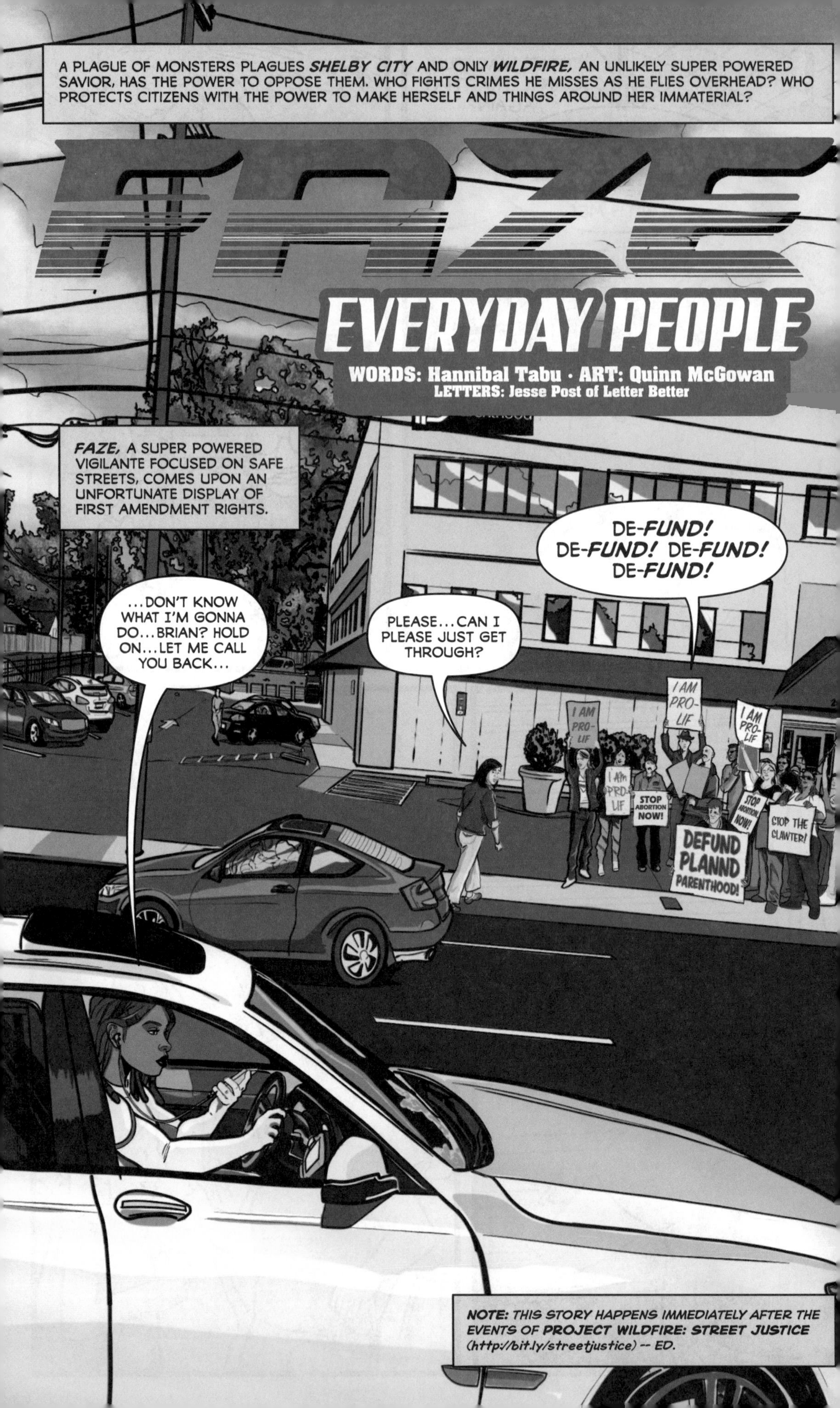
A PLAGUE OF MONSTERS PLAGUES SHELBY CITY AND ONLY WILDFIRE, AN UNLIKELY SUPER POWERED SAVIOR, HAS THE POWER TO OPPOSE THEM. WHO FIGHTS CRIMES HE MISSES AS HE FLIES OVERHEAD? WHO PROTECTS CITIZENS WITH THE POWER TO MAKE HERSELF AND THINGS AROUND HER IMMATERIAL?
FAZE
EVERYDAY PEOPLE
WORDS: Hannibal Tabu · ART: Quinn McGowan
LETTERS: Jesse Post of Letter Better
FAZE, A SUPER POWERED VIGILANTE FOCUSED ON SAFE STREETS, COMES UPON AN UNFORTUNATE DISPLAY OF FIRST AMENDMENT RIGHTS.
DE-FUND! DE-FUND! DE-FUND! DE-FUND!
...DON'T KNOW WHAT I'M GONNA DO...BRIAN? HOLD ON...LET ME CALL YOU BACK...
PLEASE...CAN I PLEASE JUST GET THROUGH?
I AM PRO-LIF
I AM PRO-LIF
I AM PRO-LIF
I AM PRO-LIF
STOP ABORTION NOW!
STOP ABORTION NOW!
DEFUND PLANND PARENTHOOD!
STOP THE CLAWTER!
NOTE: THIS STORY HAPPENS IMMEDIATELY AFTER THE EVENTS OF PROJECT WILDFIRE: STREET JUSTICE (http://bit.ly/streetjustice) -- ED.

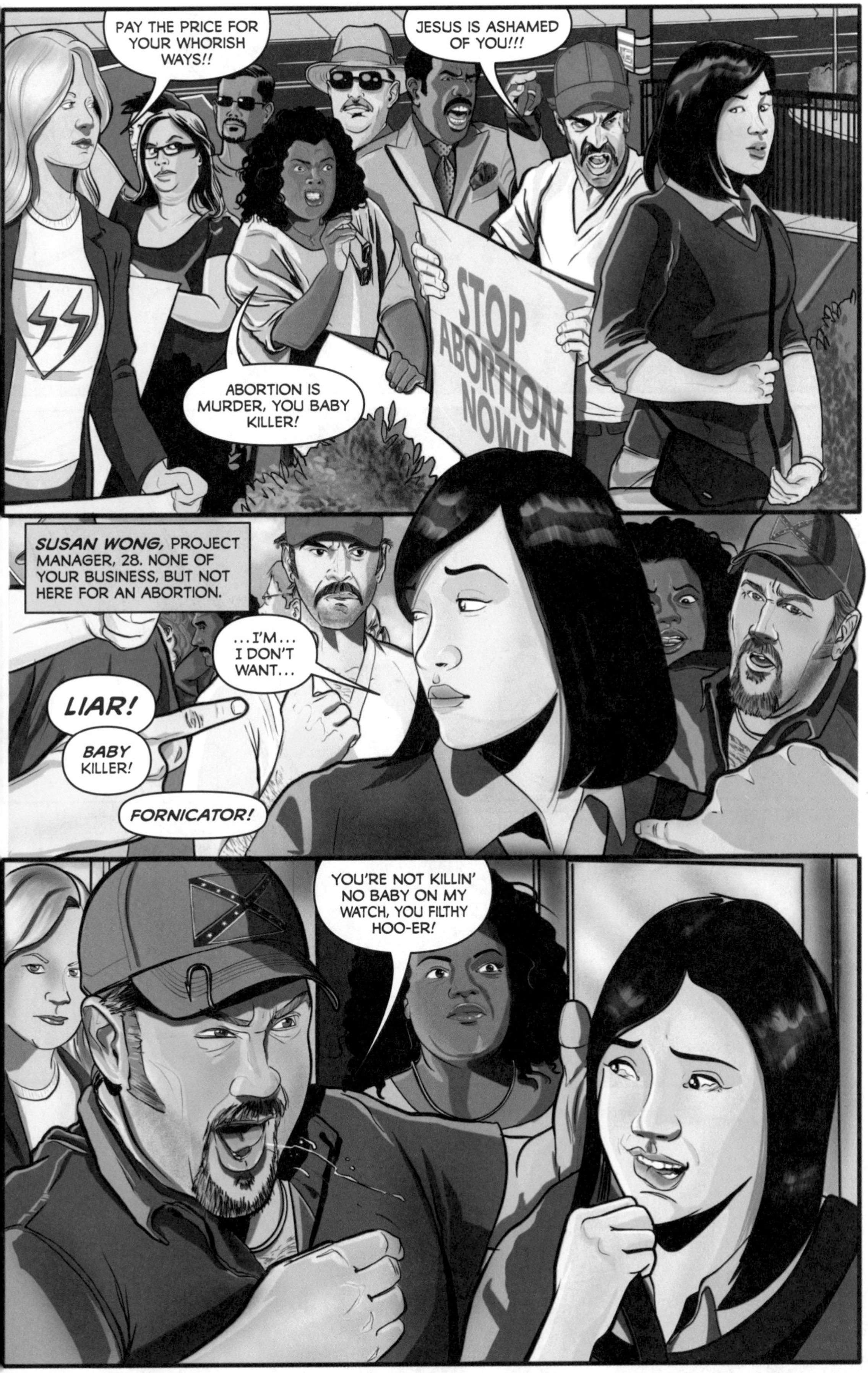
PAY THE PRICE FOR YOUR WHORISH WAYS!!
JESUS IS ASHAMED OF YOU!!!
STOP ABORTION NOW!
ABORTION IS MURDER, YOU BABY KILLER!
SUSAN WONG, PROJECT MANAGER, 28. NONE OF YOUR BUSINESS, BUT NOT HERE FOR AN ABORTION.
...I'M... I DON'T WANT...
LIAR!
BABY KILLER!
FORNICATOR!
YOU'RE NOT KILLIN' NO BABY ON MY WATCH, YOU FILTHY HOO-ER!

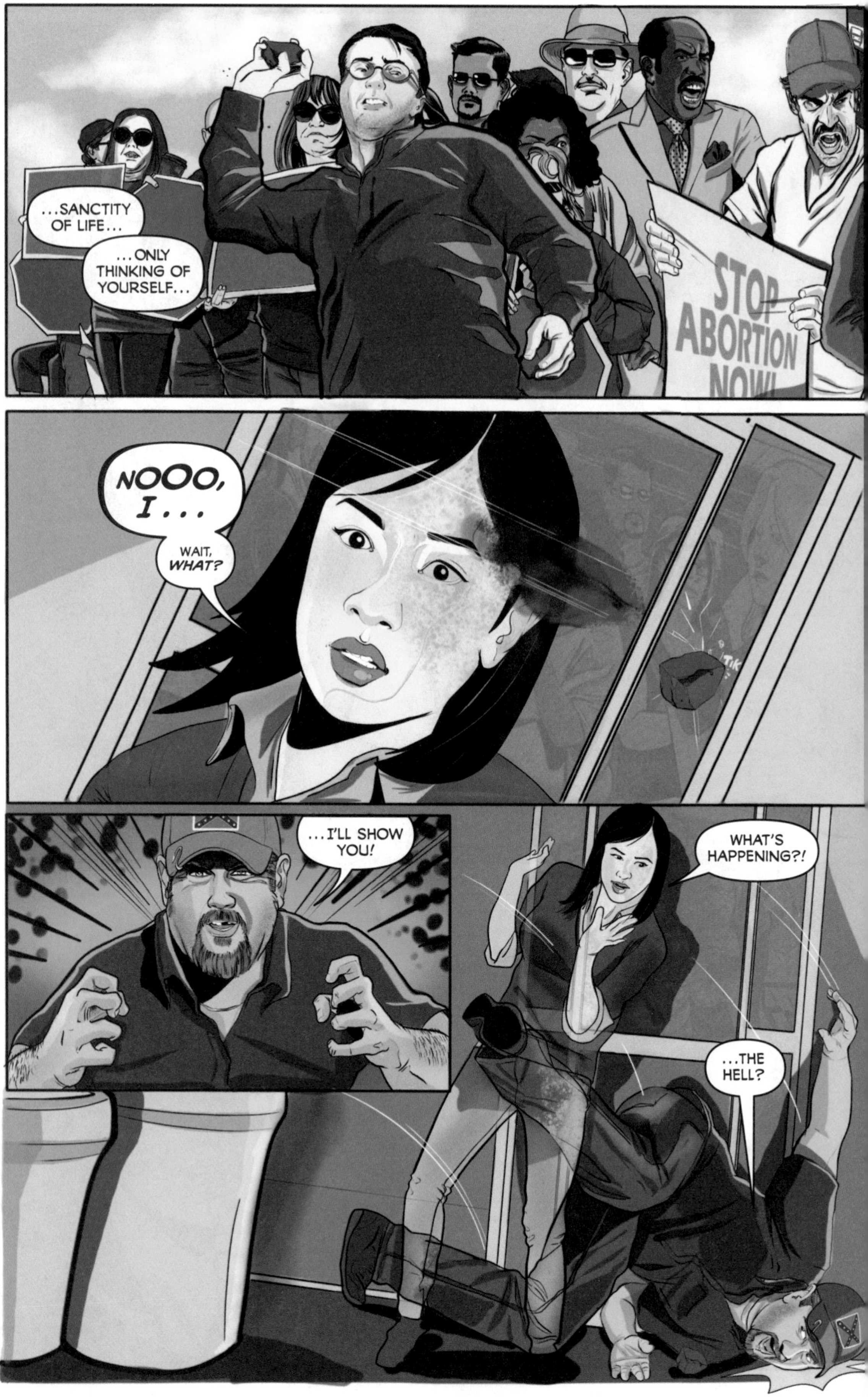
...SANCTITY OF LIFE...
...ONLY THINKING OF YOURSELF...
STOP ABORTION NOW!
NOOO, I...
WAIT, *WHAT?*
TIK
...I'LL SHOW YOU!
WHAT'S HAPPENING?!
...THE HELL?

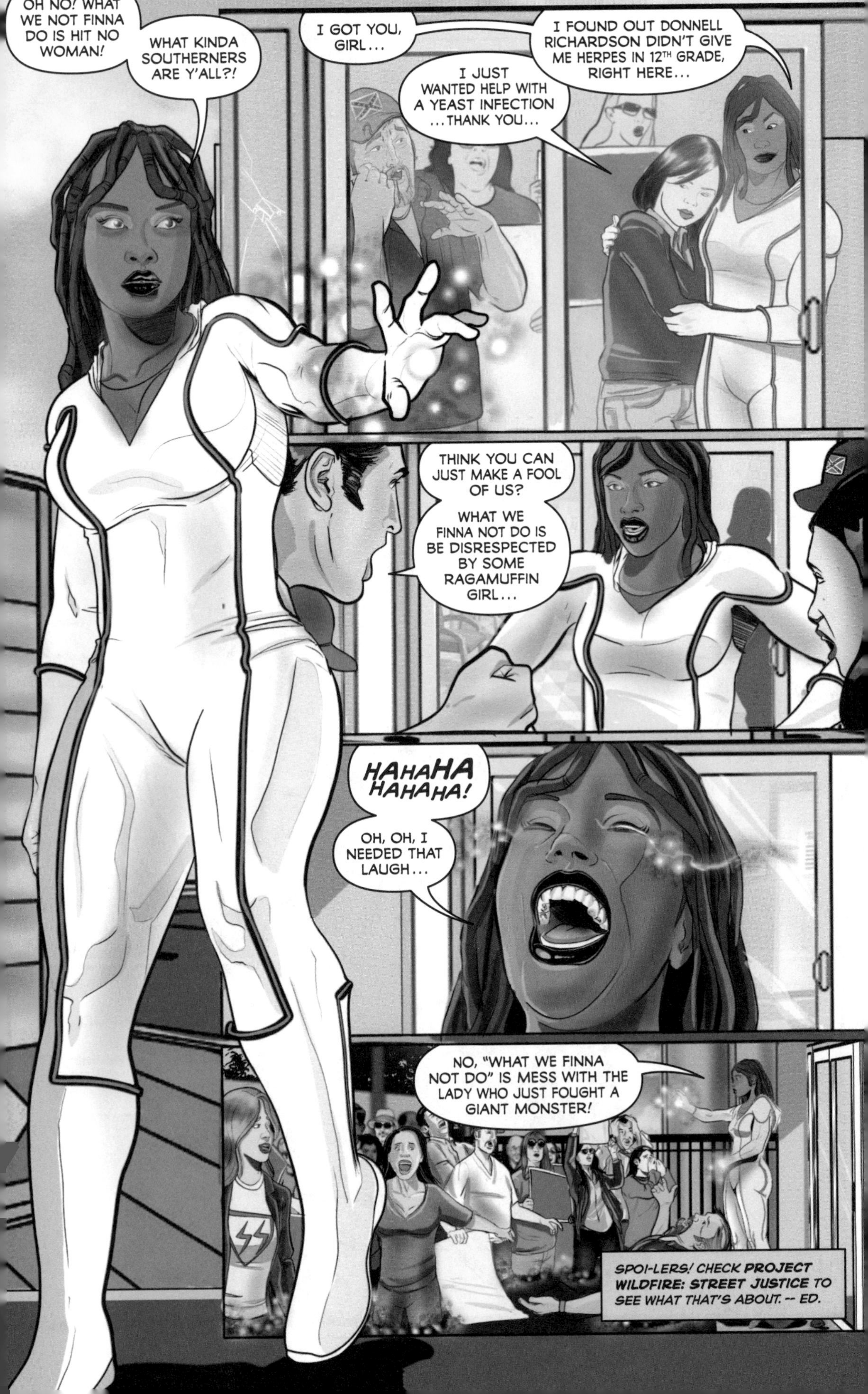
OH NO! WHAT WE NOT FINNA DO IS HIT NO WOMAN!
WHAT KINDA SOUTHERNERS ARE Y'ALL?!
I GOT YOU, GIRL...
I FOUND OUT DONNELL RICHARDSON DIDN'T GIVE ME HERPES IN 12TH GRADE, RIGHT HERE...
I JUST WANTED HELP WITH A YEAST INFECTION ...THANK YOU...
THINK YOU CAN JUST MAKE A FOOL OF US?
WHAT WE FINNA NOT DO IS BE DISRESPECTED BY SOME RAGAMUFFIN GIRL...
HAHAHA HAHAHA!
OH, OH, I NEEDED THAT LAUGH...
NO, "WHAT WE FINNA NOT DO" IS MESS WITH THE LADY WHO JUST FOUGHT A GIANT MONSTER!
SPOI-LERS! CHECK PROJECT WILDFIRE: STREET JUSTICE TO SEE WHAT THAT'S ABOUT. -- ED.

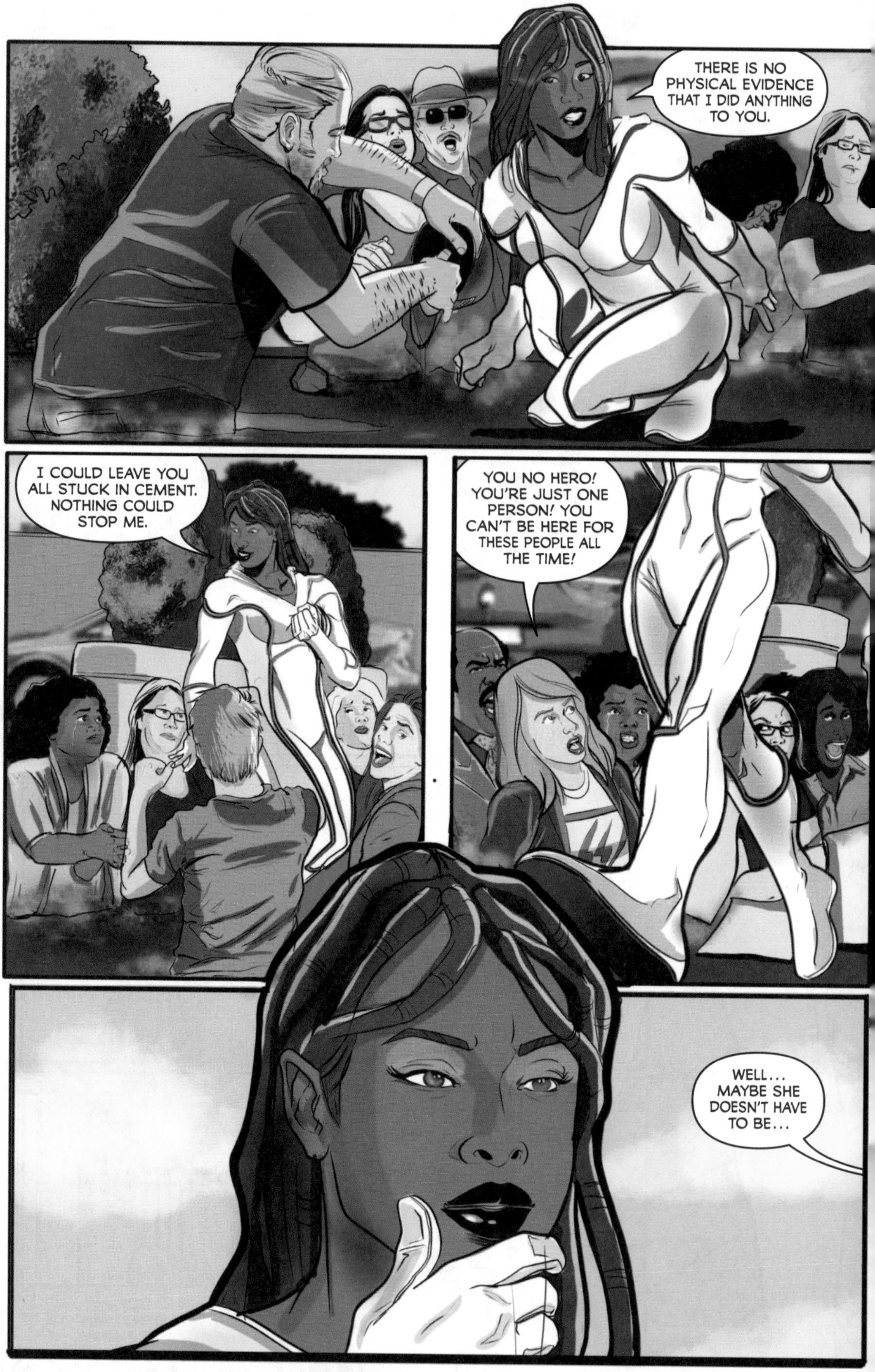
THERE IS NO PHYSICAL EVIDENCE THAT I DID ANYTHING TO YOU.
I COULD LEAVE YOU ALL STUCK IN CEMENT. NOTHING COULD STOP ME.
YOU NO HERO! YOU'RE JUST ONE PERSON! YOU CAN'T BE HERE FOR THESE PEOPLE ALL THE TIME!
WELL... MAYBE SHE DOESN'T HAVE TO BE...

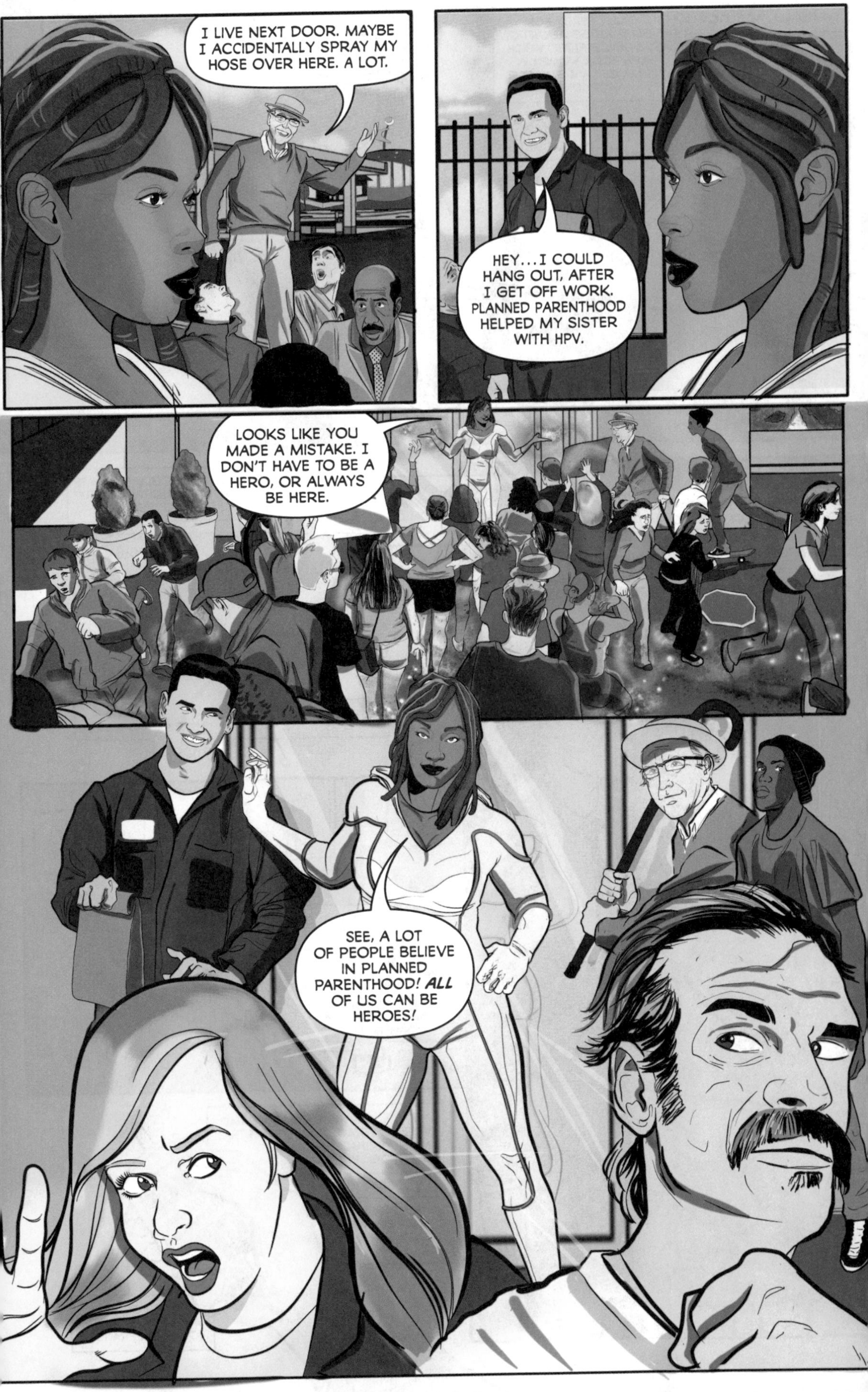

I LIVE NEXT DOOR. MAYBE I ACCIDENTALLY SPRAY MY HOSE OVER HERE. A LOT.
HEY...I COULD HANG OUT, AFTER I GET OFF WORK. PLANNED PARENTHOOD HELPED MY SISTER WITH HPV.
LOOKS LIKE YOU MADE A MISTAKE. I DON'T HAVE TO BE A HERO, OR ALWAYS BE HERE.
SEE, A LOT OF PEOPLE BELIEVE IN PLANNED PARENTHOOD! *ALL* OF US CAN BE HEROES!

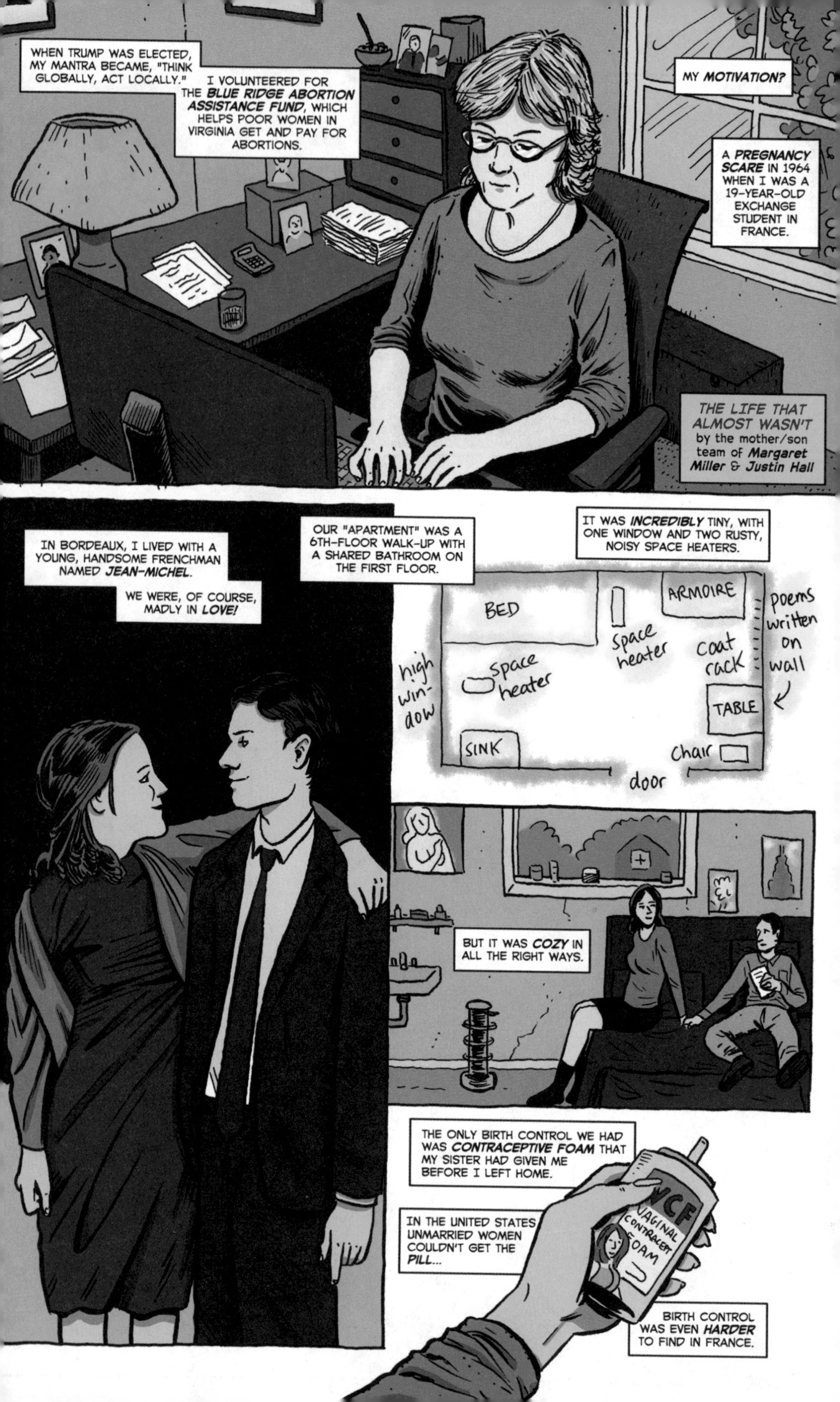

WHEN TRUMP WAS ELECTED, MY MANTRA BECAME, "THINK GLOBALLY, ACT LOCALLY."
I VOLUNTEERED FOR THE BLUE RIDGE ABORTION ASSISTANCE FUND, WHICH HELPS POOR WOMEN IN VIRGINIA GET AND PAY FOR ABORTIONS.
MY MOTIVATION?
A PREGNANCY SCARE IN 1964 WHEN I WAS A 19-YEAR-OLD EXCHANGE STUDENT IN FRANCE.
THE LIFE THAT ALMOST WASN'T by the mother/son team of Margaret Miller & Justin Hall
IN BORDEAUX, I LIVED WITH A YOUNG, HANDSOME FRENCHMAN NAMED JEAN-MICHEL.
WE WERE, OF COURSE, MADLY IN LOVE!
OUR "APARTMENT" WAS A 6TH-FLOOR WALK-UP WITH A SHARED BATHROOM ON THE FIRST FLOOR.
IT WAS INCREDIBLY TINY, WITH ONE WINDOW AND TWO RUSTY, NOISY SPACE HEATERS.
BED
ARMOIRE
space heater
poems written on wall
high win-dow
space heater
coat rack
TABLE
SINK
chair
door
BUT IT WAS COZY IN ALL THE RIGHT WAYS.
THE ONLY BIRTH CONTROL WE HAD WAS CONTRACEPTIVE FOAM THAT MY SISTER HAD GIVEN ME BEFORE I LEFT HOME.
VCF
VAGINAL CONTRACEPT FOAM
IN THE UNITED STATES UNMARRIED WOMEN COULDN'T GET THE PILL...
BIRTH CONTROL WAS EVEN HARDER TO FIND IN FRANCE.

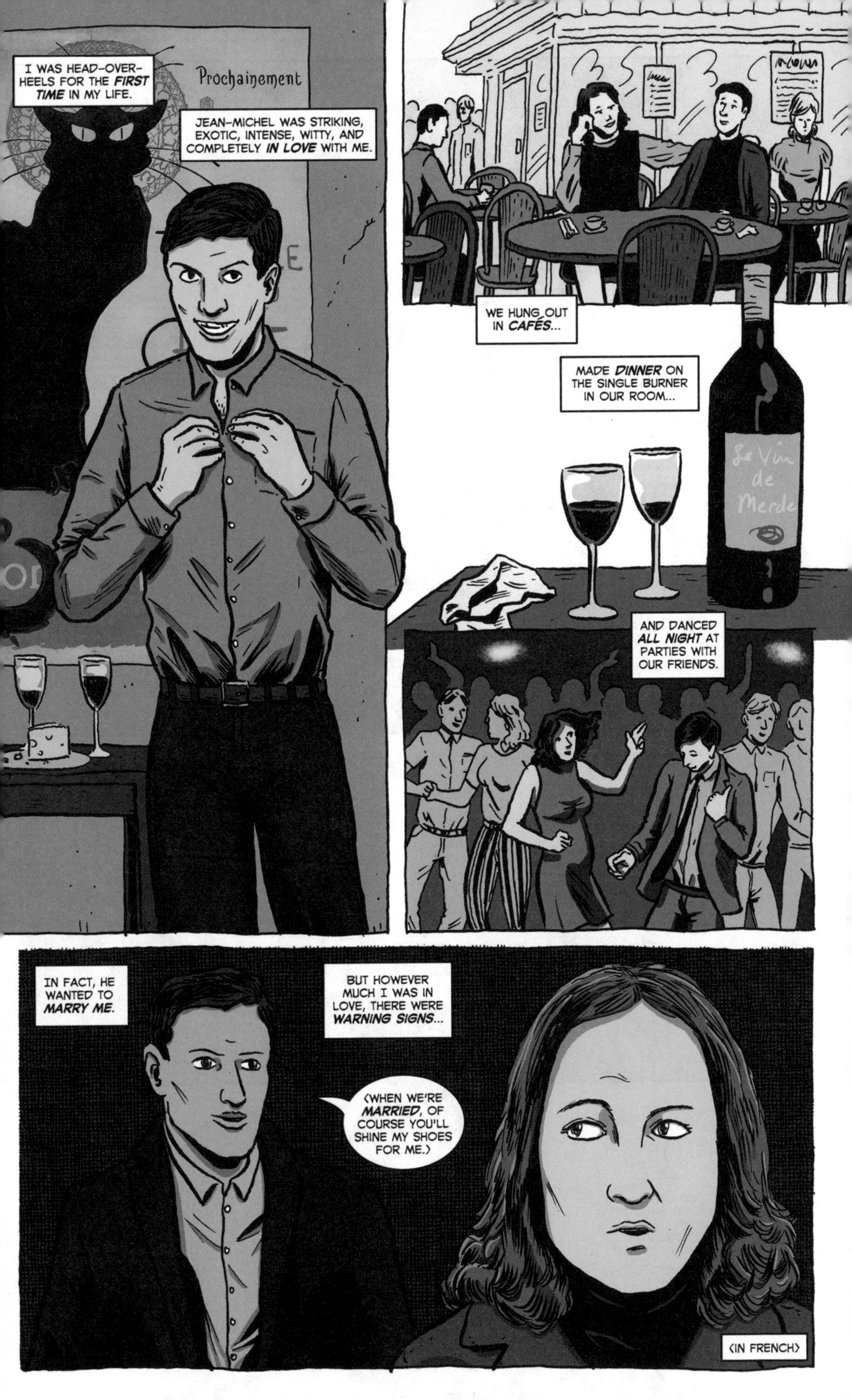
I WAS HEAD-OVER-HEELS FOR THE ***FIRST TIME*** IN MY LIFE.
Prochainement
JEAN-MICHEL WAS STRIKING, EXOTIC, INTENSE, WITTY, AND COMPLETELY ***IN LOVE*** WITH ME.
WE HUNG OUT IN ***CAFÉS***...
MADE ***DINNER*** ON THE SINGLE BURNER IN OUR ROOM...
Le Vin de Merde
AND DANCED ***ALL NIGHT*** AT PARTIES WITH OUR FRIENDS.
IN FACT, HE WANTED TO ***MARRY ME***.
BUT HOWEVER MUCH I WAS IN LOVE, THERE WERE ***WARNING SIGNS***...
〈WHEN WE'RE ***MARRIED***, OF COURSE YOU'LL SHINE MY SHOES FOR ME.〉
〈IN FRENCH〉

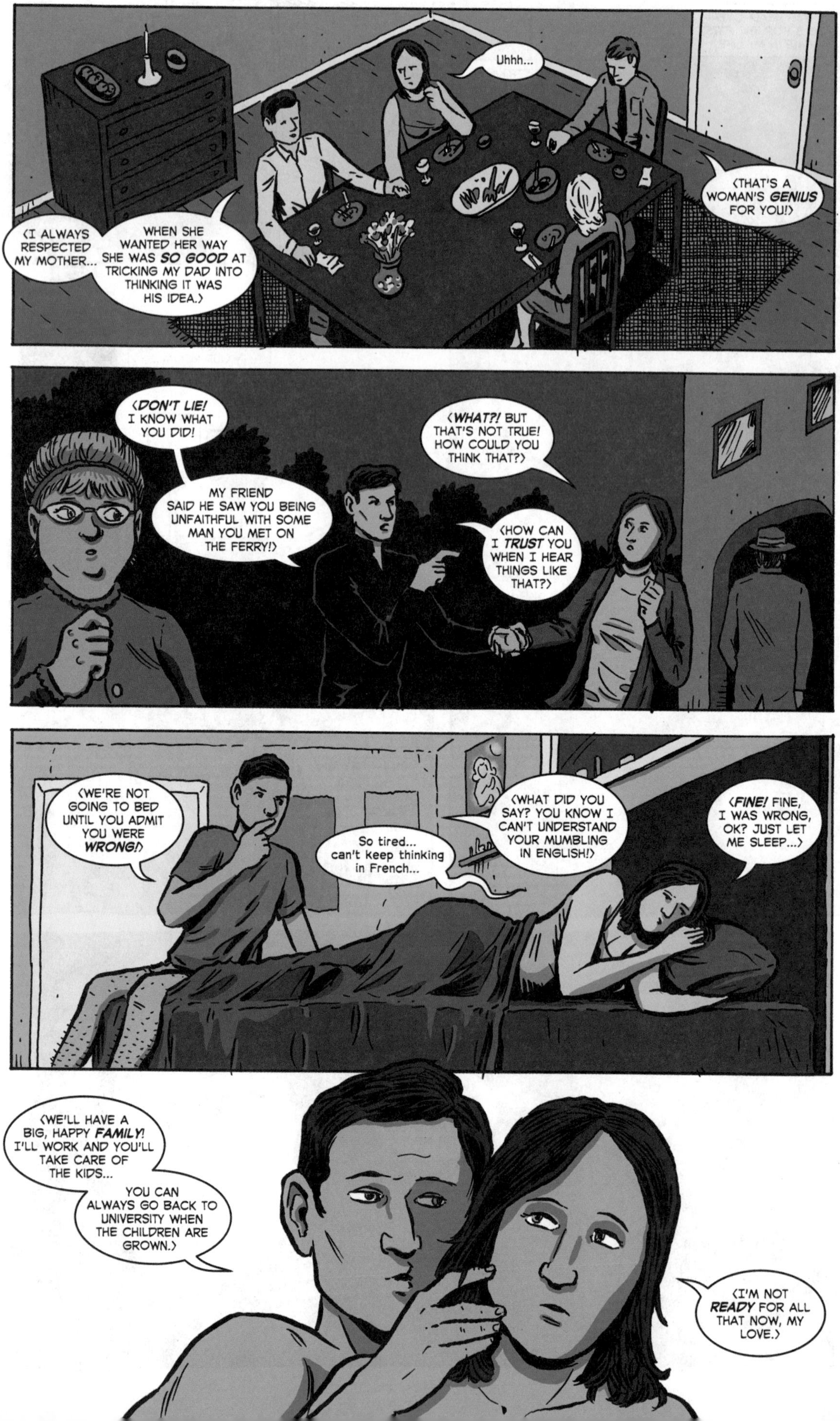
Uhhh...
⟨I ALWAYS RESPECTED MY MOTHER...
WHEN SHE WANTED HER WAY SHE WAS SO GOOD AT TRICKING MY DAD INTO THINKING IT WAS HIS IDEA.⟩
⟨THAT'S A WOMAN'S GENIUS FOR YOU!⟩
⟨DON'T LIE! I KNOW WHAT YOU DID!
MY FRIEND SAID HE SAW YOU BEING UNFAITHFUL WITH SOME MAN YOU MET ON THE FERRY!⟩
⟨WHAT?! BUT THAT'S NOT TRUE! HOW COULD YOU THINK THAT?⟩
⟨HOW CAN I TRUST YOU WHEN I HEAR THINGS LIKE THAT?⟩
⟨WE'RE NOT GOING TO BED UNTIL YOU ADMIT YOU WERE WRONG!⟩
So tired... can't keep thinking in French...
⟨WHAT DID YOU SAY? YOU KNOW I CAN'T UNDERSTAND YOUR MUMBLING IN ENGLISH!⟩
⟨FINE! FINE, I WAS WRONG, OK? JUST LET ME SLEEP...⟩
⟨WE'LL HAVE A BIG, HAPPY FAMILY! I'LL WORK AND YOU'LL TAKE CARE OF THE KIDS...
YOU CAN ALWAYS GO BACK TO UNIVERSITY WHEN THE CHILDREN ARE GROWN.⟩
⟨I'M NOT READY FOR ALL THAT NOW, MY LOVE.⟩

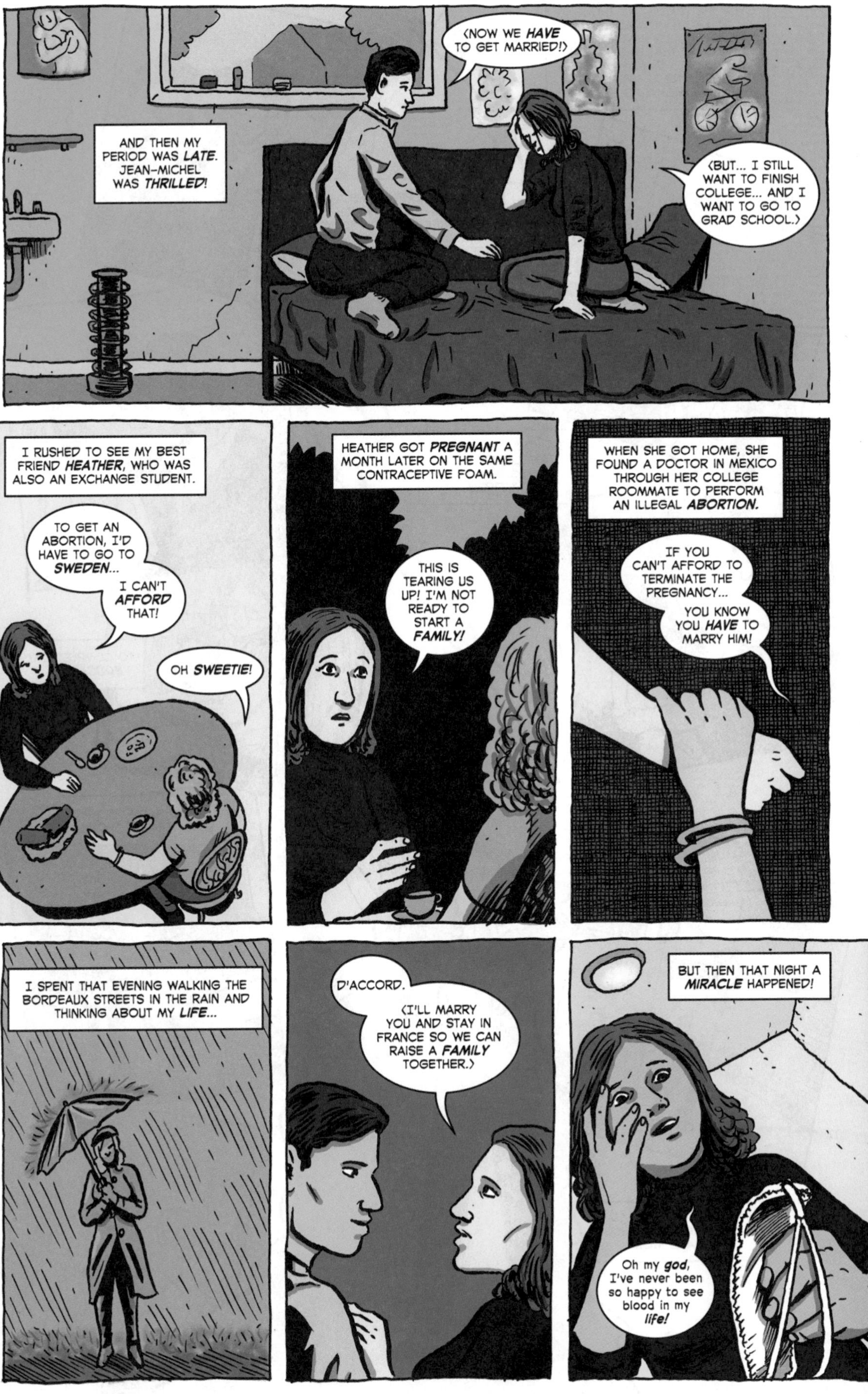
AND THEN MY PERIOD WAS LATE. JEAN-MICHEL WAS THRILLED!
‹NOW WE HAVE TO GET MARRIED!›
‹BUT... I STILL WANT TO FINISH COLLEGE... AND I WANT TO GO TO GRAD SCHOOL.›
I RUSHED TO SEE MY BEST FRIEND HEATHER, WHO WAS ALSO AN EXCHANGE STUDENT.
TO GET AN ABORTION, I'D HAVE TO GO TO SWEDEN...
I CAN'T AFFORD THAT!
OH SWEETIE!
HEATHER GOT PREGNANT A MONTH LATER ON THE SAME CONTRACEPTIVE FOAM.
THIS IS TEARING US UP! I'M NOT READY TO START A FAMILY!
WHEN SHE GOT HOME, SHE FOUND A DOCTOR IN MEXICO THROUGH HER COLLEGE ROOMMATE TO PERFORM AN ILLEGAL ABORTION.
IF YOU CAN'T AFFORD TO TERMINATE THE PREGNANCY...
YOU KNOW YOU HAVE TO MARRY HIM!
I SPENT THAT EVENING WALKING THE BORDEAUX STREETS IN THE RAIN AND THINKING ABOUT MY LIFE...
D'ACCORD.
‹I'LL MARRY YOU AND STAY IN FRANCE SO WE CAN RAISE A FAMILY TOGETHER.›
BUT THEN THAT NIGHT A MIRACLE HAPPENED!
Oh my god, I've never been so happy to see blood in my life!

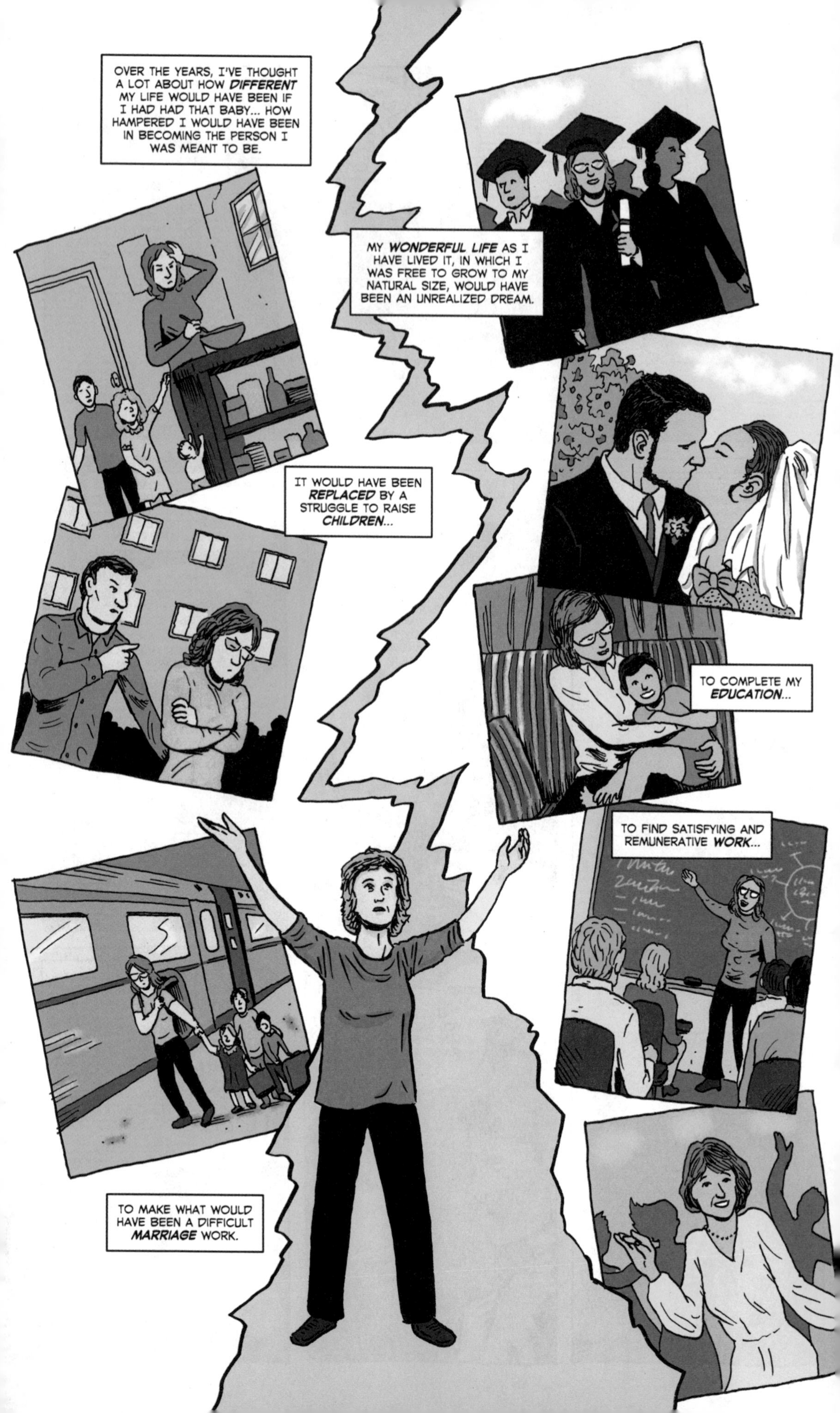

OVER THE YEARS, I'VE THOUGHT A LOT ABOUT HOW *DIFFERENT* MY LIFE WOULD HAVE BEEN IF I HAD HAD THAT BABY... HOW HAMPERED I WOULD HAVE BEEN IN BECOMING THE PERSON I WAS MEANT TO BE.
MY *WONDERFUL LIFE* AS I HAVE LIVED IT, IN WHICH I WAS FREE TO GROW TO MY NATURAL SIZE, WOULD HAVE BEEN AN UNREALIZED DREAM.
IT WOULD HAVE BEEN *REPLACED* BY A STRUGGLE TO RAISE *CHILDREN*...
TO COMPLETE MY *EDUCATION*...
TO FIND SATISFYING AND REMUNERATIVE *WORK*...
TO MAKE WHAT WOULD HAVE BEEN A DIFFICULT *MARRIAGE* WORK.

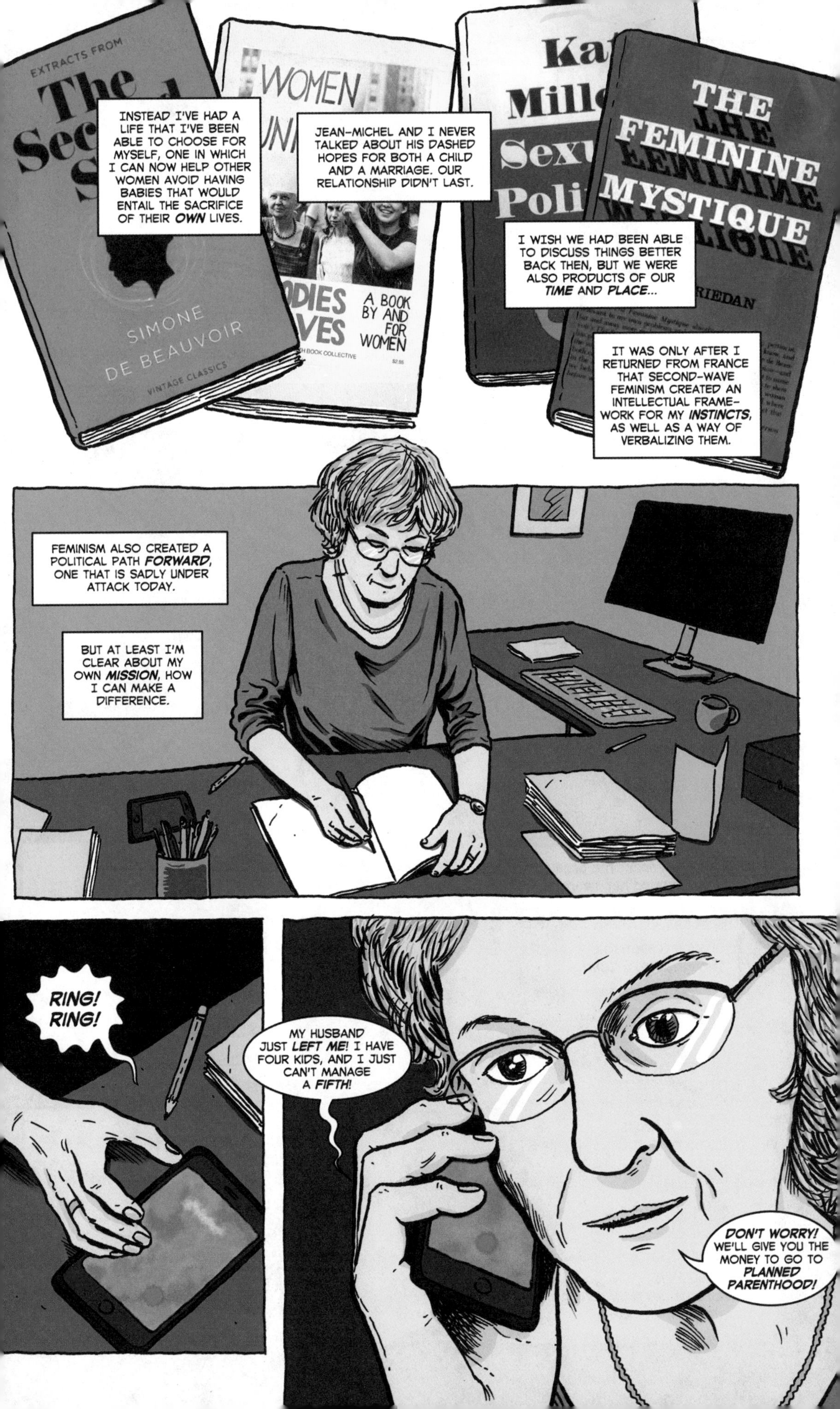

INSTEAD I'VE HAD A LIFE THAT I'VE BEEN ABLE TO CHOOSE FOR MYSELF, ONE IN WHICH I CAN NOW HELP OTHER WOMEN AVOID HAVING BABIES THAT WOULD ENTAIL THE SACRIFICE OF THEIR *OWN* LIVES.
JEAN-MICHEL AND I NEVER TALKED ABOUT HIS DASHED HOPES FOR BOTH A CHILD AND A MARRIAGE. OUR RELATIONSHIP DIDN'T LAST.
I WISH WE HAD BEEN ABLE TO DISCUSS THINGS BETTER BACK THEN, BUT WE WERE ALSO PRODUCTS OF OUR *TIME* AND *PLACE*...
IT WAS ONLY AFTER I RETURNED FROM FRANCE THAT SECOND-WAVE FEMINISM CREATED AN INTELLECTUAL FRAME-WORK FOR MY *INSTINCTS*, AS WELL AS A WAY OF VERBALIZING THEM.
FEMINISM ALSO CREATED A POLITICAL PATH *FORWARD*, ONE THAT IS SADLY UNDER ATTACK TODAY.
BUT AT LEAST I'M CLEAR ABOUT MY OWN *MISSION*, HOW I CAN MAKE A DIFFERENCE.
RING! RING!
MY HUSBAND JUST *LEFT ME*! I HAVE FOUR KIDS, AND I JUST CAN'T MANAGE A *FIFTH*!
DON'T WORRY! WE'LL GIVE YOU THE MONEY TO GO TO *PLANNED PARENTHOOD!*

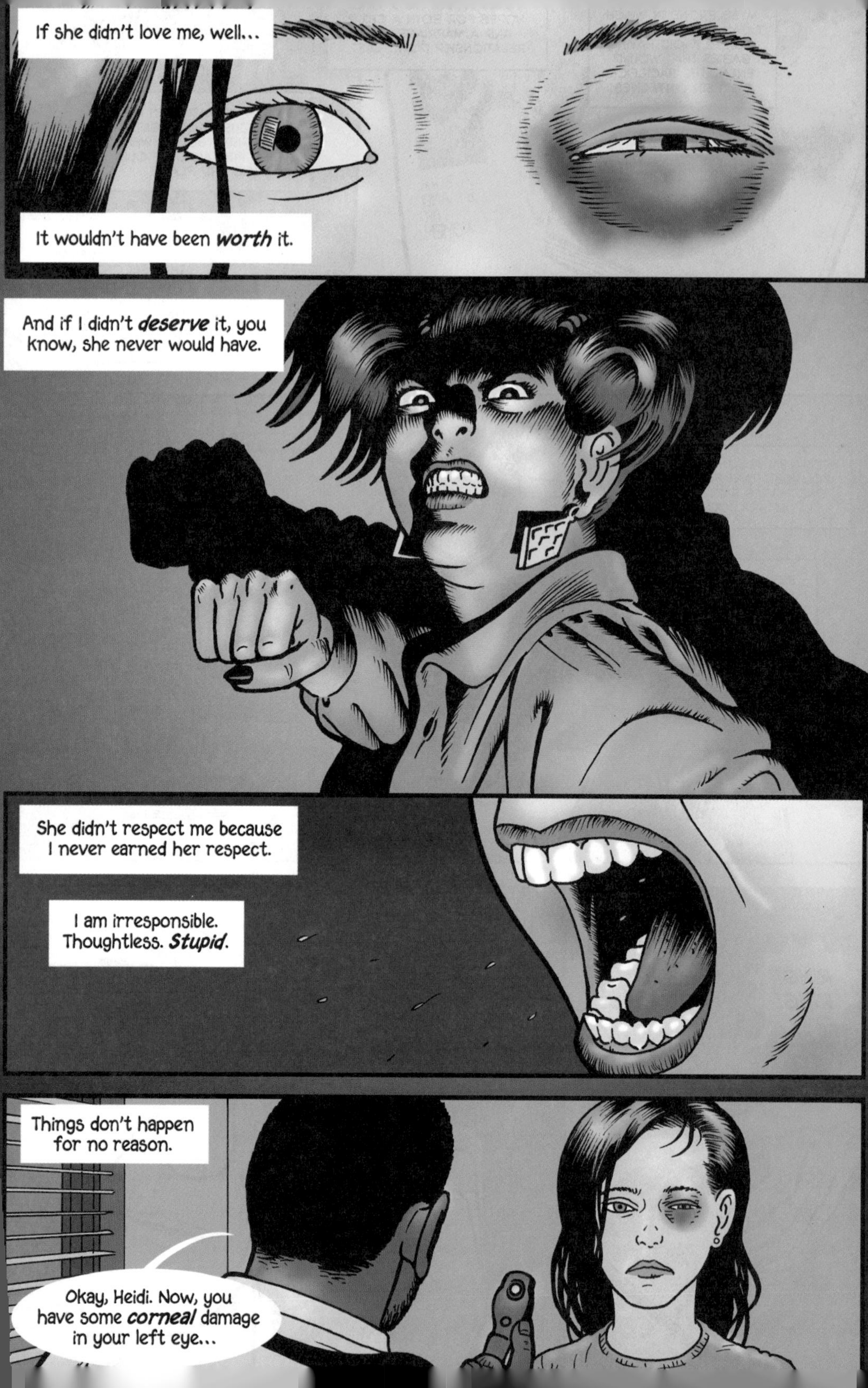
If she didn't love me, well...
It wouldn't have been *worth* it.
And if I didn't *deserve* it, you know, she never would have.
She didn't respect me because I never earned her respect.
I am irresponsible. Thoughtless. *Stupid*.
Things don't happen for no reason.
Okay, Heidi. Now, you have some *corneal* damage in your left eye...

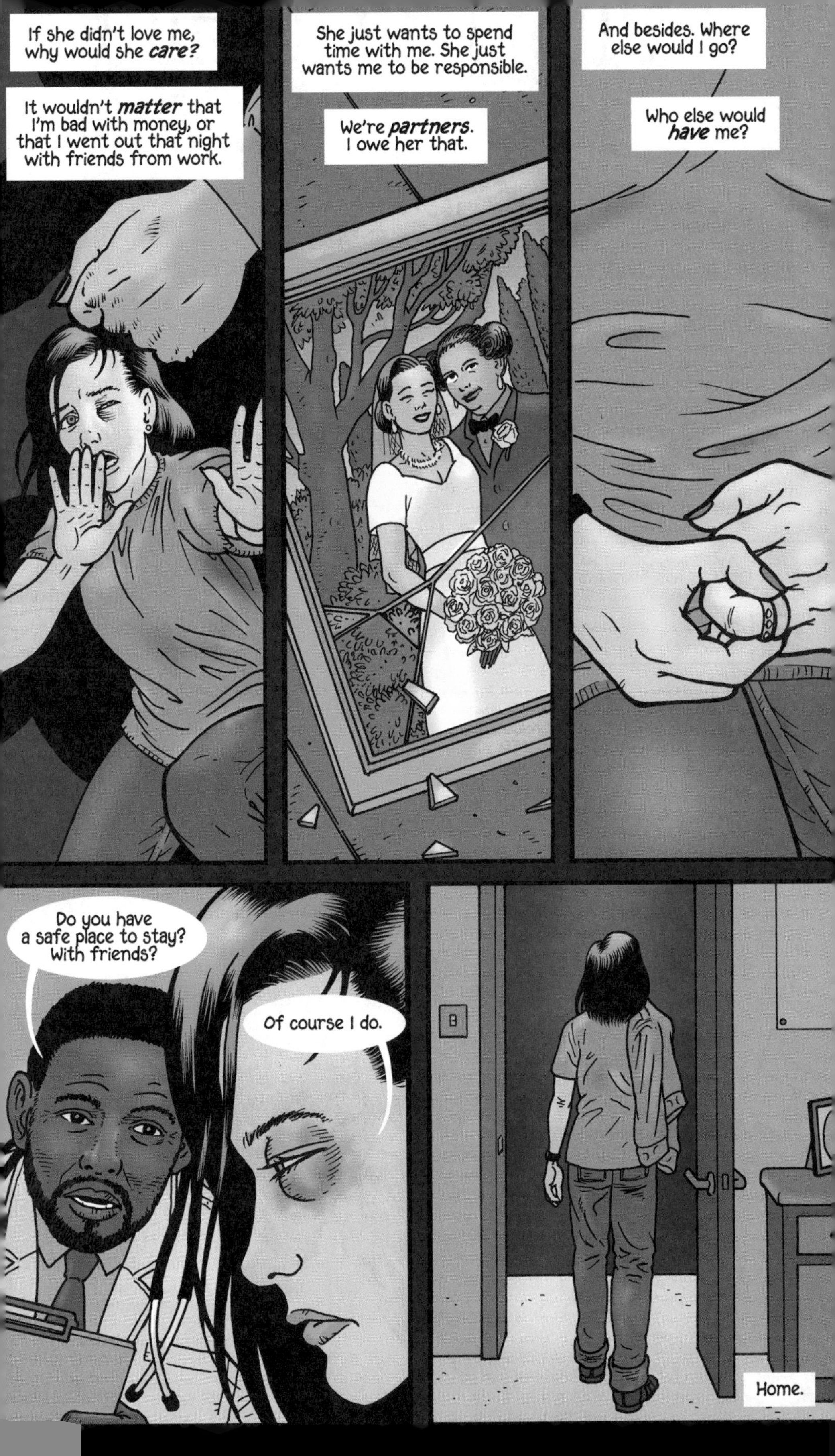
If she didn't love me, why would she *care?*
It wouldn't *matter* that I'm bad with money, or that I went out that night with friends from work.
She just wants to spend time with me. She just wants me to be responsible.
We're *partners*. I owe her that.
And besides. Where else would I go?
Who else would *have* me?
Do you have a safe place to stay? With friends?
Of course I do.
Home.

GLORIA RICHARDSON

Story by MARK WAID · Art by JOHN BROGLIA
Color by SEAN CALLAHAN
Lettering by JESSE POST OF LETTER BETTER

ANYONE WHO'S EVER BEEN AROUND ME FOR MORE THAN FIVE MINUTES KNOWS THAT I AM NOT LEVEL-HEADED AROUND BULLIES.

I GENERALLY COMBAT THEIR ABUSES IN THE MOST EFFECTIVE WAY POSSIBLE: WITH A SOUCIANT TWEET. OR PERHAPS A SCATHING FACEBOOK POST. OR SOMETIMES BY JUST SCREAMING INTO MY PILLOW. SAME RESULTS.

GLORIA RICHARDSON DIDN'T HAVE SOCIAL MEDIA AT HER FINGERTIPS, SO SHE DID SOMETHING ELSE:

SHE FACED OFF AGAINST THE GODDAMN NATIONAL GUARD.

IN 1961, THE CIVIL RIGHTS MOVEMENT CAME TO CAMBRIDGE, MARYLAND, THEN A BRUTALLY, VOMITOUSLY SEGREGATED TOWN.

NO DOGS NEGRO MEXI

GLORIA RICHARDSON WAS A BRIGHT LIGHT IN THE COMMUNITY, AN AFRICAN-AMERICAN COLLEGE GRADUATE WITH A DEGREE IN SOCIOLOGY.

DEFIANT, SHE JOINED WITH OTHERS TO CREATE (AND SUBSEQUENTLY LEAD) THE CAMBRIDGE NONVIOLENT ACTION COMMITTEE (CNAC).

SEGREGATION IS MORALLY WRONG!

WE WALK FOR HUMAN DIGNITY!

EQUAL RIGHTS FOR ALL!

EQUAL Opportunity AND HUMAN DIGNITY

SEGRE IS MORA WRO

THE CNAC, LIKE MANY OTHER BLACK PROTEST GROUPS OF THE CIVIL RIGHTS MOVEMENT, FOUGHT AGAINST EMPLOYMENT DISCRIMINATION, SEGREGATION, AND OTHER INJUSTICES.

NONVIOLENTLY. IT'S RIGHT THERE IN THEIR NAME, YES?

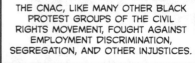

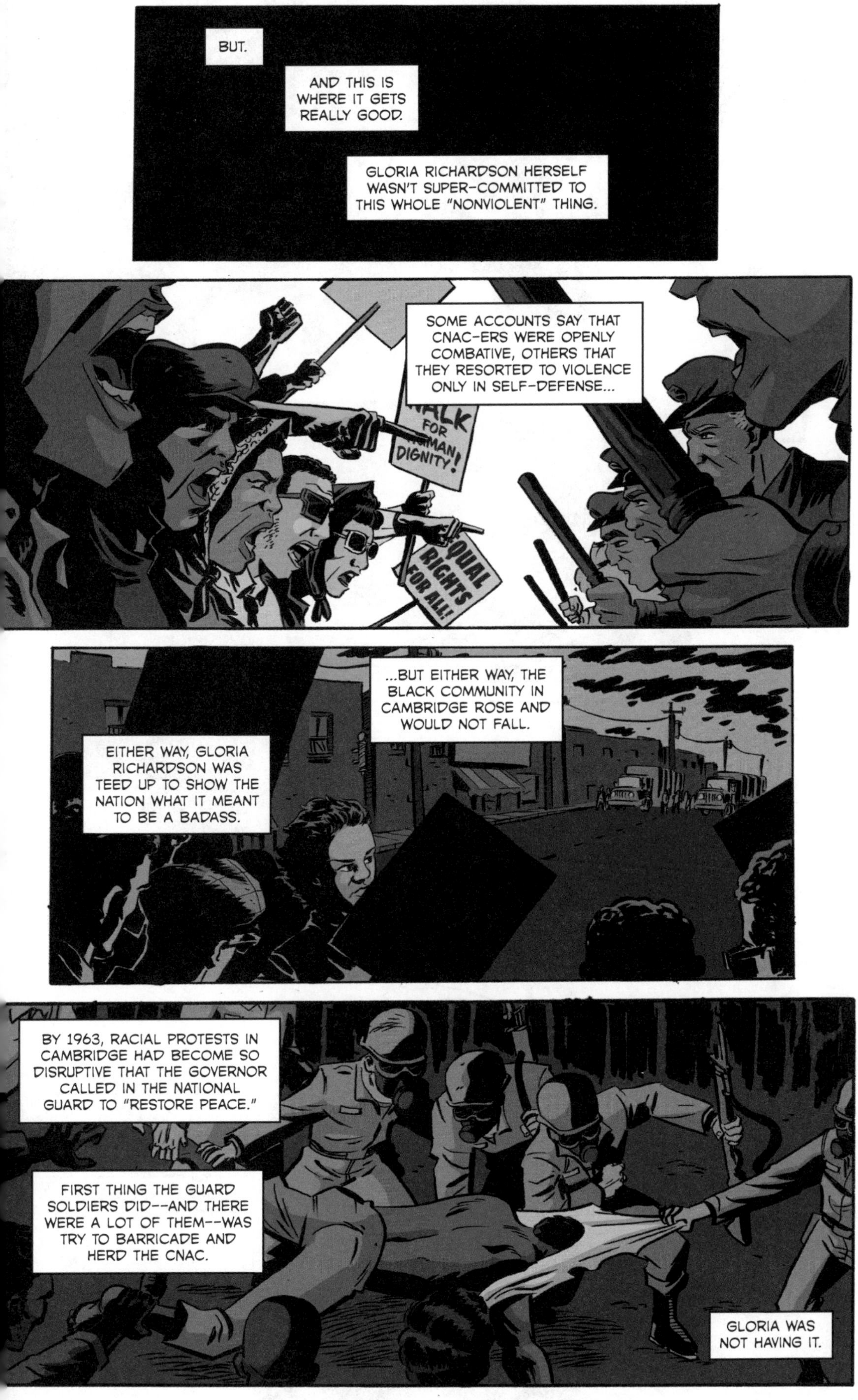
BUT.
AND THIS IS WHERE IT GETS REALLY GOOD.
GLORIA RICHARDSON HERSELF WASN'T SUPER-COMMITTED TO THIS WHOLE "NONVIOLENT" THING.
SOME ACCOUNTS SAY THAT CNAC-ERS WERE OPENLY COMBATIVE, OTHERS THAT THEY RESORTED TO VIOLENCE ONLY IN SELF-DEFENSE...
DIGNITY!
RIGHTS FOR ALL!
...BUT EITHER WAY, THE BLACK COMMUNITY IN CAMBRIDGE ROSE AND WOULD NOT FALL.
EITHER WAY, GLORIA RICHARDSON WAS TEED UP TO SHOW THE NATION WHAT IT MEANT TO BE A BADASS.
BY 1963, RACIAL PROTESTS IN CAMBRIDGE HAD BECOME SO DISRUPTIVE THAT THE GOVERNOR CALLED IN THE NATIONAL GUARD TO "RESTORE PEACE."
FIRST THING THE GUARD SOLDIERS DID--AND THERE WERE A LOT OF THEM--WAS TRY TO BARRICADE AND HERD THE CNAC.
GLORIA WAS NOT HAVING IT.

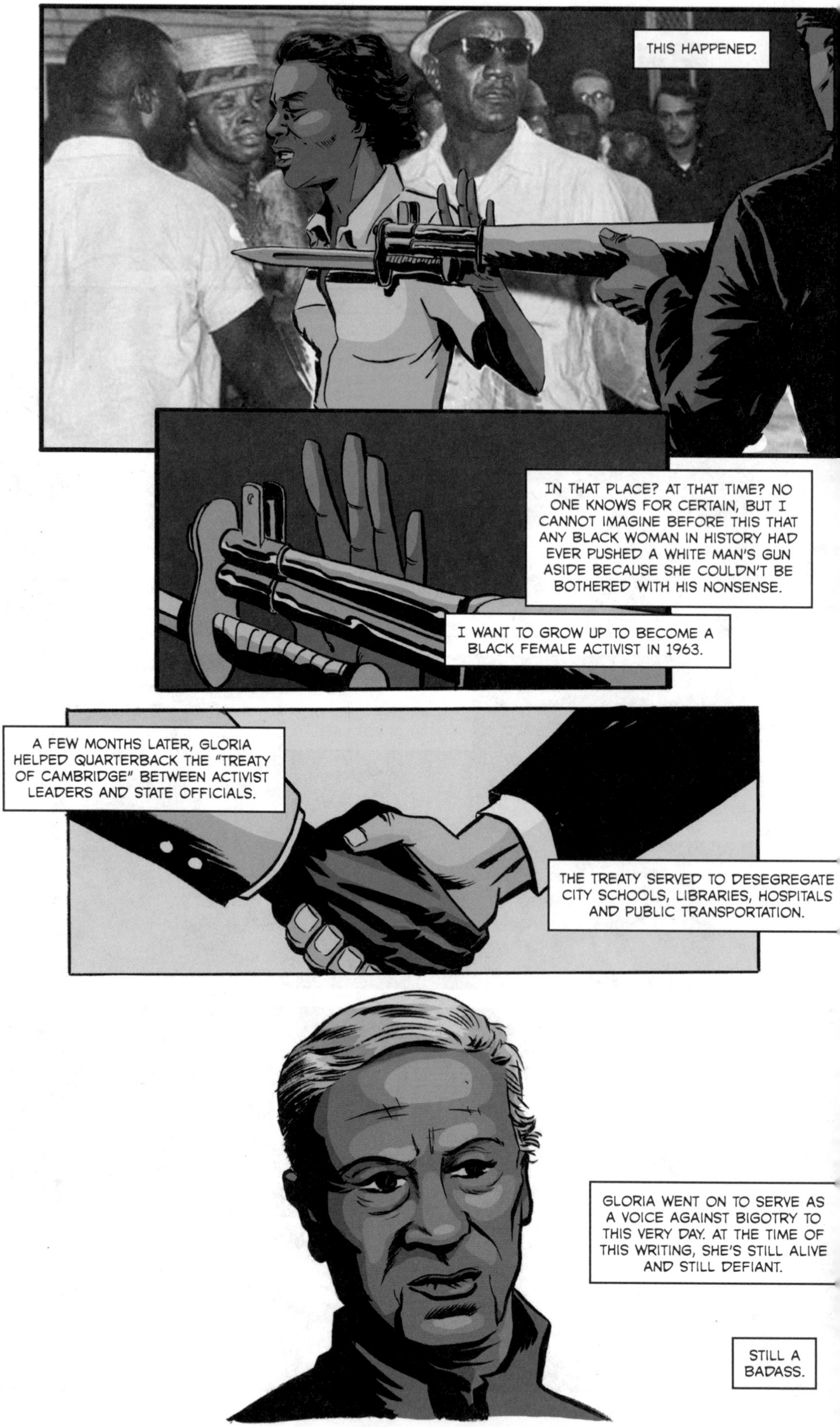
THIS HAPPENED.
IN THAT PLACE? AT THAT TIME? NO ONE KNOWS FOR CERTAIN, BUT I CANNOT IMAGINE BEFORE THIS THAT ANY BLACK WOMAN IN HISTORY HAD EVER PUSHED A WHITE MAN'S GUN ASIDE BECAUSE SHE COULDN'T BE BOTHERED WITH HIS NONSENSE.
I WANT TO GROW UP TO BECOME A BLACK FEMALE ACTIVIST IN 1963.
A FEW MONTHS LATER, GLORIA HELPED QUARTERBACK THE "TREATY OF CAMBRIDGE" BETWEEN ACTIVIST LEADERS AND STATE OFFICIALS.
THE TREATY SERVED TO DESEGREGATE CITY SCHOOLS, LIBRARIES, HOSPITALS AND PUBLIC TRANSPORTATION.
GLORIA WENT ON TO SERVE AS A VOICE AGAINST BIGOTRY TO THIS VERY DAY. AT THE TIME OF THIS WRITING, SHE'S STILL ALIVE AND STILL DEFIANT.
STILL A BADASS.

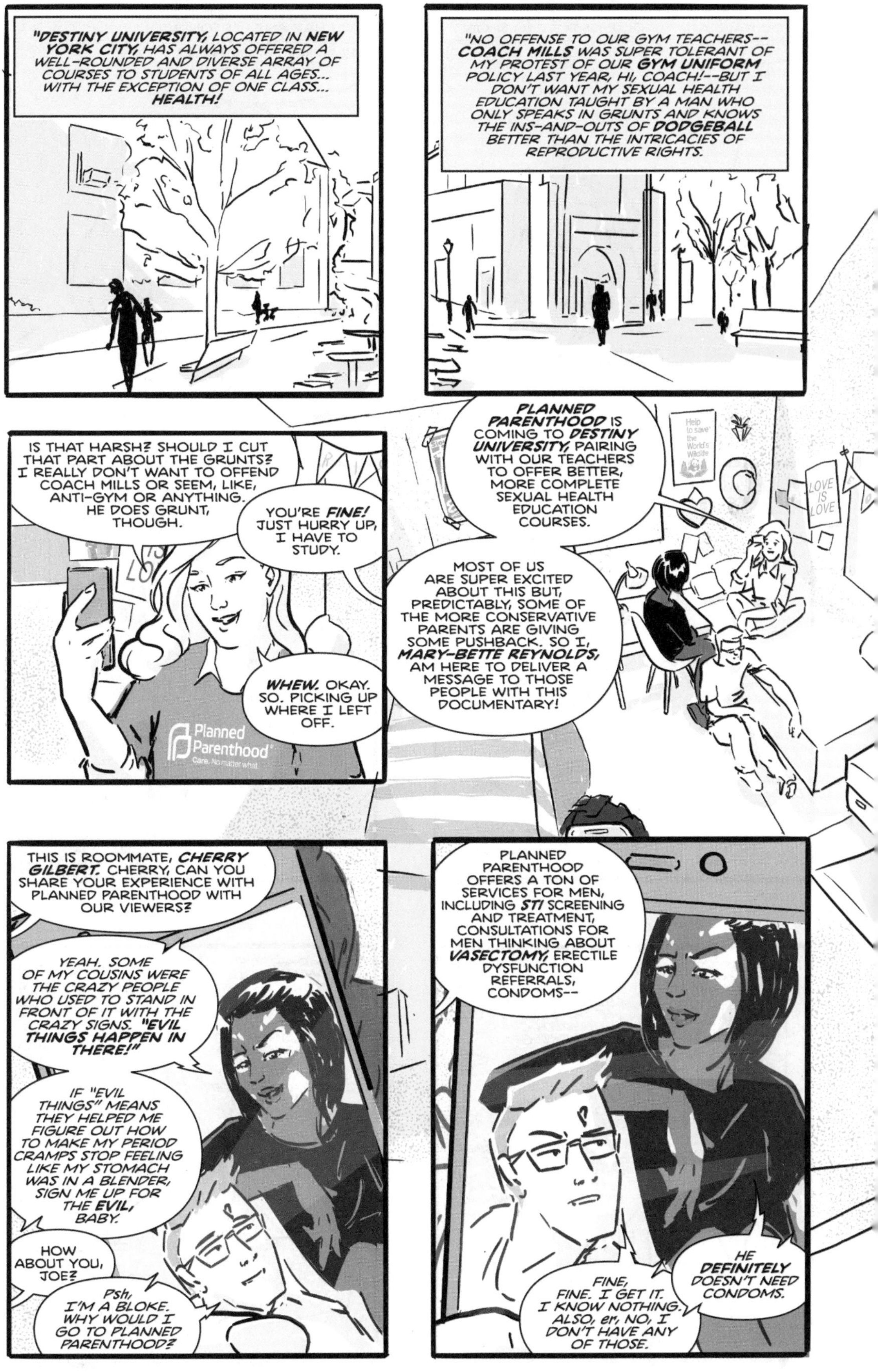
"DESTINY UNIVERSITY, LOCATED IN NEW YORK CITY, HAS ALWAYS OFFERED A WELL-ROUNDED AND DIVERSE ARRAY OF COURSES TO STUDENTS OF ALL AGES... WITH THE EXCEPTION OF ONE CLASS... HEALTH!
"NO OFFENSE TO OUR GYM TEACHERS--COACH MILLS WAS SUPER TOLERANT OF MY PROTEST OF OUR GYM UNIFORM POLICY LAST YEAR, HI, COACH!--BUT I DON'T WANT MY SEXUAL HEALTH EDUCATION TAUGHT BY A MAN WHO ONLY SPEAKS IN GRUNTS AND KNOWS THE INS-AND-OUTS OF DODGEBALL BETTER THAN THE INTRICACIES OF REPRODUCTIVE RIGHTS.
IS THAT HARSH? SHOULD I CUT THAT PART ABOUT THE GRUNTS? I REALLY DON'T WANT TO OFFEND COACH MILLS OR SEEM, LIKE, ANTI-GYM OR ANYTHING. HE DOES GRUNT, THOUGH.
YOU'RE FINE! JUST HURRY UP, I HAVE TO STUDY.
WHEW. OKAY. SO. PICKING UP WHERE I LEFT OFF.
Planned Parenthood
Care. No matter what.
PLANNED PARENTHOOD IS COMING TO DESTINY UNIVERSITY, PAIRING WITH OUR TEACHERS TO OFFER BETTER, MORE COMPLETE SEXUAL HEALTH EDUCATION COURSES.
Help to save the World's Wildlife
LOVE IS LOVE
MOST OF US ARE SUPER EXCITED ABOUT THIS BUT, PREDICTABLY, SOME OF THE MORE CONSERVATIVE PARENTS ARE GIVING SOME PUSHBACK. SO I, MARY-BETTE REYNOLDS, AM HERE TO DELIVER A MESSAGE TO THOSE PEOPLE WITH THIS DOCUMENTARY!
THIS IS ROOMMATE, CHERRY GILBERT. CHERRY, CAN YOU SHARE YOUR EXPERIENCE WITH PLANNED PARENTHOOD WITH OUR VIEWERS?
YEAH. SOME OF MY COUSINS WERE THE CRAZY PEOPLE WHO USED TO STAND IN FRONT OF IT WITH THE CRAZY SIGNS. "EVIL THINGS HAPPEN IN THERE!"
IF "EVIL THINGS" MEANS THEY HELPED ME FIGURE OUT HOW TO MAKE MY PERIOD CRAMPS STOP FEELING LIKE MY STOMACH WAS IN A BLENDER, SIGN ME UP FOR THE EVIL, BABY.
HOW ABOUT YOU, JOE?
Psh, I'M A BLOKE. WHY WOULD I GO TO PLANNED PARENTHOOD?
PLANNED PARENTHOOD OFFERS A TON OF SERVICES FOR MEN, INCLUDING STI SCREENING AND TREATMENT, CONSULTATIONS FOR MEN THINKING ABOUT VASECTOMY, ERECTILE DYSFUNCTION REFERRALS, CONDOMS--
FINE, FINE. I GET IT. I KNOW NOTHING. ALSO, er, NO, I DON'T HAVE ANY OF THOSE.
HE DEFINITELY DOESN'T NEED CONDOMS.

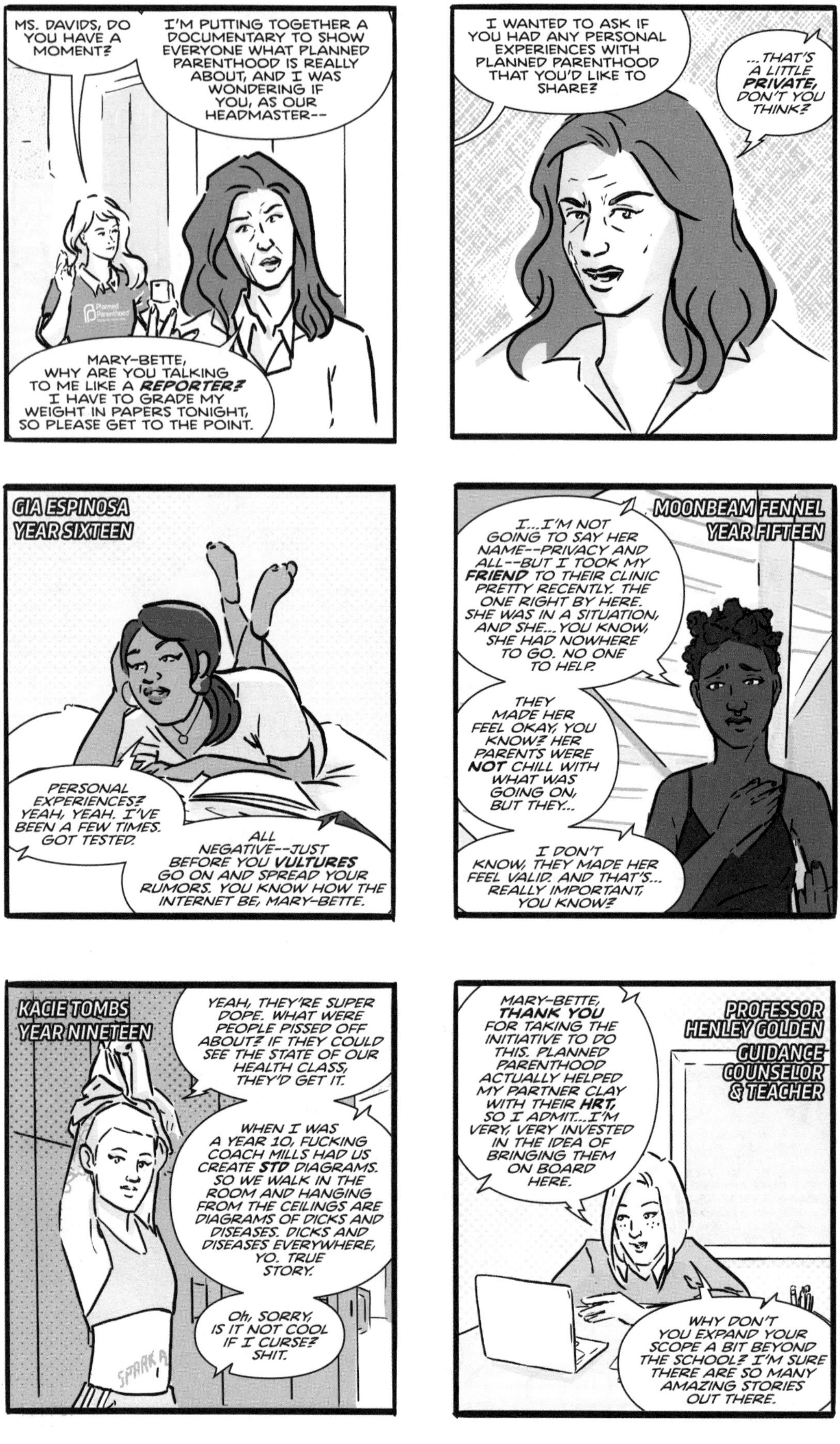
MS. DAVIDS, DO YOU HAVE A MOMENT?
I'M PUTTING TOGETHER A DOCUMENTARY TO SHOW EVERYONE WHAT PLANNED PARENTHOOD IS REALLY ABOUT, AND I WAS WONDERING IF YOU, AS OUR HEADMASTER--
MARY-BETTE, WHY ARE YOU TALKING TO ME LIKE A ***REPORTER?*** I HAVE TO GRADE MY WEIGHT IN PAPERS TONIGHT, SO PLEASE GET TO THE POINT.
I WANTED TO ASK IF YOU HAD ANY PERSONAL EXPERIENCES WITH PLANNED PARENTHOOD THAT YOU'D LIKE TO SHARE?
...THAT'S A LITTLE ***PRIVATE,*** DON'T YOU THINK?
GIA ESPINOSA
YEAR SIXTEEN
PERSONAL EXPERIENCES? YEAH, YEAH. I'VE BEEN A FEW TIMES. GOT TESTED.
ALL NEGATIVE--JUST BEFORE YOU ***VULTURES*** GO ON AND SPREAD YOUR RUMORS. YOU KNOW HOW THE INTERNET BE, MARY-BETTE.
MOONBEAM FENNEL
YEAR FIFTEEN
I...I'M NOT GOING TO SAY HER NAME--PRIVACY AND ALL--BUT I TOOK MY ***FRIEND*** TO THEIR CLINIC PRETTY RECENTLY. THE ONE RIGHT BY HERE. SHE WAS IN A SITUATION, AND SHE...YOU KNOW, SHE HAD NOWHERE TO GO. NO ONE TO HELP.
THEY MADE HER FEEL OKAY, YOU KNOW? HER PARENTS WERE ***NOT*** CHILL WITH WHAT WAS GOING ON, BUT THEY...
I DON'T KNOW, THEY MADE HER FEEL VALID. AND THAT'S... REALLY IMPORTANT, YOU KNOW?
KACIE TOMBS
YEAR NINETEEN
YEAH, THEY'RE SUPER DOPE. WHAT WERE PEOPLE PISSED OFF ABOUT? IF THEY COULD SEE THE STATE OF OUR HEALTH CLASS, THEY'D GET IT.
WHEN I WAS A YEAR 10, FUCKING COACH MILLS HAD US CREATE ***STD*** DIAGRAMS. SO WE WALK IN THE ROOM AND HANGING FROM THE CEILINGS ARE DIAGRAMS OF DICKS AND DISEASES. DICKS AND DISEASES EVERYWHERE, YO. TRUE STORY.
Oh, SORRY, IS IT NOT COOL IF I CURSE? SHIT.
PROFESSOR HENLEY GOLDEN
GUIDANCE COUNSELOR & TEACHER
MARY-BETTE, ***THANK YOU*** FOR TAKING THE INITIATIVE TO DO THIS. PLANNED PARENTHOOD ACTUALLY HELPED MY PARTNER CLAY WITH THEIR ***HRT,*** SO I ADMIT...I'M VERY, VERY INVESTED IN THE IDEA OF BRINGING THEM ON BOARD HERE.
WHY DON'T YOU EXPAND YOUR SCOPE A BIT BEYOND THE SCHOOL? I'M SURE THERE ARE SO MANY AMAZING STORIES OUT THERE.

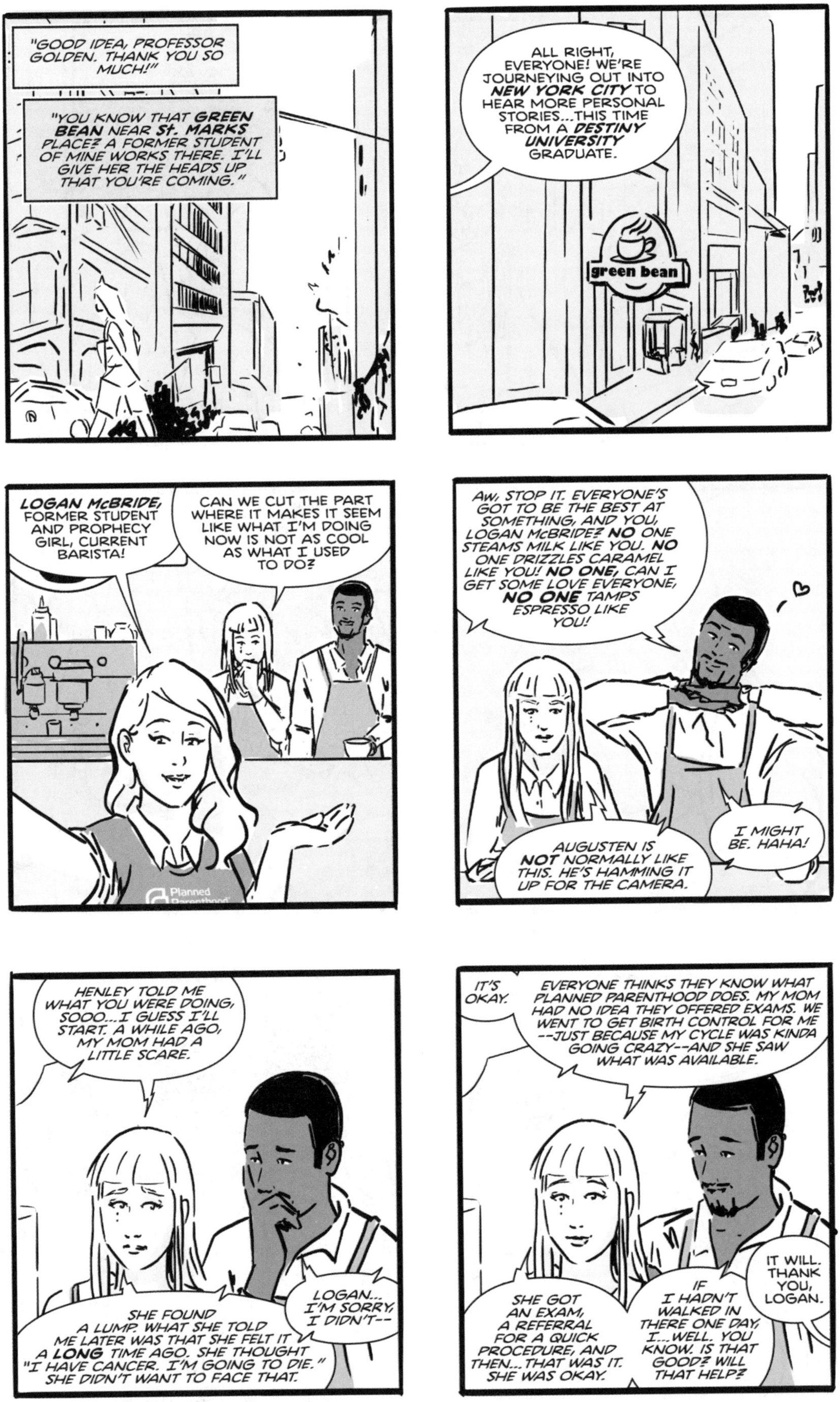
"GOOD IDEA, PROFESSOR GOLDEN. THANK YOU SO MUCH!"
"YOU KNOW THAT GREEN BEAN NEAR St. MARKS PLACE? A FORMER STUDENT OF MINE WORKS THERE. I'LL GIVE HER THE HEADS UP THAT YOU'RE COMING."
ALL RIGHT, EVERYONE! WE'RE JOURNEYING OUT INTO NEW YORK CITY TO HEAR MORE PERSONAL STORIES...THIS TIME FROM A DESTINY UNIVERSITY GRADUATE.
green bean
LOGAN McBRIDE, FORMER STUDENT AND PROPHECY GIRL, CURRENT BARISTA!
CAN WE CUT THE PART WHERE IT MAKES IT SEEM LIKE WHAT I'M DOING NOW IS NOT AS COOL AS WHAT I USED TO DO?
Planned Parenthood
AW, STOP IT. EVERYONE'S GOT TO BE THE BEST AT SOMETHING, AND YOU, LOGAN McBRIDE? NO ONE STEAMS MILK LIKE YOU. NO ONE DRIZZLES CARAMEL LIKE YOU! NO ONE, CAN I GET SOME LOVE EVERYONE, NO ONE TAMPS ESPRESSO LIKE YOU!
AUGUSTEN IS NOT NORMALLY LIKE THIS. HE'S HAMMING IT UP FOR THE CAMERA.
I MIGHT BE. HAHA!
HENLEY TOLD ME WHAT YOU WERE DOING, SOOO...I GUESS I'LL START. A WHILE AGO, MY MOM HAD A LITTLE SCARE.
SHE FOUND A LUMP. WHAT SHE TOLD ME LATER WAS THAT SHE FELT IT A LONG TIME AGO. SHE THOUGHT "I HAVE CANCER. I'M GOING TO DIE." SHE DIDN'T WANT TO FACE THAT.
LOGAN... I'M SORRY, I DIDN'T--
IT'S OKAY.
EVERYONE THINKS THEY KNOW WHAT PLANNED PARENTHOOD DOES. MY MOM HAD NO IDEA THEY OFFERED EXAMS. WE WENT TO GET BIRTH CONTROL FOR ME --JUST BECAUSE MY CYCLE WAS KINDA GOING CRAZY--AND SHE SAW WHAT WAS AVAILABLE.
SHE GOT AN EXAM, A REFERRAL FOR A QUICK PROCEDURE, AND THEN...THAT WAS IT. SHE WAS OKAY.
IF I HADN'T WALKED IN THERE ONE DAY, I...WELL. YOU KNOW. IS THAT GOOD? WILL THAT HELP?
IT WILL. THANK YOU, LOGAN.

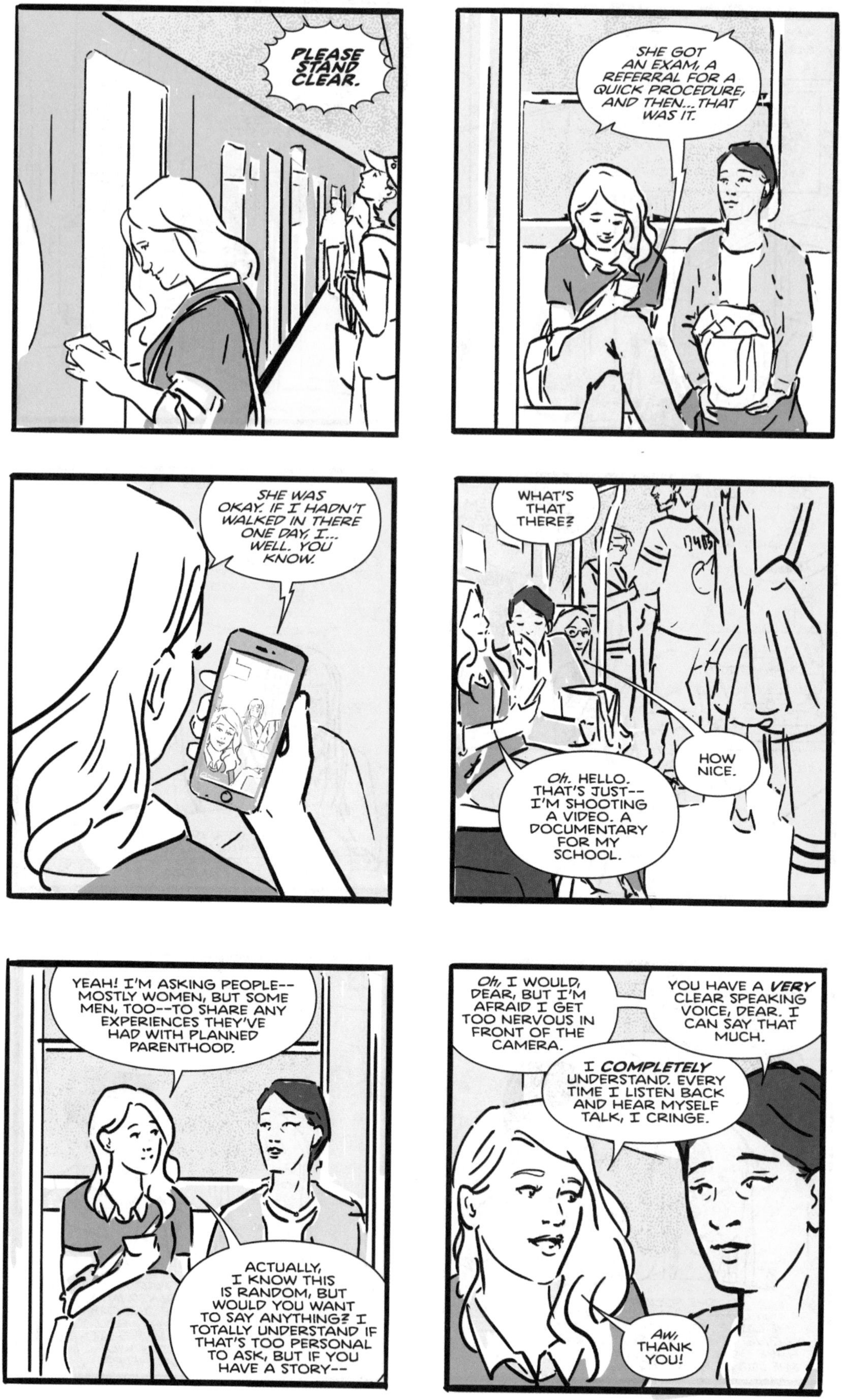
PLEASE STAND CLEAR.
SHE GOT AN EXAM, A REFERRAL FOR A QUICK PROCEDURE, AND THEN... THAT WAS IT.
SHE WAS OKAY. IF I HADN'T WALKED IN THERE ONE DAY, I... WELL. YOU KNOW.
WHAT'S THAT THERE?
Oh. HELLO. THAT'S JUST-- I'M SHOOTING A VIDEO. A DOCUMENTARY FOR MY SCHOOL.
HOW NICE.
YEAH! I'M ASKING PEOPLE-- MOSTLY WOMEN, BUT SOME MEN, TOO--TO SHARE ANY EXPERIENCES THEY'VE HAD WITH PLANNED PARENTHOOD.
ACTUALLY, I KNOW THIS IS RANDOM, BUT WOULD YOU WANT TO SAY ANYTHING? I TOTALLY UNDERSTAND IF THAT'S TOO PERSONAL TO ASK, BUT IF YOU HAVE A STORY--
Oh, I WOULD, DEAR, BUT I'M AFRAID I GET TOO NERVOUS IN FRONT OF THE CAMERA.
I **COMPLETELY** UNDERSTAND. EVERY TIME I LISTEN BACK AND HEAR MYSELF TALK, I CRINGE.
YOU HAVE A **VERY** CLEAR SPEAKING VOICE, DEAR. I CAN SAY THAT MUCH.
Aw, THANK YOU!

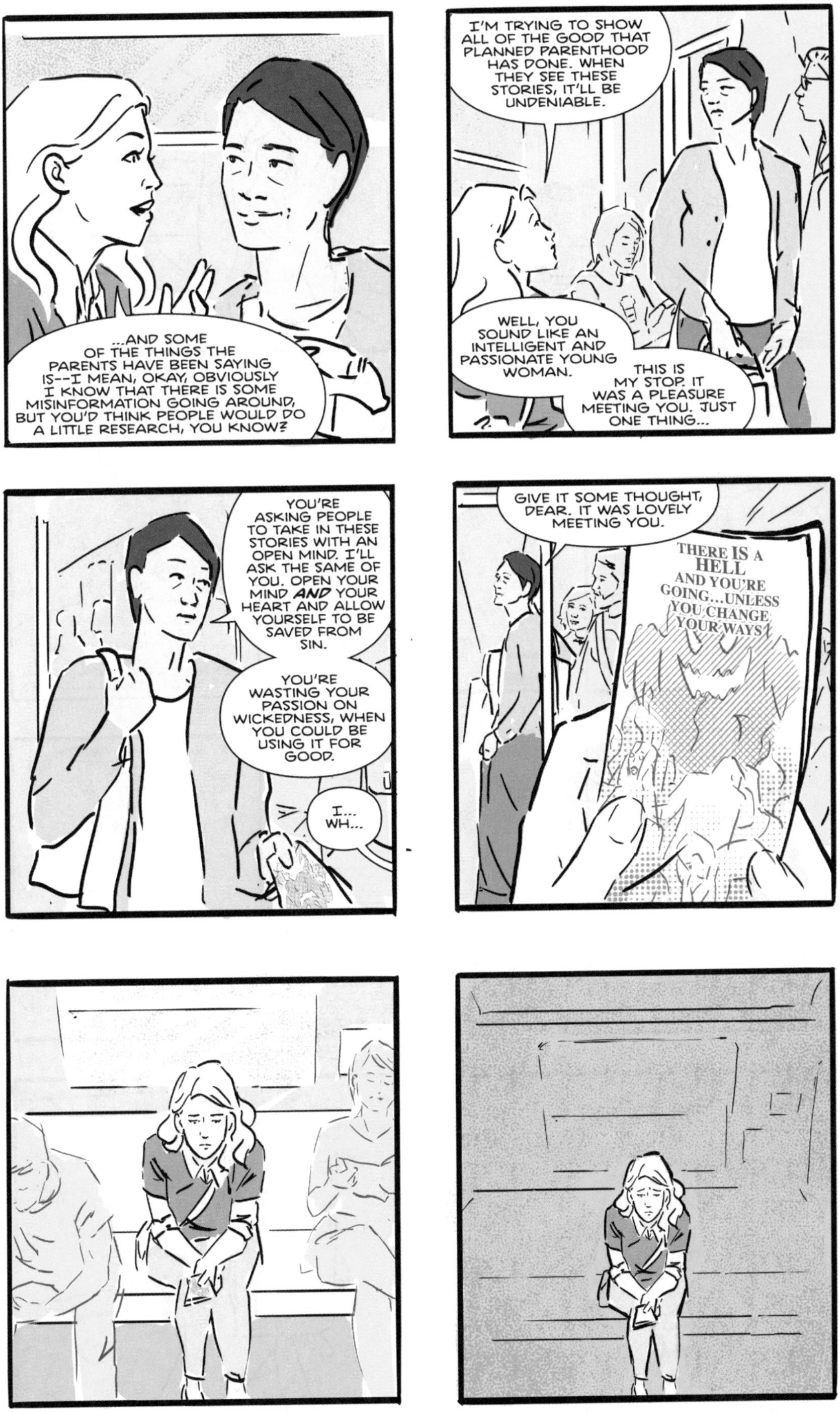
...AND SOME OF THE THINGS THE PARENTS HAVE BEEN SAYING IS--I MEAN, OKAY, OBVIOUSLY I KNOW THAT THERE IS SOME MISINFORMATION GOING AROUND, BUT YOU'D THINK PEOPLE WOULD DO A LITTLE RESEARCH, YOU KNOW?
I'M TRYING TO SHOW ALL OF THE GOOD THAT PLANNED PARENTHOOD HAS DONE. WHEN THEY SEE THESE STORIES, IT'LL BE UNDENIABLE.
WELL, YOU SOUND LIKE AN INTELLIGENT AND PASSIONATE YOUNG WOMAN.
THIS IS MY STOP. IT WAS A PLEASURE MEETING YOU. JUST ONE THING...
YOU'RE ASKING PEOPLE TO TAKE IN THESE STORIES WITH AN OPEN MIND. I'LL ASK THE SAME OF YOU. OPEN YOUR MIND AND YOUR HEART AND ALLOW YOURSELF TO BE SAVED FROM SIN.
YOU'RE WASTING YOUR PASSION ON WICKEDNESS, WHEN YOU COULD BE USING IT FOR GOOD.
I... WH...
GIVE IT SOME THOUGHT, DEAR. IT WAS LOVELY MEETING YOU.
THERE IS A HELL AND YOU'RE GOING...UNLESS YOU CHANGE YOUR WAYS!

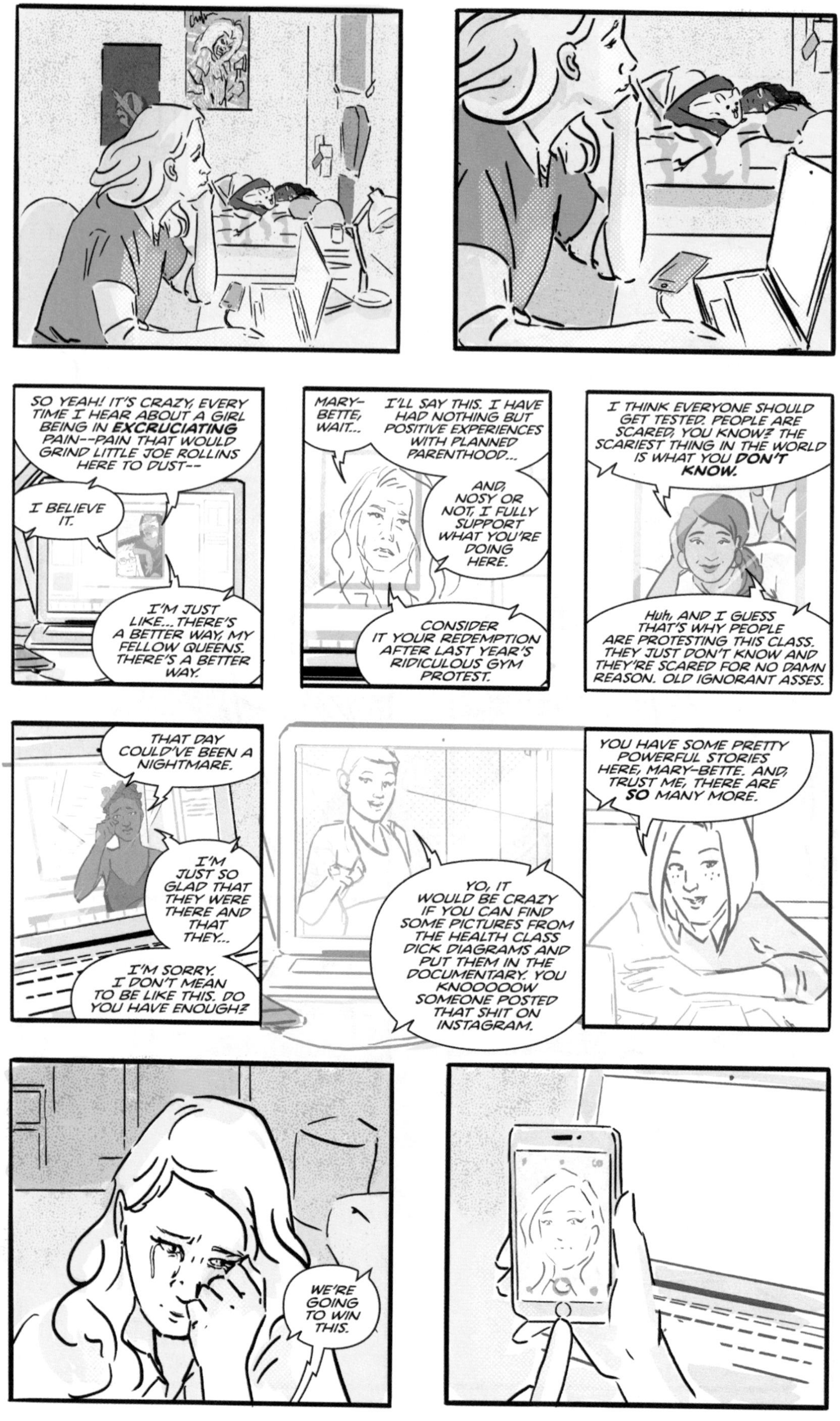

SO YEAH! IT'S CRAZY, EVERY TIME I HEAR ABOUT A GIRL BEING IN **EXCRUCIATING** PAIN--PAIN THAT WOULD GRIND LITTLE JOE ROLLINS HERE TO DUST--
I BELIEVE IT.
I'M JUST LIKE... THERE'S A BETTER WAY, MY FELLOW QUEENS. THERE'S A BETTER WAY.
MARY-BETTE, WAIT...
I'LL SAY THIS. I HAVE HAD NOTHING BUT POSITIVE EXPERIENCES WITH PLANNED PARENTHOOD...
AND, NOSY OR NOT, I FULLY SUPPORT WHAT YOU'RE DOING HERE.
CONSIDER IT YOUR REDEMPTION AFTER LAST YEAR'S RIDICULOUS GYM PROTEST.
I THINK EVERYONE SHOULD GET TESTED. PEOPLE ARE SCARED, YOU KNOW? THE SCARIEST THING IN THE WORLD IS WHAT YOU **DON'T KNOW.**
Huh, AND I GUESS THAT'S WHY PEOPLE ARE PROTESTING THIS CLASS. THEY JUST DON'T KNOW AND THEY'RE SCARED FOR NO DAMN REASON. OLD IGNORANT ASSES.
THAT DAY COULD'VE BEEN A NIGHTMARE.
I'M JUST SO GLAD THAT THEY WERE THERE AND THAT THEY...
I'M SORRY. I DON'T MEAN TO BE LIKE THIS. DO YOU HAVE ENOUGH?
YO, IT WOULD BE CRAZY IF YOU CAN FIND SOME PICTURES FROM THE HEALTH CLASS DICK DIAGRAMS AND PUT THEM IN THE DOCUMENTARY. YOU KNOOOOOW SOMEONE POSTED THAT SHIT ON INSTAGRAM.
YOU HAVE SOME PRETTY POWERFUL STORIES HERE, MARY-BETTE. AND, TRUST ME, THERE ARE **SO** MANY MORE.
WE'RE GOING TO WIN THIS.

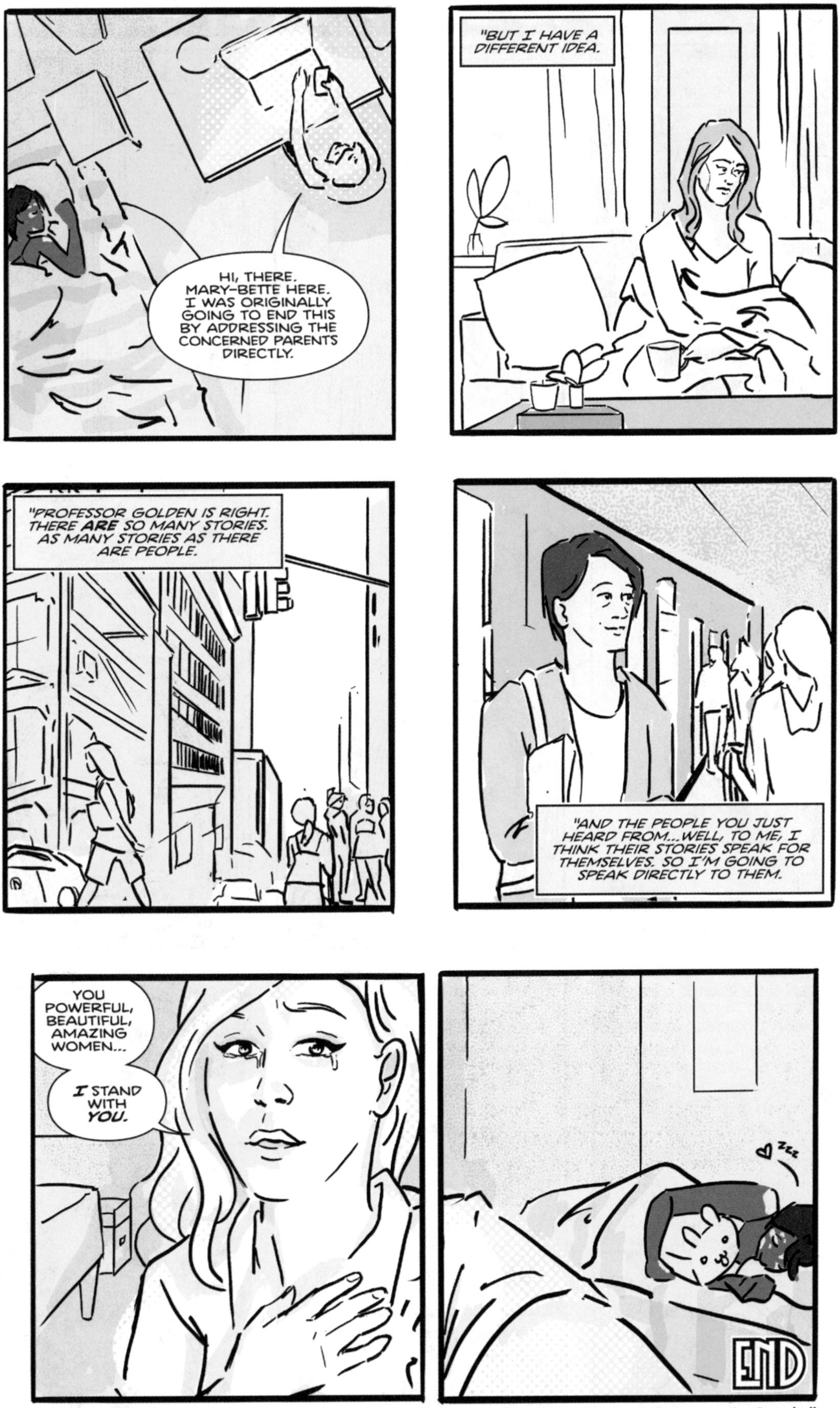

HI, THERE. MARY-BETTE HERE. I WAS ORIGINALLY GOING TO END THIS BY ADDRESSING THE CONCERNED PARENTS DIRECTLY.
"BUT I HAVE A DIFFERENT IDEA.
"PROFESSOR GOLDEN IS RIGHT. THERE ARE SO MANY STORIES. AS MANY STORIES AS THERE ARE PEOPLE.
"AND THE PEOPLE YOU JUST HEARD FROM...WELL, TO ME, I THINK THEIR STORIES SPEAK FOR THEMSELVES. SO I'M GOING TO SPEAK DIRECTLY TO THEM.
YOU POWERFUL, BEAUTIFUL, AMAZING WOMEN...
I STAND WITH YOU.
END

"I STAND WITH YOU"
A DESTINY, NY STORY

Story: **Pat Shand** Art: **Liana Kangas** Letters: **Jim Campbell**
DESTINY, NY CREATED BY PAT SHAND & MANUEL PREITANO

IN DEFENSE OF SELF

Written by KEITH R.A. DeCANDIDO
Art and letters by TOM DALY

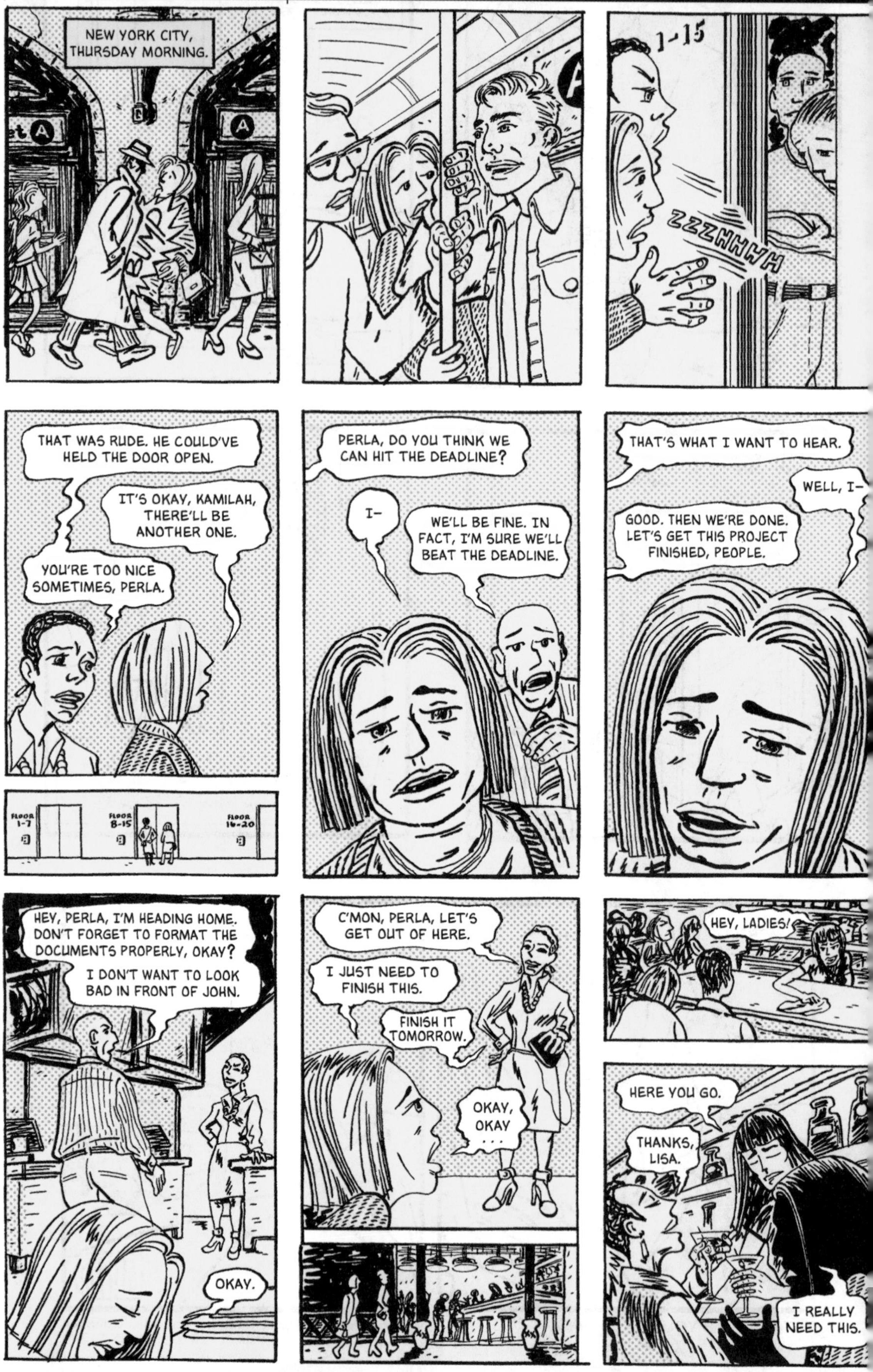
NEW YORK CITY, THURSDAY MORNING.
BUMP
1-15
ZZZHHHH
THAT WAS RUDE. HE COULD'VE HELD THE DOOR OPEN.
IT'S OKAY, KAMILAH, THERE'LL BE ANOTHER ONE.
YOU'RE TOO NICE SOMETIMES, PERLA.
FLOOR 1-7
FLOOR 8-15
FLOOR 16-20
PERLA, DO YOU THINK WE CAN HIT THE DEADLINE?
I-
WE'LL BE FINE. IN FACT, I'M SURE WE'LL BEAT THE DEADLINE.
THAT'S WHAT I WANT TO HEAR.
WELL, I-
GOOD. THEN WE'RE DONE. LET'S GET THIS PROJECT FINISHED, PEOPLE.
HEY, PERLA, I'M HEADING HOME. DON'T FORGET TO FORMAT THE DOCUMENTS PROPERLY, OKAY?
I DON'T WANT TO LOOK BAD IN FRONT OF JOHN.
OKAY.
C'MON, PERLA, LET'S GET OUT OF HERE.
I JUST NEED TO FINISH THIS.
FINISH IT TOMORROW.
OKAY, OKAY . . .
HEY, LADIES!
HERE YOU GO.
THANKS, LISA.
I REALLY NEED THIS.

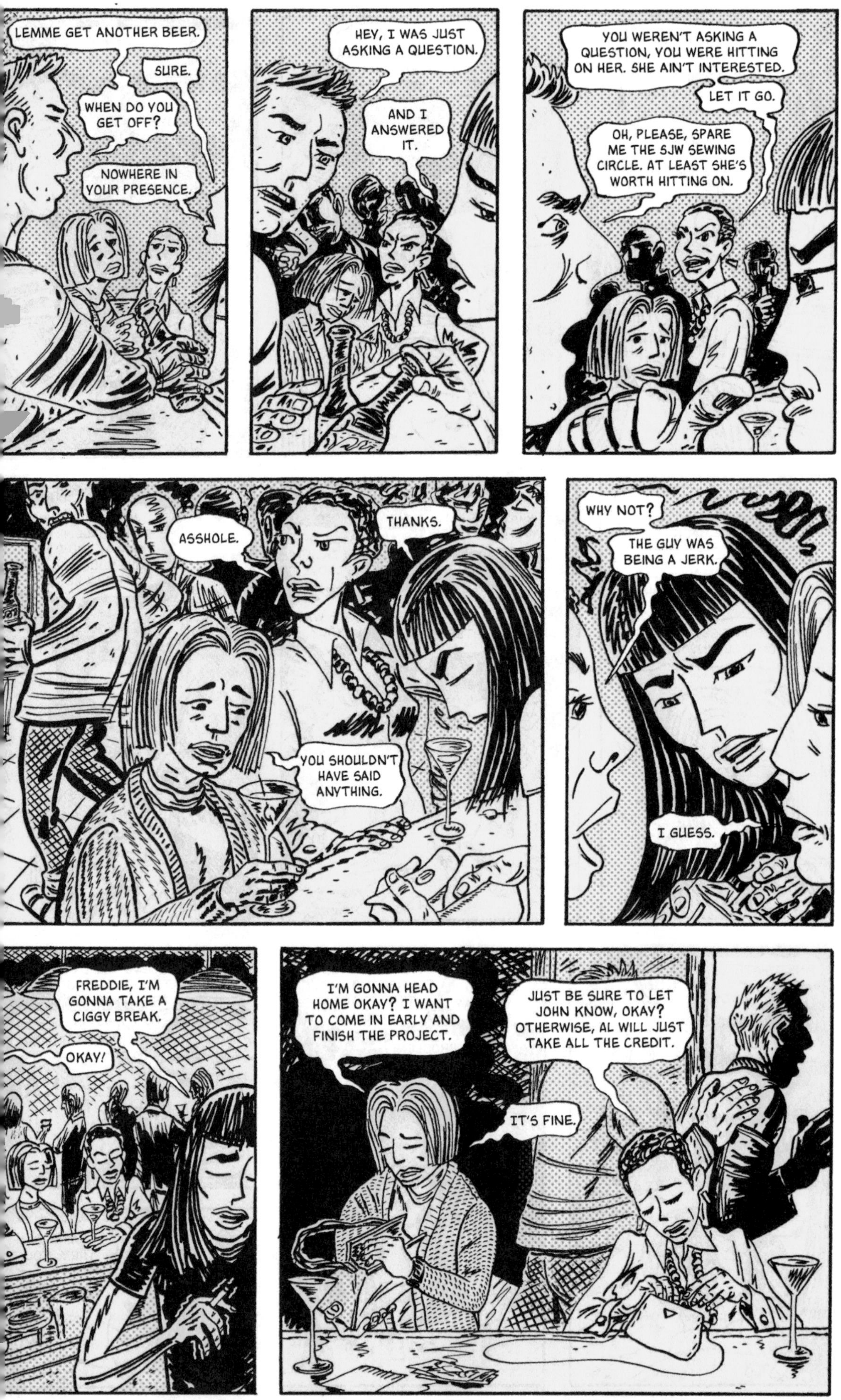
LEMME GET ANOTHER BEER.
SURE.
WHEN DO YOU GET OFF?
NOWHERE IN YOUR PRESENCE.
HEY, I WAS JUST ASKING A QUESTION.
AND I ANSWERED IT.
YOU WEREN'T ASKING A QUESTION, YOU WERE HITTING ON HER. SHE AIN'T INTERESTED.
LET IT GO.
OH, PLEASE, SPARE ME THE SJW SEWING CIRCLE. AT LEAST SHE'S WORTH HITTING ON.
ASSHOLE.
THANKS.
YOU SHOULDN'T HAVE SAID ANYTHING.
WHY NOT?
THE GUY WAS BEING A JERK.
I GUESS.
FREDDIE, I'M GONNA TAKE A CIGGY BREAK.
OKAY!
I'M GONNA HEAD HOME OKAY? I WANT TO COME IN EARLY AND FINISH THE PROJECT.
JUST BE SURE TO LET JOHN KNOW, OKAY? OTHERWISE, AL WILL JUST TAKE ALL THE CREDIT.
IT'S FINE.

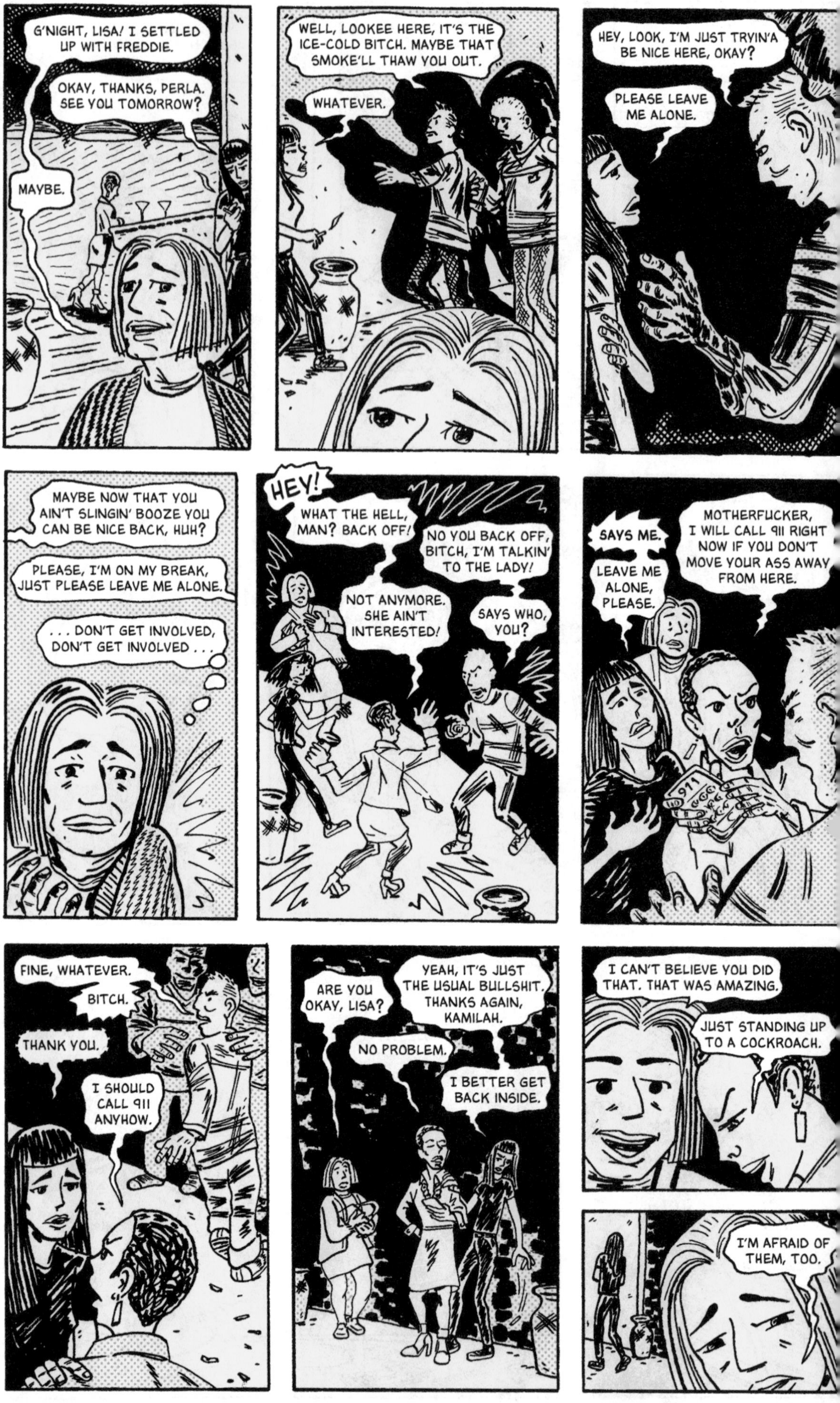
G'NIGHT, LISA! I SETTLED UP WITH FREDDIE.
OKAY, THANKS, PERLA. SEE YOU TOMORROW?
MAYBE.
WELL, LOOKEE HERE, IT'S THE ICE-COLD BITCH. MAYBE THAT SMOKE'LL THAW YOU OUT.
WHATEVER.
HEY, LOOK, I'M JUST TRYIN'A BE NICE HERE, OKAY?
PLEASE LEAVE ME ALONE.
MAYBE NOW THAT YOU AIN'T SLINGIN' BOOZE YOU CAN BE NICE BACK, HUH?
PLEASE, I'M ON MY BREAK, JUST PLEASE LEAVE ME ALONE.
. . . DON'T GET INVOLVED, DON'T GET INVOLVED . . .
HEY!
WHAT THE HELL, MAN? BACK OFF!
NO YOU BACK OFF, BITCH, I'M TALKIN' TO THE LADY!
NOT ANYMORE. SHE AIN'T INTERESTED!
SAYS WHO, YOU?
SAYS ME.
LEAVE ME ALONE, PLEASE.
MOTHERFUCKER, I WILL CALL 911 RIGHT NOW IF YOU DON'T MOVE YOUR ASS AWAY FROM HERE.
911
FINE, WHATEVER.
BITCH.
THANK YOU.
I SHOULD CALL 911 ANYHOW.
ARE YOU OKAY, LISA?
YEAH, IT'S JUST THE USUAL BULLSHIT. THANKS AGAIN, KAMILAH.
NO PROBLEM.
I BETTER GET BACK INSIDE.
I CAN'T BELIEVE YOU DID THAT. THAT WAS AMAZING.
JUST STANDING UP TO A COCKROACH.
I'M AFRAID OF THEM, TOO.

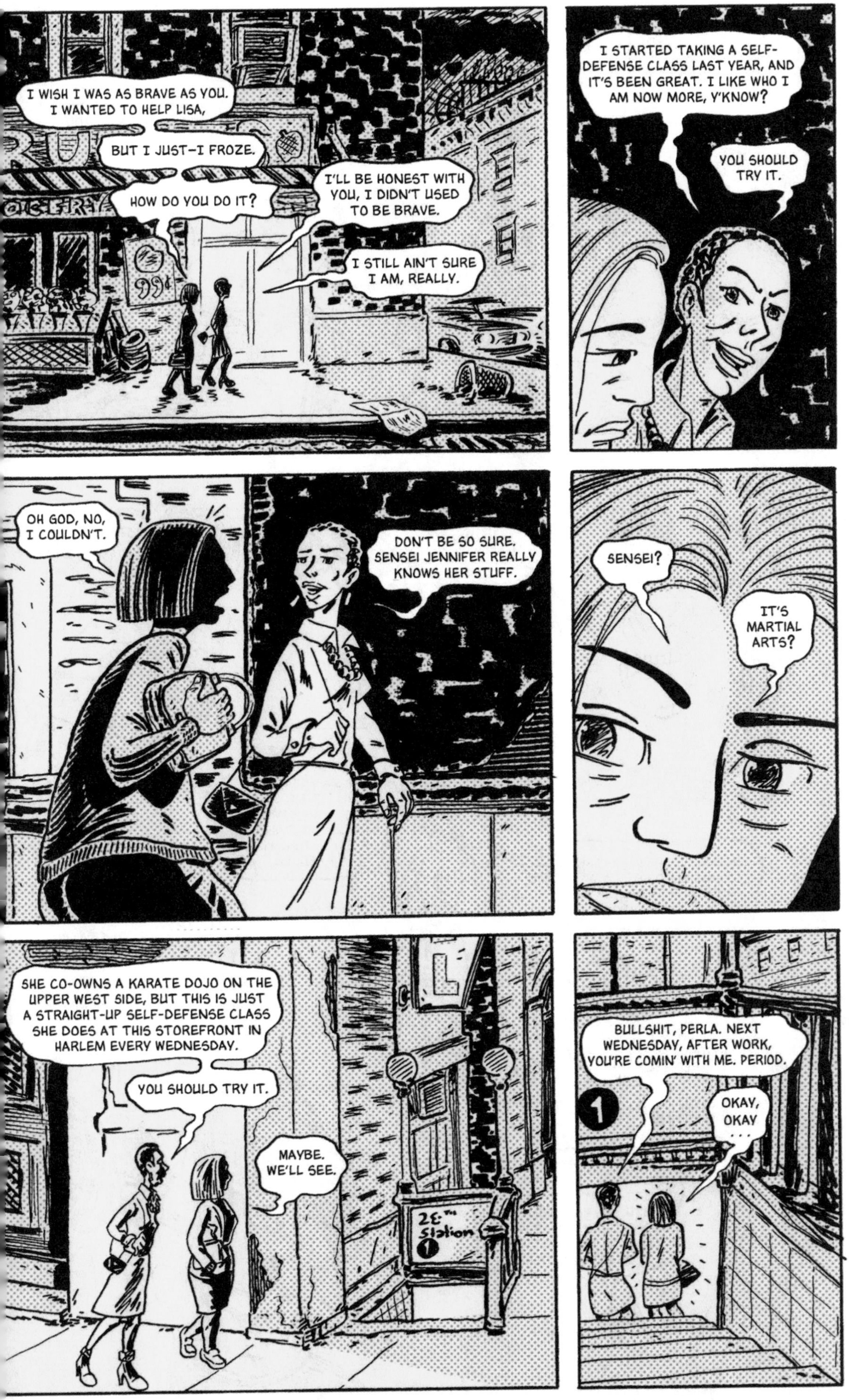
I WISH I WAS AS BRAVE AS YOU. I WANTED TO HELP LISA,
BUT I JUST—I FROZE.
HOW DO YOU DO IT?
I'LL BE HONEST WITH YOU, I DIDN'T USED TO BE BRAVE.
I STILL AIN'T SURE I AM, REALLY.
99¢
I STARTED TAKING A SELF-DEFENSE CLASS LAST YEAR, AND IT'S BEEN GREAT. I LIKE WHO I AM NOW MORE, Y'KNOW?
YOU SHOULD TRY IT.
OH GOD, NO, I COULDN'T.
DON'T BE SO SURE. SENSEI JENNIFER REALLY KNOWS HER STUFF.
SENSEI?
IT'S MARTIAL ARTS?
SHE CO-OWNS A KARATE DOJO ON THE UPPER WEST SIDE, BUT THIS IS JUST A STRAIGHT-UP SELF-DEFENSE CLASS SHE DOES AT THIS STOREFRONT IN HARLEM EVERY WEDNESDAY.
YOU SHOULD TRY IT.
MAYBE. WE'LL SEE.
L
28TH Station
1
BULLSHIT, PERLA. NEXT WEDNESDAY, AFTER WORK, YOU'RE COMIN' WITH ME. PERIOD.
OKAY, OKAY . . .

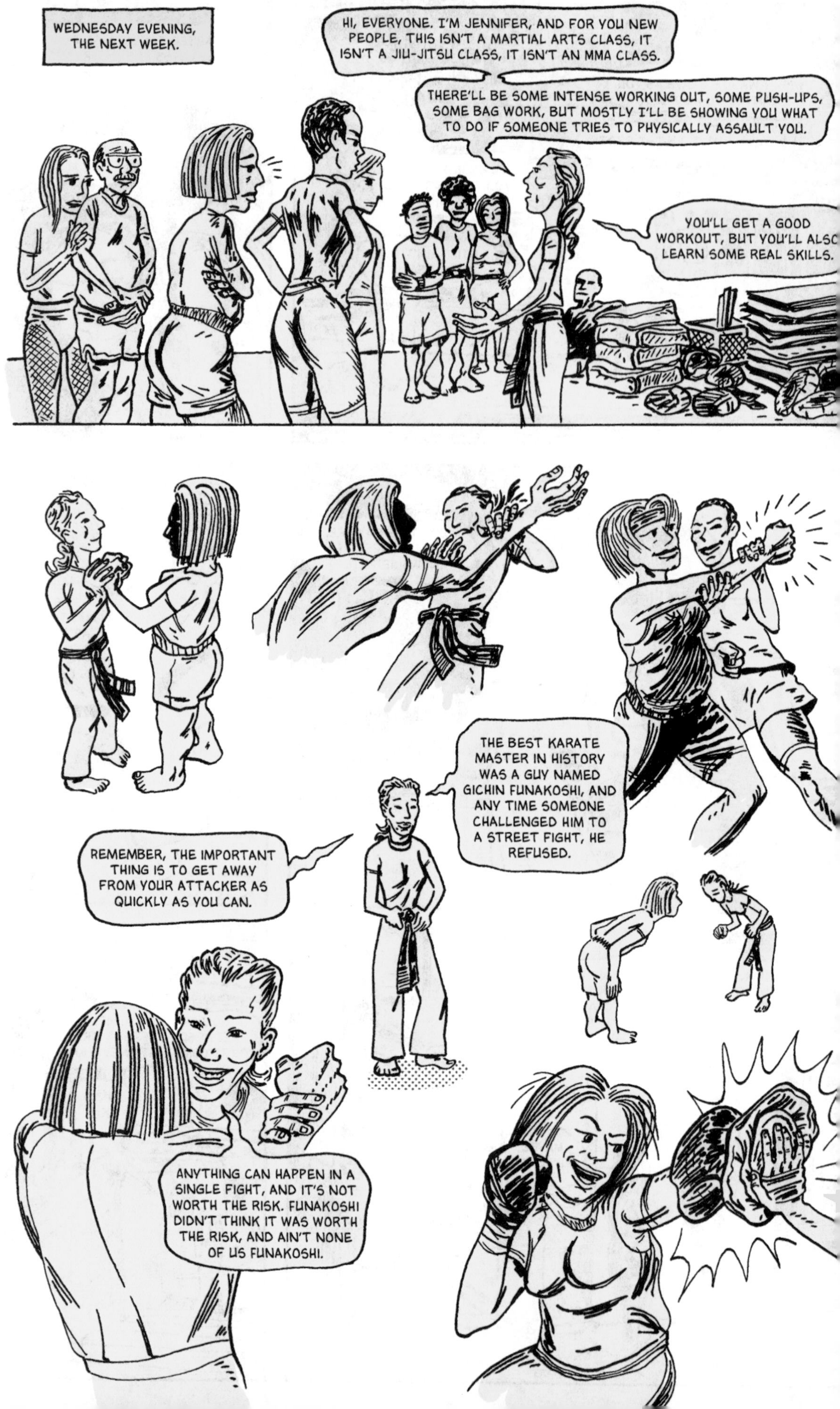
WEDNESDAY EVENING, THE NEXT WEEK.
HI, EVERYONE. I'M JENNIFER, AND FOR YOU NEW PEOPLE, THIS ISN'T A MARTIAL ARTS CLASS, IT ISN'T A JIU-JITSU CLASS, IT ISN'T AN MMA CLASS.
THERE'LL BE SOME INTENSE WORKING OUT, SOME PUSH-UPS, SOME BAG WORK, BUT MOSTLY I'LL BE SHOWING YOU WHAT TO DO IF SOMEONE TRIES TO PHYSICALLY ASSAULT YOU.
YOU'LL GET A GOOD WORKOUT, BUT YOU'LL ALSO LEARN SOME REAL SKILLS.
THE BEST KARATE MASTER IN HISTORY WAS A GUY NAMED GICHIN FUNAKOSHI, AND ANY TIME SOMEONE CHALLENGED HIM TO A STREET FIGHT, HE REFUSED.
REMEMBER, THE IMPORTANT THING IS TO GET AWAY FROM YOUR ATTACKER AS QUICKLY AS YOU CAN.
ANYTHING CAN HAPPEN IN A SINGLE FIGHT, AND IT'S NOT WORTH THE RISK. FUNAKOSHI DIDN'T THINK IT WAS WORTH THE RISK, AND AIN'T NONE OF US FUNAKOSHI.

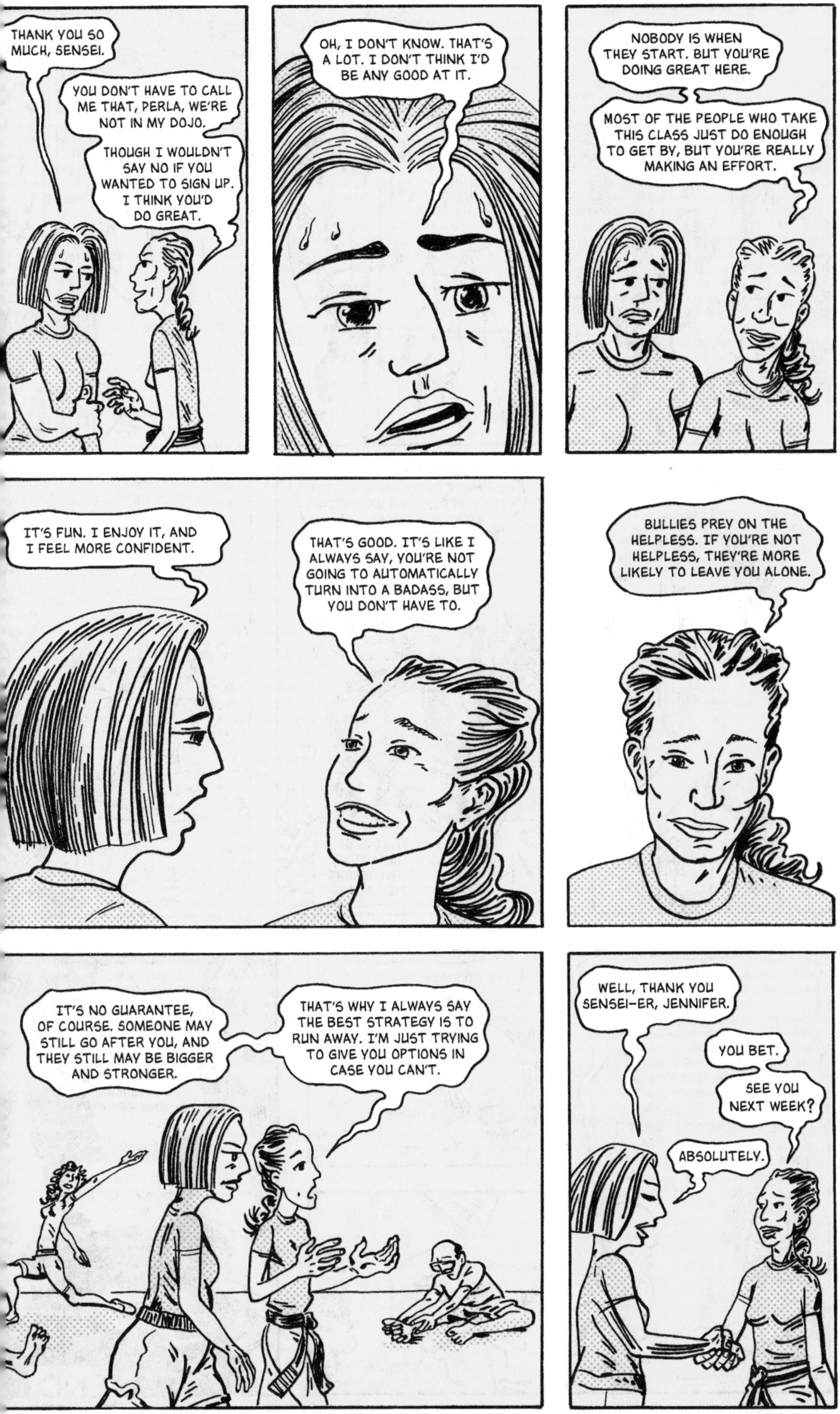

THANK YOU SO MUCH, SENSEI.
YOU DON'T HAVE TO CALL ME THAT, PERLA, WE'RE NOT IN MY DOJO.
THOUGH I WOULDN'T SAY NO IF YOU WANTED TO SIGN UP. I THINK YOU'D DO GREAT.
OH, I DON'T KNOW. THAT'S A LOT. I DON'T THINK I'D BE ANY GOOD AT IT.
NOBODY IS WHEN THEY START. BUT YOU'RE DOING GREAT HERE.
MOST OF THE PEOPLE WHO TAKE THIS CLASS JUST DO ENOUGH TO GET BY, BUT YOU'RE REALLY MAKING AN EFFORT.
IT'S FUN. I ENJOY IT, AND I FEEL MORE CONFIDENT.
THAT'S GOOD. IT'S LIKE I ALWAYS SAY, YOU'RE NOT GOING TO AUTOMATICALLY TURN INTO A BADASS, BUT YOU DON'T HAVE TO.
BULLIES PREY ON THE HELPLESS. IF YOU'RE NOT HELPLESS, THEY'RE MORE LIKELY TO LEAVE YOU ALONE.
IT'S NO GUARANTEE, OF COURSE. SOMEONE MAY STILL GO AFTER YOU, AND THEY STILL MAY BE BIGGER AND STRONGER.
THAT'S WHY I ALWAYS SAY THE BEST STRATEGY IS TO RUN AWAY. I'M JUST TRYING TO GIVE YOU OPTIONS IN CASE YOU CAN'T.
WELL, THANK YOU SENSEI—ER, JENNIFER.
YOU BET.
SEE YOU NEXT WEEK?
ABSOLUTELY.

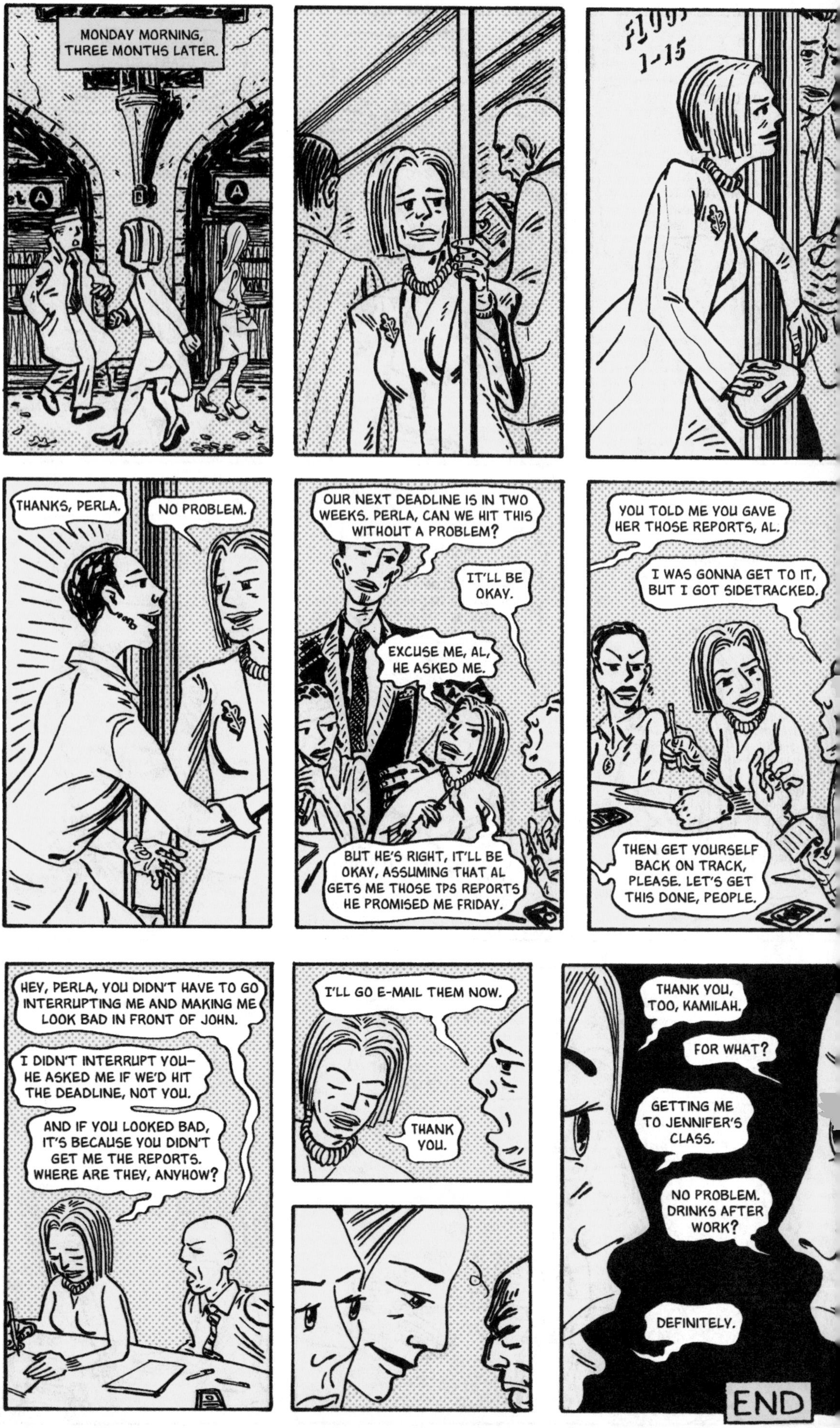
MONDAY MORNING, THREE MONTHS LATER.
THANKS, PERLA.
NO PROBLEM.
OUR NEXT DEADLINE IS IN TWO WEEKS. PERLA, CAN WE HIT THIS WITHOUT A PROBLEM?
IT'LL BE OKAY.
EXCUSE ME, AL, HE ASKED ME.
BUT HE'S RIGHT, IT'LL BE OKAY, ASSUMING THAT AL GETS ME THOSE TPS REPORTS HE PROMISED ME FRIDAY.
YOU TOLD ME YOU GAVE HER THOSE REPORTS, AL.
I WAS GONNA GET TO IT, BUT I GOT SIDETRACKED.
THEN GET YOURSELF BACK ON TRACK, PLEASE. LET'S GET THIS DONE, PEOPLE.
HEY, PERLA, YOU DIDN'T HAVE TO GO INTERRUPTING ME AND MAKING ME LOOK BAD IN FRONT OF JOHN.
I DIDN'T INTERRUPT YOU— HE ASKED ME IF WE'D HIT THE DEADLINE, NOT YOU.
AND IF YOU LOOKED BAD, IT'S BECAUSE YOU DIDN'T GET ME THE REPORTS. WHERE ARE THEY, ANYHOW?
I'LL GO E-MAIL THEM NOW.
THANK YOU.
THANK YOU, TOO, KAMILAH.
FOR WHAT?
GETTING ME TO JENNIFER'S CLASS.
NO PROBLEM. DRINKS AFTER WORK?
DEFINITELY.
END

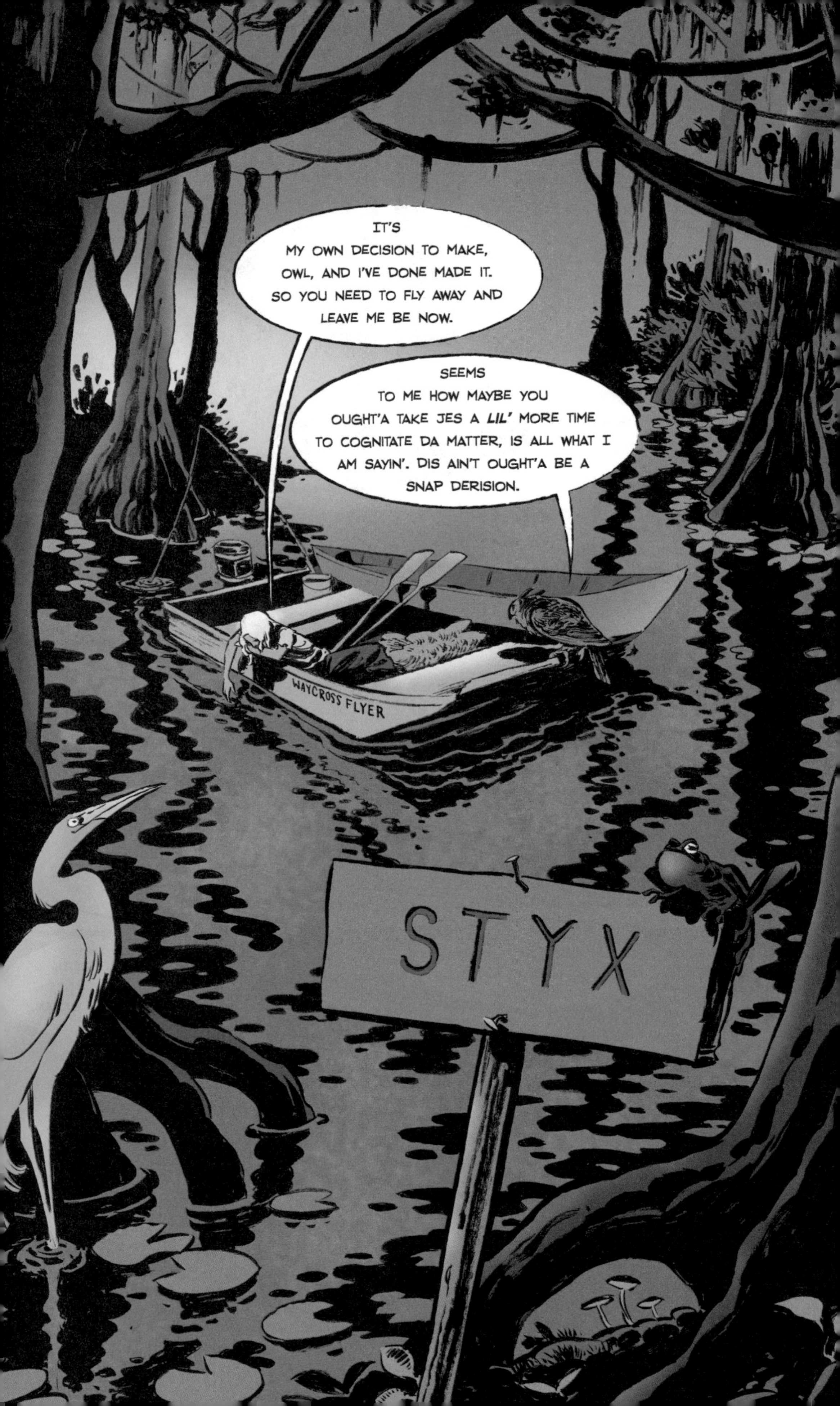
IT'S MY OWN DECISION TO MAKE, OWL, AND I'VE DONE MADE IT. SO YOU NEED TO FLY AWAY AND LEAVE ME BE NOW.
SEEMS TO ME HOW MAYBE YOU OUGHT'A TAKE JES A *LIL'* MORE TIME TO COGNITATE DA MATTER, IS ALL WHAT I AM SAYIN'. DIS AIN'T OUGHT'A BE A SNAP DERISION.
WAYCROSS FLYER
STYX

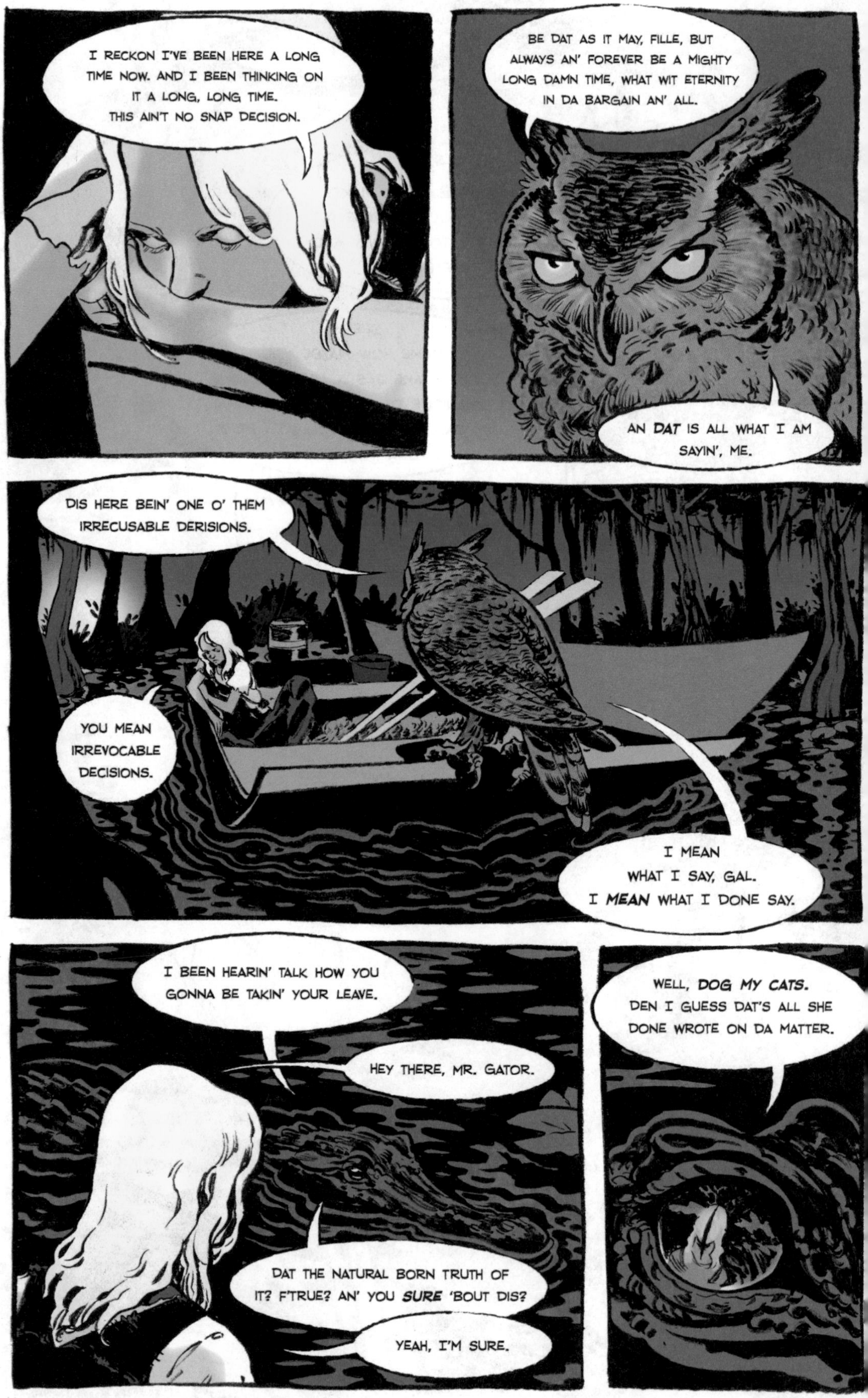
I RECKON I'VE BEEN HERE A LONG TIME NOW. AND I BEEN THINKING ON IT A LONG, LONG TIME. THIS AIN'T NO SNAP DECISION.
BE DAT AS IT MAY, FILLE, BUT ALWAYS AN' FOREVER BE A MIGHTY LONG DAMN TIME, WHAT WIT ETERNITY IN DA BARGAIN AN' ALL.
AN DAT IS ALL WHAT I AM SAYIN', ME.
DIS HERE BEIN' ONE O' THEM IRRECUSABLE DERISIONS.
YOU MEAN IRREVOCABLE DECISIONS.
I MEAN WHAT I SAY, GAL. I MEAN WHAT I DONE SAY.
I BEEN HEARIN' TALK HOW YOU GONNA BE TAKIN' YOUR LEAVE.
HEY THERE, MR. GATOR.
DAT THE NATURAL BORN TRUTH OF IT? F'TRUE? AN' YOU SURE 'BOUT DIS?
YEAH, I'M SURE.
WELL, DOG MY CATS. DEN I GUESS DAT'S ALL SHE DONE WROTE ON DA MATTER.

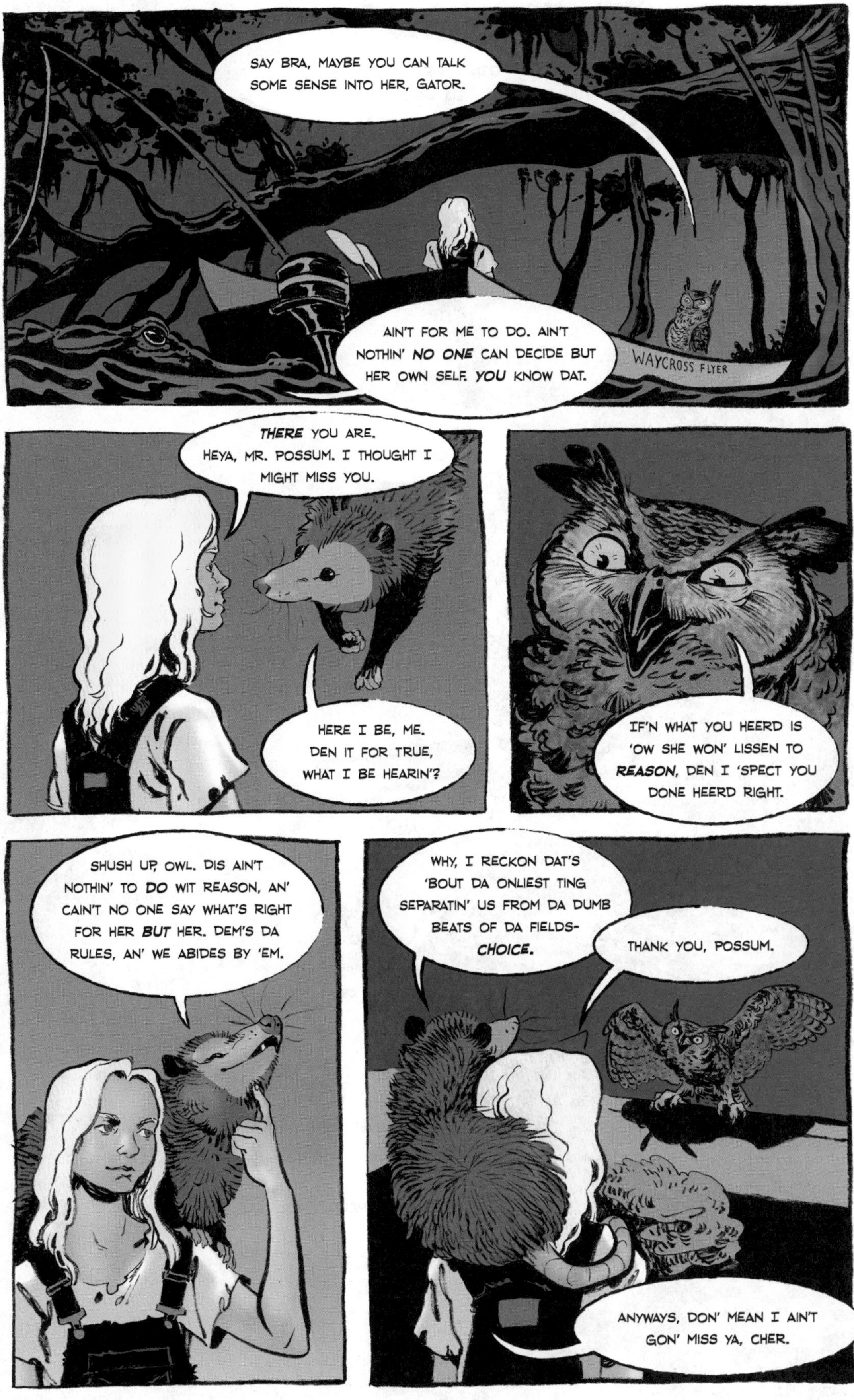
SAY BRA, MAYBE YOU CAN TALK SOME SENSE INTO HER, GATOR.
AIN'T FOR ME TO DO. AIN'T NOTHIN' NO ONE CAN DECIDE BUT HER OWN SELF. YOU KNOW DAT.
WAYCROSS FLYER
THERE YOU ARE. HEYA, MR. POSSUM. I THOUGHT I MIGHT MISS YOU.
HERE I BE, ME. DEN IT FOR TRUE, WHAT I BE HEARIN'?
IF'N WHAT YOU HEERD IS 'OW SHE WON' LISSEN TO REASON, DEN I 'SPECT YOU DONE HEERD RIGHT.
SHUSH UP, OWL. DIS AIN'T NOTHIN' TO DO WIT REASON, AN' CAIN'T NO ONE SAY WHAT'S RIGHT FOR HER BUT HER. DEM'S DA RULES, AN' WE ABIDES BY 'EM.
WHY, I RECKON DAT'S 'BOUT DA ONLIEST TING SEPARATIN' US FROM DA DUMB BEATS OF DA FIELDS- CHOICE.
THANK YOU, POSSUM.
ANYWAYS, DON' MEAN I AIN'T GON' MISS YA, CHER.

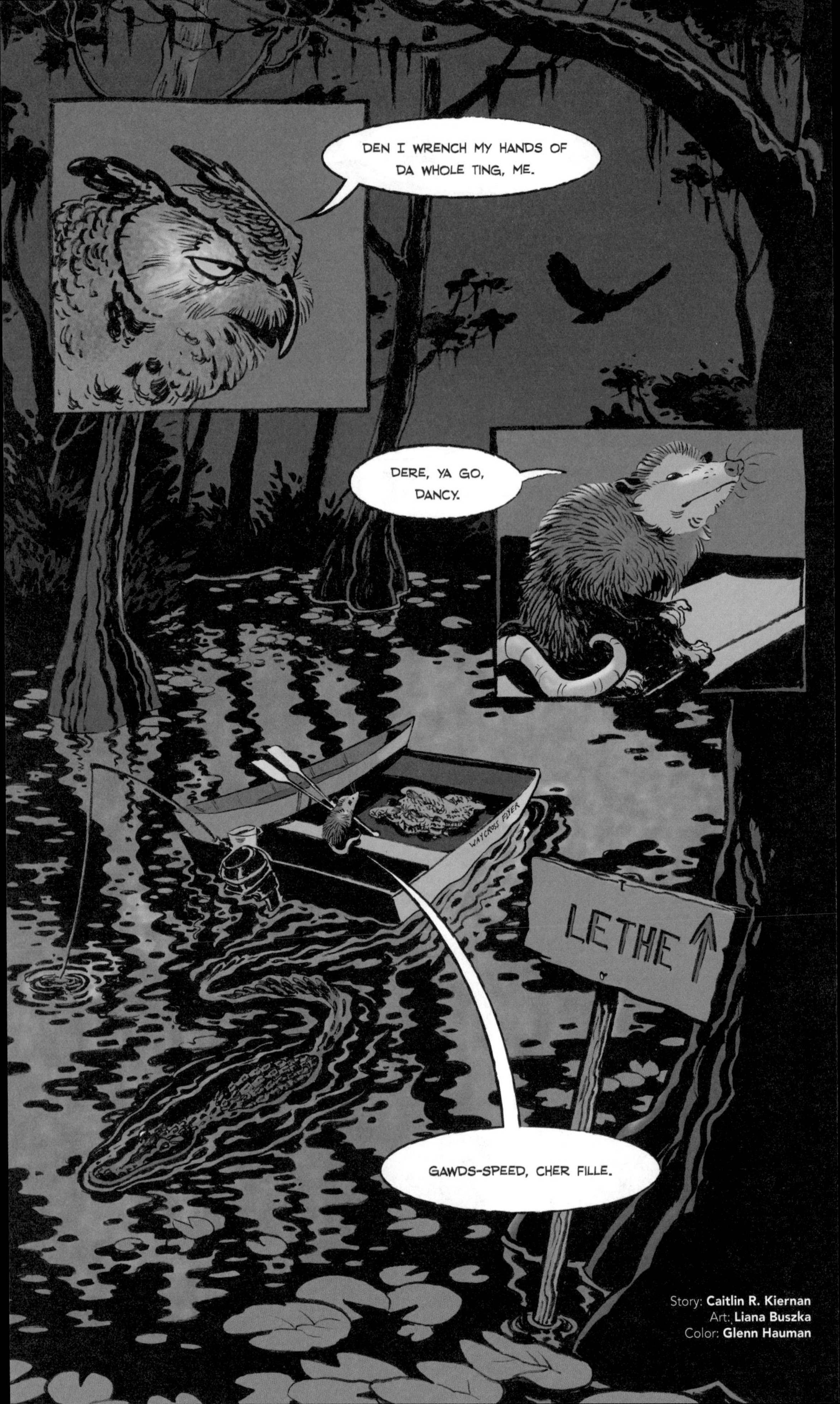
DEN I WRENCH MY HANDS OF DA WHOLE TING, ME.
DERE, YA GO, DANCY.
WAYCROSS FLYER
LETHE
GAWDS-SPEED, CHER FILLE.

Story: **Caitlin R. Kiernan**
Art: **Liana Buszka**
Color: **Glenn Hauman**

Because of you

by: Madeline Zuluaga

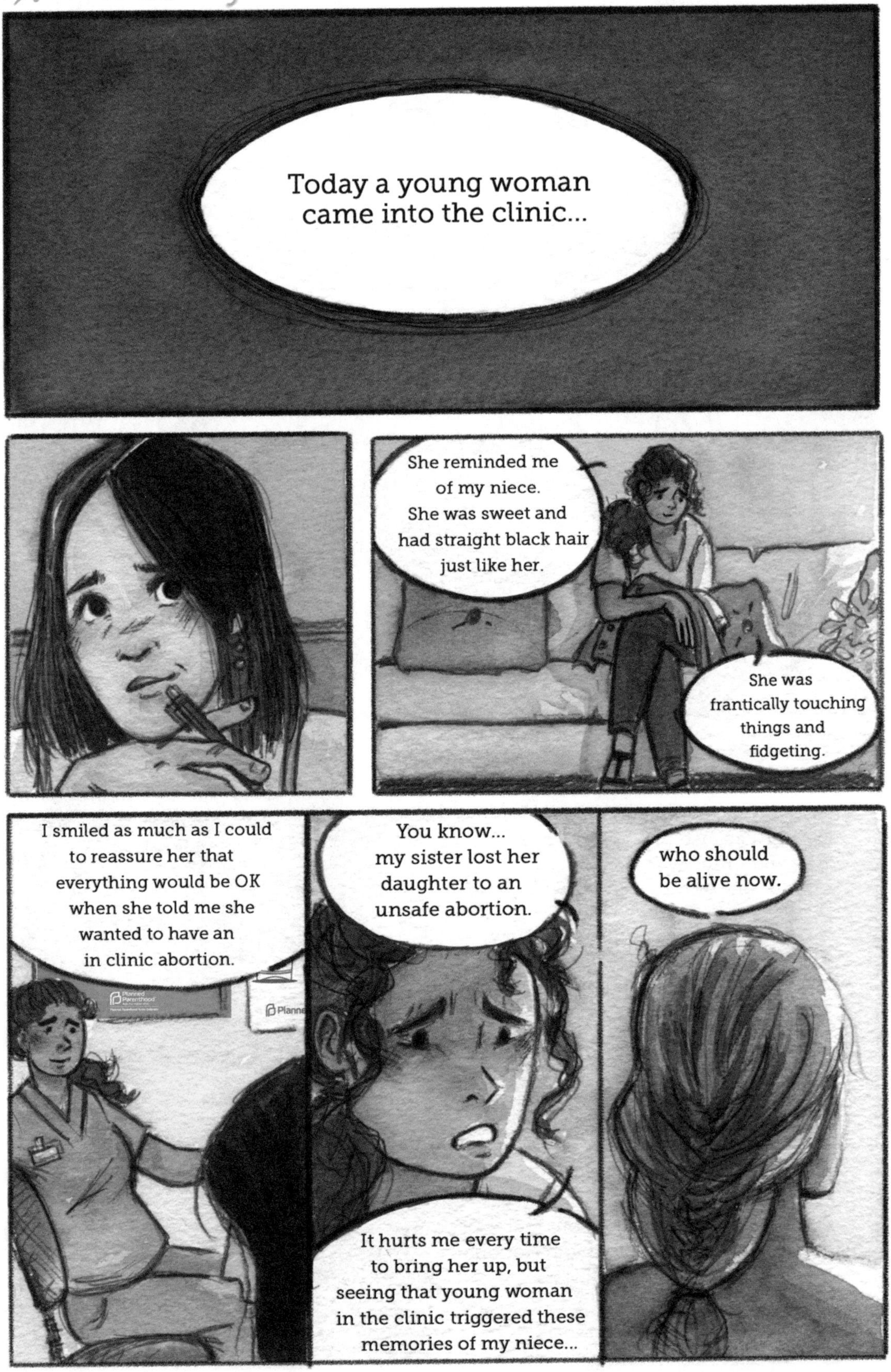
Today a young woman came into the clinic...
She reminded me of my niece. She was sweet and had straight black hair just like her.
She was frantically touching things and fidgeting.
I smiled as much as I could to reassure her that everything would be OK when she told me she wanted to have an in clinic abortion.
You know... my sister lost her daughter to an unsafe abortion.
It hurts me every time to bring her up, but seeing that young woman in the clinic triggered these memories of my niece...
who should be alive now.

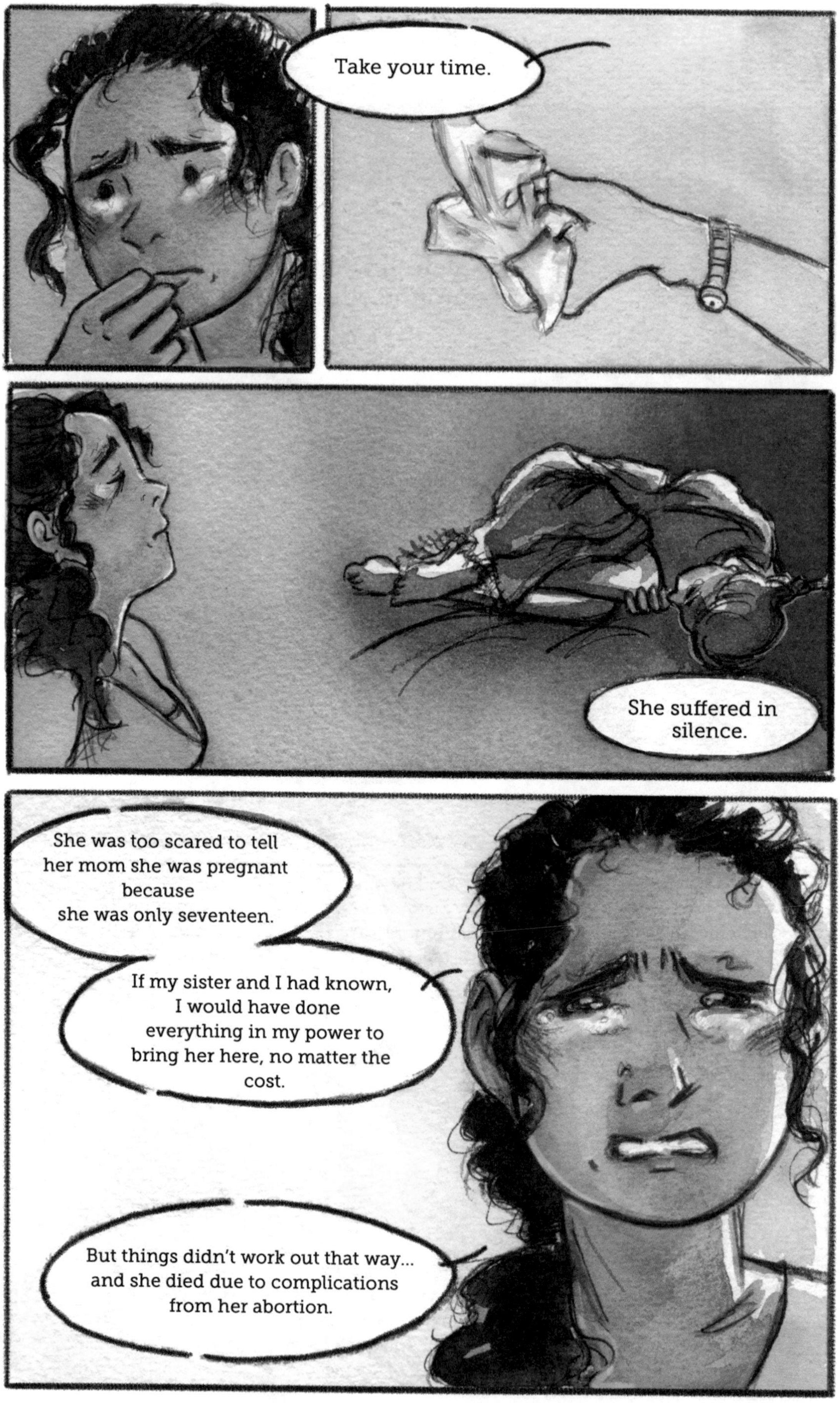
Take your time.
She suffered in silence.
She was too scared to tell her mom she was pregnant because she was only seventeen.
If my sister and I had known, I would have done everything in my power to bring her here, no matter the cost.
But things didn't work out that way... and she died due to complications from her abortion.

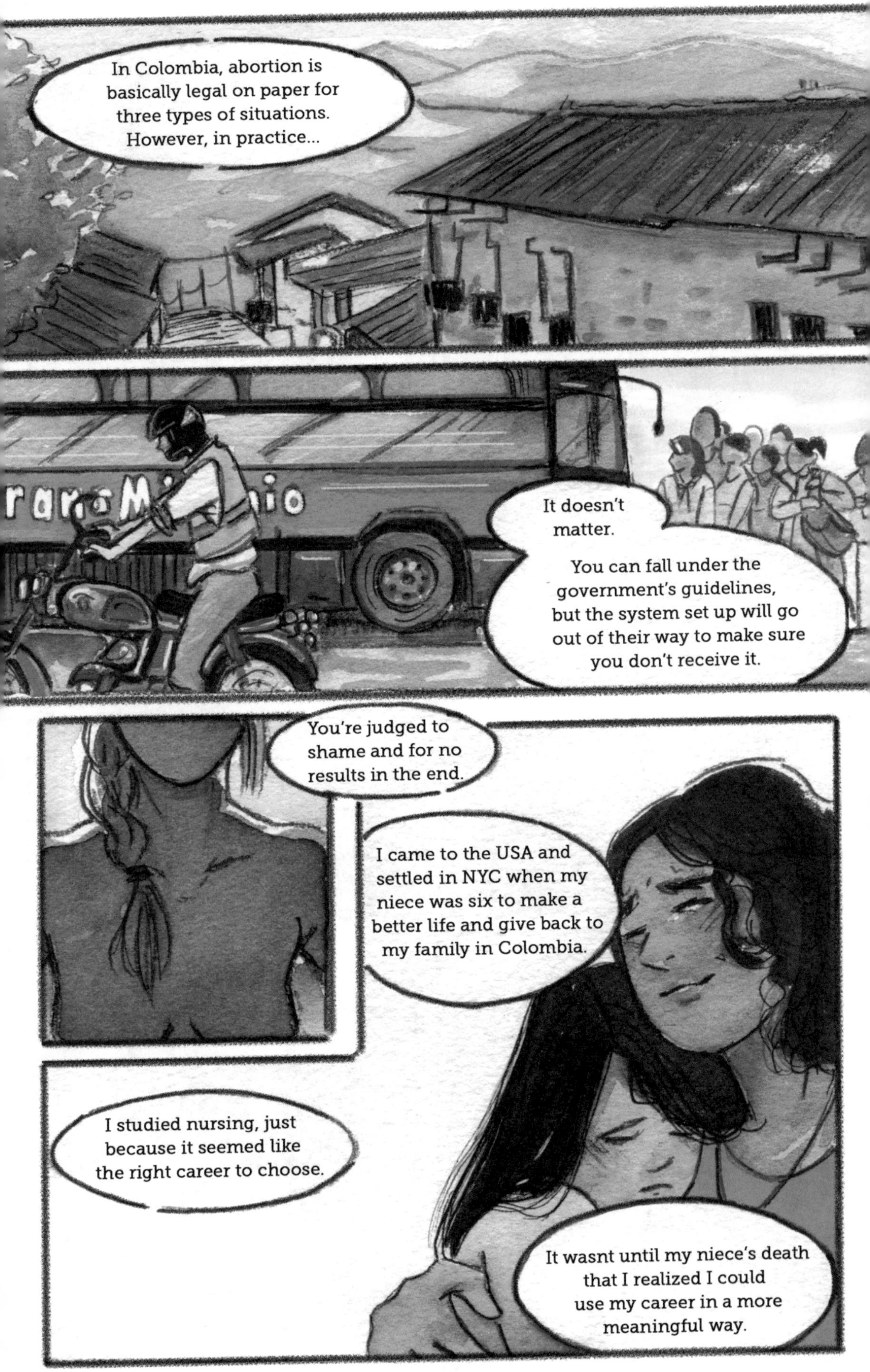
In Colombia, abortion is basically legal on paper for three types of situations. However, in practice...
It doesn't matter.
You can fall under the government's guidelines, but the system set up will go out of their way to make sure you don't receive it.
You're judged to shame and for no results in the end.
I came to the USA and settled in NYC when my niece was six to make a better life and give back to my family in Colombia.
I studied nursing, just because it seemed like the right career to choose.
It wasnt until my niece's death that I realized I could use my career in a more meaningful way.

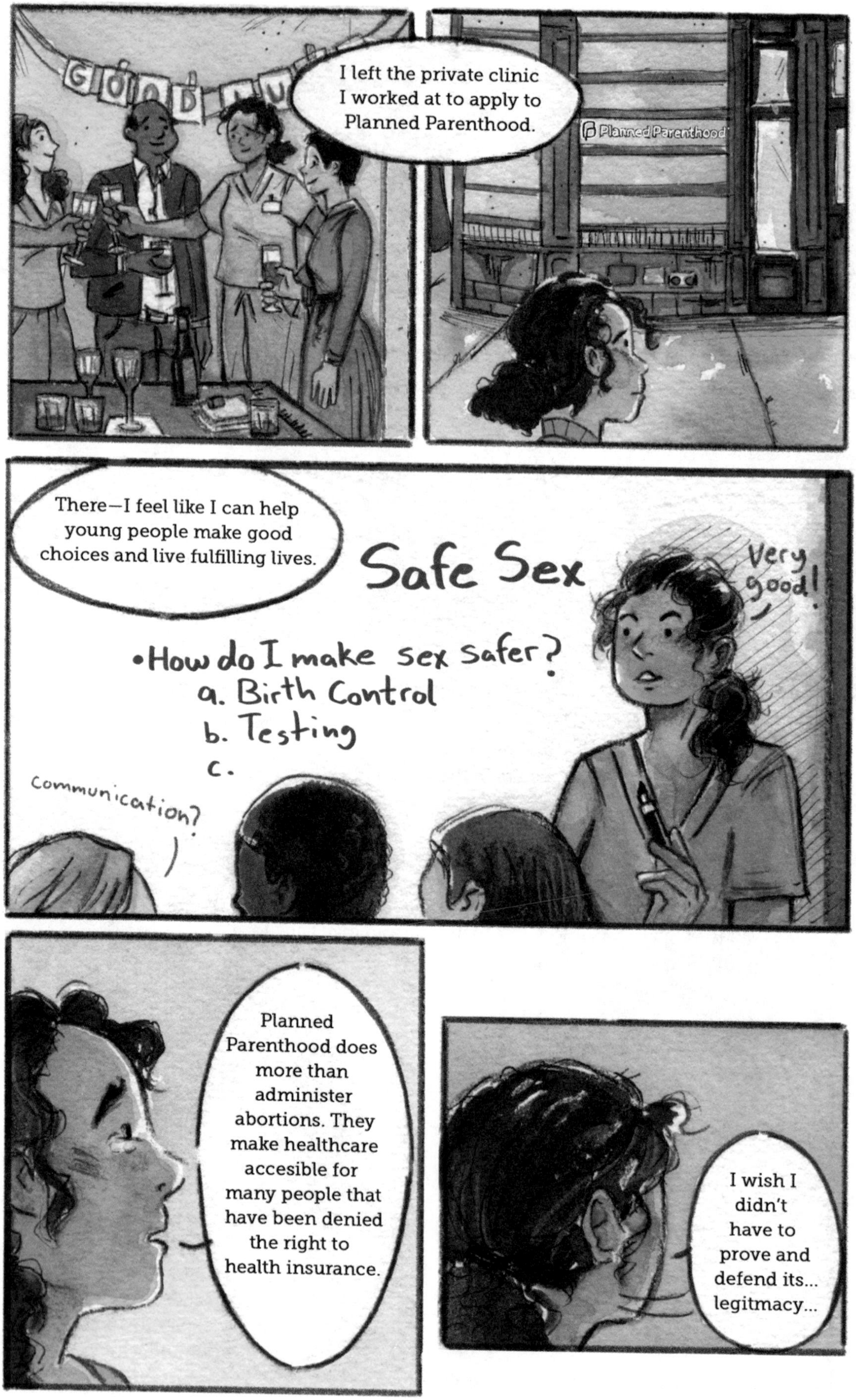

GOOD LU
I left the private clinic I worked at to apply to Planned Parenthood.
Planned Parenthood
There—I feel like I can help young people make good choices and live fulfilling lives.
Safe Sex
•How do I make sex safer?
a. Birth Control
b. Testing
c.
Very good!
communication?
Planned Parenthood does more than administer abortions. They make healthcare accesible for many people that have been denied the right to health insurance.
I wish I didn't have to prove and defend its... legitmacy...

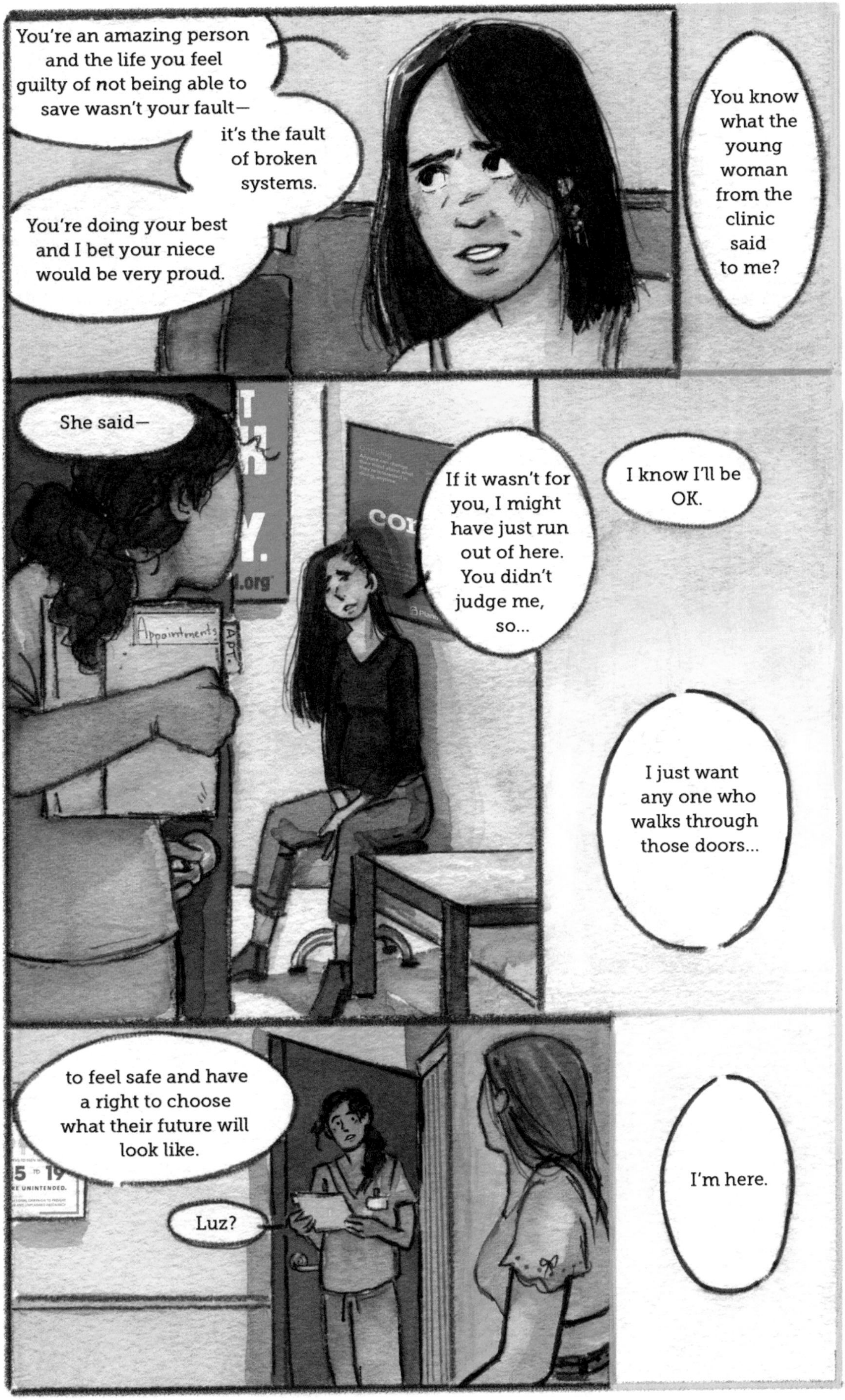
You're an amazing person and the life you feel guilty of *n*ot being able to save wasn't your fault—
it's the fault of broken systems.
You're doing your best and I bet your niece would be very proud.
You know what the young woman from the clinic said to me?
She said—
If it wasn't for you, I might have just run out of here. You didn't judge me, so...
I know I'll be OK.
Appointments
APT.
I just want any one who walks through those doors...
to feel safe and have a right to choose what their future will look like.
Luz?
I'm here.

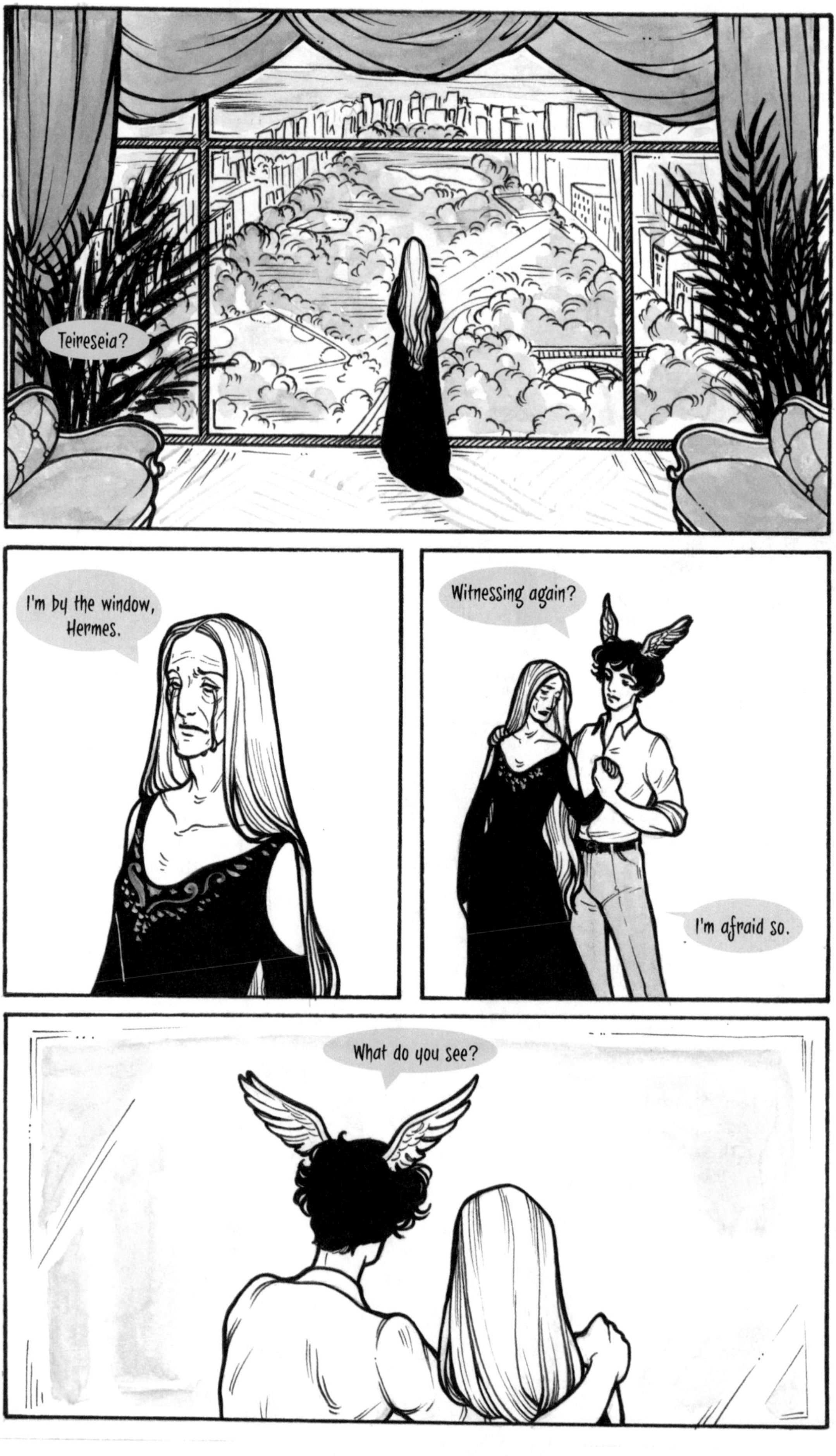
Teireseia?
I'm by the window, Hermes.
Witnessing again?
I'm afraid so.
What do you see?

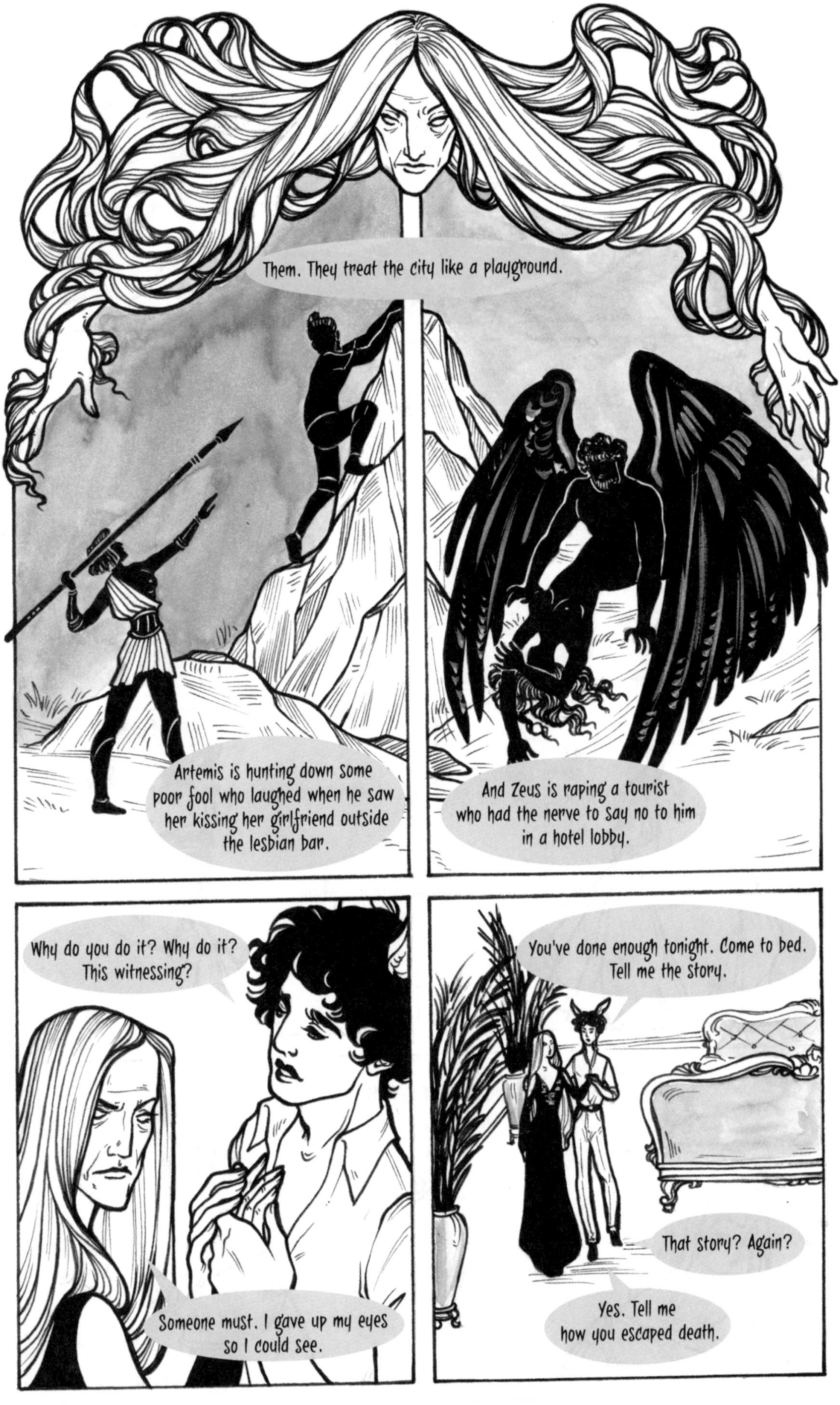

Them. They treat the city like a playground.
Artemis is hunting down some poor fool who laughed when he saw her kissing her girlfriend outside the lesbian bar.
And Zeus is raping a tourist who had the nerve to say no to him in a hotel lobby.
Why do you do it? Why do it? This witnessing?
Someone must. I gave up my eyes so I could see.
You've done enough tonight. Come to bed. Tell me the story.
That story? Again?
Yes. Tell me how you escaped death.

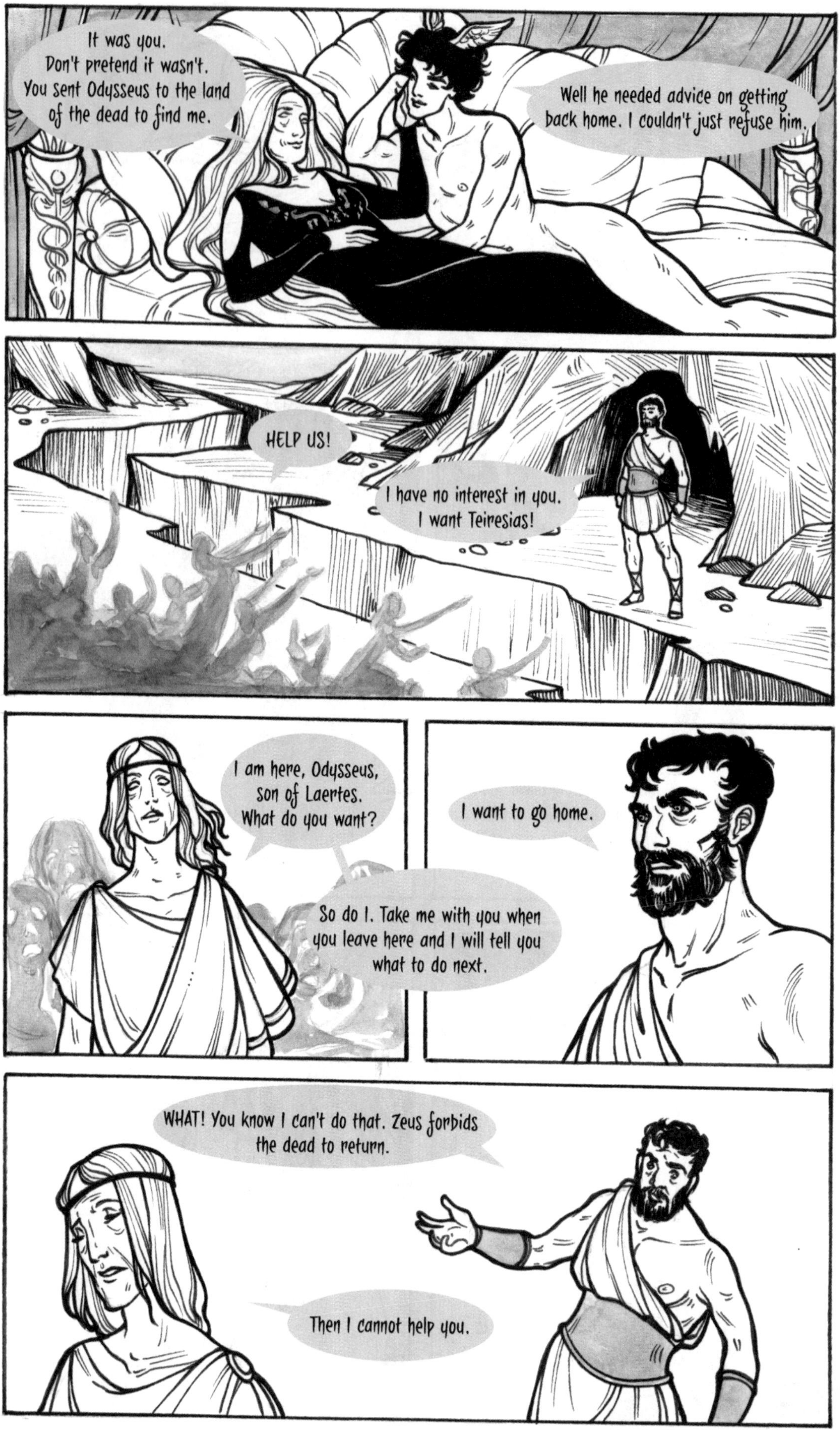
It was you. Don't pretend it wasn't. You sent Odysseus to the land of the dead to find me.
Well he needed advice on getting back home. I couldn't just refuse him.
HELP US!
I have no interest in you. I want Teiresias!
I am here, Odysseus, son of Laertes. What do you want?
I want to go home.
So do I. Take me with you when you leave here and I will tell you what to do next.
WHAT! You know I can't do that. Zeus forbids the dead to return.
Then I cannot help you.

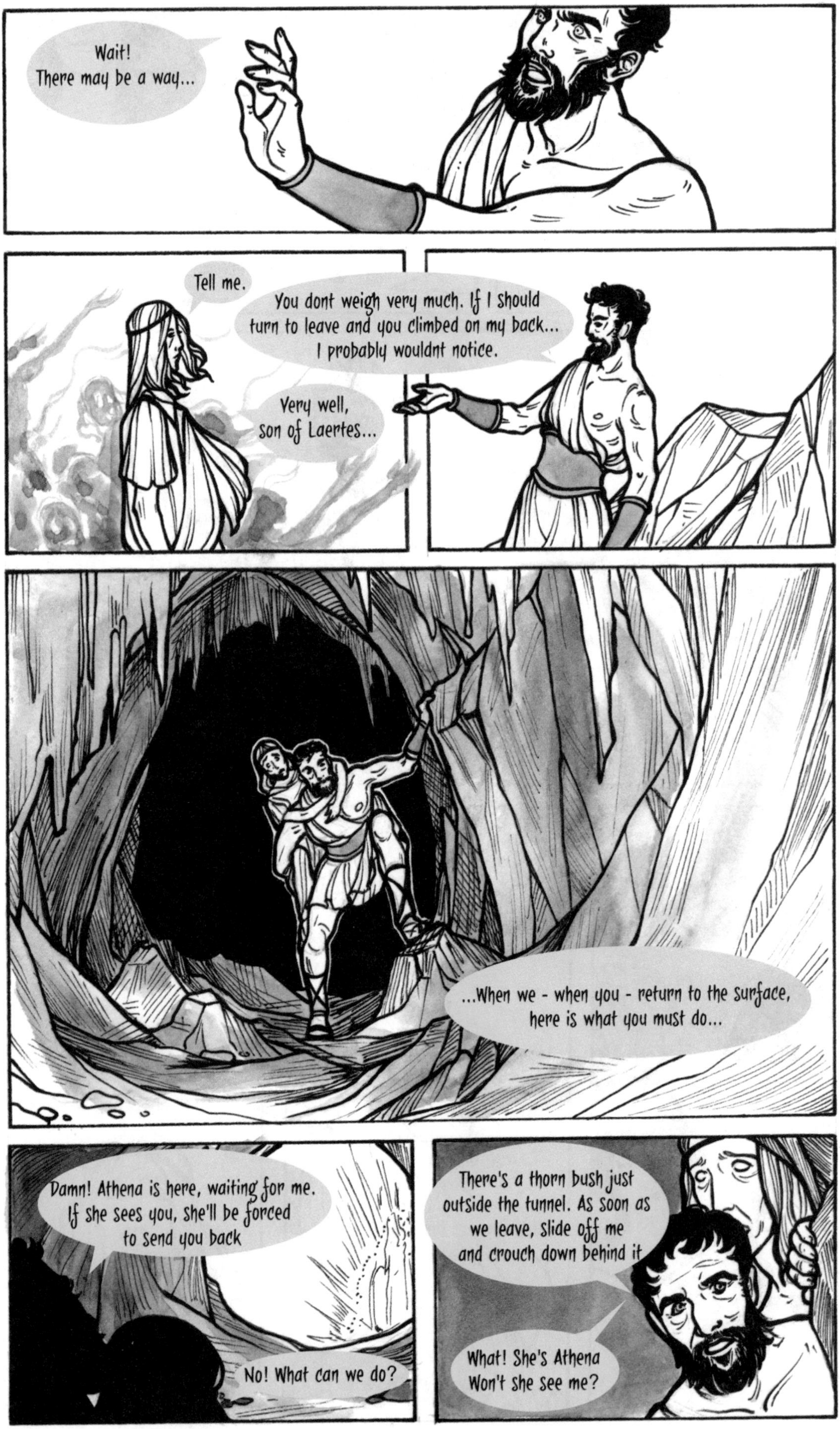
Wait!
There may be a way...
Tell me.
You dont weigh very much. If I should turn to leave and you climbed on my back... I probably wouldnt notice.
Very well, son of Laertes...
...When we - when you - return to the surface, here is what you must do...
Damn! Athena is here, waiting for me. If she sees you, she'll be forced to send you back
No! What can we do?
There's a thorn bush just outside the tunnel. As soon as we leave, slide off me and crouch down behind it
What! She's Athena Won't she see me?

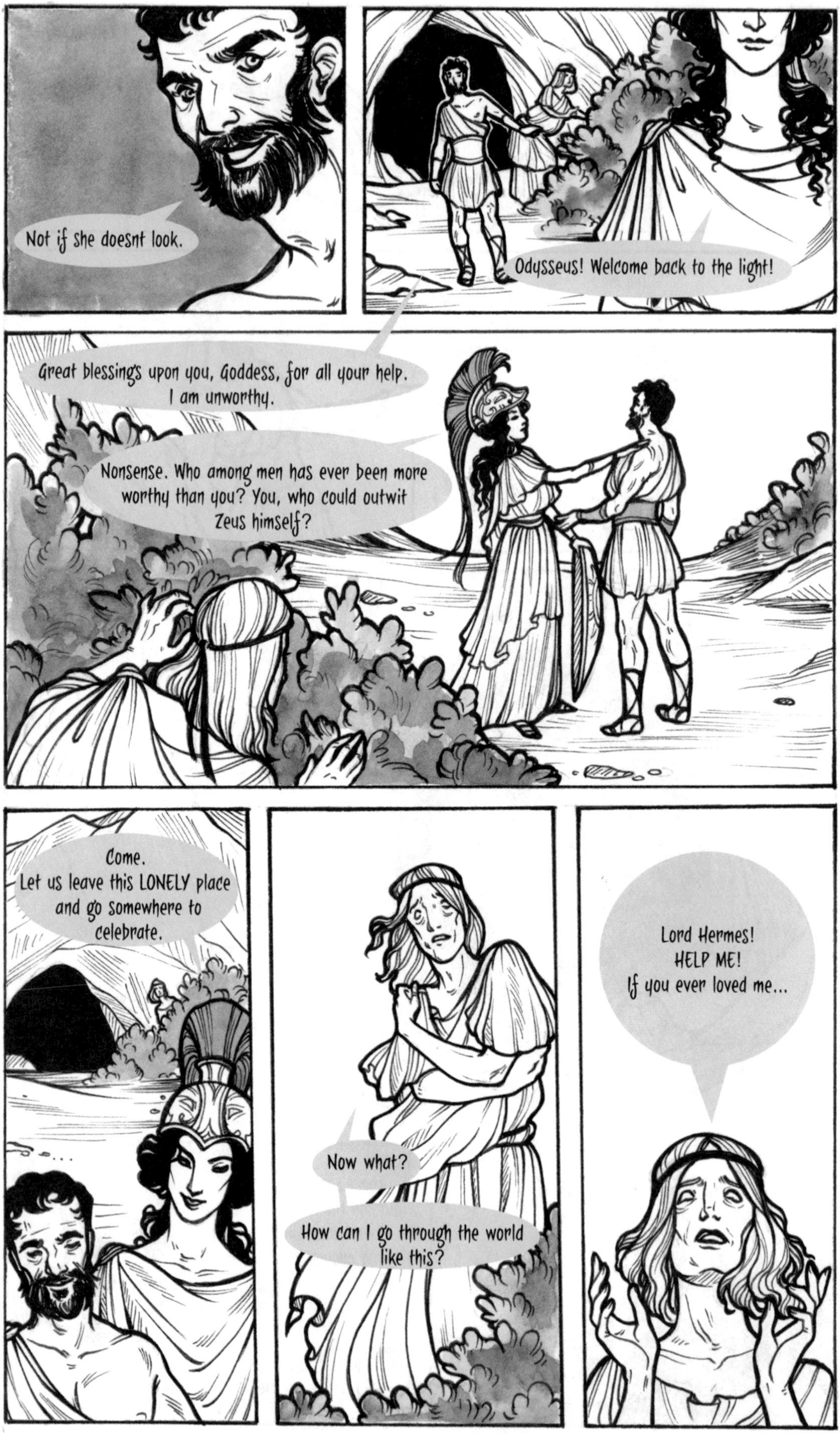
Not if she doesnt look.
Odysseus! Welcome back to the light!
Great blessings upon you, Goddess, for all your help. I am unworthy.
Nonsense. Who among men has ever been more worthy than you? You, who could outwit Zeus himself?
Come. Let us leave this LONELY place and go somewhere to celebrate.
Now what?
How can I go through the world like this?
Lord Hermes! HELP ME! If you ever loved me...

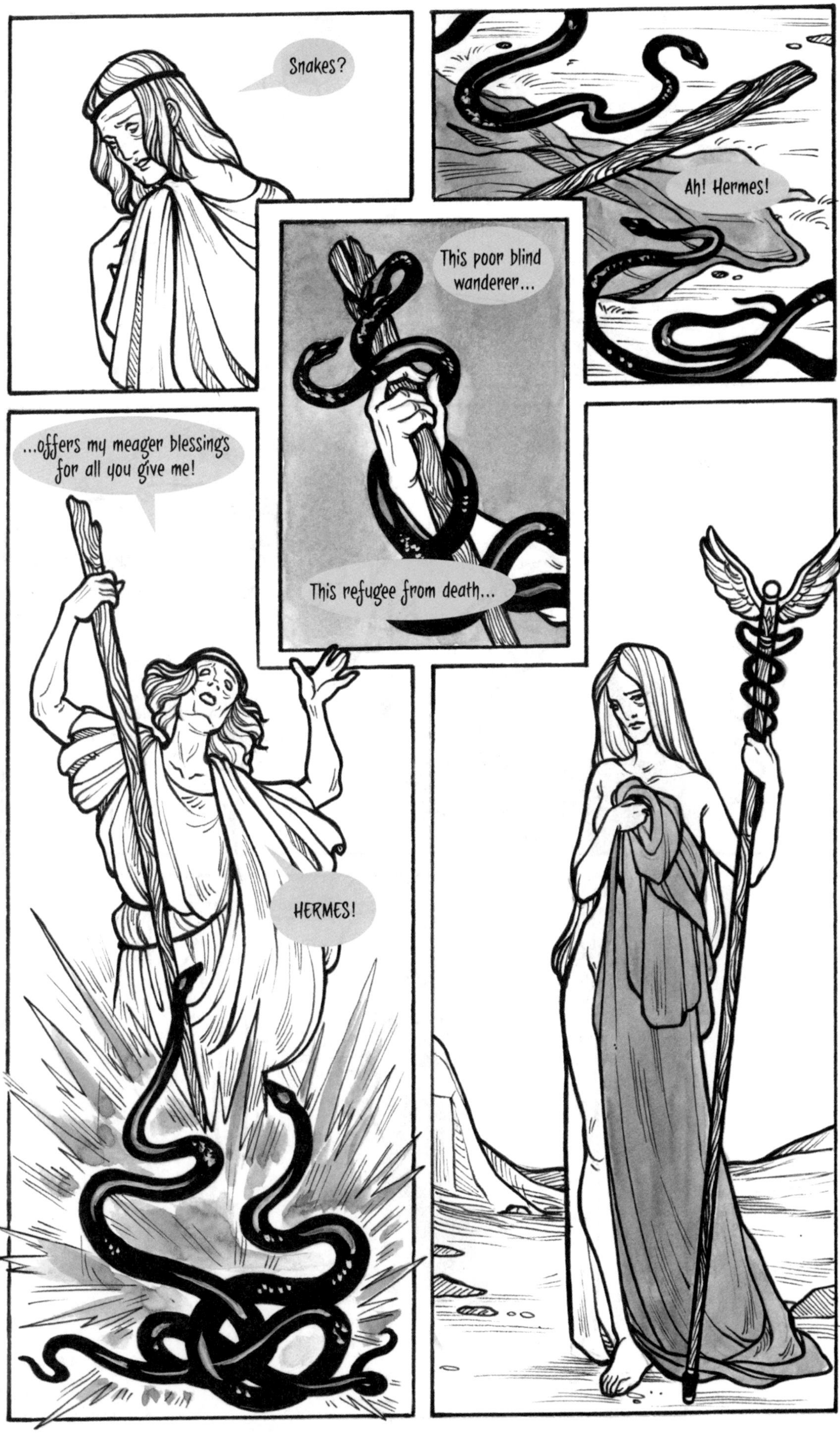
Snakes?
Ah! Hermes!
This poor blind wanderer...
This refugee from death...
...offers my meager blessings for all you give me!
HERMES!

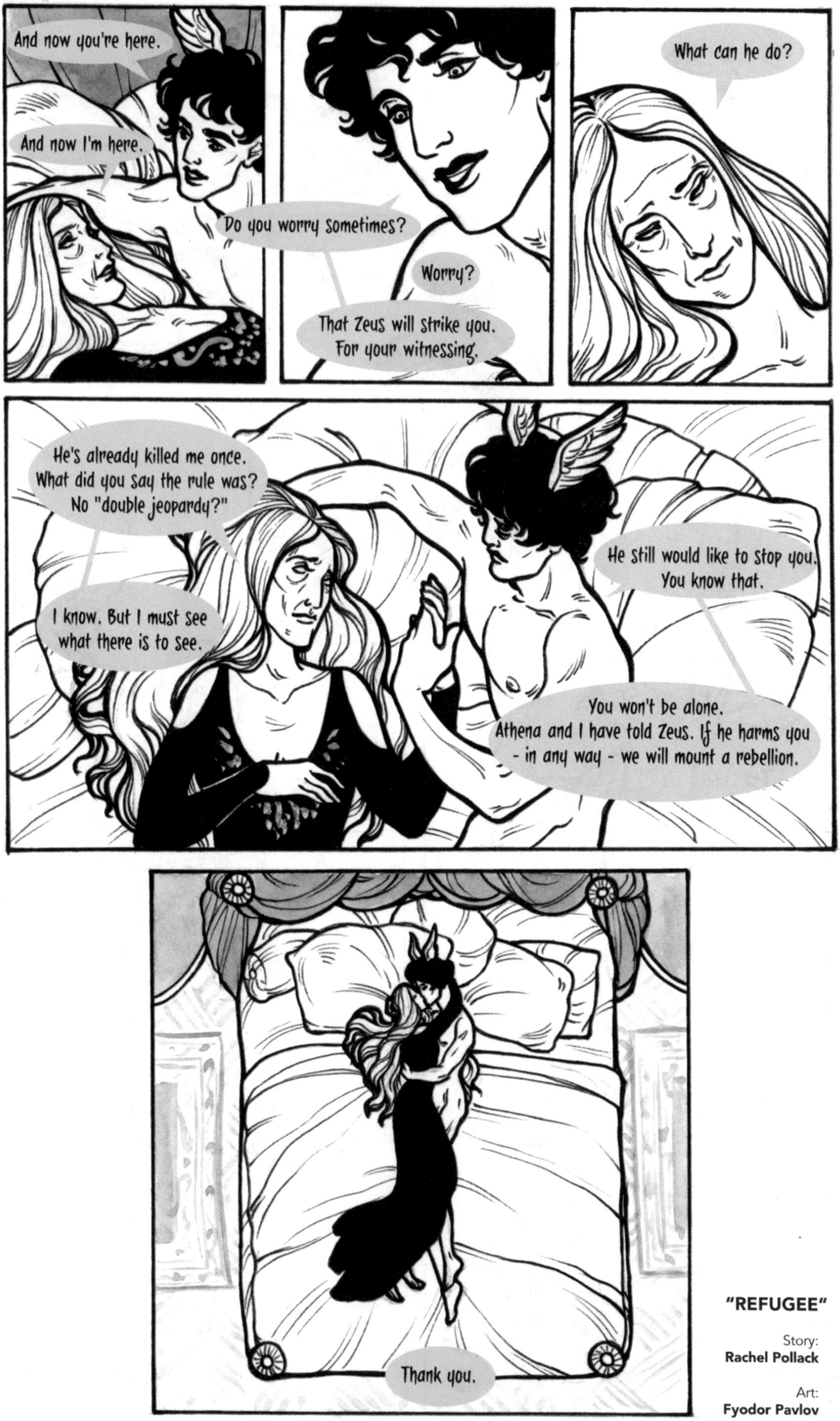
And now you're here.
And now I'm here.
Do you worry sometimes?
Worry?
That Zeus will strike you. For your witnessing.
What can he do?
He's already killed me once. What did you say the rule was? No "double jeopardy?"
He still would like to stop you. You know that.
I know. But I must see what there is to see.
You won't be alone. Athena and I have told Zeus. If he harms you - in any way - we will mount a rebellion.
Thank you.

"REFUGEE"

Story:
Rachel Pollack

Art:
Fyodor Pavlov

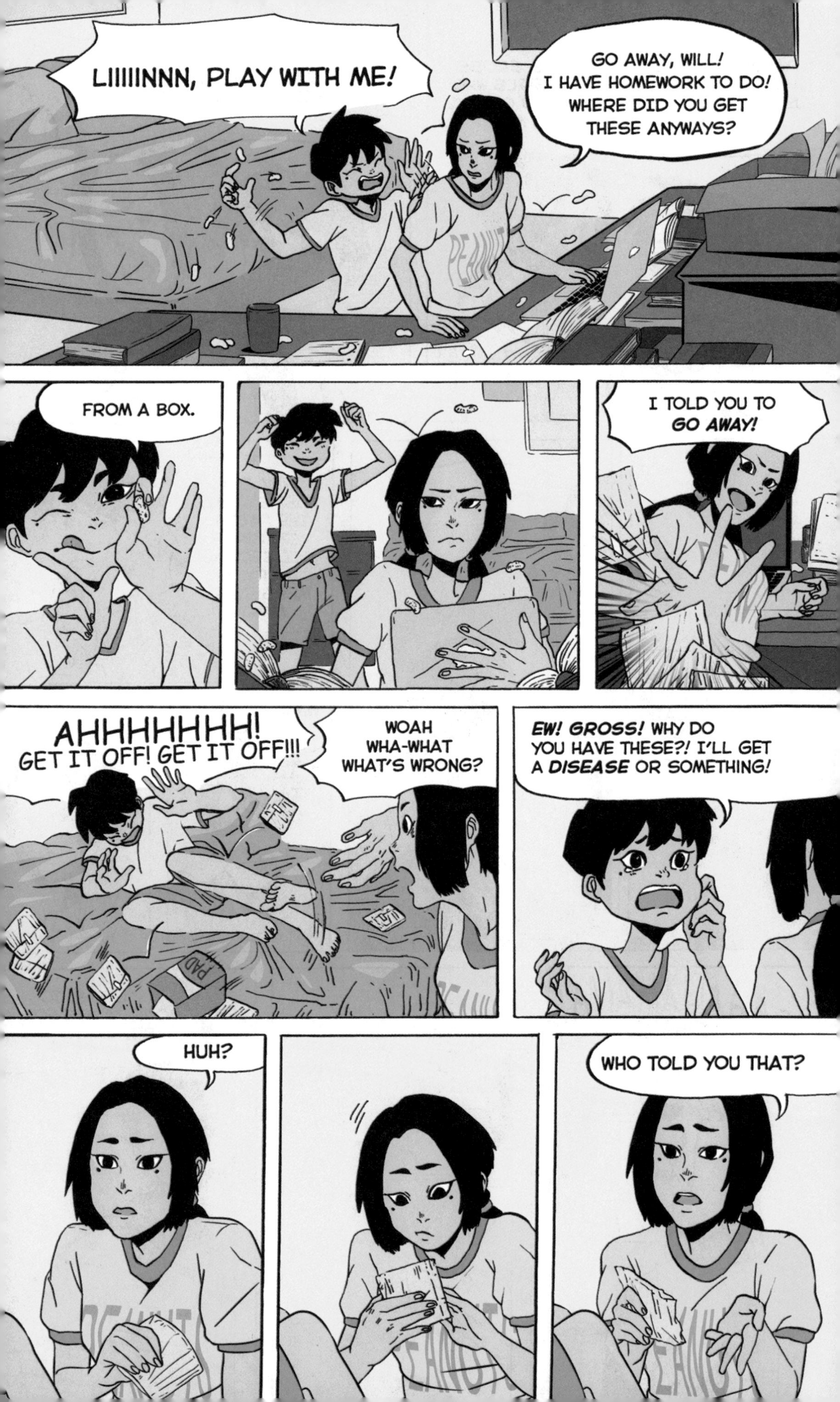
LIIIIINNN, PLAY WITH ME!
GO AWAY, WILL! I HAVE HOMEWORK TO DO! WHERE DID YOU GET THESE ANYWAYS?
FROM A BOX.
I TOLD YOU TO GO AWAY!
AHHHHHHH! GET IT OFF! GET IT OFF!!!
WOAH WHA-WHAT WHAT'S WRONG?
PAD
EW! GROSS! WHY DO YOU HAVE THESE?! I'LL GET A DISEASE OR SOMETHING!
HUH?
WHO TOLD YOU THAT?

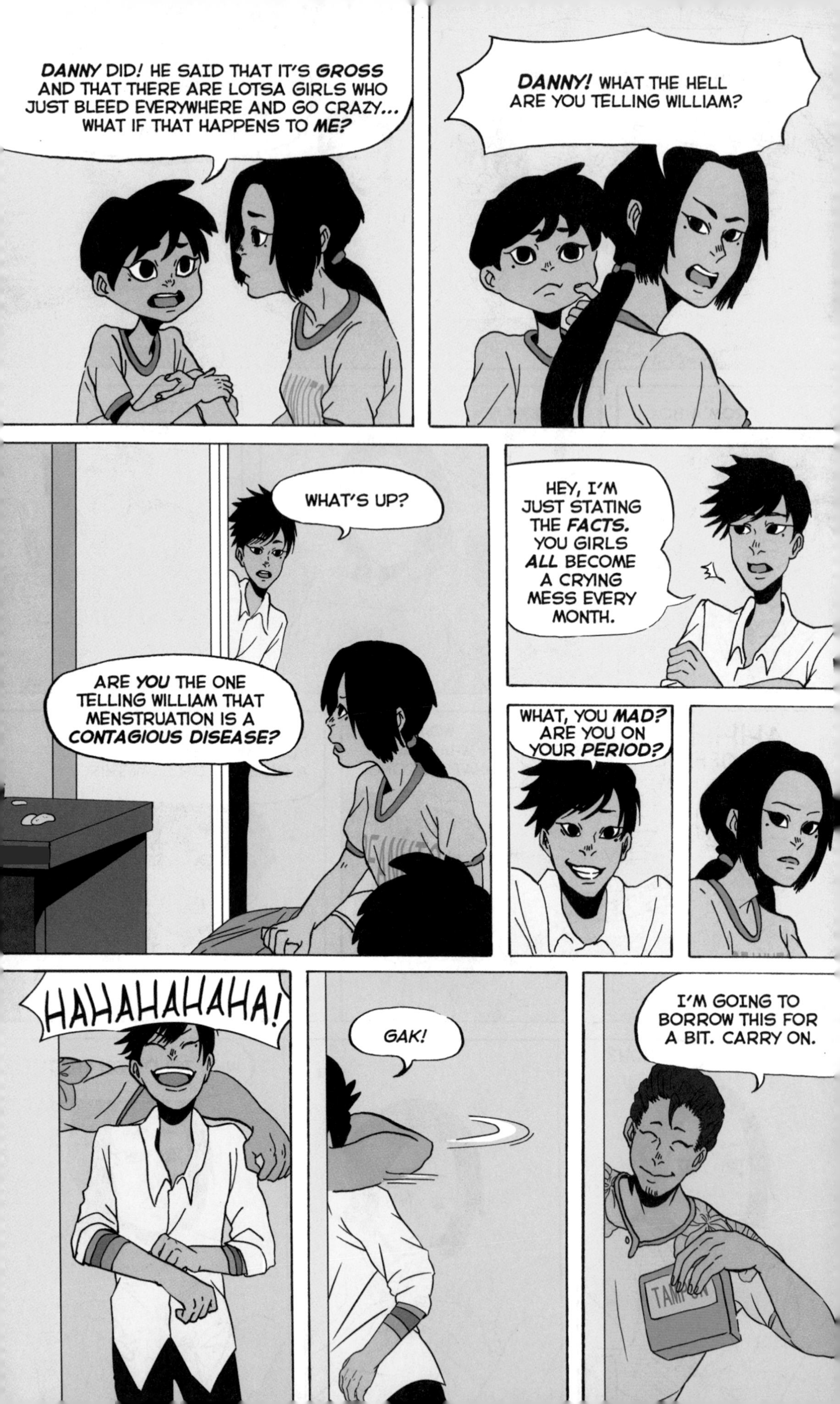
DANNY DID! HE SAID THAT IT'S GROSS AND THAT THERE ARE LOTSA GIRLS WHO JUST BLEED EVERYWHERE AND GO CRAZY... WHAT IF THAT HAPPENS TO ME?
DANNY! WHAT THE HELL ARE YOU TELLING WILLIAM?
WHAT'S UP?
ARE YOU THE ONE TELLING WILLIAM THAT MENSTRUATION IS A CONTAGIOUS DISEASE?
HEY, I'M JUST STATING THE FACTS. YOU GIRLS ALL BECOME A CRYING MESS EVERY MONTH.
WHAT, YOU MAD? ARE YOU ON YOUR PERIOD?
HAHAHAHAHA!
GAK!
I'M GOING TO BORROW THIS FOR A BIT. CARRY ON.
TAMPON

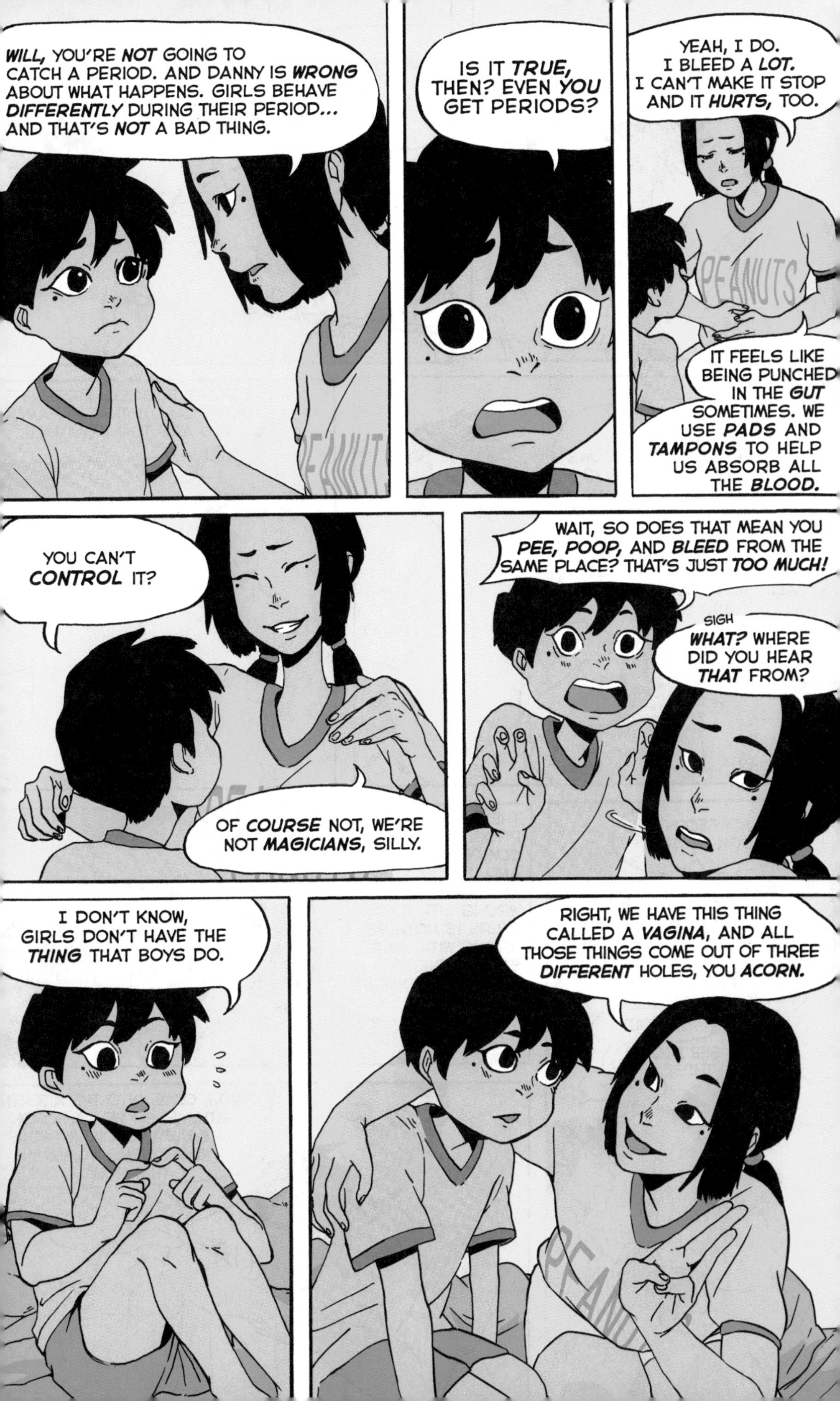

WILL, YOU'RE NOT GOING TO CATCH A PERIOD. AND DANNY IS WRONG ABOUT WHAT HAPPENS. GIRLS BEHAVE DIFFERENTLY DURING THEIR PERIOD... AND THAT'S NOT A BAD THING.
IS IT TRUE, THEN? EVEN YOU GET PERIODS?
YEAH, I DO. I BLEED A LOT. I CAN'T MAKE IT STOP AND IT HURTS, TOO.
PEANUTS
IT FEELS LIKE BEING PUNCHED IN THE GUT SOMETIMES. WE USE PADS AND TAMPONS TO HELP US ABSORB ALL THE BLOOD.
YOU CAN'T CONTROL IT?
OF COURSE NOT, WE'RE NOT MAGICIANS, SILLY.
WAIT, SO DOES THAT MEAN YOU PEE, POOP, AND BLEED FROM THE SAME PLACE? THAT'S JUST TOO MUCH!
SIGH
WHAT? WHERE DID YOU HEAR THAT FROM?
I DON'T KNOW, GIRLS DON'T HAVE THE THING THAT BOYS DO.
RIGHT, WE HAVE THIS THING CALLED A VAGINA, AND ALL THOSE THINGS COME OUT OF THREE DIFFERENT HOLES, YOU ACORN.

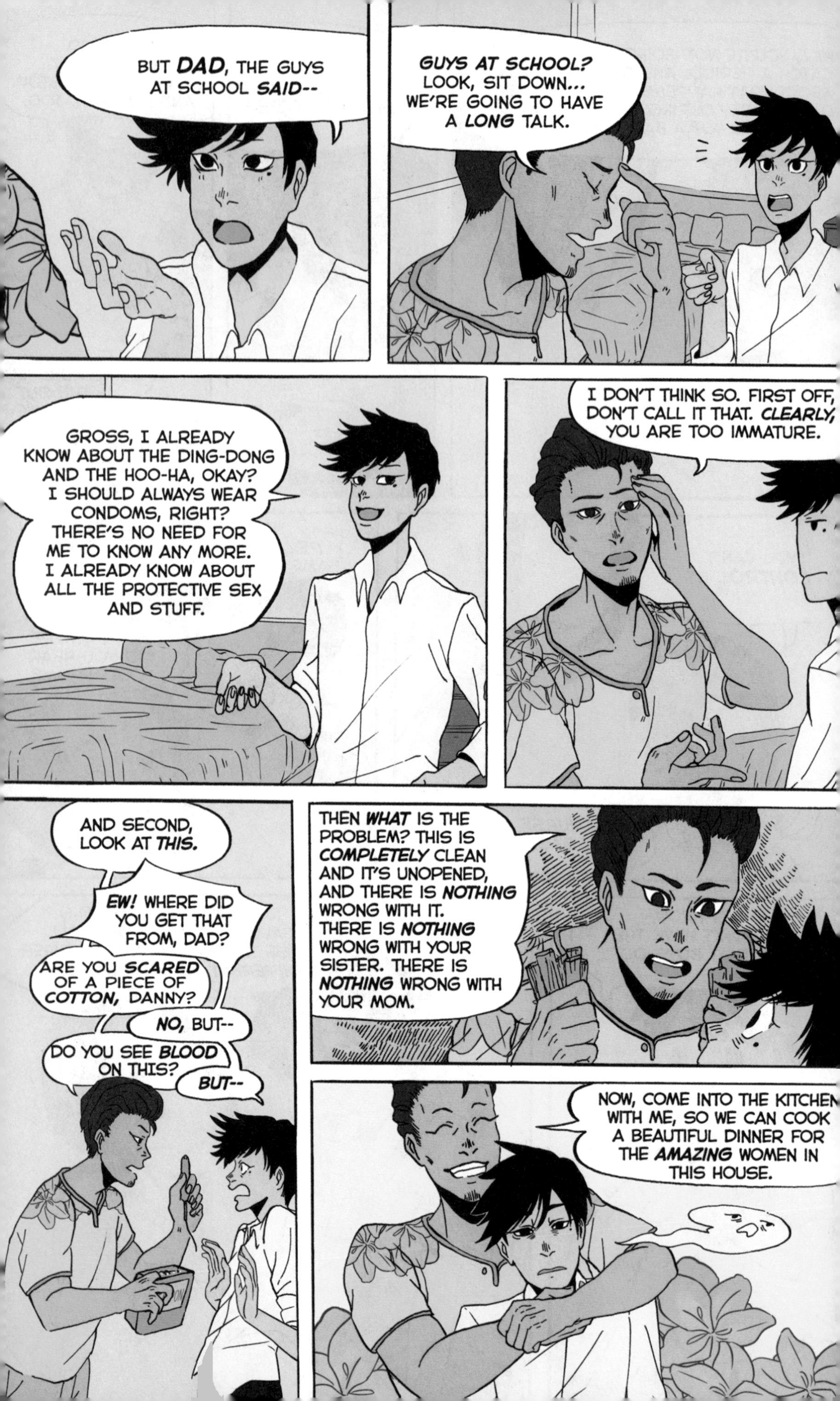

BUT DAD, THE GUYS AT SCHOOL SAID--
GUYS AT SCHOOL? LOOK, SIT DOWN... WE'RE GOING TO HAVE A LONG TALK.
GROSS, I ALREADY KNOW ABOUT THE DING-DONG AND THE HOO-HA, OKAY? I SHOULD ALWAYS WEAR CONDOMS, RIGHT? THERE'S NO NEED FOR ME TO KNOW ANY MORE. I ALREADY KNOW ABOUT ALL THE PROTECTIVE SEX AND STUFF.
I DON'T THINK SO. FIRST OFF, DON'T CALL IT THAT. CLEARLY, YOU ARE TOO IMMATURE.
AND SECOND, LOOK AT THIS.
EW! WHERE DID YOU GET THAT FROM, DAD?
ARE YOU SCARED OF A PIECE OF COTTON, DANNY?
NO, BUT--
DO YOU SEE BLOOD ON THIS?
BUT--
THEN WHAT IS THE PROBLEM? THIS IS COMPLETELY CLEAN AND IT'S UNOPENED, AND THERE IS NOTHING WRONG WITH IT. THERE IS NOTHING WRONG WITH YOUR SISTER. THERE IS NOTHING WRONG WITH YOUR MOM.
NOW, COME INTO THE KITCHEN WITH ME, SO WE CAN COOK A BEAUTIFUL DINNER FOR THE AMAZING WOMEN IN THIS HOUSE.

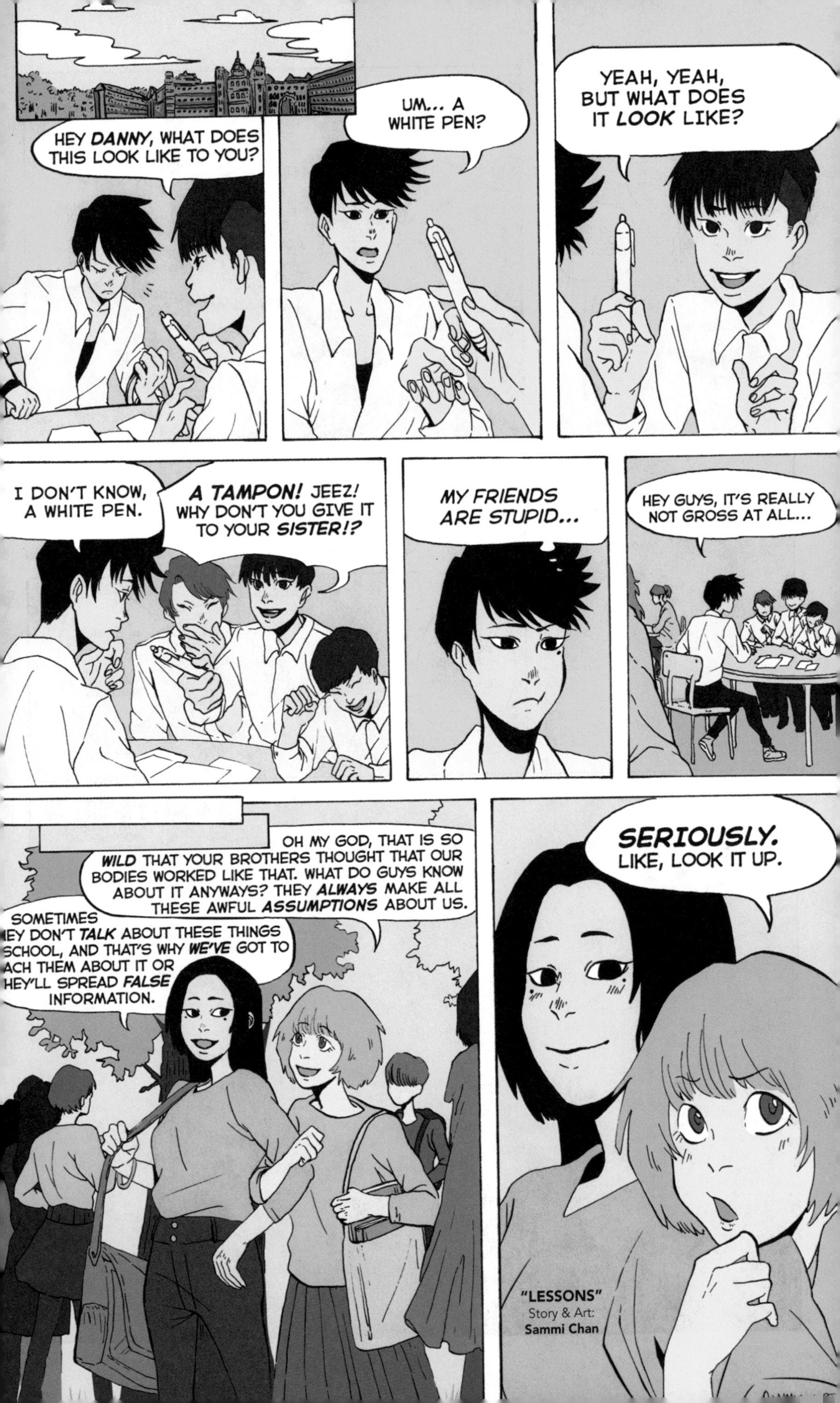
HEY DANNY, WHAT DOES THIS LOOK LIKE TO YOU?
UM... A WHITE PEN?
YEAH, YEAH, BUT WHAT DOES IT LOOK LIKE?
I DON'T KNOW, A WHITE PEN.
A TAMPON! JEEZ! WHY DON'T YOU GIVE IT TO YOUR SISTER!?
MY FRIENDS ARE STUPID...
HEY GUYS, IT'S REALLY NOT GROSS AT ALL...
OH MY GOD, THAT IS SO WILD THAT YOUR BROTHERS THOUGHT THAT OUR BODIES WORKED LIKE THAT. WHAT DO GUYS KNOW ABOUT IT ANYWAYS? THEY ALWAYS MAKE ALL THESE AWFUL ASSUMPTIONS ABOUT US.
SOMETIMES
EY DON'T TALK ABOUT THESE THINGS
SCHOOL, AND THAT'S WHY WE'VE GOT TO
ACH THEM ABOUT IT OR
HEY'LL SPREAD FALSE
INFORMATION.
SERIOUSLY. LIKE, LOOK IT UP.
"LESSONS"
Story & Art:
Sammi Chan

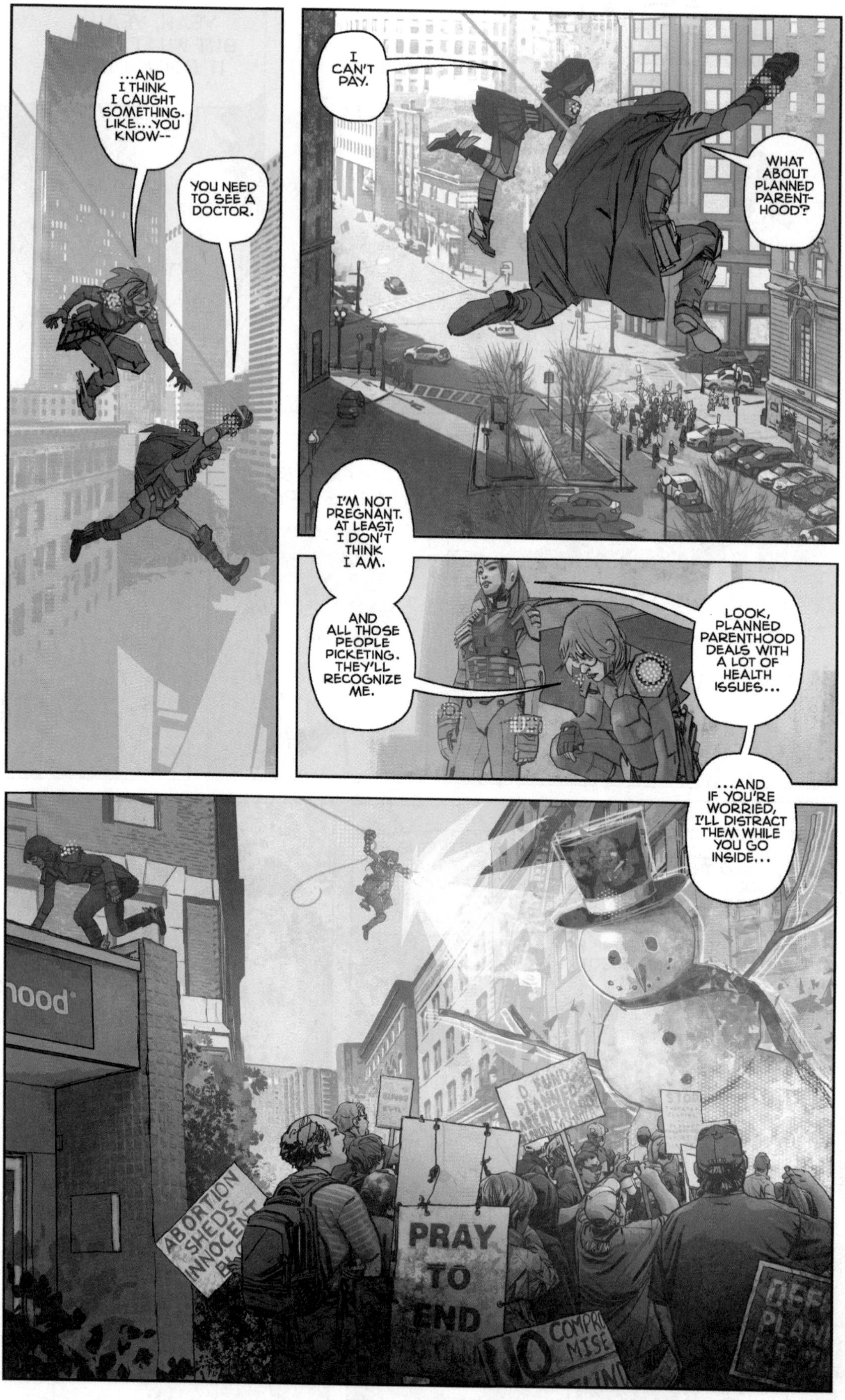
...AND I THINK I CAUGHT SOMETHING. LIKE...YOU KNOW--
YOU NEED TO SEE A DOCTOR.
I CAN'T PAY.
WHAT ABOUT PLANNED PARENT-HOOD?
I'M NOT PREGNANT. AT LEAST, I DON'T THINK I AM.
AND ALL THOSE PEOPLE PICKETING. THEY'LL RECOGNIZE ME.
LOOK, PLANNED PARENTHOOD DEALS WITH A LOT OF HEALTH ISSUES...
...AND IF YOU'RE WORRIED, I'LL DISTRACT THEM WHILE YOU GO INSIDE...
hood
ABORTION SHEDS INNOCENT
PRAY TO END
NO COMPROMISE

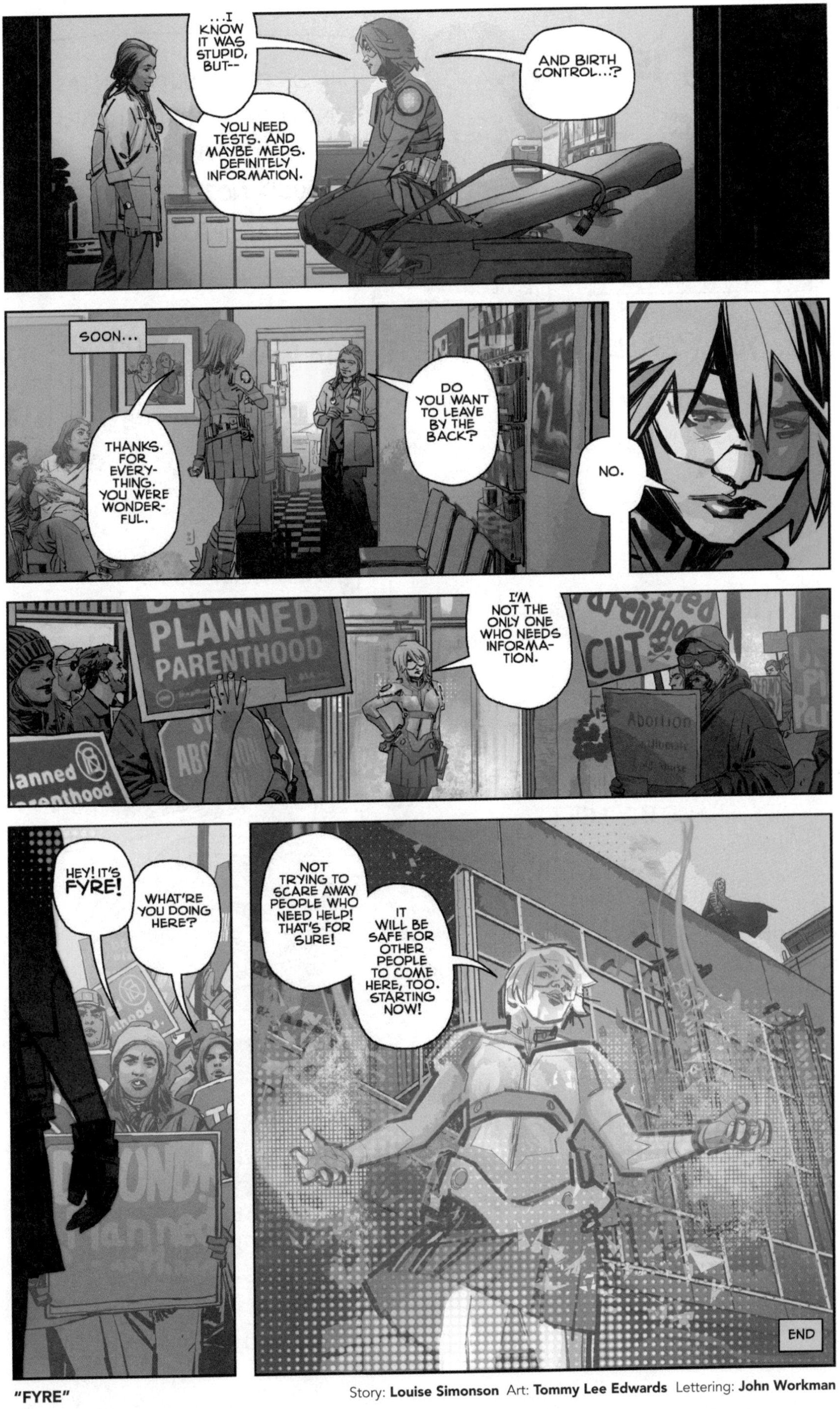
...I KNOW IT WAS STUPID, BUT--
YOU NEED TESTS. AND MAYBE MEDS. DEFINITELY INFORMATION.
AND BIRTH CONTROL...?
SOON...
THANKS. FOR EVERY-THING. YOU WERE WONDER-FUL.
DO YOU WANT TO LEAVE BY THE BACK?
NO.
PLANNED PARENTHOOD
I'M NOT THE ONLY ONE WHO NEEDS INFORMA-TION.
CUT
Abortion
HEY! IT'S FYRE!
WHAT'RE YOU DOING HERE?
NOT TRYING TO SCARE AWAY PEOPLE WHO NEED HELP! THAT'S FOR SURE!
IT WILL BE SAFE FOR OTHER PEOPLE TO COME HERE, TOO. STARTING NOW!
END

"FYRE" Story: **Louise Simonson** Art: **Tommy Lee Edwards** Lettering: **John Workman**

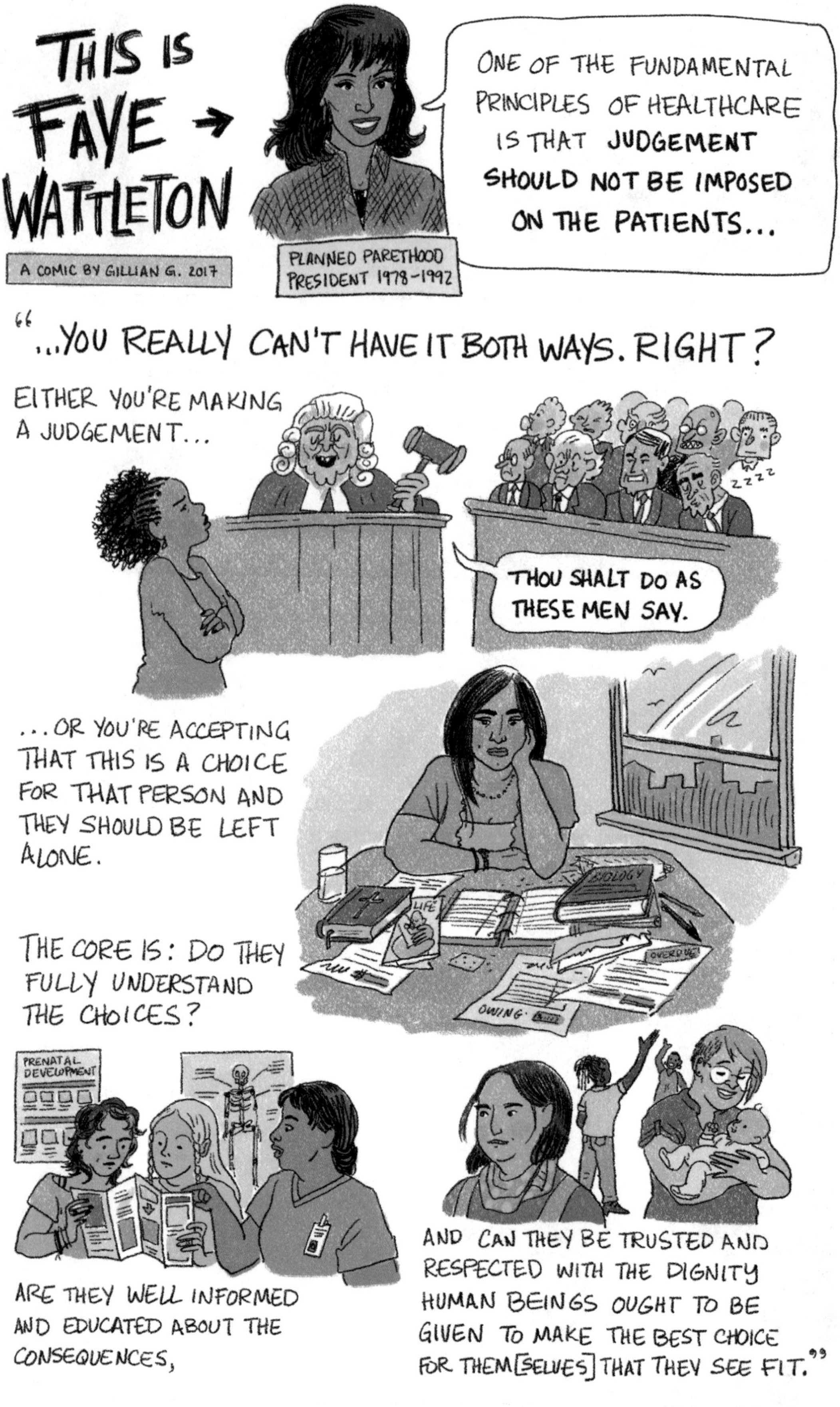
THIS IS FAYE WATTLETON
A COMIC BY GILLIAN G. 2017
PLANNED PARETHOOD PRESIDENT 1978-1992
ONE OF THE FUNDAMENTAL PRINCIPLES OF HEALTHCARE IS THAT JUDGEMENT SHOULD NOT BE IMPOSED ON THE PATIENTS...
"...YOU REALLY CAN'T HAVE IT BOTH WAYS. RIGHT?
EITHER YOU'RE MAKING A JUDGEMENT...
ZZZZ
THOU SHALT DO AS THESE MEN SAY.
...OR YOU'RE ACCEPTING THAT THIS IS A CHOICE FOR THAT PERSON AND THEY SHOULD BE LEFT ALONE.
BIOLOGY
LIFE
OVERDUE!
OWING
THE CORE IS: DO THEY FULLY UNDERSTAND THE CHOICES?
PRENATAL DEVELOPMENT
ARE THEY WELL INFORMED AND EDUCATED ABOUT THE CONSEQUENCES,
AND CAN THEY BE TRUSTED AND RESPECTED WITH THE DIGNITY HUMAN BEINGS OUGHT TO BE GIVEN TO MAKE THE BEST CHOICE FOR THEM[SELVES] THAT THEY SEE FIT."

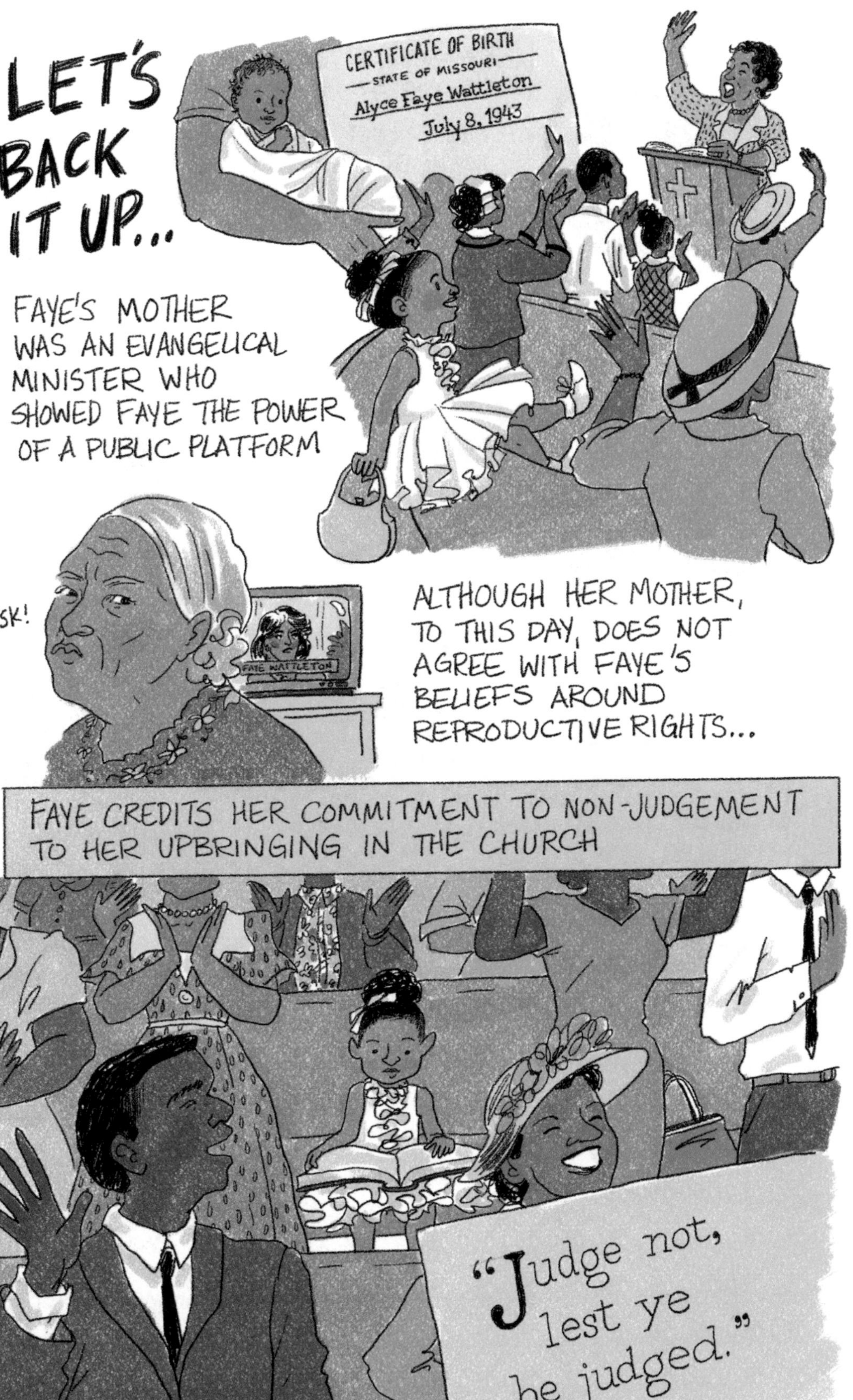

LET'S BACK IT UP...
CERTIFICATE OF BIRTH
STATE OF MISSOURI
Alyce Faye Wattleton
July 8, 1943
FAYE'S MOTHER WAS AN EVANGELICAL MINISTER WHO SHOWED FAYE THE POWER OF A PUBLIC PLATFORM
TSK!
FAYE WATTLETON
ALTHOUGH HER MOTHER, TO THIS DAY, DOES NOT AGREE WITH FAYE'S BELIEFS AROUND REPRODUCTIVE RIGHTS...
FAYE CREDITS HER COMMITMENT TO NON-JUDGEMENT TO HER UPBRINGING IN THE CHURCH
"Judge not, lest ye be judged."

BY AGE 16 FAYE WAS ENROLLED IN NURSING AT OHIO STATE UNIVERSITY.

SHE EARNED A FULL SCHOLARSHIP TO COLUMBIA, AND EARNED HER MASTERS IN MATERNAL & INFANT CARE, SPECIALIZING IN MIDWIFERY.

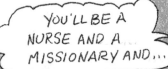

YOU'LL BE A NURSE AND A MISSIONARY AND...

WHILE HER MOTHER'S HOPES MAY HAVE LED HER TO NURSING, AN INTERSHIP IN HARLEM OPENED HER EYES TO THE REALITY OF ILLEGAL ABORTION

I TOOK CARE OF A GIRL WHO INSTILLED BLEACH & LYSOL INTO HER UTERUS TO END HER UNWANTED PREGNANCY - IT WAS HORRIFYING.

RICH WOMEN WILL ALWAYS HAVE ACCESS TO ABORTION, BUT IF THE LAW DOESN'T PROVIDE A SAFE WAY, POOR AND MARGINALIZED WOMEN WOULD SUFFER.

HER ADVOCACY BEGAN.

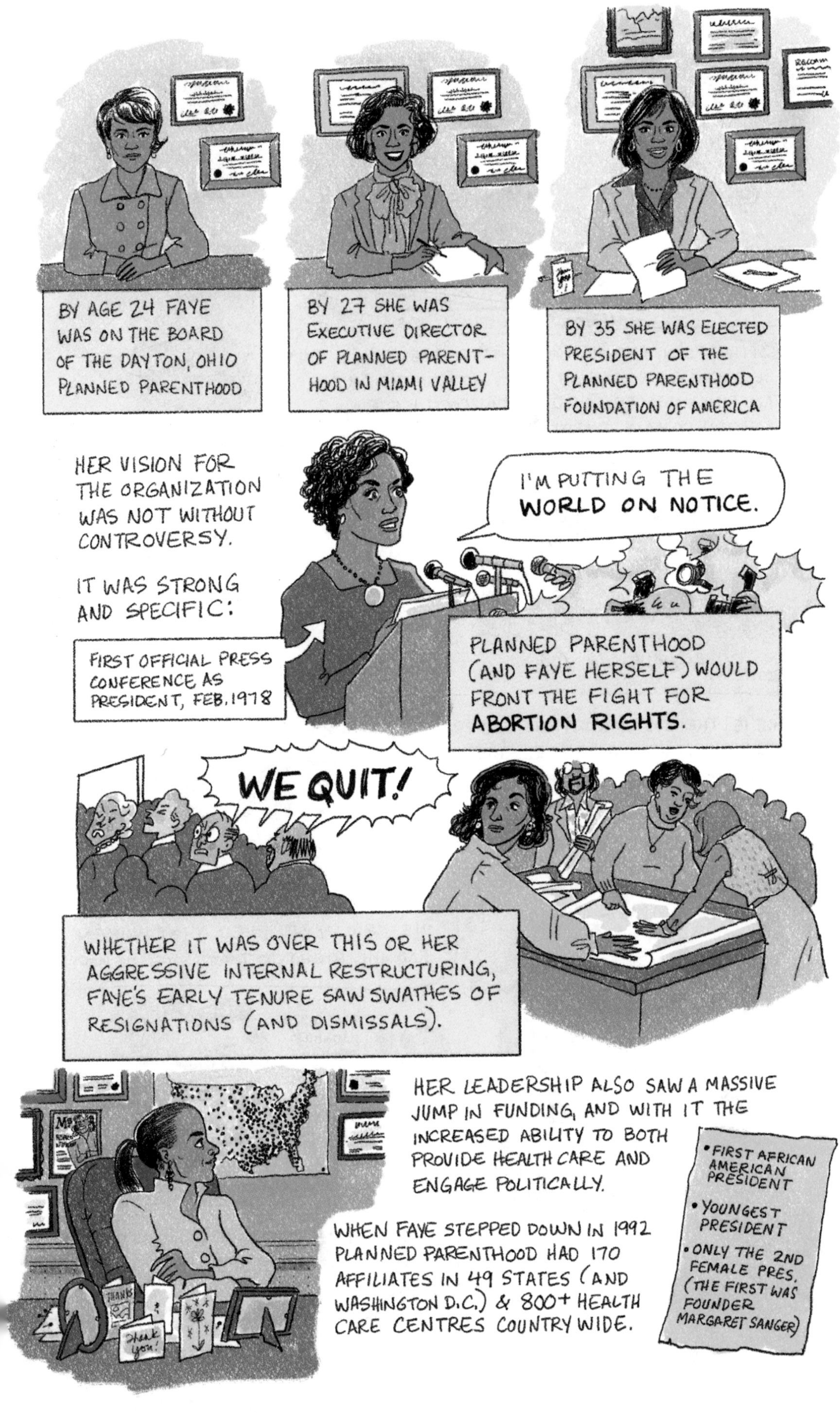
BY AGE 24 FAYE WAS ON THE BOARD OF THE DAYTON, OHIO PLANNED PARENTHOOD
BY 27 SHE WAS EXECUTIVE DIRECTOR OF PLANNED PARENT-HOOD IN MIAMI VALLEY
BY 35 SHE WAS ELECTED PRESIDENT OF THE PLANNED PARENTHOOD FOUNDATION OF AMERICA
HER VISION FOR THE ORGANIZATION WAS NOT WITHOUT CONTROVERSY.
IT WAS STRONG AND SPECIFIC:
I'M PUTTING THE WORLD ON NOTICE.
FIRST OFFICIAL PRESS CONFERENCE AS PRESIDENT, FEB. 1978
PLANNED PARENTHOOD (AND FAYE HERSELF) WOULD FRONT THE FIGHT FOR ABORTION RIGHTS.
WE QUIT!
WHETHER IT WAS OVER THIS OR HER AGGRESSIVE INTERNAL RESTRUCTURING, FAYE'S EARLY TENURE SAW SWATHES OF RESIGNATIONS (AND DISMISSALS).
HER LEADERSHIP ALSO SAW A MASSIVE JUMP IN FUNDING, AND WITH IT THE INCREASED ABILITY TO BOTH PROVIDE HEALTH CARE AND ENGAGE POLITICALLY.
WHEN FAYE STEPPED DOWN IN 1992 PLANNED PARENTHOOD HAD 170 AFFILIATES IN 49 STATES (AND WASHINGTON D.C.) & 800+ HEALTH CARE CENTRES COUNTRY WIDE.
• FIRST AFRICAN AMERICAN PRESIDENT
• YOUNGEST PRESIDENT
• ONLY THE 2ND FEMALE PRES. (THE FIRST WAS FOUNDER MARGARET SANGER)
THANKS
Thank you!

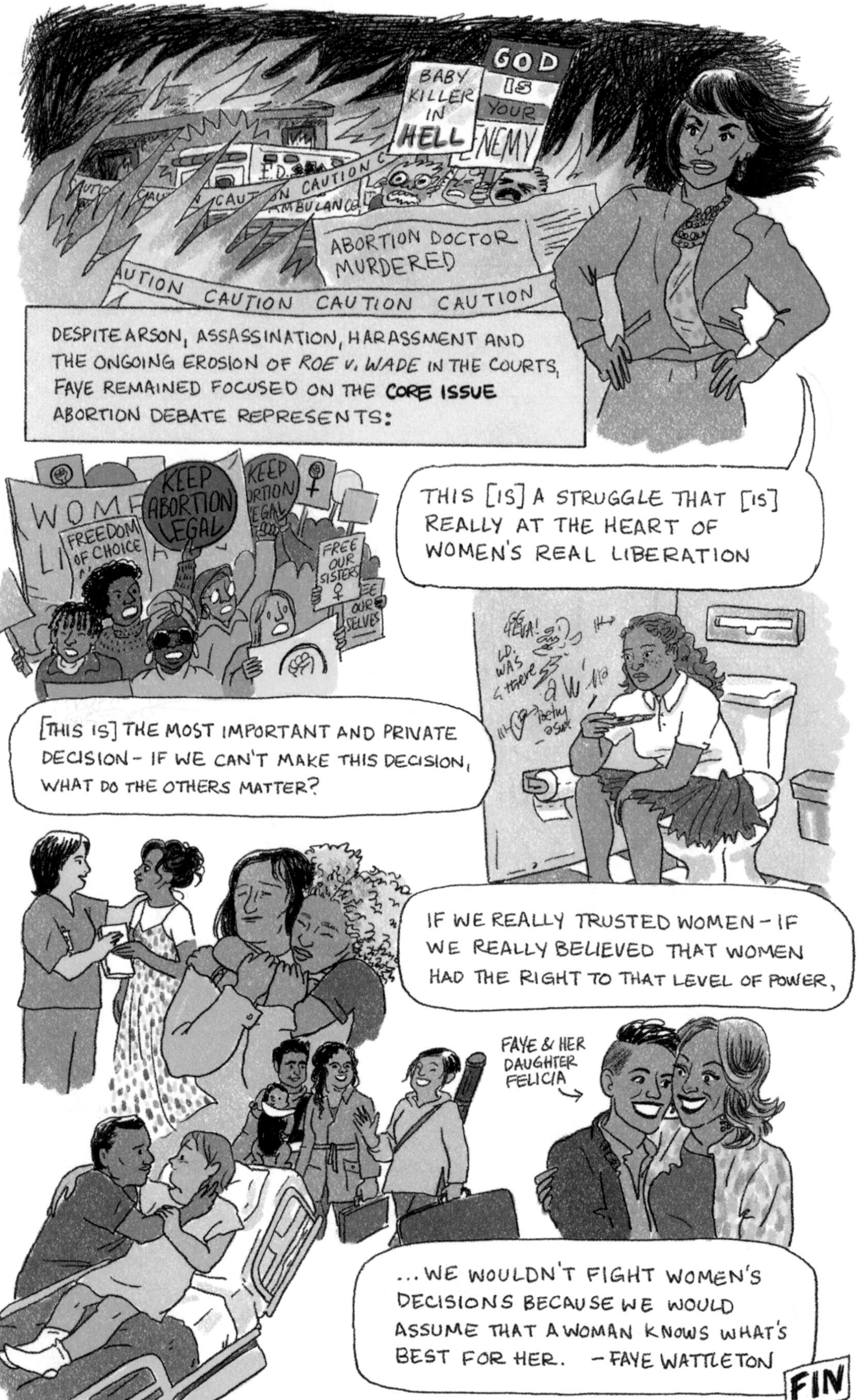
BABY KILLER IN HELL
GOD IS YOUR ENEMY
CAUTION CAUTION
AMBULANCE
ABORTION DOCTOR MURDERED
CAUTION CAUTION CAUTION CAUTION
DESPITE ARSON, ASSASSINATION, HARASSMENT AND THE ONGOING EROSION OF *ROE v. WADE* IN THE COURTS, FAYE REMAINED FOCUSED ON THE **CORE ISSUE** ABORTION DEBATE REPRESENTS:
THIS [IS] A STRUGGLE THAT [IS] REALLY AT THE HEART OF WOMEN'S REAL LIBERATION
KEEP ABORTION LEGAL
FREEDOM OF CHOICE
FREE OUR SISTERS
OUR SELVES
[THIS IS] THE MOST IMPORTANT AND PRIVATE DECISION - IF WE CAN'T MAKE THIS DECISION, WHAT DO THE OTHERS MATTER?
IF WE REALLY TRUSTED WOMEN - IF WE REALLY BELIEVED THAT WOMEN HAD THE RIGHT TO THAT LEVEL OF POWER,
FAYE & HER DAUGHTER FELICIA
...WE WOULDN'T FIGHT WOMEN'S DECISIONS BECAUSE WE WOULD ASSUME THAT A WOMAN KNOWS WHAT'S BEST FOR HER. - FAYE WATTLETON
FIN

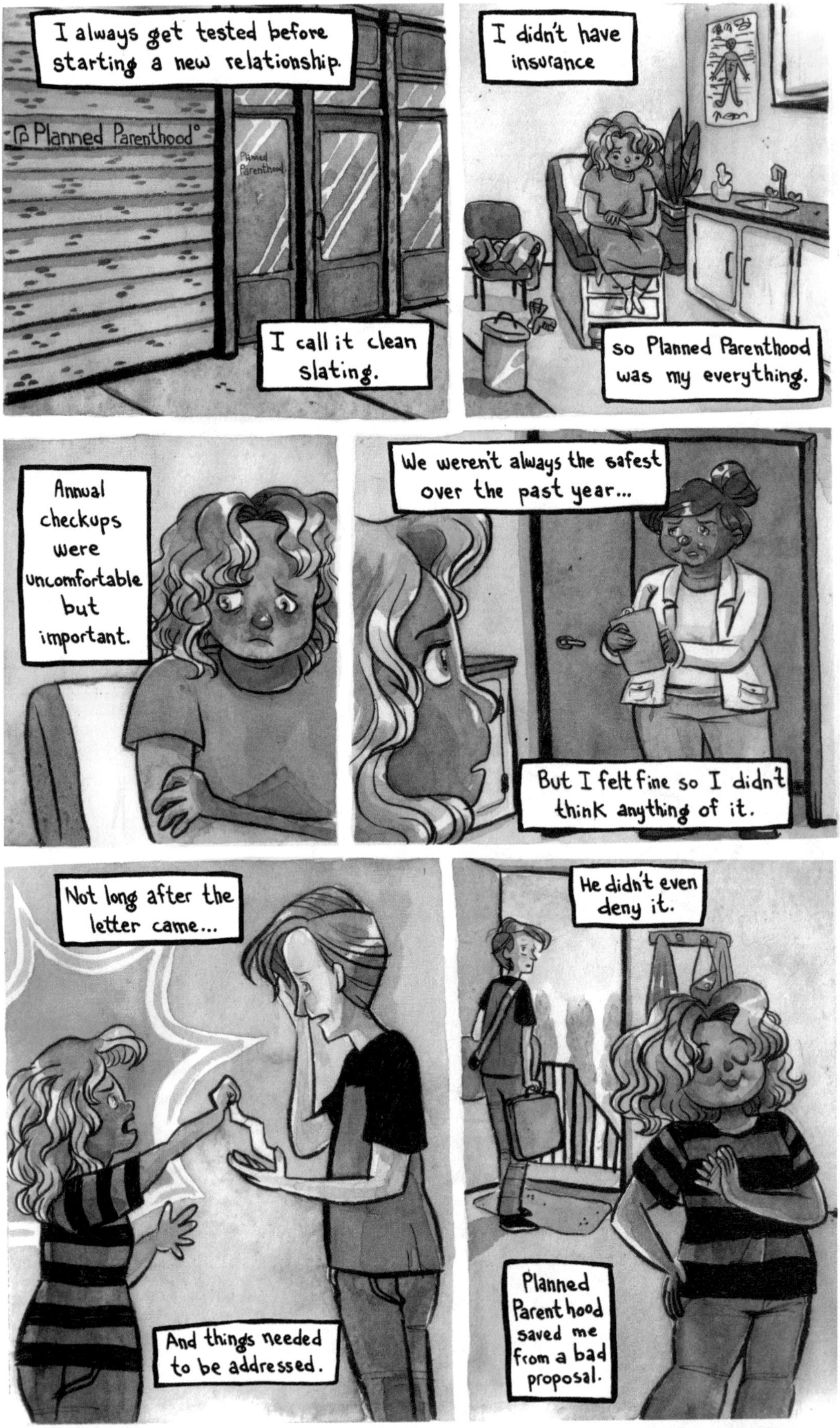
I always get tested before starting a new relationship.
Planned Parenthood
Planned Parenthood
I call it clean slating.
I didn't have insurance
so Planned Parenthood was my everything.
Annual checkups were uncomfortable but important.
We weren't always the safest over the past year...
But I felt fine so I didn't think anything of it.
Not long after the letter came...
And things needed to be addressed.
He didn't even deny it.
Planned Parenthood saved me from a bad proposal.

"BAD PROPOSAL"

Story: **Sheliah Villari** Art: **Robby Barrett**

I feel like I'm in a movie. Starring me.

What would happen if I just turn around and walk back down the aisle and out the door, out of the temple? Like Katherine Ross at the end of The Graduate.

I should do it. Do it now, before it's too late.

It's not him. He's a nice guy, I like him. And he looks amazing in his tux. (He gives me a wink and smile.) Maybe I could love him. I don't know.

The only thing I do know is that I don't want to get married now. To anybody. There are places to go, people to see, like Ann Margaret sang in Bye Bye Birdie.

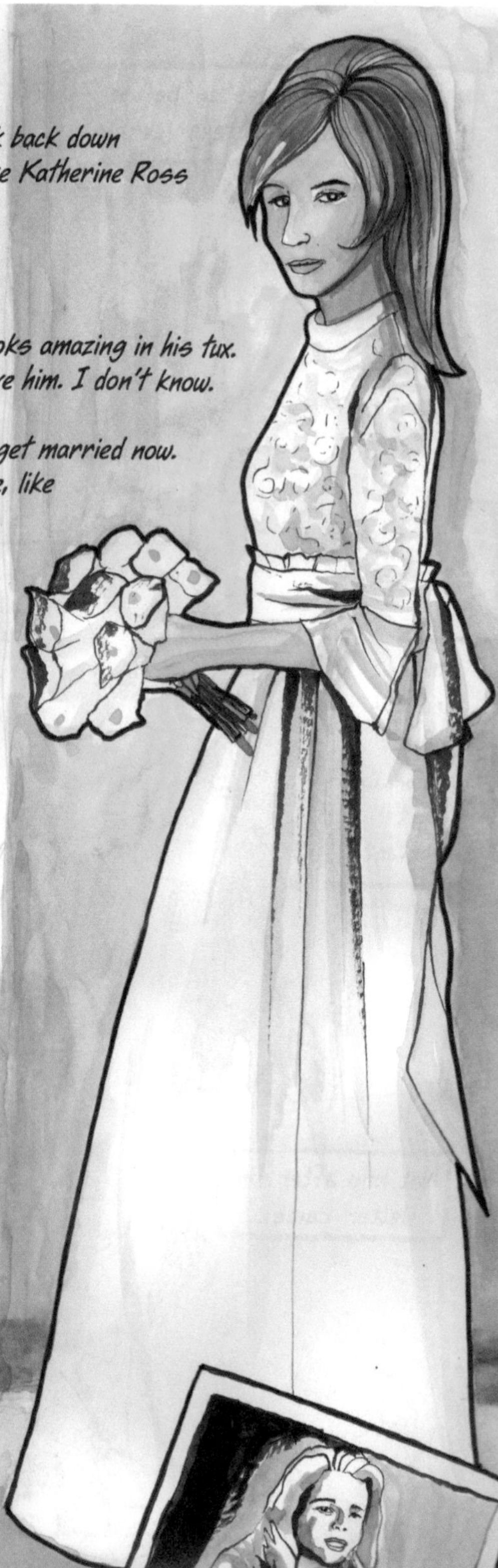

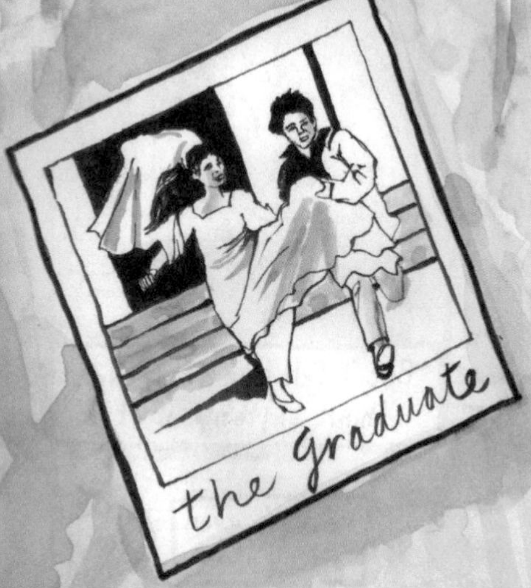
the Graduate

Everything is storybook beautiful. The chuppa made of roses, the white beeswax candles in filigreed silver candlesticks, the red wine in her grandfather's goblet that he brought all the way from Poland. Her parents, and his, proud and happy and weepy in their gowns and tuxedos. The rabbi, with a twinkle in his eye. The guests, dressed up and ready to party.

How did I end up here?

I should have said no.

But I didn't.

I never do.

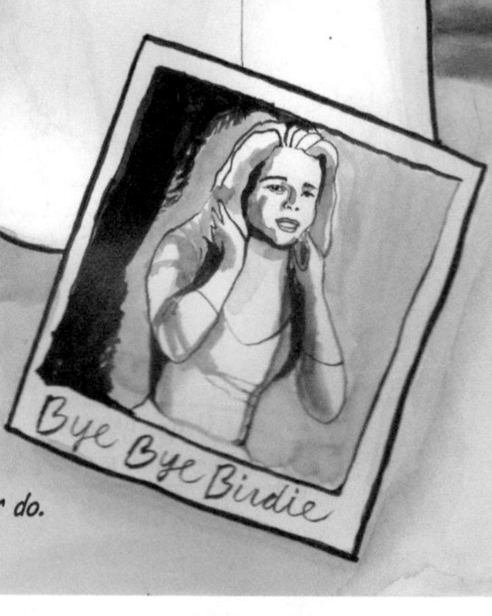
Bye Bye Birdie

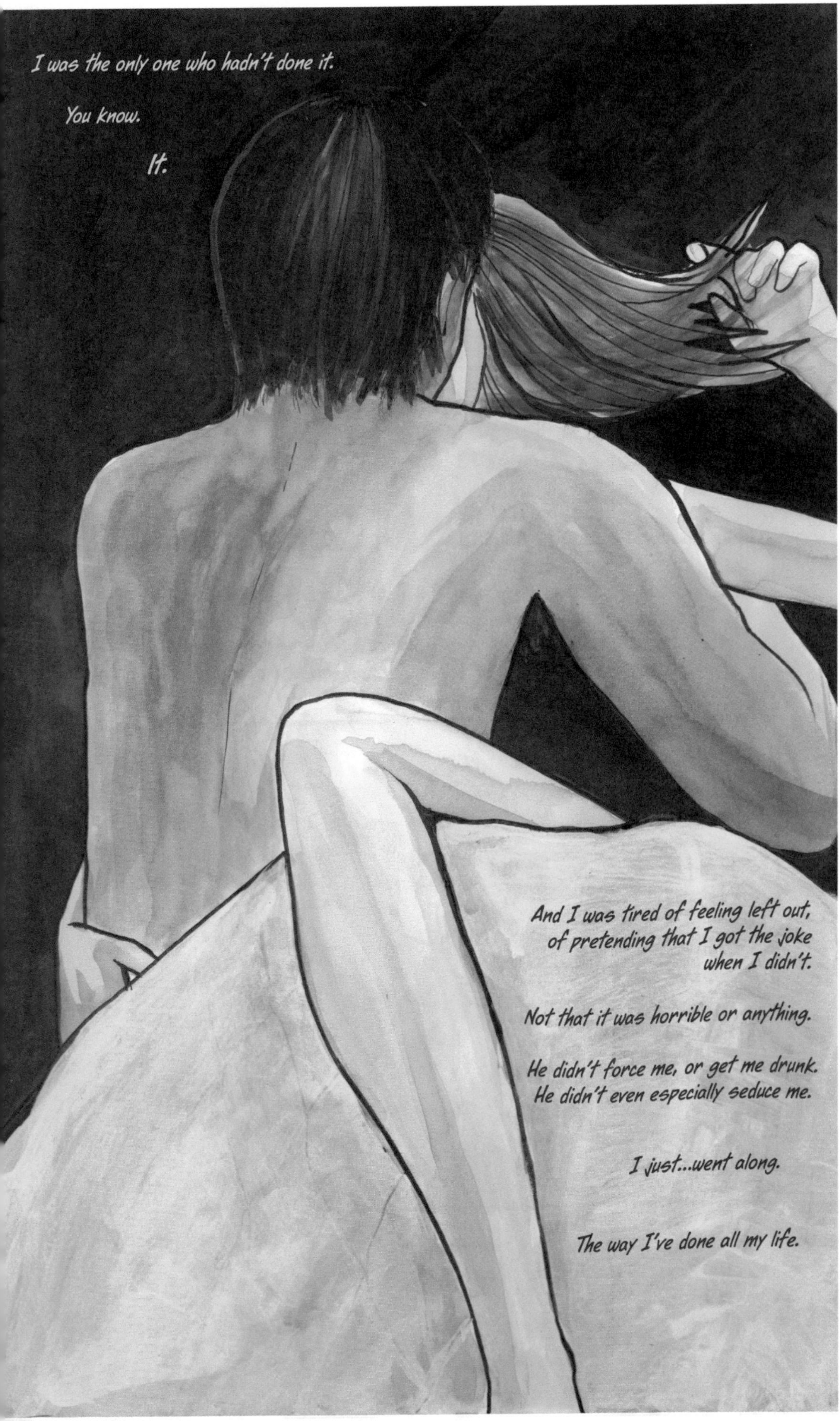
I was the only one who hadn't done it.
You know.
It.
And I was tired of feeling left out, of pretending that I got the joke when I didn't.
Not that it was horrible or anything.
He didn't force me, or get me drunk. He didn't even especially seduce me.
I just...went along.
The way I've done all my life.

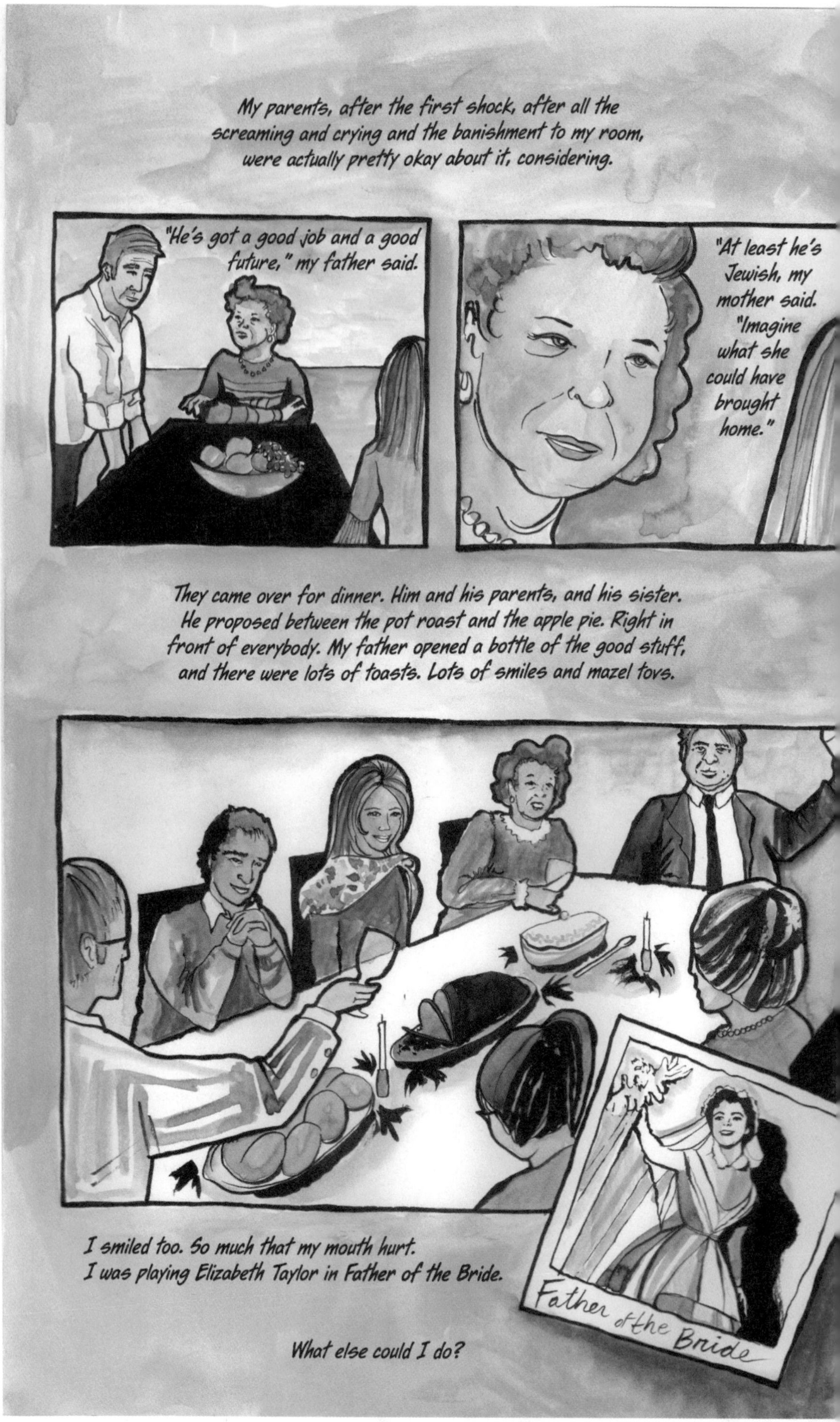
My parents, after the first shock, after all the screaming and crying and the banishment to my room, were actually pretty okay about it, considering.
"He's got a good job and a good future," my father said.
"At least he's Jewish, my mother said. "Imagine what she could have brought home."
They came over for dinner. Him and his parents, and his sister. He proposed between the pot roast and the apple pie. Right in front of everybody. My father opened a bottle of the good stuff, and there were lots of toasts. Lots of smiles and mazel tovs.
I smiled too. So much that my mouth hurt. I was playing Elizabeth Taylor in Father of the Bride.
Father of the Bride
What else could I do?

Barefoot in the Park

We talked about the honeymoon. I wanted to go to New York City. Stay at the Plaza like Robert Redford and Jane Fonda in Barefoot in the Park. Go to plays and Radio City Music Hall and ride the Staten Island Ferry.

He wanted to go to Miami Beach. Stay at the Fontainebleau.

"We were there when I was a kid. Daddy taught me how to swim in the hotel pool."

"Well, we weren't rich like you."

"We're not rich."

"Poor little rich girl. Has to get married to a poor schmuck like me."

"You're not a poor schmuck."

It was a huge fight.

I went to the diner and had three cups of coffee. I called Peggy.

"I want a divorce."

"You're not even married yet."

"I can't marry him."

"Well, you gotta. What else can you do?"

"I can get rid of it."

"Are you nuts? It's illegal."

"I can't do this, Peggy."

"Yeah, you can. So you had a fight. Big deal. You should be there when Drew and I go at it. You want to see a fight? I'll show you a fight.

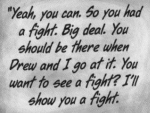

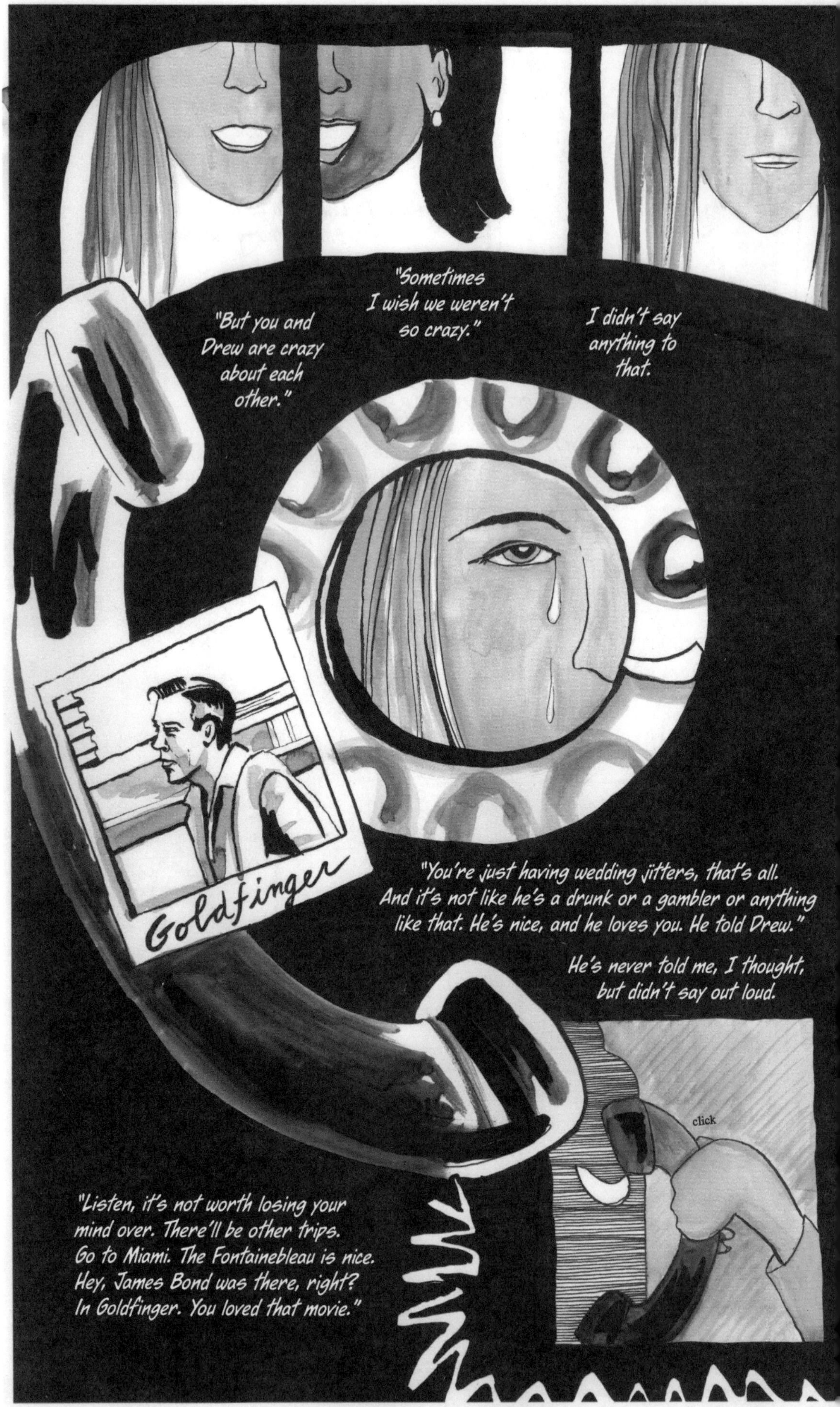

"But you and Drew are crazy about each other."
"Sometimes I wish we weren't so crazy."
I didn't say anything to that.
Goldfinger
"You're just having wedding jitters, that's all. And it's not like he's a drunk or a gambler or anything like that. He's nice, and he loves you. He told Drew."
He's never told me, I thought, but didn't say out loud.
click
"Listen, it's not worth losing your mind over. There'll be other trips. Go to Miami. The Fontainebleau is nice. Hey, James Bond was there, right? In Goldfinger. You loved that movie."

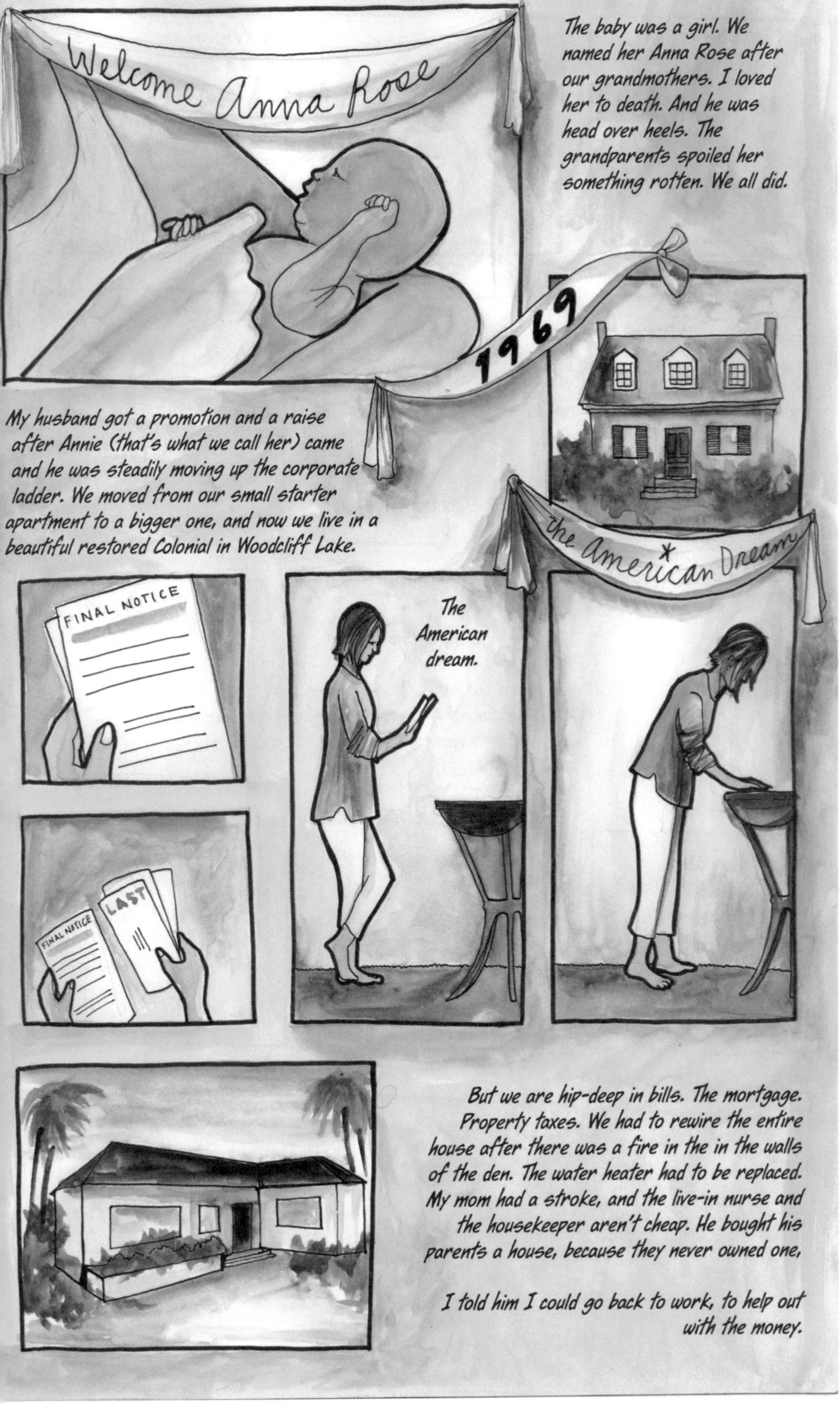
Welcome Anna Rose
The baby was a girl. We named her Anna Rose after our grandmothers. I loved her to death. And he was head over heels. The grandparents spoiled her something rotten. We all did.
1969
My husband got a promotion and a raise after Annie (that's what we call her) came and he was steadily moving up the corporate ladder. We moved from our small starter apartment to a bigger one, and now we live in a beautiful restored Colonial in Woodcliff Lake.
the American* Dream
FINAL NOTICE
FINAL NOTICE
LAST
The American dream.
But we are hip-deep in bills. The mortgage. Property taxes. We had to rewire the entire house after there was a fire in the in the walls of the den. The water heater had to be replaced. My mom had a stroke, and the live-in nurse and the housekeeper aren't cheap. He bought his parents a house, because they never owned one,
I told him I could go back to work, to help out with the money.

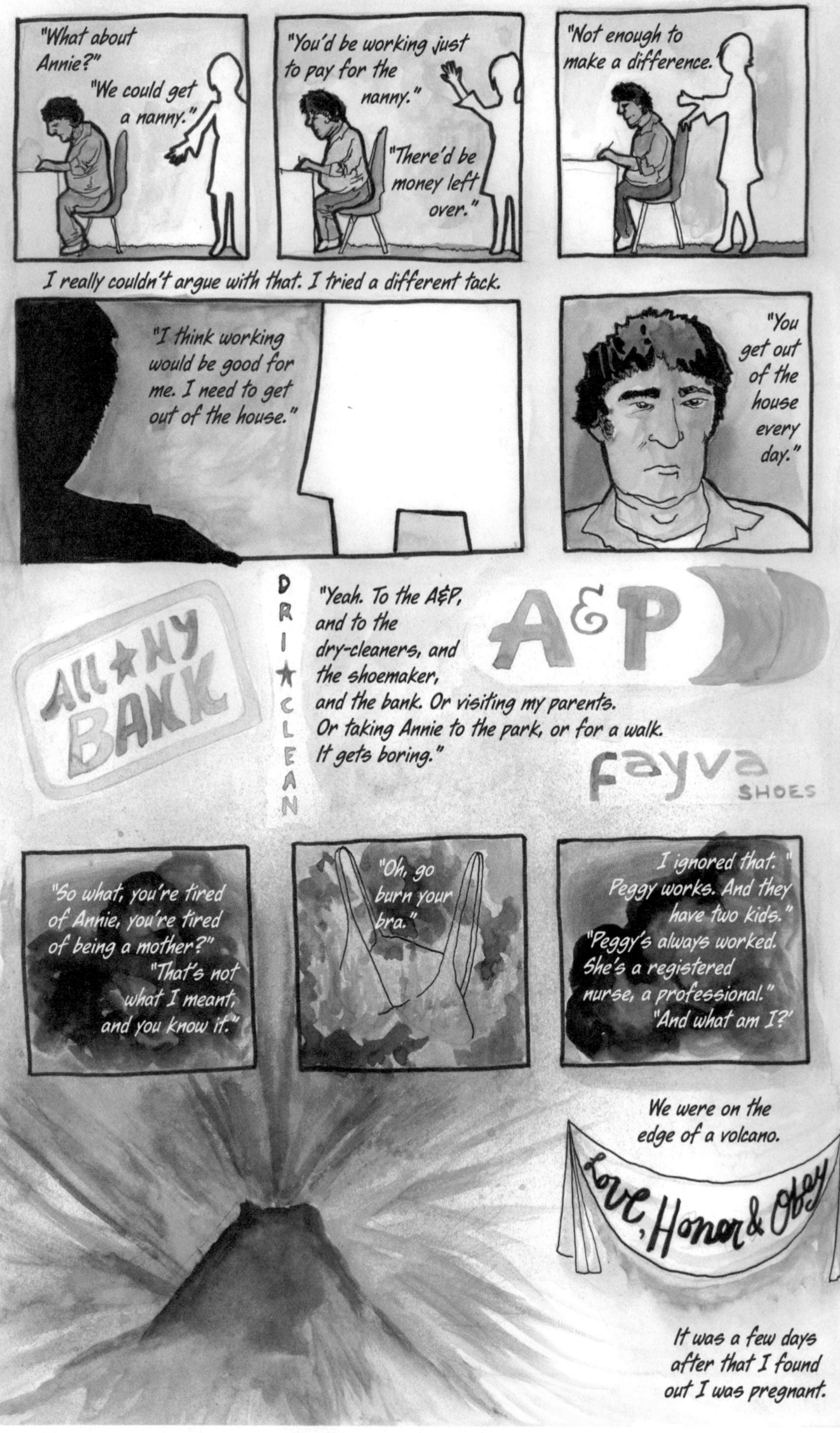

"What about Annie?"
"We could get a nanny."
"You'd be working just to pay for the nanny."
"There'd be money left over."
"Not enough to make a difference."
I really couldn't argue with that. I tried a different tack.
"I think working would be good for me. I need to get out of the house."
"You get out of the house every day."
"Yeah. To the A&P, and to the dry-cleaners, and the shoemaker, and the bank. Or visiting my parents. Or taking Annie to the park, or for a walk. It gets boring."
All★NY BANK
DRI★CLEAN
A&P
fayva SHOES
"So what, you're tired of Annie, you're tired of being a mother?"
"That's not what I meant, and you know it."
"Oh, go burn your bra."
I ignored that. "Peggy works. And they have two kids."
"Peggy's always worked. She's a registered nurse, a professional."
"And what am I?"
We were on the edge of a volcano.
Love, Honor & Obey
It was a few days after that I found out I was pregnant.

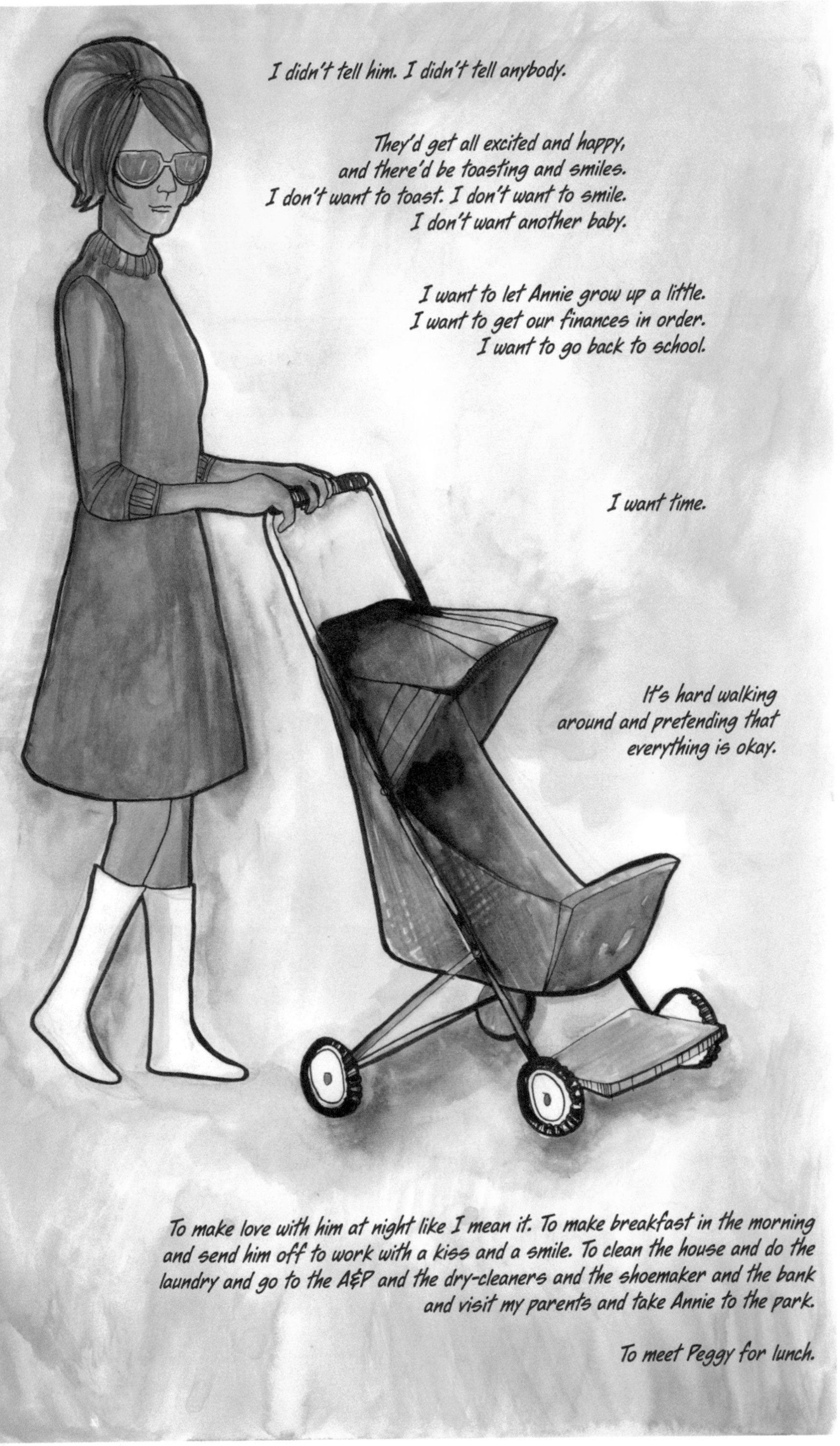
I didn't tell him. I didn't tell anybody.
They'd get all excited and happy, and there'd be toasting and smiles. I don't want to toast. I don't want to smile. I don't want another baby.
I want to let Annie grow up a little. I want to get our finances in order. I want to go back to school.
I want time.
It's hard walking around and pretending that everything is okay.
To make love with him at night like I mean it. To make breakfast in the morning and send him off to work with a kiss and a smile. To clean the house and do the laundry and go to the A&P and the dry-cleaners and the shoemaker and the bank and visit my parents and take Annie to the park.
To meet Peggy for lunch.

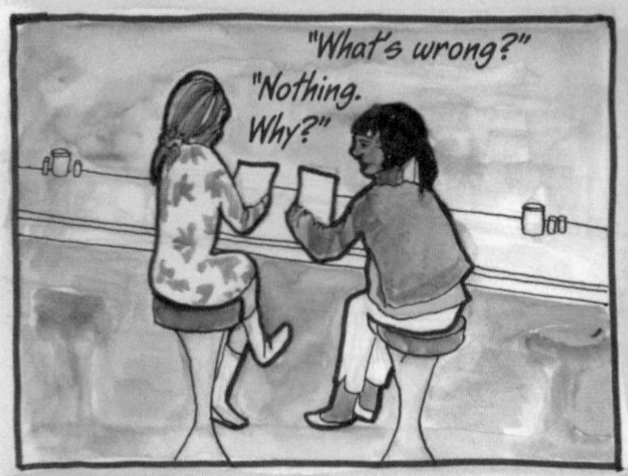
"What's wrong?"
"Nothing.
Why?"

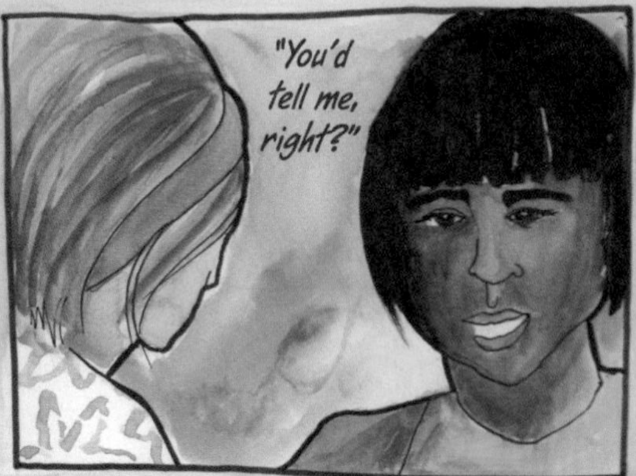
"You'd
tell me,
right?"

"Peggy, stop being my mother.
Everything's fine. Where's the
waitress, I'm hungry."

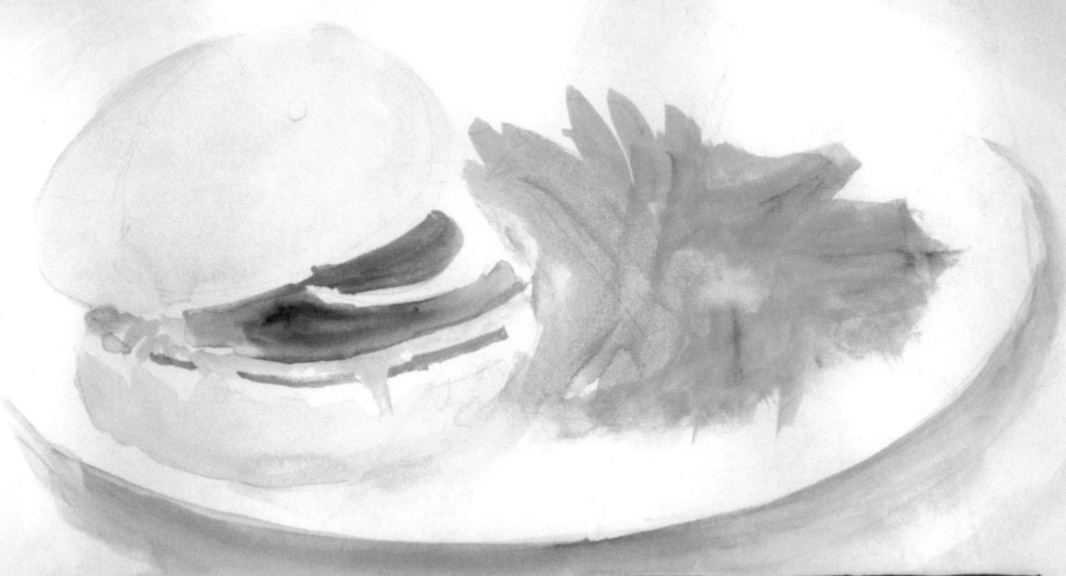

What I really am is nauseous, and
the diner smells are making it worse.
Food is the last thing I want.

I order the Hamburger Deluxe.
I force myself to eat
everything on the plate.

And I make a decision.

I wish Peggy would stop looking at
me like that.

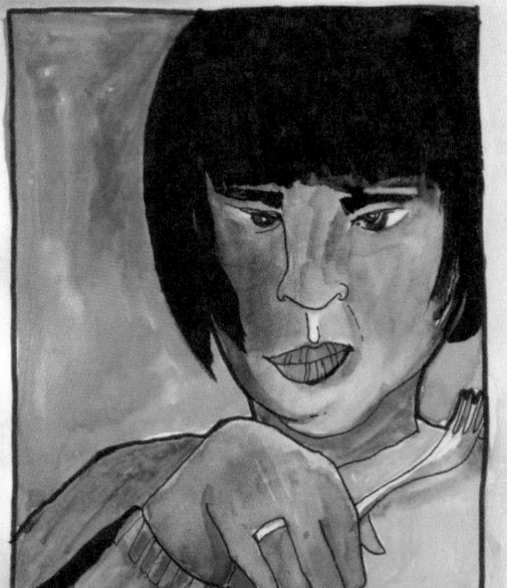

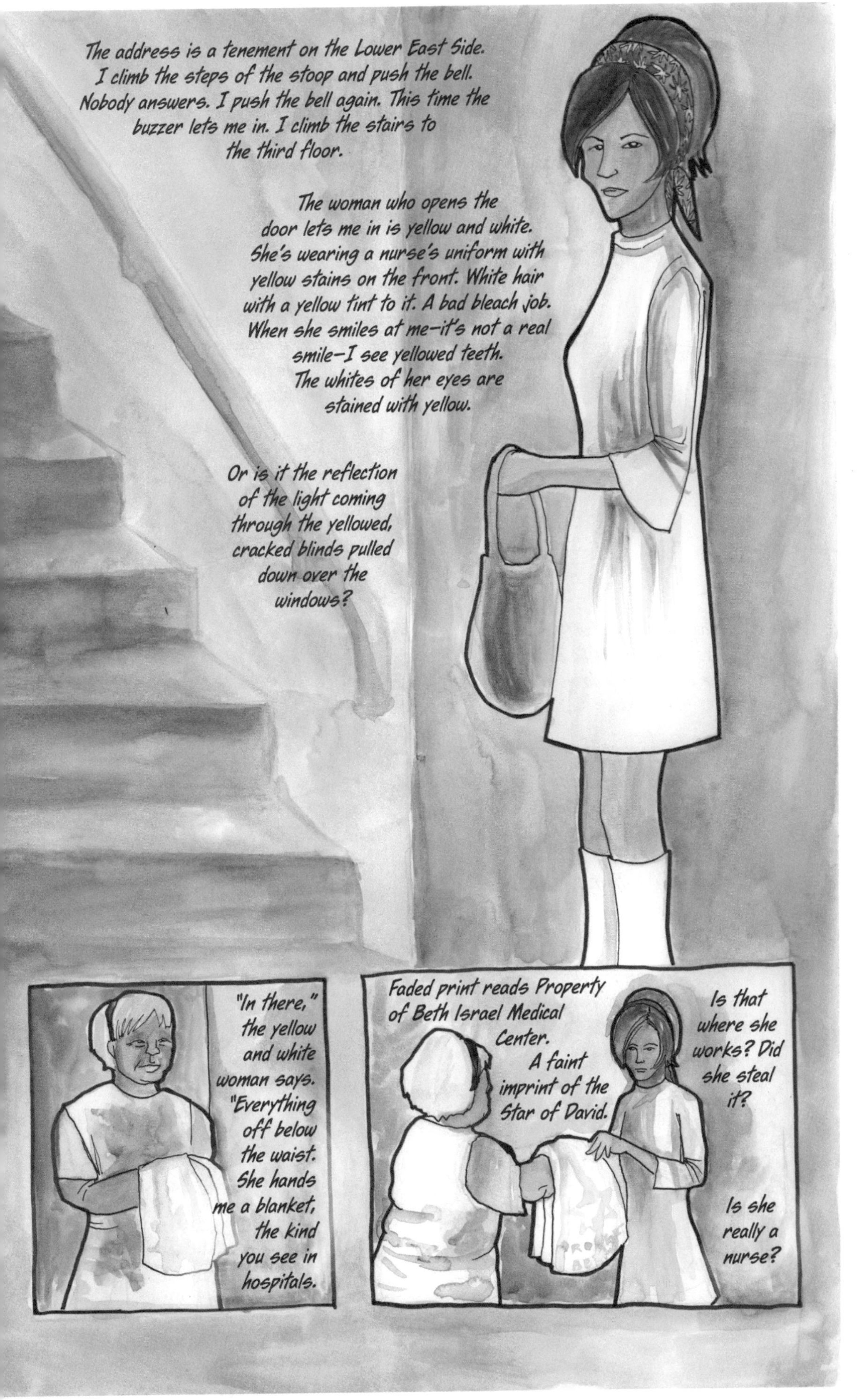

The address is a tenement on the Lower East Side. I climb the steps of the stoop and push the bell. Nobody answers. I push the bell again. This time the buzzer lets me in. I climb the stairs to the third floor.
The woman who opens the door lets me in is yellow and white. She's wearing a nurse's uniform with yellow stains on the front. White hair with a yellow tint to it. A bad bleach job. When she smiles at me—it's not a real smile—I see yellowed teeth. The whites of her eyes are stained with yellow.
Or is it the reflection of the light coming through the yellowed, cracked blinds pulled down over the windows?
"In there," the yellow and white woman says. "Everything off below the waist. She hands me a blanket, the kind you see in hospitals.
Faded print reads Property of Beth Israel Medical Center.
A faint imprint of the Star of David.
Is that where she works? Did she steal it?
Is she really a nurse?

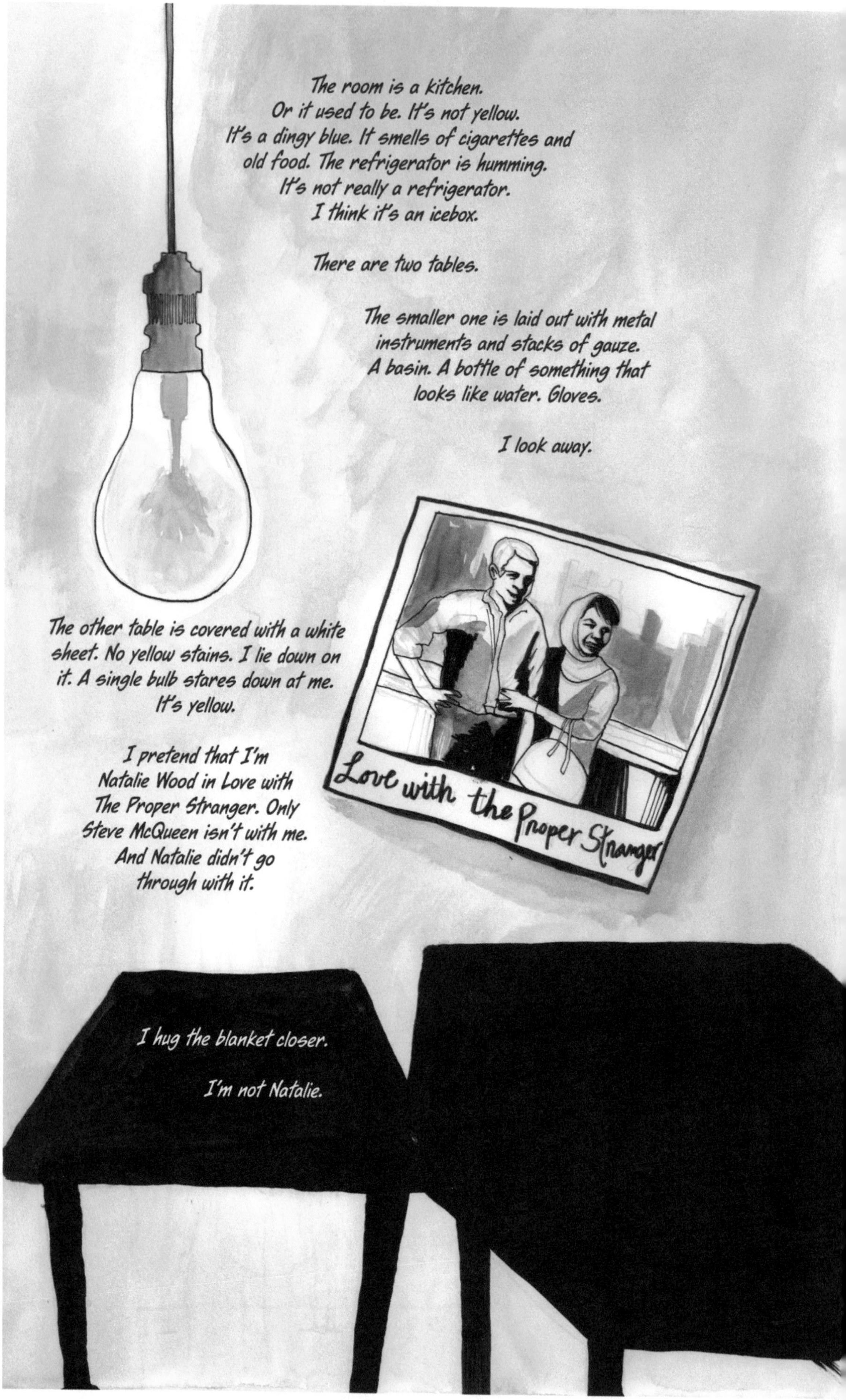

The room is a kitchen. Or it used to be. It's not yellow. It's a dingy blue. It smells of cigarettes and old food. The refrigerator is humming. It's not really a refrigerator. I think it's an icebox.
There are two tables.
The smaller one is laid out with metal instruments and stacks of gauze. A basin. A bottle of something that looks like water. Gloves.
I look away.
Love with the Proper Stranger
The other table is covered with a white sheet. No yellow stains. I lie down on it. A single bulb stares down at me. It's yellow.
I pretend that I'm Natalie Wood in Love with The Proper Stranger. Only Steve McQueen isn't with me. And Natalie didn't go through with it.
I hug the blanket closer.
I'm not Natalie.

I stare up at the yellow bulb,
but out of the corner of my eye I see the woman come in,
go to the sink and wash her hands.

I have an impression of rust-tinged water, but I'm not sure.
She wipes her hands with a dish towel.

"Open your legs and
bend your knees."
I obey.

"Wider."
I spread them.

"Move down so you're on the edge of the table."
I shimmy down. She fiddles down there. I feel her fingers entering me, and
her hand is pushing down on my stomach. She pours something between my
legs, cold and wet. I hear it dripping onto the floor.

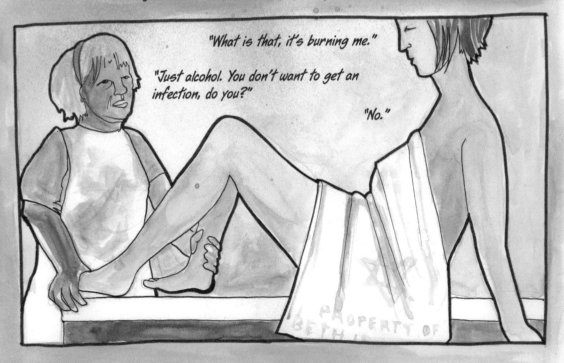

"What is that, it's burning me."

"Just alcohol. You don't want to get an
infection, do you?"

"No."

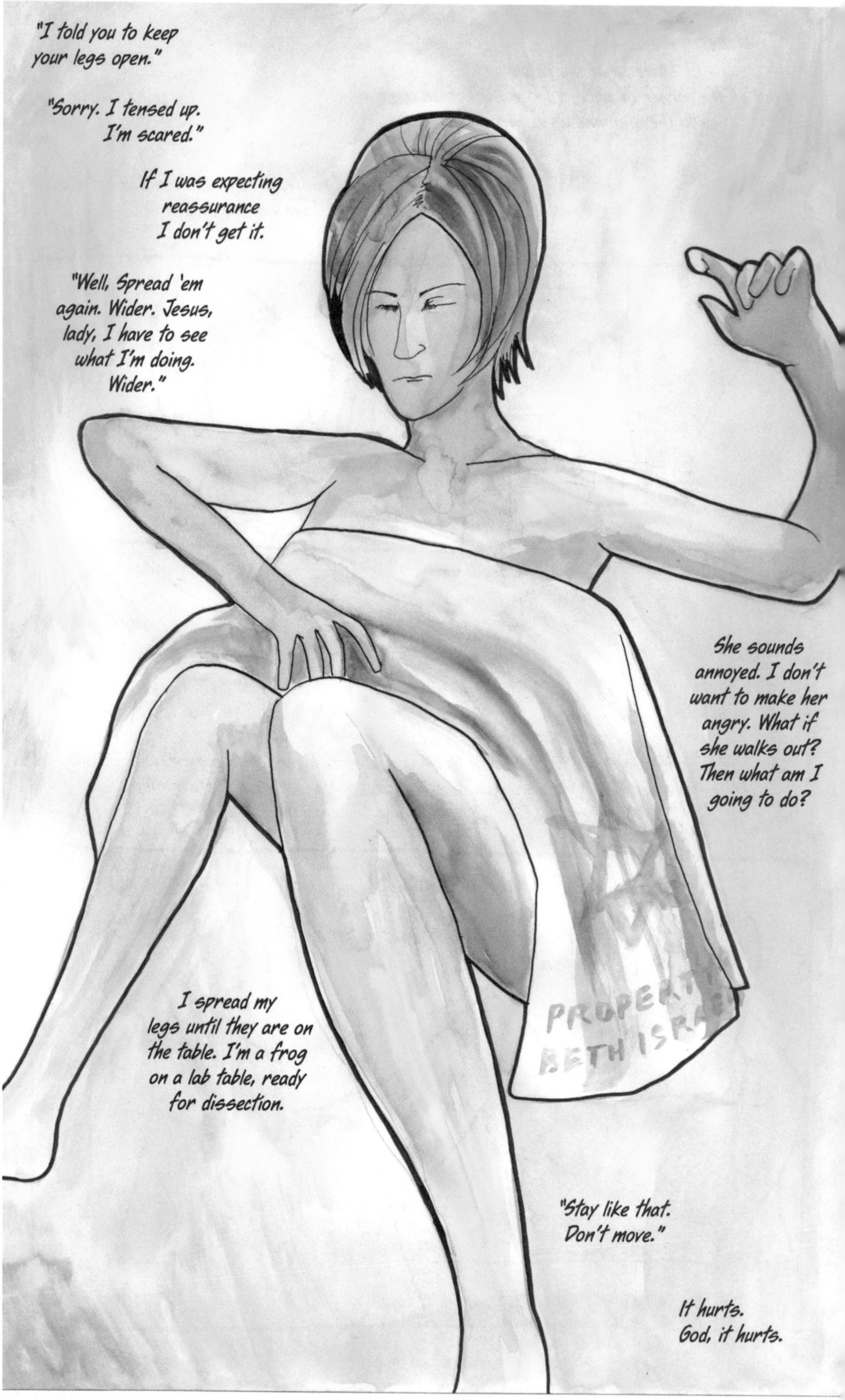
"I told you to keep your legs open."
"Sorry. I tensed up. I'm scared."
If I was expecting reassurance I don't get it.
"Well, Spread 'em again. Wider. Jesus, lady, I have to see what I'm doing. Wider."
She sounds annoyed. I don't want to make her angry. What if she walks out? Then what am I going to do?
I spread my legs until they are on the table. I'm a frog on a lab table, ready for dissection.
"Stay like that. Don't move."
It hurts. God, it hurts.

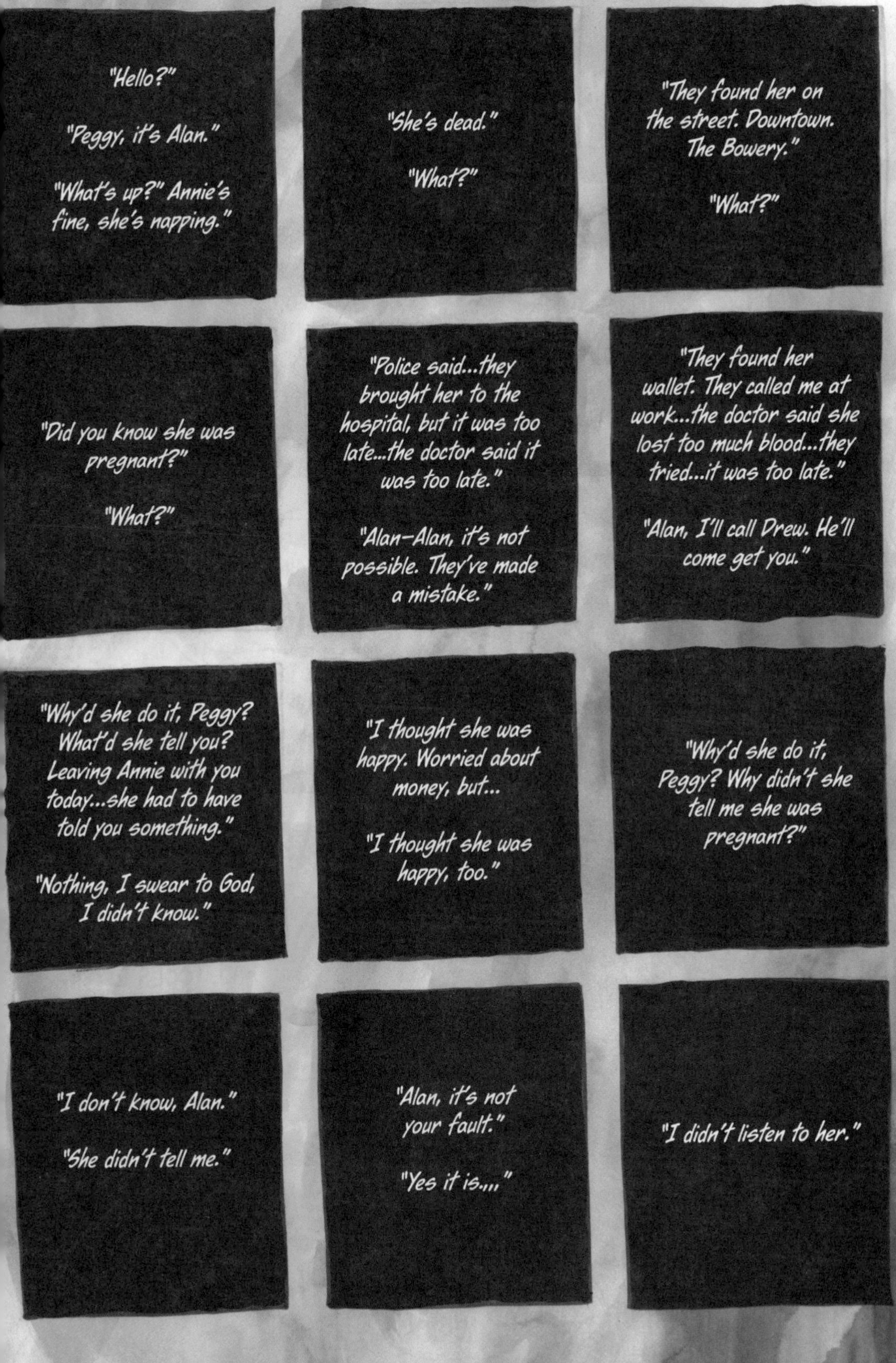
"Hello?"
"Peggy, it's Alan."
"What's up?" Annie's fine, she's napping."
"She's dead."
"What?"
"They found her on the street. Downtown. The Bowery."
"What?"
"Did you know she was pregnant?"
"What?"
"Police said...they brought her to the hospital, but it was too late...the doctor said it was too late."
"Alan—Alan, it's not possible. They've made a mistake."
"They found her wallet. They called me at work...the doctor said she lost too much blood...they tried...it was too late."
"Alan, I'll call Drew. He'll come get you."
"Why'd she do it, Peggy? What'd she tell you? Leaving Annie with you today...she had to have told you something."
"Nothing, I swear to God, I didn't know."
"I thought she was happy. Worried about money, but...
"I thought she was happy, too."
"Why'd she do it, Peggy? Why didn't she tell me she was pregnant?"
"I don't know, Alan."
"She didn't tell me."
"Alan, it's not your fault."
"Yes it is...."
"I didn't listen to her."

"THE BRIDE"

Story: **Mindy Newell** Art: **Andrea Shockling** Lettering: **Christy Sawyer**

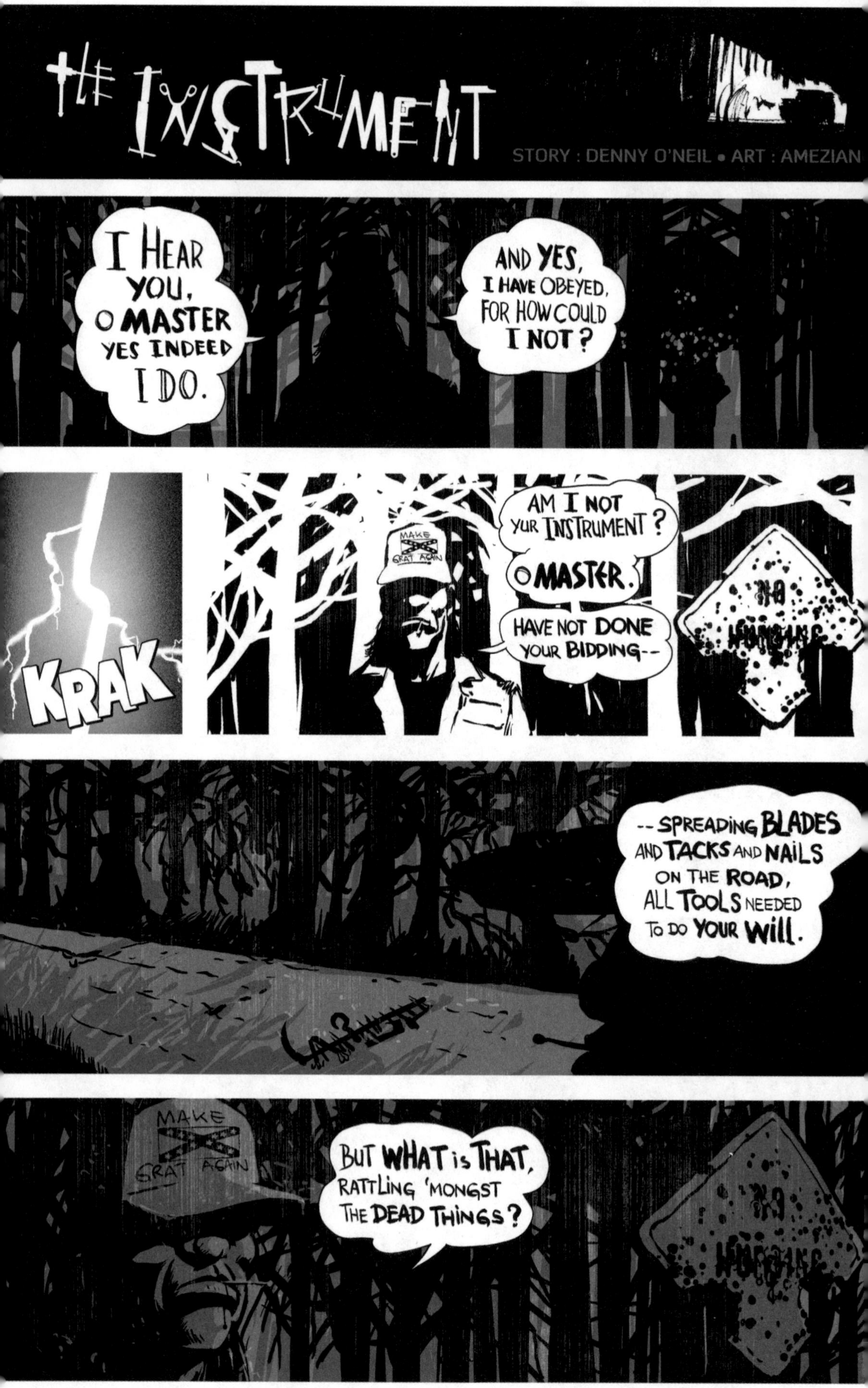
THE INSTRUMENT
STORY : DENNY O'NEIL • ART : AMEZIAN
I HEAR YOU, O MASTER YES INDEED I DO.
AND YES, I HAVE OBEYED, FOR HOW COULD I NOT?
KRAK
MAKE GRAT AGAIN
AM I NOT YUR INSTRUMENT?
O MASTER.
HAVE NOT DONE YOUR BIDDING--
--SPREADING BLADES AND TACKS AND NAILS ON THE ROAD, ALL TOOLS NEEDED TO DO YOUR WILL.
MAKE GRAT AGAIN
BUT WHAT IS THAT, RATTLING 'MONGST THE DEAD THINGS?

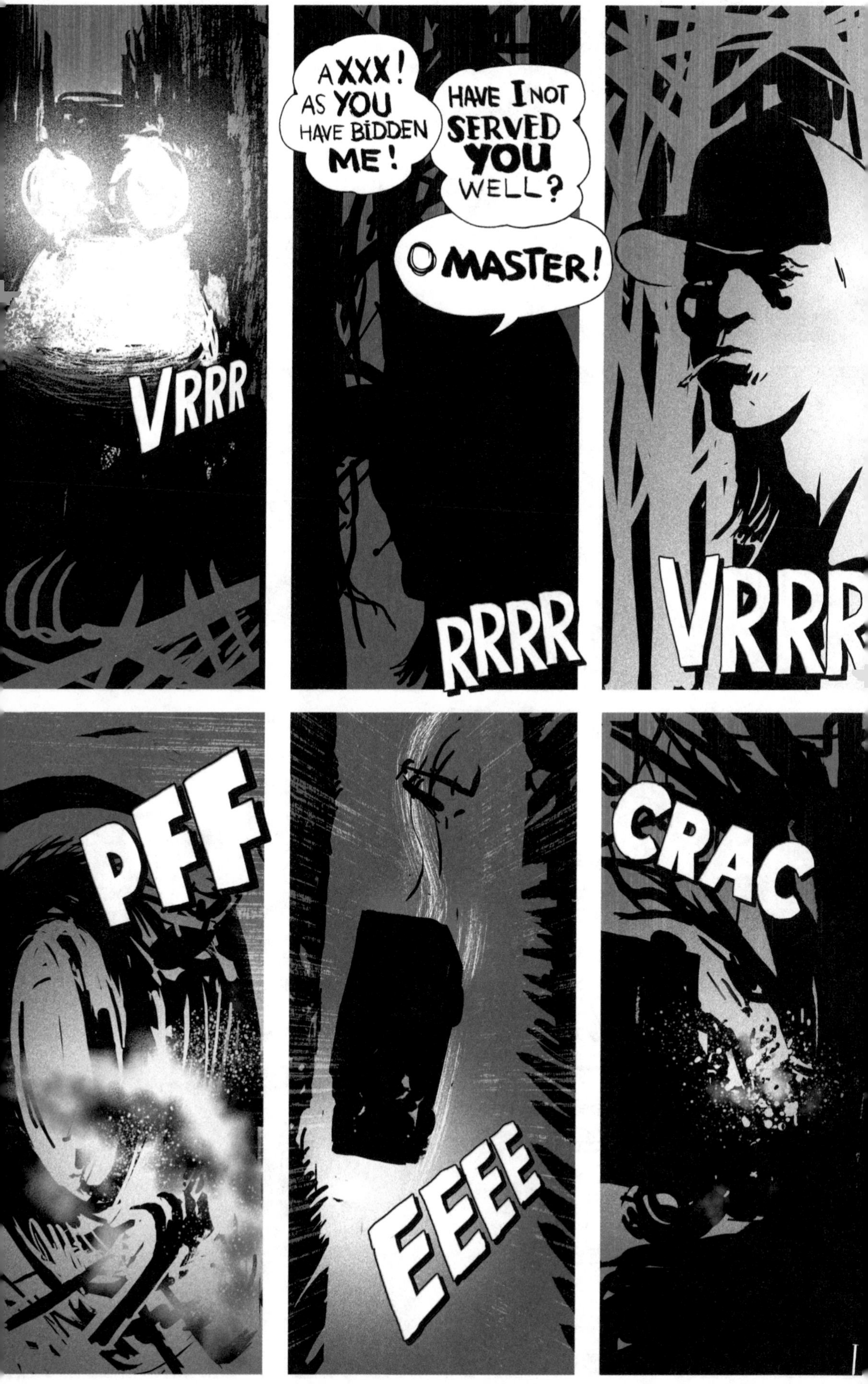
VRRR
AXXX! AS YOU HAVE BIDDEN ME!
HAVE I NOT SERVED YOU WELL?
O MASTER!
RRRR
VRRR
PFF
EEEE
CRAC

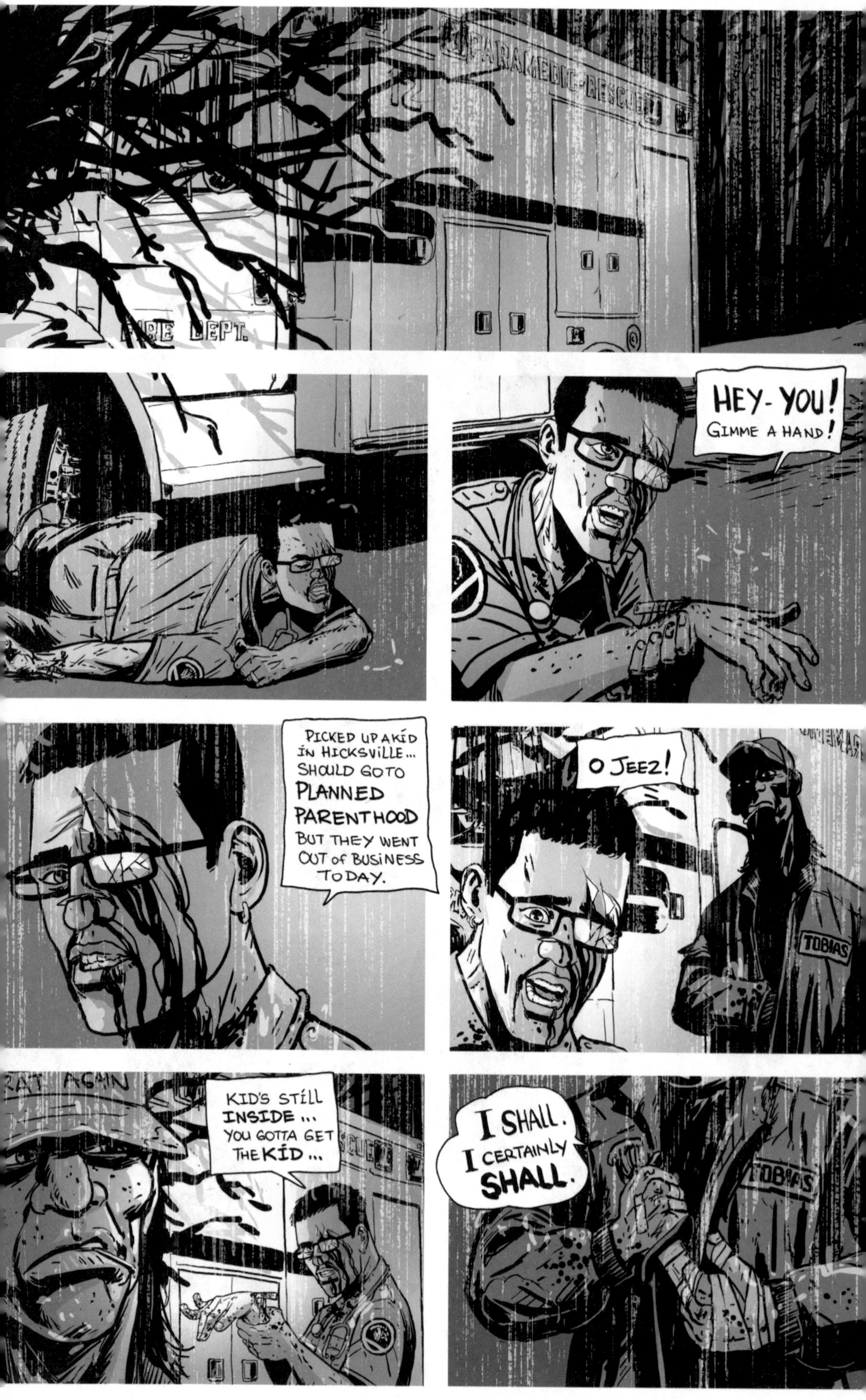
PARAMEDIC-RESCUE
FIRE DEPT.
HEY- YOU! GIMME A HAND!
PICKED UP A KID IN HICKSVILLE... SHOULD GO TO PLANNED PARENTHOOD BUT THEY WENT OUT OF BUSINESS TODAY.
O JEEZ!
TOBIAS
KID'S STILL INSIDE... YOU GOTTA GET THE KID...
I SHALL. I CERTAINLY SHALL.
TOBIAS

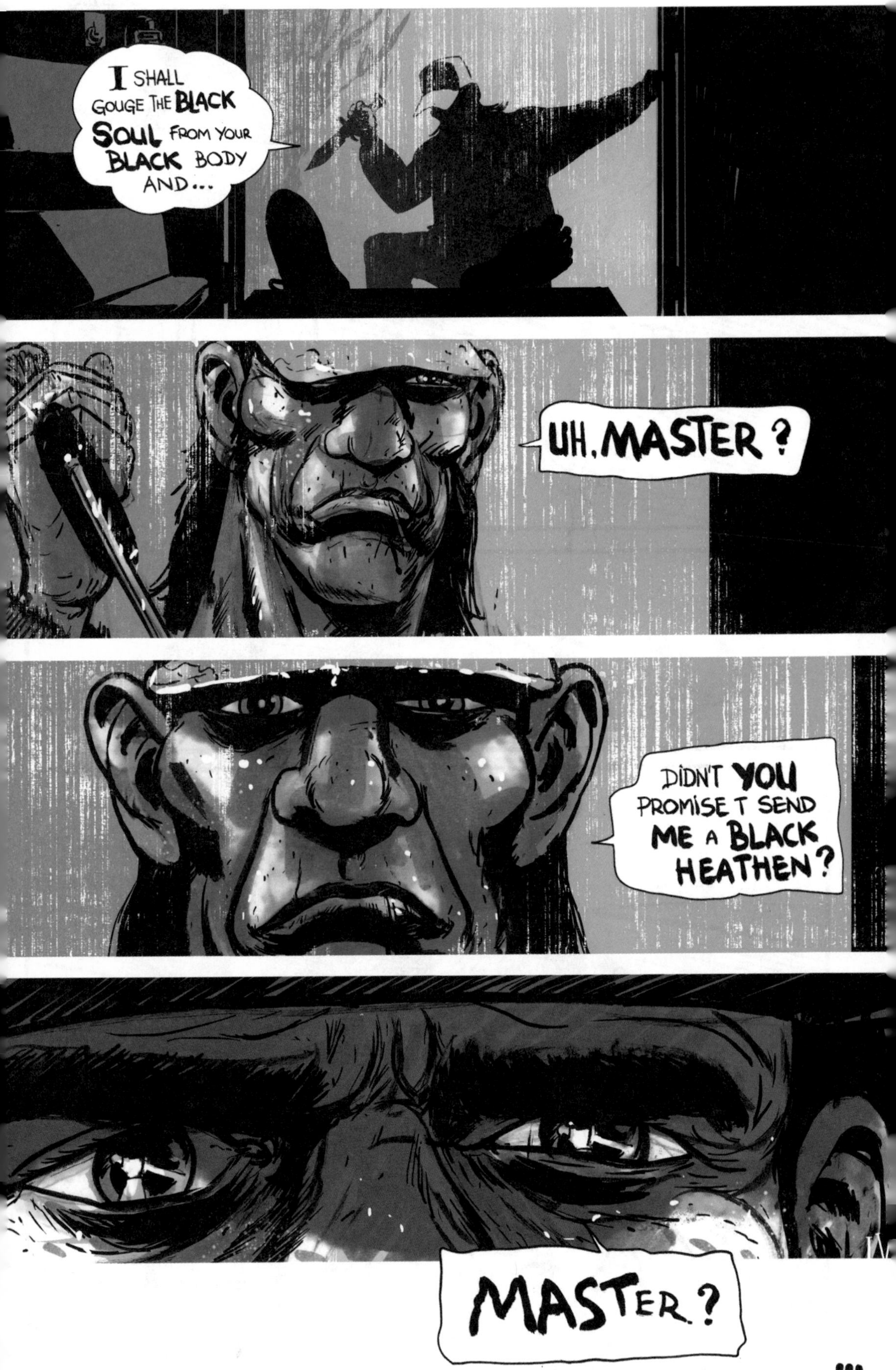
I SHALL GOUGE THE BLACK SOUL FROM YOUR BLACK BODY AND...
UH, MASTER?
DIDN'T YOU PROMISE T SEND ME A BLACK HEATHEN?
MASTER?

CRAMPS

AMY SHAND • EMILY PEARSON
JIM CAMPBELL

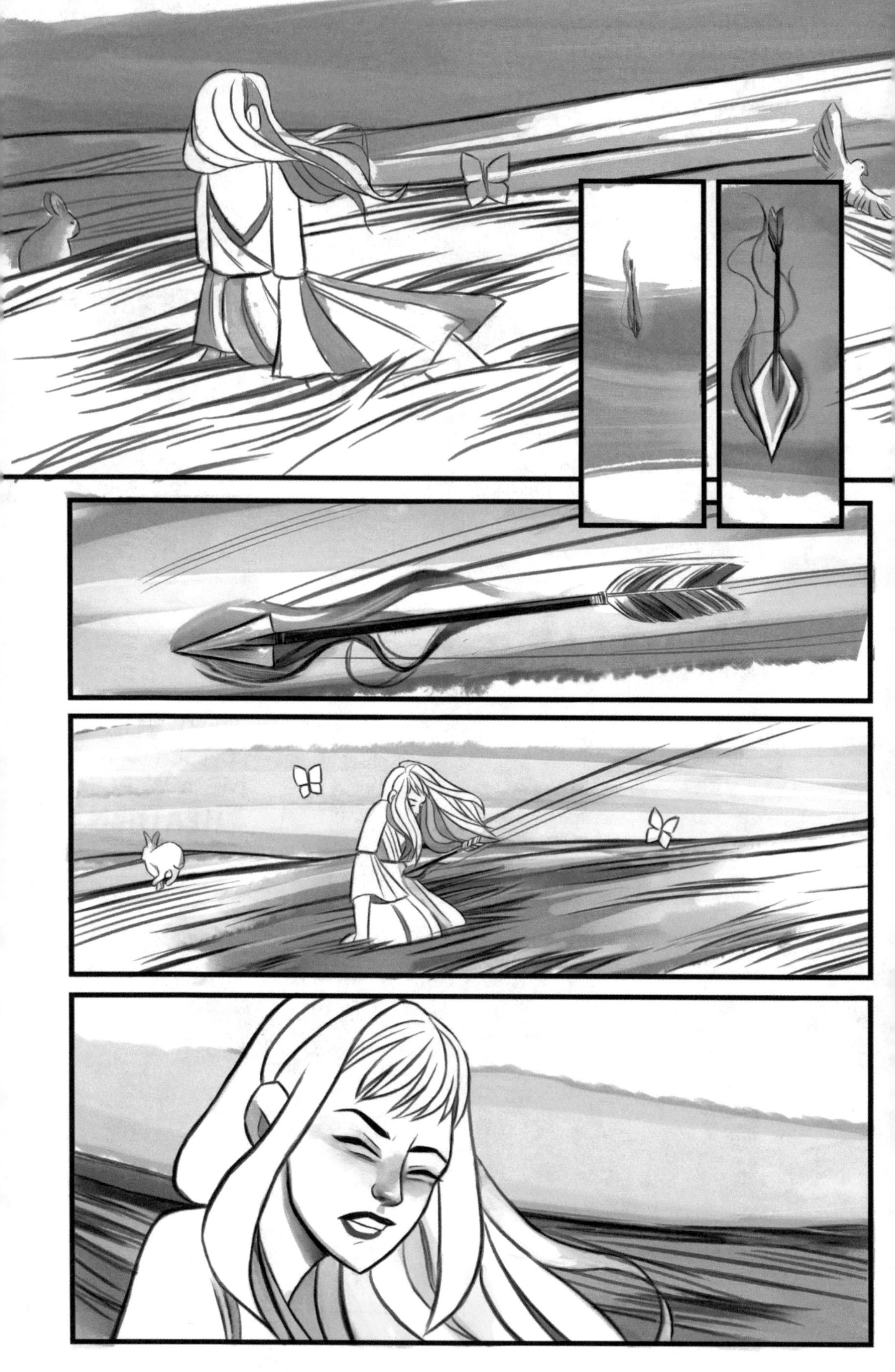

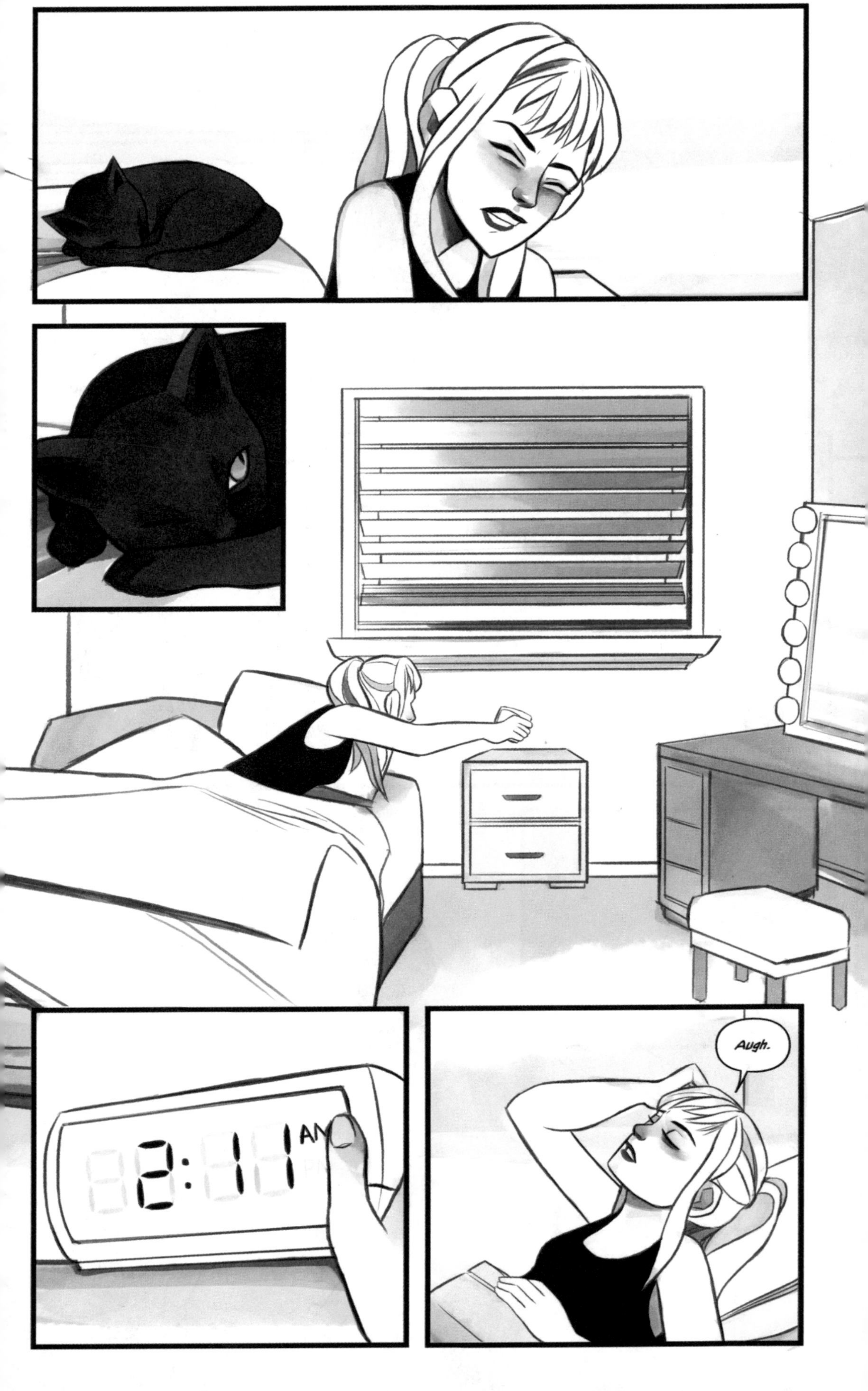
AM
Augh.

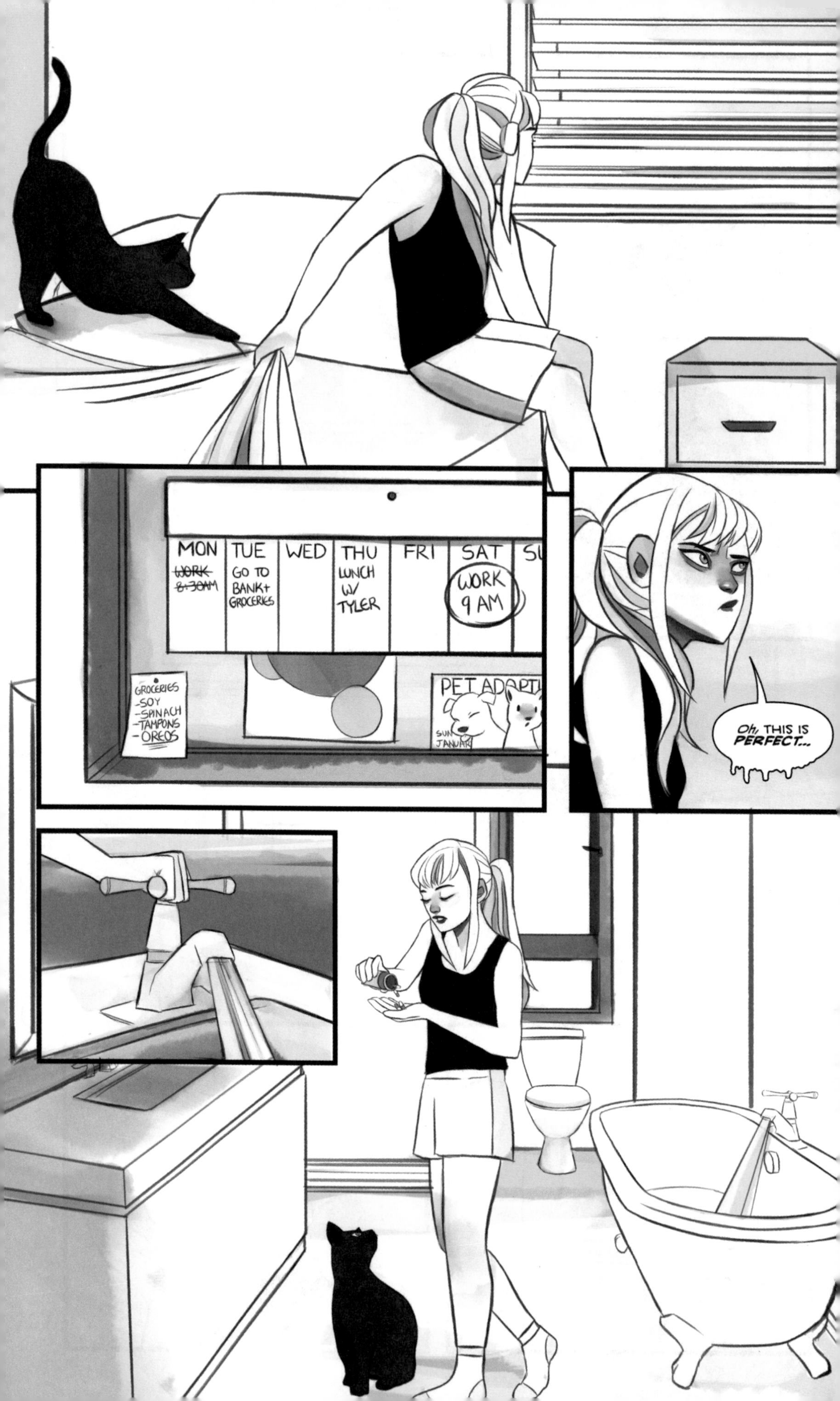

MON
WORK 8:30AM
TUE
GO TO BANK+ GROCERIES
WED
THU
LUNCH W/ TYLER
FRI
SAT
WORK 9 AM
GROCERIES
-SOY
-SPINACH
-TAMPONS
-OREOS
PET ADOPT
Oh, THIS IS PERFECT...

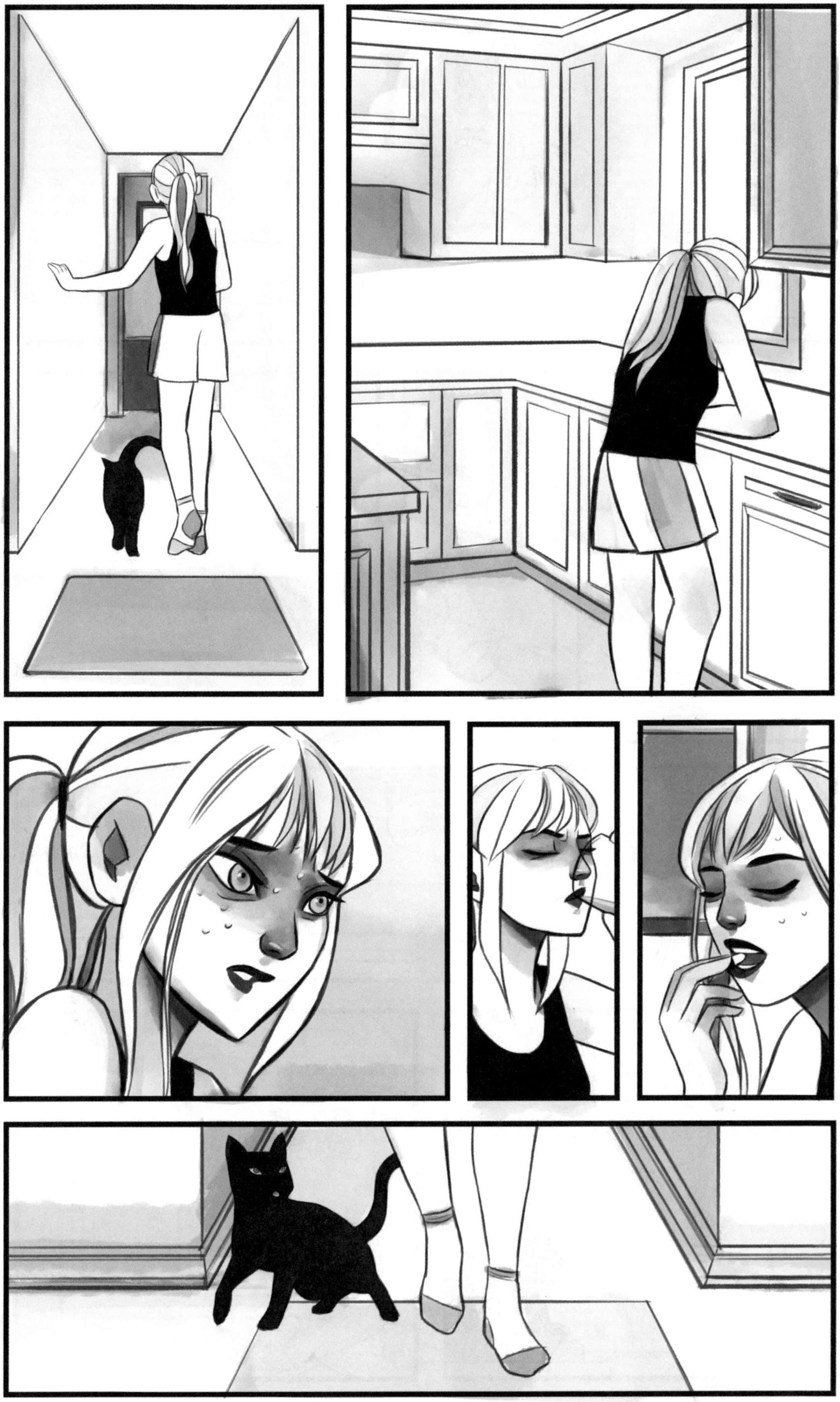

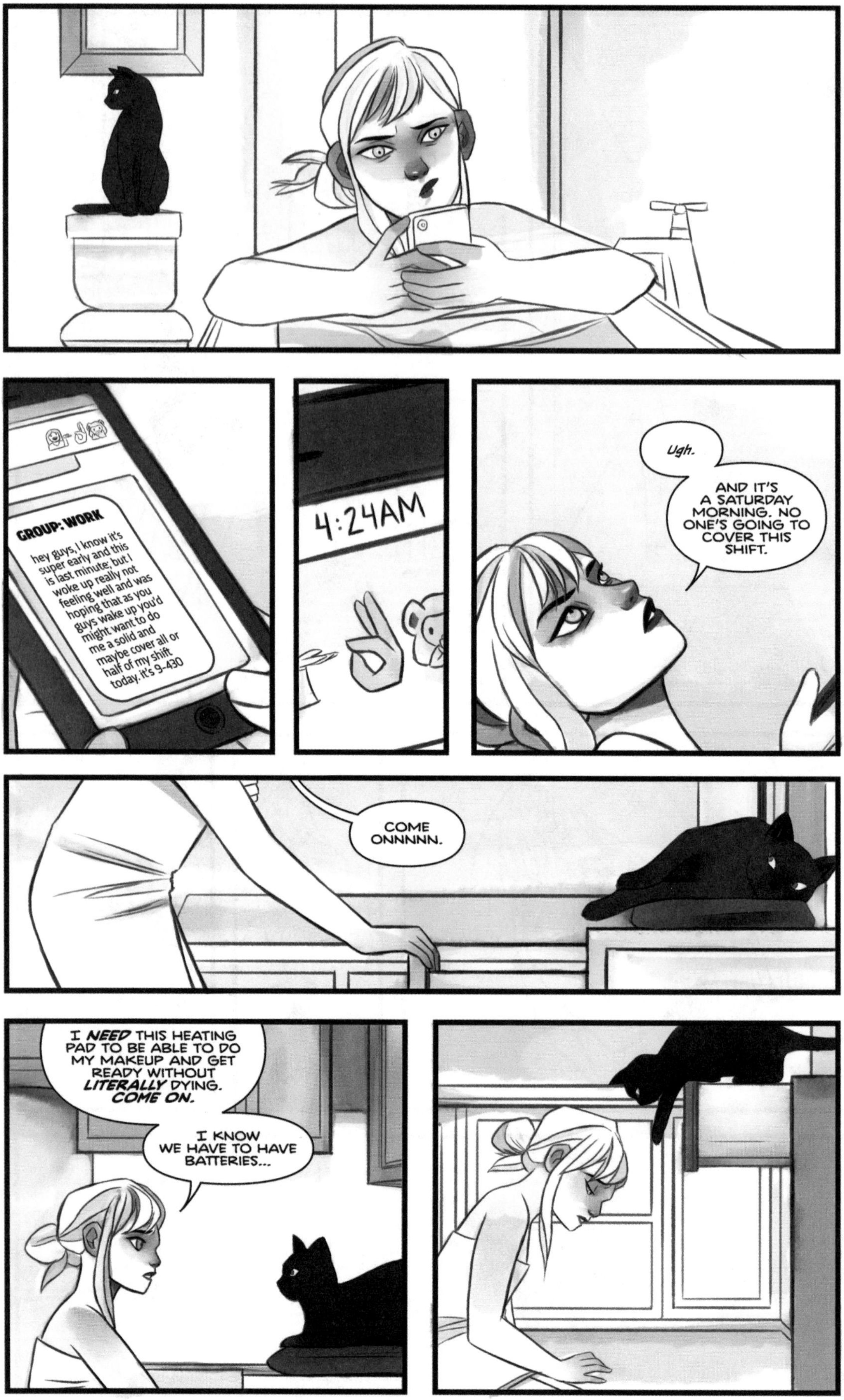
GROUP: WORK
hey guys, I know it's super early and this is last minute; but I woke up really not feeling well and was hoping that as you guys wake up you'd might want to do me a solid and maybe cover all or half of my shift today. it's 9-430
4:24AM
Ugh.
AND IT'S A SATURDAY MORNING. NO ONE'S GOING TO COVER THIS SHIFT.
COME ONNNNN.
I NEED THIS HEATING PAD TO BE ABLE TO DO MY MAKEUP AND GET READY WITHOUT LITERALLY DYING. COME ON.
I KNOW WE HAVE TO HAVE BATTERIES...

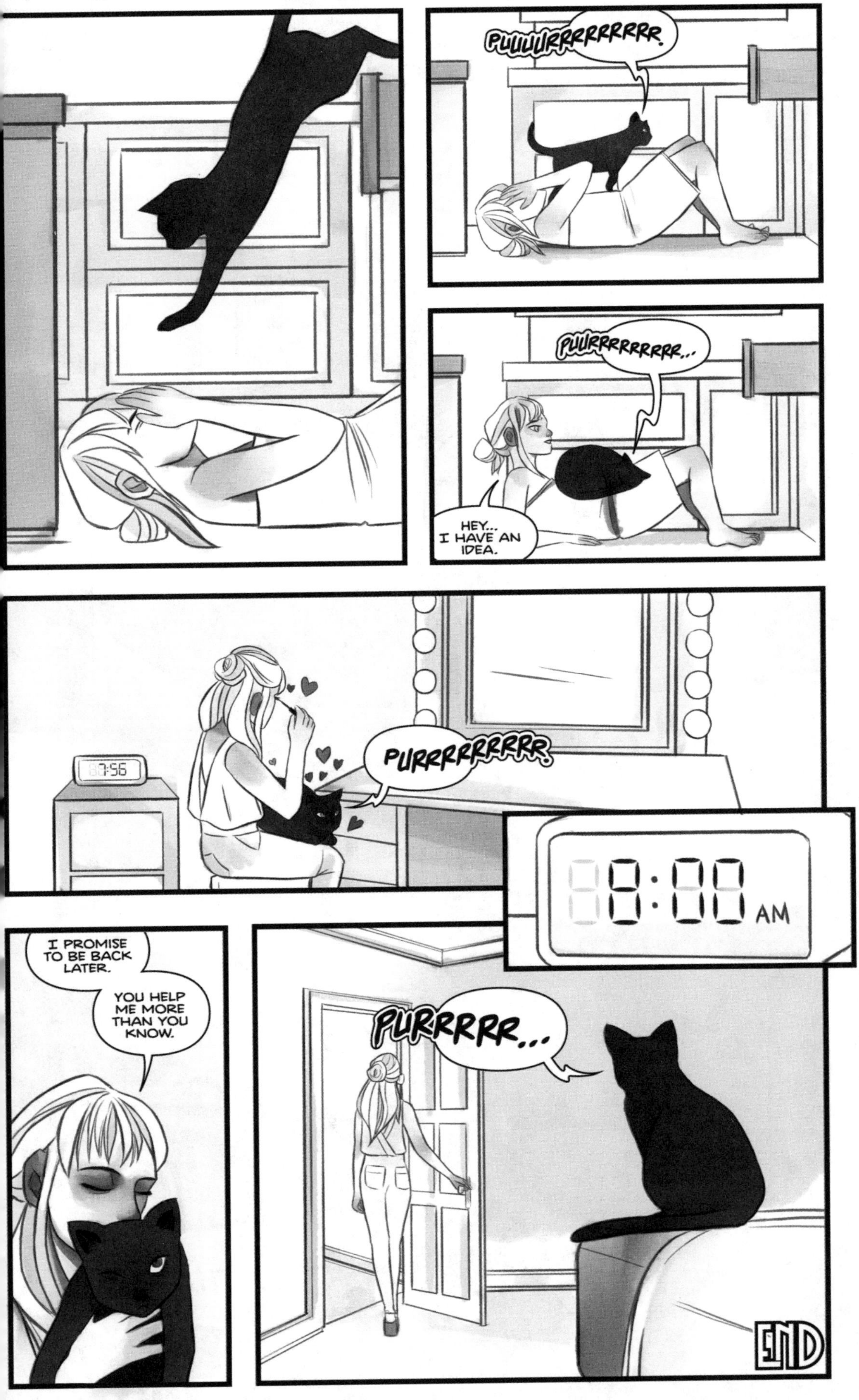
PUUUURRRRRRRR.
PUURRRRRRRRR...
HEY... I HAVE AN IDEA.
PURRRRRRRRR.
09:00 AM
I PROMISE TO BE BACK LATER.
YOU HELP ME MORE THAN YOU KNOW.
PURRRRR...
END

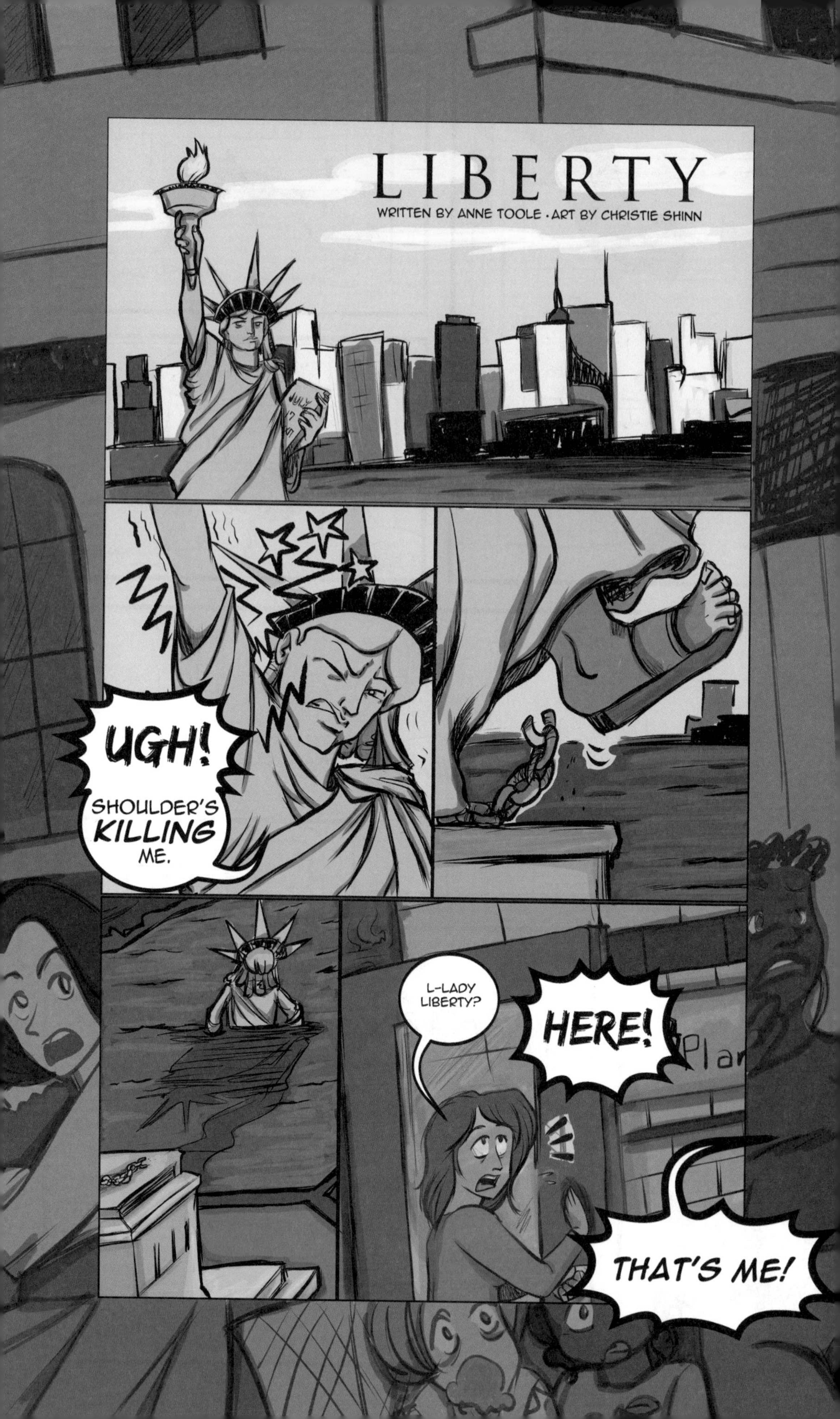
LIBERTY
WRITTEN BY ANNE TOOLE • ART BY CHRISTIE SHINN
UGH!
SHOULDER'S KILLING ME.
L-LADY LIBERTY?
HERE!
THAT'S ME!

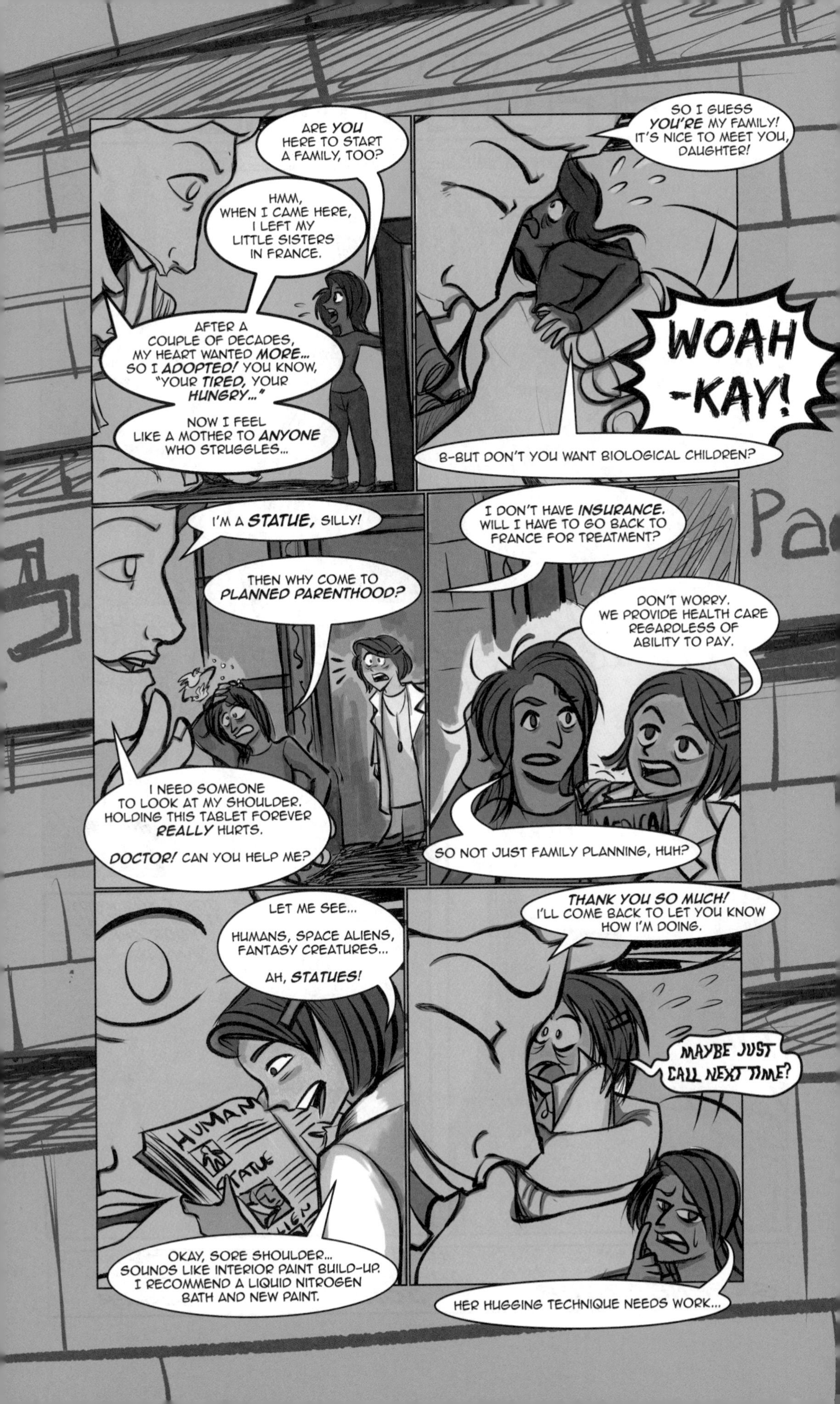
ARE *YOU* HERE TO START A FAMILY, TOO?
HMM, WHEN I CAME HERE, I LEFT MY LITTLE SISTERS IN FRANCE.
AFTER A COUPLE OF DECADES, MY HEART WANTED *MORE*... SO I *ADOPTED!* YOU KNOW, "YOUR *TIRED,* YOUR *HUNGRY*..."
NOW I FEEL LIKE A MOTHER TO *ANYONE* WHO STRUGGLES...
SO I GUESS *YOU'RE* MY FAMILY! IT'S NICE TO MEET YOU, DAUGHTER!
WOAH -KAY!
B-BUT DON'T YOU WANT BIOLOGICAL CHILDREN?
I'M A *STATUE,* SILLY!
THEN WHY COME TO *PLANNED PARENTHOOD?*
I NEED SOMEONE TO LOOK AT MY SHOULDER. HOLDING THIS TABLET FOREVER *REALLY* HURTS.
DOCTOR! CAN YOU HELP ME?
I DON'T HAVE *INSURANCE.* WILL I HAVE TO GO BACK TO FRANCE FOR TREATMENT?
DON'T WORRY. WE PROVIDE HEALTH CARE REGARDLESS OF ABILITY TO PAY.
SO NOT JUST FAMILY PLANNING, HUH?
LET ME SEE...
HUMANS, SPACE ALIENS, FANTASY CREATURES...
AH, *STATUES!*
HUMAN
STATUE
ALIEN
OKAY, SORE SHOULDER... SOUNDS LIKE INTERIOR PAINT BUILD-UP. I RECOMMEND A LIQUID NITROGEN BATH AND NEW PAINT.
THANK YOU SO MUCH! I'LL COME BACK TO LET YOU KNOW HOW I'M DOING.
MAYBE JUST CALL NEXT TIME?
HER HUGGING TECHNIQUE NEEDS WORK...

THE APPOINTMENT

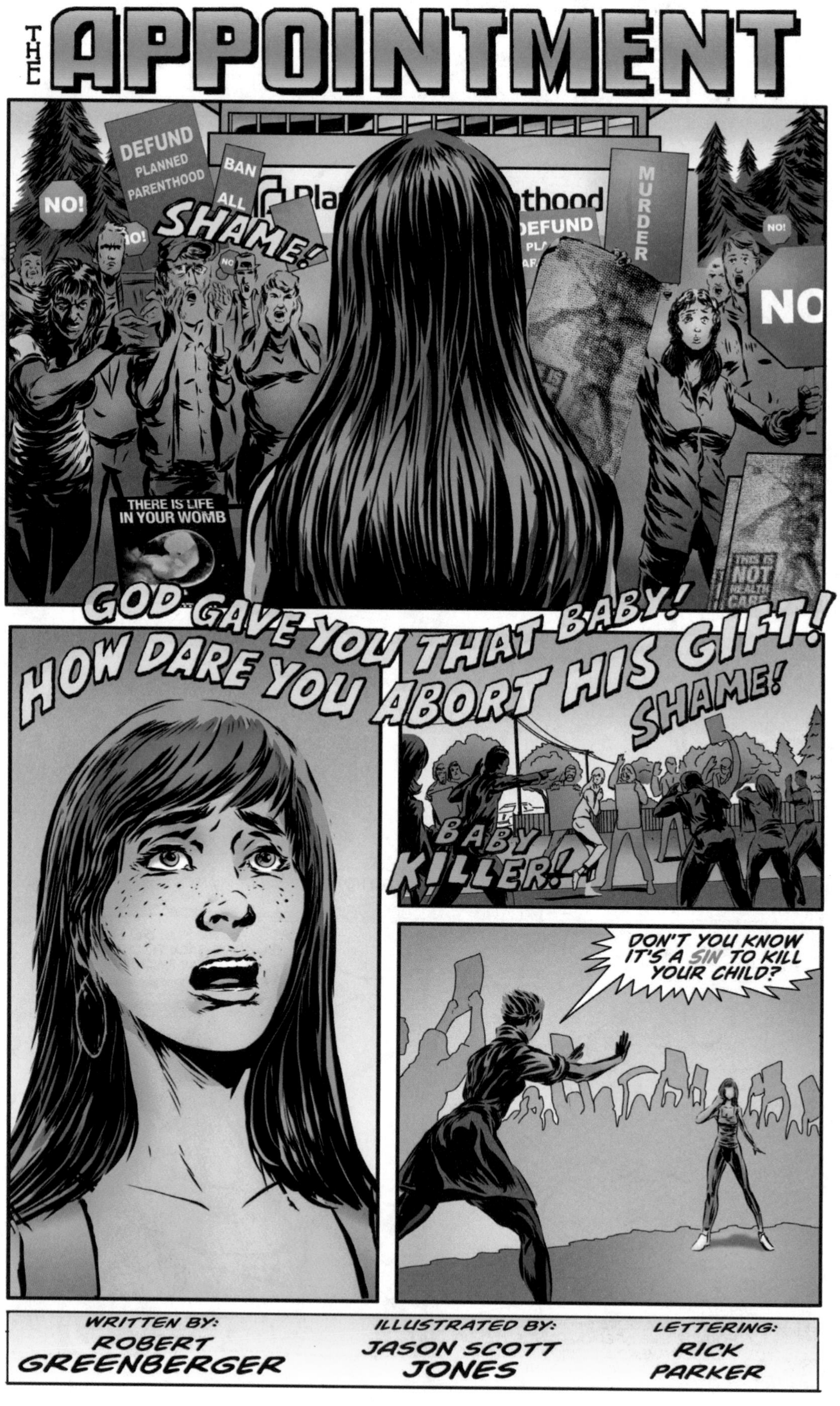
DEFUND PLANNED PARENTHOOD
BAN ALL
NO!
SHAME!
MURDER
DEFUND
NO!
NO
THERE IS LIFE IN YOUR WOMB
GOD GAVE YOU THAT BABY!
HOW DARE YOU ABORT HIS GIFT!
SHAME!
BABY KILLER!
DON'T YOU KNOW IT'S A SIN TO KILL YOUR CHILD?

WRITTEN BY: ROBERT GREENBERGER

ILLUSTRATED BY: JASON SCOTT JONES

LETTERING: RICK PARKER

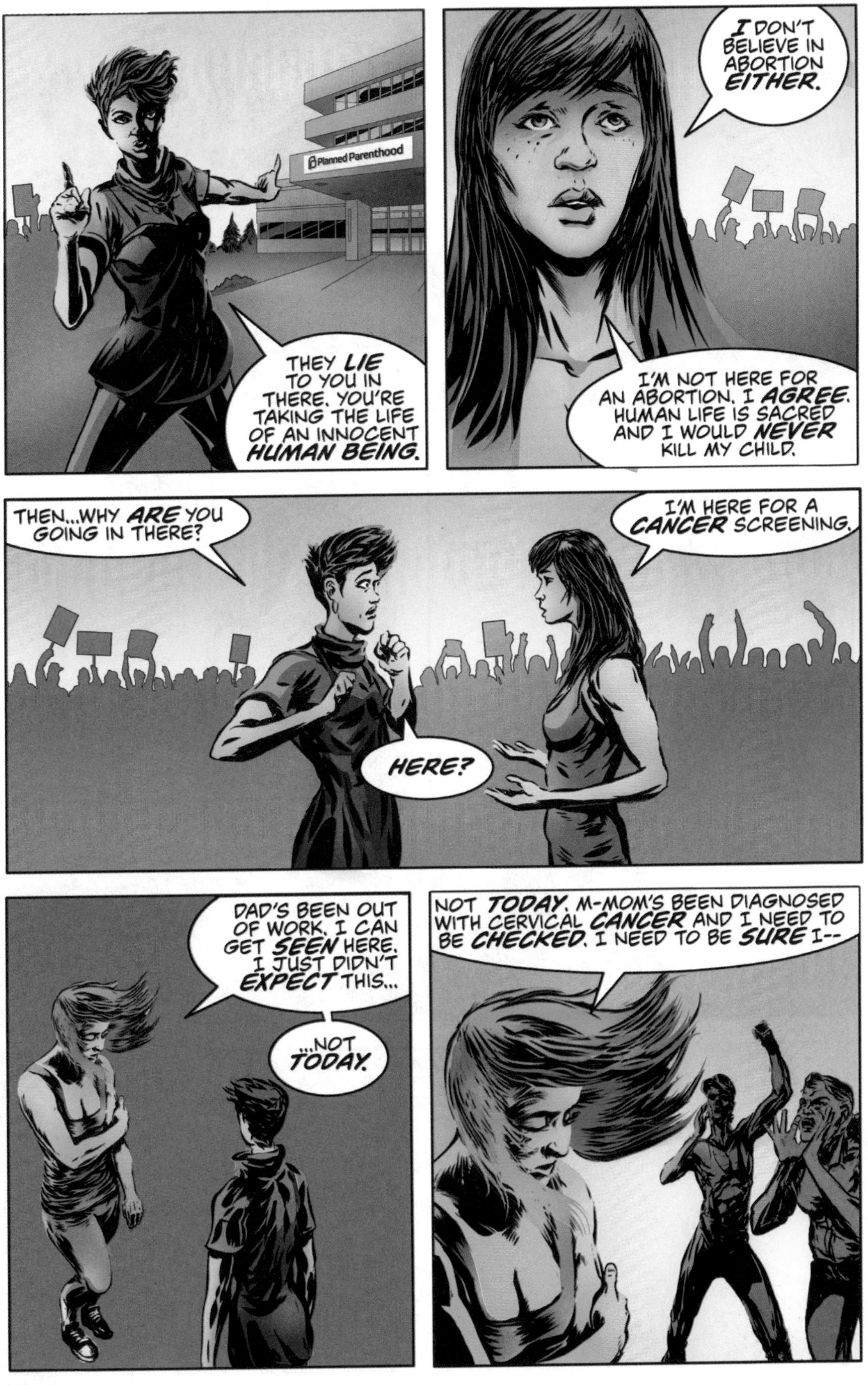
Planned Parenthood
THEY LIE TO YOU IN THERE. YOU'RE TAKING THE LIFE OF AN INNOCENT HUMAN BEING.
I DON'T BELIEVE IN ABORTION EITHER.
I'M NOT HERE FOR AN ABORTION. I AGREE. HUMAN LIFE IS SACRED AND I WOULD NEVER KILL MY CHILD.
THEN...WHY ARE YOU GOING IN THERE?
I'M HERE FOR A CANCER SCREENING.
HERE?
DAD'S BEEN OUT OF WORK. I CAN GET SEEN HERE. I JUST DIDN'T EXPECT THIS...
...NOT TODAY.
NOT TODAY. M-MOM'S BEEN DIAGNOSED WITH CERVICAL CANCER AND I NEED TO BE CHECKED. I NEED TO BE SURE I--

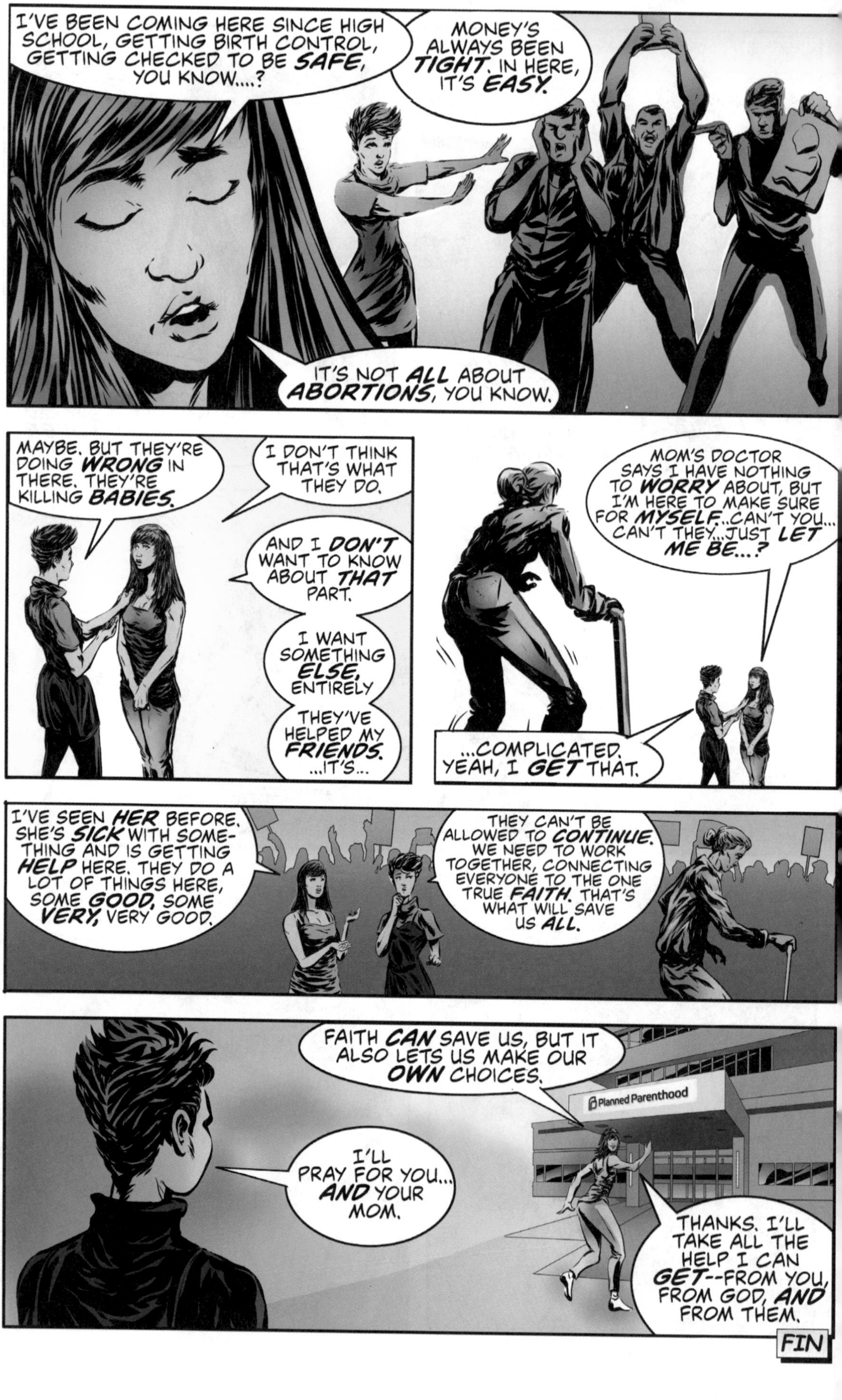

I'VE BEEN COMING HERE SINCE HIGH SCHOOL, GETTING BIRTH CONTROL, GETTING CHECKED TO BE SAFE, YOU KNOW....?
MONEY'S ALWAYS BEEN TIGHT. IN HERE, IT'S EASY.
IT'S NOT ALL ABOUT ABORTIONS, YOU KNOW.
MAYBE. BUT THEY'RE DOING WRONG IN THERE. THEY'RE KILLING BABIES.
I DON'T THINK THAT'S WHAT THEY DO.
AND I DON'T WANT TO KNOW ABOUT THAT PART.
I WANT SOMETHING ELSE, ENTIRELY
THEY'VE HELPED MY FRIENDS. ...IT'S...
...COMPLICATED. YEAH, I GET THAT.
MOM'S DOCTOR SAYS I HAVE NOTHING TO WORRY ABOUT, BUT I'M HERE TO MAKE SURE FOR MYSELF...CAN'T YOU... CAN'T THEY...JUST LET ME BE...?
I'VE SEEN HER BEFORE. SHE'S SICK WITH SOME-THING AND IS GETTING HELP HERE. THEY DO A LOT OF THINGS HERE, SOME GOOD, SOME VERY, VERY GOOD.
THEY CAN'T BE ALLOWED TO CONTINUE. WE NEED TO WORK TOGETHER, CONNECTING EVERYONE TO THE ONE TRUE FAITH. THAT'S WHAT WILL SAVE US ALL.
FAITH CAN SAVE US, BUT IT ALSO LETS US MAKE OUR OWN CHOICES.
Planned Parenthood
I'LL PRAY FOR YOU... AND YOUR MOM.
THANKS. I'LL TAKE ALL THE HELP I CAN GET--FROM YOU, FROM GOD, AND FROM THEM.
FIN

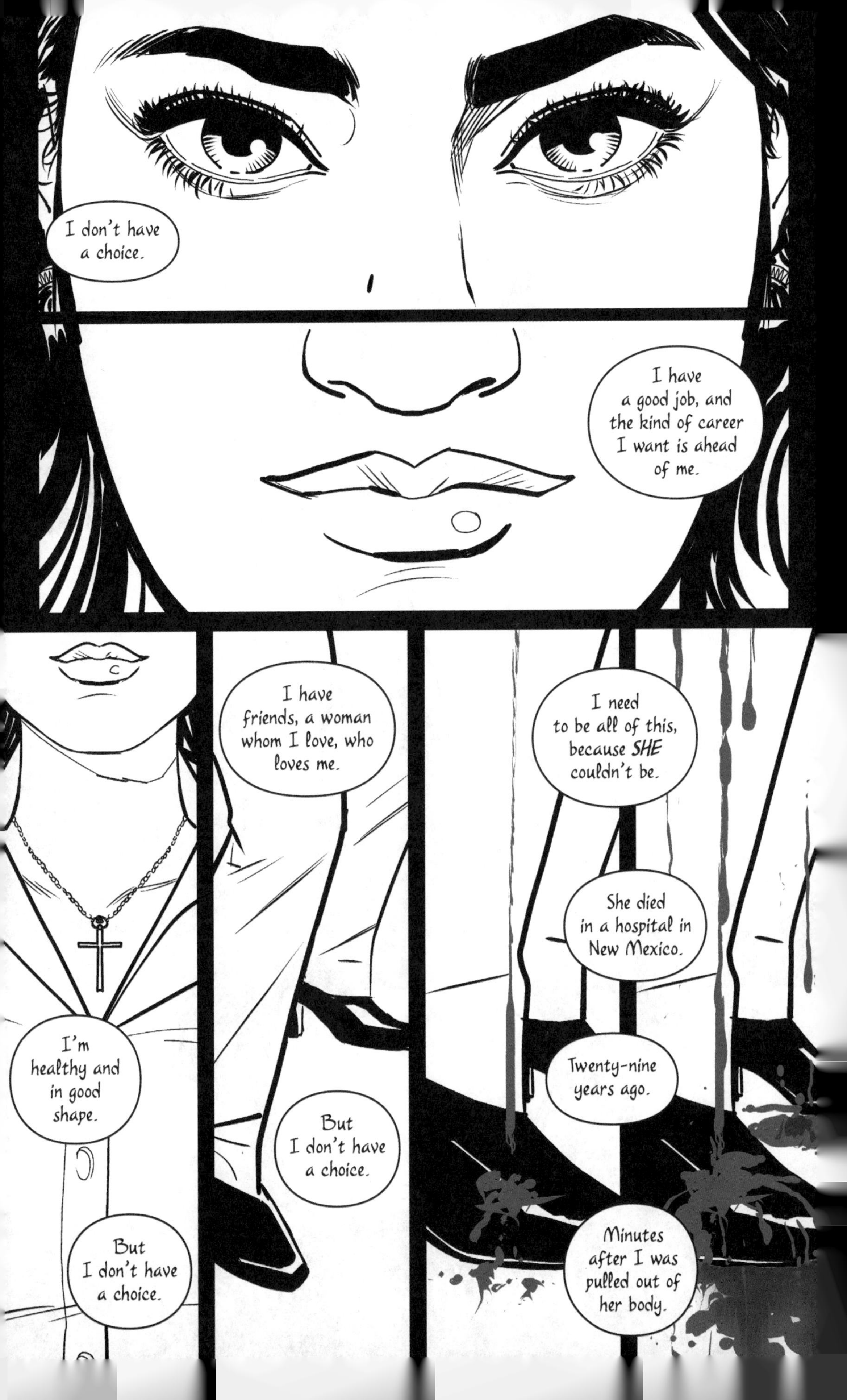

I don't have a choice.
I have a good job, and the kind of career I want is ahead of me.
I have friends, a woman whom I love, who loves me.
I need to be all of this, because SHE couldn't be.
She died in a hospital in New Mexico.
I'm healthy and in good shape.
Twenty-nine years ago.
But I don't have a choice.
But I don't have a choice.
Minutes after I was pulled out of her body.

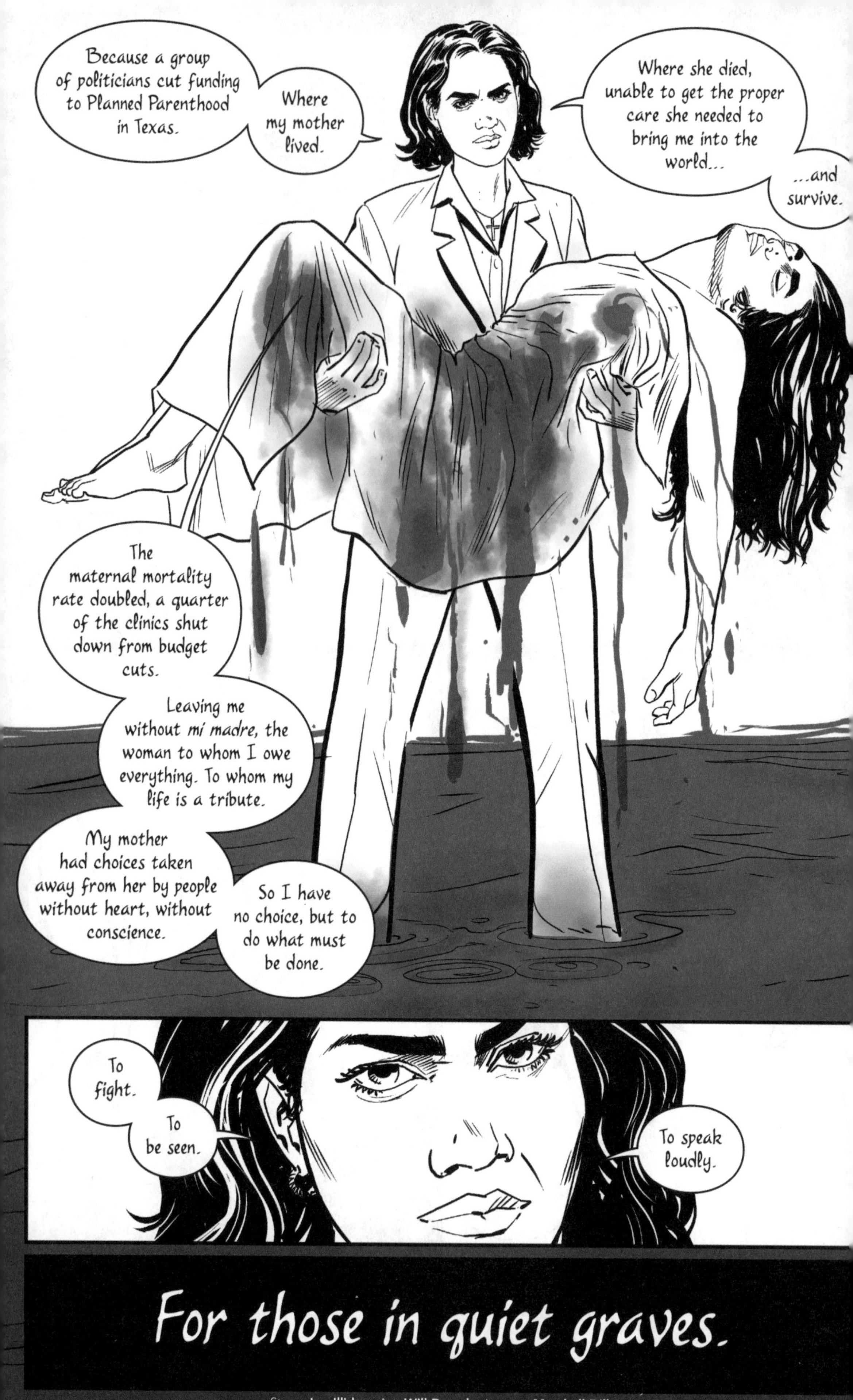
Because a group of politicians cut funding to Planned Parenthood in Texas.
Where my mother lived.
Where she died, unable to get the proper care she needed to bring me into the world...
...and survive.
The maternal mortality rate doubled, a quarter of the clinics shut down from budget cuts.
Leaving me without *mi madre*, the woman to whom I owe everything. To whom my life is a tribute.
My mother had choices taken away from her by people without heart, without conscience.
So I have no choice, but to do what must be done.
To fight.
To be seen.
To speak loudly.
For those in quiet graves.

Story: **Joe Illidge** Art: **Will Rosado** Letters: **Marshall Dillon**

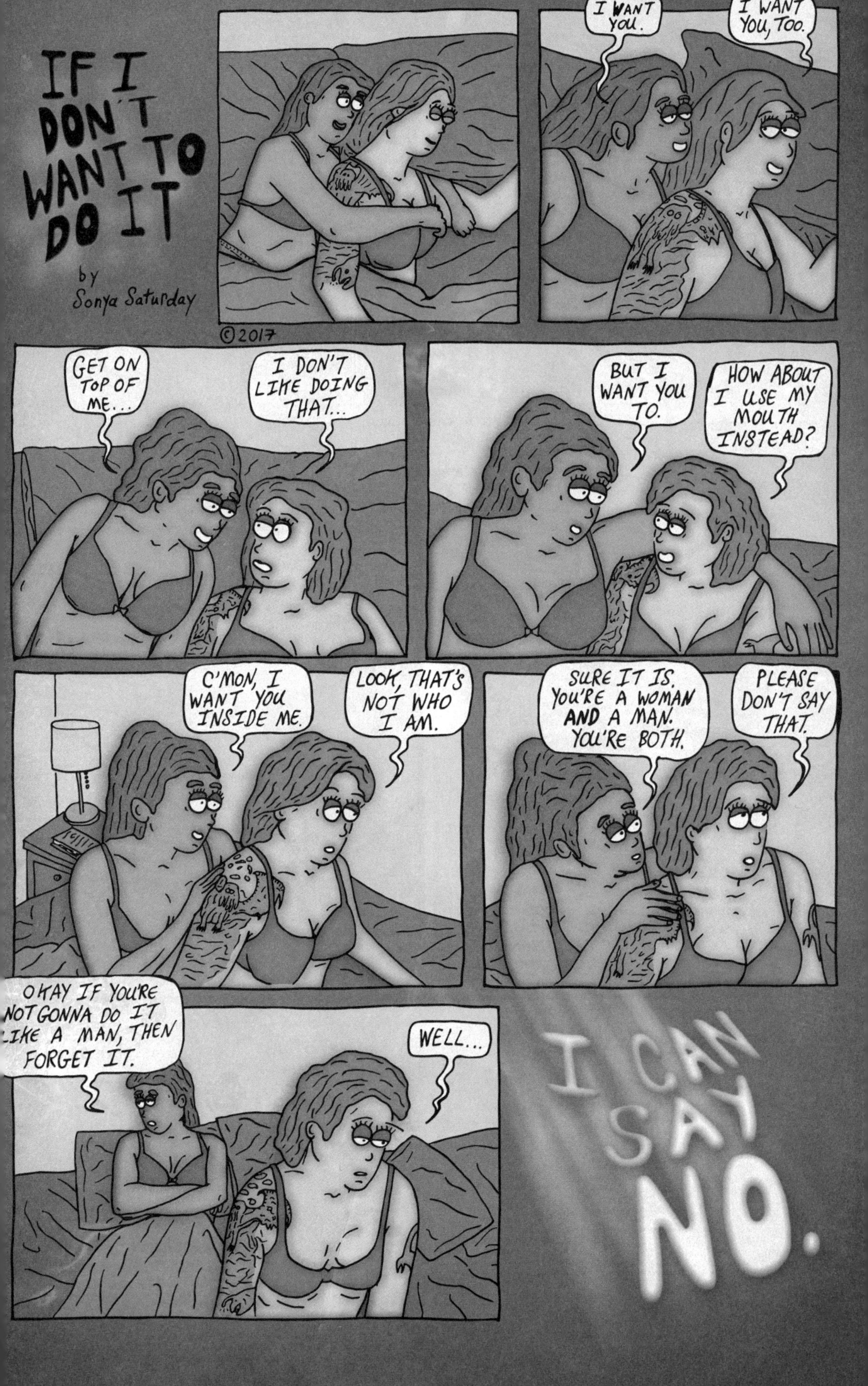
IF I DON'T WANT TO DO IT
by Sonya Saturday
©2017
I WANT YOU.
I WANT YOU, TOO.
GET ON TOP OF ME...
I DON'T LIKE DOING THAT...
BUT I WANT YOU TO.
HOW ABOUT I USE MY MOUTH INSTEAD?
C'MON, I WANT YOU INSIDE ME.
LOOK, THAT'S NOT WHO I AM.
SURE IT IS. YOU'RE A WOMAN AND A MAN. YOU'RE BOTH.
PLEASE DON'T SAY THAT.
OKAY IF YOU'RE NOT GONNA DO IT LIKE A MAN, THEN FORGET IT.
WELL...
I CAN SAY NO.

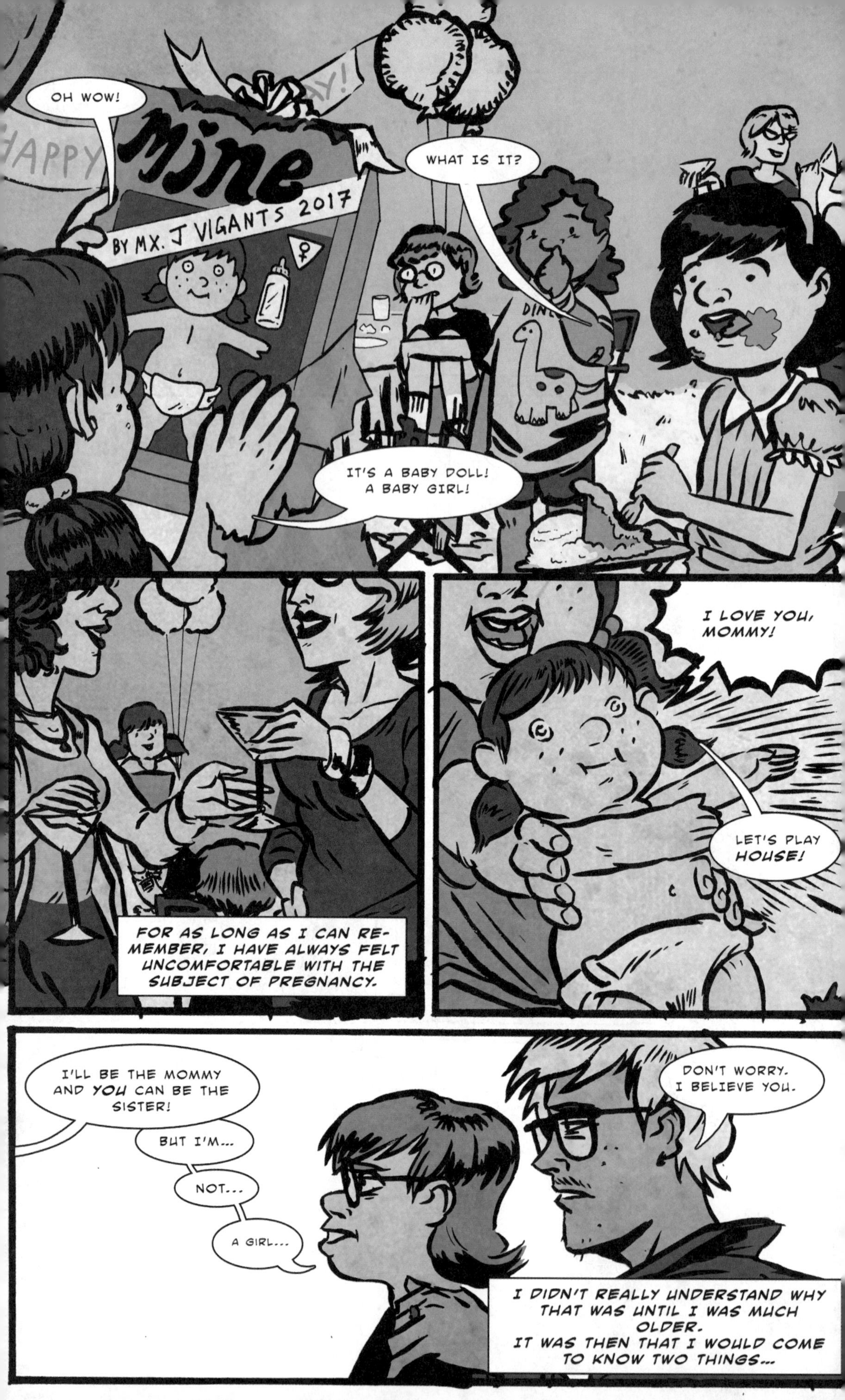
OH WOW!
HAPPY
mine
BY MX. J VIGANTS 2017
WHAT IS IT?
DINO
IT'S A BABY DOLL! A BABY GIRL!
FOR AS LONG AS I CAN REMEMBER, I HAVE ALWAYS FELT UNCOMFORTABLE WITH THE SUBJECT OF PREGNANCY.
I LOVE YOU, MOMMY!
LET'S PLAY HOUSE!
I'LL BE THE MOMMY AND YOU CAN BE THE SISTER!
BUT I'M...
NOT...
A GIRL...
DON'T WORRY. I BELIEVE YOU.
I DIDN'T REALLY UNDERSTAND WHY THAT WAS UNTIL I WAS MUCH OLDER.
IT WAS THEN THAT I WOULD COME TO KNOW TWO THINGS...

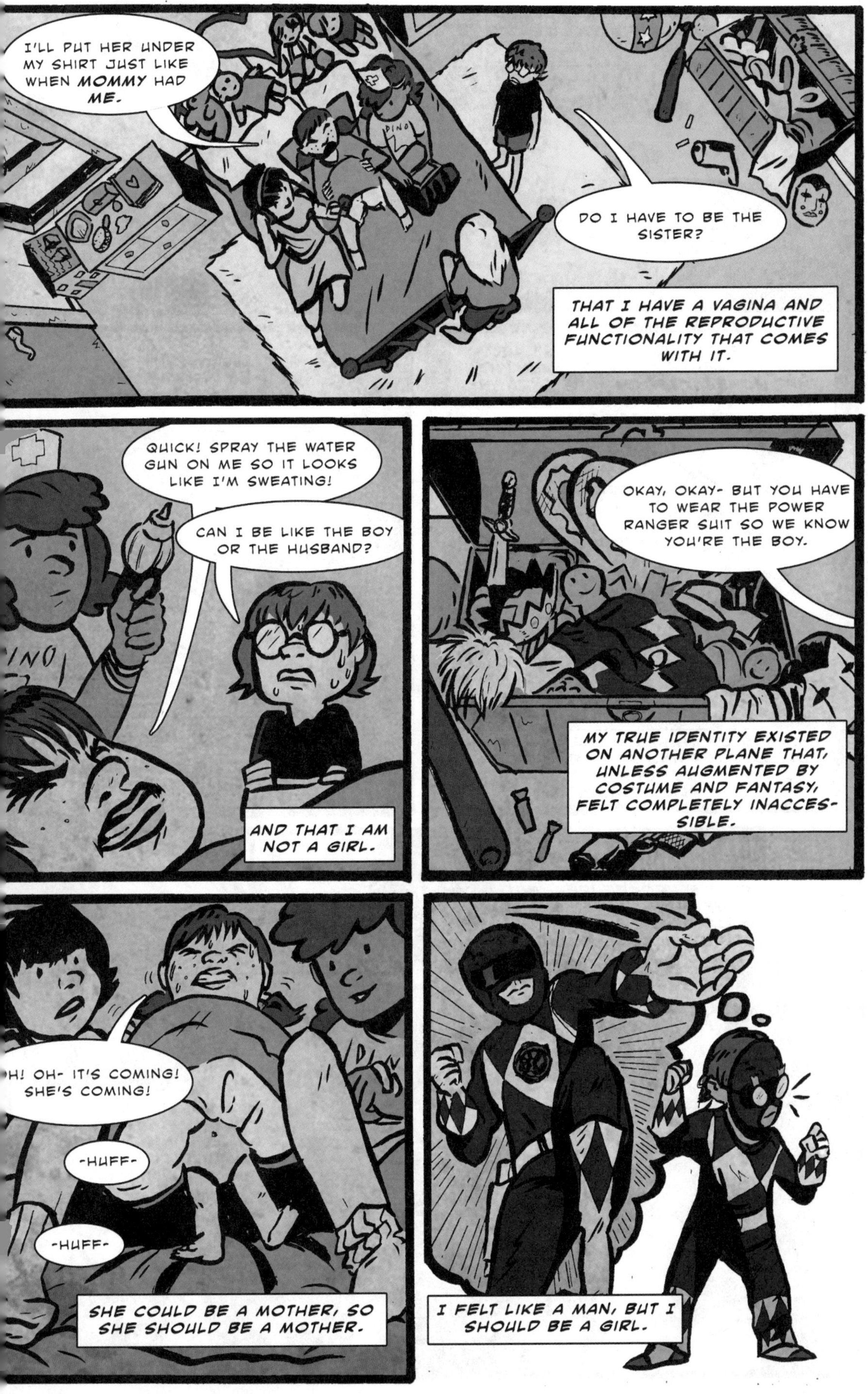
I'LL PUT HER UNDER MY SHIRT JUST LIKE WHEN MOMMY HAD ME.
DO I HAVE TO BE THE SISTER?
THAT I HAVE A VAGINA AND ALL OF THE REPRODUCTIVE FUNCTIONALITY THAT COMES WITH IT.
QUICK! SPRAY THE WATER GUN ON ME SO IT LOOKS LIKE I'M SWEATING!
CAN I BE LIKE THE BOY OR THE HUSBAND?
AND THAT I AM NOT A GIRL.
OKAY, OKAY- BUT YOU HAVE TO WEAR THE POWER RANGER SUIT SO WE KNOW YOU'RE THE BOY.
MY TRUE IDENTITY EXISTED ON ANOTHER PLANE THAT, UNLESS AUGMENTED BY COSTUME AND FANTASY, FELT COMPLETELY INACCES-SIBLE.
H! OH- IT'S COMING! SHE'S COMING!
-HUFF-
-HUFF-
SHE COULD BE A MOTHER, SO SHE SHOULD BE A MOTHER.
I FELT LIKE A MAN, BUT I SHOULD BE A GIRL.

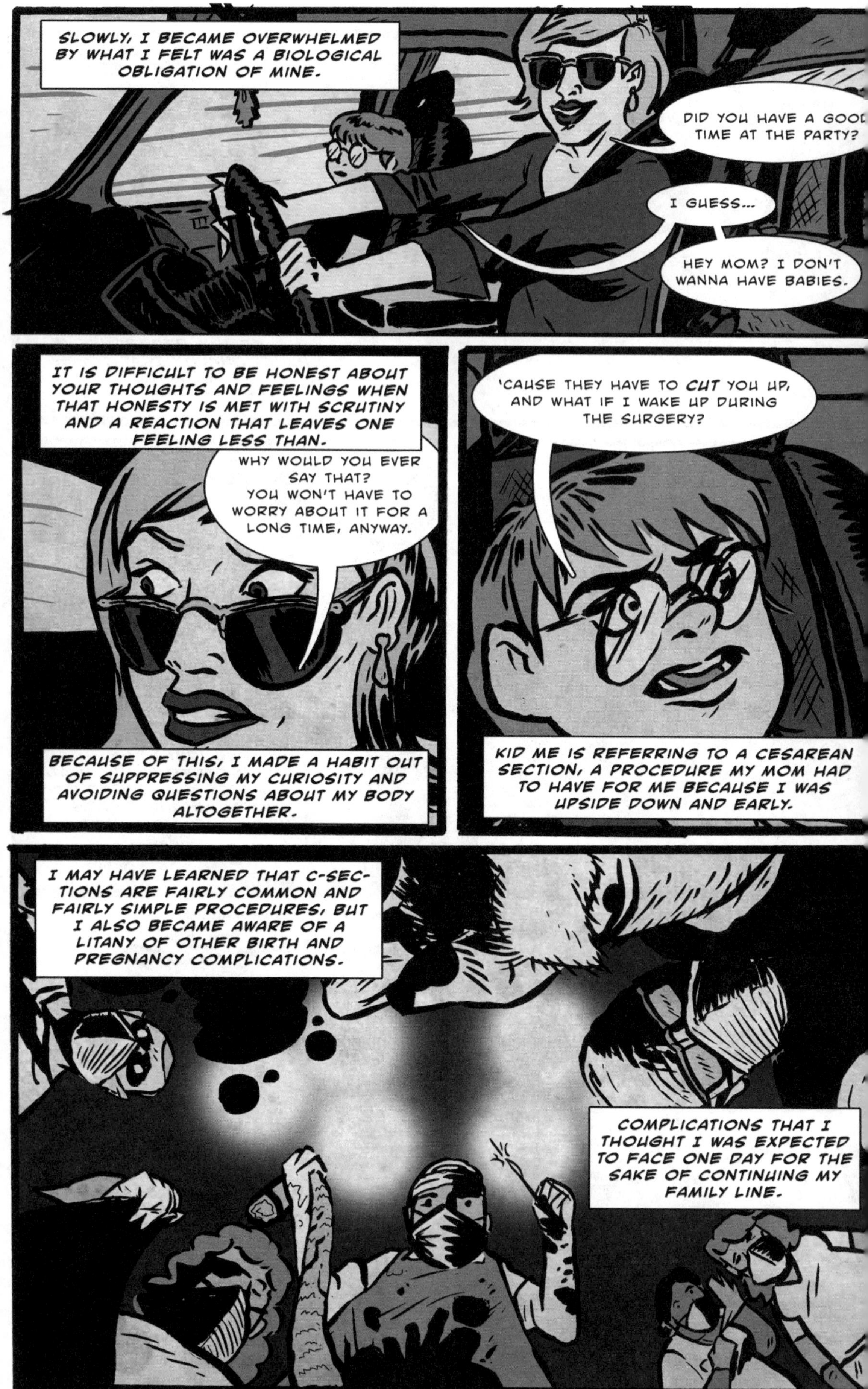
SLOWLY, I BECAME OVERWHELMED BY WHAT I FELT WAS A BIOLOGICAL OBLIGATION OF MINE.
DID YOU HAVE A GOOD TIME AT THE PARTY?
I GUESS...
HEY MOM? I DON'T WANNA HAVE BABIES.
IT IS DIFFICULT TO BE HONEST ABOUT YOUR THOUGHTS AND FEELINGS WHEN THAT HONESTY IS MET WITH SCRUTINY AND A REACTION THAT LEAVES ONE FEELING LESS THAN.
WHY WOULD YOU EVER SAY THAT? YOU WON'T HAVE TO WORRY ABOUT IT FOR A LONG TIME, ANYWAY.
BECAUSE OF THIS, I MADE A HABIT OUT OF SUPPRESSING MY CURIOSITY AND AVOIDING QUESTIONS ABOUT MY BODY ALTOGETHER.
'CAUSE THEY HAVE TO CUT YOU UP, AND WHAT IF I WAKE UP DURING THE SURGERY?
KID ME IS REFERRING TO A CESAREAN SECTION, A PROCEDURE MY MOM HAD TO HAVE FOR ME BECAUSE I WAS UPSIDE DOWN AND EARLY.
I MAY HAVE LEARNED THAT C-SECTIONS ARE FAIRLY COMMON AND FAIRLY SIMPLE PROCEDURES, BUT I ALSO BECAME AWARE OF A LITANY OF OTHER BIRTH AND PREGNANCY COMPLICATIONS.
COMPLICATIONS THAT I THOUGHT I WAS EXPECTED TO FACE ONE DAY FOR THE SAKE OF CONTINUING MY FAMILY LINE.

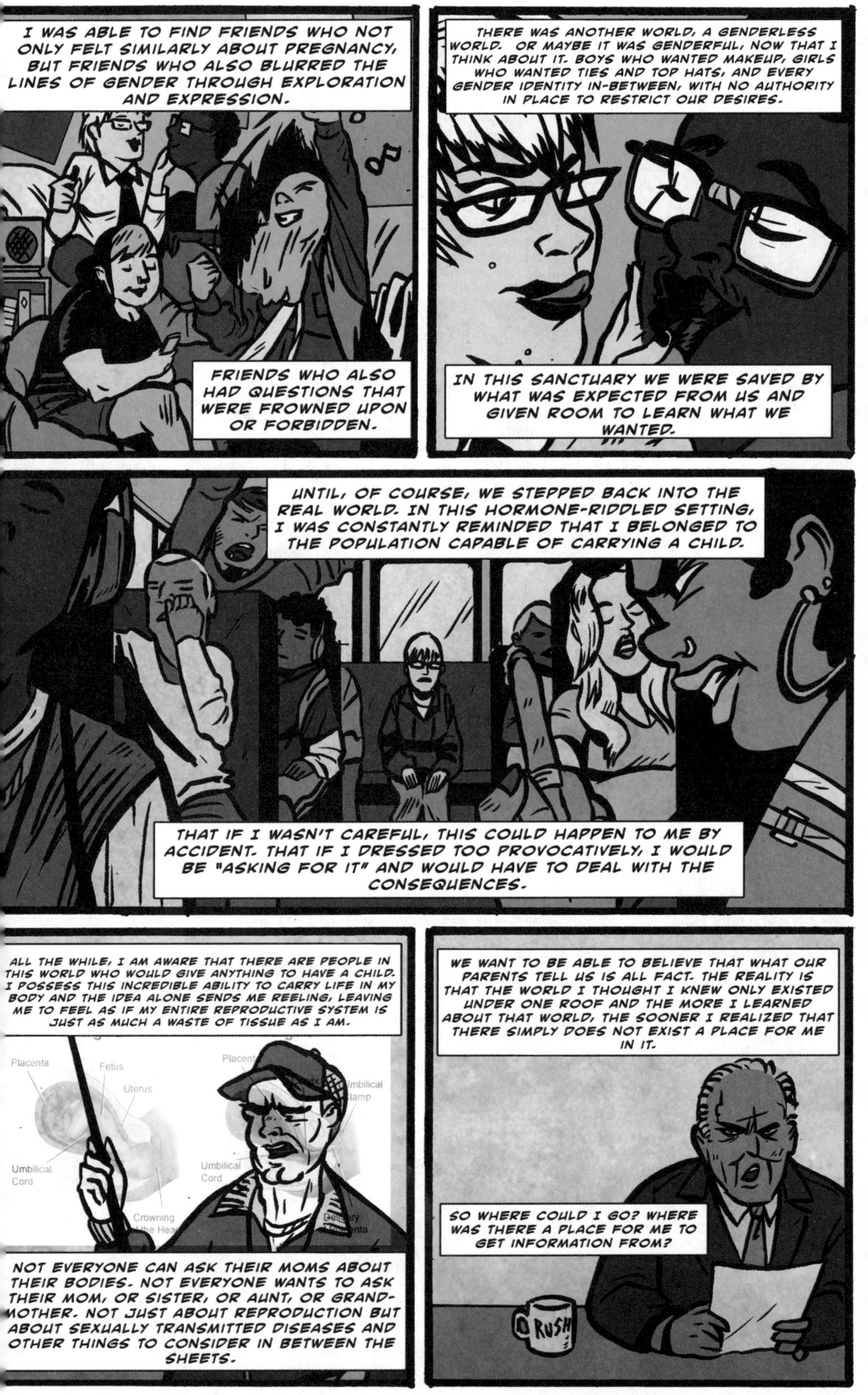
I WAS ABLE TO FIND FRIENDS WHO NOT ONLY FELT SIMILARLY ABOUT PREGNANCY, BUT FRIENDS WHO ALSO BLURRED THE LINES OF GENDER THROUGH EXPLORATION AND EXPRESSION.
FRIENDS WHO ALSO HAD QUESTIONS THAT WERE FROWNED UPON OR FORBIDDEN.
THERE WAS ANOTHER WORLD, A GENDERLESS WORLD. OR MAYBE IT WAS GENDERFUL, NOW THAT I THINK ABOUT IT. BOYS WHO WANTED MAKEUP, GIRLS WHO WANTED TIES AND TOP HATS, AND EVERY GENDER IDENTITY IN-BETWEEN, WITH NO AUTHORITY IN PLACE TO RESTRICT OUR DESIRES.
IN THIS SANCTUARY WE WERE SAVED BY WHAT WAS EXPECTED FROM US AND GIVEN ROOM TO LEARN WHAT WE WANTED.
UNTIL, OF COURSE, WE STEPPED BACK INTO THE REAL WORLD. IN THIS HORMONE-RIDDLED SETTING, I WAS CONSTANTLY REMINDED THAT I BELONGED TO THE POPULATION CAPABLE OF CARRYING A CHILD.
THAT IF I WASN'T CAREFUL, THIS COULD HAPPEN TO ME BY ACCIDENT. THAT IF I DRESSED TOO PROVOCATIVELY, I WOULD BE "ASKING FOR IT" AND WOULD HAVE TO DEAL WITH THE CONSEQUENCES.
ALL THE WHILE, I AM AWARE THAT THERE ARE PEOPLE IN THIS WORLD WHO WOULD GIVE ANYTHING TO HAVE A CHILD. I POSSESS THIS INCREDIBLE ABILITY TO CARRY LIFE IN MY BODY AND THE IDEA ALONE SENDS ME REELING, LEAVING ME TO FEEL AS IF MY ENTIRE REPRODUCTIVE SYSTEM IS JUST AS MUCH A WASTE OF TISSUE AS I AM.
Placenta
Fetus
Uterus
Umbilical Cord
Umbilical Cord
NOT EVERYONE CAN ASK THEIR MOMS ABOUT THEIR BODIES. NOT EVERYONE WANTS TO ASK THEIR MOM, OR SISTER, OR AUNT, OR GRANDMOTHER. NOT JUST ABOUT REPRODUCTION BUT ABOUT SEXUALLY TRANSMITTED DISEASES AND OTHER THINGS TO CONSIDER IN BETWEEN THE SHEETS.
WE WANT TO BE ABLE TO BELIEVE THAT WHAT OUR PARENTS TELL US IS ALL FACT. THE REALITY IS THAT THE WORLD I THOUGHT I KNEW ONLY EXISTED UNDER ONE ROOF AND THE MORE I LEARNED ABOUT THAT WORLD, THE SOONER I REALIZED THAT THERE SIMPLY DOES NOT EXIST A PLACE FOR ME IN IT.
SO WHERE COULD I GO? WHERE WAS THERE A PLACE FOR ME TO GET INFORMATION FROM?
RUSH

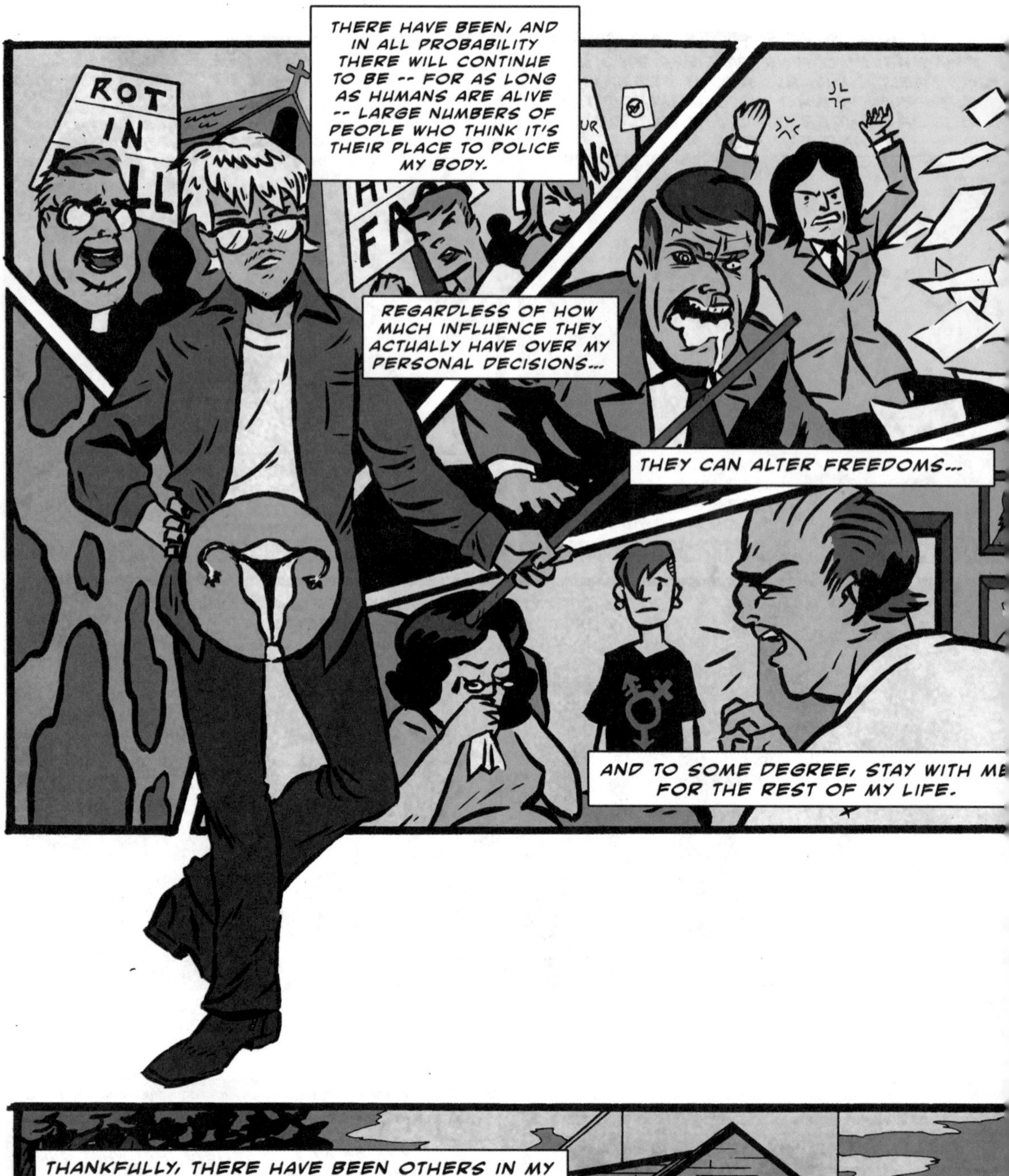
THERE HAVE BEEN, AND IN ALL PROBABILITY THERE WILL CONTINUE TO BE -- FOR AS LONG AS HUMANS ARE ALIVE -- LARGE NUMBERS OF PEOPLE WHO THINK IT'S THEIR PLACE TO POLICE MY BODY.
ROT IN
REGARDLESS OF HOW MUCH INFLUENCE THEY ACTUALLY HAVE OVER MY PERSONAL DECISIONS...
THEY CAN ALTER FREEDOMS...
AND TO SOME DEGREE, STAY WITH ME FOR THE REST OF MY LIFE.

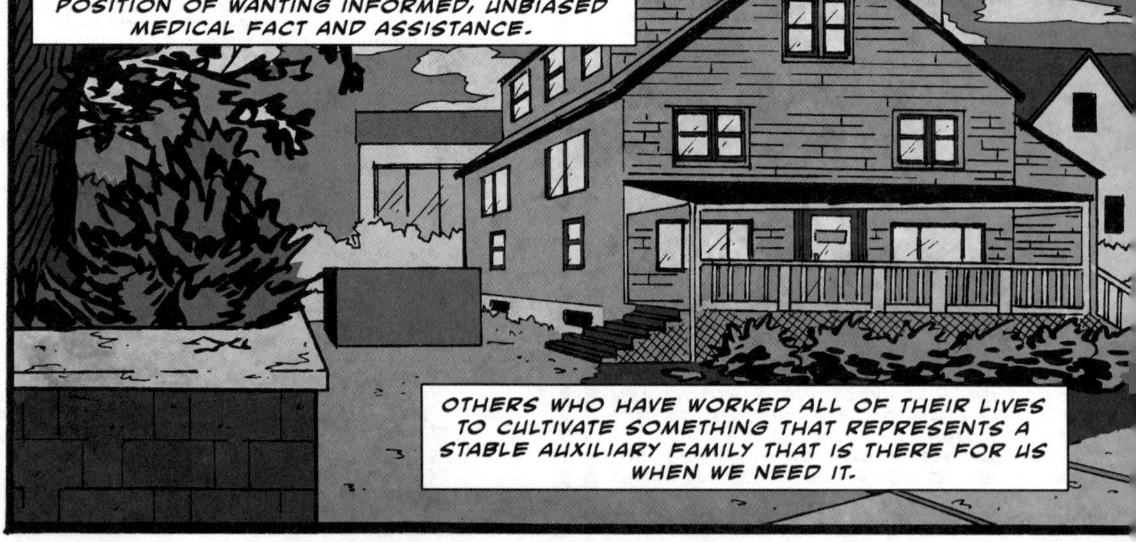
THANKFULLY, THERE HAVE BEEN OTHERS IN MY POSITION OF WANTING INFORMED, UNBIASED MEDICAL FACT AND ASSISTANCE.
OTHERS WHO HAVE WORKED ALL OF THEIR LIVES TO CULTIVATE SOMETHING THAT REPRESENTS A STABLE AUXILIARY FAMILY THAT IS THERE FOR US WHEN WE NEED IT.

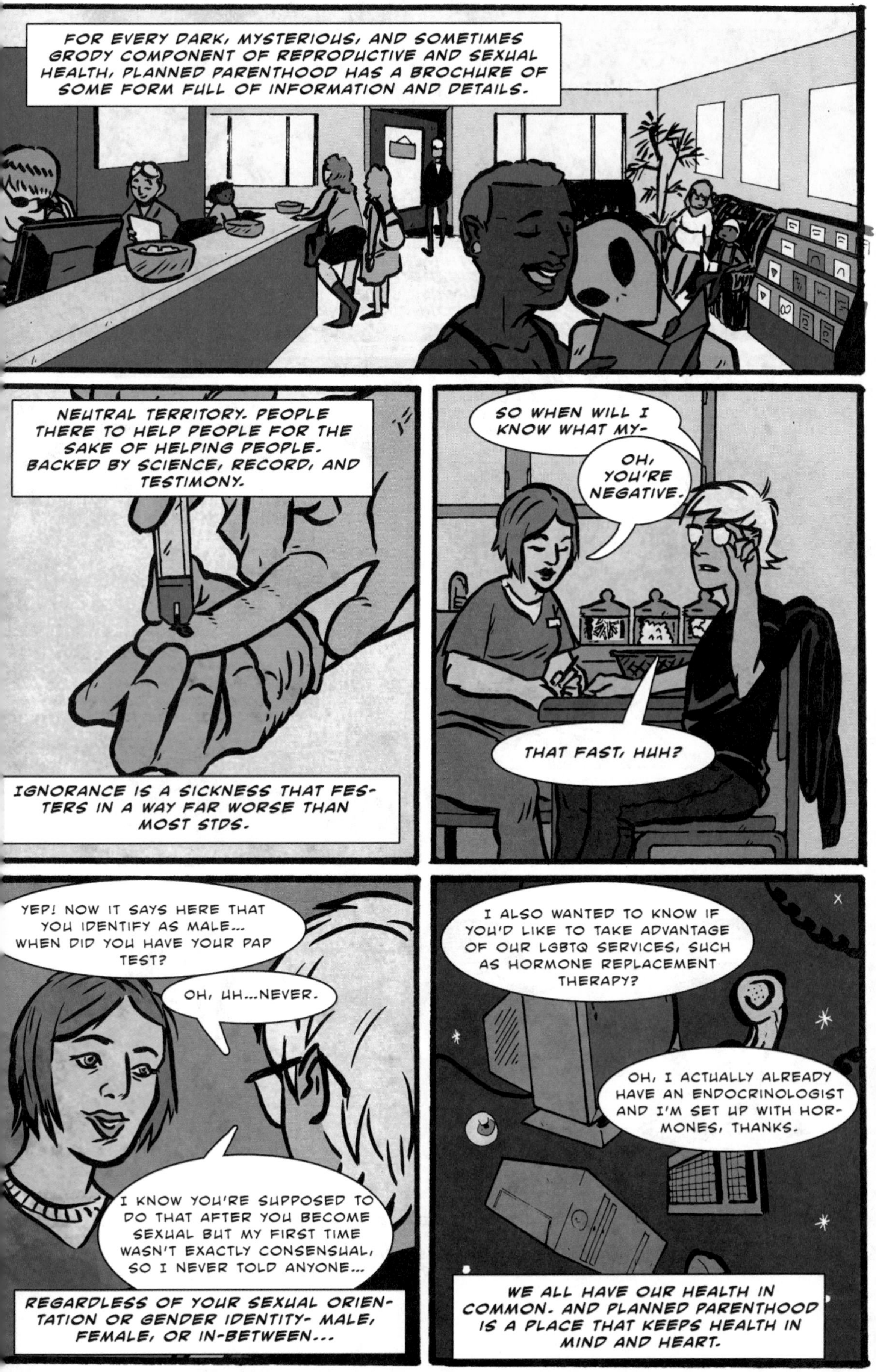

FOR EVERY DARK, MYSTERIOUS, AND SOMETIMES GRODY COMPONENT OF REPRODUCTIVE AND SEXUAL HEALTH, PLANNED PARENTHOOD HAS A BROCHURE OF SOME FORM FULL OF INFORMATION AND DETAILS.
NEUTRAL TERRITORY. PEOPLE THERE TO HELP PEOPLE FOR THE SAKE OF HELPING PEOPLE. BACKED BY SCIENCE, RECORD, AND TESTIMONY.
IGNORANCE IS A SICKNESS THAT FESTERS IN A WAY FAR WORSE THAN MOST STDS.
SO WHEN WILL I KNOW WHAT MY-
OH, YOU'RE NEGATIVE.
THAT FAST, HUH?
YEP! NOW IT SAYS HERE THAT YOU IDENTIFY AS MALE... WHEN DID YOU HAVE YOUR PAP TEST?
OH, UH...NEVER.
I KNOW YOU'RE SUPPOSED TO DO THAT AFTER YOU BECOME SEXUAL BUT MY FIRST TIME WASN'T EXACTLY CONSENSUAL, SO I NEVER TOLD ANYONE...
REGARDLESS OF YOUR SEXUAL ORIENTATION OR GENDER IDENTITY- MALE, FEMALE, OR IN-BETWEEN...
I ALSO WANTED TO KNOW IF YOU'D LIKE TO TAKE ADVANTAGE OF OUR LGBTQ SERVICES, SUCH AS HORMONE REPLACEMENT THERAPY?
OH, I ACTUALLY ALREADY HAVE AN ENDOCRINOLOGIST AND I'M SET UP WITH HORMONES, THANKS.
WE ALL HAVE OUR HEALTH IN COMMON. AND PLANNED PARENTHOOD IS A PLACE THAT KEEPS HEALTH IN MIND AND HEART.

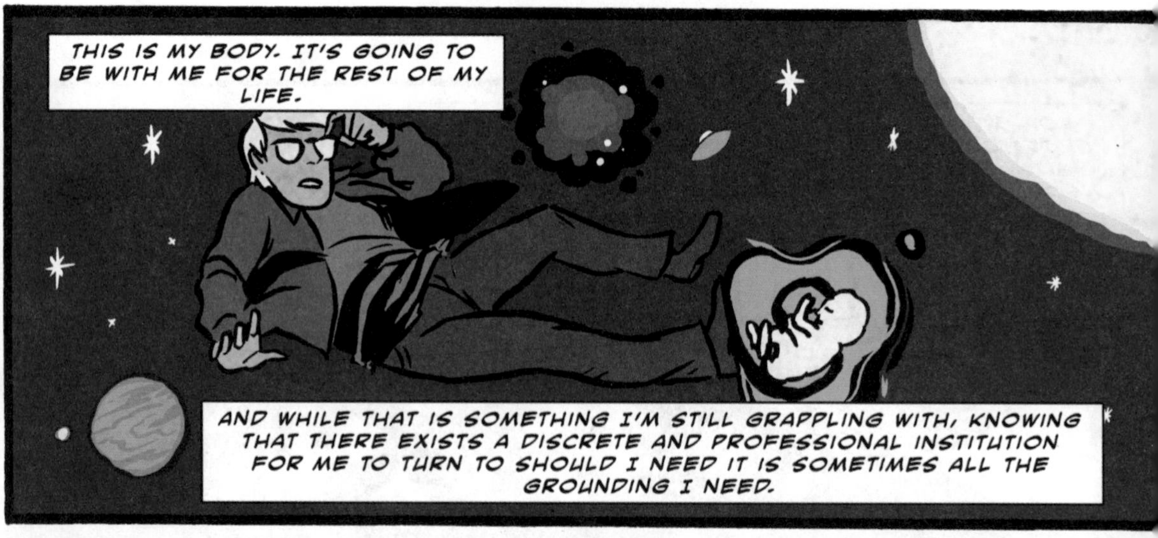
THIS IS MY BODY. IT'S GOING TO BE WITH ME FOR THE REST OF MY LIFE.
AND WHILE THAT IS SOMETHING I'M STILL GRAPPLING WITH, KNOWING THAT THERE EXISTS A DISCRETE AND PROFESSIONAL INSTITUTION FOR ME TO TURN TO SHOULD I NEED IT IS SOMETIMES ALL THE GROUNDING I NEED.

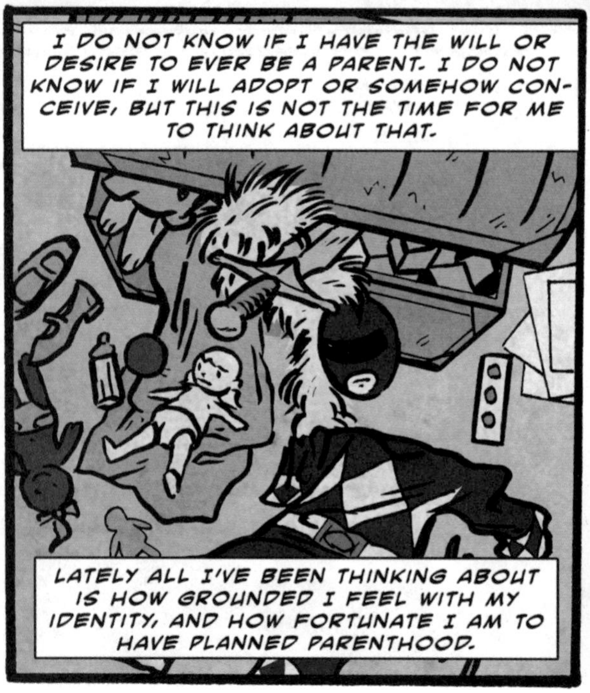
I DO NOT KNOW IF I HAVE THE WILL OR DESIRE TO EVER BE A PARENT. I DO NOT KNOW IF I WILL ADOPT OR SOMEHOW CONCEIVE, BUT THIS IS NOT THE TIME FOR ME TO THINK ABOUT THAT.
LATELY ALL I'VE BEEN THINKING ABOUT IS HOW GROUNDED I FEEL WITH MY IDENTITY, AND HOW FORTUNATE I AM TO HAVE PLANNED PARENTHOOD.

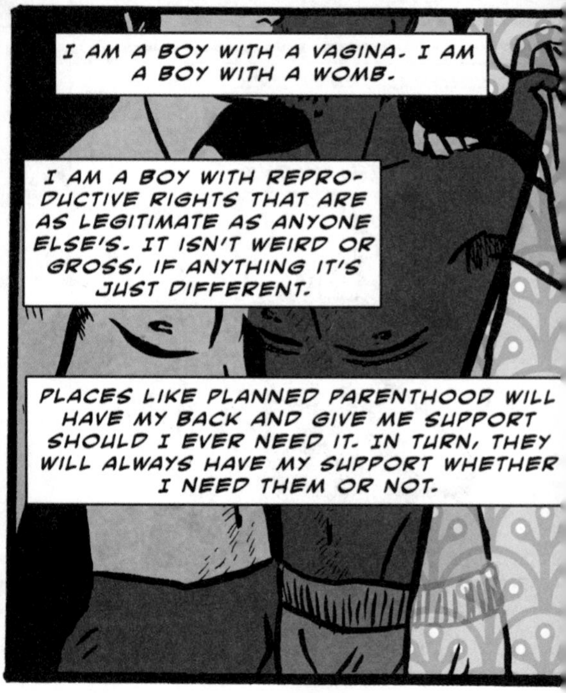
I AM A BOY WITH A VAGINA. I AM A BOY WITH A WOMB.
I AM A BOY WITH REPRODUCTIVE RIGHTS THAT ARE AS LEGITIMATE AS ANYONE ELSE'S. IT ISN'T WEIRD OR GROSS, IF ANYTHING IT'S JUST DIFFERENT.
PLACES LIKE PLANNED PARENTHOOD WILL HAVE MY BACK AND GIVE ME SUPPORT SHOULD I EVER NEED IT. IN TURN, THEY WILL ALWAYS HAVE MY SUPPORT WHETHER I NEED THEM OR NOT.

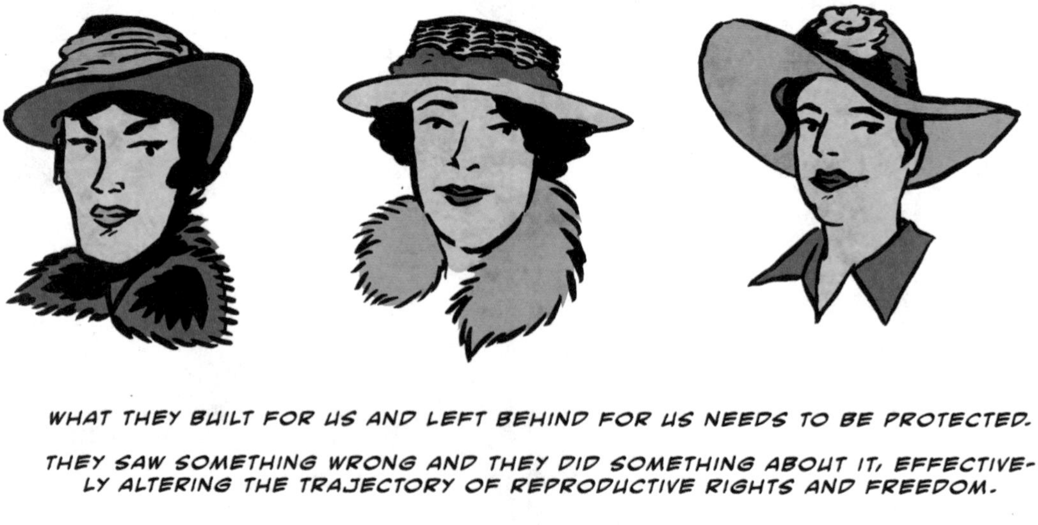

WHAT THEY BUILT FOR US AND LEFT BEHIND FOR US NEEDS TO BE PROTECTED.

THEY SAW SOMETHING WRONG AND THEY DID SOMETHING ABOUT IT, EFFECTIVELY ALTERING THE TRAJECTORY OF REPRODUCTIVE RIGHTS AND FREEDOM.

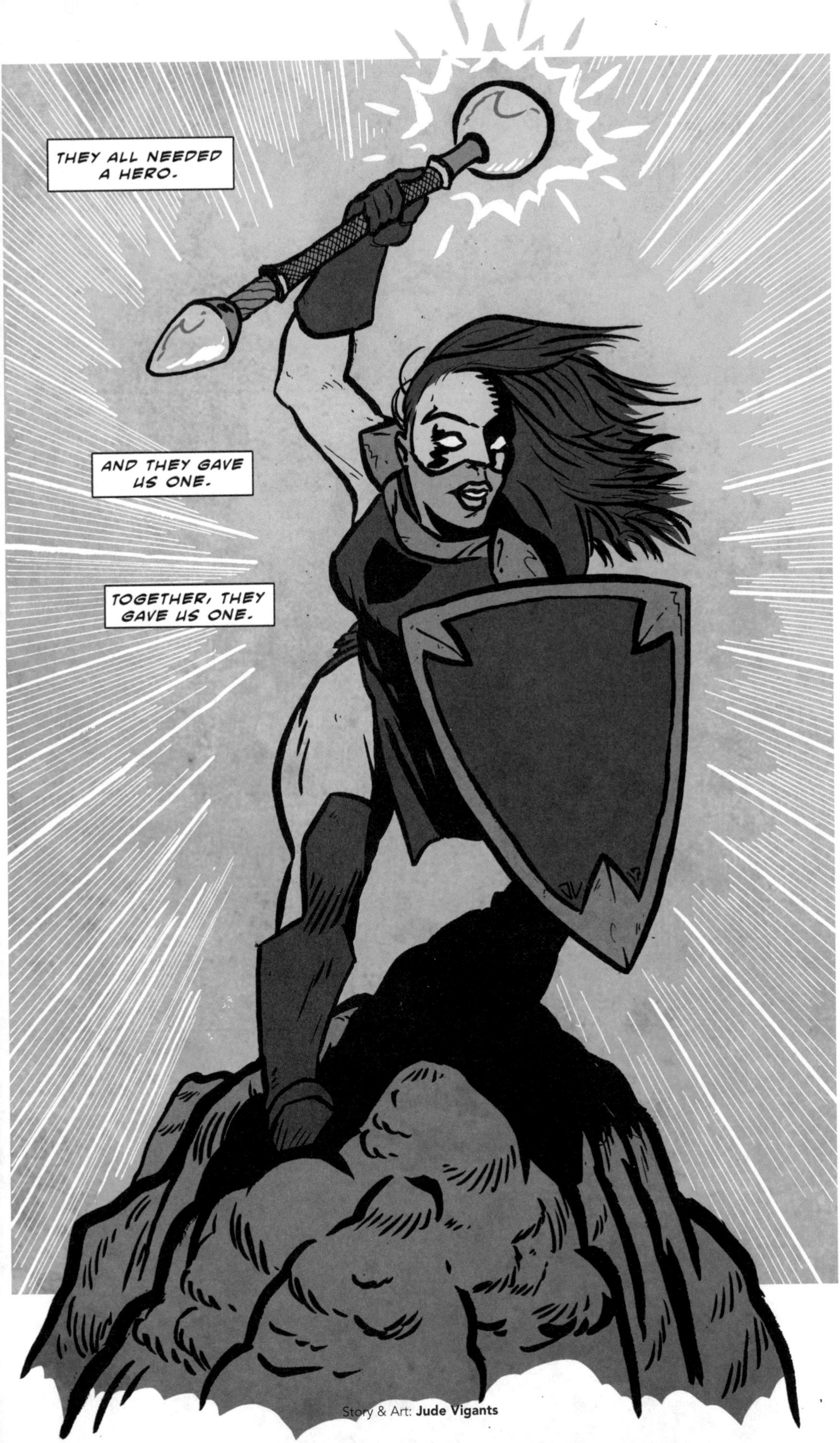
THEY ALL NEEDED A HERO.
AND THEY GAVE US ONE.
TOGETHER, THEY GAVE US ONE.

Story & Art: **Jude Vigants**

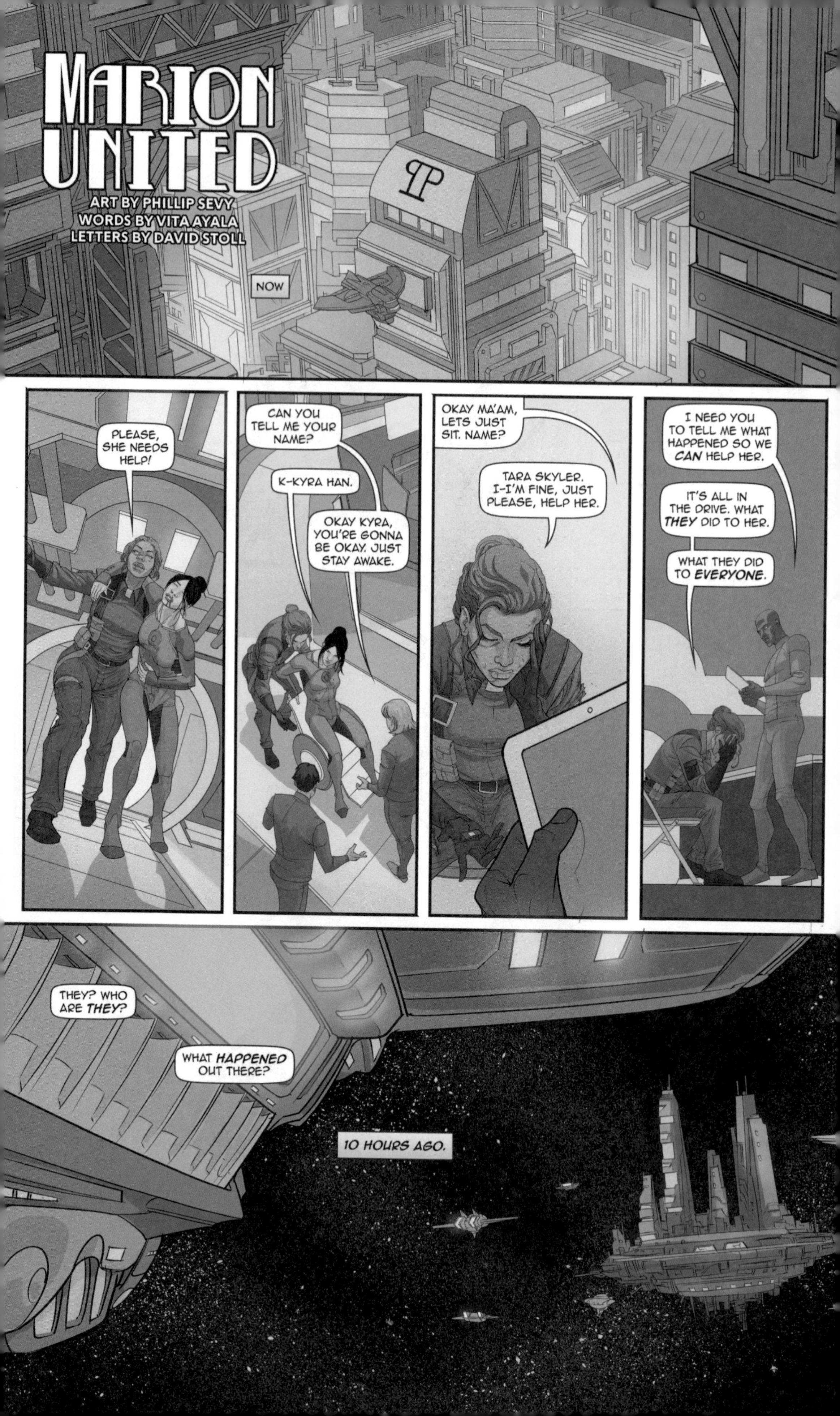
MARION UNITED
ART BY PHILLIP SEVY
WORDS BY VITA AYALA
LETTERS BY DAVID STOLL
NOW
PLEASE, SHE NEEDS HELP!
CAN YOU TELL ME YOUR NAME?
K-KYRA HAN.
OKAY KYRA, YOU'RE GONNA BE OKAY. JUST STAY AWAKE.
OKAY MA'AM, LETS JUST SIT. NAME?
TARA SKYLER. I-I'M FINE, JUST PLEASE, HELP HER.
I NEED YOU TO TELL ME WHAT HAPPENED SO WE CAN HELP HER.
IT'S ALL IN THE DRIVE. WHAT THEY DID TO HER.
WHAT THEY DID TO EVERYONE.
THEY? WHO ARE THEY?
WHAT HAPPENED OUT THERE?
10 HOURS AGO.

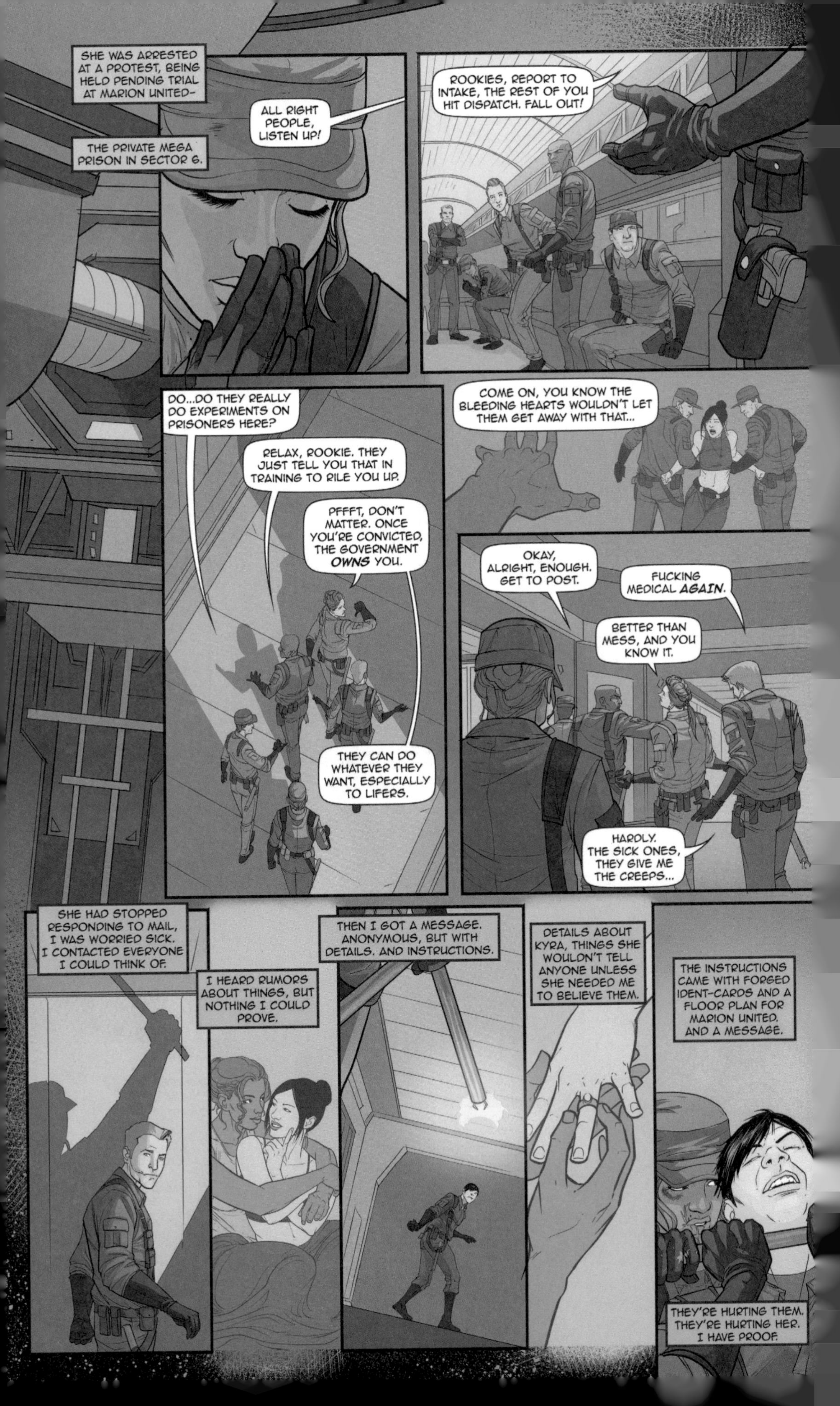
SHE WAS ARRESTED AT A PROTEST, BEING HELD PENDING TRIAL AT MARION UNITED-
THE PRIVATE MEGA PRISON IN SECTOR 6.
ALL RIGHT PEOPLE, LISTEN UP!
ROOKIES, REPORT TO INTAKE, THE REST OF YOU HIT DISPATCH. FALL OUT!
DO...DO THEY REALLY DO EXPERIMENTS ON PRISONERS HERE?
RELAX, ROOKIE. THEY JUST TELL YOU THAT IN TRAINING TO RILE YOU UP.
PFFFT, DON'T MATTER. ONCE YOU'RE CONVICTED, THE GOVERNMENT OWNS YOU.
THEY CAN DO WHATEVER THEY WANT, ESPECIALLY TO LIFERS.
COME ON, YOU KNOW THE BLEEDING HEARTS WOULDN'T LET THEM GET AWAY WITH THAT...
OKAY, ALRIGHT, ENOUGH. GET TO POST.
FUCKING MEDICAL AGAIN.
BETTER THAN MESS, AND YOU KNOW IT.
HARDLY. THE SICK ONES, THEY GIVE ME THE CREEPS...
SHE HAD STOPPED RESPONDING TO MAIL, I WAS WORRIED SICK. I CONTACTED EVERYONE I COULD THINK OF.
I HEARD RUMORS ABOUT THINGS, BUT NOTHING I COULD PROVE.
THEN I GOT A MESSAGE. ANONYMOUS, BUT WITH DETAILS. AND INSTRUCTIONS.
DETAILS ABOUT KYRA, THINGS SHE WOULDN'T TELL ANYONE UNLESS SHE NEEDED ME TO BELIEVE THEM.
THE INSTRUCTIONS CAME WITH FORGED IDENT-CARDS AND A FLOOR PLAN FOR MARION UNITED. AND A MESSAGE.
THEY'RE HURTING THEM. THEY'RE HURTING HER. I HAVE PROOF.

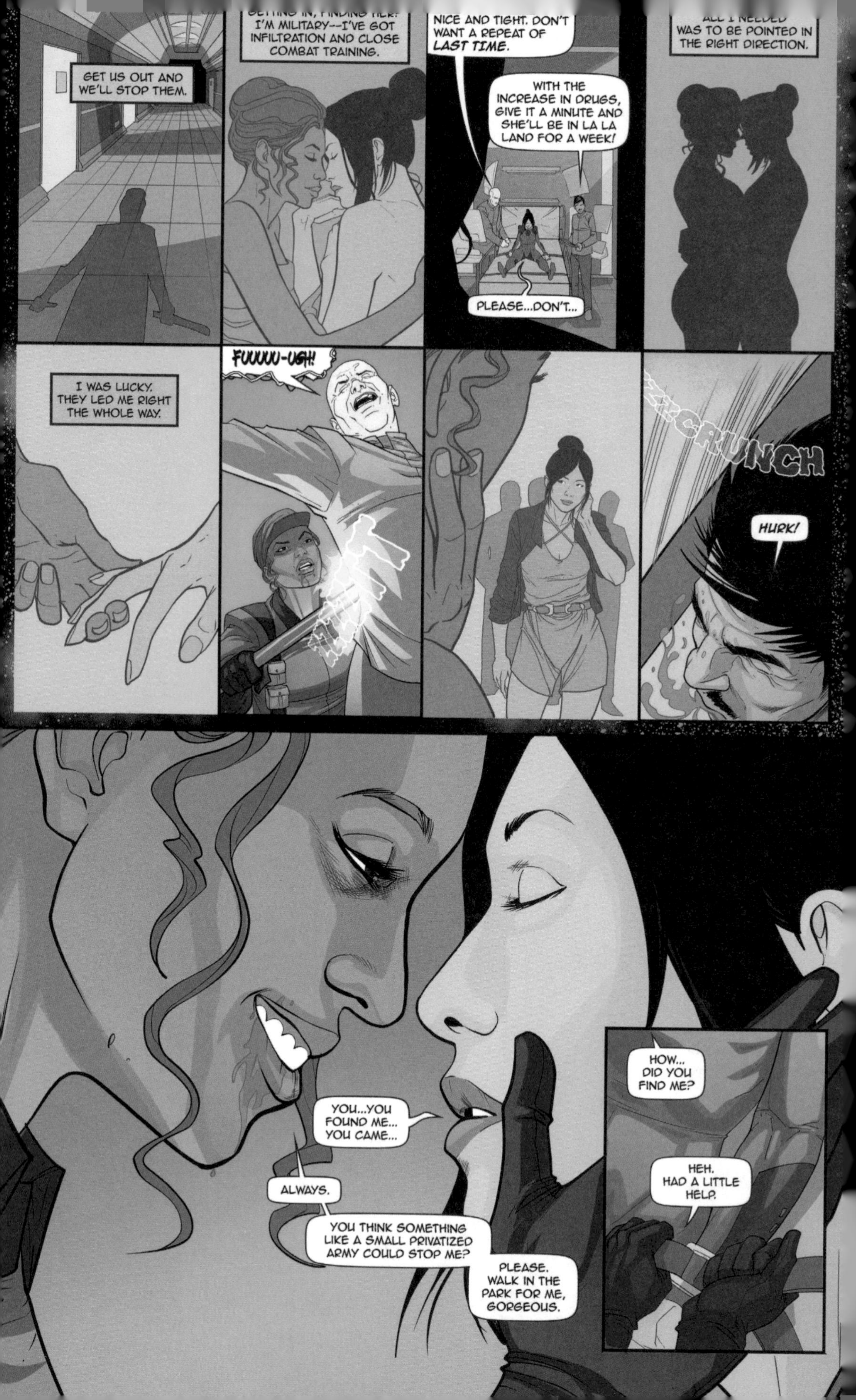
GET US OUT AND WE'LL STOP THEM.
I'M MILITARY--I'VE GOT INFILTRATION AND CLOSE COMBAT TRAINING.
NICE AND TIGHT. DON'T WANT A REPEAT OF LAST TIME.
WITH THE INCREASE IN DRUGS, GIVE IT A MINUTE AND SHE'LL BE IN LA LA LAND FOR A WEEK!
PLEASE...DON'T...
WAS TO BE POINTED IN THE RIGHT DIRECTION.
I WAS LUCKY. THEY LED ME RIGHT THE WHOLE WAY.
FUUUUU-UGH!
CRUNCH
HURK!
YOU...YOU FOUND ME... YOU CAME...
ALWAYS.
YOU THINK SOMETHING LIKE A SMALL PRIVATIZED ARMY COULD STOP ME?
PLEASE. WALK IN THE PARK FOR ME, GORGEOUS.
HOW... DID YOU FIND ME?
HEH. HAD A LITTLE HELP.

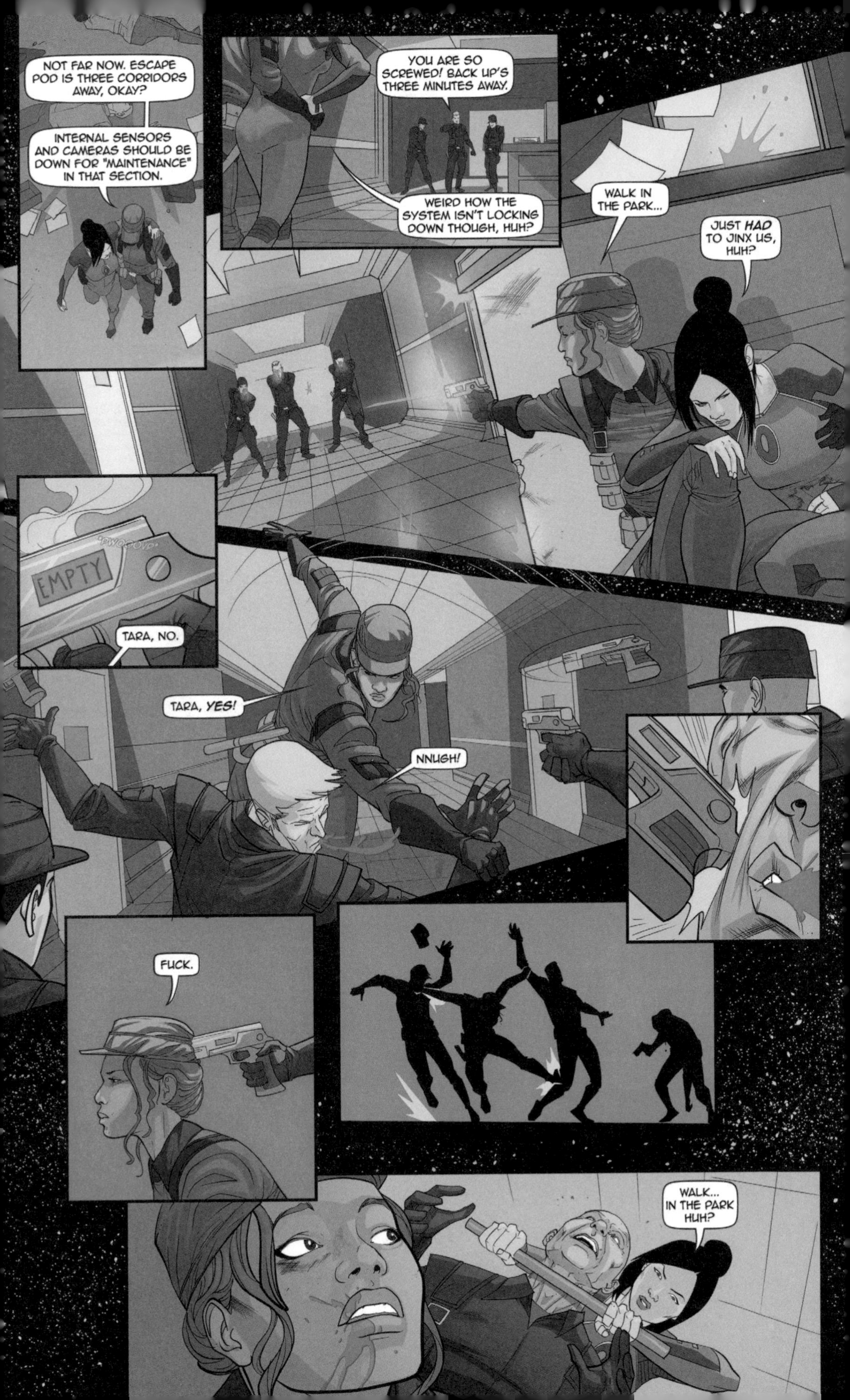
NOT FAR NOW. ESCAPE POD IS THREE CORRIDORS AWAY, OKAY?
INTERNAL SENSORS AND CAMERAS SHOULD BE DOWN FOR "MAINTENANCE" IN THAT SECTION.
YOU ARE SO SCREWED! BACK UP'S THREE MINUTES AWAY.
WEIRD HOW THE SYSTEM ISN'T LOCKING DOWN THOUGH, HUH?
WALK IN THE PARK...
JUST HAD TO JINX US, HUH?
EMPTY
TARA, NO.
TARA, YES!
NNUGH!
FUCK.
WALK... IN THE PARK HUH?

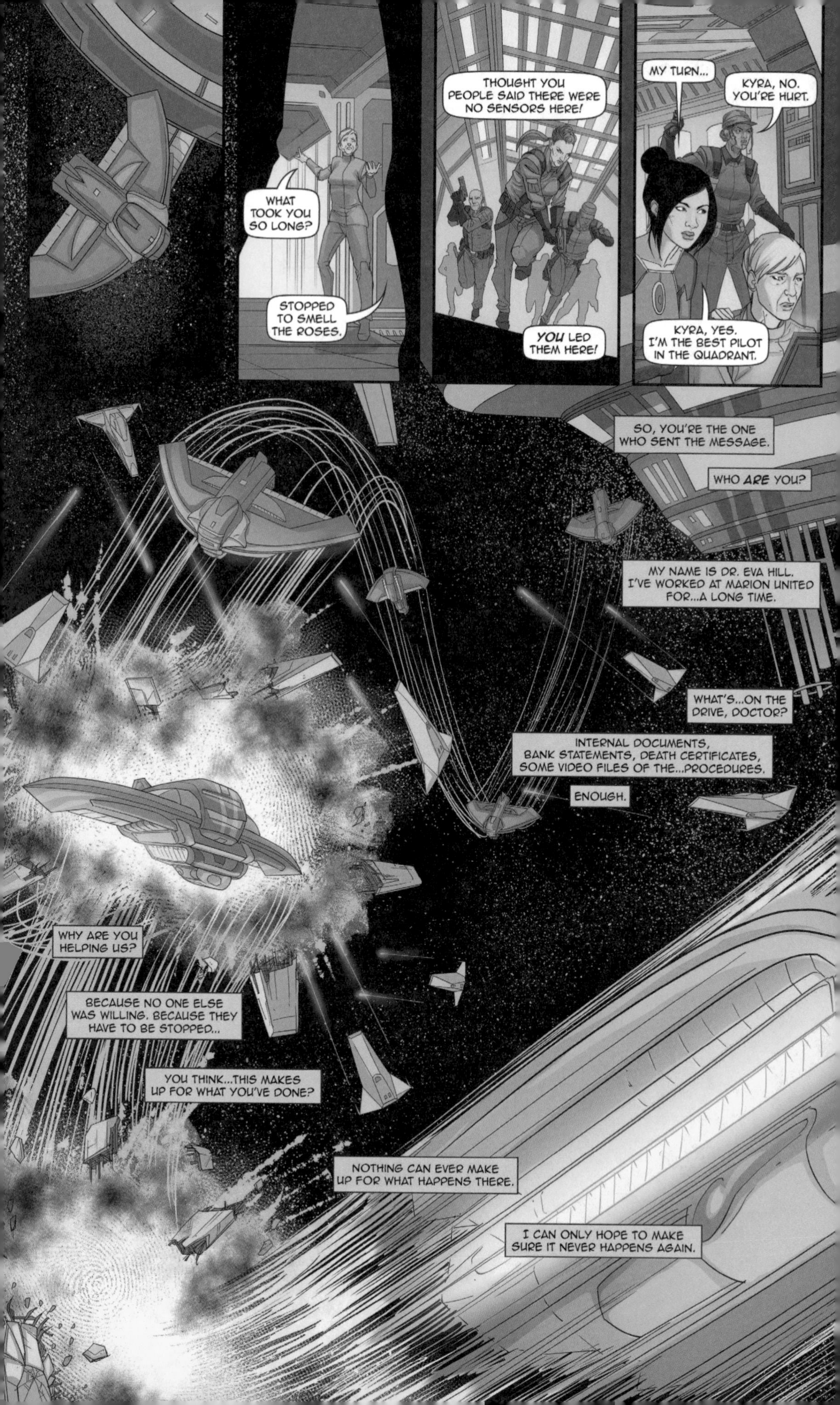
WHAT TOOK YOU SO LONG?
STOPPED TO SMELL THE ROSES.
THOUGHT YOU PEOPLE SAID THERE WERE NO SENSORS HERE!
YOU LED THEM HERE!
MY TURN...
KYRA, NO. YOU'RE HURT.
KYRA, YES. I'M THE BEST PILOT IN THE QUADRANT.
SO, YOU'RE THE ONE WHO SENT THE MESSAGE.
WHO ARE YOU?
MY NAME IS DR. EVA HILL. I'VE WORKED AT MARION UNITED FOR...A LONG TIME.
WHAT'S...ON THE DRIVE, DOCTOR?
INTERNAL DOCUMENTS, BANK STATEMENTS, DEATH CERTIFICATES, SOME VIDEO FILES OF THE...PROCEDURES.
ENOUGH.
WHY ARE YOU HELPING US?
BECAUSE NO ONE ELSE WAS WILLING. BECAUSE THEY HAVE TO BE STOPPED...
YOU THINK...THIS MAKES UP FOR WHAT YOU'VE DONE?
NOTHING CAN EVER MAKE UP FOR WHAT HAPPENS THERE.
I CAN ONLY HOPE TO MAKE SURE IT NEVER HAPPENS AGAIN.

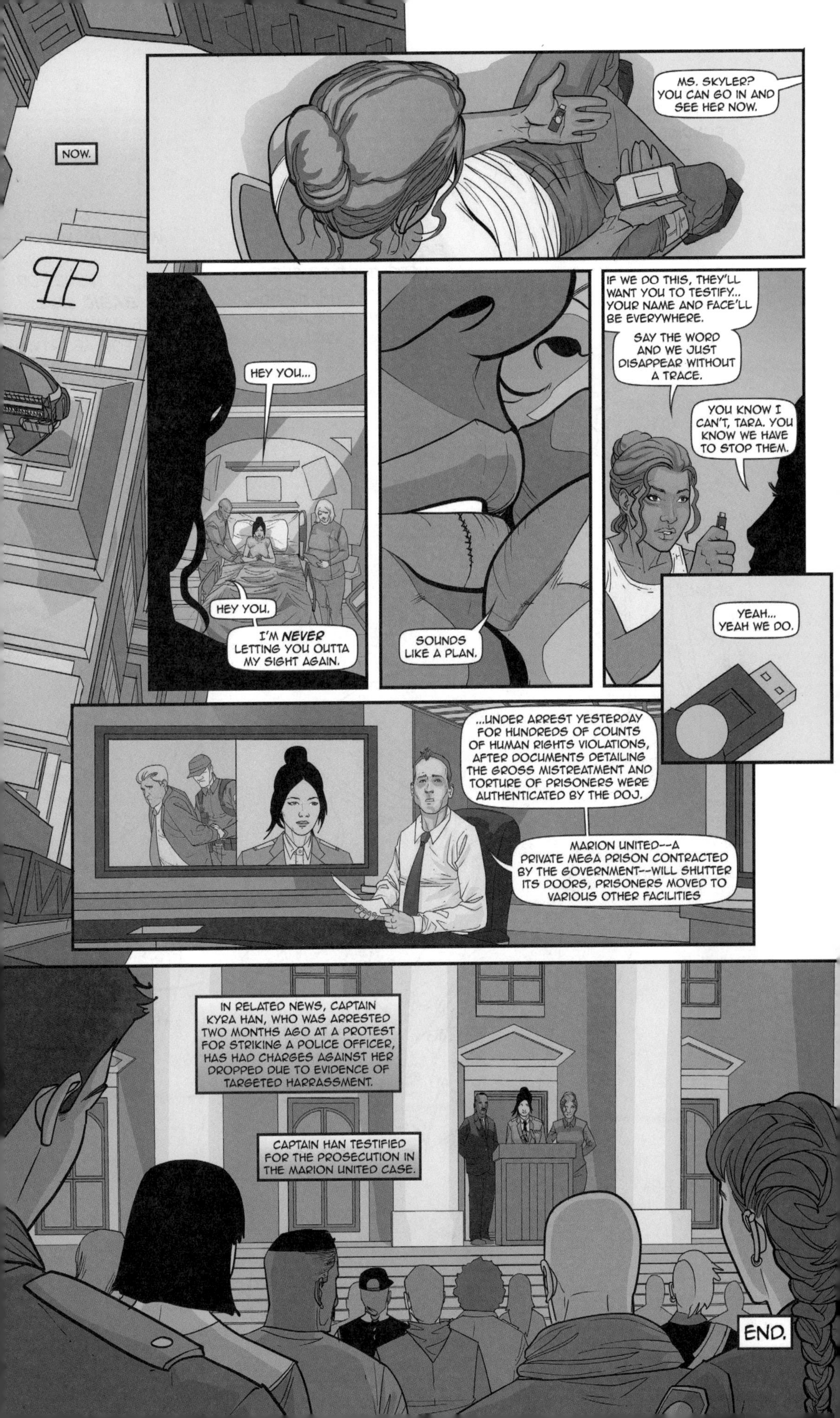
NOW.
MS. SKYLER? YOU CAN GO IN AND SEE HER NOW.
HEY YOU...
HEY YOU.
I'M **NEVER** LETTING YOU OUTTA MY SIGHT AGAIN.
SOUNDS LIKE A PLAN.
IF WE DO THIS, THEY'LL WANT YOU TO TESTIFY... YOUR NAME AND FACE'LL BE EVERYWHERE.
SAY THE WORD AND WE JUST DISAPPEAR WITHOUT A TRACE.
YOU KNOW I CAN'T, TARA. YOU KNOW WE HAVE TO STOP THEM.
YEAH... YEAH WE DO.
...UNDER ARREST YESTERDAY FOR HUNDREDS OF COUNTS OF HUMAN RIGHTS VIOLATIONS, AFTER DOCUMENTS DETAILING THE GROSS MISTREATMENT AND TORTURE OF PRISONERS WERE AUTHENTICATED BY THE DOJ.
MARION UNITED--A PRIVATE MEGA PRISON CONTRACTED BY THE GOVERNMENT--WILL SHUTTER ITS DOORS, PRISONERS MOVED TO VARIOUS OTHER FACILITIES
IN RELATED NEWS, CAPTAIN KYRA HAN, WHO WAS ARRESTED TWO MONTHS AGO AT A PROTEST FOR STRIKING A POLICE OFFICER, HAS HAD CHARGES AGAINST HER DROPPED DUE TO EVIDENCE OF TARGETED HARRASSMENT.
CAPTAIN HAN TESTIFIED FOR THE PROSECUTION IN THE MARION UNITED CASE.
END.

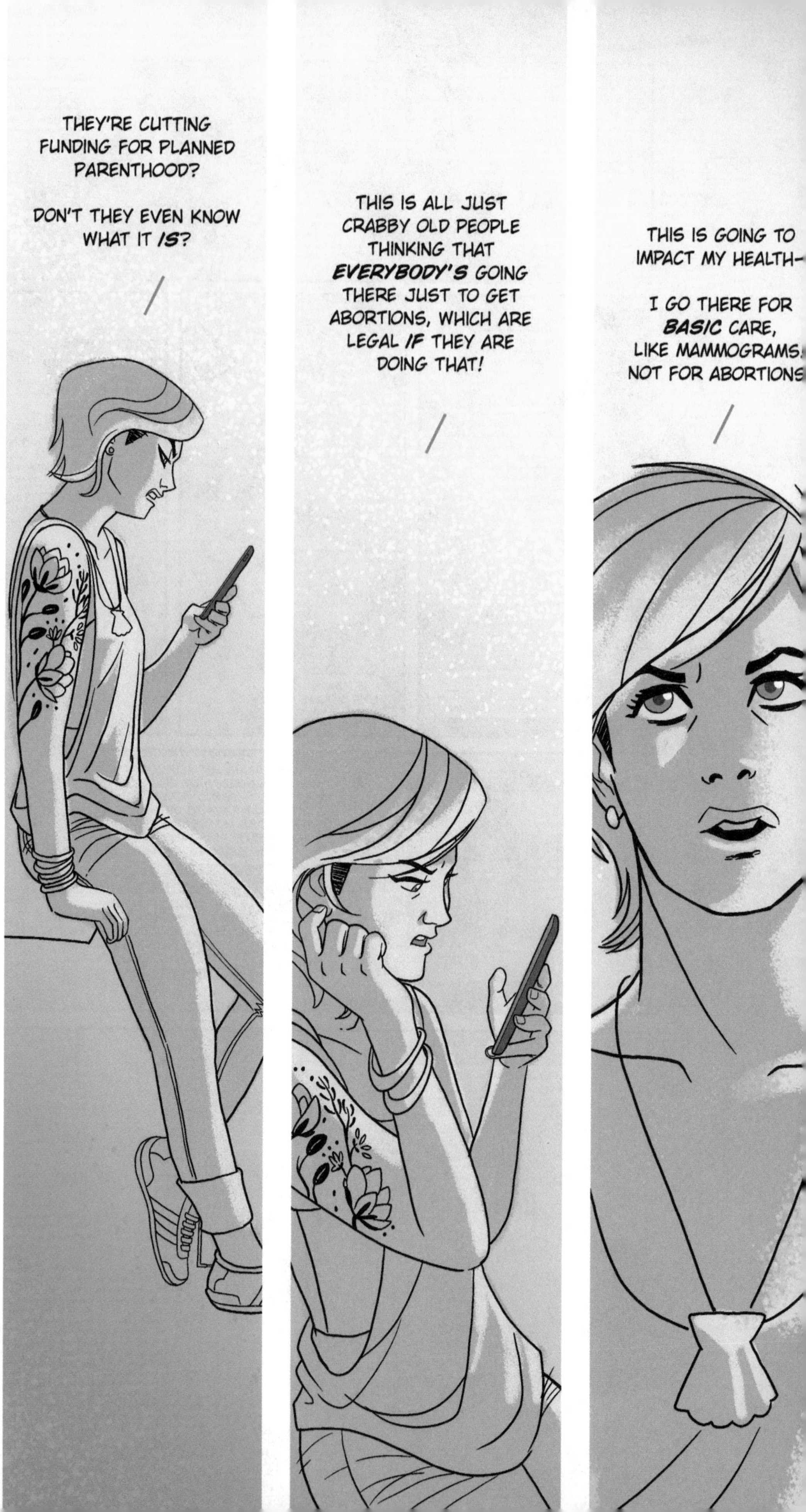
THEY'RE CUTTING FUNDING FOR PLANNED PARENTHOOD?
DON'T THEY EVEN KNOW WHAT IT *IS*?
THIS IS ALL JUST CRABBY OLD PEOPLE THINKING THAT ***EVERYBODY'S*** GOING THERE JUST TO GET ABORTIONS, WHICH ARE LEGAL *IF* THEY ARE DOING THAT!
THIS IS GOING TO IMPACT MY HEALTH-
I GO THERE FOR ***BASIC*** CARE, LIKE MAMMOGRAMS, NOT FOR ABORTIONS

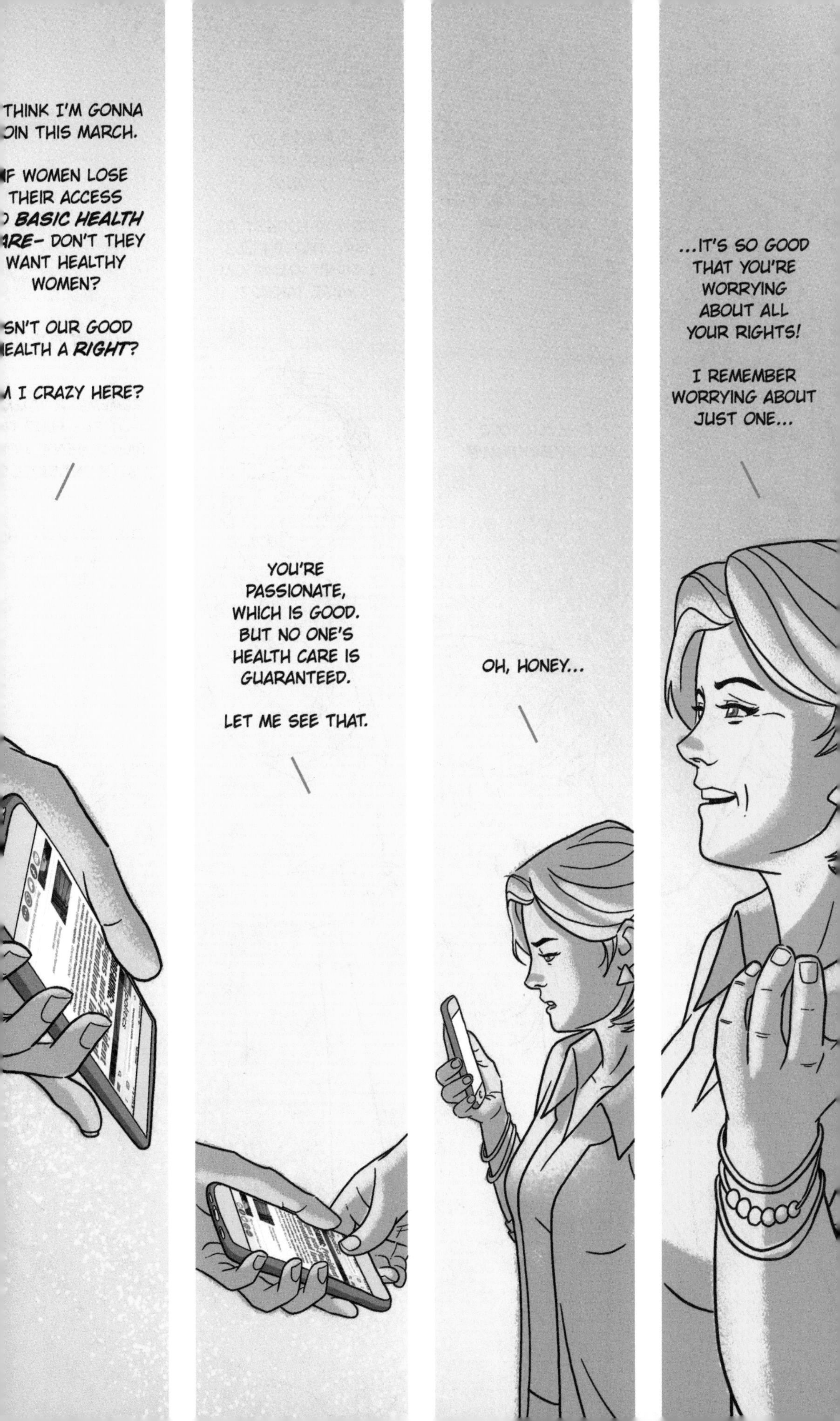

THINK I'M GONNA
JOIN THIS MARCH.

IF WOMEN LOSE
THEIR ACCESS
TO *BASIC HEALTH
CARE*– DON'T THEY
WANT HEALTHY
WOMEN?

ISN'T OUR GOOD
HEALTH A *RIGHT*?

AM I CRAZY HERE?

YOU'RE
PASSIONATE,
WHICH IS GOOD.
BUT NO ONE'S
HEALTH CARE IS
GUARANTEED.

LET ME SEE THAT.

OH, HONEY...

...IT'S SO GOOD
THAT YOU'RE
WORRYING
ABOUT ALL
YOUR RIGHTS!

I REMEMBER
WORRYING ABOUT
JUST ONE...

BIRTH CONTROL!

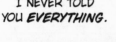

CALLIE! I DIDN'T KNOW YOU DID THAT SO EARLY!

I NEVER TOLD YOU *EVERYTHING*.

BUT YOU GOT PREGNANT SO YOUNG!

DID YOU FORGET TO TAKE THOSE PILLS I DIDN'T KNOW YOU WERE TAKING?

I DIDN'T FORGE

REMEMBER WHEN GOT THE FLU? TI PILL DOESN'T WOI WITH ANTIBIOTIC!

THEY TOLD ME, B I JUST DIDN'T LISTEN.

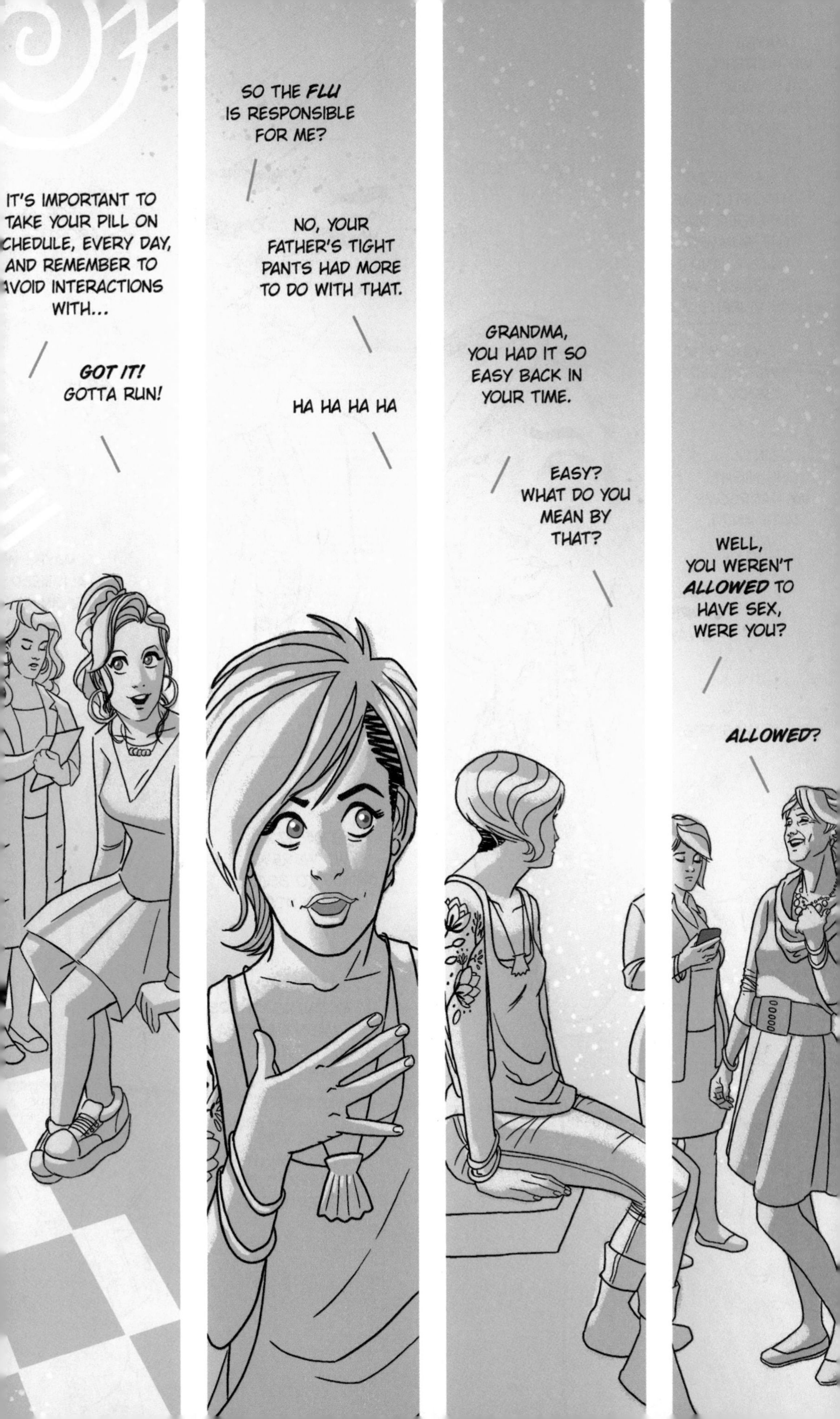
IT'S IMPORTANT TO TAKE YOUR PILL ON CHEDULE, EVERY DAY, AND REMEMBER TO VOID INTERACTIONS WITH...
GOT IT! GOTTA RUN!
SO THE FLU IS RESPONSIBLE FOR ME?
NO, YOUR FATHER'S TIGHT PANTS HAD MORE TO DO WITH THAT.
HA HA HA HA
GRANDMA, YOU HAD IT SO EASY BACK IN YOUR TIME.
EASY? WHAT DO YOU MEAN BY THAT?
WELL, YOU WEREN'T ALLOWED TO HAVE SEX, WERE YOU?
ALLOWED?

MAYBE WE WEREN'T "ALLOWED", BUT KIDS DID IT.

AND EVEN THOUGH I WAS A TEENAGER DURING THE SUMMER OF LOVE, AND I REMEMBER WHEN ROE VERSUS WADE WAS PASSED, I WAS WHAT WE CALLED A "GOOD GIRL."

UNTIL ONE NIGHT. MY HANDSOME DATE AND I, WE...

...WE GOT CARRIED AWAY.

IT WAS 1975.

BUT I WASN'T BORN UNTIL '79?

EXACTLY! WE WERE'NT READY TO BECOME PARENTS.

AFTER THE NEXT MORNING, THERE WASN'T EVEN A "WE."

I WAS THE GIRL WHO NEEDED PLANNED PARENTHOOD...

...FOR AN ABORTION.

GRANDMA!

MAYBE W ALL NEED JOIN YOU MARCH!

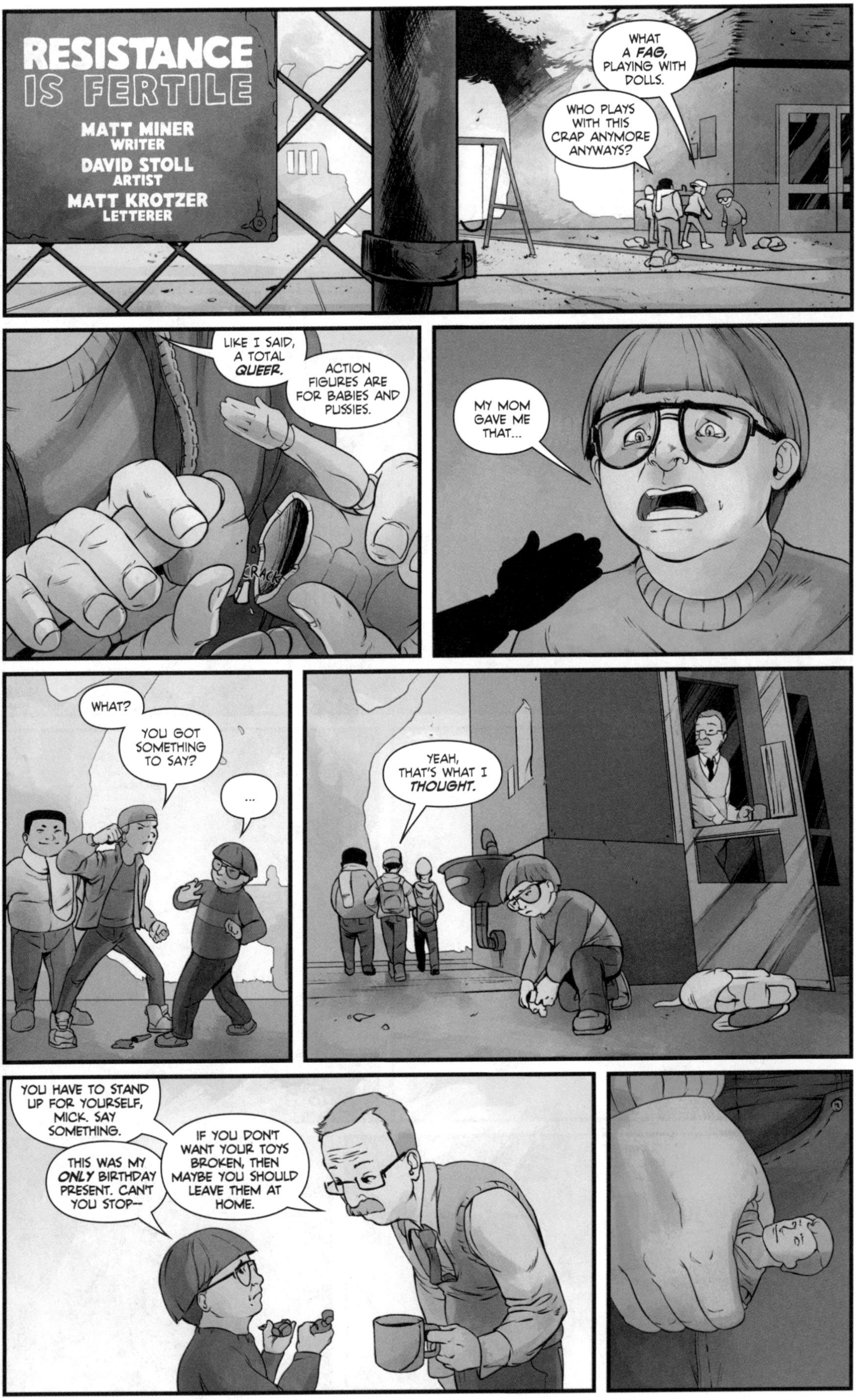
RESISTANCE IS FERTILE
MATT MINER
WRITER
DAVID STOLL
ARTIST
MATT KROTZER
LETTERER
WHAT A *FAG,* PLAYING WITH DOLLS.
WHO PLAYS WITH THIS CRAP ANYMORE ANYWAYS?
LIKE I SAID, A TOTAL *QUEER.*
ACTION FIGURES ARE FOR BABIES AND PUSSIES.
CRACK
MY MOM GAVE ME THAT...
WHAT?
YOU GOT SOMETHING TO SAY?
...
YEAH, THAT'S WHAT I *THOUGHT.*
YOU HAVE TO STAND UP FOR YOURSELF, MICK. SAY SOMETHING.
THIS WAS MY *ONLY* BIRTHDAY PRESENT. CAN'T YOU STOP--
IF YOU DON'T WANT YOUR TOYS BROKEN, THEN MAYBE YOU SHOULD LEAVE THEM AT HOME.

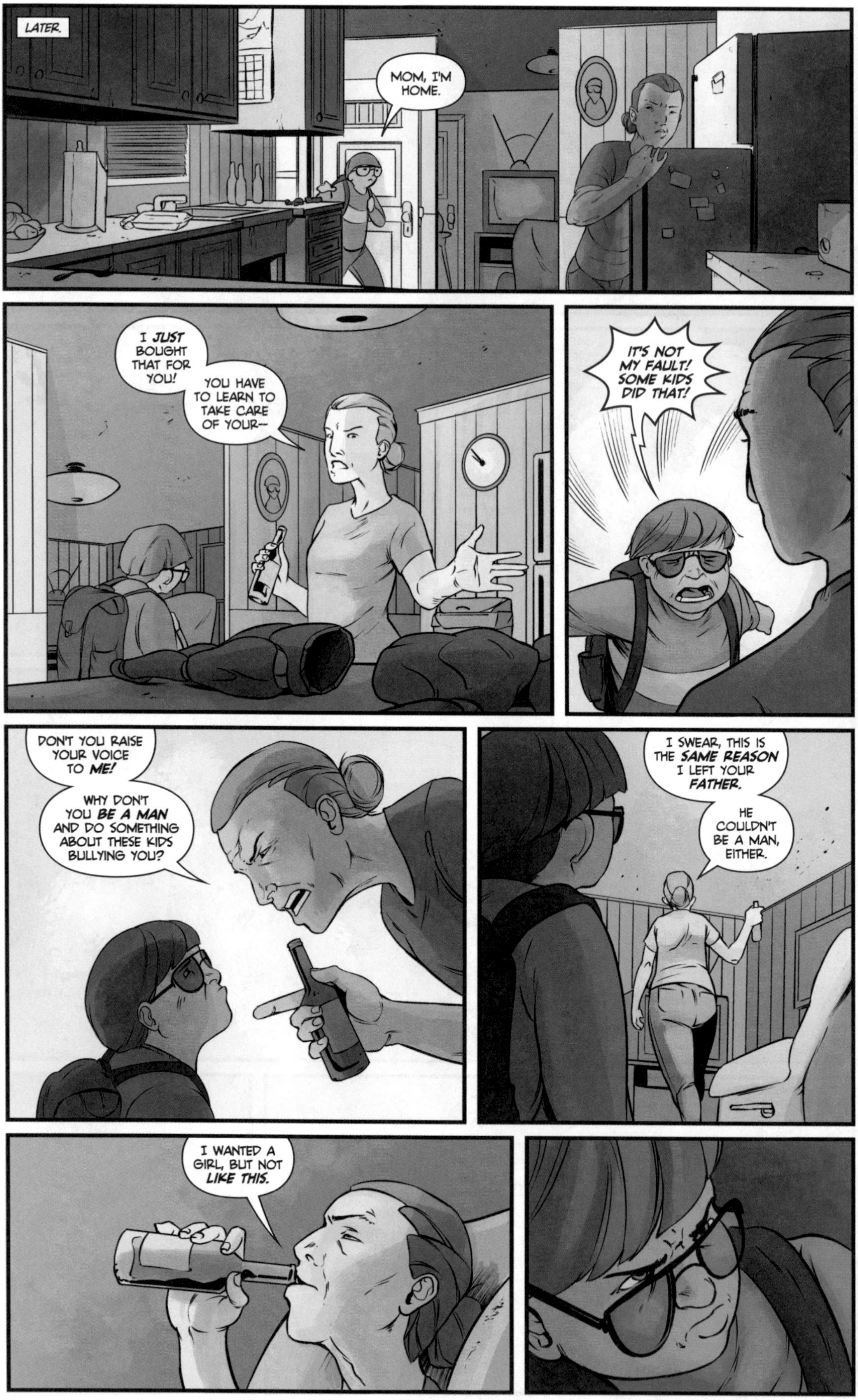
LATER.
MOM, I'M HOME.
I JUST BOUGHT THAT FOR YOU!
YOU HAVE TO LEARN TO TAKE CARE OF YOUR--
IT'S NOT MY FAULT! SOME KIDS DID THAT!
DON'T YOU RAISE YOUR VOICE TO ME!
WHY DON'T YOU BE A MAN AND DO SOMETHING ABOUT THESE KIDS BULLYING YOU?
I SWEAR, THIS IS THE SAME REASON I LEFT YOUR FATHER.
HE COULDN'T BE A MAN, EITHER.
I WANTED A GIRL, BUT NOT LIKE THIS.

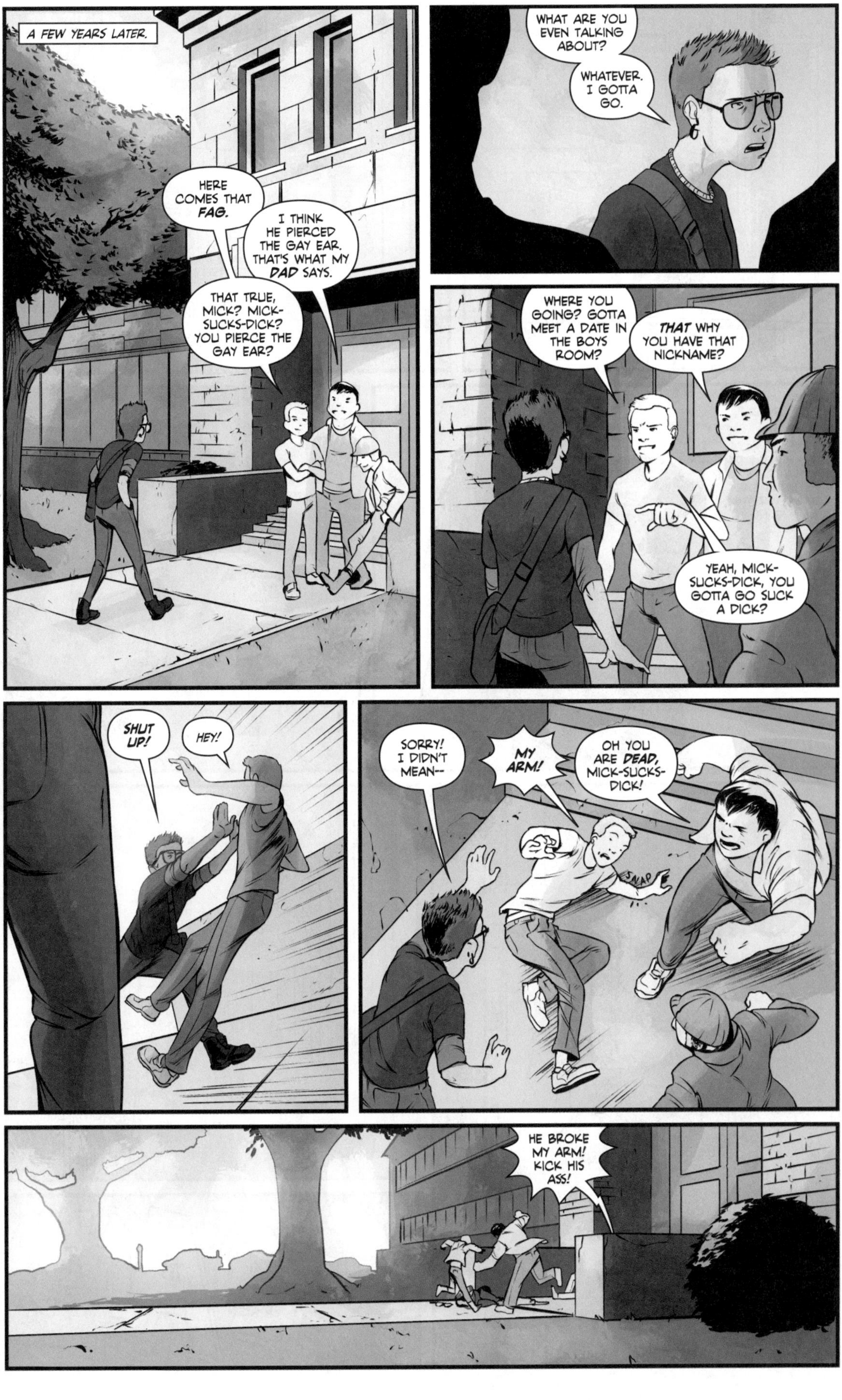

A FEW YEARS LATER.
HERE COMES THAT *FAG.*
I THINK HE PIERCED THE GAY EAR. THAT'S WHAT MY *DAD* SAYS.
THAT TRUE, MICK? MICK-SUCKS-DICK? YOU PIERCE THE GAY EAR?
WHAT ARE YOU EVEN TALKING ABOUT?
WHATEVER. I GOTTA GO.
WHERE YOU GOING? GOTTA MEET A DATE IN THE BOYS ROOM?
THAT WHY YOU HAVE THAT NICKNAME?
YEAH, MICK-SUCKS-DICK, YOU GOTTA GO SUCK A DICK?
SHUT UP!
HEY!
SORRY! I DIDN'T MEAN--
MY ARM!
OH YOU ARE *DEAD,* MICK-SUCKS-DICK!
SNAP
HE BROKE MY ARM! KICK HIS ASS!

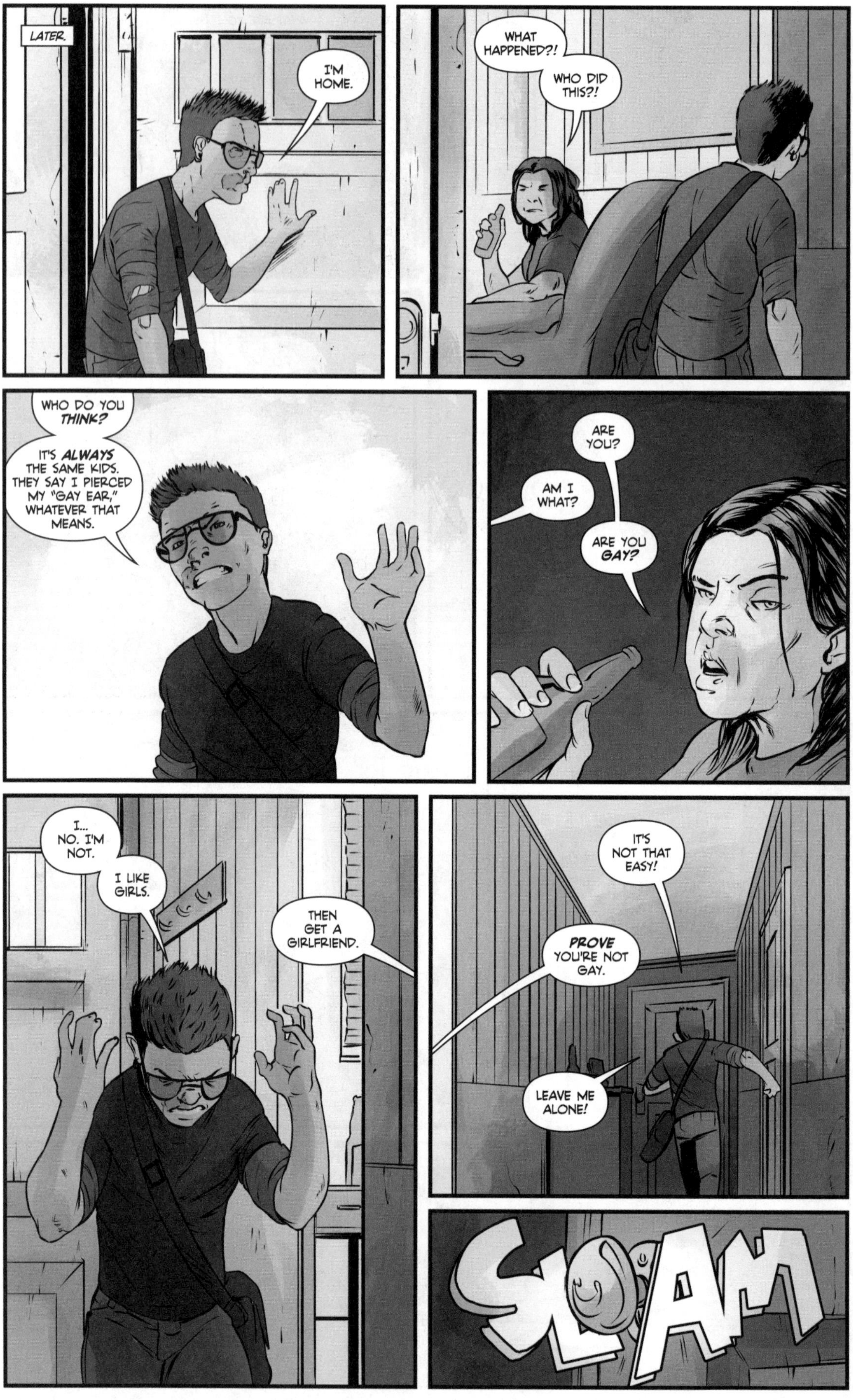
LATER.
I'M HOME.
WHAT HAPPENED?!
WHO DID THIS?!
WHO DO YOU THINK?
IT'S ALWAYS THE SAME KIDS. THEY SAY I PIERCED MY "GAY EAR," WHATEVER THAT MEANS.
ARE YOU?
AM I WHAT?
ARE YOU GAY?
I... NO. I'M NOT.
I LIKE GIRLS.
THEN GET A GIRLFRIEND.
IT'S NOT THAT EASY!
PROVE YOU'RE NOT GAY.
LEAVE ME ALONE!
SLAM

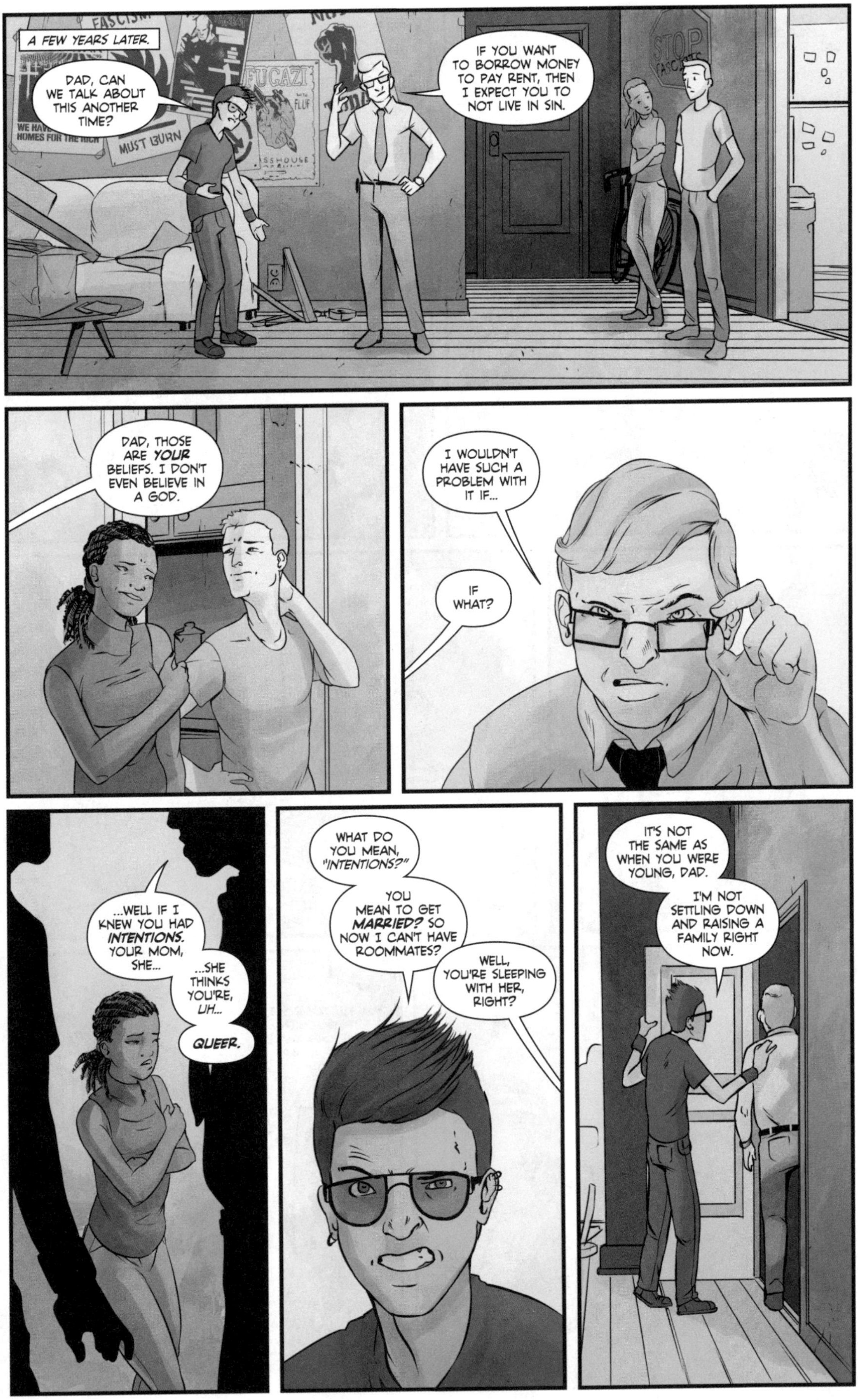
A FEW YEARS LATER.
DAD, CAN WE TALK ABOUT THIS ANOTHER TIME?
IF YOU WANT TO BORROW MONEY TO PAY RENT, THEN I EXPECT YOU TO NOT LIVE IN SIN.
FASCISM
FUGAZI
MUST BURN
WE HAVE HOMES FOR THE RICH
STOP FASCISM
DAD, THOSE ARE *YOUR* BELIEFS. I DON'T EVEN BELIEVE IN A GOD.
I WOULDN'T HAVE SUCH A PROBLEM WITH IT IF...
IF WHAT?
...WELL IF I KNEW YOU HAD *INTENTIONS.* YOUR MOM, SHE...
...SHE THINKS YOU'RE, UH...
QUEER.
WHAT DO YOU MEAN, *"INTENTIONS?"*
YOU MEAN TO GET *MARRIED?* SO NOW I CAN'T HAVE ROOMMATES?
WELL, YOU'RE SLEEPING WITH HER, RIGHT?
IT'S NOT THE SAME AS WHEN YOU WERE YOUNG, DAD.
I'M NOT SETTLING DOWN AND RAISING A FAMILY RIGHT NOW.

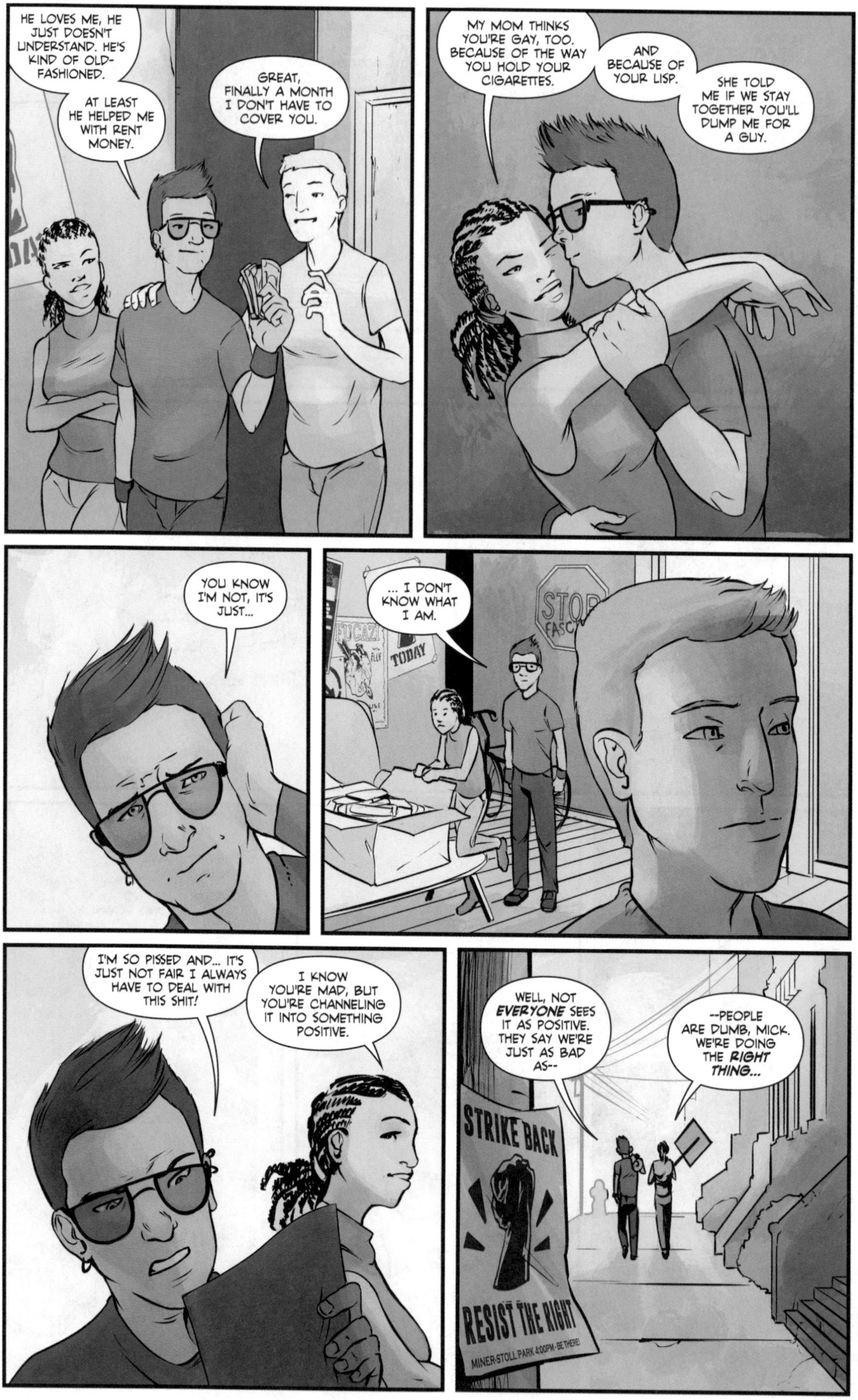

HE LOVES ME, HE JUST DOESN'T UNDERSTAND. HE'S KIND OF OLD-FASHIONED.
AT LEAST HE HELPED ME WITH RENT MONEY.
GREAT, FINALLY A MONTH I DON'T HAVE TO COVER YOU.
MY MOM THINKS YOU'RE GAY, TOO. BECAUSE OF THE WAY YOU HOLD YOUR CIGARETTES.
AND BECAUSE OF YOUR LISP.
SHE TOLD ME IF WE STAY TOGETHER YOU'LL DUMP ME FOR A GUY.
YOU KNOW I'M NOT, IT'S JUST...
... I DON'T KNOW WHAT I AM.
FUGAZI
TODAY
I'M SO PISSED AND... IT'S JUST NOT FAIR I ALWAYS HAVE TO DEAL WITH THIS SHIT!
I KNOW YOU'RE MAD, BUT YOU'RE CHANNELING IT INTO SOMETHING POSITIVE.
WELL, NOT ***EVERYONE*** SEES IT AS POSITIVE. THEY SAY WE'RE JUST AS BAD AS--
--PEOPLE ARE DUMB, MICK. WE'RE DOING THE ***RIGHT THING...***
STRIKE BACK
RESIST THE RIGHT
MINER-STOLL PARK 4:00PM - BE THERE!

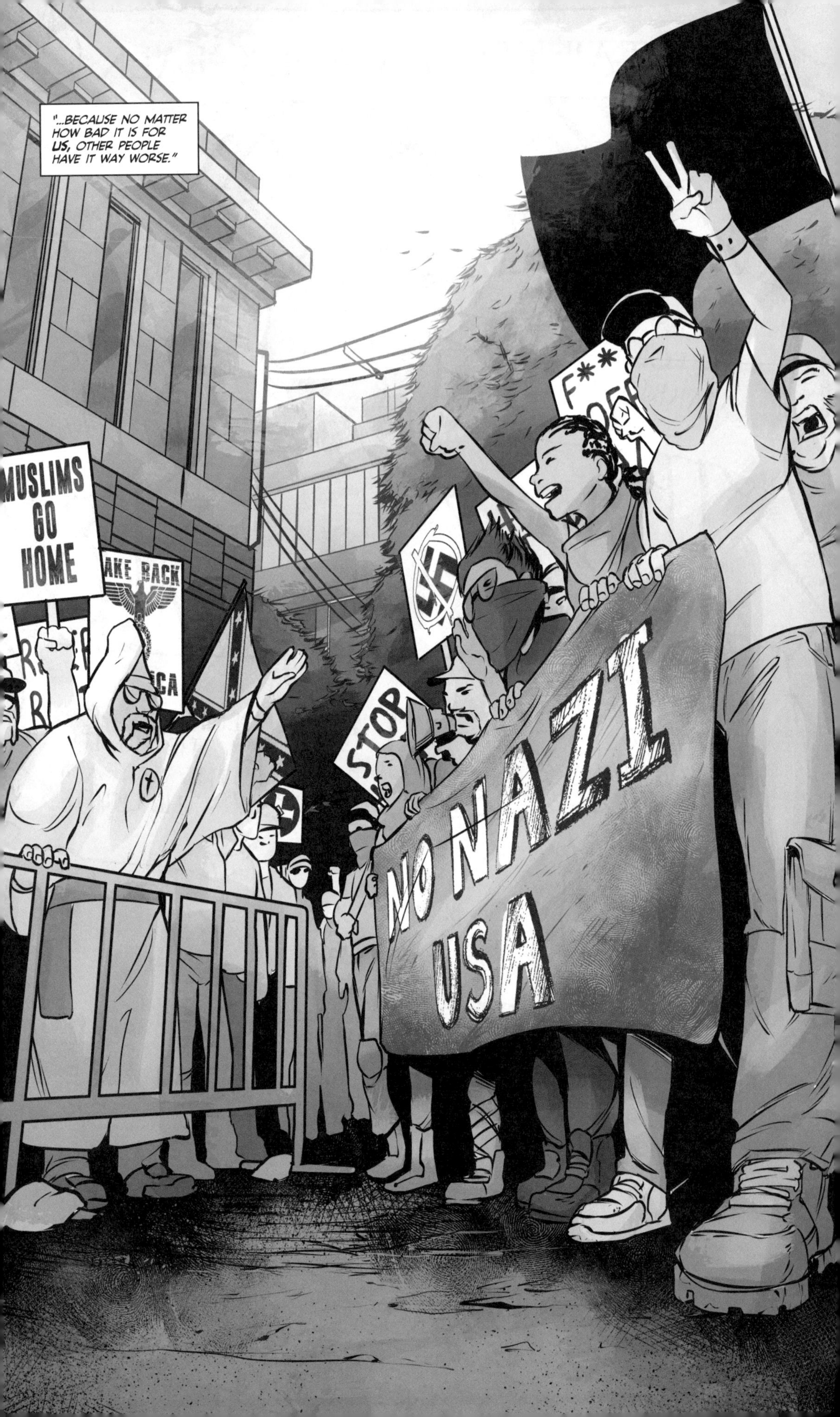
"...BECAUSE NO MATTER HOW BAD IT IS FOR US, OTHER PEOPLE HAVE IT WAY WORSE."
MUSLIMS GO HOME
AKE BACK
F**
STOP
NO NAZI USA

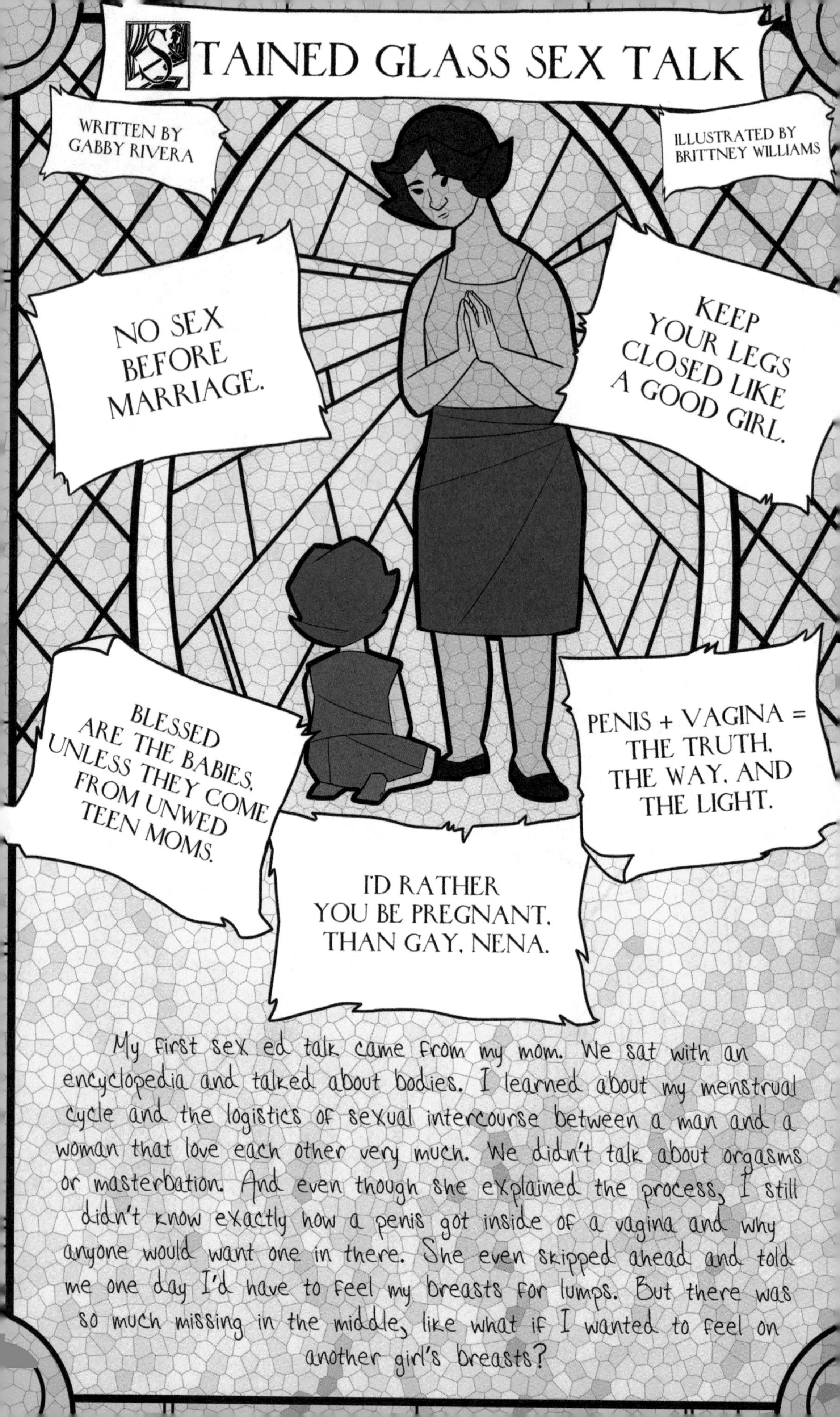
STAINED GLASS SEX TALK
WRITTEN BY GABBY RIVERA
ILLUSTRATED BY BRITTNEY WILLIAMS
NO SEX BEFORE MARRIAGE.
KEEP YOUR LEGS CLOSED LIKE A GOOD GIRL.
BLESSED ARE THE BABIES, UNLESS THEY COME FROM UNWED TEEN MOMS.
PENIS + VAGINA = THE TRUTH, THE WAY, AND THE LIGHT.
I'D RATHER YOU BE PREGNANT, THAN GAY, NENA.
My first sex ed talk came from my mom. We sat with an encyclopedia and talked about bodies. I learned about my menstrual cycle and the logistics of sexual intercourse between a man and a woman that love each other very much. We didn't talk about orgasms or masterbation. And even though she explained the process, I still didn't know exactly how a penis got inside of a vagina and why anyone would want one in there. She even skipped ahead and told me one day I'd have to feel my breasts for lumps. But there was so much missing in the middle, like what if I wanted to feel on another girl's breasts?

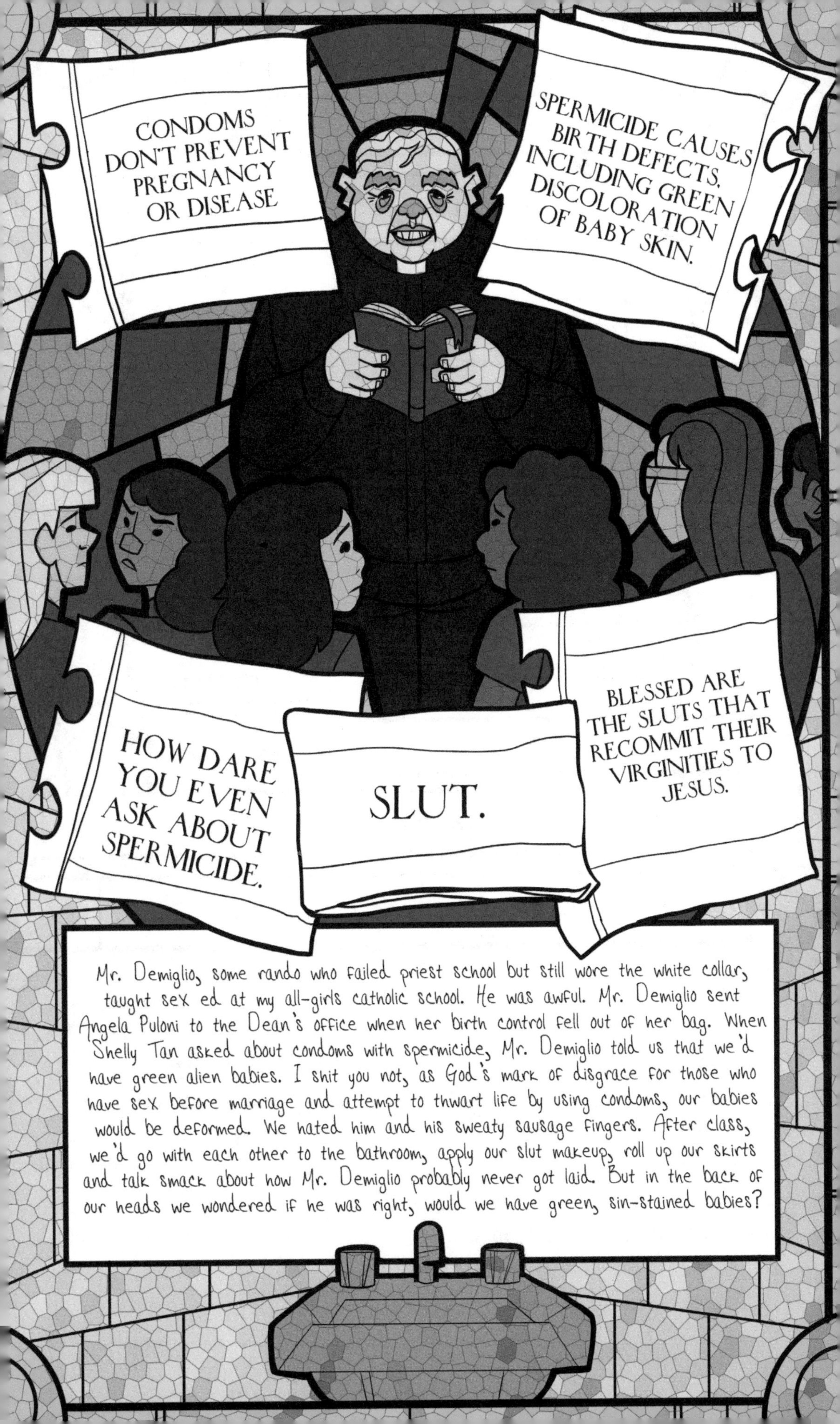
CONDOMS DON'T PREVENT PREGNANCY OR DISEASE
SPERMICIDE CAUSES BIRTH DEFECTS, INCLUDING GREEN DISCOLORATION OF BABY SKIN.
HOW DARE YOU EVEN ASK ABOUT SPERMICIDE.
SLUT.
BLESSED ARE THE SLUTS THAT RECOMMIT THEIR VIRGINITIES TO JESUS.
Mr. Demiglio, some rando who failed priest school but still wore the white collar, taught sex ed at my all-girls catholic school. He was awful. Mr. Demiglio sent Angela Puloni to the Dean's office when her birth control fell out of her bag. When Shelly Tan asked about condoms with spermicide, Mr. Demiglio told us that we'd have green alien babies. I shit you not, as God's mark of disgrace for those who have sex before marriage and attempt to thwart life by using condoms, our babies would be deformed. We hated him and his sweaty sausage fingers. After class, we'd go with each other to the bathroom, apply our slut makeup, roll up our skirts and talk smack about how Mr. Demiglio probably never got laid. But in the back of our heads we wondered if he was right, would we have green, sin-stained babies?

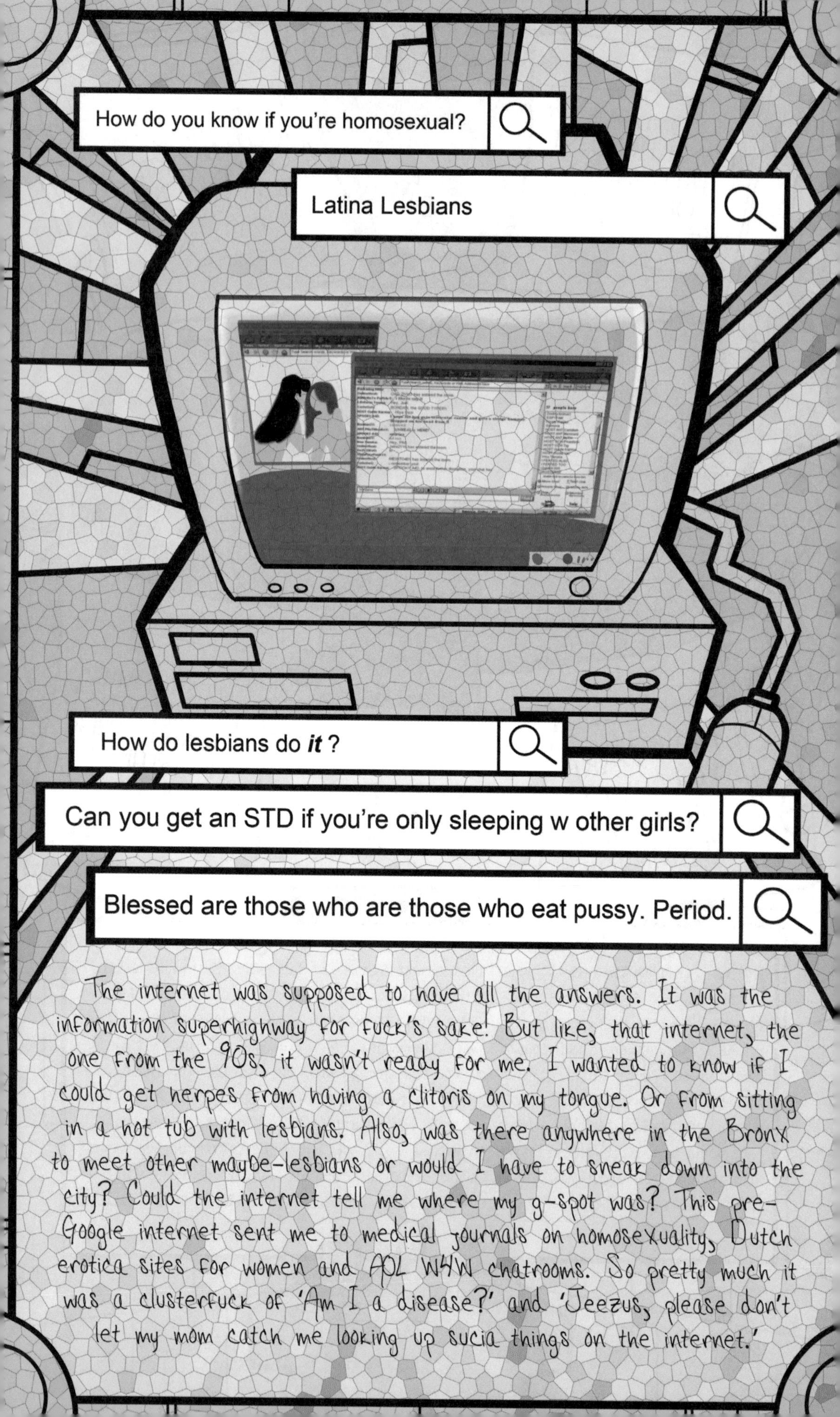
How do you know if you're homosexual?
Latina Lesbians
How do lesbians do *it* ?
Can you get an STD if you're only sleeping w other girls?
Blessed are those who are those who eat pussy. Period.

The internet was supposed to have all the answers. It was the information superhighway for fuck's sake! But like, that internet, the one from the 90s, it wasn't ready for me. I wanted to know if I could get herpes from having a clitoris on my tongue. Or from sitting in a hot tub with lesbians. Also, was there anywhere in the Bronx to meet other maybe-lesbians or would I have to sneak down into the city? Could the internet tell me where my g-spot was? This pre-Google internet sent me to medical journals on homosexuality, Dutch erotica sites for women and AOL W4W chatrooms. So pretty much it was a clusterfuck of 'Am I a disease?' and 'Jeezus, please don't let my mom catch me looking up sucia things on the internet.'

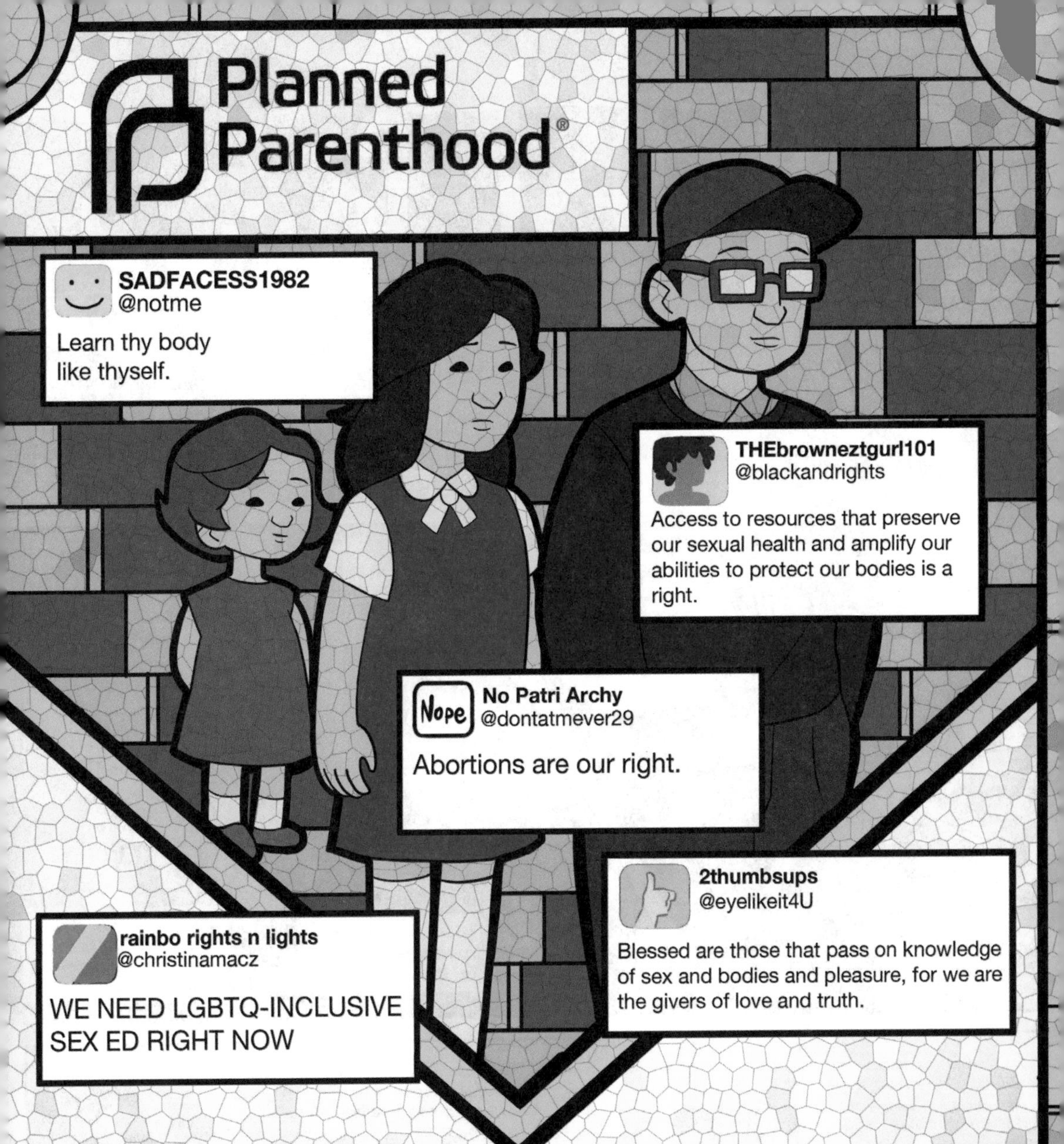
Planned Parenthood®
SADFACESS1982
@notme
Learn thy body like thyself.
THEbrowneztgurl101
@blackandrights
Access to resources that preserve our sexual health and amplify our abilities to protect our bodies is a right.
Nope
No Patri Archy
@dontatmever29
Abortions are our right.
2thumbsups
@eyelikeit4U
Blessed are those that pass on knowledge of sex and bodies and pleasure, for we are the givers of love and truth.
rainbo rights n lights
@christinamacz
WE NEED LGBTQ-INCLUSIVE SEX ED RIGHT NOW

I wanted the sexy/dirty facts about sex and bodies, minus the unnecessary religious guilt and blatant lies. I still don't get why it's so taboo for us to talk to each other about sex, gender, genitals, fucking, pleasure, consent, and all the rest of the sweaty beautiful things that bodies can do. I mean, it's definitely part of the scam hetero-patriarchy sells us, like abstinence-only sex-ed programs.

Why do folks have to gatekeep so hard?

We need unbiased sexual health information and access to resources like Planned Parenthood. And we gotta give it to the kids when they ask, and the teens when they're afraid to ask but so so desperately in need of the truth, and we need it when we're adults and act like we know everything but we're still out here catching genital warts and not knowing what a vulva is, you feel me?

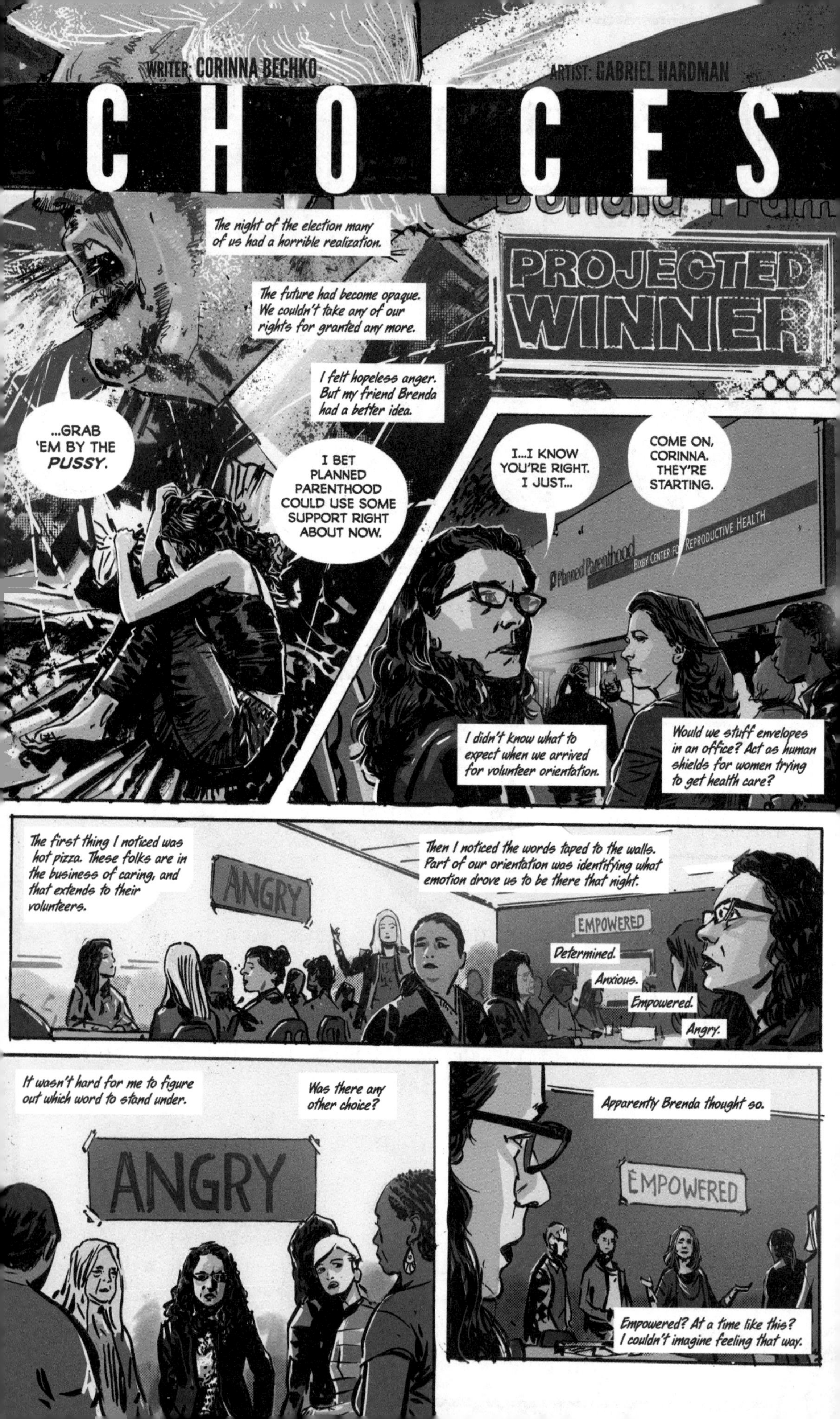
WRITER: CORINNA BECHKO
ARTIST: GABRIEL HARDMAN
CHOICES
The night of the election many of us had a horrible realization.
PROJECTED WINNER
The future had become opaque. We couldn't take any of our rights for granted any more.
I felt hopeless anger. But my friend Brenda had a better idea.
...GRAB 'EM BY THE *PUSSY*.
I BET PLANNED PARENTHOOD COULD USE SOME SUPPORT RIGHT ABOUT NOW.
COME ON, CORINNA. THEY'RE STARTING.
I...I KNOW YOU'RE RIGHT. I JUST...
Planned Parenthood
BIXBY CENTER FOR REPRODUCTIVE HEALTH
I didn't know what to expect when we arrived for volunteer orientation.
Would we stuff envelopes in an office? Act as human shields for women trying to get health care?
The first thing I noticed was hot pizza. These folks are in the business of caring, and that extends to their volunteers.
ANGRY
Then I noticed the words taped to the walls. Part of our orientation was identifying what emotion drove us to be there that night.
EMPOWERED
Determined.
Anxious.
Empowered.
Angry.
It wasn't hard for me to figure out which word to stand under.
Was there any other choice?
ANGRY
Apparently Brenda thought so.
EMPOWERED
Empowered? At a time like this? I couldn't imagine feeling that way.

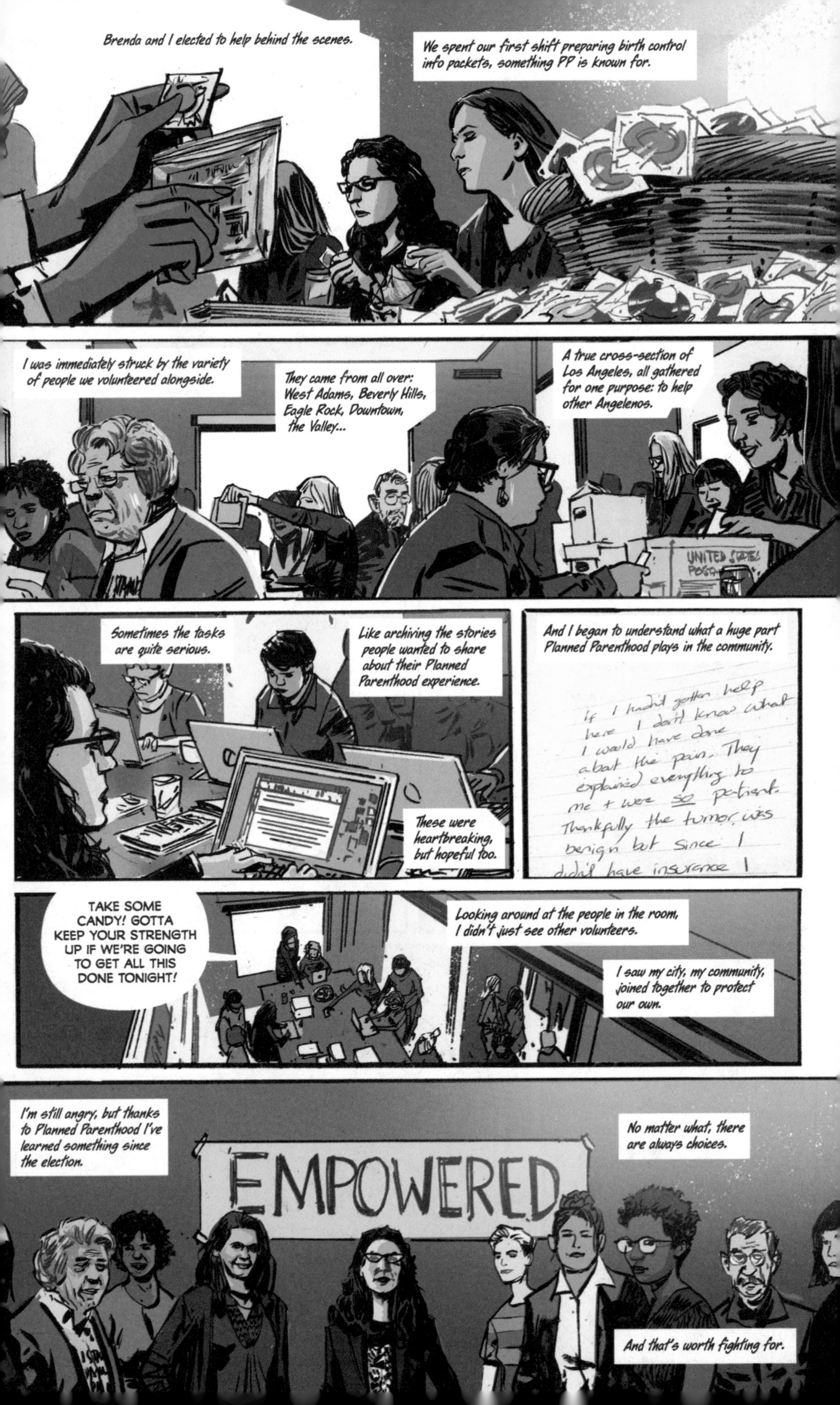
Brenda and I elected to help behind the scenes.
We spent our first shift preparing birth control info packets, something PP is known for.
I was immediately struck by the variety of people we volunteered alongside.
They came from all over: West Adams, Beverly Hills, Eagle Rock, Downtown, the Valley...
A true cross-section of Los Angeles, all gathered for one purpose: to help other Angelenos.
UNITED STATES POST
Sometimes the tasks are quite serious.
Like archiving the stories people wanted to share about their Planned Parenthood experience.
These were heartbreaking, but hopeful too.
And I began to understand what a huge part Planned Parenthood plays in the community.
If I hadn't gotten help here I don't know what I would have done about the pain. They explained everything to me + were so patient. Thankfully the tumor was benign but since I didn't have insurance I
TAKE SOME CANDY! GOTTA KEEP YOUR STRENGTH UP IF WE'RE GOING TO GET ALL THIS DONE TONIGHT!
Looking around at the people in the room, I didn't just see other volunteers.
I saw my city, my community, joined together to protect our own.
I'm still angry, but thanks to Planned Parenthood I've learned something since the election.
EMPOWERED
No matter what, there are always choices.
And that's worth fighting for.

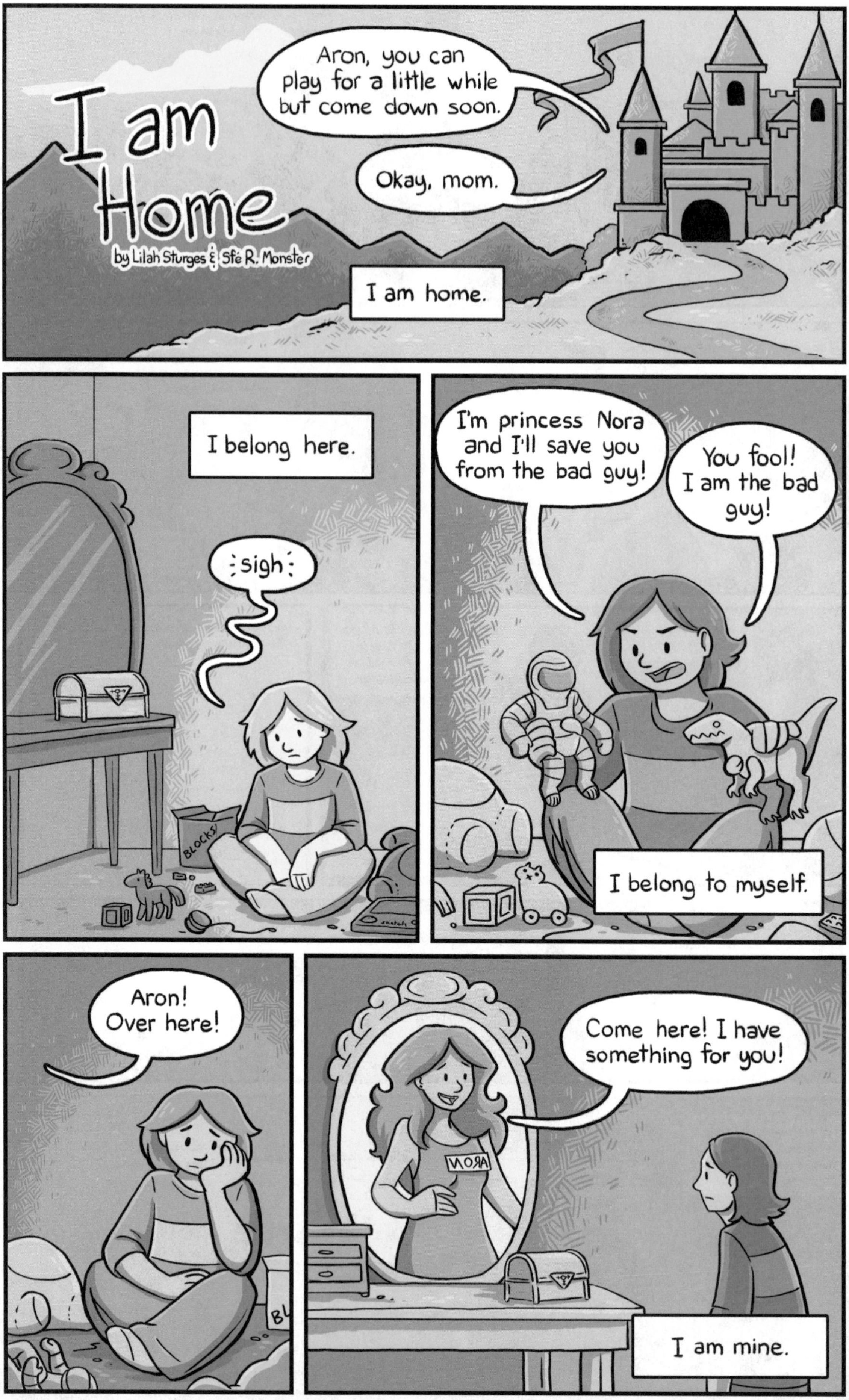

I am Home
by Lilah Sturges & Sfé R. Monster
Aron, you can play for a little while but come down soon.
Okay, mom.
I am home.
I belong here.
sigh
BLOCKS
I'm princess Nora and I'll save you from the bad guy!
You fool! I am the bad guy!
I belong to myself.
Aron! Over here!
Come here! I have something for you!
I am mine.

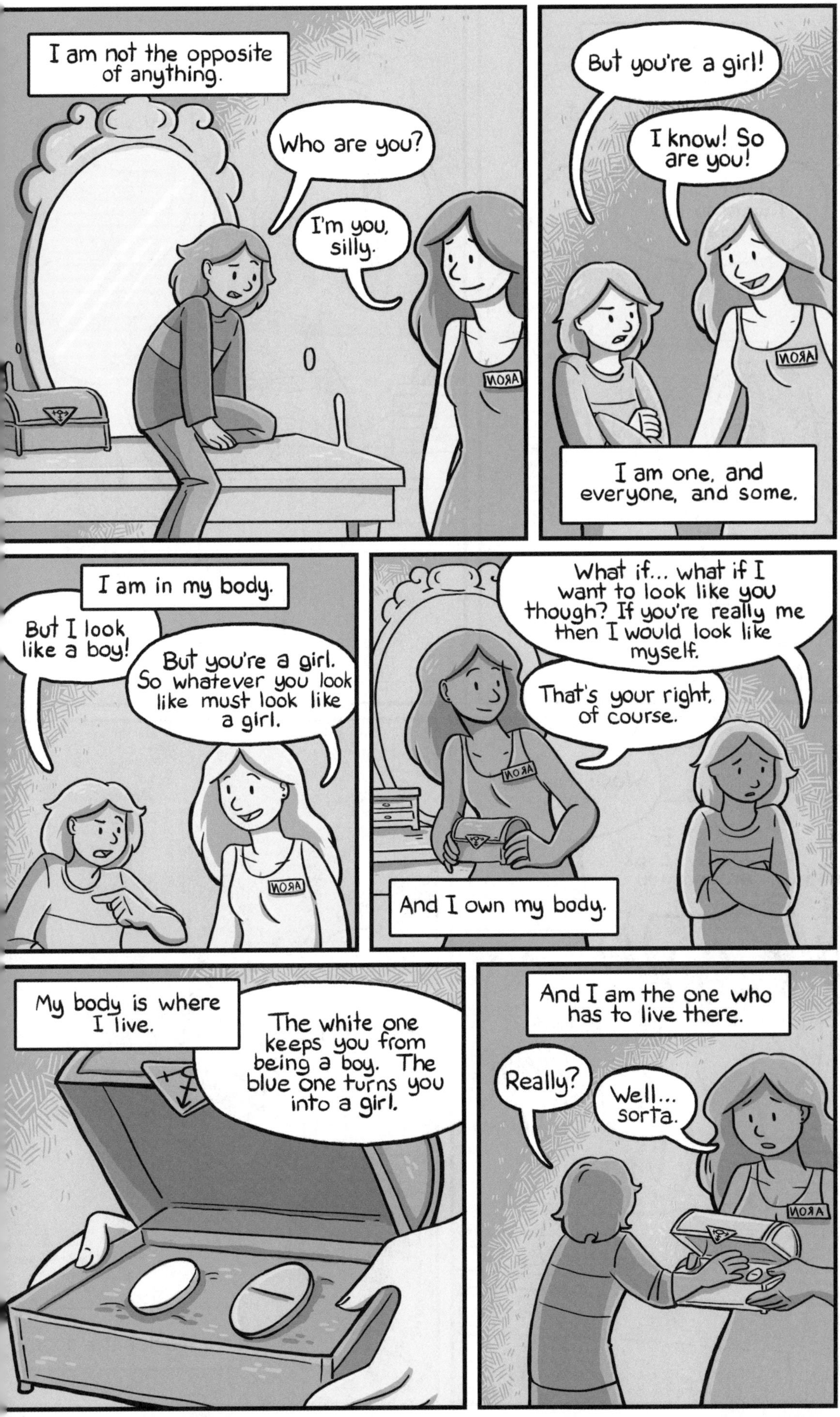
I am not the opposite of anything.
Who are you?
I'm you, silly.
NORA
But you're a girl!
I know! So are you!
ARON
I am one, and everyone, and some.
I am in my body.
But I look like a boy!
But you're a girl. So whatever you look like must look like a girl.
What if... what if I want to look like you though? If you're really me then I would look like myself.
That's your right, of course.
And I own my body.
My body is where I live.
The white one keeps you from being a boy. The blue one turns you into a girl.
And I am the one who has to live there.
Really?
Well... sorta.

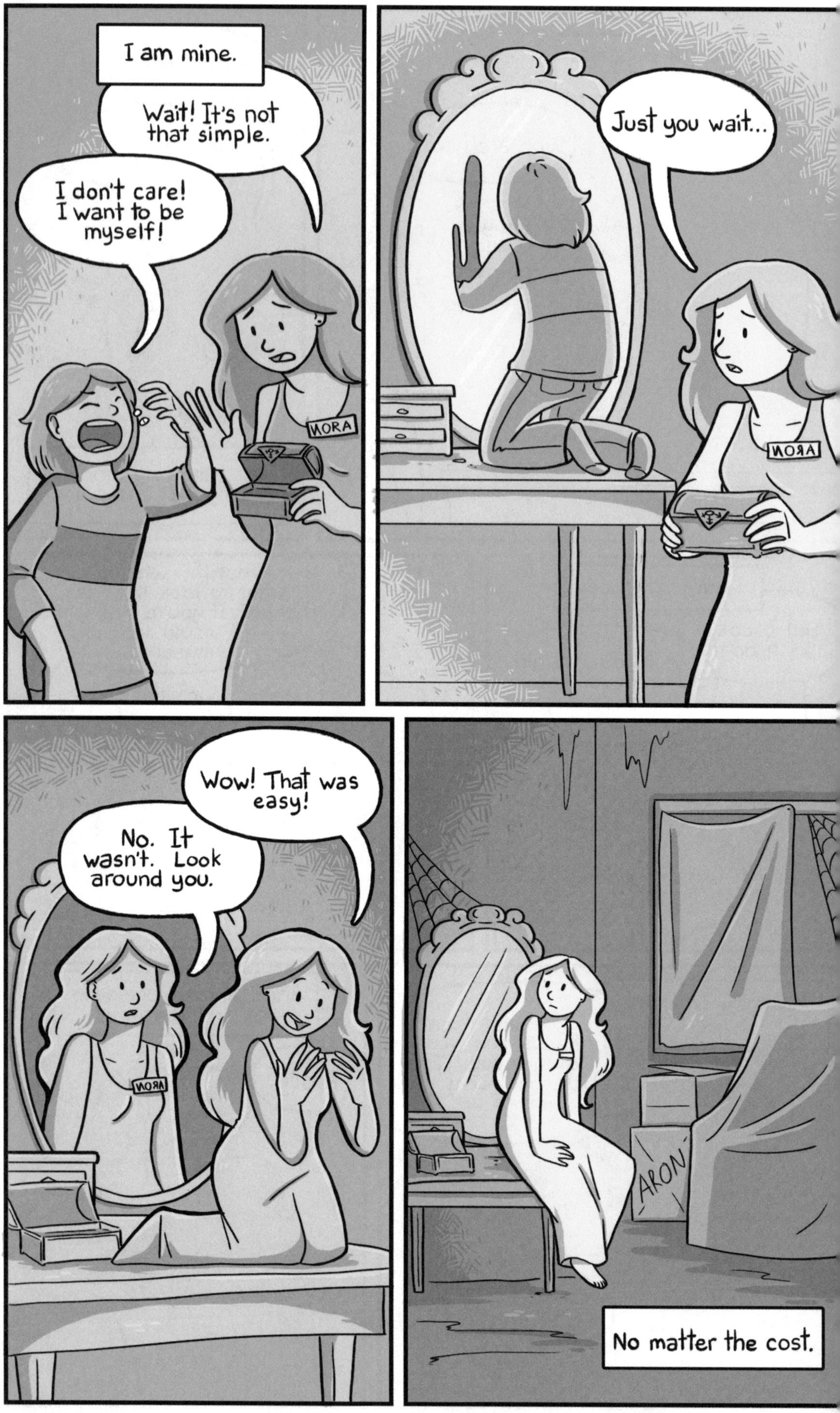

I am mine.
Wait! It's not that simple.
I don't care! I want to be myself!
NORA
Just you wait...
NORA
Wow! That was easy!
No. It wasn't. Look around you.
NORA
ARON
No matter the cost.

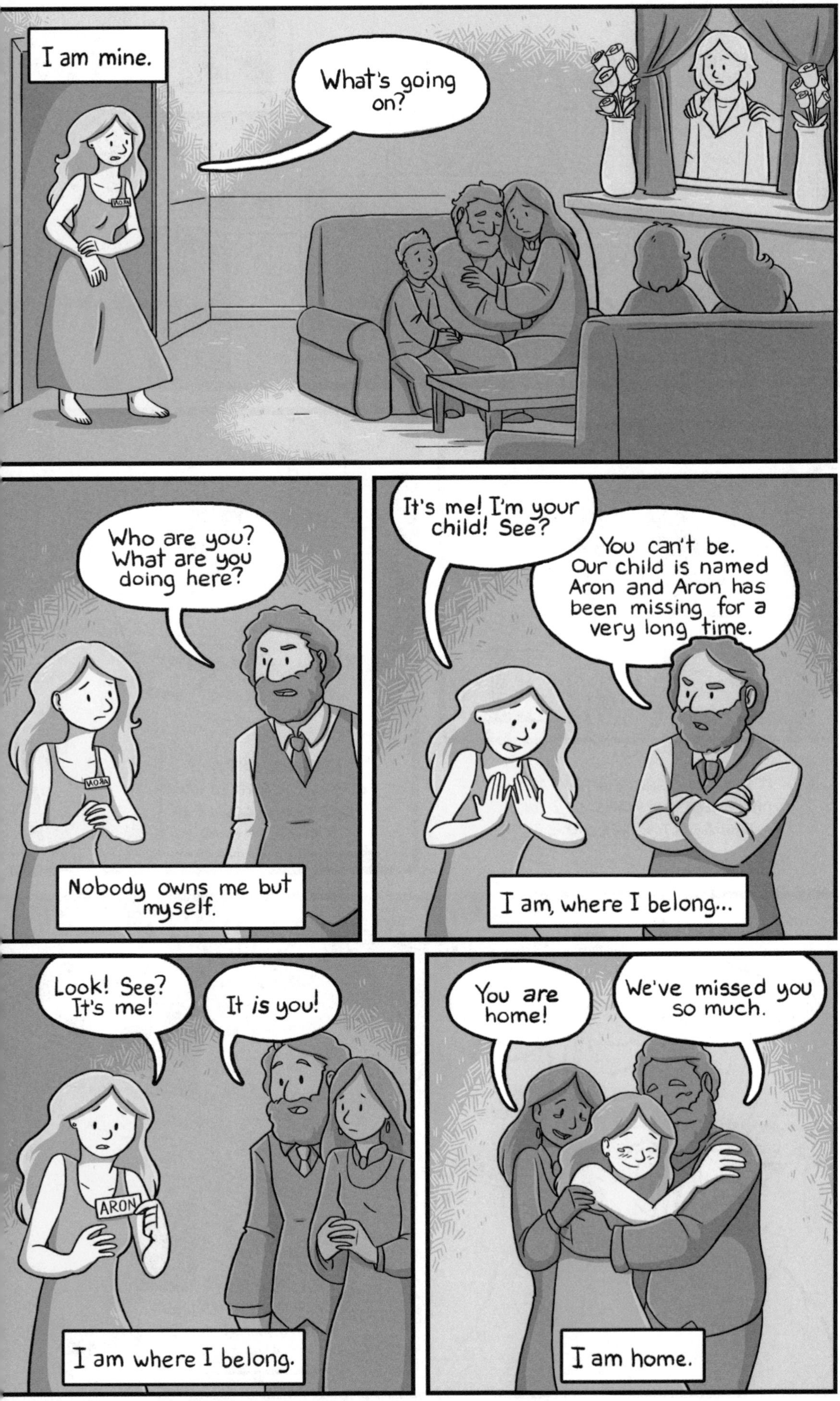
I am mine.
What's going on?
Who are you? What are you doing here?
Nobody owns me but myself.
It's me! I'm your child! See?
You can't be. Our child is named Aron and Aron has been missing for a very long time.
I am, where I belong...
Look! See? It's me!
It *is* you!
ARON
I am where I belong.
You are home!
We've missed you so much.
I am home.

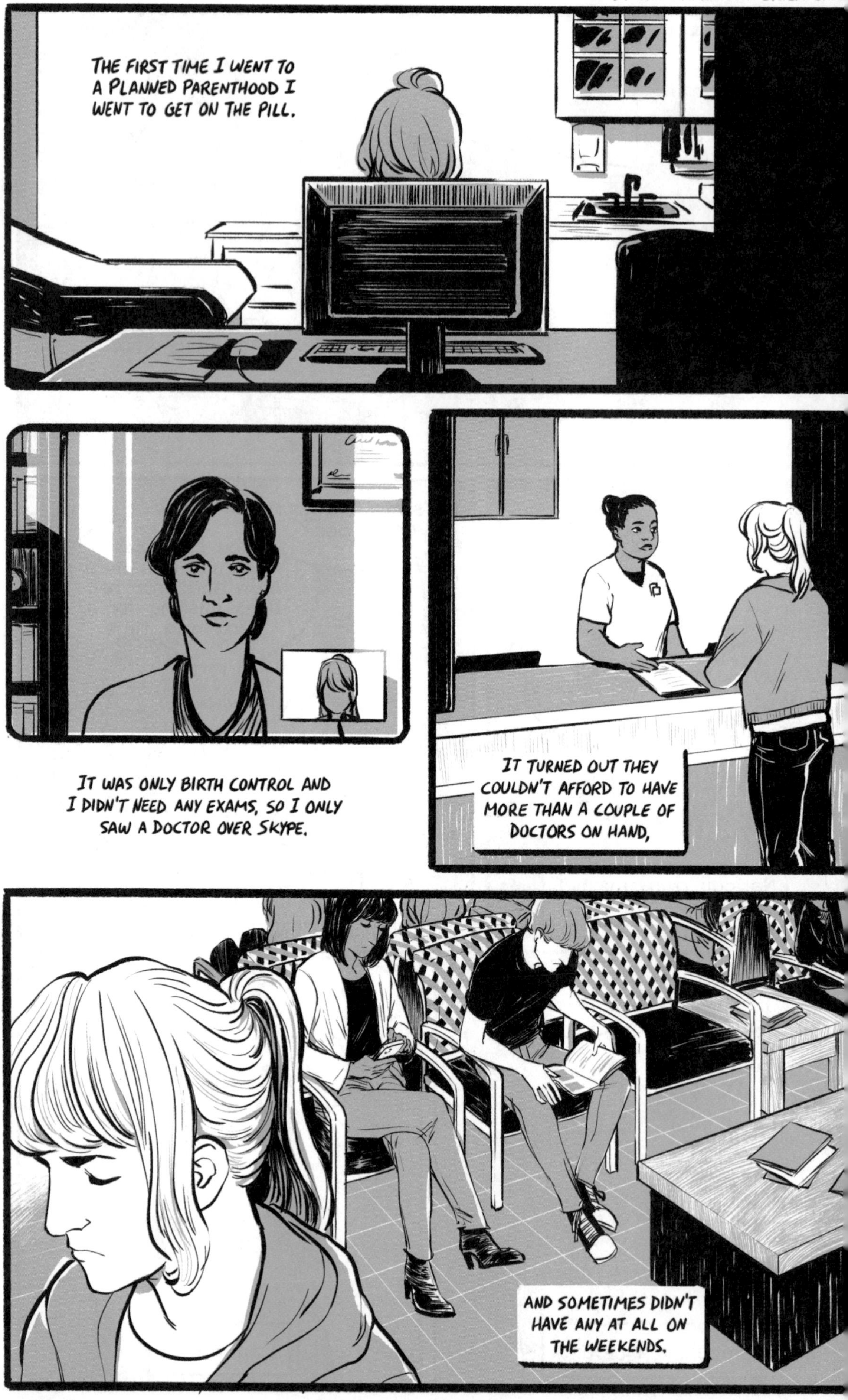
The first time I went to a Planned Parenthood I went to get on the pill.
It was only birth control and I didn't need any exams, so I only saw a Doctor over Skype.
It turned out they couldn't afford to have more than a couple of Doctors on hand,
and sometimes didn't have any at all on the weekends.

BUT DESPITE THIS ALL OF THE NURSES AND THE DOCTOR MADE SURE TO CHECK WITH ME TO SEE IF I NEEDED ANY EXAMS OR OTHER CARE.

BECAUSE THEY CARED.

BECAUSE THEY'RE DOING WHAT THEY BELIEVE IN.

THERE ARE A LOT OF CLINICS OUT THERE WORKING WITH EVEN LESS, BUT DESPITE PROTESTS AND POLITICIANS THEY'RE MAKING IT WORK.

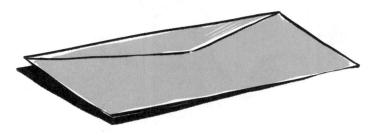

THE SECOND TIME I WENT TO PLANNED PARENTHOOD WAS TO MAKE A DONATION.

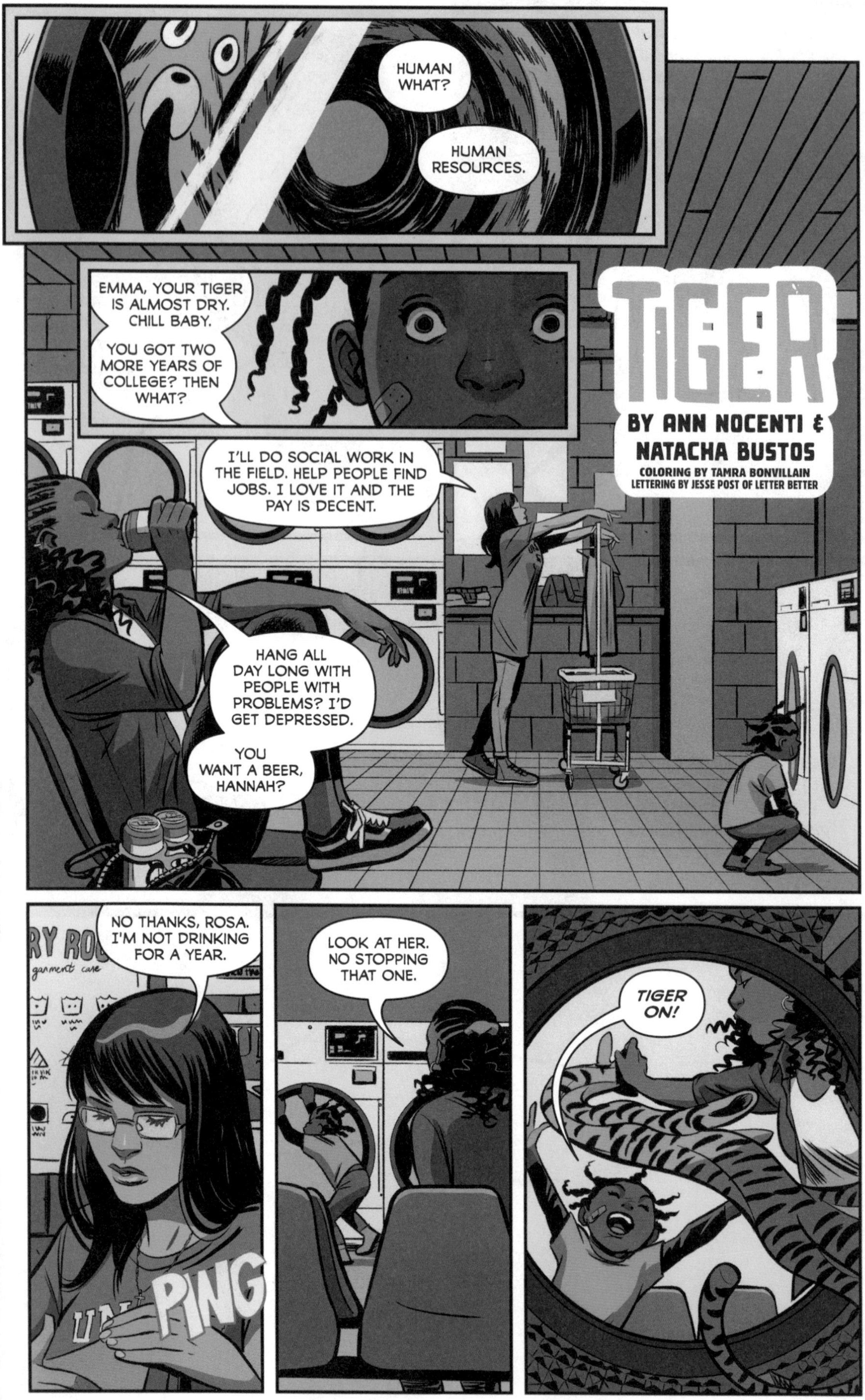
HUMAN WHAT?
HUMAN RESOURCES.
TIGER
BY ANN NOCENTI & NATACHA BUSTOS
COLORING BY TAMRA BONVILLAIN
LETTERING BY JESSE POST OF LETTER BETTER
EMMA, YOUR TIGER IS ALMOST DRY. CHILL BABY.
YOU GOT TWO MORE YEARS OF COLLEGE? THEN WHAT?
I'LL DO SOCIAL WORK IN THE FIELD. HELP PEOPLE FIND JOBS. I LOVE IT AND THE PAY IS DECENT.
HANG ALL DAY LONG WITH PEOPLE WITH PROBLEMS? I'D GET DEPRESSED.
YOU WANT A BEER, HANNAH?
NO THANKS, ROSA. I'M NOT DRINKING FOR A YEAR.
PING
LOOK AT HER. NO STOPPING THAT ONE.
TIGER ON!

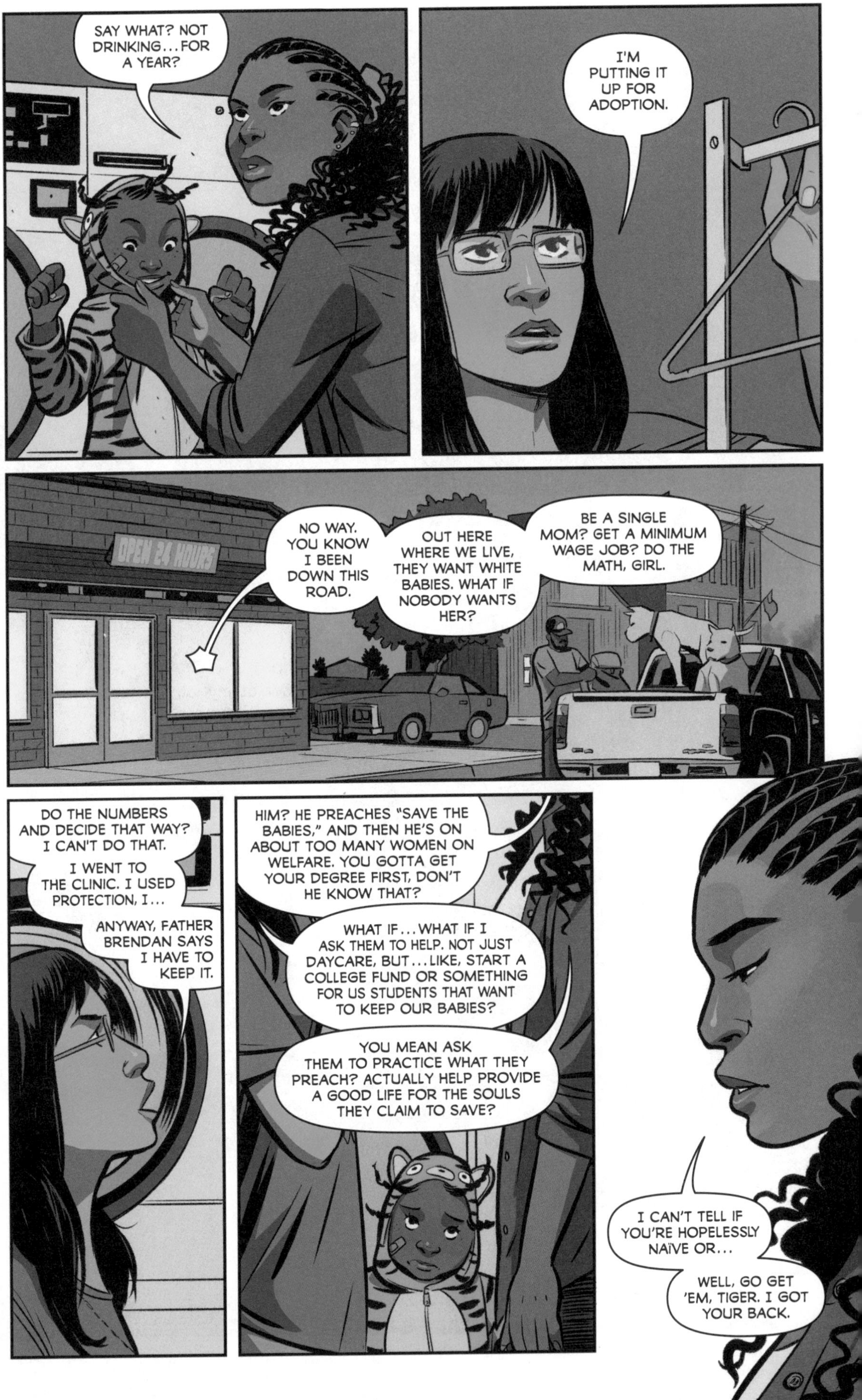
SAY WHAT? NOT DRINKING...FOR A YEAR?
I'M PUTTING IT UP FOR ADOPTION.
OPEN 24 HOURS
NO WAY. YOU KNOW I BEEN DOWN THIS ROAD.
OUT HERE WHERE WE LIVE, THEY WANT WHITE BABIES. WHAT IF NOBODY WANTS HER?
BE A SINGLE MOM? GET A MINIMUM WAGE JOB? DO THE MATH, GIRL.
DO THE NUMBERS AND DECIDE THAT WAY? I CAN'T DO THAT.
I WENT TO THE CLINIC. I USED PROTECTION, I...
ANYWAY, FATHER BRENDAN SAYS I HAVE TO KEEP IT.
HIM? HE PREACHES "SAVE THE BABIES," AND THEN HE'S ON ABOUT TOO MANY WOMEN ON WELFARE. YOU GOTTA GET YOUR DEGREE FIRST, DON'T HE KNOW THAT?
WHAT IF...WHAT IF I ASK THEM TO HELP. NOT JUST DAYCARE, BUT...LIKE, START A COLLEGE FUND OR SOMETHING FOR US STUDENTS THAT WANT TO KEEP OUR BABIES?
YOU MEAN ASK THEM TO PRACTICE WHAT THEY PREACH? ACTUALLY HELP PROVIDE A GOOD LIFE FOR THE SOULS THEY CLAIM TO SAVE?
I CAN'T TELL IF YOU'RE HOPELESSLY NAÏVE OR...
WELL, GO GET 'EM, TIGER. I GOT YOUR BACK.

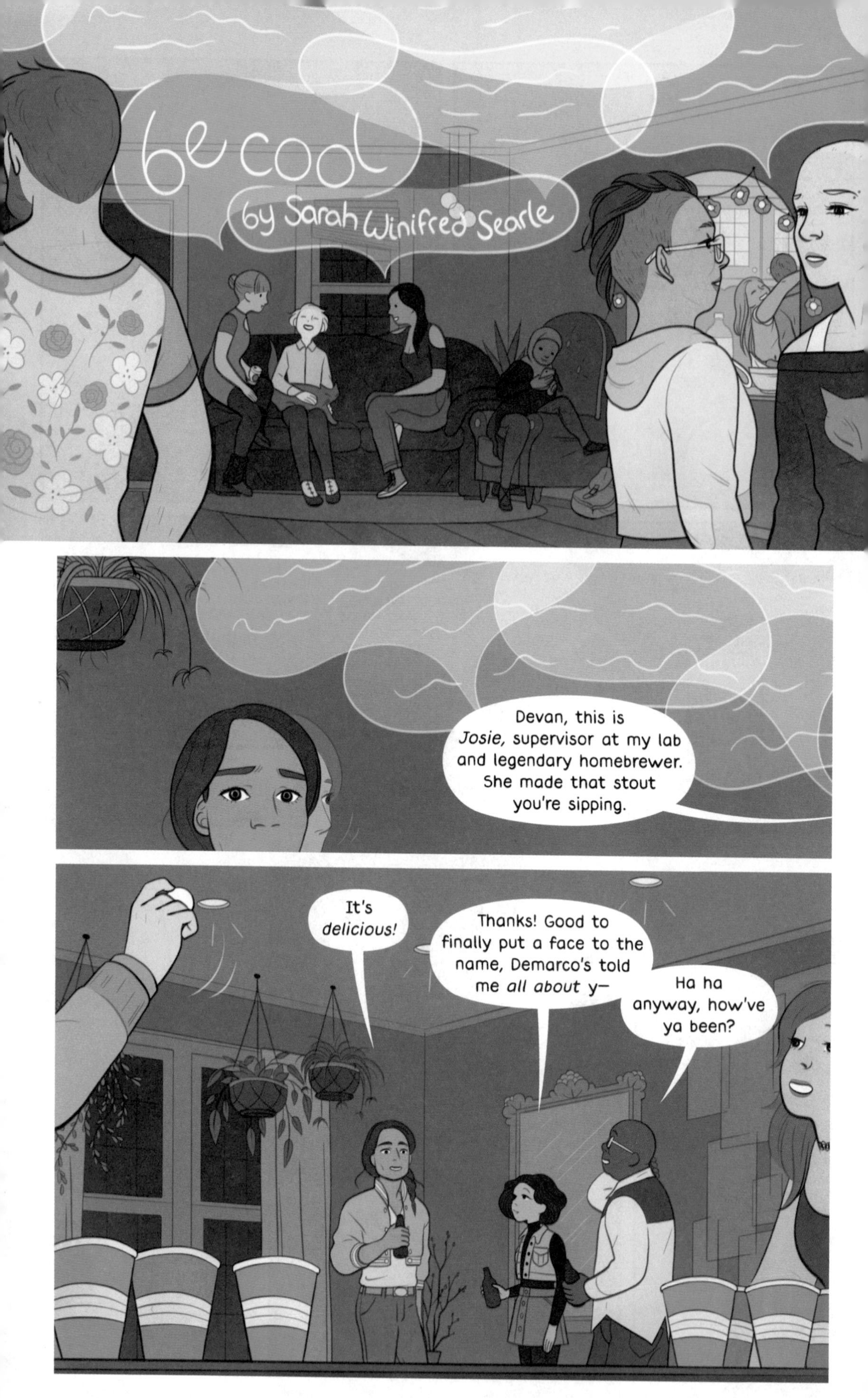
be cool
by Sarah Winifred Searle
Devan, this is *Josie,* supervisor at my lab and legendary homebrewer. She made that stout you're sipping.
It's *delicious!*
Thanks! Good to finally put a face to the name, Demarco's told me *all about* y—
Ha ha anyway, how've ya been?

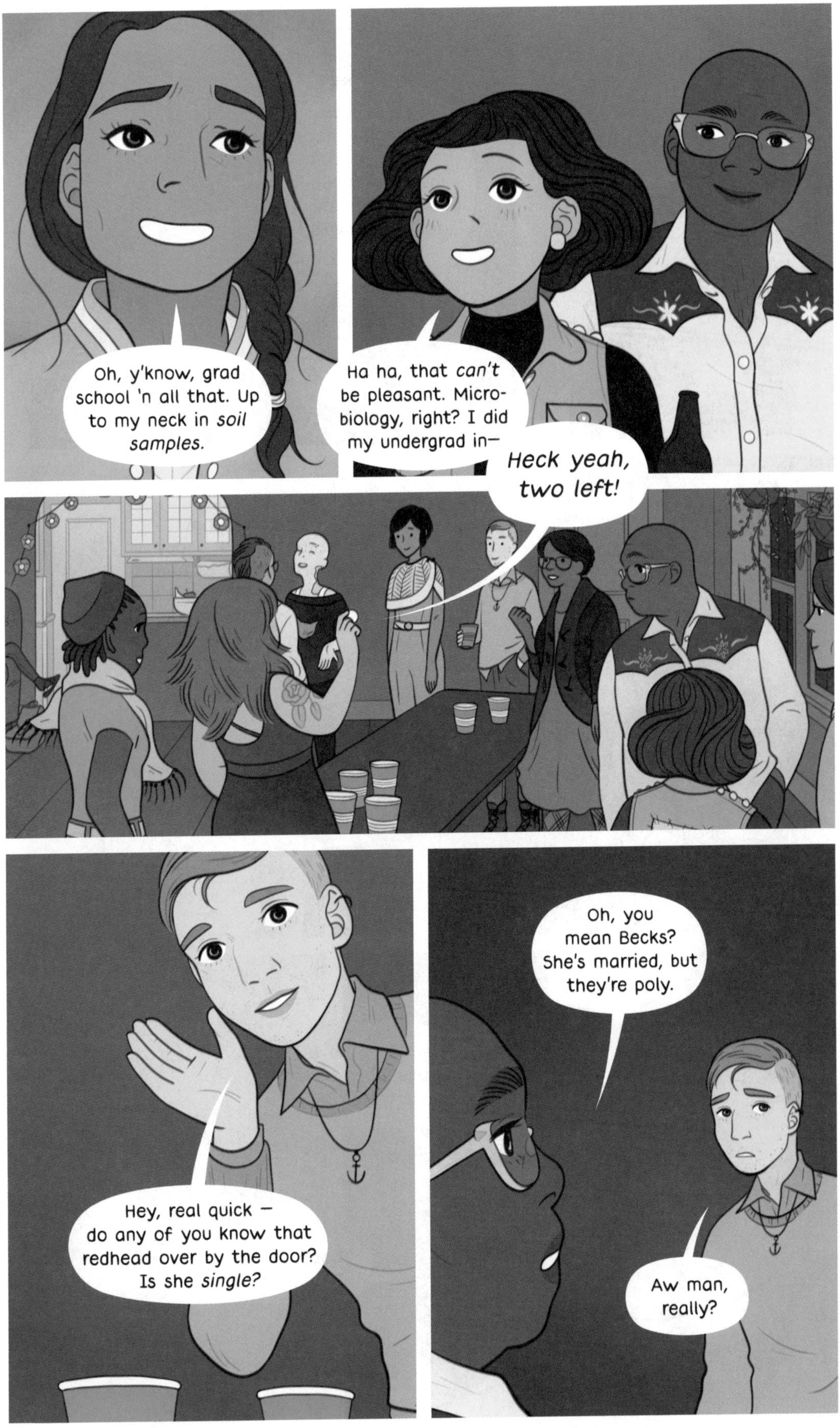
Oh, y'know, grad school 'n all that. Up to my neck in *soil samples.*
Ha ha, that *can't* be pleasant. Microbiology, right? I did my undergrad in—
Heck yeah, two left!
Hey, real quick — do any of you know that redhead over by the door? Is she *single?*
Oh, you mean Becks? She's married, but they're poly.
Aw man, really?

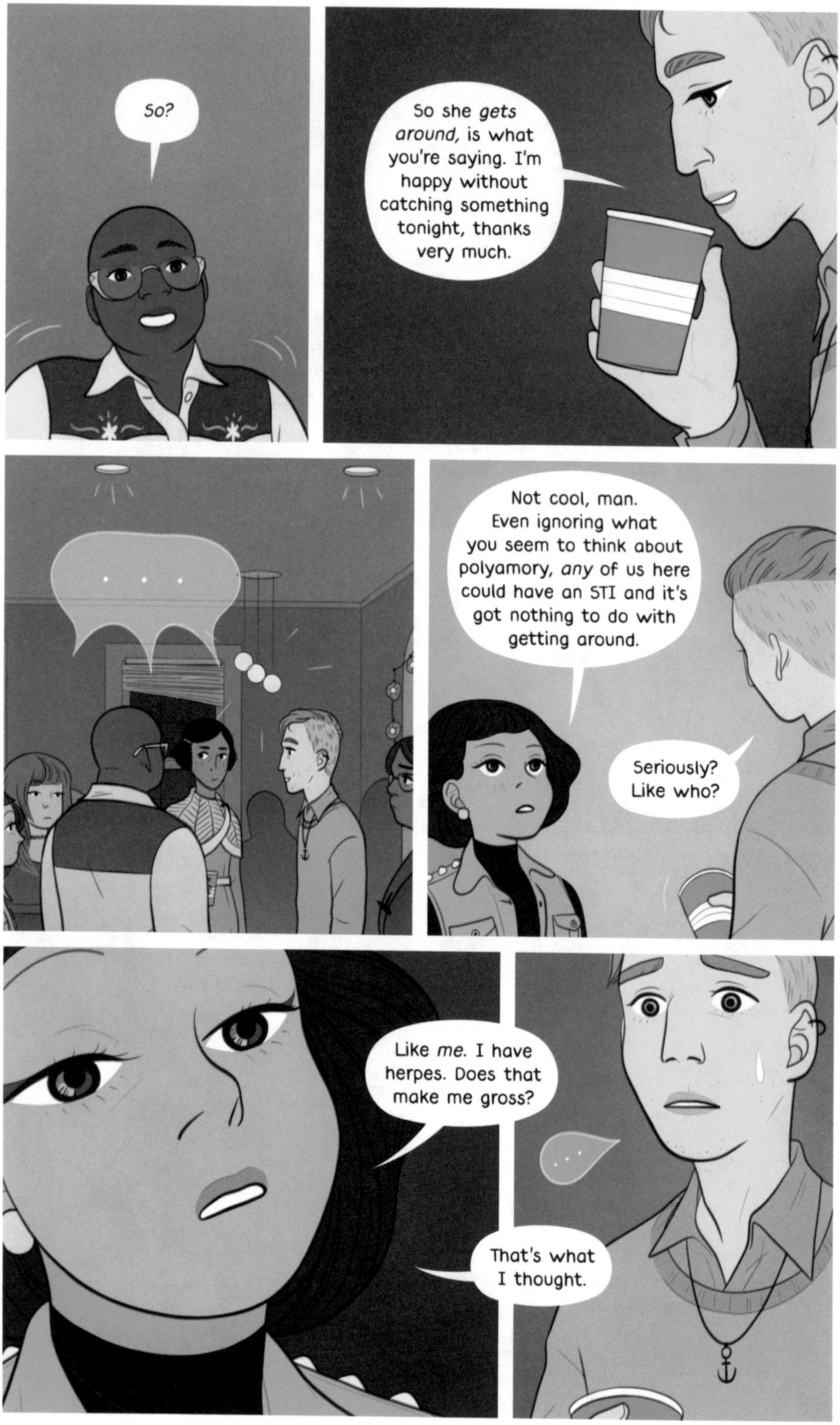

So?
So she *gets around,* is what you're saying. I'm happy without catching something tonight, thanks very much.
. . .
Not cool, man. Even ignoring what you seem to think about polyamory, *any* of us here could have an STI and it's got nothing to do with getting around.
Seriously? Like who?
Like *me.* I have herpes. Does that make me gross?
. . .
That's what I thought.

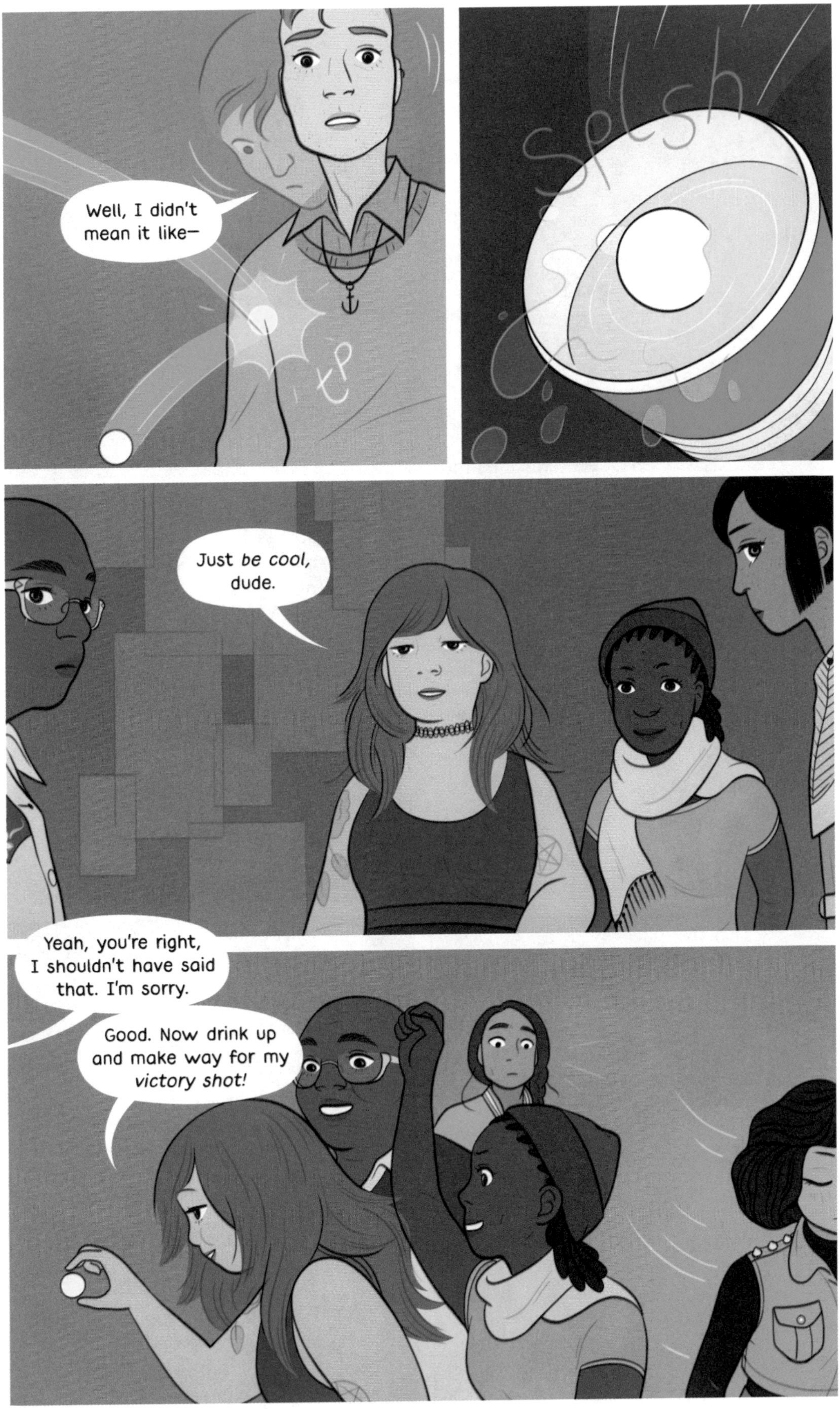
Well, I didn't mean it like—
Splsh
Just *be cool,* dude.
Yeah, you're right, I shouldn't have said that. I'm sorry.
Good. Now drink up and make way for my *victory shot!*

Thanks for what you said back there.

I was diagnosed with HPV earlier this week, and it... it feels *bad,* y' know? Like some *dirty secret.* I've even been too scared to tell Demarco. You're so brave.

Not brave, just *angry.* It's always scary to say it, but it's worse to let people think and talk like that.

So, did you go to Planned Parenthood?

Yeah, Forest Ave.

Me too!

Semira's my favorite nurse there. She helped me educate myself, put things into perspective.

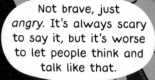

And her voice is so soothing! I felt like it was the end of the world, but she just handed me some tissues and told me it wasn't a big deal, and I believed her.

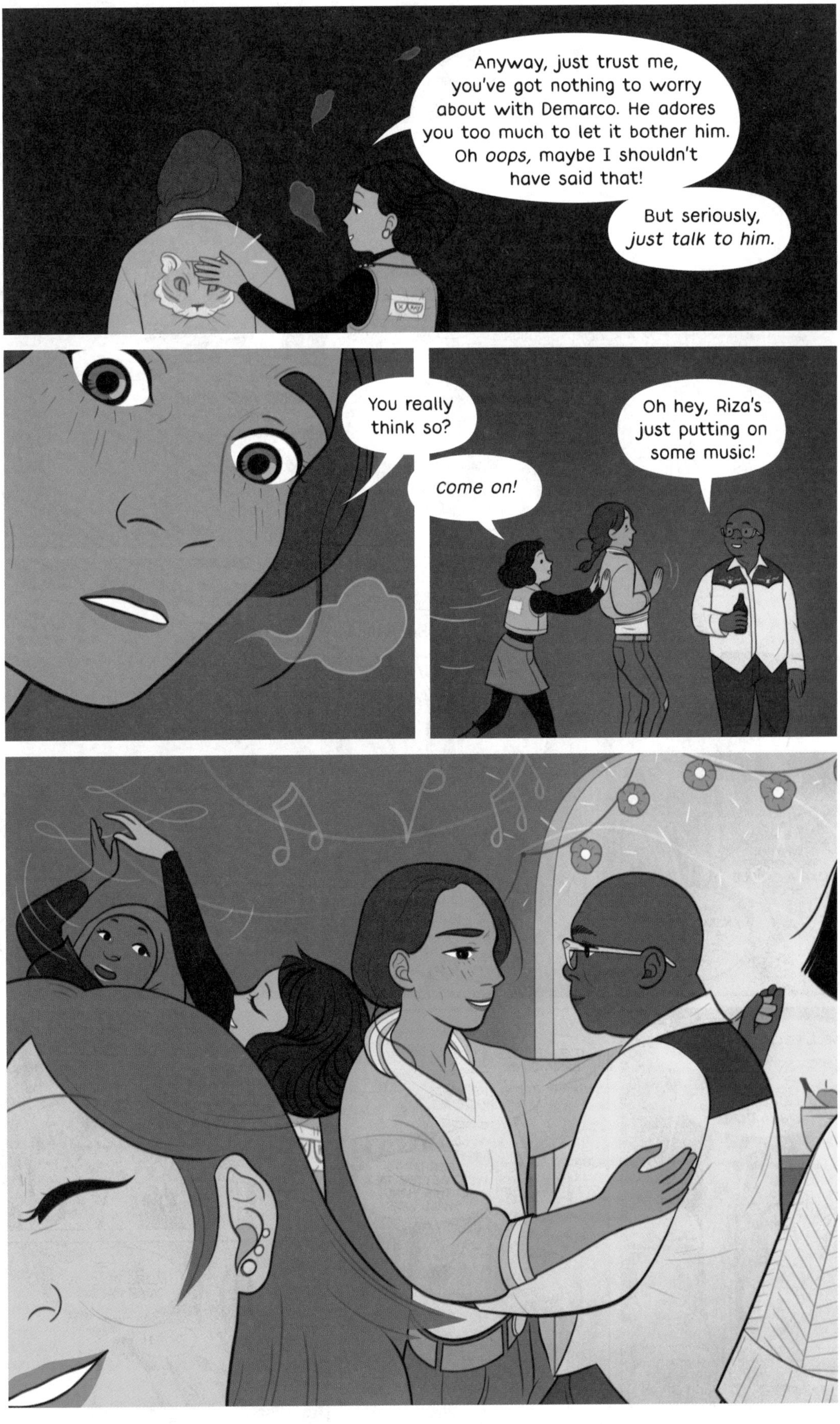
Anyway, just trust me, you've got nothing to worry about with Demarco. He adores you too much to let it bother him. Oh *oops,* maybe I shouldn't have said that!
But seriously, *just talk to him.*
You really think so?
Come on!
Oh hey, Riza's just putting on some music!

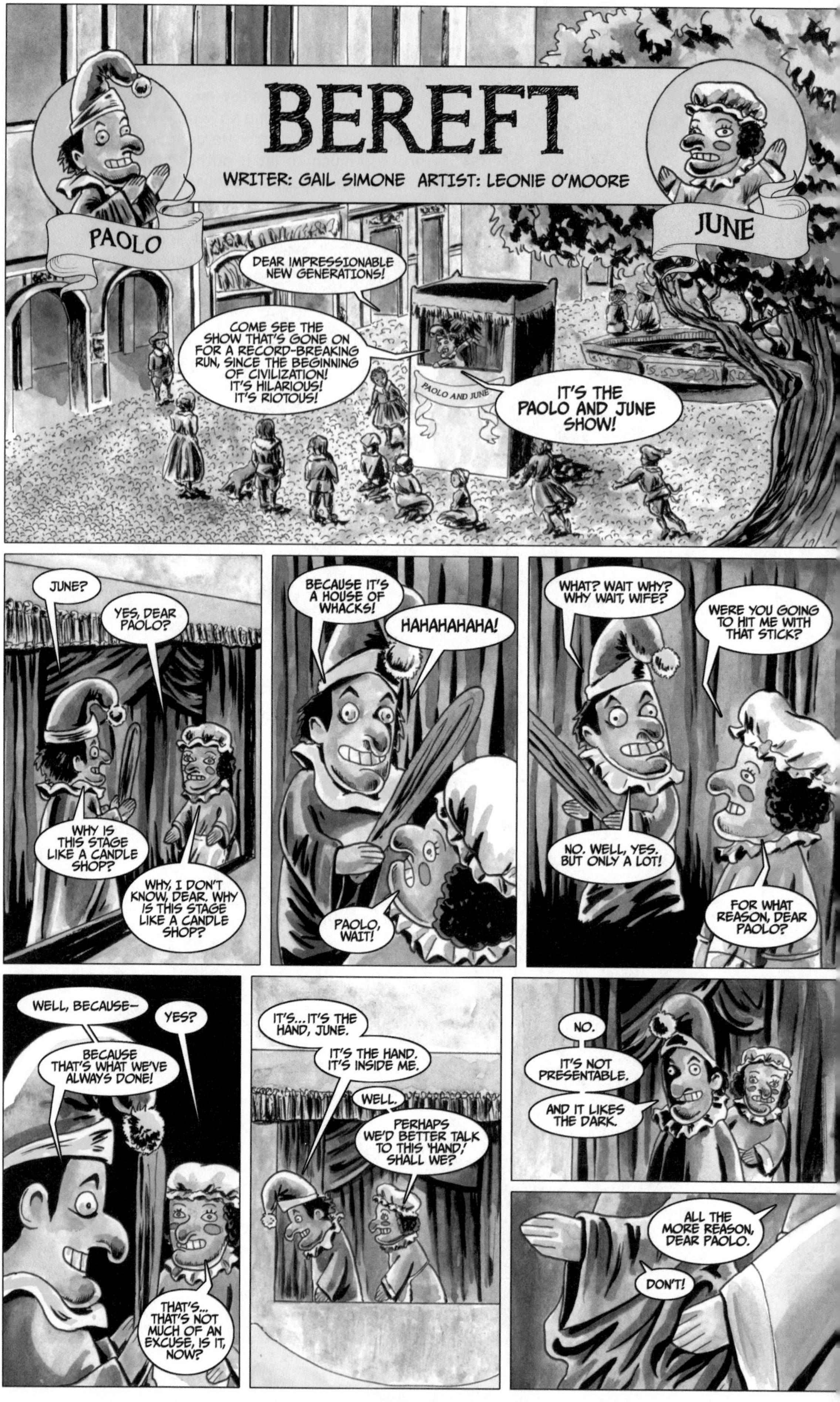
BEREFT
WRITER: GAIL SIMONE ARTIST: LEONIE O'MOORE
PAOLO
JUNE
DEAR IMPRESSIONABLE NEW GENERATIONS!
COME SEE THE SHOW THAT'S GONE ON FOR A RECORD-BREAKING RUN, SINCE THE BEGINNING OF CIVILIZATION! IT'S HILARIOUS! IT'S RIOTOUS!
PAOLO AND JUNE
IT'S THE PAOLO AND JUNE SHOW!
JUNE?
YES, DEAR PAOLO?
WHY IS THIS STAGE LIKE A CANDLE SHOP?
WHY, I DON'T KNOW, DEAR. WHY IS THIS STAGE LIKE A CANDLE SHOP?
BECAUSE IT'S A HOUSE OF WHACKS!
HAHAHAHAHA!
PAOLO, WAIT!
WHAT? WAIT WHY? WHY WAIT, WIFE?
WERE YOU GOING TO HIT ME WITH THAT STICK?
NO. WELL, YES. BUT ONLY A LOT!
FOR WHAT REASON, DEAR PAOLO?
WELL, BECAUSE—
YES?
BECAUSE THAT'S WHAT WE'VE ALWAYS DONE!
THAT'S... THAT'S NOT MUCH OF AN EXCUSE, IS IT, NOW?
IT'S...IT'S THE HAND, JUNE.
IT'S THE HAND. IT'S INSIDE ME.
WELL.
PERHAPS WE'D BETTER TALK TO THIS 'HAND,' SHALL WE?
NO.
IT'S NOT PRESENTABLE.
AND IT LIKES THE DARK.
ALL THE MORE REASON, DEAR PAOLO.
DON'T!

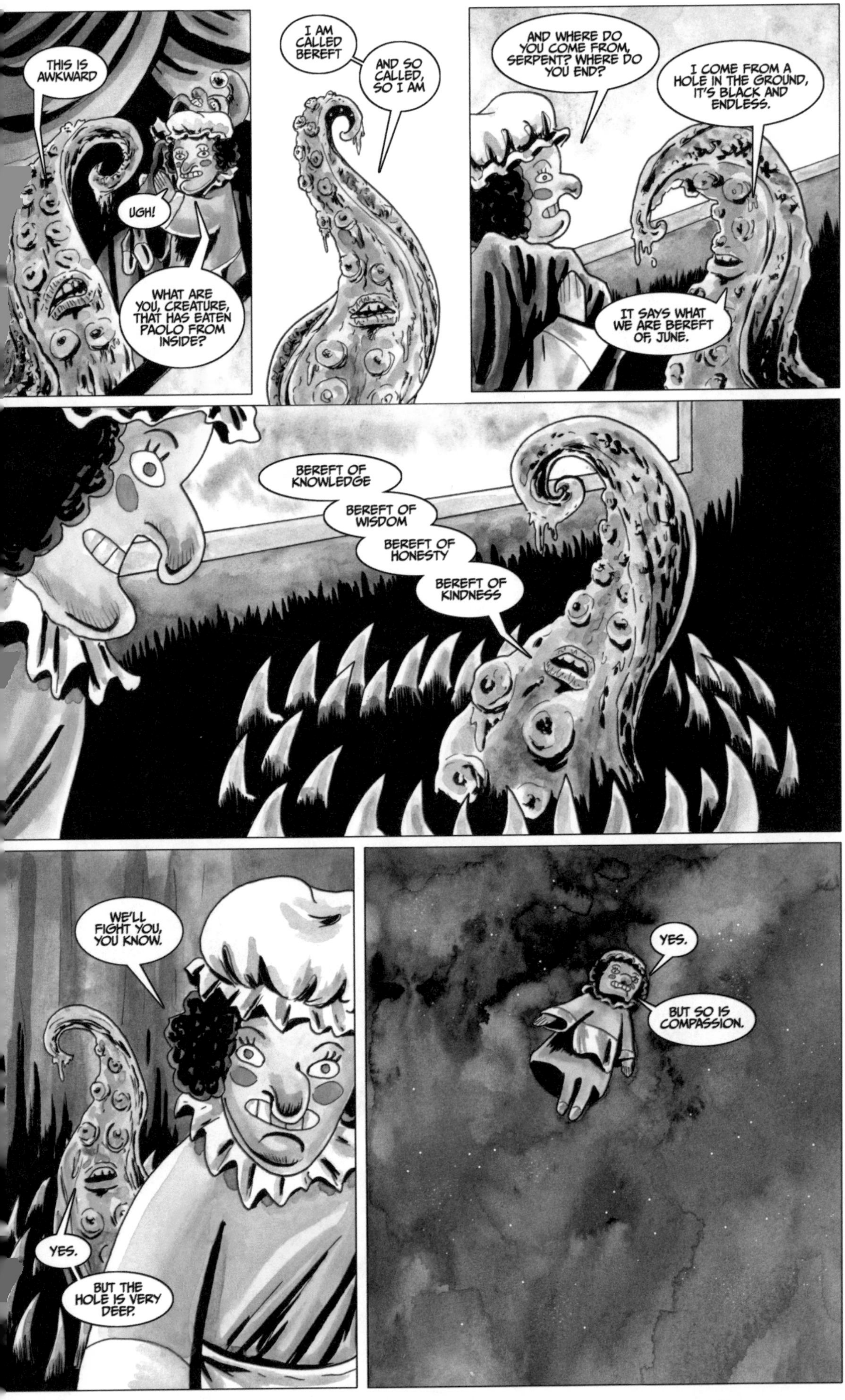
THIS IS AWKWARD
UGH!
WHAT ARE YOU, CREATURE, THAT HAS EATEN PAOLO FROM INSIDE?
I AM CALLED BEREFT
AND SO CALLED, SO I AM
AND WHERE DO YOU COME FROM, SERPENT? WHERE DO YOU END?
I COME FROM A HOLE IN THE GROUND, IT'S BLACK AND ENDLESS.
IT SAYS WHAT WE ARE BEREFT OF, JUNE.
BEREFT OF KNOWLEDGE
BEREFT OF WISDOM
BEREFT OF HONESTY
BEREFT OF KINDNESS
WE'LL FIGHT YOU, YOU KNOW.
YES.
BUT THE HOLE IS VERY DEEP.
YES.
BUT SO IS COMPASSION.

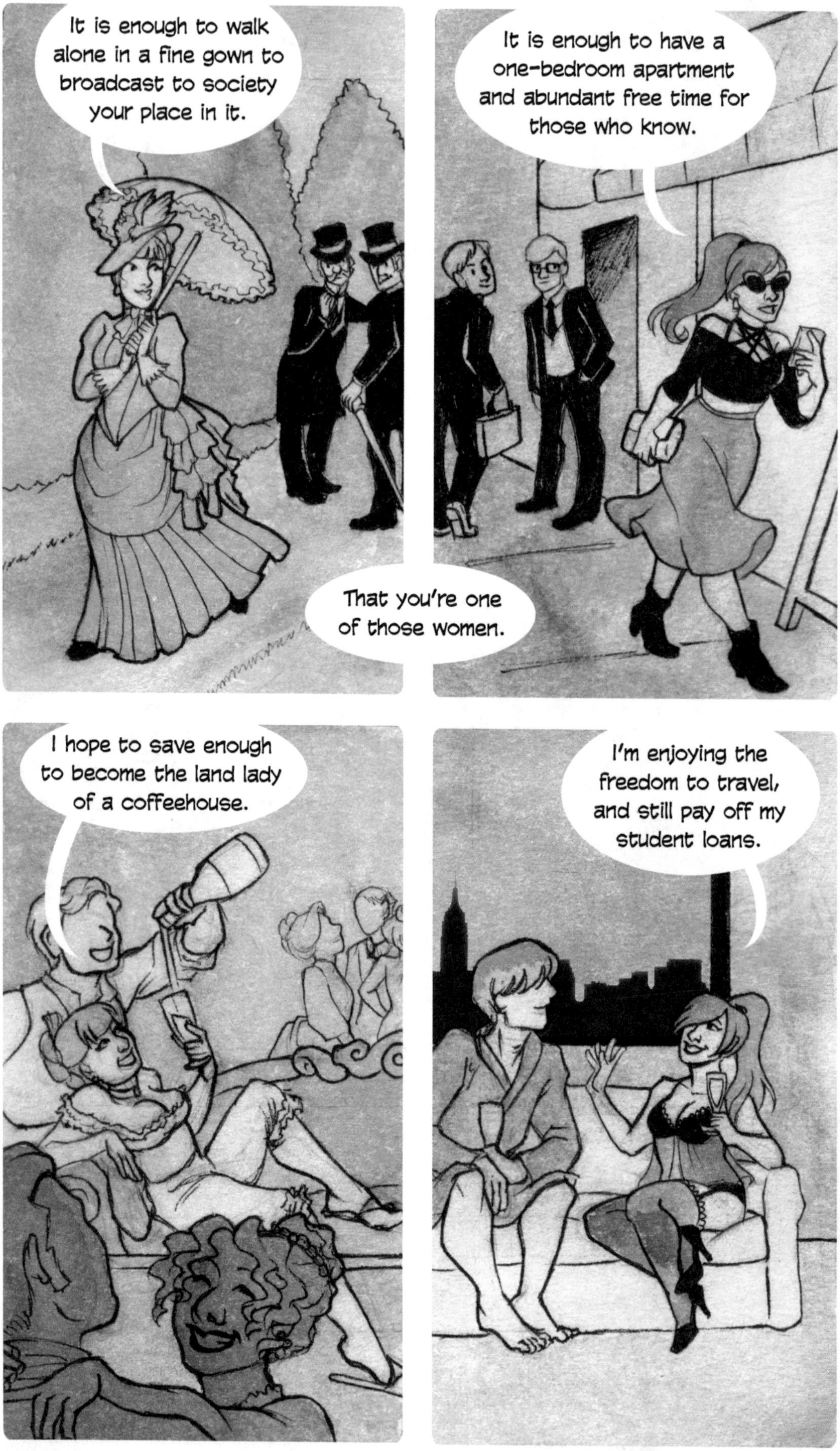
It is enough to walk alone in a fine gown to broadcast to society your place in it.
It is enough to have a one-bedroom apartment and abundant free time for those who know.
That you're one of those women.
I hope to save enough to become the land lady of a coffeehouse.
I'm enjoying the freedom to travel, and still pay off my student loans.

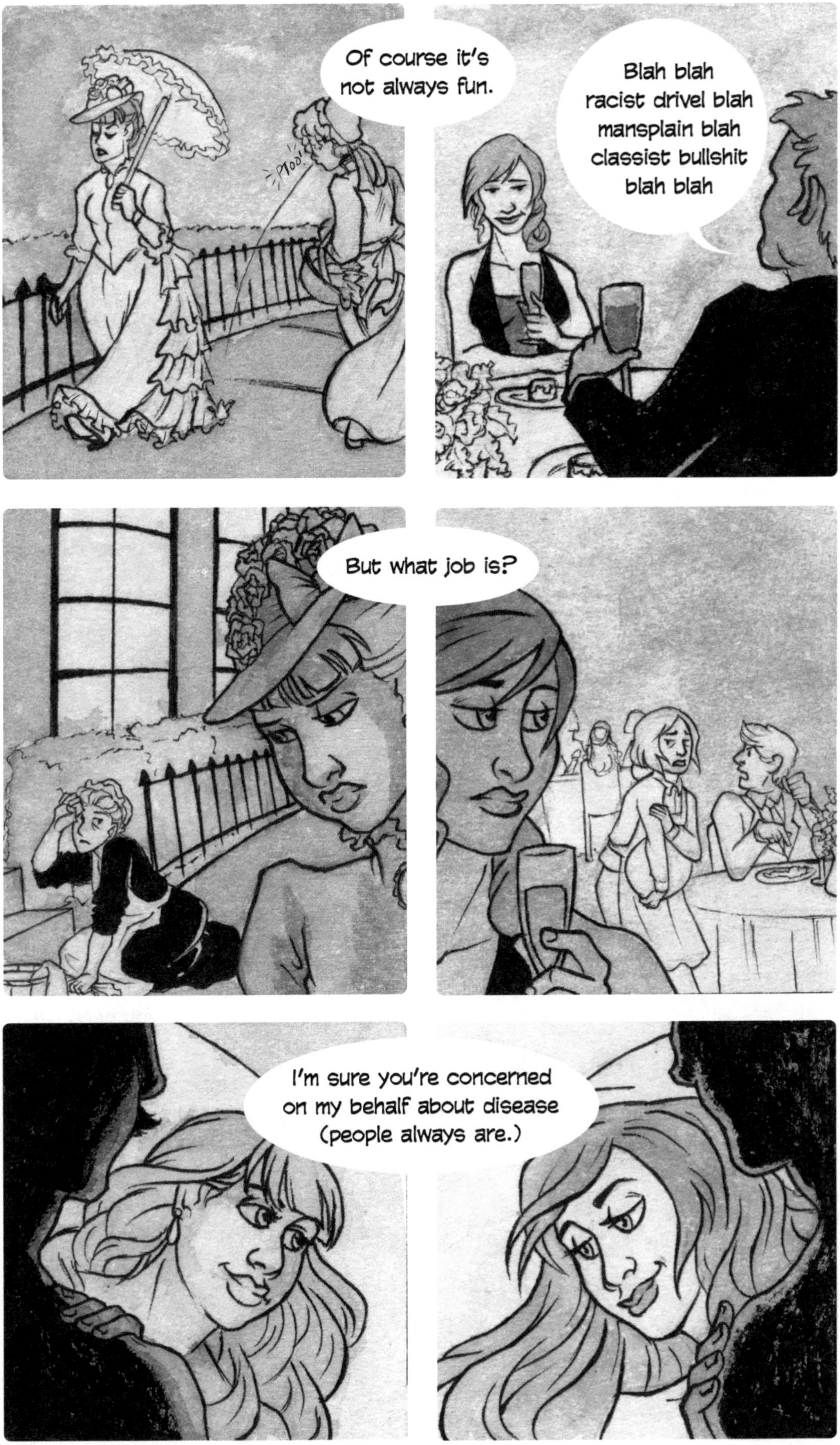
PTOO!
Of course it's not always fun.
Blah blah racist drivel blah mansplain blah classist bullshit blah blah
But what job is?
I'm sure you're concerned on my behalf about disease (people always are.)

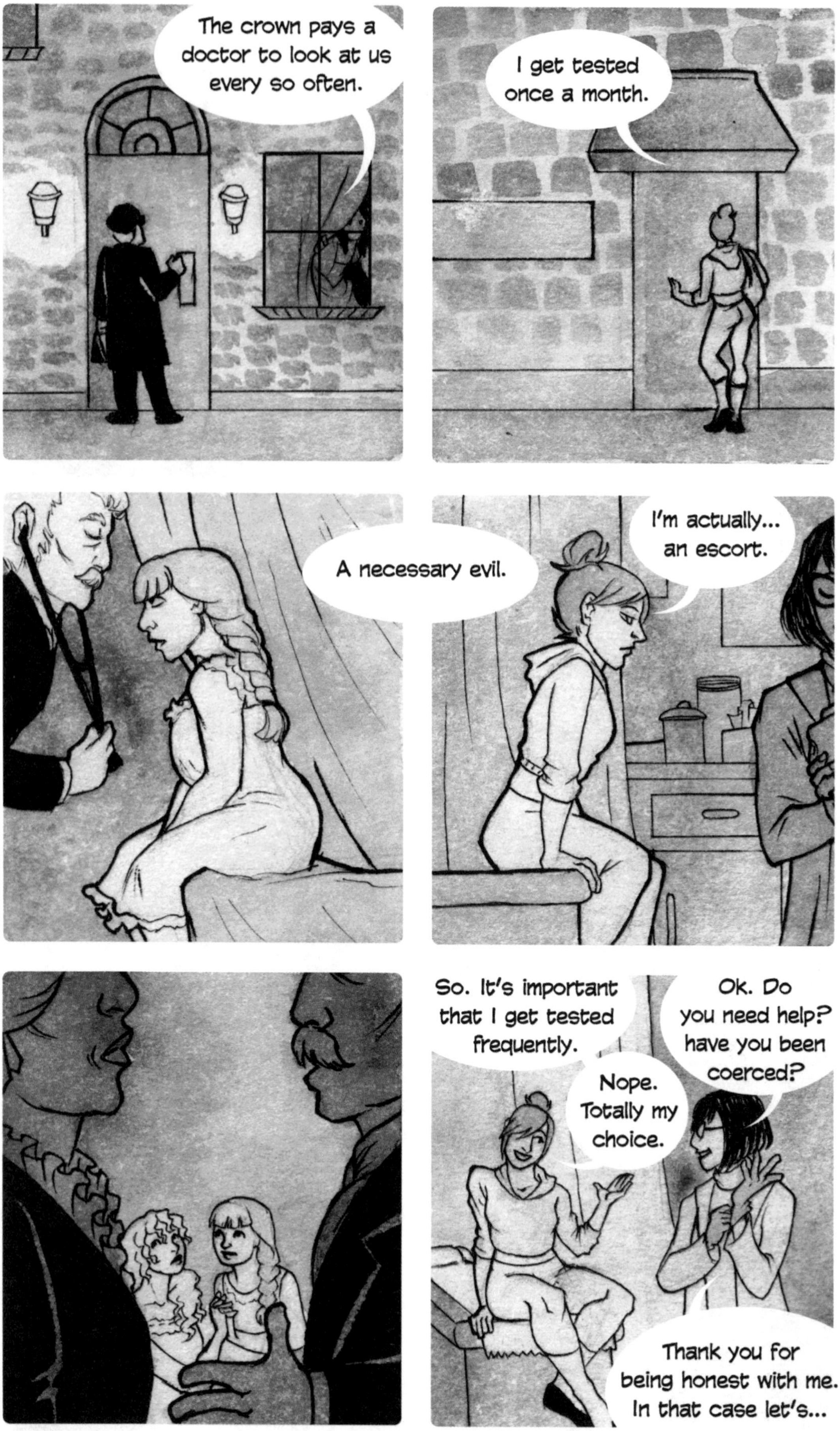
The crown pays a doctor to look at us every so often.
I get tested once a month.
A necessary evil.
I'm actually... an escort.
So. It's important that I get tested frequently.
Ok. Do you need help? have you been coerced?
Nope. Totally my choice.
Thank you for being honest with me. In that case let's...

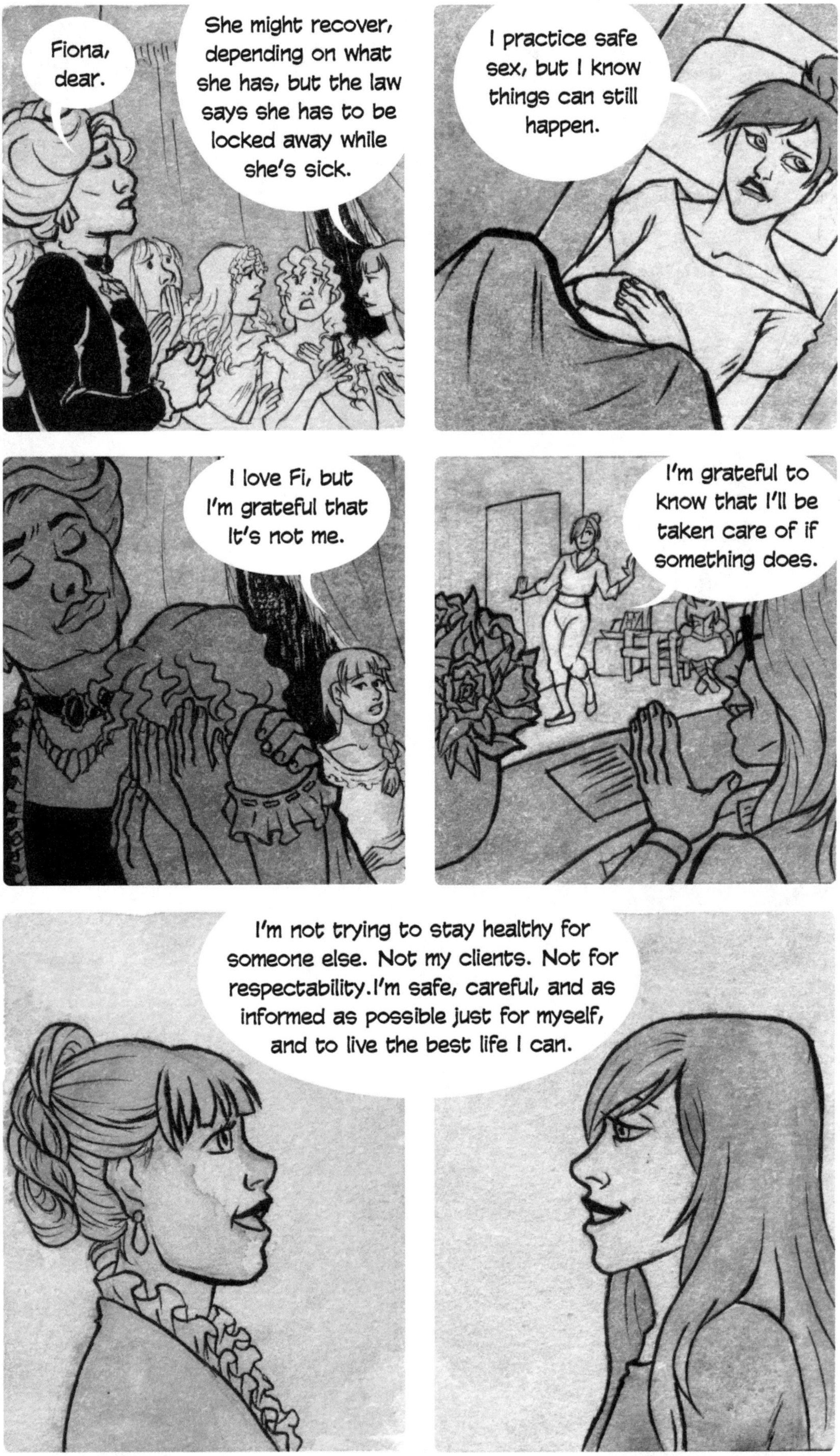
Fiona, dear.
She might recover, depending on what she has, but the law says she has to be locked away while she's sick.
I practice safe sex, but I know things can still happen.
I love Fi, but I'm grateful that it's not me.
I'm grateful to know that I'll be taken care of if something does.
I'm not trying to stay healthy for someone else. Not my clients. Not for respectability. I'm safe, careful, and as informed as possible just for myself, and to live the best life I can.

"I CAN" Story: **Kelsey Hercs** Art: **Jessi Jordan**

THE FUTURE IS STILL NOW!

by ANNA WILSON

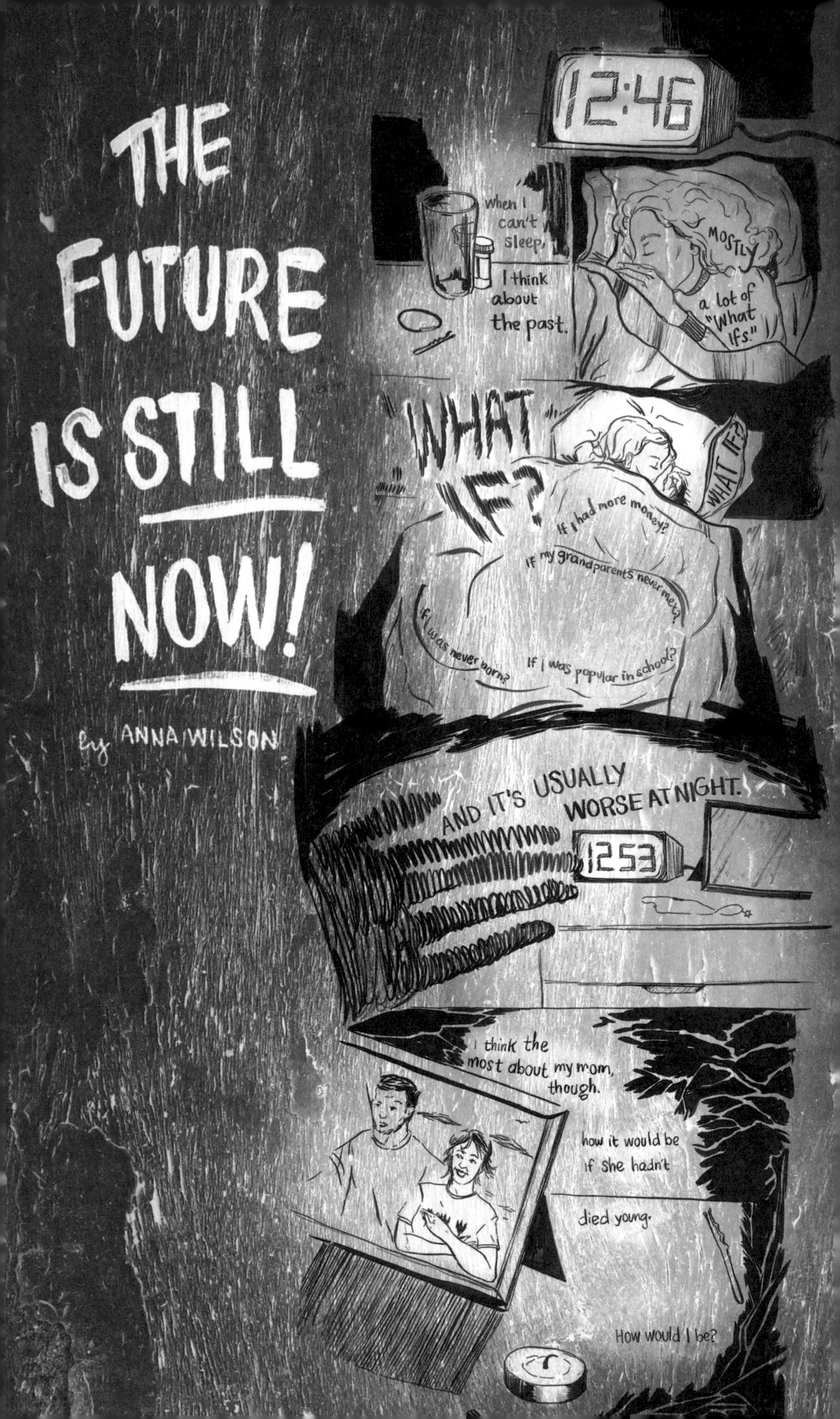
12:46
when I can't sleep,
I think about the past.
MOSTLY
a lot of "What Ifs."
WHAT IF?
WHAT IF?
If I had more money?
If my grandparents never met?
If I was never born?
If I was popular in school?
AND IT'S USUALLY WORSE AT NIGHT.
12:53
I think the most about my mom, though.
how it would be if she hadn't
died young.
How would I be?

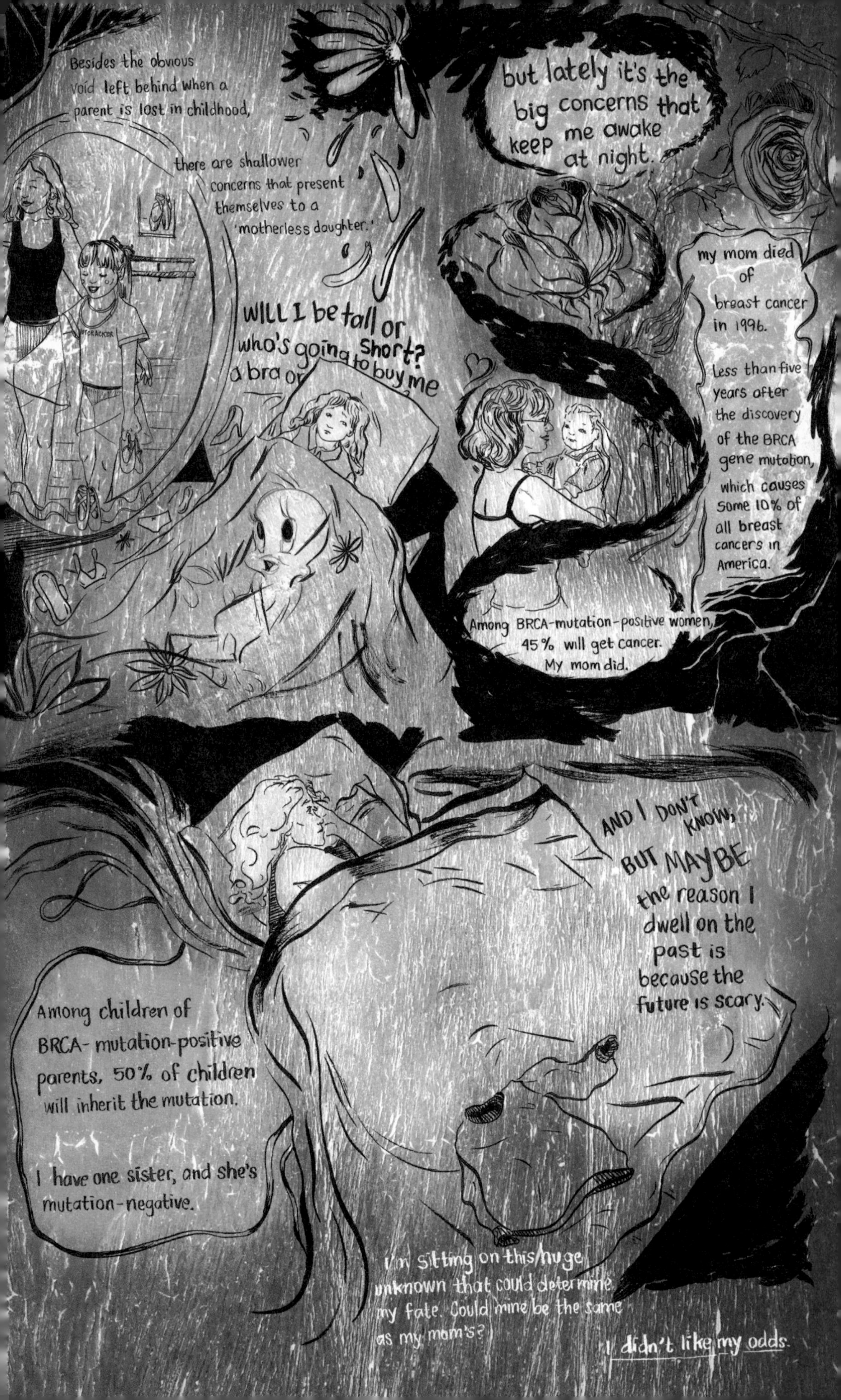

Besides the obvious void left behind when a parent is lost in childhood,
there are shallower concerns that present themselves to a 'motherless daughter.'
WILL I be tall or short? who's going to buy me a bra or
but lately it's the big concerns that keep me awake at night.
my mom died of breast cancer in 1996.
Less than five years after the discovery of the BRCA gene mutation, which causes some 10% of all breast cancers in America.
Among BRCA-mutation-positive women, 45% will get cancer. My mom did.
AND I DON'T KNOW, BUT MAYBE the reason I dwell on the past is because the future is scary.
Among children of BRCA-mutation-positive parents, 50% of children will inherit the mutation.
I have one sister, and she's mutation-negative.
I'm sitting on this huge unknown that could determine my fate. Could mine be the same as my mom's?
I didn't like my odds.

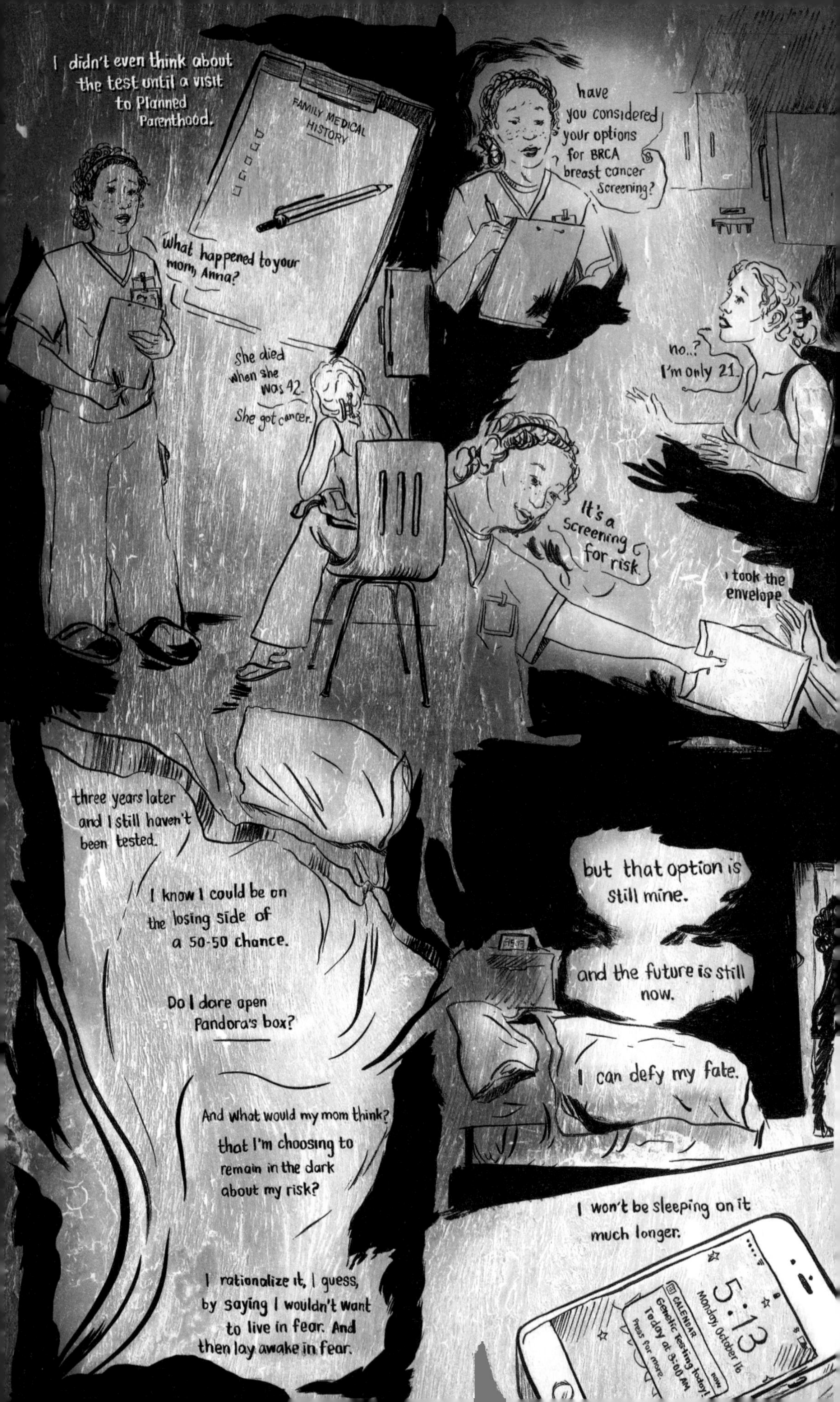
I didn't even think about the test until a visit to Planned Parenthood.
FAMILY MEDICAL HISTORY
What happened to your mom, Anna?
She died when she was 42.
She got cancer.
have you considered your options for BRCA breast cancer screening?
no..? I'm only 21.
It's a screening for risk.
I took the envelope
three years later and I still haven't been tested.
I know I could be on the losing side of a 50-50 chance.
Do I dare open Pandora's box?
And what would my mom think?
that I'm choosing to remain in the dark about my risk?
I rationalize it, I guess, by saying I wouldn't want to live in fear. And then lay awake in fear.
but that option is still mine.
and the future is still now.
I can defy my fate.
I won't be sleeping on it much longer.
5:13
Monday, October 16
CALENDAR
now
Genetic Testing today!
Today at 8:00 AM
Press for more.

WHITE COAT SYNDROME

WRITTEN BY: ANDREW AYDIN
COLORS BY: GLENN HAUMAN
ART BY: FABIAN LELAY
LETTERS BY: TAYLOR ESPOSITO

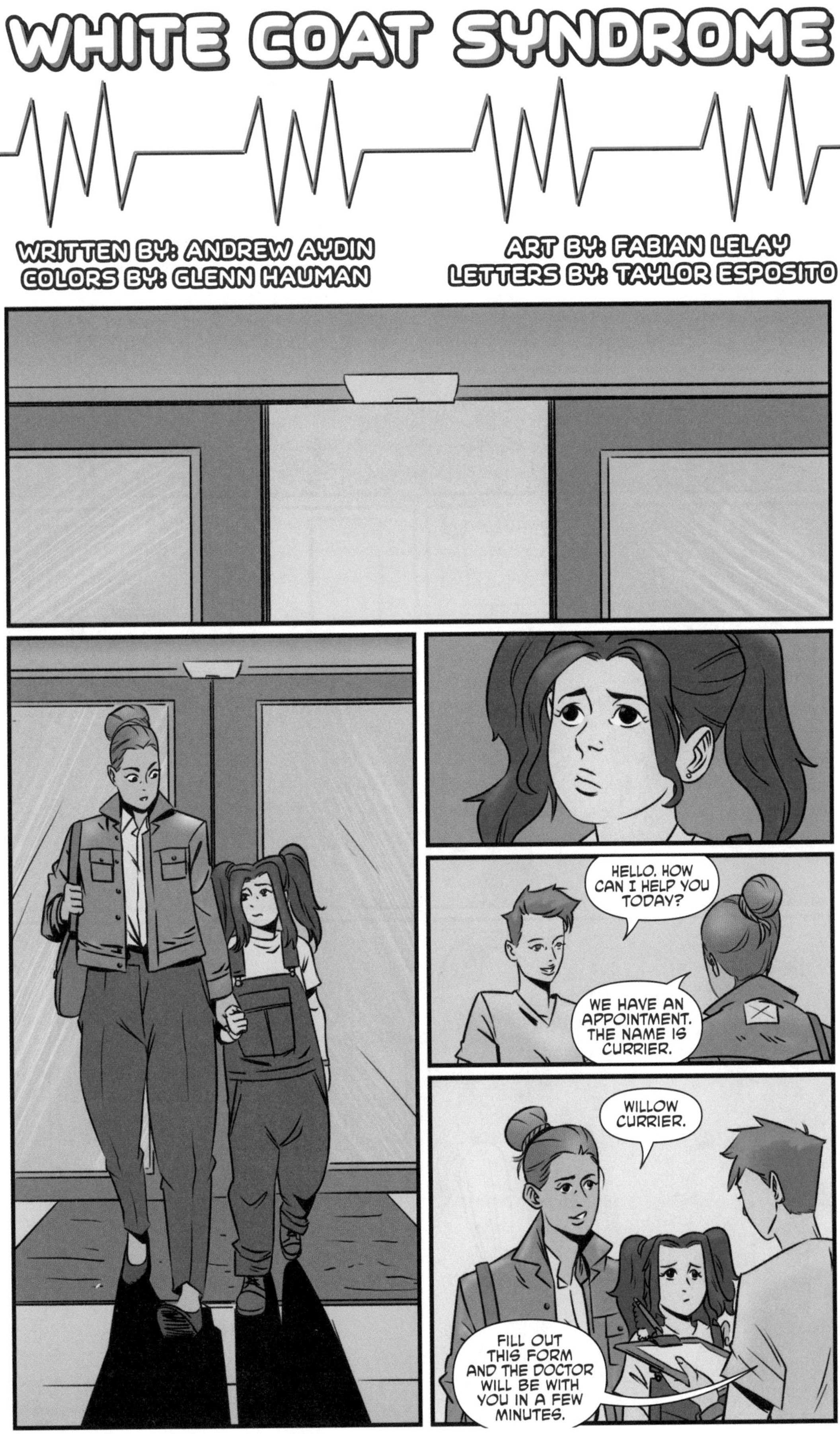
HELLO. HOW CAN I HELP YOU TODAY?
WE HAVE AN APPOINTMENT. THE NAME IS CURRIER.
WILLOW CURRIER.
FILL OUT THIS FORM AND THE DOCTOR WILL BE WITH YOU IN A FEW MINUTES.

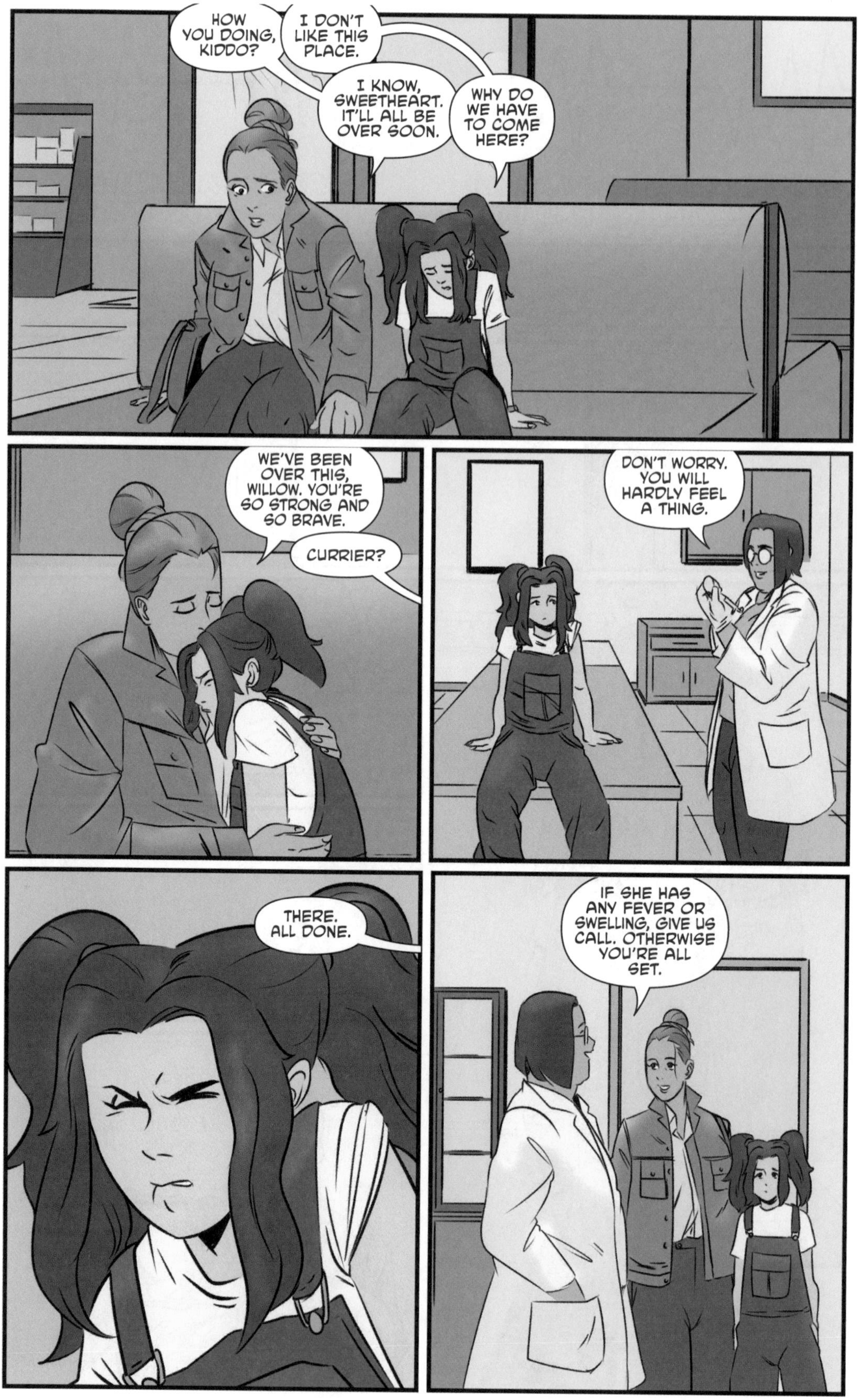
HOW YOU DOING, KIDDO?
I DON'T LIKE THIS PLACE.
I KNOW, SWEETHEART. IT'LL ALL BE OVER SOON.
WHY DO WE HAVE TO COME HERE?
WE'VE BEEN OVER THIS, WILLOW. YOU'RE SO STRONG AND SO BRAVE.
CURRIER?
DON'T WORRY. YOU WILL HARDLY FEEL A THING.
THERE. ALL DONE.
IF SHE HAS ANY FEVER OR SWELLING, GIVE US CALL. OTHERWISE YOU'RE ALL SET.

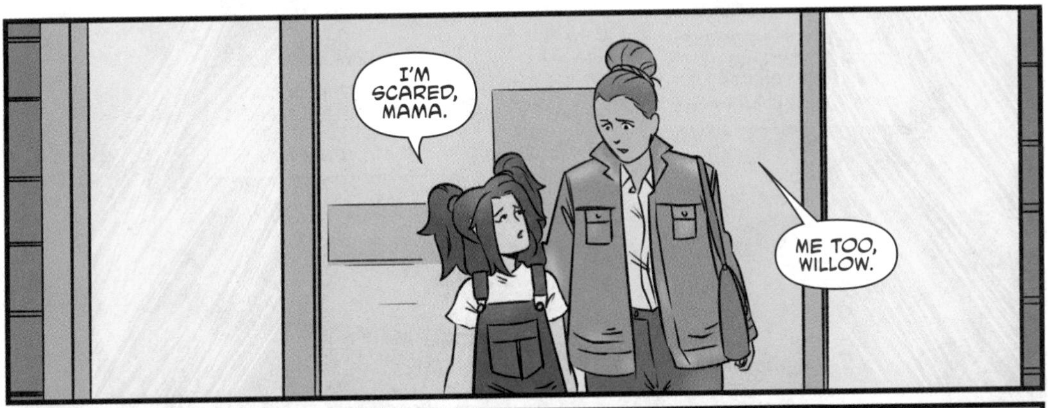
I'M SCARED, MAMA.
ME TOO, WILLOW.

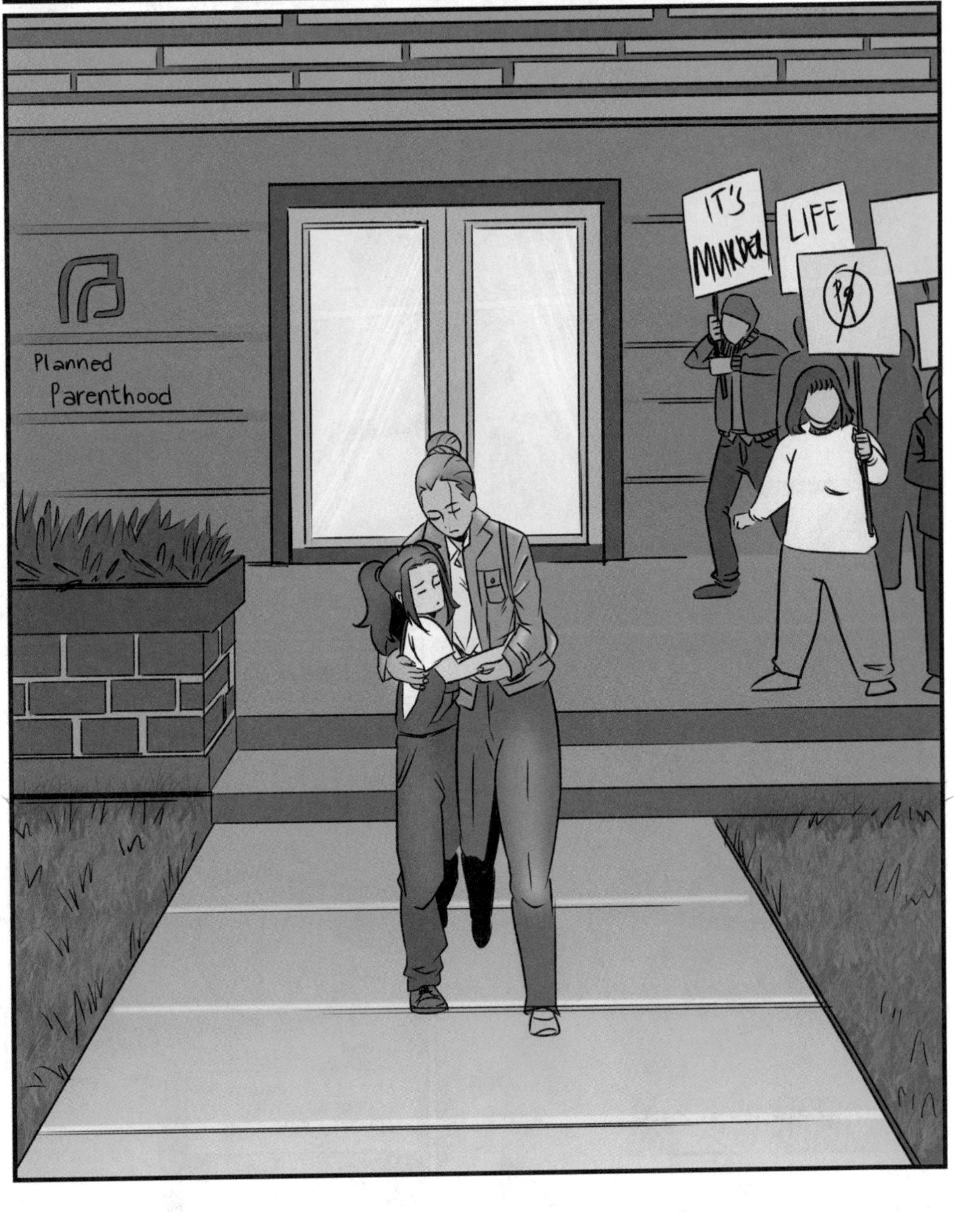
Planned Parenthood
IT'S MURDER
LIFE

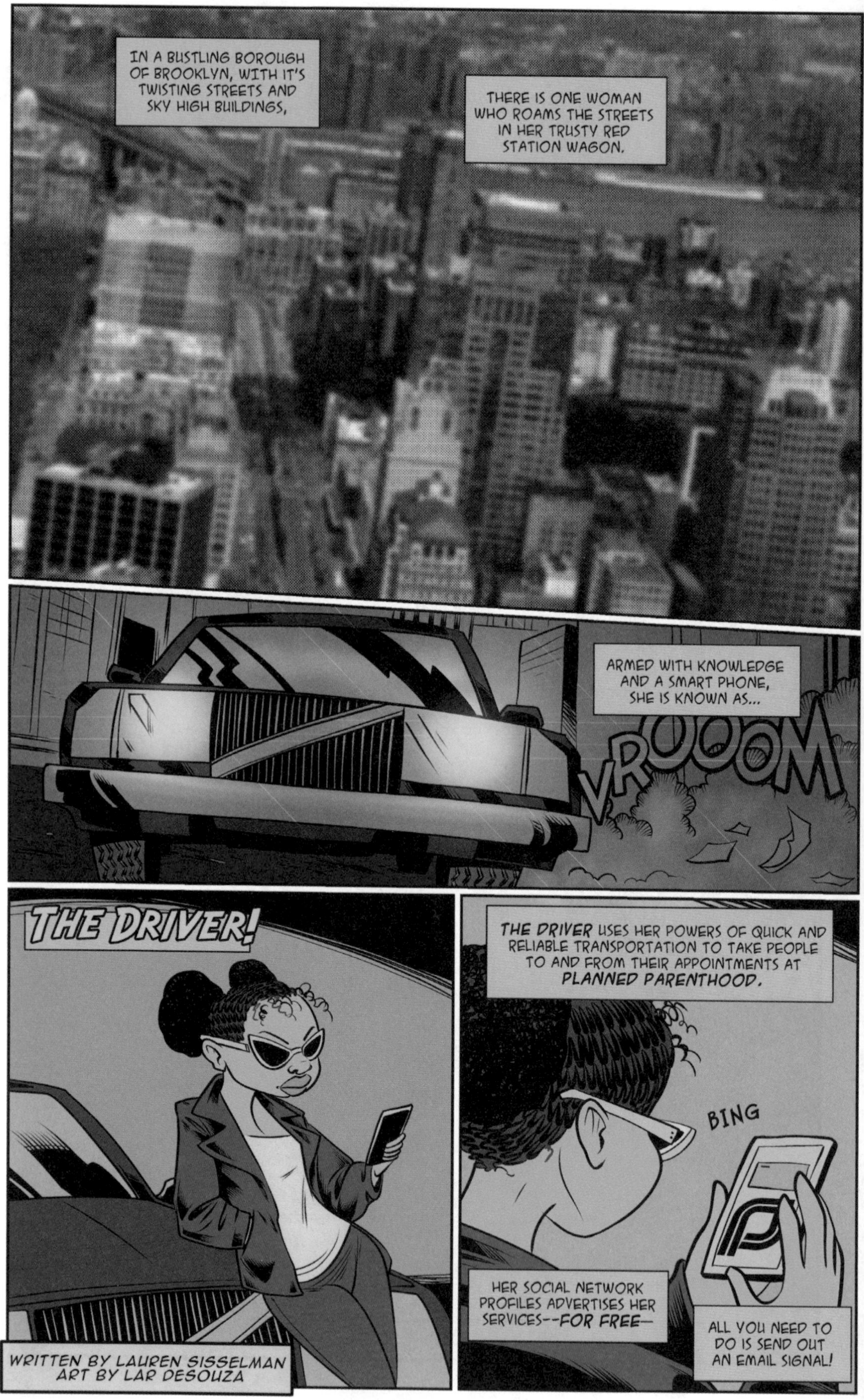

IN A BUSTLING BOROUGH OF BROOKLYN, WITH IT'S TWISTING STREETS AND SKY HIGH BUILDINGS,
THERE IS ONE WOMAN WHO ROAMS THE STREETS IN HER TRUSTY RED STATION WAGON.
ARMED WITH KNOWLEDGE AND A SMART PHONE, SHE IS KNOWN AS...
VROOOM
THE DRIVER!
WRITTEN BY LAUREN SISSELMAN
ART BY LAR DESOUZA
THE DRIVER USES HER POWERS OF QUICK AND RELIABLE TRANSPORTATION TO TAKE PEOPLE TO AND FROM THEIR APPOINTMENTS AT PLANNED PARENTHOOD.
BING
HER SOCIAL NETWORK PROFILES ADVERTISES HER SERVICES--FOR FREE--
ALL YOU NEED TO DO IS SEND OUT AN EMAIL SIGNAL!

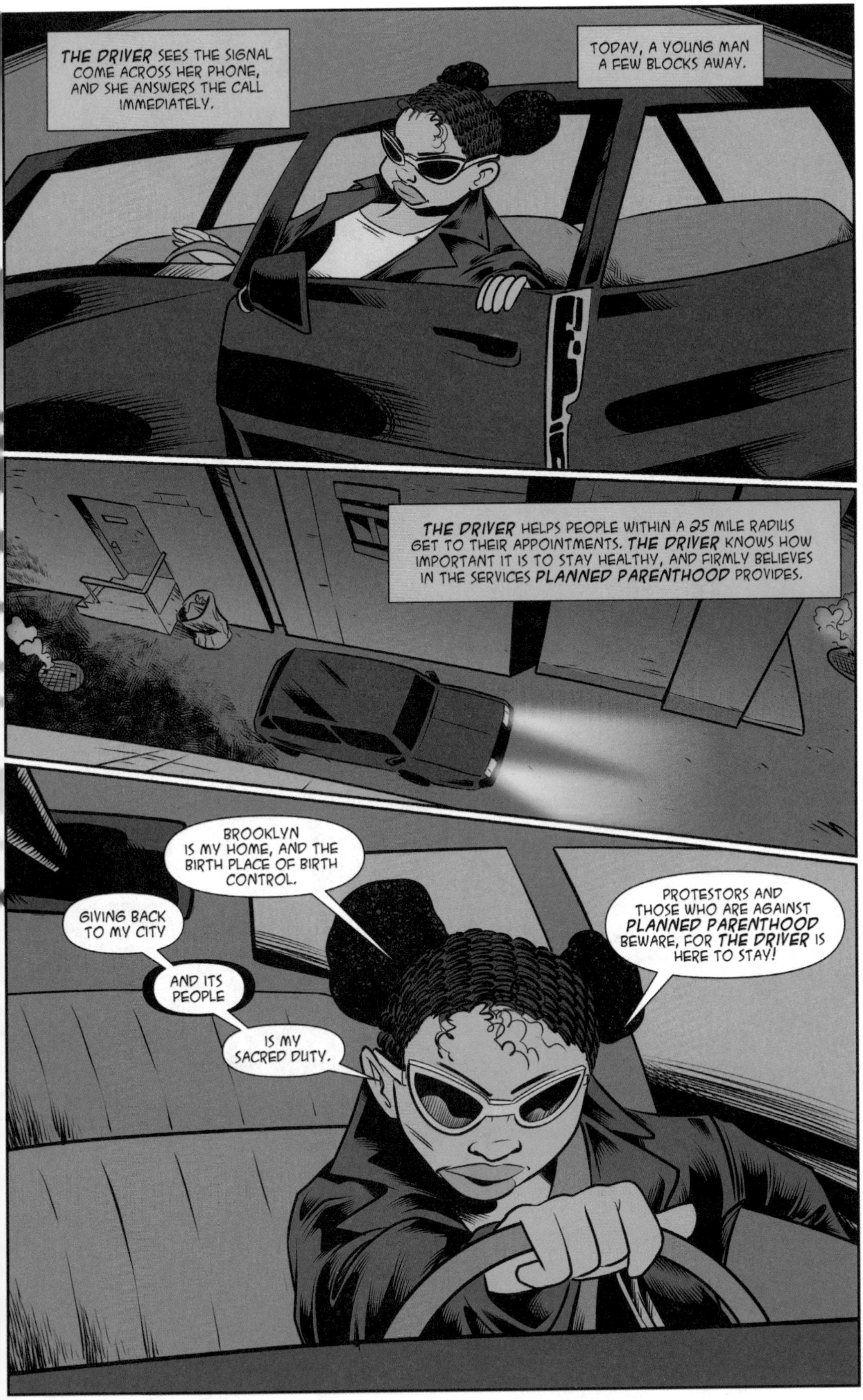
THE DRIVER SEES THE SIGNAL COME ACROSS HER PHONE, AND SHE ANSWERS THE CALL IMMEDIATELY.
TODAY, A YOUNG MAN A FEW BLOCKS AWAY.
THE DRIVER HELPS PEOPLE WITHIN A 25 MILE RADIUS GET TO THEIR APPOINTMENTS. THE DRIVER KNOWS HOW IMPORTANT IT IS TO STAY HEALTHY, AND FIRMLY BELIEVES IN THE SERVICES PLANNED PARENTHOOD PROVIDES.
BROOKLYN IS MY HOME, AND THE BIRTH PLACE OF BIRTH CONTROL.
GIVING BACK TO MY CITY
AND ITS PEOPLE
IS MY SACRED DUTY.
PROTESTORS AND THOSE WHO ARE AGAINST PLANNED PARENTHOOD BEWARE, FOR THE DRIVER IS HERE TO STAY!

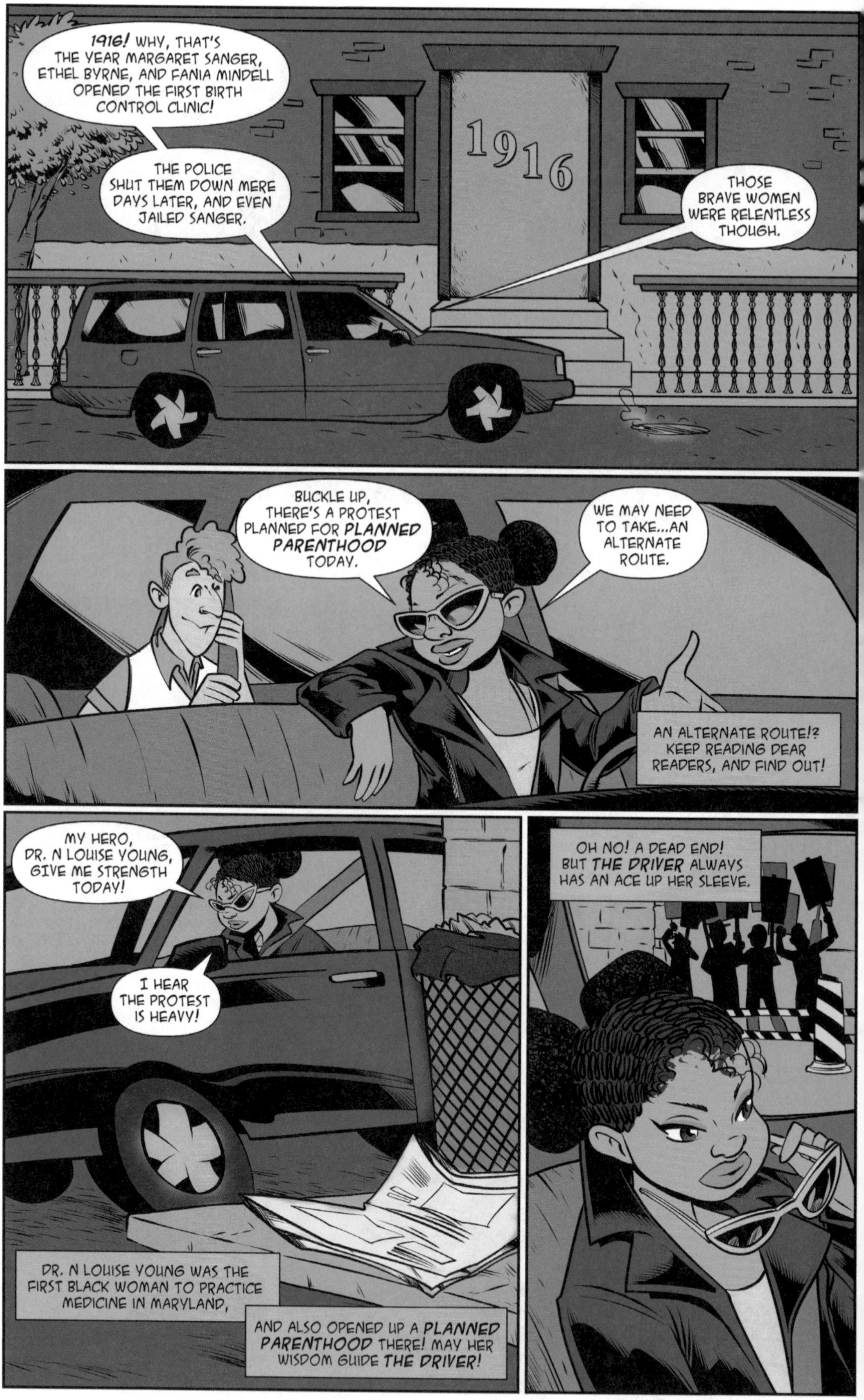
1916! WHY, THAT'S THE YEAR MARGARET SANGER, ETHEL BYRNE, AND FANIA MINDELL OPENED THE FIRST BIRTH CONTROL CLINIC!
THE POLICE SHUT THEM DOWN MERE DAYS LATER, AND EVEN JAILED SANGER.
1916
THOSE BRAVE WOMEN WERE RELENTLESS THOUGH.
BUCKLE UP, THERE'S A PROTEST PLANNED FOR PLANNED PARENTHOOD TODAY.
WE MAY NEED TO TAKE...AN ALTERNATE ROUTE.
AN ALTERNATE ROUTE!? KEEP READING DEAR READERS, AND FIND OUT!
MY HERO, DR. N LOUISE YOUNG, GIVE ME STRENGTH TODAY!
I HEAR THE PROTEST IS HEAVY!
DR. N LOUISE YOUNG WAS THE FIRST BLACK WOMAN TO PRACTICE MEDICINE IN MARYLAND,
AND ALSO OPENED UP A PLANNED PARENTHOOD THERE! MAY HER WISDOM GUIDE THE DRIVER!
OH NO! A DEAD END! BUT THE DRIVER ALWAYS HAS AN ACE UP HER SLEEVE.

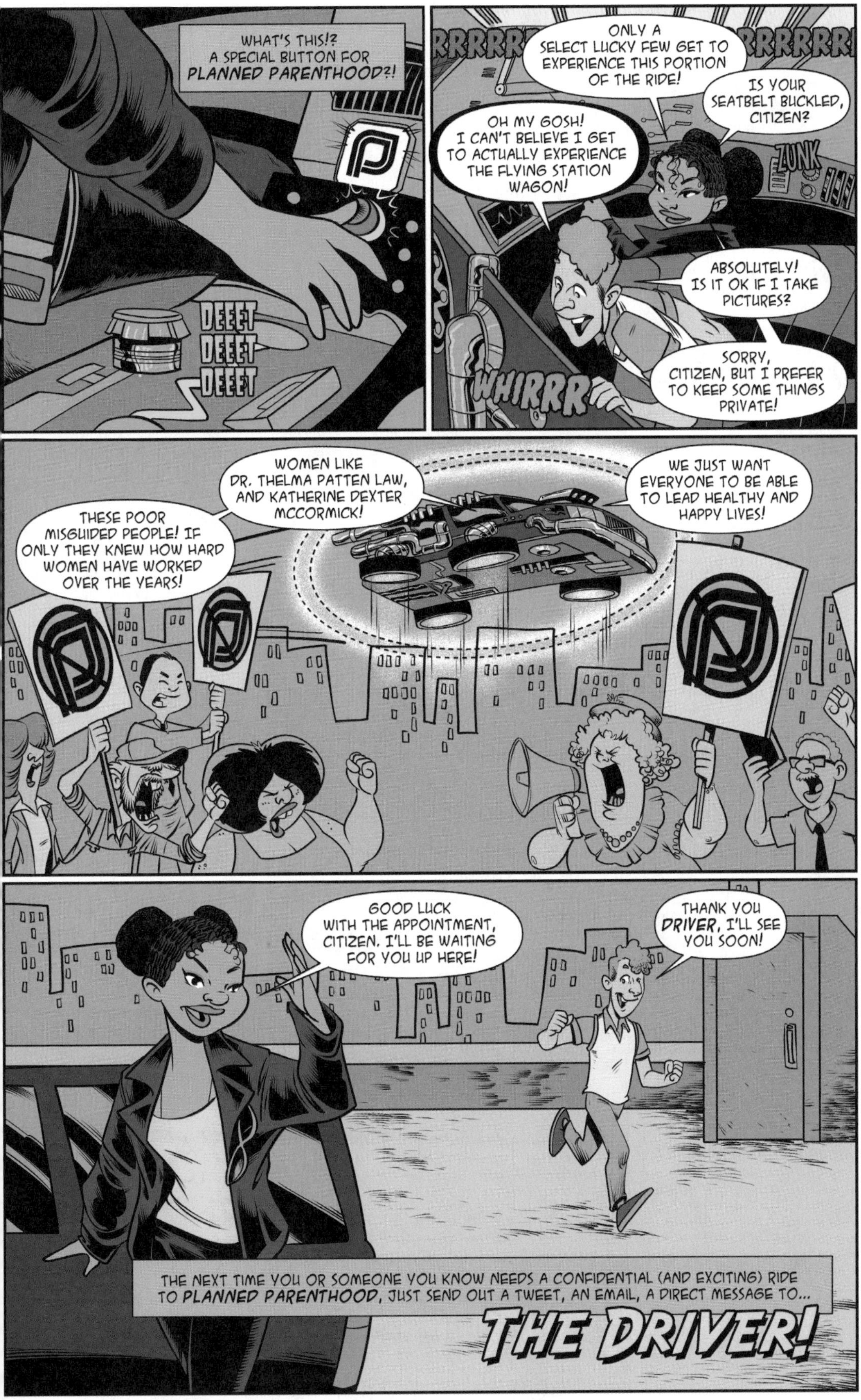
WHAT'S THIS!? A SPECIAL BUTTON FOR PLANNED PARENTHOOD?!
DEEET DEEET DEEET
RRRRRR
ONLY A SELECT LUCKY FEW GET TO EXPERIENCE THIS PORTION OF THE RIDE!
RRRRRR
IS YOUR SEATBELT BUCKLED, CITIZEN?
OH MY GOSH! I CAN'T BELIEVE I GET TO ACTUALLY EXPERIENCE THE FLYING STATION WAGON!
ZUNK
ABSOLUTELY! IS IT OK IF I TAKE PICTURES?
WHIRRR
SORRY, CITIZEN, BUT I PREFER TO KEEP SOME THINGS PRIVATE!
THESE POOR MISGUIDED PEOPLE! IF ONLY THEY KNEW HOW HARD WOMEN HAVE WORKED OVER THE YEARS!
WOMEN LIKE DR. THELMA PATTEN LAW, AND KATHERINE DEXTER MCCORMICK!
WE JUST WANT EVERYONE TO BE ABLE TO LEAD HEALTHY AND HAPPY LIVES!
GOOD LUCK WITH THE APPOINTMENT, CITIZEN. I'LL BE WAITING FOR YOU UP HERE!
THANK YOU DRIVER, I'LL SEE YOU SOON!
THE NEXT TIME YOU OR SOMEONE YOU KNOW NEEDS A CONFIDENTIAL (AND EXCITING) RIDE TO PLANNED PARENTHOOD, JUST SEND OUT A TWEET, AN EMAIL, A DIRECT MESSAGE TO...
THE DRIVER!

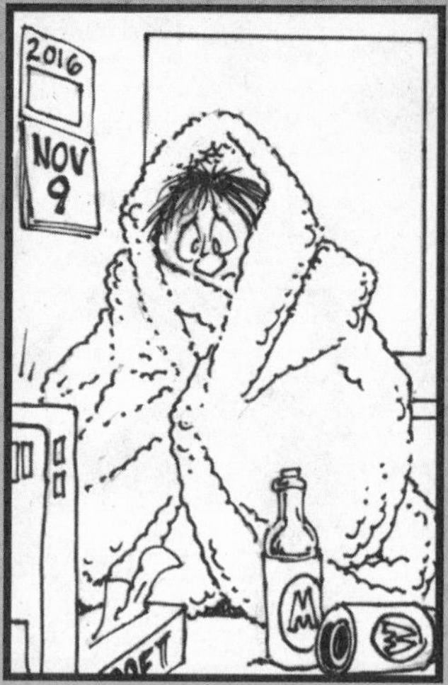
2016
NOV
9

Less than one week after Donald Trump was elected, I sat in the atrium of an office building in Midtown with about ten people, all but one of whom were women, listening to a list of things I could do to help.

I'd spent the day after the election huddled under a blanket, crying on and off, feeling afraid to go outside and see the shock in other peoples' eyes. Like everyone else in New York City, I was jovial the night before, eating brie and drinking Malbec with my friends as we waited to celebrate the first woman president. Like everyone else, my joy gave way to half-panic as states swung red. Afraid – and drunk – I went home and to bed, hoping for a miracle that didn't come.

I awoke to a world that seemed different overnight; that night, still in pajamas, I watched the news like a junkie and saw my friend's face suddenly appear in the midst of a protest outside Trump Tower. He spoke bravely into the mic thrust into his face, and I felt the first glimmer of something like hope.

With Thursday's sunrise came the knowledge I had to do something real, something tangible. I thought of the empty seat on the Supreme Court. I'd said before I was willing to put my body on the line to defend Roe v Wade – march, protest, take up physical space, refuse to move. Somewhere, I found an online list – Five Things You Can Do About the Election Right Now – something like that. On the list, it said, "Become an abortion escort."

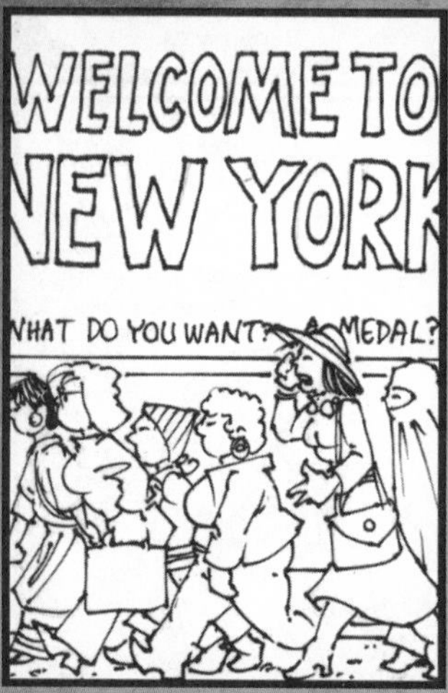
WELCOME TO
NEW YORK
HAT DO YOU WANT?
A MEDAL?

Yes. This was a real action that would involve time and my actual self, motivated by peace and a desire to help. Somehow, I wound through the internet and found the Haven Coalition – a non-profit group that offers both places to stay for women traveling to New York for abortions and escorts from the clinic for women who go alone to terminate their pregnancies. Sitting in that Midtown atrium with others who had found Haven in their post-election desperation, I knew I was among kindred people. The volunteers who led the meeting said it was the biggest one they'd had yet.

Women travel to New York from all over the country for their abortions, even flying from places like Texas or the Bahamas. I could use the free time I had while I was on sabbatical from my middle school teaching job to pick women up after their procedures, when they awoke from anesthesia and would not be permitted to leave alone. I could do that. I wanted to do that.

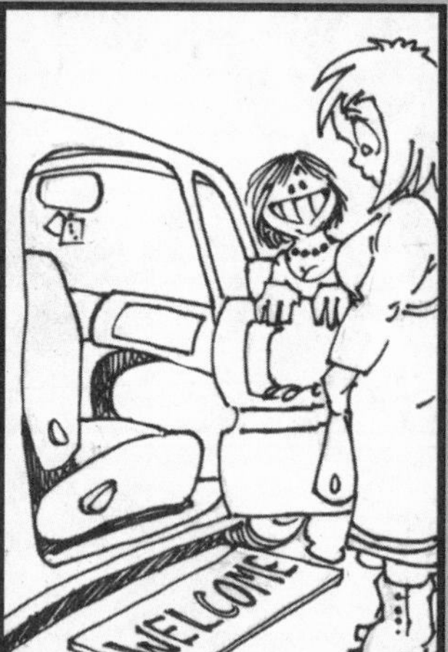
WELCOME

I was nervous the first time I pulled up outside the Manhattan clinic. It would be me and a stranger alone in my car. I thought of how my car's seat warmers help when I have back pain or menstrual cramps and clicked on the passenger seat warmer, wondering if this woman would be in any pain. I fretted about if it was ok to listen to a podcast or if I should drive in silence or with music, and what kind. I worried I might say something stupid. I wasn't worried about encountering protesters or anything – I knew I'd be able to face them. I knew if they had anything to say to the patient, I would protect her from them. What I was more nervous about was the emotional state of the woman I would meet, and whether or not I was doing right by her.

But my first patient, a 20-year-old from Baltimore, had brought her uncle with her at the last minute, then decided she would rest at his apartment and catch the bus home that night, instead of going to the Haven volunteer's home in Brooklyn. "I wanna get home to my baby girl," she said. So I was off the hook.

The next week, I picked up a woman in Queens, walked with her to the pharmacy to pick up her antibiotics, and then drove her a few miles to an auto shop near her house. I don't know why I was surprised she was about my age, in her late 30s or so, but I was. She tried to give me money for gas and we talked about her car troubles, her boyfriend, her three teenaged kids. "I didn't know there were people who did stuff like this," she said to me. "Thank you so much!"

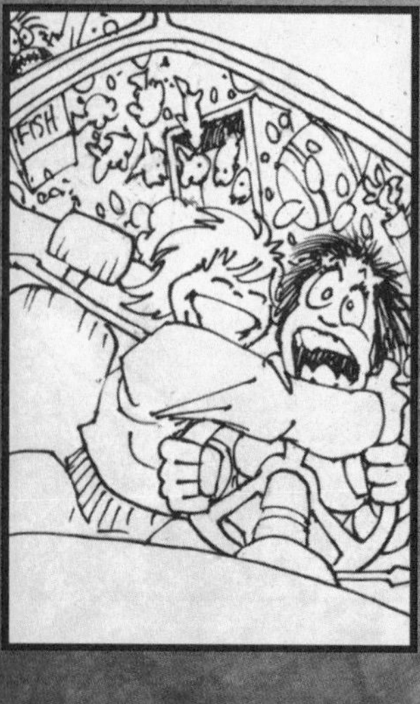
FISH

But really, I wanted to thank her. I wasn't nervous anymore. I remembered once reading that studies show the most common emotional response a woman has after an abortion is relief. Each time I volunteer, I find it's true. The women I drive home from their appointments are light, friendly. They want to chat. They smile a lot. And they cut across every demographic imaginable.

I have driven home black, white, Asian, and Latina women. I have driven home a sixteen-year-old girl from Bushwick, a twenty-three-year-old woman from the Bronx, and that first maybe forty-year-old woman who could have been my friend, who reminded me of women I have taught with, women who are my friends. Many of the women I have sat next to in my Subaru with the heated seats already have kids – and they like to talk about them.

One woman and I shared funny stories about how to get kids to behave. She said the thing that makes her sons most sorry is when she won't hug them after they've misbehaved. "I'm so lucky they're so good," she said. When I pulled up at the fish market near her house so she could buy something to make her boys for dinner, she said, "I'm a hugger, so I'm just gonna go ahead and hug you."

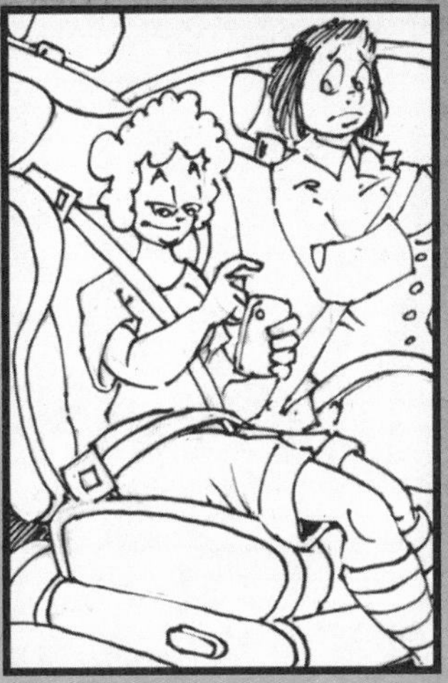

Another was a sixteen-year-old who looked about thirteen. We talked about school. I told her I'm a teacher. She said she wants to go to college for nursing. We talked about how much her Brooklyn neighborhood has changed as we drove past the cafes and bars that gentrification has brought there. All I could think was, "Where's the guy who got you pregnant?" even though I was afraid to think about it; she didn't even look like she was through with puberty, like a sexually mature woman.

One was an Army cadet, who was staying at a Bed and Breakfast in Astoria. She told me how much she loved seeing poetry on the subway, and quoted a poem she'd seen: "A strange, beautiful woman / met me in the mirror / the other night. / Hey, / I said, / What are you doing here? / She asked me / the same thing."

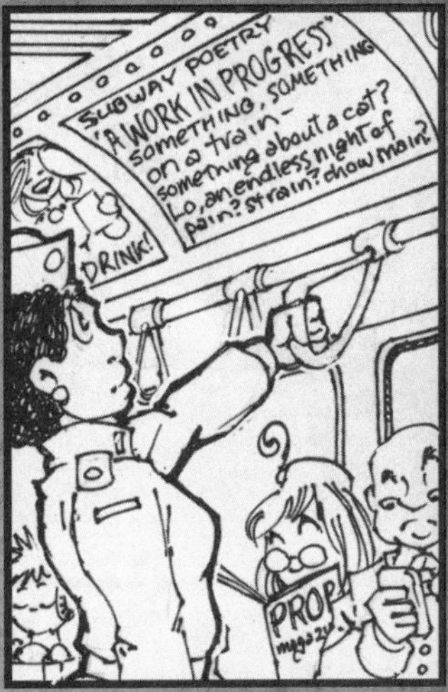
SUBWAY POETRY
"A WORK IN PROGRESS"
SOMETHING, SOMETHING
on a train -
something about a cat?
Lo, an endless night of
pain? strain? chow main?
DRINK!
PROP
magazine

"Oh, yes," I said. "That's Marilyn Nelson."

She told me she wrote poetry. I told her I was a poet, too. A Phantogram song was playing on Spotify. "I love this song," she said, and I said, "So do I."

And last week, I picked up two teenaged sisters in Queens. The younger one, the patient, was fifteen and in eighth grade – the grade I teach – shy and gorgeous, with lustrous black hair. Her sister, one year older, though shorter with a rounder, more childish face, wore a turquoise hijab. I walked with them to the pharmacy. The young girl holding the slip didn't know what to do, had never filled a prescription before, so I brought her prescription to the window myself, and then we sat and waited, an unlikely trio. I recognized their last name from having taught many kids with the same one. "Are you from Bangladesh?" I asked, and they nodded and smiled, some of the tension dripping away.

"We can take the bus home," the older sister said. "Really."

"If it's all right with you," I said, "I'd prefer to drive you. I teach girls your age. Will you humor me? Will you let me drive you?"

They nodded. The older, veiled sister sat in the front seat, and her younger sister stayed quiet in the back. She spoke to me with an accent about how tricky it is to learn English, how that's the reason her sister and she had each repeated a grade. "What do you teach?" she asked.

"English!" I said, and she laughed, "Oh, no!" but I assured her she was speaking well, I could understand her perfectly.

"I can tell you're a good teacher," she said.

Almost to their block, she turned and said, "I like you."

My heart swelled. "I like you, too," I said.

When her sister got out first, I took the chance to say, "Take care of her. She's so lucky to have a sister like you," before I called out to them both, "Be good to yourselves!"

I wonder who will be next.

I don't know whom those protesters outside Planned Parenthood every weekend believe are the wrong-doers (clue: it's them), or who politicians have in their minds when they picture the type of woman who gets an abortion. But the women and girls who sit in my passenger seat continue to defy any expectation I ever had. It's a challenge to rally and get into the car and get myself to the clinic, then drive to a part of the city I've usually not seen before, even though I've lived here for 26 of my 40 years. But each time I escort someone home from her appointment, I am thankful for the chance to have served even the smallest purpose in her life, and for the ways each of them show me – again – that there is not one definition of a woman or a girl.

Every one of them has thanked me before they closed the car door behind them, after our lives made brief contact. But I always drive away thinking, "No, thank *you*, thank *you*, thank *you*."

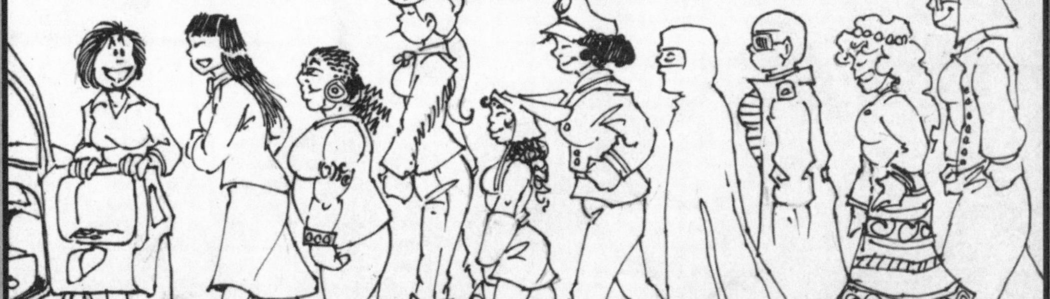

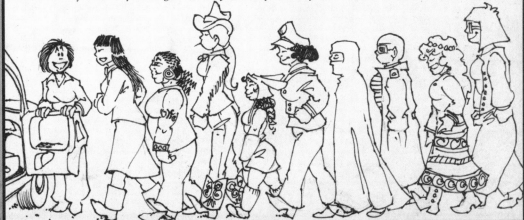

"NOT ONE DEFINITION" Story: **Rachel Rear** Art: **Phil Foglio**

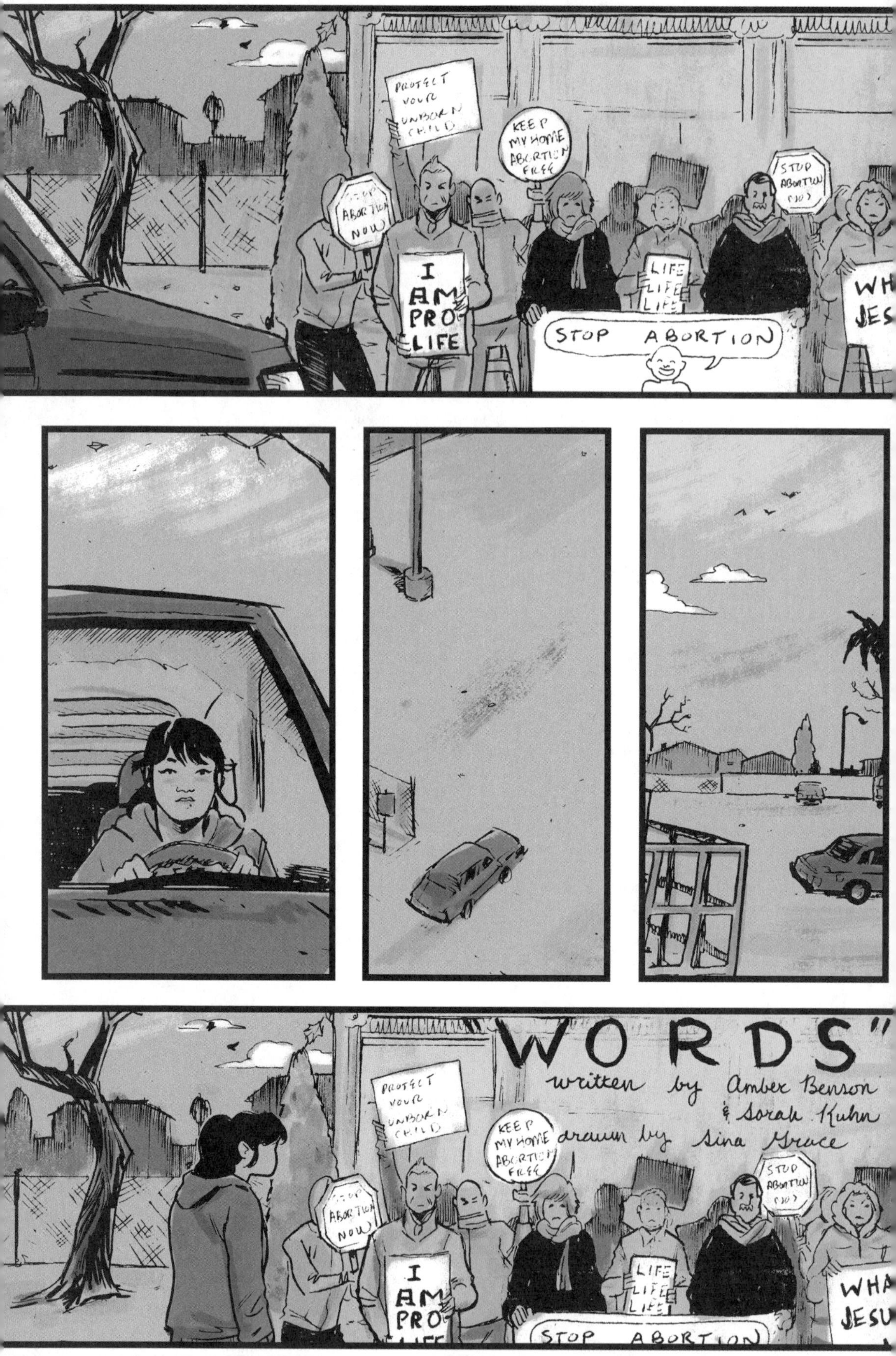
PROTECT YOUR UNBORN CHILD
KEEP MY HOME ABORTION FREE
STOP ABORTION NOW
STOP ABORTION NOW
I AM PRO-LIFE
LIFE LIFE LIFE
STOP ABORTION
"WORDS"
written by Amber Benson & Sarah Kuhn
drawn by Sina Grace

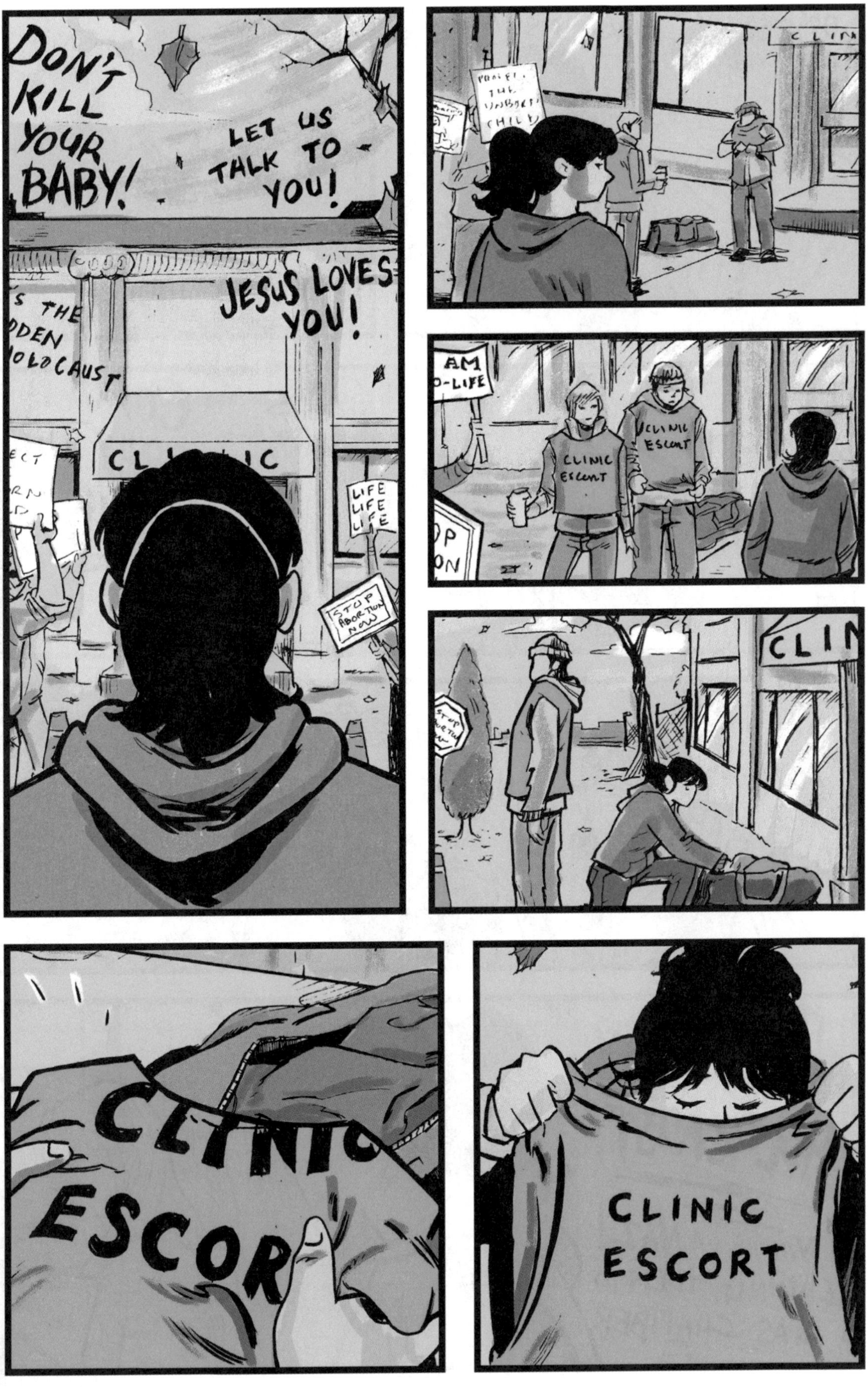

DON'T KILL YOUR BABY!
LET US TALK TO YOU!
JESUS LOVES YOU!
LIFE LIFE LIFE
STOP ABORTION NOW
CLINIC ESCORT
CLINIC ESCORT
CLINIC ESCORT

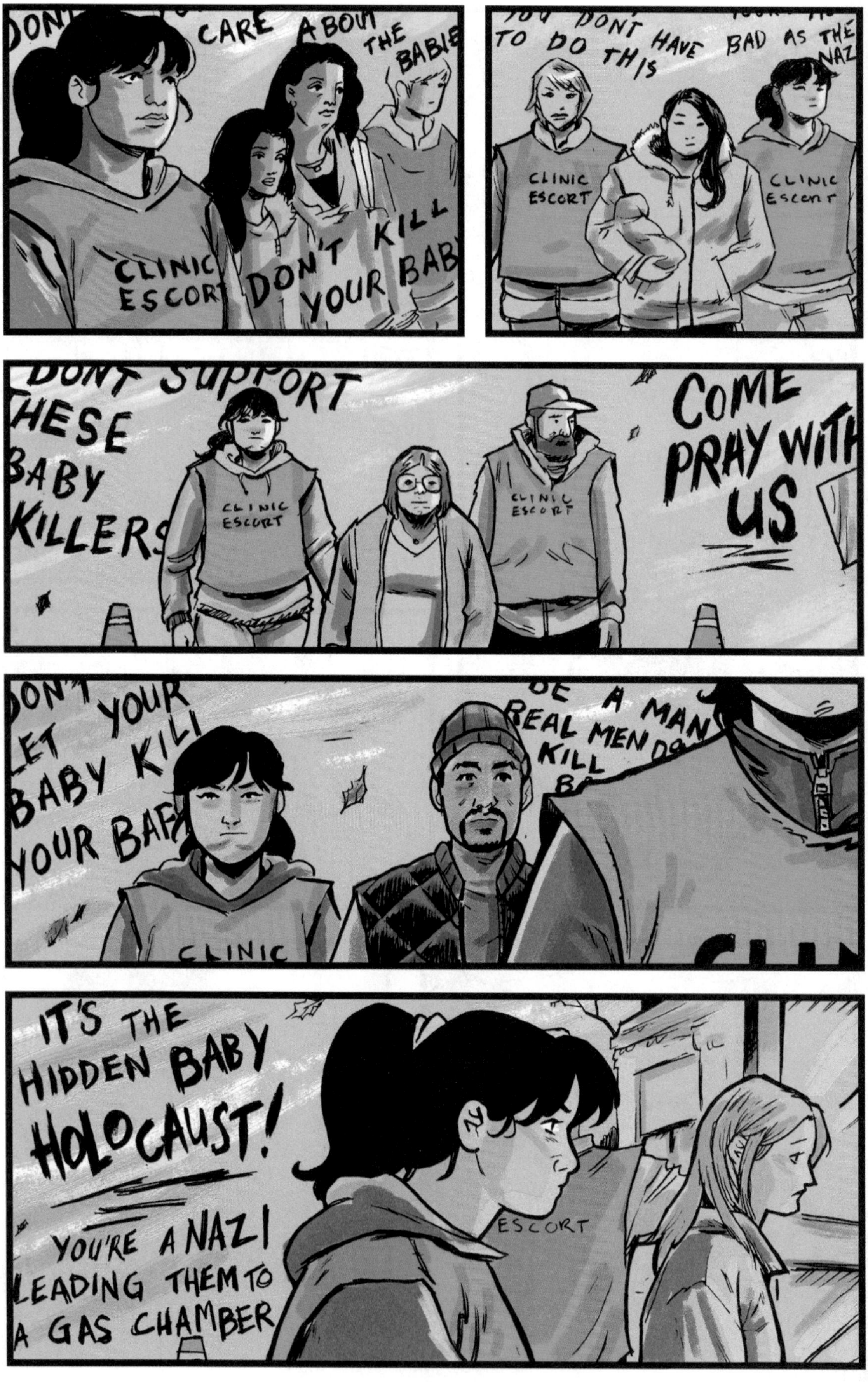
CARE ABOUT THE BABIE
CLINIC ESCORT
DON'T KILL YOUR BAB
TO DO THIS
YOU DONT HAVE
BAD AS THE NAZ
CLINIC ESCORT
CLINIC ESCORT
THESE BABY KILLERS
CLINIC ESCORT
CLINIC ESCORT
COME PRAY WITH US
BABY KILL
YOUR BAB
REAL MEN
KILL
CLINIC
IT'S THE HIDDEN BABY HOLOCAUST!
YOU'RE A NAZI LEADING THEM TO A GAS CHAMBER
ESCORT

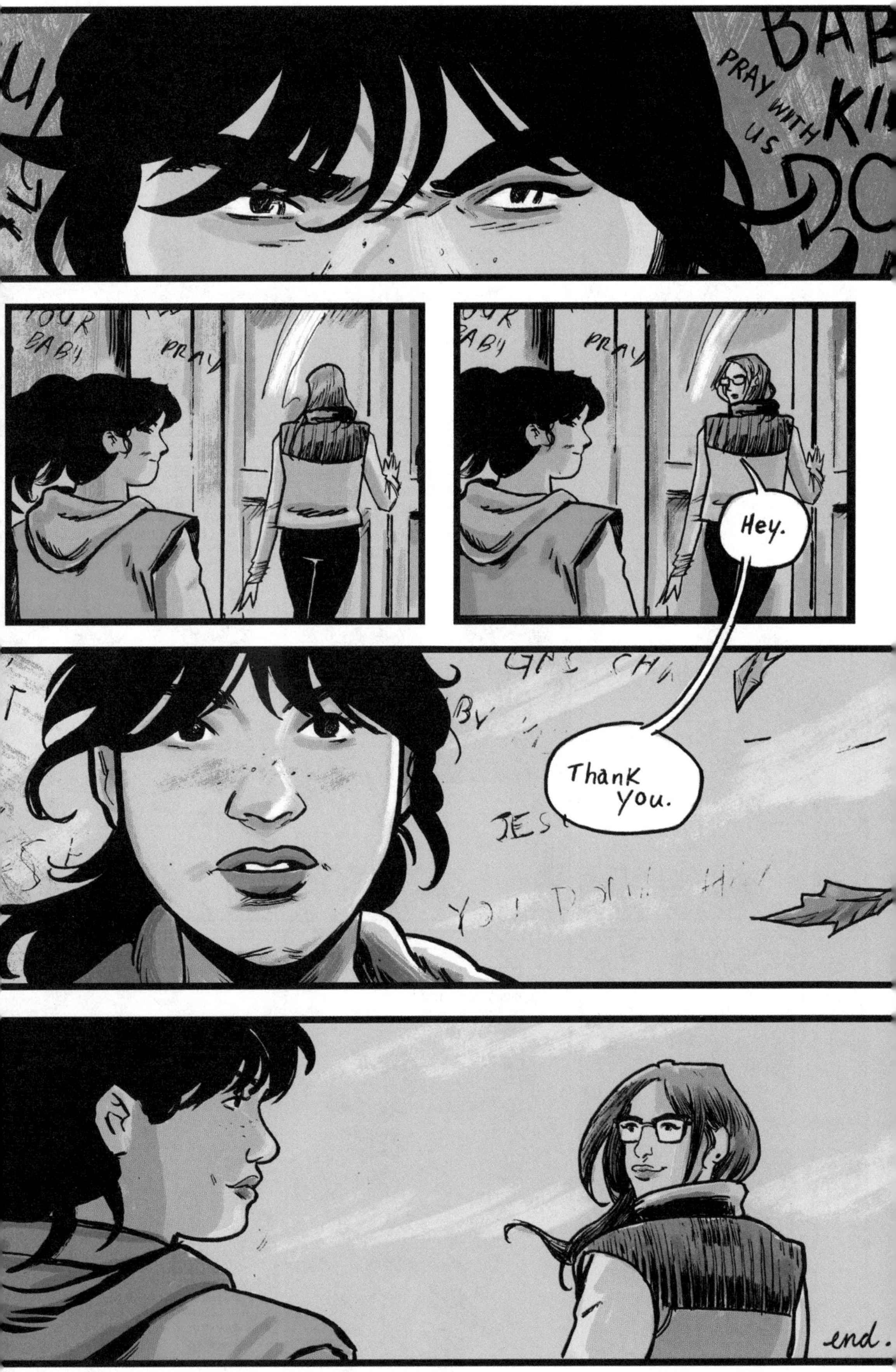
PRAY WITH US
YOUR BABY
PRAY
Hey.
Thank you.
end.

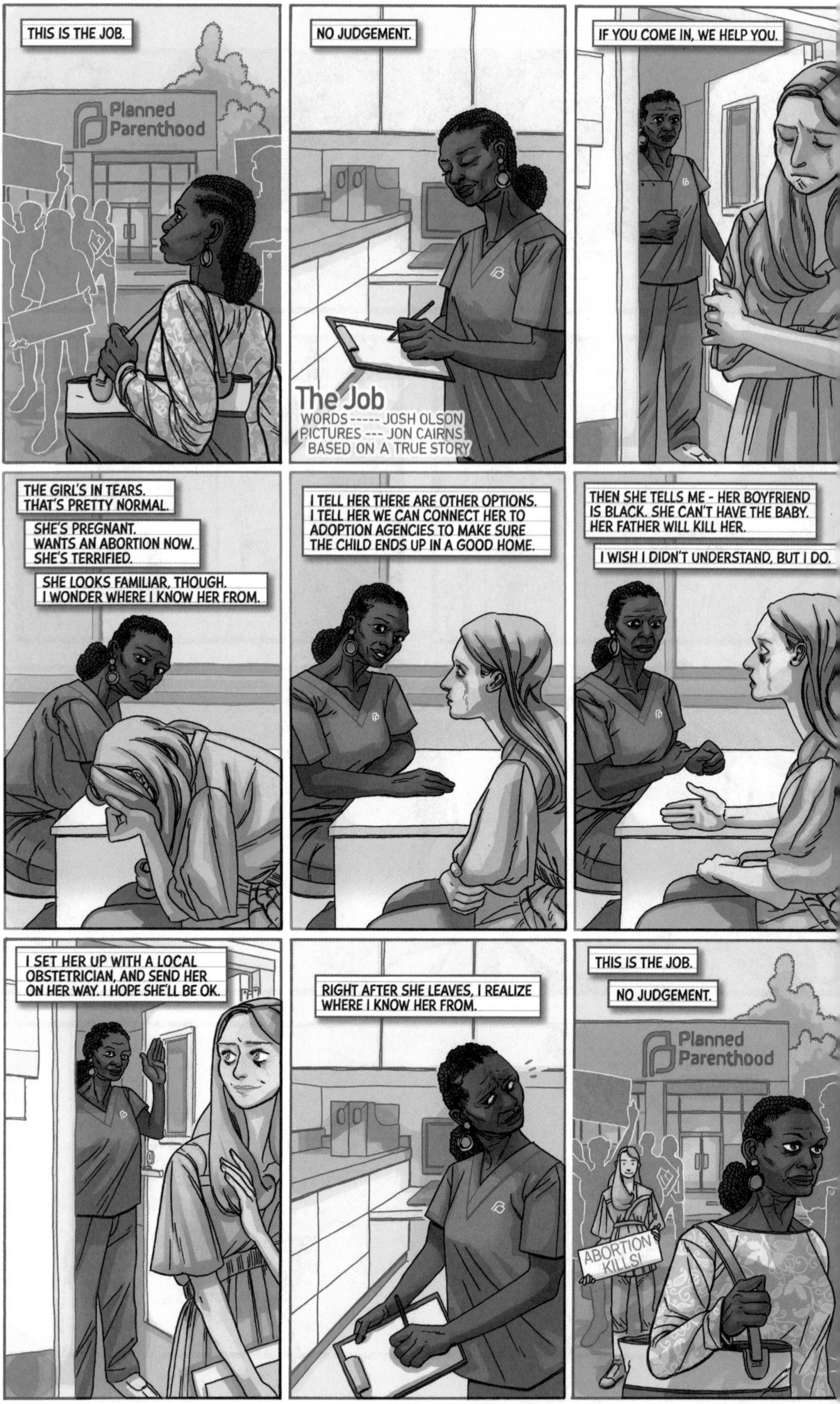
THIS IS THE JOB.
Planned Parenthood
NO JUDGEMENT.
The Job
WORDS ----- JOSH OLSON
PICTURES --- JON CAIRNS
BASED ON A TRUE STORY
IF YOU COME IN, WE HELP YOU.
THE GIRL'S IN TEARS. THAT'S PRETTY NORMAL.
SHE'S PREGNANT. WANTS AN ABORTION NOW. SHE'S TERRIFIED.
SHE LOOKS FAMILIAR, THOUGH. I WONDER WHERE I KNOW HER FROM.
I TELL HER THERE ARE OTHER OPTIONS. I TELL HER WE CAN CONNECT HER TO ADOPTION AGENCIES TO MAKE SURE THE CHILD ENDS UP IN A GOOD HOME.
THEN SHE TELLS ME - HER BOYFRIEND IS BLACK. SHE CAN'T HAVE THE BABY. HER FATHER WILL KILL HER.
I WISH I DIDN'T UNDERSTAND, BUT I DO.
I SET HER UP WITH A LOCAL OBSTETRICIAN, AND SEND HER ON HER WAY. I HOPE SHE'LL BE OK.
RIGHT AFTER SHE LEAVES, I REALIZE WHERE I KNOW HER FROM.
THIS IS THE JOB.
NO JUDGEMENT.
Planned Parenthood
ABORTION KILLS!

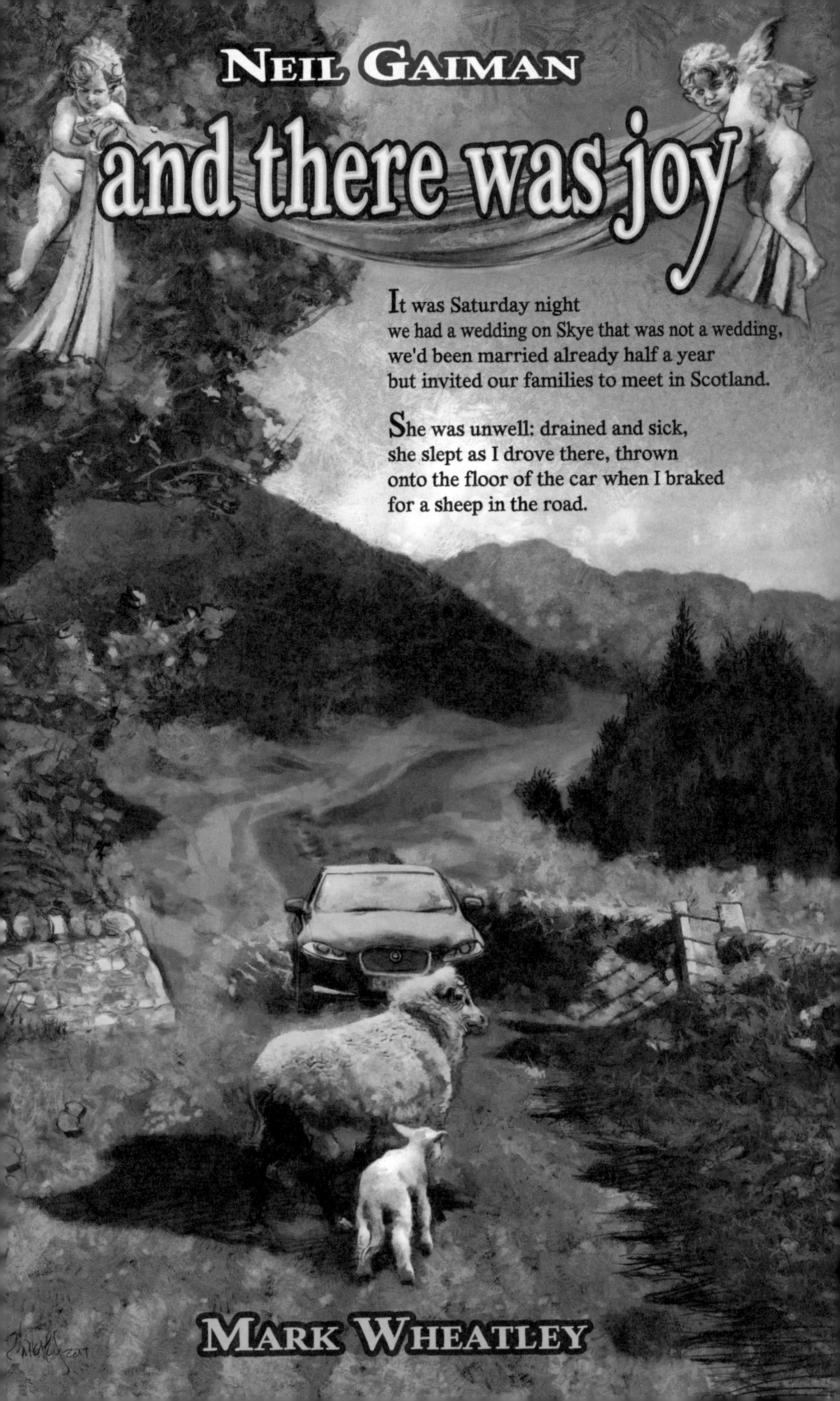

NEIL GAIMAN
and there was joy
It was Saturday night
we had a wedding on Skye that was not a wedding,
we'd been married already half a year
but invited our families to meet in Scotland.
She was unwell: drained and sick,
she slept as I drove there, thrown
onto the floor of the car when I braked
for a sheep in the road.
MARK WHEATLEY

On Monday she went to the hospital. They
told her she had a kidney infection and
prescribed her drugs. "You aren't pregnant?"
they asked her, and she laughed
and told them she wasn't.
"Good," they said. "You can't take these
if you're pregnant."

Ten days later, in Edinburgh,
she peed on a stick in a shop
And there was joy,
And then our world went dark. Doctors explained that
the drugs would probably have had
a teratalogical effect on the foetus:
teratology, the study of monsters.
We had to make a choice.

She cried a lot. I did not cry when I was with her,
thought I was staying strong for her.
She thought I was cold and distant.
I cried on phones, and when alone.
We met with a doctor whose mother had Alzheimer's,
something I only realised when we had
the same conversation
three times through.

The day of the abortion,
we thought pills would be easier than surgery.
I watched my wife shake and sleep, and vomit and sleep again,
I sat by her side and held her hand,
willing her to know in her unconsciousness that I loved her
and was there for her
and didn't cry.
Until it was time to leave, and the doctor drove us away.

I went onstage in front of 800 people and talked about books
and remember nothing I said that night, nothing I was asked,
nothing. And she went home to our friends' house,
and miscarried into their toilet bowl alone.

That was six years ago. Our son is two now, and he smiles
a smile as big as his mother's,
his eyes are as blue as tropical lagoons. He loves music,
books, dolls, cows, bears and swings. He laughs a lot,
is kind to other children,
and cries freely when the world disappoints him.
We chose to have him.
We choose so little in this world,
but we chose him as he perhaps chose us.

Some choices are unfair, impossible, and hard.
Nobody chooses pain and grief for themselves.
Nobody chooses the hard choices.
The best that we can do, when faced with them,
Is to have compassion.
To have wisdom. To forgive. To be kind.

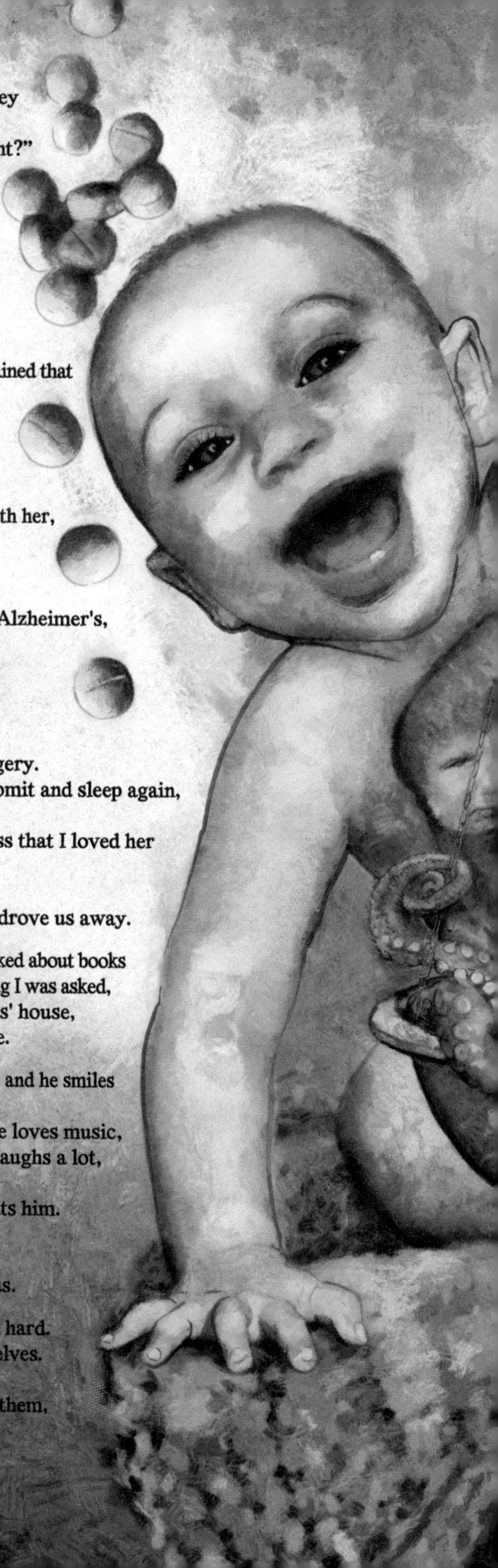

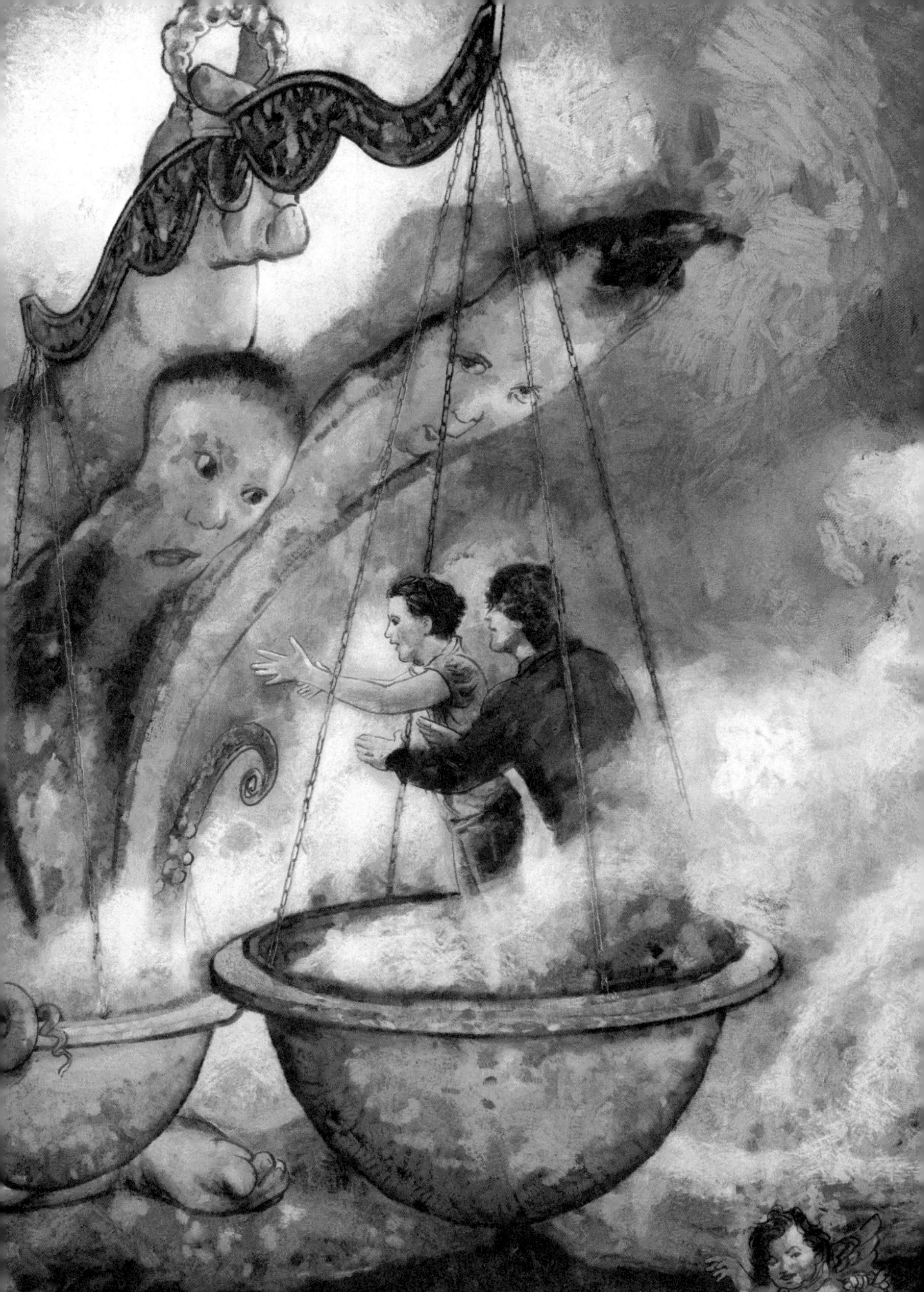

And for every hour, there's another me and she,
talking in their bed late at night, through tears and doubt.
Or a her alone,
who stares at the rain coming down on the window glass
turning the world outside into a blurry question
and wonders how the hell she'll get through tomorrow.

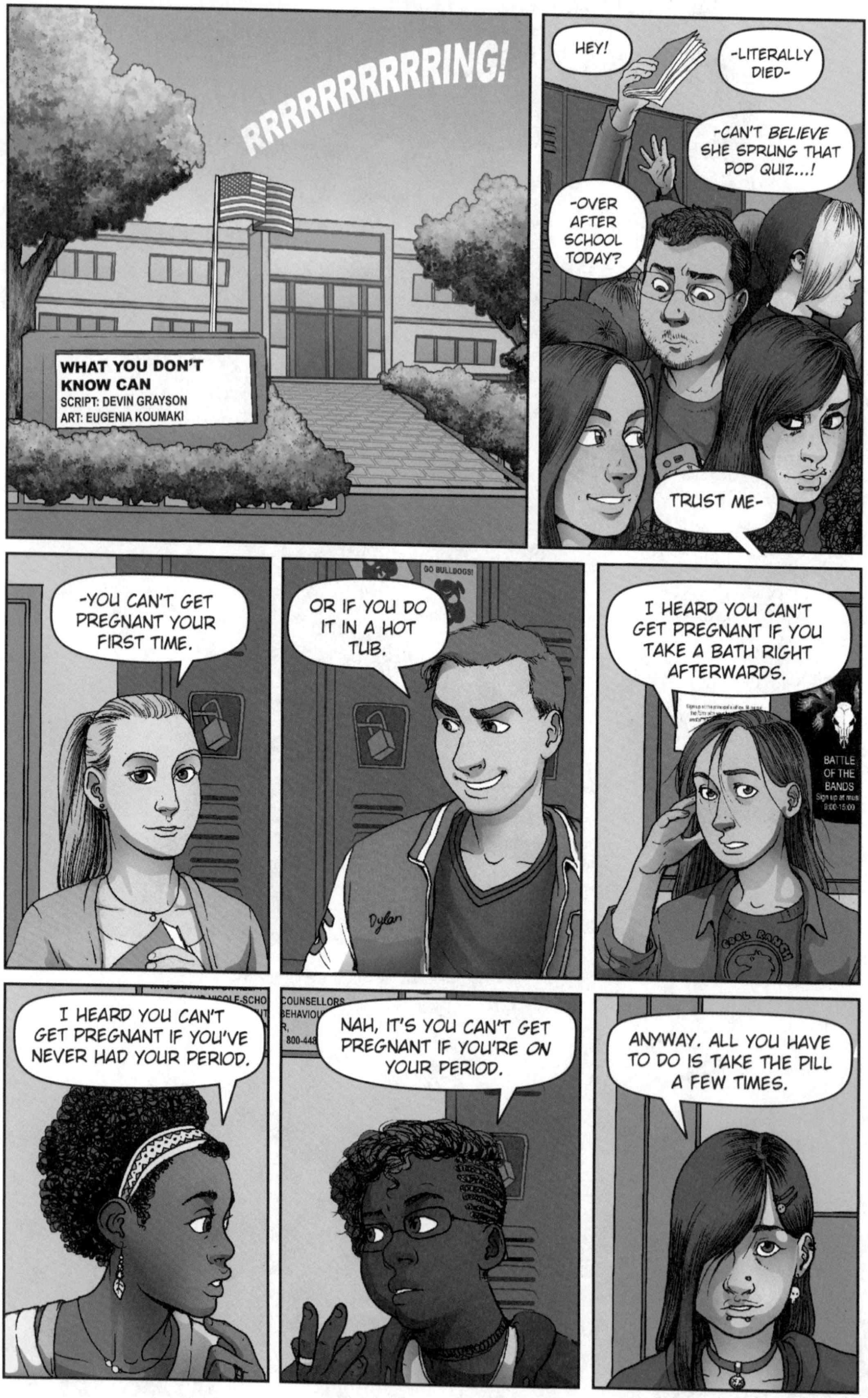
RRRRRRRRRRING!
WHAT YOU DON'T KNOW CAN
SCRIPT: DEVIN GRAYSON
ART: EUGENIA KOUMAKI
HEY!
-LITERALLY DIED-
-CAN'T *BELIEVE* SHE SPRUNG THAT POP QUIZ...!
-OVER AFTER SCHOOL TODAY?
TRUST ME-
-YOU CAN'T GET PREGNANT YOUR FIRST TIME.
GO BULLDOGS!
OR IF YOU DO IT IN A HOT TUB.
Dylan
I HEARD YOU CAN'T GET PREGNANT IF YOU TAKE A BATH RIGHT AFTERWARDS.
BATTLE OF THE BANDS
COOL RANCH
I HEARD YOU CAN'T GET PREGNANT IF YOU'VE NEVER HAD YOUR PERIOD.
COUNSELLORS
NAH, IT'S YOU CAN'T GET PREGNANT IF YOU'RE *ON* YOUR PERIOD.
ANYWAY. ALL YOU HAVE TO DO IS TAKE THE PILL A FEW TIMES.

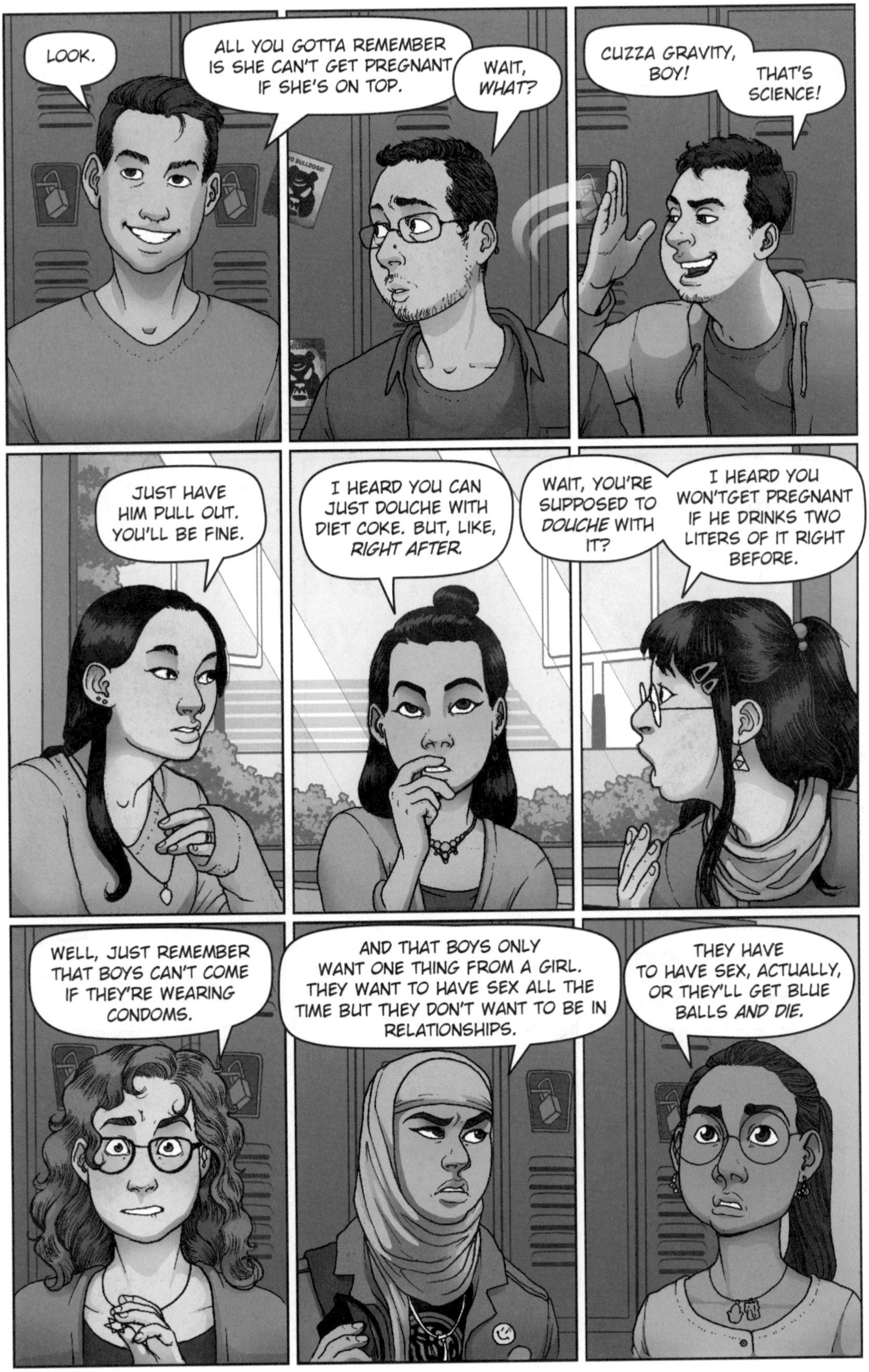
LOOK.
ALL YOU GOTTA REMEMBER IS SHE CAN'T GET PREGNANT IF SHE'S ON TOP.
WAIT, *WHAT?*
CUZZA GRAVITY, BOY!
THAT'S SCIENCE!
JUST HAVE HIM PULL OUT. YOU'LL BE FINE.
I HEARD YOU CAN JUST DOUCHE WITH DIET COKE. BUT, LIKE, *RIGHT AFTER.*
WAIT, YOU'RE SUPPOSED TO *DOUCHE* WITH IT?
I HEARD YOU WON'TGET PREGNANT IF HE DRINKS TWO LITERS OF IT RIGHT BEFORE.
WELL, JUST REMEMBER THAT BOYS CAN'T COME IF THEY'RE WEARING CONDOMS.
AND THAT BOYS ONLY WANT ONE THING FROM A GIRL. THEY WANT TO HAVE SEX ALL THE TIME BUT THEY DON'T WANT TO BE IN RELATIONSHIPS.
THEY HAVE TO HAVE SEX, ACTUALLY, OR THEY'LL GET BLUE BALLS *AND DIE.*

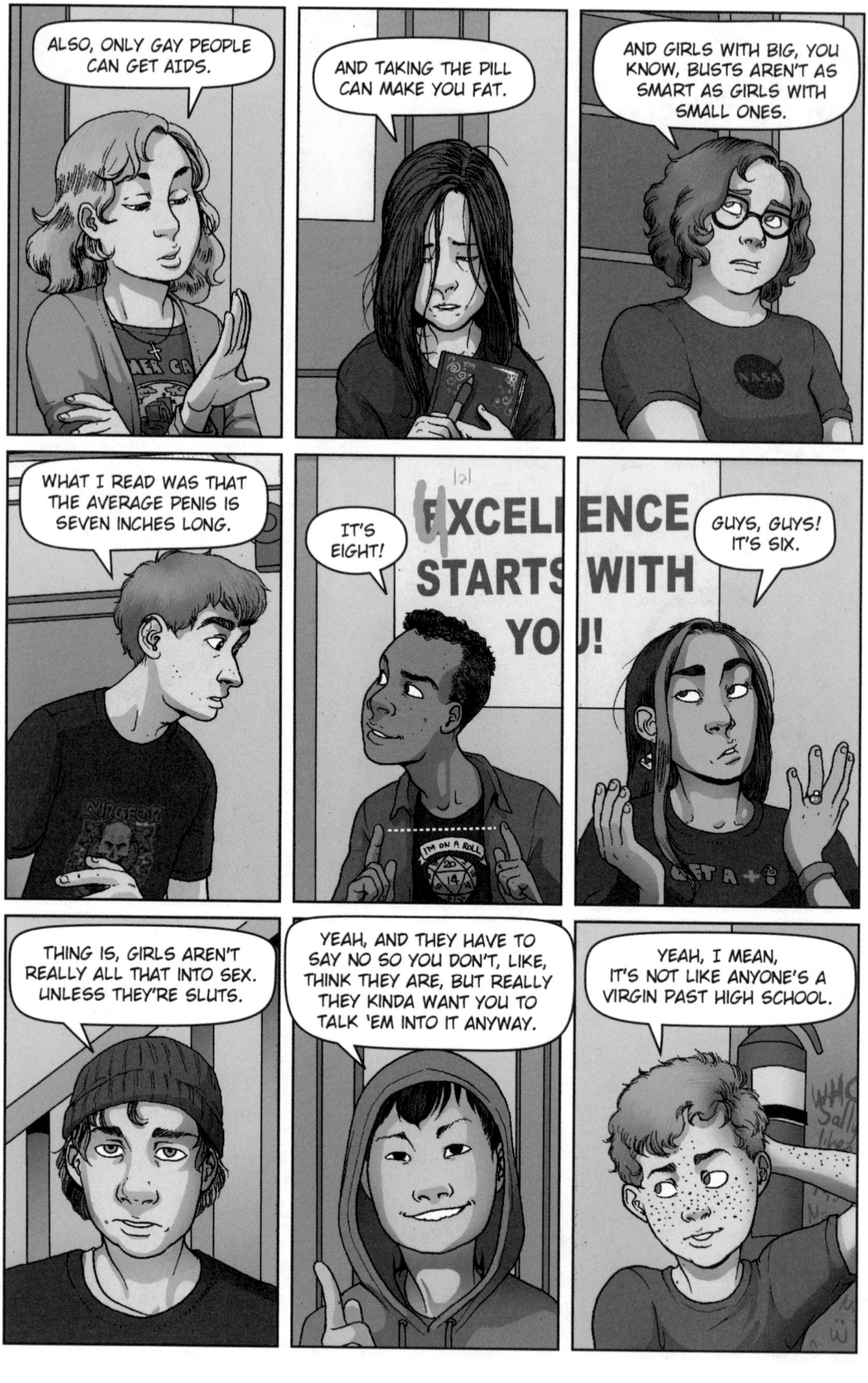

ALSO, ONLY GAY PEOPLE CAN GET AIDS.
AND TAKING THE PILL CAN MAKE YOU FAT.
AND GIRLS WITH BIG, YOU KNOW, BUSTS AREN'T AS SMART AS GIRLS WITH SMALL ONES.
NASA
WHAT I READ WAS THAT THE AVERAGE PENIS IS SEVEN INCHES LONG.
IT'S EIGHT!
EXCELLENCE STARTS WITH YOU!
GUYS, GUYS! IT'S SIX.
I'M ON A ROLL
THING IS, GIRLS AREN'T REALLY ALL THAT INTO SEX. UNLESS THEY'RE SLUTS.
YEAH, AND THEY HAVE TO SAY NO SO YOU DON'T, LIKE, THINK THEY ARE, BUT REALLY THEY KINDA WANT YOU TO TALK 'EM INTO IT ANYWAY.
YEAH, I MEAN, IT'S NOT LIKE ANYONE'S A VIRGIN PAST HIGH SCHOOL.

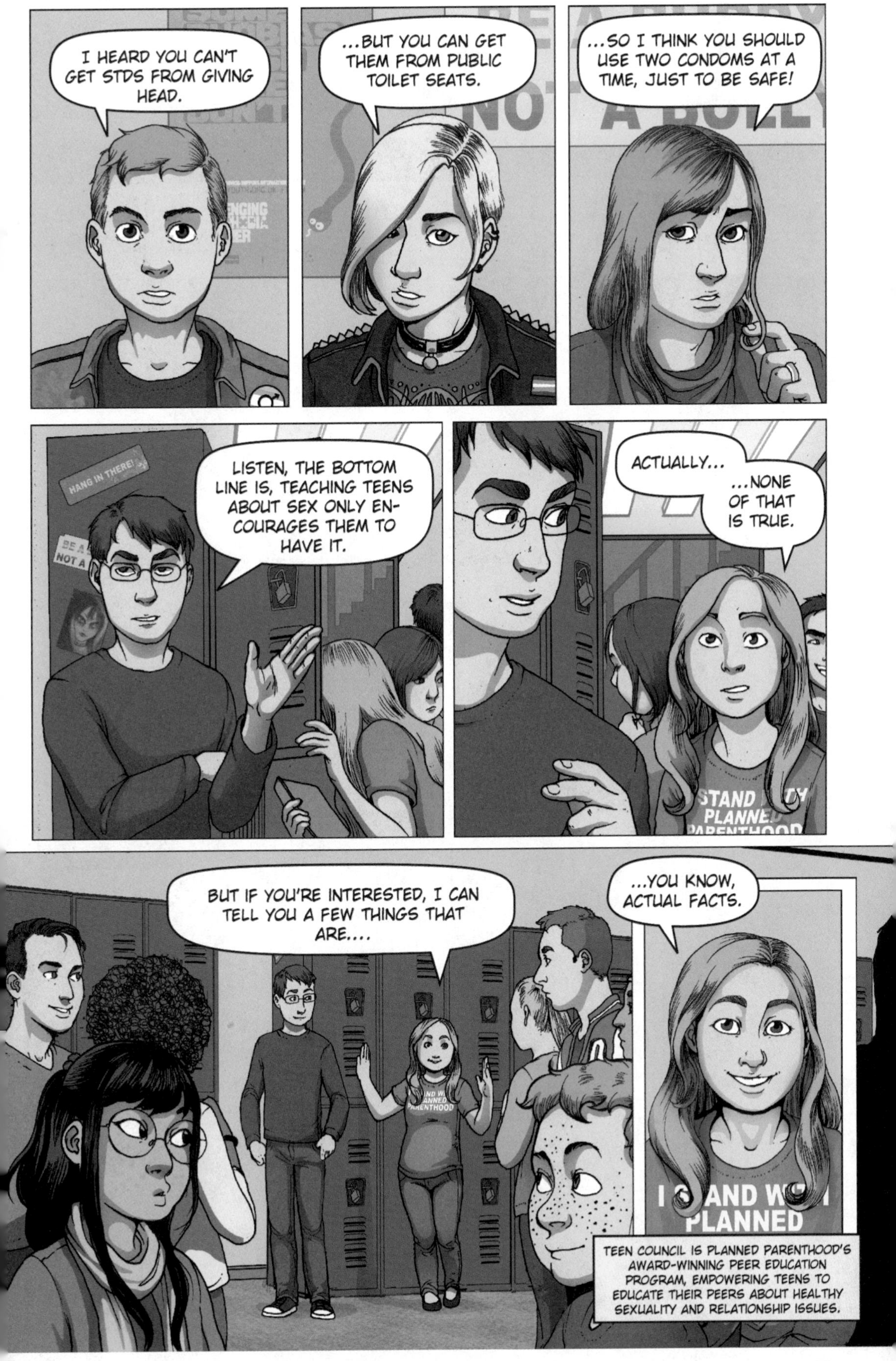

I HEARD YOU CAN'T GET STDS FROM GIVING HEAD.
...BUT YOU CAN GET THEM FROM PUBLIC TOILET SEATS.
...SO I THINK YOU SHOULD USE TWO CONDOMS AT A TIME, JUST TO BE SAFE!
HANG IN THERE!
LISTEN, THE BOTTOM LINE IS, TEACHING TEENS ABOUT SEX ONLY ENCOURAGES THEM TO HAVE IT.
ACTUALLY...
...NONE OF THAT IS TRUE.
BUT IF YOU'RE INTERESTED, I CAN TELL YOU A FEW THINGS THAT ARE....
...YOU KNOW, ACTUAL FACTS.
TEEN COUNCIL IS PLANNED PARENTHOOD'S AWARD-WINNING PEER EDUCATION PROGRAM, EMPOWERING TEENS TO EDUCATE THEIR PEERS ABOUT HEALTHY SEXUALITY AND RELATIONSHIP ISSUES.

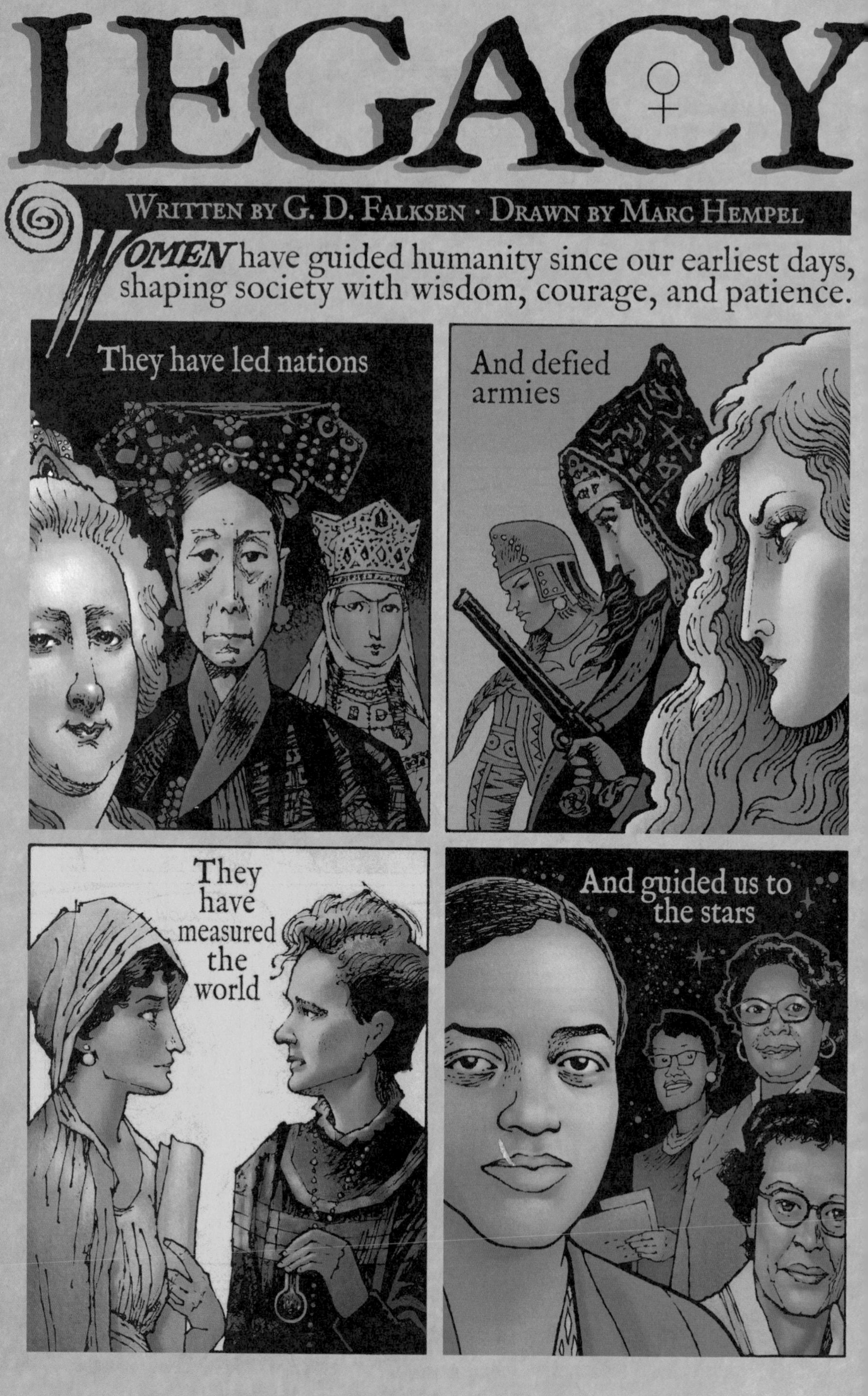
LEGACY
Written by G. D. Falksen · Drawn by Marc Hempel
Women have guided humanity since our earliest days, shaping society with wisdom, courage, and patience.
They have led nations
And defied armies
They have measured the world
And guided us to the stars